Volume IX

Petrarch and the Literary Culture of Nineteenth-Century France

ISSN 2043–8230

Series Editors
Karl Fugelso
Chris Jones

Medievalism aims to provide a forum for monographs and collections devoted to the burgeoning and highly dynamic multi-disciplinary field of medievalism studies: that is, work investigating the influence and appearance of 'the medieval' in the society and culture of later ages. Titles within the series will investigate the post-medieval construction and manifestations of the Middle Ages – attitudes towards, and uses and meanings of, 'the medieval' – in all fields of culture, from politics and international relations, literature, history, architecture, and ceremonial ritual to film and the visual arts. It welcomes a wide range of topics, from historiographical subjects to revivalism, with the emphasis always firmly on what the idea of 'the medieval' has variously meant and continues to mean; it is founded on the belief that scholars interested in the Middle Ages can and should communicate their research both beyond and within the academic community of medievalists, and on the continuing relevance and presence of 'the medieval' in the contemporary world.

New proposals are welcomed. They may be sent directly to the editors or the publishers at the addresses given below.

Professor Karl Fugelso
Art Department
Towson University
3103 Center for the Arts
8000 York Road
Towson, MD 21252–0001
USA

Dr Chris Jones
School of English
University of St Andrews
St Andrews
Fife KY16 9AL
UK

Boydell & Brewer Ltd
PO Box 9
Woodbridge
Suffolk IP12 3DF
UK

Previous volumes in this series are printed at the back of this book

Petrarch and the Literary Culture of Nineteenth-Century France

Translation, Appropriation, Transformation

Jennifer Rushworth

THE BOYDELL PRESS

First published 2017

The Boydell Press, Woodbridge

ISBN 978 1 84384 456 3

The Boydell Press is an imprint of Boydell & Brewer Ltd
PO Box 9, Woodbridge, Suffolk IP12 3DF, UK
and of Boydell & Brewer Inc.
668 Mt Hope Avenue, Rochester, NY 14620-2731, USA
website: www.boydellandbrewer.com
A CIP catalogue record for this book is available
from the British Library

For 'My Dee'

Contents

Acknowledgements

I have incurred many debts in the writing of this book. I would like to express my thanks to colleagues, librarians, friends, and family who helped and advised me during this project, as well as the organizers of the various conferences where I presented material from this work. For unstinting, insightful, and often creative comments on the final draft, I am particularly indebted to the kindness of Simon Park, David Bowe, and Francesca Southerden. Julia Hartley, for her part, was always there to share with me her love of nineteenth-century French literature. My understanding of Petrarch has long been challenged and enriched by Francesca Southerden, and it has been a pleasure more recently to meet Unn Falkeid, with whom I share an interest in the relations between Petrarch and Avignon.

For guidance, not to mention constant companionship throughout, I am grateful to Matthew Salisbury, who sets a fine example of archival patience and attention to detail. Without Matthew's parents, I would never have made it to Cornell to consult the amazing Fiske Petrarch Collection; I thank them for taking care of me and for happy memories of that lovely spring visit. On this subject I am also grateful to all the librarians at Cornell who made my visit so productive, in particular Patrick Joseph Stevens. At other libraries I thank Elisabeth Morger and Stefanie Lind at the Museumsgesellschaft Bibliothek, Zurich, and Leslie Morris at Harvard University. For generous advice on specific matters I thank David Hook and Louise Esher.

The later part of this project was invigorated by discussions and dialogue as part of the Petrarch project led by Carole Birkan-Berz, 'Métamorphoses d'un genre migrateur: Traduction et adaptation du sonnet anglais de la Renaissance à aujourd'hui', Jeunes Chercheurs de Paris 3 – Sorbonne Paris Cité. It has been a pleasure to work with such a lovely team of researchers on this project, and also to meet Riccardo Raimondo, whose ambitious thesis proposes to study French translations of Petrarch across many centuries. I would also like to signal here Guillaume Coatalen's even more ambitious work-in-progress online database of translations of Petrarch across a number of European languages: Europetrarca.

Significant parts of this book were written in the splendid company of Gertie, whose owners Richard and Ela are to be thanked for their endless hospitality and support. Finally, I am immensely grateful to Boydell & Brewer for taking on this book, with especial thanks to Caroline Palmer and Robert Kinsey, to the editors of the Medievalism series, Karl Fugelso and Chris Jones, and to the anonymous reader. My greatest debt, however, is to St John's College, Oxford, which, through a very generous Junior Research Fellowship, provided me with a home and haven for this project.

Note on English Translations

English translations are the author's own, unless otherwise indicated. For foreign language material in prose, English translations are given in the main text with the original in footnotes, and the same is true for short extracts of verse, unless there is a desire to highlight a particular word or phrase. However, longer verse extracts (typically indented) are instead given both in the original and in English translation in the main text. The awkwardness of translating translations is not lost on the author; such an activity is undertaken for the sake of accessibility of the material. Titles, if cited in the main text, are given in translation on their first mention, and thereafter only in their original form.

Quotations from Petrarch's *Canzoniere* in the original follow the text and ordering of Francesco Petrarca, *Canzoniere*, ed. Marco Santagata, 4th edn (Milan: Arnoldo Mondadori, 2010), preceded by the abbreviation *RVF* (with reference to the original Latin title of the work, *Rerum vulgarium fragmenta* [*Fragments of Things in the Vernacular*]).

Introduction: Local History, Local Stories

The nineteenth century needed its own Petrarch.[1]

(Alphonse de Lamartine)

THE MEDIEVAL ITALIAN poet Francesco Petrarca (known in English as Petrarch, in French as Pétrarque) is a chameleon-like, nomadic figure. Temporally, his life spanned the end of the Middle Ages and the start of the Renaissance, and he has accordingly been hailed both as 'the last troubadour' and 'the first modern man'.[2] Geographically, he was a wanderer, 'a restless tourist', born in exile in Arezzo on 20 July 1304, raised in Carpentras, educated at Montpellier and Bologna, and a frequent presence alternately at the papal court of Avignon and in the rural idyll of Fontaine-de-Vaucluse, this last known to Petrarch simply as Vaucluse.[3] In September 1340, Petrarch received invitations to receive the laurel crown from both Rome and Paris, a sign of his growing reputation even in his life-

[1] 'Il fallait au 19ème siècle son Pétrarque.' *Correspondance d'Alphonse de Lamartine (1830–1867)*, ed. Christian Croisille, 7 vols (Paris: Honoré Champion, 2000–3), VI (2003), 232.

[2] Charles Singleton, *An Essay on the 'Vita nuova'* (Cambridge, MA: Publication for the Dante Society by Harvard University Press, 1949), p. 66; Ferdinand Loise, *Histoire de la poésie mise en rapport avec la civilisation en Italie depuis les origines jusqu'à nos jours* (Brussels: Alfred Castaigne; Paris: Thorin & fils, A. Fontemoing, 1895), p. 140; William D. Paden, 'Petrarch as a Poet of Provence', in *Petrarch and the European Lyric Tradition*, ed. Dino S. Cervigni (= *Annali d'Italianistica*, 22 (2004)), pp. 19–44 (p. 21); Jean Bartholoni, *Le Roman de Pétrarque et de Laure (1327–1348)* (Paris: Albert Messein, 1927), p. 18. See also Albert Russell Ascoli, 'Petrarch's Middle Age: Memory, Imagination, History, and "The Ascent of Mont Ventoux"', *Stanford Italian Review*, 10.1 (1991), 5–43 (repr. in Albert Russell Ascoli, *A Local Habitation and a Name: Imagining Histories in the Italian Renaissance* (New York: Fordham University Press, 2011), pp. 21–58).

[3] The phrase 'irrequieto turista' is from Gianfranco Contini, 'Preliminari sulla lingua del Petrarca [1951]', in *Varianti e altra linguistica: una raccolta di saggi (1938–1968)* (Turin: Einaudi, 1970), pp. 169–92 (p. 175). On Petrarch's travels, see Theodore J. Cachey, '"Peregrinus (quasi) ubique": Petrarca e la storia del viaggio', *Intersezioni: rivista di storia delle idee*, 27 (December 1997), 369–84; E. H. Wilkins, 'Peregrinus Ubique', *Studies in Philology*, 45.3 (1948), 445–53 (repr. in E. H. Wilkins, *The Making of the 'Canzoniere' and Other Petrarchan Studies* (Rome: Edizioni di storia e letteratura, 1951), pp. 1–8); Annalisa Cipollone, 'Peregrinus ubique. Petrarca viaggiatore (nello spazio e nel tempo)', in *Il viaggio e le arti: il contesto italiano*, ed. Lucia Bertolini and Annalisa Cipollone (Pescara: Edizioni dell'Orso, 2009), pp. 61–88.

time.[4] In later life he made a home for himself in a variety of northern Italian cities, particularly Milan, Padua, Parma, Pavia, and Venice. He spent his final years in Arquà, a village in the Euganean Hills, where he died on 19 July 1374, on the eve of his seventieth birthday, and where he was also laid to rest. In his writings, similarly, Petrarch crossed boundaries of both language and genre, producing work in Italian and Latin, in poetry and prose, with regard to matters in turn religious, historical, poetic, and moral.[5] The editor and translator of Petrarch's *Bucolicum carmen* (*Bucolic Poem*), a series of twelve allegorical poems in Latin, wrote that in these texts 'there is something for everyone', and we might well extend this statement to the whole of Petrarch's varied *œuvre*, thanks to its breadth of scope and interest.[6] Yet despite this variety and richness, the Petrarch that has been handed down by tradition is Petrarch the love poet, author of celebrated sonnets in Italian. It is the Petrarchan sonnet, more than any other part of his work, which has entranced and seduced readers, writers, and translators over the centuries.

The aims of this volume are to explore the specifically French motivation behind the reception of Petrarch in the nineteenth century and to investigate the different forms that this reception took. Within the field of reception studies, this book takes a twofold methodological approach. It begins with a study of French translations of Petrarch's Italian and Latin works throughout the nineteenth century (Part I: Translations) and proceeds to an analysis of French poetry and prose inspired and informed by Petrarch in this same period (Part II: Rewritings). I group both parts— translations and rewritings—under the final sub-titular term 'transformation'. For Walter Benjamin, translation is a process of transformation: 'Translation is removal from one language into another through a continuum of transformations.'[7] Yet at the heart of the concept of trans*form*ation there also lies the potential for formal innovation.[8] Transformation in this sense, that of a 'movement from one form to another', encompasses rewritings of Petrarch, especially in the transition from poetry to prose of the 'novelization' of Petrarch, that is, the varied adoption of Petrarch in the nineteenth-century French novel.[9] The following rare mention of Petrarch by

---

[4]   This point is discussed in the Conclusion.

[5]   For an introduction to Petrarch's corpus, see *Petrarch: A Critical Guide to the Complete Works*, ed. Victoria Kirkham and Armando Maggi (Chicago: University of Chicago Press, 2009) as well as *The Cambridge Companion to Petrarch*, ed. Albert Russell Ascoli and Unn Falkeid (Cambridge: Cambridge University Press, 2015).

[6]   Thomas G. Bergin, 'Introduction', in *Petrarch's Bucolicum carmen*, ed. and trans. Thomas G. Bergin (New Haven, CT: Yale University Press, 1974), pp. ix–xvii (p. xi).

[7]   Walter Benjamin, 'On Language as Such and on the Language of Man', trans. Edmund Jephcott, in *Selected Writings*, ed. Marcus Bullock, Michael W. Jennings, Howard Eiland, and Gary Smith, 4 vols (Cambridge, MA: The Belknap Press of Harvard University Press, 1996–2003), I, 62–74 (p. 70).

[8]   For a similar pun on trans*form*ation, see Clive Scott, *Translating Baudelaire* (Exeter: University of Exeter Press, 2000), especially Ch. 5, 'Translation and Transformation', pp. 94–119.

[9]   I take the phrase 'passage d'une forme à une autre' from the definition of 'transformation' in Pierre Larousse, *Grand dictionnaire universel du XIXe siècle*, 17 vols in 34 (Geneva: Slatkine, 1982 [originally Paris: Administration du Grand dictionnaire universel, 1866–79]), xv (première partie), 416. While the term 'novelization' derives from the work of Mikhail

Marcel Proust in a letter from September 1921 resonates beautifully with the present project in its recognition of the variety of forms which the Petrarchan story can take: 'Alas I know that the eternal (hi)story [*histoire*] of Petrarch and of Laura takes all sorts of forms, but remains true.'[10] In this quotation, the French *histoire*—both history and story—leaves an ambiguous space between fact and fiction that runs through much nineteenth-century French writing about the poet and his beloved.

In this introduction I will first briefly situate this investigation of the nineteenth-century French Petrarch within the wider critical discourses to which it belongs, namely Petrarchism and medievalism. I will then explain the reasons for the novel focus on French Petrarchism of the nineteenth century, and the temporal bookmarks of the project. Finally, the remainder of the introduction is dedicated to some initial reflections on the important questions of who Petrarch was and what he represented for French readers, writers, and translators of the nineteenth century, questions which necessitate a consideration of the associated conundrum of the disputed identity of Petrarch's beloved, Laura.

Critical Background

French Petrarchism has typically been associated with Renaissance poets such as Pierre de Ronsard and Joachim du Bellay.[11] As such it is part of a European-wide adoption of Petrarch as a lyric model, leading to an explosion of Petrarchist love sonnets in the sixteenth century and beyond.[12] In the words of Jonathan Culler,

Bakhtin (see Chapter 6), the notion of a French Petrarchan novel (*roman pétrarquiste*) belongs to Ève Duperray, 'Le mythe littéraire de Vaucluse dans le roman pétrarquiste de *L'Astrée* (1607–1628) à *Adriani* (1853)', in *Dynamique d'une expansion culturelle: Pétrarque en Europe XIVe–XXe siècle: actes du XXVIe congrès international du CEFI, Turin et Chambéry, 11–15 décembre 1995: à la mémoire de Franco Simone*, ed. Pierre Blanc (Paris: Honoré Champion, 2001), pp. 417–27, and *L'Or des mots: une lecture de Pétrarque et du mythe littéraire de Vaucluse des origines à l'orée du XXe siècle: histoire du pétrarquisme en France* (Paris: Publications de la Sorbonne, 1997), pp. 109–23.

[10] 'Hélas ! je sais que l'éternelle histoire de Pétrarque et de Laure prend toutes les formes, mais reste vraie.' Marcel Proust, *Correspondance*, ed. Philip Kolb, 21 vols (Paris: Plon, 1970–93), xx (1992), 473.

[11] Amongst many such studies, see: Marius Piéri, *Le Pétrarquisme au XVIe siècle: Pétrarque & Ronsard, ou, De l'influence de Pétrarque sur la Pléiade française* (Marseille: Lafitte, 1896); Joseph Vianey, *Le Pétrarquisme en France au XVIe siècle* (Montpellier: Coulet et fils, 1909); Dario Cecchetti, *Il petrarchismo in Francia* (Turin: G. Giappichelli, 1970); *Petrarch and Petrarchism: The English and French Traditions*, ed. Stephen Minta (Manchester: Manchester University Press, 1980); Sara Sturm-Maddox, *Ronsard, Petrarch and the 'Amours'* (Gainesville: University Press of Florida, 1999) and idem, 'The French Petrarch', in *Petrarch and the European Lyric Tradition*, pp. 171–87; William J. Kennedy, *The Site of Petrarchism: Early Modern National Sentiment in Italy, France, and England* (Baltimore: Johns Hopkins University Press, 2003); *Les Poètes français de la Renaissance et Pétrarque*, ed. Jean Balsamo (Geneva: Droz, 2004); Jean Balsamo, 'Le "premier cercle" du pétrarquisme français (1533–1540)', in *La Postérité répond à Pétrarque: sept siècles de fortune pétrarquienne en France: actes du colloque tenu à l'Hôtel de Sade et à l'Université d'Avignon et des Pays de Vaucluse les 22, 23, 24 janvier 2004*, ed. Ève Duperray (Paris: Beauchesne, 2006), pp. 127–45; *Petrarch and his Readers in the Renaissance*, ed. Karl A.E. Enenkel and Jan Papy (Leiden: Brill, 2006).

[12] See Leonard Forster, *The Icy Fire: Five Studies in European Petrarchism* (Cambridge:

'Petrarch's *Canzoniere* established a grammar for the European love lyric: a set of tropes, images, oppositions (fire and ice), and typical scenarios that permitted generations of poets throughout Europe to exercise their ingenuity in the construction of love sonnets.'[13] That the nineteenth century, in contrast, might constitute a similarly fertile Petrarchan moment has been obscured both by justified preoccupation with sixteenth-century Petrarchism and by the productive if typically all-engrossing critical interest in the nineteenth-century reception of that other great medieval Italian poet, Dante Alighieri.[14] Key exceptions to this general rule include: Edoardo Zuccato's *Petrarch in Romantic England*, which, however, overstates the claim for England as the unique site of nineteenth-century Petrarchism; Carmelina Naselli's early but comprehensive work on the legacy and reception of Petrarch in nineteenth-century Italy; and Gerhart Hoffmeister's postulation of a wider Petrarchism in European poetry of this period.[15] In terms of the specifically French reception of Petrarch in the nineteenth century, most illuminating has been the work of Ève Duperray in the context of a wider study of the myths of Petrarch and Vaucluse in France through the ages, following in the footsteps of earlier but now dated work by Lide Bertoli.[16] Yet the specific topic of Petrarch in nineteenth-century France has still not received the attention and recognition it deserves.

Besides the history of European Petrarchism, this volume is firmly situated within the broader field of medievalism, and more particularly within the already

---

Cambridge University Press, 1969), as well as *Il petrarchismo: un modello di poesia per l'Europa*, ed. Loredana Chines, Floriana Calitti, and Roberto Gigliucci, 2 vols (Rome: Bulzoni, 2006). English Petrarchism is also studied more broadly in both *Petrarch in English*, ed. Thomas P. Roche (London: Penguin, 2005) and *Petrarch in Britain: Interpreters, Imitators, and Translators over 700 Years*, ed. Martin McLaughlin and Letizia Panizza with Peter Hainsworth (Oxford: Oxford University Press for the British Academy, 2007).

[13] Jonathan Culler, *Theory of the Lyric* (Cambridge, MA: Harvard University Press, 2015), p. 69.

[14] See for essential introductions to this topic: Michael Pitwood, *Dante and the French Romantics* (Geneva: Droz, 1985); *Dante in the Nineteenth Century: Reception, Canonicity, Popularization*, ed. Nick Havely (Oxford: Peter Lang, 2011); *Dante in the Long Nineteenth Century: Nationality, Identity, and Appropriation*, ed. Aida Audeh and Nick Havely (Oxford: Oxford University Press, 2012). On the French reception of Dante more broadly, see Albert Counson, *Dante en France* (Erlangen: Fr. Junge, 1906).

[15] Edoardo Zuccato, *Petrarch in Romantic England* (Basingstoke: Palgrave Macmillan, 2008); Carmelina Naselli, *Il Petrarca nell'ottocento* (Naples: Società anonima editrice Francesco Perrella, 1923); Gerhart Hoffmeister, 'The Petrarchan Mode in European Romanticism', in *European Romanticism: Literary Cross-Currents, Modes, and Models*, ed. Gerhart Hoffmeister (Detroit: Wayne State University Press, 1990), pp. 97–111. While Zuccato's work in particular is an important cross-channel mirror for my own project, I cannot concur with his opening statement that 'Few readers, or even scholars, would think of Romanticism as a Petrarchan age. And they would be right for every European country except England': Zuccato, *Petrarch in Romantic England*, p. ix.

[16] Duperray, *L'Or des mots* and 'Le pétrarquisme en Provence (1804–1937): heures de gloire et crépuscule', in *La Postérité répond à Pétrarque*, pp. 209–17; Lide Bertoli, *La Fortuna del Petrarca in Francia nella prima metà del secolo XIX: note ed appunti* (Livorno: Raffaello Giusti, 1916) and 'I traduttori francesi del Petrarca nel secolo XIX', in *Raccolta di studi di storia e critica letteraria dedicata a Francesco Flamini da' suoi discepoli* (Pisa: Mariotti, 1918), pp. 653–79.

well-established topic of Romantic, nineteenth-century medievalism.[17] Medievalism is typically understood as heed paid by later writers to the Middle Ages, often motivated by a quest for origins, and as a mode of attention which ultimately reveals as much if not more about the values and concerns of the later, more modern age as about the medieval period itself. In Leslie Workman's foundational definition, medievalism is described as a form of revival that is predicated on irreversible distance from its object of desire: 'medievalism could only begin, not simply when the Middle Ages had ended, whenever that may have been, but when the Middle Ages were perceived to have been something in the past, something it was necessary to revive or desirable to imitate'.[18] Despite this unifying theoretical backdrop, medievalism, even in its nineteenth-century incarnation, is a concept and phenomenon that can only with difficulty be reduced to a stable, static, or homogeneous whole. As Claude Foucart warns:

> The assumption that there is only one '*return to the Middle Ages*' throughout the whole of the nineteenth century is definitely an error in as much as the past evoked by the myth is not chosen for itself, but rather in accordance with contemporary realities and even visions of the future.[19]

The nineteenth-century French return to Petrarch discussed in this book is, as we shall see, similarly varied in form according to the demands and desires of each successive generation of readers and writers.

In recent years, medievalism has been the subject of renewed interest, in part because of a will to challenge the academic and disciplinary barriers at times erected between Medieval Studies and Medievalism, and in part because of an allied

---

[17] See, of particular relevance to the present volume, *La Fabrique du Moyen Âge au XIXe siècle: représentations du moyen âge dans la culture et la littérature françaises du XIXe siècle*, ed. Simone Bernard-Griffiths, Pierre Glaudes, and Bertrand Vibert (Paris: Honoré Champion, 2006); Janine R. Dakyns, *The Middle Ages in French Literature, 1851–1900* (London: Oxford University Press, 1973); Barbara G. Keller, *The Middle Ages Reconsidered: Attitudes in France from the Eighteenth Century through the Romantic Movement* (New York: Peter Lang, 1994); *Medievalism and the Modernist Temper*, ed. R. Howard Bloch and Stephen G. Nichols (Baltimore and London: Johns Hopkins University Press, 1996); Kathleen Biddick, *The Shock of Medievalism* (Durham, NC: Duke University Press, 1998). Essential for background to nineteenth-century French medievalism are Alicia C. Montoya, *Medievalist Enlightenment from Charles Perrault to Jean-Jacques Rousseau* (Cambridge: D.S. Brewer, 2013) and Lionel Gossman, *Medievalism and the Ideologies of the Enlightenment: The World and Work of La Curne de Sainte-Palaye* (Baltimore: Johns Hopkins University Press, 1968).

[18] Leslie J. Workman, 'Editorial', *Studies in Medievalism* 1.1 (Spring 1979), 1–3 (p. 1).

[19] 'Présupposer qu'il n'existe ainsi que ce seul "*retour au Moyen Age*" durant tout le dix-neuvième siècle est à coup sûr une erreur dans l'exacte mesure où le passé évoqué par le mythe n'est point choisi pour lui-même, mais bien en fonction de réalités contemporaines et même de visions d'avenir.' Claude Foucart, 'Les grandes tendances du mythe du Moyen Âge dans la littérature française à la fin du XIXème siècle', in *L'Image du Moyen Âge dans la littérature française: colloque organisé par le département de français de l'U.E.R. de Lettres et Langues à l'occasion du 550ème anniversaire de l'Université de Poitiers, 7-8-9 mai 1981*, ed. Michel Autrand, 2 vols (= *La Licorne*, 6.1-2 (1982)), II, 145-75 (p. 145).

discomfort over strict distinctions between professional and amateur spheres.[20] The relationship between Medieval Studies and Medievalism has typically been characterized antithetically, along the following lines summarized by Clare Simmons:

> *Medieval Studies*: Professional; within the academy; research-based, objective; committed to discovering the authentic past.

> *Medievalism*: Amateur, outside the academy; based on cultural preconceptions; subjective; shaped by the individual's needs and desires.[21]

We are, of course, becoming ever more aware of how all research is inevitably 'shaped by the individual's needs and desires'.[22] Thus medievalism is no longer defined in strict opposition to Medieval Studies, but is, rather, understood as part of the history of this same discipline. As David Matthews suggests, 'what tends to happen over time is that medieval studies passes into medievalism; as it ceaselessly updates itself, medieval studies expels what it no longer wishes to recognize as part of itself'.[23] The recent academic turn towards medievalism is typically a move to reintegrate and to embrace rather than to reject both what lies in the past and that which might formerly have been considered at the margins of the institutionalized study of the Middle Ages. The greater openness and respect underlying this turn are at the heart of this book, which seeks to approach nineteenth-century French Petrarchism and its promulgators in an attentive, open, and receptive fashion, even if—or, indeed, especially when—the Petrarch expounded by these readers and writers differs more or less radically from present-day scholarly views.

This volume also, then, affirms the interest and importance of reception studies

---

[20] I should also signal here the recent burgeoning interest in other, newer forms of medievalism, whether these are concerned with non-literary media (comics, films, or videogames) or with non-European examples. Neither of these approaches pertains directly to the present book, but see, nonetheless, amongst an increasing number of such studies: *Metamorphosing Dante: Appropriations, Manipulations, and Rewritings in the Twentieth and Twenty-First Centuries*, ed. Manuele Gragnolati, Fabio Camilletti, and Fabian Lampart (Vienna and Berlin: Turia + Kant, 2011); *Médiévalisme, modernité du Moyen Âge*, ed. Vincent Ferré (Paris: L'Harmattan, 2010); *Mass Market Medieval: Essays on the Middle Ages in Popular Culture*, ed. David Marshall (Jefferson, NC: McFarland, 2007); *Medievalisms in the Postcolonial World: The Idea of the 'Middle Ages' Outside Europe*, ed. Kathleen Davis and Nadia Altschul (Baltimore: Johns Hopkins University Press, 2009).

[21] Clare A. Simmons, 'Introduction', in *Medievalism and the Quest for the 'Real' Middle Ages*, ed. Clare A. Simmons (Oxford: Taylor and Francis, 2001), pp. 1–28 (p. 12), cited in Pam Clements, 'Authenticity', in *Medievalism: Key Critical Terms*, ed. Elizabeth Emery and Richard Utz (Cambridge: D.S. Brewer, 2014), pp. 19–26 (p. 20).

[22] By way of example, see Norman F. Cantor, *Inventing the Middle Ages: The Lives, Works, and Ideas of the Great Medievalists of the Twentieth Century* (New York: W. Morrow, 1991) and Carolyn Dinshaw, *How Soon is Now? Medieval Texts, Amateur Readers, and the Queerness of Time* (Durham, NC: Duke University Press, 2012).

[23] David Matthews, 'Chaucer's American Accent', *American Literary History* 22.4 (Winter 2010), 758–72 (p. 759), again cited in Clements, 'Authenticity', p. 21. See also Richard Utz, 'Coming to Terms with Medievalism', *European Journal of English Studies*, 15.2 (August 2011), 101–13 (p. 109), for the suggestion that 'medievalism and medieval studies might become coterminous at some future moment'.

in shaping our understanding of the past and in constructing a history of particular authors and their readership. As Susan Gillingham has recently argued in relation to Biblical studies, even if reception studies at times may have been considered a form of scholarship 'on holiday' (in the sense of transporting scholars to a different space and time from their usual, more habitual haunts), it ought also to be recognized that this type of 'holiday' provides a welcome and much needed 'total change of perspective' and 'a different set of priorities'.[24] Reception studies are vital in revealing to us the filters through which we ordinarily view the past; we are led to be wary about our present assumptions as a result of encounters with different narratives and different explanations of past events and texts. As Zuccato concludes his *Petrarch in Romantic England*, 'it would be naïve to believe that our sight is more impartial and unprejudiced than the Romantic-era fascination with the romance of Petrarch and Laura'.[25] Reception studies also demonstrate the enduring fascination of particular texts and authors, and the variety of reasons that underpin this long-lasting though often fluctuating and intermittent fascination. Finally, reception studies, like medievalism, shed light not only on the past, but also on modern concerns and desires. In this regard, this book advances not only our understanding of Petrarch and Petrarchism, but also our understanding of nineteenth-century French literary culture, from an oblique and perhaps unexpected angle.

Temporal and Geographical Parameters

While the focal time period of this project is the nineteenth century, one has to go back a little further in time, to the 1750s and 1760s and to Voltaire, Jean-Jacques Rousseau, and the abbé de Sade, in order to find the foundations of modern French Petrarchism. The first, Voltaire, ushered in a new era of Petrarch translation by translating the first stanza of *RVF* 126 (the celebrated *canzone* 'Chiare, fresche et dolci acque', 'Clear, fresh, and sweet waters') in his *Essai sur les mœurs et l'esprit des nations* (1756; *Essay on the Customs and Spirit of the Nations*).[26] As I show at the end of Chapter 2, Voltaire's knowingly incomplete rendition was foundational for many later translators, and acted as a sort of bookmark within the *Canzoniere* of a poem particularly ripe for French translation and retranslation. The second, Rousseau, inaugurated the tradition of Petrarchism in the French novel by citing from Petrarch

---

[24] Susan Gillingham, 'Biblical Studies on Holiday? A Personal View of Reception History', in *Reception History and Biblical Studies: Theory and Practice*, ed. William John Lyons and Emma England (London: Bloomsbury, 2015), pp. 17–30 (p. 17).

[25] Zuccato, *Petrarch in Romantic England*, p. 156.

[26] Voltaire, *Essai sur les mœurs et l'esprit des nations*, ed. Bruno Bernard, John Renwick, Nicholas Cronk, and Janet Godden, 9 vols (Oxford: Voltaire Foundation, 2009–), IV (2011), 274. Voltaire has more typically been considered in relation to Dante rather than Petrarch: see Russell Goulbourne, '"Bizarre, mais brillant de beautés naturelles": Voltaire and Dante's *Commedia*', in *Dante in France*, ed. Russell Goulbourne, Claire Honess, and Matthew Treherne (= *La Parola del testo: rivista internazionale di letteratura italiana e comparata*, 17.1–2 (2013)), pp. 31–43, and 'Voltaire, Dante and the Dynamics of Influence', in *Questions of Influence in Modern French Literature*, ed. Thomas Baldwin, James Fowler, and Ana de Medeiros (Basingstoke: Palgrave Macmillan, 2013), pp. 18–31.

in his epistolary novel of 1761, *Julie, ou la Nouvelle Héloïse* (*Julie, or the New Heloise*), from the title page (in the form of a Petrarchan epigraph) onwards.[27] Finally, the abbé de Sade's three-volume *Mémoires pour la vie de François Pétrarque* (1764–7; *Memoirs for the Life of Francis Petrarch*) attracted new attention to the Italian poet in both France and England, the latter via an abridged English translation of the *Mémoires* by Susannah Dobson.[28] In these *Mémoires*, the abbé de Sade, uncle to the more famous marquis de Sade, provided copious translations of Petrarch's Italian poetry and Latin letters, as well as lengthy swathes of historical information about the context of Petrarch's life, particularly Avignon, Sade's own home town, and a shared point of reference between biographer and subject.[29] I consider Sade to be the principal starting point for French translations of Petrarch in the nineteenth century, both in Part I and in Appendix 1, the latter of which offers a detailed biblio-graphical survey in chronological order of French translations of Petrarch's Italian poetry published between 1764 (the date of Sade's first volume) and 1903. At the end of Chapter 2, however, as in Appendix 2, Voltaire's earlier translation of the first stanza of *RVF* 126 (1756) is taken to be a similarly crucial model for later translators.

At the other end of the temporal spectrum, the upper limit of this investigation is marked by 1904, a year which saw the third in a series of key Petrarchan anniversary celebrations held in Avignon and Fontaine-de-Vaucluse:

1804, the five-hundredth anniversary of Petrarch's birth;
1874, the five-hundredth anniversary of Petrarch's death;
1904, the six-hundredth anniversary of Petrarch's birth.[30]

These three dates, particularly the 1874 celebrations, were the catalyst for public festivities, poetry competitions, and many publications relating to Petrarch, in critical, biographical, and translational veins, as subsequent chapters will explore. A fourth date, difficult to verify historically besides Petrarch's own account, is sometimes added to this trio: 1927, the six-hundredth anniversary of Petrarch's

---

[27] See Chapter 6.

[28] Jacques François Paul Aldonce de Sade (abbé), *Mémoires pour la vie de François Pétrarque, tirés de ses œuvres et des auteurs contemporains, avec des notes ou dissertations, & les pieces justificatives*, 3 vols (Amsterdam: Arskée & Mercus, 1764–7); Susannah Dobson, *The Life of Petrarch*, 2 vols (London: James Buckland, 1775). See Julie Candler Hayes, 'Petrarch/Sade: Writing the Life', in *Representations of the Self from the Renaissance to Romanticism*, ed. Patrick Coleman, Jayne Lewis, and Jill Kowalik (Cambridge: Cambridge University Press, 2000), pp. 117–34; Zuccato, *Petrarch in Romantic England*, pp. 1–6; Martin McLaughlin, 'Nineteenth-Century British Biographies of Petrarch', in *Petrarch in Britain*, pp. 319–40.

[29] For the marquis de Sade's reading of his uncle's *Mémoires*, a subject requiring separate consideration, see, for instance, Duperray, *L'Or des mots*, pp. 192–8.

[30] On these centenary celebrations, see Harald Hendrix, 'Petrarch 1804–1904: Nation-Building and Glocal Identities', in *Commemorating Writers in Nineteenth-Century Europe: Nation-Building and Centenary Fever*, ed. Joseph Leerssen and Ann Rigney (Basingstoke: Palgrave Macmillan, 2014), pp. 117–133, and Duperray, *L'Or des mots*, pp. 222–57. On the comparable phenomenon of nineteenth-century Dantean festivities in Italy, see Mahnaz Yousefzadeh, *City and Nation in the Italian Unification: The National Festivals of Dante Alighieri* (Basingstoke: Palgrave Macmillan, 2011).

first sight of Laura.[31] This last date itself also anticipates one of the most striking, if belated, results of nineteenth-century French Petrarchism: the opening of the Musée Pétrarque on 7 October 1928, on the purported site of Petrarch's own house in Fontaine-de-Vaucluse.[32] The foundation of this museum is both a culminating point and a new beginning for nineteenth-century French Petrarchism, and manifests an ever-increasing desire for an actual encounter with Petrarch's life and works on French soil, in competition both with Petrarch's transalpine birthplace (in Arezzo) and his final resting place (at Arquà).[33] Nonetheless, this book remains largely bounded by the three principal Petrarchan anniversaries which span the preceding century (1804–1874–1904). Within this span, moreover, many of the examples of French poetry and prose inspired by Petrarch come from the first half of the nineteenth century, in particular the 1830s. Around that time, a distinctively French Romantic Petrarch emerges against a wider backdrop of French Romantic medievalism and Italophilia.

These Petrarchan anniversary dates provide a different, idiosyncratic way of navigating the socio-political turmoil of nineteenth-century France, which, in the aftermath of the Revolution, was host to various, alternating, and competing forms of governance, between republic, empire, and monarchy. As regards this socio-political backdrop, I consider the unification of Avignon with France during the Revolution as decisive for nineteenth-century French Petrarchism. This unification was ratified on 14 September 1791 by the Assemblée nationale, and definitively decided by the surrender of the papal states to the French at the Treaty of Tolentino on 19 February 1797.[34] Thus came to an end Avignon's status as a papal annex, a status it had retained since the days of the Avignon Papacy back in the fourteenth century (1309–77). It was this papal Avignon with which Petrarch had been familiar, indeed perhaps too familiar; Petrarch's distinctly voiced antipathy towards the city's supplanting of Rome as papal seat was a source of tension, however hidden, in nineteenth-century Avignon's attempted adoption of the poet as her own.[35] At the

---

[31] On the importance of the 1927 anniversary, see *Pétrarque: mélanges de littérature et d'histoire publiés par l'Union intellectuelle franco-italienne* (Paris: Librairie Ernest Leroux, 1928).

[32] See Pierre de Nolhac, *Inauguration de la maison de Pétrarque à Vaucluse: le dimanche 7 octobre, 1928: discours de M. Pierre de Nolhac au nom de l'Académie française* (Paris: Typographie de Firmin-Didot et Cie, 1928).

[33] See Harald Hendrix, 'The Early Modern Invention of Literary Tourism: Petrarch's Houses in France and Italy', in *Writers' Houses and the Making of Memory*, ed. Harald Hendrix (New York and London: Routledge, 2008), pp. 15–29, and Harald Hendrix, 'From Early Modern to Romantic Literary Tourism: A Diachronical Perspective', in *Literary Tourism and Nineteenth-Century Culture*, ed. Nicola Watson (Basingstoke: Palgrave Macmillan, 2009), pp. 13–24. The inauguration of the Musée Pétrarque is deemed the end of a certain form or brand of French Petrarchism by Duperray, *L'Or des mots*, p. 157.

[34] For more detailed information see René Moulinas, *Histoire de la Révolution d'Avignon* (Avignon: Aubanel, 1986).

[35] On Petrarch and Avignon, see Unn Falkeid, *The Avignon Papacy Contested: Power and Politics in Fourteenth-Century Literature* (Cambridge, MA: Harvard University Press, forthcoming), and, on the tension between Avignon's nineteenth-century adoption of Petrarch and Petrarch's original antipathy towards the city, Chapter 4 of the present book.

end of the eighteenth century, Avignon became the capital of the newly formed *département* of Vaucluse, an appellation which was even attributed to the region's earlier associations with Petrarch: 'When the Comtat became French again and formed one of our *départements*, the first act of France was a tribute to Petrarch. The name of the modest village distinguished by his poems became that of the new *département*.'[36] If, according to Theodore Cachey, 'the contrast between France and Italy' was 'like a hinge' 'around which Petrarch's career turned',[37] it is—I contend— after the unification of Avignon that this hinge becomes particularly audible and even a sticking point. Petrarch, through his nineteenth-century reception, is pulled back towards and firmly anchored in newly French soil.

At the turn of the century, claiming Avignon as French politically was reinforced by claiming Petrarch as culturally French, and a means of recuperating Avignon's medieval past more generally as part of French heritage. Treating Petrarch as a French poet was a way to integrate Avignon's particular history into a wider narrative of nation-building and an emerging sense of national culture. At this time, moreover, French claims on the Italian Petrarch were also consonant with and a cultural extension of French political, military advances on Italy in the aftermath of the Revolution and during the Napoleonic Wars. Later in the century, however, local readers and translators often claimed Petrarch not as French, but rather specifically as Avignonese or Provençal, to the greater glory of the city and region in the face of cultural and linguistic domination from the north after Avignon's unification. In this respect, while the editors of *The Cambridge Companion to Petrarch* comment that 'we have tended to underestimate the influence of Avignon—where Petrarch spent much of the first half of his life—on his early formation', the opposite is usefully true of Petrarch's nineteenth-century French readers.[38] National and local tensions thus emerge in the nineteenth-century French adoption of Petrarch, and these tensions are particularly evident in the special case of Occitan translations of Petrarch in the later nineteenth century.[39] Through translations, biographies, and festivals, Avignon showcased its illustrious past to the rest of France as well as to Italy.

In this book, Petrarch emerges as a chameleon figure, in the sense that his

---

[36] 'Lorsque le Comtat redevint français et forma un de nos départements, le premier acte de la France fut un hommage à Pétrarque. Le nom de la modeste bourgade illustrée par ses rimes devint celui du département nouveau.' *Fête séculaire et internationale de Pétrarque célébrée en Provence 1874: procès-verbaux & vers inédits*, ed. Léon de Berluc-Perussis and Hippolyte Guillibert (Aix-en-Provence: Vve Remondet-Aubin, 1875), p. 23. This explanation is reiterated, for instance, in *Les Sonnets de Pétrarque: traduction complète en sonnets réguliers, avec introduction et commentaire par Philibert Le Duc*, 2 vols (Paris: Leon Willem, 1877–9), II, 353.

[37] Theodore J. Cachey, 'Introduction', in *Petrarch's Guide to the Holy Land: Itinerary to the Sepulcher of Our Lord Jesus Christ*, ed. and trans. Theodore J. Cachey (Notre Dame: University of Notre Dame Press, 2002) pp. 1–50 (p. 6).

[38] Albert Russell Ascoli and Unn Falkeid, 'Introduction', in *The Cambridge Companion to Petrarch*, pp. 1–9 (p. 3).

[39] See Chapter 4 and the Conclusion. Note that the terms Occitan and Provençal are typically interchangeable, though Provençal is more specifically the form of Occitan found in Provence. A distinction is also to be made between medieval Occitan and the modern form adopted and promoted by the Félibrige.

coloration (or appearance) changes depending on the geographical and political background against which he is placed. As a consequence, we might speak not of nineteenth-century France as having its own, particular Petrarch (*son Pétrarque*, echoing Lamartine's words), but rather of its having several or many Petrarchs, that it is the task of this book to trace. Petrarch, in his reception as in his lifetime, remains a protean figure of contradiction and plurality. Nonetheless, the remainder of this Introduction will be devoted to outlining some of the key, recurrent features of the version of Petrarch promoted by French writers from Sade onwards, firstly through an exploration of the repeated declaration of Petrarch's Frenchness in this period, and secondly through the competing claims made for the true, historical identity of Petrarch's beloved Laura.

The French Petrarch

French and often specifically Avignonese readers of Petrarch had a vested interest in claiming the poet as somehow French, whether because of his reading (which likely included the troubadours), biography and education (his upbringing and early adult life in Avignon and Vaucluse), or love interest (the French Laure, discussed below).[40] This claim had historical weight, traceable back to sixteenth-century Petrarchism and puns on Petrarch's French name, François (*Français*, French) Pétrarque. The author of the first complete French translation of Petrarch's *Canzoniere*, dating from the middle of the sixteenth century, dedicated Book One of his work to the Florentine Catherine de' Medici-turned-French Queen, with the lines: 'Thus Petrarch will have new renown / When he will be *Françoys* under your name.'[41] The translator, Vasquin Philieul, offered his Franco-Italian patron a *Pétrarque français* of *François Pétrarque*. Indeed, the very habit of translating Francesco Petrarca's name into other

---

[40] On Petrarch and the troubadour tradition see: Perugi, *Trovatori a Valchiusa: un frammento della cultura provenzale del Petrarca* (Padua: Editrice Antenore, 1985); Alessio Fontana, 'La filologia romanza e il problema del rapporto Petrarca–trovatori (premesse per una ripresa del problema secondo nuove prospettive)', in *Petrarca 1304–1374: Beiträge zu Werk und Wirkung*, ed. Fritz Schalk (Frankfurt am Main: Vittorio Klostermann, 1975), pp. 51–70; Charles Gidel, *Les troubadours et Pétrarque: thèse présentée à la Faculté des lettres de Paris* (Angers: Cosnier et Lachèse, 1857). Within the *Canzoniere* itself, of particular note is Petrarch's citing of a *canzone* attributed to Arnaut Daniel at the end of the first stanza of *RVF* 70 (v. 10); on this citation, see Sarah Kay, *Parrots and Nightingales: Troubadour Quotations and the Development of European Poetry* (Philadelphia: University of Pennsylvania Press, 2013), pp. 189–95.

[41] 'Aussi Pétrarque aura nouveau renom / Quand il sera Françoys dessoubz ton nom.' Vasquin Philieul, *Toutes les euvres vulgaires de Françoys Pétrarque, contenans quatre Livres de M.D. Laure d'Avignon sa maistresse* (Avignon: De l'Imprimerie de Barthelemy Bonhomme, 1555), p. 4. On these lines, see Cécile Alduy, *Politique des 'Amours': poétique et genèse d'un genre français nouveau (1544–1560)* (Geneva: Droz, 2007), p. 59, and Kennedy, *The Site of Petrarchism*, p. 113. On the translator, see Marcel Françon, 'Vasquin Philieul, traducteur de Pétrarque', *French Studies*, 4.3 (1950), 216–26, and Giovanna Bellati, 'Il primo traduttore del *Canzoniere* petrarchesco nel Rinascimento francese: Vasquin Philieul', *Aevum*, 59.2 (1985), 371–98.

languages (at least, as is evident from this book, in both French and English) may be a sign of a deeper urge to appropriate the poet into new national literary canons.

The Frenchness of Petrarch is courteously promoted by the abbé de Sade in his introductory address to Italian readers at the start of the first volume of his *Mémoires pour la vie de François Pétrarque*:

> What would you say if someone dared to dispute your claim to Petrarch? He first saw the light of day in the heart of your beautiful land, of that there can be no doubt; the town of Arezzo witnessed his birth, none other one can compete for this honour; but he studied in Carpentras, Avignon, and Montpellier. His best works were conceived, begun, and many also completed on the banks of the river Sorgue; the rocks of Vaucluse have repeated a thousand times the harmonious sounds of his lyre; in these beautiful *canzoni* which you admire so much, he calls as witness the springs, woods, mountains, and meadows of this solitary place: lastly, it is here that he conceived the epic poem to which he owes his crown.
>
> It is necessary, then, to consider now whether a man of letters does not belong more to the country where he was brought up, formed, and educated, and where he composed his best works, than to the earth where he received life and whence he departed the same. It is a problem that I leave you to resolve amongst yourselves. I would rather refrain from speaking my mind on this matter; I would fear to incite your wrath, by depriving you of one of the greatest ornaments of your country.[42]

This type of assertion was to be repeated throughout the nineteenth century, especially around dates of particular Petrarchan significance.

On the occasion of a planning meeting for the fifth centenary celebrations in honour of Petrarch's birth organized by the Athénée de Vaucluse (a recently formed society charged with the promotion of local culture), it was, for instance, much less tentatively asserted by one of the Athénée's members, 'Citoyen' Piot, that:

> Though Petrarch was born and died beyond the Alps, he does not belong any less to this hospitable land. In Carpentras, he found teachers; in Avignon, a muse; in Vaucluse, the enthusiasm which produces poets. Without our schools, without Laura, without our happy sites, he might perhaps never have

---

[42] 'Que diriez-vous, si on osoit vous disputer Pétrarque ? Il a reçu le jour dans le sein de votre belle contrée, cela n'est pas douteux ; la Ville d'Arezzo l'a vu naître, on ne peut pas lui contester cet honneur ; mais il a fait ses études à Carpentras, à Avignon, à Montpellier. Ses meilleurs Ouvrages ont été conçus, commencés, plusieurs même achevés sur les bords de la Sorgue ; les rochers de Vaucluse ont répété mille fois les sons harmonieux de sa lyre ; dans ces belles Odes que vous admirez tant, il prend à témoin les sources, les bois, les monts & les prés de cette solitude : enfin, c'est là qu'il a conçu ce Poëme épique auquel il doit la couronne.

Il s'agit à présent de sçavoir, si un homme de Lettres n'appartient pas plus au Pays où il a été élevé, formé, instruit, où il a composé ses meilleurs Ouvrages, qu'à la terre où il a reçu & quitté la vie. C'est un problème que je vous laisse à résoudre. Je me garderois bien de dire sur cela ce que je pense : je craindrois d'exciter votre courroux, en vous enlevant un des plus grands ornemens de votre patrie.' Sade, *Mémoires*, i, pp. lxxi–lxxii.

become the glory of Italy nor the delight of the learned world. If homeland [*la patrie*] means above all the places where the mind is formed and the heart cultivated, Petrarch belongs to no one but us.[43]

In a surprising confluence of Petrarchism and politics, the pro-Petrarch Athénée de Vaucluse (from 1815, rebranded the Académie de Vaucluse) had, in fact, been founded only a few years earlier by none other than Napoleon himself, on 20 July 1801.[44] Napoleon's patronage of the society prompted the same Piot also to wonder:

If he had lived nowadays, Petrarch, so profound a politician, a skilful nego-tiator, and an ardent friend of wise liberty, would have looked on the rich and varied scene of France regenerated; what would he not have left to posterity on the inexhaustible subject of the great Napoleon, that sublime genius?[45]

Nineteenth-century French Petrarchism thus emerges as intimately bound up with political matters and motivations, and the same remains true of later Petrarchan anniversary celebrations, in particular those of 1874.

After the bold, Napoleon-inspired claims around the first Petrarchan centenary marked in this period (1804), later nineteenth-century French readers were to undertake a continued diminishment of Petrarch's Italianness, in favour of the same, reiterated proposal that Petrarch was, at heart, French. Hyacinthe d'Olivier Vitalis, for instance, declared in 1842 that 'Petrarch hardly owes his birth to Italy; France, which offered his parents a refuge, became the theatre of his celebrity'.[46] Events to celebrate the next significant Petrarchan date (1874) were, however, also shaped by an attempt to render the occasion a key moment of political unity and harmony between France and Italy, in the aftermath both of the Franco-Prussian war (a time of depression for the defeated France) and of the Risorgimento (the Unification of Italy, marking the emergence of a new, stronger, united neighbour for France). The

---

[43] 'Si Pétrarque naquit et mourut au-delà des Alpes, il n'appartient pas moins à cette terre hospitalière. À Carpentras, il trouva des instituteurs ; à Avignon, une muse ; à Vaucluse, l'enthousiasme qui fait les poètes. Sans nos écoles, sans Laure, sans nos heureux sites, il n'eût peut-être jamais fait la gloire de l'Italie, ni les délices du monde savant. Si la patrie est sur-tout aux lieux où l'esprit se forma, où se développa le cœur, Pétrarque n'est pas à d'autres qu'à nous.' Citoyen Piot, 'Proposition d'ériger à Vaucluse un monument public à la gloire de Pétrarque, le 20 juillet 1804 (1er Thermidor an 12), jour séculaire de sa naissance', in *Mémoires de l'Athénée de Vaucluse, contenant le compte rendu des travaux de cette Société depuis son institution, et le Recueil des ouvrages en prose et en vers, lus à sa séance publique le 2 Brumaire an XII* (Avignon: Alph. Berenguier, an XII (1804)), pp. 105–13 (pp. 105–6).
[44] See Duperray, *L'Or des mots*, p. 224.
[45] 'S'il eût vécu de nos jours, Pétrarque, si politique profond, négociateur habile, ami brûlant d'une liberté sage, il eût promené ses regards sur le tableau riche et varié de la France régénérée ; que n'eût-il pas laissé à la postérité, sur le sujet inépuisable du grand Napoléon, génie sublime ?' Piot, 'Proposition', p. 108.
[46] 'Pétrarque doit à peine sa naissance à l'Italie, et la France, qui offre à ses parents un asile, devient le théâtre de sa célébrité.' Hyacinthe d'Olivier-Vitalis, *L'Illustre Chatelaine des environs de Vaucluse, la Laure de Pétrarque: dissertation et examen critique* (Paris: Librairie historique et curieuse de J. Teschener, 1842), p. x.

desired expression of solidarity between France and Italy at this time is emphasized in Victor Hugo's commentary on the proceedings, *in absentia*:

> I congratulate Avignon. Avignon, which during these three memorable days, is going to put on an illustrious spectacle. We might say that Rome and Paris are going to meet there; Rome who crowned Petrarch, Paris who razed the Bastille to the ground; Rome who crowns poets, Paris who dethrones kings; Rome who glorifies human thought; Paris who frees it.
>
> This accolade of two mother cities is superb. It is the coming together of two ideas. There is nothing more moving nor more comforting. Rome and Paris fraternizing in saintly democratic communion is a beautiful thing. Your acclamations will give to this meeting all due meaning. Avignon, a city both pontifical and popular, is a lynchpin between the two capitals of the past and the future.[47]

In this vision, Petrarch is a mutual friend who can unite rather than antagonize relations between France and the newly formed Italy, even if, more polemically, Hugo concludes by proposing that the future is French, led by Paris rather than Rome. Yet the 1874 celebrations were, as I discuss in Chapter 4, also marked by intense local and regional pride, as is evident from the involvement of the Occitan poetic group the Félibrige. In this respect, the 1874 festivities were, despite Hugo's perspective, as much, perhaps even more, a chance to consolidate historical links between Petrarch and Avignon and to defend modern Occitan culture, as they were a meeting ground for the twin powers of Paris and Rome.

On the eve of the six-hundredth anniversary of Petrarch's birth, the scholar and translator Henry Cochin reiterated that Petrarch did indeed belong at least in part to France, through his patrons, friends, correspondents, poetry (citing the *incipit* of *RVF* 126), and even family:

> Petrarch belongs a little to France, whatever he might have said or thought himself; he belongs through King Robert of Anjou, his great patron, through our poor King Jean [John], who admired him, through all his French and Provençal friends, who loved him, from Pope Urban V, the cardinals of Boulogne and Cabassole, Bishop Philippe de Vitry, the monks Jean Birelle, Pierre de Bressuire, and Pierre Abbé de Saint-Bénigne de Dijon, down to the humble peasant Monet; but he belongs to us especially because of Provence, where the murmur can still be heard of the 'Clear, fresh, and sweet waters',

---

[47] 'Je félicite Avignon. Avignon, pendant ces trois jours mémorables, va donner un illustre spectacle. On pourrait dire que Rome et Paris vont s'y rencontrer ; Rome qui a sacré Pétrarque, Paris qui a jeté bas la Bastille ; Rome qui couronne les poëtes, Paris qui détrône les rois ; Rome qui glorifie la pensée humaine, Paris qui la délivre.
Cette accolade des deux cités mères est superbe. C'est l'embrassement de deux idées. Rien de plus pathétique et de plus rassurant. Rome et Paris fraternisant dans la sainte communion démocratique, c'est beau. Vos acclamations donneront à cette rencontre toute sa signification. Avignon, ville pontificale et ville populaire, est un trait d'union entre les deux capitales du passé et de l'avenir.' Victor Hugo, 'Le centenaire de Pétrarque', in *Œuvres complètes de Victor Hugo: Actes et paroles: III: Depuis l'exil 1870–1876* (Paris: J. Hetzel & Cie/A. Quantin, 1884), pp. 317–20 (p. 319).

Provence, where he left behind him, by moving away, his better half, his beloved brother.[48]

The political context might have changed since the words of Piot back in 1803, and the evidence may display greater familiarity with Petrarch's life and works, but the sentiment remains much the same. The only surprising detail is the final assertion that Gherardo and not Laura was Petrarch's beloved 'better half', and this detail is understandable given that Cochin is here introducing a work devoted—as the first part of the title proclaims—to *Le Frère de Pétrarque* (1903; *Petrarch's Brother*).

These claims for a Provençal Petrarch or 'Petrarch as a Poet of Provence' form a consistent accompaniment to the various manifestations of nineteenth-century French Petrarchism examined in this book.[49] In this way, Petrarch is seen as peculiarly and uniquely relevant to French nineteenth-century culture, particularly in southern climes. Moreover, as I have already begun to outline, it is my contention that such claims are particularly acute and urgent after the unification of Avignon with France, as a consequence of the bifocal, often divergent need both to preserve the specificity of Avignon's illustrious past and to integrate this past into part of a wider, national inheritance. From this perspective, it is hardly coincidental that both Sade and Piot, writing in Avignon, emphasize Petrarch's local connections (Carpentras, Avignon, Montpellier, the Sorgue river, Vaucluse), while the Parisian Cochin is keener to widen the perspective to France in general. Indeed, in a footnote to the passage cited above, Cochin defends himself against those who would seek to undermine as anachronistic his view of Provence as part of France, asserting that for Petrarch medieval Provence was already perceived as essentially French: 'In vain will people inform me that Provence was at that time hardly French at all. Petrarch did not judge matters thus.'[50] For the Parisian Cochin, it is desirable that Petrarch be subsumed into a larger whole, even at the cost of historical revisionism.

The debate over Petrarch's true identity amongst French writers raises further questions: what are the key parts of a person's identity? How can we know someone who is long dead? One recurrent answer is that Petrarch can only be understood

[48] 'Pétrarque appartient un peu à la France, quoi qu'il ait pu en dire et en penser lui-même ; il lui appartient par le roi Robert d'Anjou, son grand patron, par notre pauvre roi Jean, qui l'admira, par tous les amis Français ou Provençaux, qui l'aimèrent, depuis le pape Urbain V, les cardinaux de Boulogne et de Cabassole, l'évêque Philippe de Vitry, les religieux Jean Birelle, Pierre de Bressuire, Pierre Abbé de Saint-Bénigne de Dijon, jusqu'à l'humble paysan Monet ; mais il nous appartient surtout par la Provence, où murmurent encore les "Claires, fraîches et douces eaux", la Provence, où il laissa derrière lui, en s'éloignant, la meilleure moitié de lui-même, son frère bien-aimé.' Henry Cochin, *Le Frère de Pétrarque et le livre 'Du repos des religieux'* (Paris: Librairie Émile Bouillon, 1903), pp. 1–2.

[49] For these appellations in more recent scholarship see Maurizio Perugi, 'Petrarca provenzale', *Quaderni petrarcheschi*, 7 (1990), 109–81, and Paden, 'Petrarch as a Poet of Provence'.

[50] 'En vain me dira-t-on que la Provence était alors bien peu Française. Pétrarque n'en jugeait pas ainsi.' Cochin, *Le Frère de Pétrarque*, p. 2. Technically, Provence only became part of France in 1486, when it came under the control of Louis XI, although it is true that Petrarch tended to refer to France according to the general concept of Gaul, inherited from Roman times.

with reference to those he loved, namely, for Cochin, his brother Gherardo (as cited above), and for most other readers, his beloved Laura. In this respect, discussion of Petrarch's identity leads inevitably to the question: who was Petrarch's Laura?

The French Beloved

'Every age claims its own Beatrice', the Dante scholar Guglielmo Gorni once declared.[51] The same is true of Petrarch's Laura, and no more so than in the nineteenth century, which was obsessed—to borrow another phrase from Dante studies—by a 'quest for the historical' Laura behind the poetic figure.[52] This quest was particularly vital for French readers of Petrarch, for whom Laure as a French lady was a key component of the postulation of the poet's own Frenchness. Yet despite the certainty that Laura did exist and was French or Provençal, other facets of her character remained murky and a source of contention: was she married? Or a virgin? Did she have any children? Which city, town, or village can truly claim the honour of her birthplace and/or place of burial? As one French reader commented in the late eighteenth century, Petrarch's Italian poetry inevitably led to 'the desire to know who was this beautiful Laura who made his lyre produce such tender and passionate airs'.[53]

Petrarch himself provided vital information about Laura in a handwritten note on the flyleaf of his copy of Virgil, preserved in the Biblioteca Ambrosiana in Milan:

> Laura, illustrious through her own virtues, and long famed through my verses, first appeared to my eyes in my youth, in the year of our Lord 1327, on the sixth day of April, in the church of St. Clare in Avignon, at matins; and in the same city, also on the sixth day of April, at the same first hour, but in the year 1348, the light of her life was withdrawn from the light of day, while I, as it chanced, was in Verona, unaware of my fate. The sad tidings reached me in Parma, in the same year, on the morning of the 19th day of May, in a letter from my Ludovicus. Her chaste and lovely form was laid to rest at vesper time, on the same day on which she died, in the burial place of the Brothers Minor. I am persuaded that her soul returned to the heaven from which it came, as Seneca says of Africanus. I have thought to write this, in bitter memory, yet with a certain bitter sweetness, here in this place that is often before my eyes, so that I may be admonished, by the sight of these words and by the consideration of

---

[51] 'Ogni età reclama una sua propria Beatrice'. Guglielmo Gorni, 'Beatrice agli inferi', in *Omaggio a Beatrice 1290–1990*, ed. Rudy Abardo (Florence: Le Lettere, 1997), pp. 143–58 (p. 146).

[52] I model this phrase on 'The quest for the historical Beatrice' in Alison Milbank, *Dante and the Victorians* (Manchester: Manchester University Press, 1998), pp. 102–16. For a summary of the various historical figures proposed as Petrarch's Laura, not limited to the nineteenth century, see Emmanuel Davin, 'Les différentes Laure de Pétrarque', *Bulletin de l'Association Guillaume Budé: lettres d'humanité*, 15 (December 1956), 83–104.

[53] 'le désir de connoître quelle fut cette belle Laure qui fit naître sur sa lyre des airs si tendres & si passionnés', Alexandre Delon, *Les Vies de Pétrarque et de Laure, et description de la Fontaine de Vaucluse; et 'Laure et Pétrarque', poème* (Nismes: Buchet, 1788), p. 12.

the swift flight of time, that there is nothing in this life in which I should find pleasure; and that it is time, now that the strongest tie is broken, to flee from Babylon; and this, by the prevenient grace of God, should be easy for me, if I meditate deeply and manfully on the futile cares, the empty hopes, and the unforeseen events of my past years.[54]

Despite the information here provided about Laura by Petrarch himself, this note was considered throughout the nineteenth century to be of dubious authenticity, and so its contents were typically discounted by readers. Questions about all aspects of Laura's identity remained, then, open to discussion and debate, as I will discuss with particular reference to the polarized views of the abbé de Sade's *Mémoires* and the abbé Costaing de Pusignan's *La Muse de Pétrarque* (1819; *Petrarch's Muse*). These two writers represent a wider tension, even a literary *querelle*, between competing views of Laura in the late eighteenth and nineteenth centuries: virgin or mother; Avignonese or Vauclusian.[55]

A preoccupation with the historical personage of Laura was hardly new to the nineteenth century. As early as 1525, the influential early modern commentator and editor of Petrarch's poetry, Alessandro Vellutello, had argued that Petrarch's Laura was a certain Laure de Chiabau from Cabrières, setting a trend for scholarly claims for the historical identity of Petrarch's beloved, often rooted in a specific geographical landscape.[56] Soon afterwards, in 1533, the French poet Maurice Scève claimed to have found Laura's tomb and remains in a church in Avignon. In confirmation of this discovery, he reported that the grave contained a poem and a medallion featuring the image of a lady and inscribed with the initials M.L.M.I. (interpreted

---

[54] 'Laurea, propriis uirtutibus illustris et meis longum celebrata carminibus, primum oculis meis apparuit sub primum adolescentie mee tempus, anno Domini m° iij^c xxviij die vj° mensis Aprilis in ecclesia sancte Clare Auin. hora matutina; et in eadem ciuitate eodem mense Aprili eodem die sexto eadem hora prima, anno autem m° iij^c xlviij° ab hac luce lux illa subtracta est, cum ego forte tunc Verone essem, heu! fati mei nescius. Rumor autem infelix per literas Ludouici mei me Parme repperit, anno eodem mense Maio die xix° mane. Corpus illud castissimum atque pulcerrimum in loco Fratrum Minorum repositum est, ipso die mortis ad uesperam. Animam quidem eius, ut de Africano ait Seneca, in celum, unde erat, rediisse persuadeo michi. Hec autem ad acerbam rei memoriam amara quadam dulcedine scribere uisum est, hoc potissimum loco qui sepe sub oculis meis redit, ut scilicet nichil esse debere quod amplius mihi placeat in hac uita et, effracto maiori laqueo, tempus esse de Babilone fugiendi crebra horum inspectione ac fugacissime etatis estimatione conmonear, quod, preuia Dei gratia, facile erit preteriti temporis curas superuacuas spes inanes et inexpectatos exitus acriter ac uiriliter cogitanti.' English translation from E. H. Wilkins, *The Life of Petrarch* (Chicago: University of Chicago Press, 1961), p. 77; Latin transcription from Pierre de Nolhac, *Pétrarque et l'humanisme*, 2 vols (Paris: Honoré Champion, 1907), II, 286–7, where it is introduced as authentic.

[55] On the *querelle* as a motivating force in intellectual and literary history, see Alain Viala, 'Un temps de querelles', *Littératures classiques*, 8 (2013), 5–22.

[56] *Le volgari opere del Petrarcha con la espositione di Alessandro Vellutello da Lucca* (Venice: Giovanni Antonio et Fratelli da Sabbio, 1525). On Vellutello, see William J. Kennedy, *Authorizing Petrarch* (Ithaca, NY: Cornell University Press, 1994) and Gino Belloni, *Laura tra Petrarca e Bembo: studi sul commento umanistico-rinascimentale al 'Canzoniere'* (Padua: Editrice Antenore, 1992).

by Scève as 'Madonna Laura Morta Iace', 'Here lies the deceased lady Laura'). The veracity of this claim was sealed by a visit to the site by none other than François Ier, who composed a poem to mark the occasion.[57]

Following in the wake of illustrious historical precedent for such contentions, questions about Laura's identity became newly pressing for French readers of Petrarch in the nineteenth century as a result of various controversial claims made about Petrarch's Laura by the abbé de Sade in his *Mémoires*. Alongside his bid for a Provençal Petrarch (cited above), Sade was also the committed spokesperson for a Laura who had been not only French but more specifically Avignonese, and indeed from the author's own family. Notes at the end of the first volume trace the Sade family genealogy back to Hugues de Sade, Laure's husband, and also affirm Laura's birthplace as Avignon.[58] Similarly, the third and final volume ends with a number of 'justificatory documents' (*pieces justificatives*), including a marriage contract between Hugues de Sade and Laure de Noves, as well as the will of Laure de Noves, wife of Hugues de Sade, dated 3 April 1348, only days before the death date (6 April 1348) given by Petrarch for his beloved.[59] These valuable documents were, until the Revolution, preserved in the family archive, whence Sade transcribed their contents; since then, the published *Mémoires* have been their only witness. This is not to say that Sade necessarily invented these documents. Rather, more open to scrutiny may be the assumption that somebody called Laure, living contemporaneously with Petrarch and from Avignon, must automatically have been Petrarch's Laura. Yet Sade's proposed identification made good use of available, convincing textual evidence, and his version of events was to prove persuasive and long-lasting, despite subsequent challenges.

Sade revived interest in Petrarch in France in part by claiming that he was a descendant of Laura and therefore peculiarly placed to write an authoritative history of Petrarch drawing on unique material from his family archive. For Sade, it was literally true that, as Gaston Paris was later to affirm, 'the literature of the Middle Ages [...] is the first chapter of our family memoirs'.[60] It is as if Sade had taken to heart Benjamin's later advice that translators should aim not merely for 'likeness' but rather for 'kinship' with their chosen original.[61] Sade's claim of genealogical descent from Petrarch's Laura was to be reiterated by the French poet Alphonse de

---

[57]   On this key episode of French Petrarchism, see: Olivier Millet, 'Le tombeau de la morte et la voix du poète: la mémoire de Pétrarque en France autour de 1533', in *Regards sur le passé dans l'Europe des XVIe et XVIIe siècles: actes du colloque organisé par l'Université de Nancy II (14 au 16 décembre 1995)*, ed. Francine Wild (Bern: Peter Lang, 1997), pp. 183–95; Enzo Giudici, 'Bilancio di un'annosa questione: Maurice Scève e "la scoperta" della tomba di Laura', *Quaderni di filologia e lingue romanze*, 2 (1980), 3–70; Duperray, *L'Or des mots*, pp. 160–5.

[58]   Sade, *Mémoires*, I, 29–39 and 40–9 (from the 'Notes' section).

[59]   Sade, *Mémoires*, III, 22–5 and 83–5 (also from the 'Notes' section).

[60]   'La littérature du moyen âge [...] est le premier chapitre de nos mémoires de famille.' Gaston Paris, *La Poésie du Moyen Âge: leçons et lectures*, 2 vols (Paris: Librairie Hachette, 1885–95), I, p. xiv.

[61]   Walter Benjamin, 'The Task of the Translator: An Introduction to the Translation of Baudelaire's *Tableaux parisiens*', in *Illuminations*, ed. Hannah Arendt and trans. Harry Zorn (London: Pimlico, 1999), pp. 70–82 (p. 74).

Lamartine, in his *Cours familier de littérature* (1856–69; *Informal Course in Literature*), from a similarly personal perspective:

> The (hi)story [again, *histoire*] of Laure has been written with the pride of kinship by the abbé de Sade, a descendent of this angelic lady; by a chance of fate, my maternal family also goes back to this same source. The chronological family tree leaves no shred of doubt in this regard. My mother had the blood of Laura in her veins just as she had Laura's charm and piety. I do not boast about this, because there is no glory in chance; but I have always been pleased about it, because poetry and beauty have always been in my eyes the true nobility of women.[62]

Zrinka Stahuljak has argued that nineteenth-century genealogy tended to insist much more on biological bloodline than did its medieval counterpart, and this observation certainly rings true for Lamartine's celebration of his material affinity to Laura via his mother's blood (*sang*).[63] A further figure in this Sadean family tree is the comtesse de Chevigné, née Laure de Sade, to whom Proust wrote, no doubt flattering her august descent (and shared first name), of the enduring truth of 'the eternal (hi)story of Petrarch and of Laura', cited above. To the question posed in Honoré de Balzac's *Le Lys dans la vallée* (1836; *The Lily in the Valley*)—'Can Petrarch's Laura be again renewed?'—the genealogical connection insisted on by Sade, Lamartine, and Proust answers in the affirmative.[64]

Sade's identification of Petrarch's Laura was to prove popular and influential, even beyond later family members such as Lamartine, for whom the literary ancestry was understandably tempting.[65] Yet Sade's thesis was not without its detractors,

---

[62] 'L'histoire de Laure a été écrite avec l'orgueil de la parenté par l'abbé de Sades [*sic*], descendant de cette femme angélique ; par un hasard de la destinée, ma famille maternelle remonte également à cette source. L'arbre chronologique de cette famille ne laisse à cet égard aucun doute. Ma mère avait du sang de Laure dans les veines comme elle en avait le charme et la piété. Je ne m'en glorifie pas, car il n'y a point de gloire dans le hasard ; mais je m'en suis toujours félicité, car la poésie et la beauté ont été toujours à mes yeux les vraies noblesses des femmes.' 'XXXIe entretien: vie et œuvres de Pétrarque', in Lamartine, *Cours familier de littérature*, 28 vols (Paris: Chez l'auteur, 1856–69), VI (1858), 1–79 (p. 14). I return to Lamartine in Chapter 5. A further poetic chain in the family tree traced by Sade back to Laura is Christina Rossetti: see Zuccato, *Petrarch in Romantic England*, p. 153.

[63] See Zrinka Stahuljak, *Pornographic Archeology: Medicine, Medievalism, and the Invention of the French Nation* (Philadelphia: University of Pennsylvania Press, 2013); idem, *Bloodless Genealogies of the French Middle Ages: Translatio, Kinship, and Metaphor* (Gainesville: University Press of Florida, 2005); idem, 'Genealogy', in *Medievalism: Key Critical Terms*, pp. 71–8.

[64] 'La Laure de Pétrarque peut-elle se recommencer ?' Honoré de Balzac, *Le Lys dans la vallée*, ed. Jean-Hervé Donnard, in *La Comédie humaine*, ed. Pierre-Georges Castex, 12 vols (Paris: Gallimard, 1976–81), IX (1978), 873–1229 (p. 1035), with English translation from Balzac, *The Lily in the Valley* (London: The Caxton Publishing Company, 1897), p. 110. All subsequent quotations in French and English are from these editions. On the role of invocations of Petrarch in this novel, see Chapter 6.

[65] For instance, Morris Bishop, writing in the early 1960s, still believes the identification of Petrarch's Laura with Laure de Sade to be certain: Bishop, *Petrarch and his World* (London: Chatto & Windus, 1964), p. 65. See also: Gennaro Ferrante, 'Laura de Sade tra leggenda e

who often countered his claims with suggestions of their own. Sade's critics were often themselves abbés, confirming the truth of the somewhat caustic remark by the president of the Académie de Vaucluse on the occasion of the festivities for the sixth centenary of Petrarch's birth in 1904: 'the extent to which our abbés have been preoccupied by Laura is unbelievable.'[66] Duperray offers the following explanation of this abbé-led Laura-mania: 'For many Petrarchist priests who carried out their ministry in the area of Vaucluse, she was the only temptation to which they could succumb without sin. All their hours of leisure were spent on erudite research concerning the poet's mystical lover.'[67] Sade's Laura was an urban, noble construct, born in Avignon, deceased and buried there likewise, married to his ancestral Hugues de Sade, and mother to eleven children. Subsequent readers (often, abbés) would take issue with Sade's narrative on all of these points.

The first refutation of note came from the abbé Costaing de Pusignan, in a volume dating from 1819, entitled *La Muse de Pétrarque*. In this work, Costaing had an uphill struggle in his quest to convince readers that many cherished facts of Petrarchan biography, especially as promulgated by Sade, were in fact fallacious. Costaing's justifications clearly demonstrate the ways in which both philology and translation involve ideological choices and are inevitably permeated by desire. Against Sade's Avignonese ancestor, Costaing presented an alternative narrative, that of Petrarch's love for a virgin, Laure des Baux, in the rustic setting of Vaucluse. Costaing also denied that Petrarch had had two illegitimate children, a fact discussed by Sade (and accepted by modern scholarship), since this would, in his eyes, have rendered Petrarch, unacceptably, 'an utter libertine' (*un libertin achevé*).[68] Faced with the compelling evidence of a Jean (Giovanni) and a Françoise (Francesca) close to Petrarch, as testified by letters written by the poet himself, Costaing decided that Jean was an adopted (not biological) son, and that Françoise was the name of both Petrarch's sister and her daughter (i.e. Petrarch's niece). In this way, Costaing purged Petrarch of charges of immoderate, forbidden lust and Laura of the taint of sexual relations, even within the context of marriage. Costaing's assessment of the value of Petrarch's poetry relies heavily on the moral integrity of the poet, and he thus takes

identificazione storica: la testimonianza inedita di un biografo di Petrarca', *Annali dell'Istituto italiano per gli studi storici*, 24 (2009), 169–99; Frederic J. Jones, 'Further Evidence of the Identity of Laura', *Italian Studies*, 39 (1984), 27–46, and 'I rapporti tra la Laure de Sade e la Laura del Petrarca', *Italianistica: rivista di letteratura italiana*, 21.2–3 (1992), 485–501; Thibault de Sade, 'Les Sade et Pétrarque', in *La Postérité répond à Pétrarque*, pp. 187–96.

[66] 'Il est incroyable combien les abbés chez nous se sont intéressés à Laure.' Le baron de Vissac, 'Discours du président de l'Académie', in Académie de Vaucluse, *Sixième centenaire de la naissance de Pétrarque célébré à Vaucluse et Avignon les 16, 17, et 18 juillet 1904* (Avignon: François Seguin, 1904), pp. 60–8 (p. 64).

[67] 'Pour de nombreux curés pétrarquistes qui exercèrent leur ministère dans l'environnement de Vaucluse, elle fut la seule tentation à laquelle ils pouvaient succomber sans faillir. Toutes leurs heures de loisir étaient consacrées à des recherches érudites sur l'amante mystique du poète.' Duperray, *L'Or des mots*, p. 198.

[68] Costaing de Pusignan (abbé) *La Muse de Pétrarque dans les collines de Vaucluse, ou Laure des Baux, sa solitude et son tombeau dans le vallon de Galas* (Paris: Chez Rapet; Avignon: Chez Bonnet fils, 1819), p. 245.

pains to clear Petrarch's name of indecency both in relation to putative illegitimate offspring and to the Sadean thesis of Petrarch's love for a married woman.

From this perspective, the foundational moment of Petrarch's love at first sight, in the church of St Clare in Avignon on Good Friday, had also to be relocated. There is good textual evidence in support of Good Friday, given not only the previously cited note in Petrarch's copy of Virgil (discounted, at this time, as inauthentic) but also *RVF* 3, which situates the first sight of Laura on that holiest of days: 'It was the day the sun's rays lost their colour [*si scoloraro*] out of pity for their Creator.'[69] For Costaing, however, the idea that Petrarch could have fallen in love in church, on a Good Friday, was impossible: 'Would the most libertine poet have wanted to write a sonnet to publicize his blindness for a woman, if this had taken place in a church one Good Friday, on a day which is so little suited to dissipation?'[70] As a result, Costaing insisted on reading the end of the opening line of *RVF* 3 not as a reference to the sun's pallor or loss of colour (drawing on Gospel accounts of the darkening of the sky on the day of Christ's Crucifixion), but rather as the much more anodyne meteorological detail 'under a sun of rare colour' (*al sol di color raro*).[71]

A similarly new reading lay behind Costaing's rejection of the idea that Petrarch's beloved, virginal Laura might be described as *fera*, either as an adjective ('proud') or a noun ('wild beast').[72] Instead, despite lyric precedent for such descriptors, Costaing proposed in each case the reading *sfera* ('sphere'), in line with other angelic qualities of the lady. As Costaing explained, rendering the reader complicit in his argumentation: 'Everybody knows, moreover, that the word *fera*, in Italian, is applicable only to a wild beast, and that the word *fiera*, is that which expresses a proud person in the meaning of these authors; but Petrarch never has recourse to low or vulgar expressions.'[73] Costaing deliberately attacks the typically Petrarchan oxymoronic force of phrases such as 'this angelic innocent wild creature' (*questa fera angelica innocente*, *RVF* 134, v. 45), reading them instead as purely celestially orientated by substituting for *fera*, *sfera* ('sphere').

Costaing's principal desire to overturn Sade's proposal of a married Laura, mother of many children, could not be resolved merely by discrediting the *Mémoires* and arguing from purported common sense that such beautiful poetry could only

[69] 'Era il giorno ch'al sol si scoloraro / per la pietà del suo fattore i rai.' *RVF* 3, vv. 1–2. Note that throughout this book all Italian quotations marked *RVF* are from Francesco Petrarca, *Canzoniere*, ed. Marco Santagata, 4th edn (Milan: Arnoldo Mondadori, 2010), with English translations my own.

[70] 'Le poëte le plus libertin aurait-il voulu faire un sonnet pour publier son aveuglement pour une femme, si la chose se fût passée dans une église un vendredi saint, jour qui prête si peu à la dissipation ?' Costaing, *La Muse de Pétrarque*, pp. 107–8.

[71] Costaing, *La Muse de Pétrarque*, p. 106. In contrast, for more recent critical discussion of the Biblical intertexts for *scoloraro*, see Sabrina Stroppa, '"Obscuratus est sol". Codice lirico e codice biblico in *RVF* III', *Lettere italiane*, 56.2 (April–June 2004), 165–89.

[72] For the adjective, see, for instance, *RVF* 174 (with anaphora on 'fera', including 'fera donna', 'cruel lady', v. 5), and for the noun, *RVF* 135, v. 45.

[73] 'Tout le monde sait d'ailleurs que le mot *fera*, en italien, n'est applicable qu'à une bête sauvage, et que le mot *fiera*, est celui qui exprime une personne fière dans le sens de ces auteurs ; mais Pétrarque n'a jamais recours aux expressions basses et vulgaires.' Costaing, *La Muse de Pétrarque*, p. 205.

have been the response of an entirely chaste poet to an entirely chaste lady. Instead, Costaing also had to overcome evidence from Book Three of Petrarch's *Secretum* (*My Secret Book*), a Latin prose dialogue between two figures named as Franciscus and Augustinus. In the *Secretum*, it is stated that Laura's body had been weakened and compromised by having given birth a number of times: 'That wonderful body, worn out by illness and frequent childbirth, has already lost much of its former health and strength'.[74] This passage, given in French translation by Sade in his *Mémoires*, includes the detail that Laura's beautiful body had been exhausted by *plusieurs couches* ('repeated childbirth').[75] To this translation Sade added a footnote with the relevant Latin (identical to the modern edition), stressing that his reading of *partubus* (from *partus*, 'birth') ought to replace the typical reading in printed editions of *perturbationibus* (from *perturbatio*, a somewhat vaguer ailment denoting disturbance or confusion of either a physical or a mental nature): 'The printed books have *perturbationibus*, instead of *partubus*: this, however, is a mistake. Two reliable manuscripts of the *Bibliothèque du roi*, 6502 and 6728, contain *ptubs*, which is without doubt the abbreviation of *partubus*.'[76]

Costaing, like Sade, disagrees with the earlier reading of *perturbationibus* in various printings of the *Secretum*, although he rejects Sade's proposed interpretation of *partubus* (incontrovertible evidence that Petrarch's Laura was not a virgin), substituting in turn his own alternative. Costaing wants to clarify his own view of the precise cause of Laura's death, neither childbirth nor even the plague (another commonly adduced reason), but, in a classic nineteenth-century twist to the tale, consumption:

> All the editions contain the word *perturbationibus*, instead of *ptysmatibus*, the manuscript reads *ptūbs*, and the same can be read in the manuscript of the royal library. Now, the only possible expansion of this abbreviation is *phtysmatibus*, if we follow the meaning of the text which establishes the loss of energy and the languorous state into which the body of the sick lady had fallen, exhausted by frequent expectoration, indicated by the word *phtysma*. Laura died of consumption.[77]

---

[74] 'Corpus illud egregium, morbis ac crebris partubus exhaustum, multum pristini vigoris amisit.' Latin text cited from Petrarca, *Secretum* [*De secreto conflictu curarum mearum*], ed. Enrico Carrara, in *Prose* (Milan and Naples: Riccardo Ricciardi, 1955), pp. 22–215 (p. 138), with English translation from Petrarch, *My Secret Book*, trans. J. G. Nichols (London: Hesperus Press, 2002), p. 59.

[75] 'Ce beau corps [...], épuisé par les maladies & *par plusieurs couches*, a déjà perdu beaucoup de sa force, & de son éclat.' Sade, *Mémoires*, II, 114 (emphasis in the original).

[76] 'Dans les imprimés il y a *perturbationibus*, au lieu de *partubus*; mais c'est une faute. Dans deux Mss. très-bons de la bibliothèque du Roi, 6502. & 6728. il y a *ptubs*. qui est certainement l'abbréviation de *partubus*.' Sade, *Mémoires*, II, 114. Many early printed editions of the *Secretum* do seem to have *perturbationibus*: see, for instance, Petrarch, *De contemptu mundi, colloquiorum liber quem Secretum suum inscripsit; De VII. psalmi poenitentiales* (Bern: Ioannes le Preux, 1604), bound with *De vita solitaria* (Bern: Ioannes le Preux, 1605) [Bodleian Toynbee 1885], p. 102.

[77] 'On lit dans toutes les éditions, le mot : *perturbationibus*, au lieu de *ptysmatibus*, il est écrit dans le manuscrit *ptūbs*, et de même dans le manuscrit de la bibliothèque du roi.

Costaing's designation of Petrarch's Laura not merely as a virgin and not Laure de Sade, but more specifically as Laure des Baux, relied not only on philological and paleographical evidence, but also on translation. One striking example is his insistence on the connection between Laura and the orange tree (*oranger*), essential to his claim that Petrarch's Laura was Laure des Baux of the *maison d'Orange*. Thus Costaing's translation of *canzone RVF* 325 renders the detail in line 32 of 'the green ensign of victory' (*la victorïosa insegna verde*) as 'this victorious and beautiful green–orange [*verd–orange*] ensign'.[78] This type of translation is more potent and persuasive in the absence of the original Italian corresponding to this section of the poem. Costaing consistently interprets Petrarch's laurel as a *laurier orange*, ignoring mythological precedents (in particular, the story of Apollo and Daphne) in favour of a genealogical explanation of the connection between Laura and the here orange laurel.

Costaing's defence of a virginal Laura against Sade's married Laure de Sade was motivated by sentiments of morality and propriety, and was to be reiterated throughout the nineteenth century, even if the specific historical identity of the virgin often varied.[79] Subsequent Petrarch enthusiasts, who sided with Costaing against Sade in terms of Laura's likely marital status, ultimately proposed other virgins in competition with Costaing's Laure des Baux. One common solution that combined aspects of the theses of both Sade and Costaing was that Laura might well have been Laure de Sade, but that this person was either the daughter of Paul de Sade or the sister rather than the wife of Hugues de Sade.[80] This last interpretation

---

Or, on ne peut rendre cette abréviation que par *phtysmatibus*, si l'on veut suivre le sens du texte qui établit la perte des forces et l'état de langueur dans lequel était tombé le corps de la malade, fatigué des fréquentes expectorations, désignées par le mot *phtysma*. Laure mourut de consumption.' Costaing, *La Muse de Pétrarque*, p. 158. The only two French translations of the *Secretum* in the nineteenth century, both towards the end of the century, entirely ignore Costaing's machinations over these lines, and though neither translation is published with facing Latin, one can assume from the French that both translators are taking the word to be *partubus*. In the first French translation, Victor Develay writes that 'ce beau corps, épuisé par des maladies et des couches fréquentes, a beaucoup perdu de sa première vigueur', and the translation in Pompée Mabille is almost identical apart from punctuation: see *Mon secret, ou du conflit de mes passions, traduit pour la première fois par Victor Develay*, 3 vols (Paris: Librairie des Bibliophiles, 1879), III, 25, and *Mon secret, ou du mépris du monde: confessions de Pétrarque translaté du latin en quasi français par le docteur Pompée Mabille* (Angers: Imprimerie P. Lachèse et Dolbeau, 1886), p. 84. Further, Develay clearly sides with Sade rather than Costaing, given his footnote to these lines: 'Laure de Noves, épouse de Hugues de Sade, a eu neuf enfants' ('Laure de Noves, wife of Hugues de Sade, had nine children'). On the translation of the Latin Petrarch into French, see Chapter 3.

[78] 'cette victorieuse et belle enseigne verd–orange', Costaing, *La Muse de Pétrarque*, p. 58.

[79] See, for instance, the findings of Olivier-Vitalis, *L'Illustre Chatelaine des environs de Vaucluse*, as well as those of Théodore Pierre, *Abrégé de l'histoire de Pétrarque contenant les principaux traits de sa vie et les différents phases de son amour avec la belle Laure d'après ses propres écrits et ceux des meilleurs auteurs et traducteurs anciens* (Vaucluse: Maria Brun; Avignon: Seguin frères, 1879).

[80] Frédéric Mistral, *Lou tresor dóu Felibrige, ou, Dictionnaire provençal-français: embrassant les divers dialectes de la langue d'oc moderne*, 2 vols (Aix-en-Provence: Vve Remondet-Aubin, 1878–86), II, 831 (entry on 'Sado' specifying that Laure de Sade was the daughter of

received the approval of Léon de Berluc-Pérussis, the chief organizer of the 1874 celebrations on the anniversary of Petrarch's death, who explained the importance of Laura's virginity in the following terms:

> Was the Laura beloved of the immortal dreamer of Vaucluse the sister or the wife of Hugues de Sade? Did Petrarch fall in love with an ideal young girl or a prosaic matron? In other words, placing the question on the elevated ground which it deserves, was the poet's love pure or adulterous?
>
> This problem, as we know, has provoked much research and passionate debate, neither of which seems anywhere near coming to an end. The celebration of the centenary festival of Petrarch has given this question new relevance and importance which no one could fail to notice.
>
> If, in effect, the ancient deceased whom Latin nations have just glorified owed his inspiration and immortality to nothing more than a perverse desire, would he really deserve the posthumous honours that after five hundred years have been lavished on his tomb?
>
> If, in contrast, his passion was legitimate, would it not be essential, for the honour of literature, to proclaim as much as soon as possible? Should we any longer allow people to believe that a despicable thought could have inspired such noble and splendid accents? Is it not our duty to disillusion those who, through an error that is aesthetically and morally monstrous, have believed that Evil could engender Good?[81]

In the mocking description of Laura, wife of Hugues de Sade, as 'a prosaic matron', Berluc-Pérussis from the start of this passage aligns poetic truth with youth and virginity (the 'ideal young girl') and rejects as unpoetic, that is, prosaic, the belief in a married Laura. As the conclusion of the passage makes very clear, Berluc-Pérussis, like Costaing before him, refuses to believe that 'Evil' (an adulterous love) can produce 'Good' (immortal poetry).

In contrast to these arguments in favour of Laura as virgin, the translator

---

Paul de Sade); A. Bruce-Whyte, *Histoire des langues romanes et de leur littérature, depuis leur origine jusqu'au XIV siècle*, 3 vols (Paris: Treuttel et Würtz, 1841), III, 338–96.

[81]   'La Laure aimée de l'immortel rêveur de Vaucluse, était-elle la sœur ou la femme d'Hugues de Sade ? Pétrarque s'éprit-il d'une idéale jeune fille, ou d'une prosaïque matrone ? En d'autres termes, et pour placer la question sur le terrain élevé qui lui convient, l'amour du poète fut-il pur ou adultère ?

Ce problème, on le sait, a provoqué des recherches nombreuses, des discussions passionnées, et qui ne semblent pas près de finir. La célébration de la fête séculaire de Pétrarque lui a donné une actualité et une importance qui ne peuvent échapper à personne.

Si, en effet, le vieux mort que les nations latines viennent de glorifier n'a dû ses inspirations et son immortalité qu'à une ardeur perverse, mériterait-il bien les honneurs posthumes qu'après cinq cents ans nous avons prodigués sur sa tombe ?

Si, au contraire, sa passion fut légitime, ne faut-il pas, pour l'honneur des lettres, le proclamer bien vite ? Doit-on plus longtemps laisser croire qu'une pensée détestable a pu inspirer de nobles et splendides accents ? N'est-ce pas un devoir de désillusionner ceux qui, par une erreur monstrueuse en esthétique comme en morale, ont cru que le Mal pouvait engendrer le Beau ?' Léon de Berluc-Pérussis, *Un document inédit sur Laure de Sade: extrait des Mémoires de l'Académie d'Aix* (Aix-en-Provence: Chez Marius Illy, 1876), pp. 3–4.

Philibert Le Duc, around the same time that Berluc-Pérussis was writing, instead recommended reading Petrarch with the mores of courtly love in mind. According to the model of *amour courtois*, a term coined by Gaston Paris and itself as much an invention of the nineteenth century as the Middle Ages, love could not exist inside marriage, and love for a married lady was supposed to lead not to adultery but to a necessary preservation of chastity, in an idealized form of love often from afar (*amor de lonh*).[82] For Philibert Le Duc, therefore, love for a virgin (the thesis of Costaing et al.) would be more shocking, inappropriate, and potentially sinful, than love for a married lady (such as Laure de Sade, in the abbé de Sade's narrative), precisely because of the lack of marriage as a barrier to intimate relations. As Le Duc explained, 'We can have no doubt that Petrarch, in taking the wife of Hugues de Sade as the lady of his thoughts, was merely following the laws of chivalry, which must not be judged according to our modern ideas.'[83] In all these readings of Petrarch post-Sade, the precise identity of the lady may vary, but the desire to found poetry on moral ground (albeit variously defined and justified) is consistently voiced.

Costaing's proposal of Laure des Baux as the true identity of Petrarch's Laura was not, however, merely a matter of moral and aesthetic taste, but was equally motivated by geographical preference. In essence, Sade had proposed an Avignonese Laura who had been both born and buried in the city. In contrast, Costaing opposed to Sade's *Laure de Provence* his own *Laure de Vaucluse*, whose life, encounters with Petrarch, and eventual death and burial were all played out against an idyllic, rural backdrop.[84] This tension mirrored Petrarch's own alternation between Avignon and Vaucluse, that is, between hectic city life and solitary country retreat. Yet the history of Petrarch's Laura as told by nineteenth-century French—and typically much more local—readers tended to be uncomfortable with this instability and contradiction, preferring instead to imagine Laura as either wholly urban (Sade) or wholly rural (Costaing). In this manner, French readers from Sade throughout the nineteenth century created their own Petrarchan myths, in which place and the memory of place (Pierre Nora's *lieux de mémoire*) played a vital role in shaping, situating, and authenticating their narratives.[85] Crucially, both sides of the debate over Laura's birthplace of necessity ignored words recorded by Petrarch as uttered by Laura in

---

[82] See Isabel DiVanna, *Reconstructing the Middle Ages: Gaston Paris and the Development of Nineteenth-Century Medievalism* (Newcastle upon Tyne: Cambridge Scholars, 2008) and Ji-hyun Philippa Kim, *Pour une littérature médiévale moderne: Gaston Paris, l'amour courtois et les enjeux de la modernité* (Paris: Honoré Champion, 2012).

[83] 'On n'en peut douter, Pétrarque, en prenant la femme de Hugues de Sade pour dame de ses pensées, ne fit que suivre les lois de la chevalerie, et ne doit pas être jugé avec nos idées modernes.' Le Duc, *Les Sonnets de Pétrarque*, I, p. xli.

[84] Costaing, *La Muse de Pétrarque*, p. 64 (emphases in the original).

[85] See *Les Lieux de mémoire*, ed. Pierre Nora, 4 vols (Paris: Gallimard, 1984–6) and, for other and earlier examples of the role of place in Petrarchism, Kennedy, *The Site of Petrarchism*; J. B. Trapp, 'Petrarchan Places: An Essay in the Iconography of Commemoration', *Journal of the Warburg and Courtauld Institutes*, 69 (2006), 1–50; Louisa Mackenzie, *The Poetry of Place: Lyric, Landscape, and Ideology in Renaissance France* (Toronto: University of Toronto Press, 2011).

the *Triumphus Mortis* (*Triumph of Death*), to the effect that she would have wished to have been born nearer to Petrarch's 'flowery nest', that is Florence.[86]

Up to this point, arguments about the identity of Petrarch's Laura have been seen to be founded on often explicit moral and geographical motives. Typically, readers proposed a specific historical personage for the missing beloved, with Laure de Sade (whether wife, sister, or daughter), possibly née Laure de Noves (Sade's claim), and Laure des Baux (Costaing's suggestion) being popular candidates among a number of other contenders. Such readings were common from the time of Sade's *Mémoires* onwards, and had new impetus around anniversary dates. However, early twentieth-century French readers often refused to follow the examples of their predecessors, and typically rejected entirely the idea that Laura might ever be able to be identified correctly or persuasively with a specific, historical individual. Against the desire, evinced in the late eighteenth century and throughout the nineteenth, to find the precise historical, familial identity of Petrarch's Laura, early twentieth-century readers of Petrarch were much more likely to accept that although Laura certainly existed, her identity would remain forever a mystery. This latter acceptance—the enduring mystery of Laura—is the thesis of many important translators and scholars in the early decades of the twentieth century. On the occasion of the 1904 celebrations in honour of Petrarch, Émile Gebhart, for instance, declared unambiguously: 'No, never will we decipher the mystery of this veiled lady, who was like the symbol of Petrarch's love for our ancient Provence. [...] It is history's secret, which will never be revealed.'[87] While extending Petrarch's love of Laura to encompass a love for the whole of Provence, Gebhart steps back from specifying the historical identity of Petrarch's Provençal beloved.

Two decades later Cochin concurred that despite the certainty of Laura's existence, her precise identity was unknowable and indeed unimportant:

> That Madame Laura was the wife of Hugues de Sade, as the abbé de Sade ingeniously claimed for the glory of his family, or rather that she was an entirely different lady, matters a great deal to history, and not at all to lyric

---

[86] See *Triumphus Mortis II*, vv. 166–7: 'Duolmi anchor veramente ch'i' non nacqui / almen più presso al tuo fiorito nido' ('It grieves me truly still more that I was not born at least nearer to your flowery nest'), cited from *Trionfi, rime estravaganti, codice degli abbozzi*, ed. Vinicio Pacca and Laura Paolino (Milan: Arnoldo Mondadori, 1996), p. 42. All subsequent citations of the *Triumphi* in Italian are from this edition. Directly preceding these lines is Laura's description of her birthplace as 'troppo humil terren' ('too humble a land'), *Triumphus Mortis II*, v. 165 (*Trionfi, rime estravaganti, codice degli abbozzi*, p. 340), an appellation which has not helped to shed much light on the issue of the specific site in question, though it has at times been adduced in order to rule out Avignon. On Petrarch's own birthplace as ideally Florence but really Arezzo, see the Conclusion.

[87] 'Non, jamais on ne déchiffrera le mystère de cette femme voilée, qui fut comme le symbole de l'amour de Pétrarque pour notre vieille Provence. [...] C'est le secret de l'histoire, qui jamais ne sera révélé.' Émile Gebhart, 'Liminaire', in Académie de Vaucluse, *Sixième centenaire de la naissance de Pétrarque*, pp. 1–3 (p. 2). The motif of Laura as veiled no doubt stems from her presentation in the *Canzoniere*, in poems such as *RVF* 11.

poetry. Let's be content to know only that Madame Laura existed, and that the lady loved by Petrarch was real, and not a shadow.[88]

By 1927, the anniversary of Petrarch's first sight of Laura, such a view had become widespread and prevalent. In a volume published as a result of the 1927 festivities, Pierre de Nolhac declared that 'The ideal feminine figure, which fills the *Canzoniere* with her sweet reality, will no doubt remain forever surrounded by the mystery bestowed on her by the poet.'[89] Henri Hauvette's contribution to this same publication, a lecture on the subject of 'What we know about Laura', concluded, similarly, that we know very little.[90]

The views of Nolhac, Cochin, and Hauvette may represent a greater reticence towards historical speculation, in a way that can be considered broadly typical (though no doubt reductively so) of a shift from Romantic, nineteenth-century to modern, twentieth-century sensibilities and historiographies. However, it is also worth noting, as has already been discussed in the case of Cochin, that these later critics were in fact Parisian and therefore at least partly removed from the desires to conduct research into local history and to tell local stories. These Paris-based critics were not detained by scholarly feuds concerning Laura's origins conducted between Avignon and surrounding villages. Instead, from their northern point of view, Laura had certainly existed, but her (hi)story ought to be subsumed into a more broadly French narrative about the whole country's medieval past. It might only be a short step from the distrust of the proposed historical identities of Laura to a distrust of the historical reality of Laura *tout court*, but this was a step that lies beyond the boundaries of the present study.[91]

*

[88] 'Que Madame Laure fut l'épouse de Hugues de Sade, comme l'abbé de Sade l'a ingénieusement soutenu pour la gloire de sa famille, ou bien qu'elle fût toute autre dame, cela importe fort à l'histoire, point à la poésie lyrique. Sachons seulement que Madame Laure a existé, et que la dame aimée de Pétrarque fut une réalité, et non une ombre.' Henry Cochin, 'Le traducteur au lecteur: préface', in Petrarch, *Les Triomphes traduits par Henry Cochin et ornés de vignettes gravées sur bois par Alfred Latour* (Paris: Léon Pichon, 1923), pp. vii–xxiv (p. x).

[89] 'L'idéale figure de femme, qui remplit le *Canzoniere* de sa douce réalité, gardera sans doute à jamais le mystère dont l'a entourée son poète. Le nom de sa famille demeurera inconnu à nos futiles curiosités.' Pierre de Nolhac, 'L'Année de Pétrarque', in *Pétrarque: mélanges de littérature et d'histoire*, pp. 5–8 (p. 5).

[90] Henri Hauvette, 'Ce que nous savons de Laure (lecture faite à la Sorbonne le 6 avril 1927)', in *Pétrarque: mélanges de littérature et d'histoire*, pp. 10–25. Hauvette, however, does believe, *pace* Costaing and others, that based on the *partubus* reading of the *Secretum*, Laura must have been married and have had children.

[91] Already by the 1930s, there was a marked backlash against obsession with the historical Laura, with Enrico Carrara, for instance, arguing that Laura's birthplace was nowhere but in Petrarch's poetry: Carrara, 'La leggenda di Laura (1934)', in *Studi petrarcheschi ed altri scritti: raccolta a cura di amici e discepoli* (Turin: Bottega d'Erasmo, 1959), pp. 77–111 (p. 80). In truth, however, the jury may still be out as to the reality of Petrarch's Laura, since we tend, rather than entirely discarding such a presupposition, merely to assume that even were Laura to have been a living individual known to Petrarch, this reality is not especially useful or necessary as an approach to Petrarch's poetry. As Cochin already asserted in 1923, Laura's identity

In the early decades of the twentieth century, Bertoli correctly commented that 'for many inhabitants of Provence, the cult of Petrarch was the cult of their own region'.[92] Yet Bertoli's dismissal of this cult as an uninteresting, better forgotten product of 'local vanity' (*vanità locale*) overlooks the ways in which the forms of local history and local stories charted in this Introduction reveal some of the essential motives at the heart of the various and often competing manifestations of nineteenth-century French Petrarchism.[93] The tensions uncovered in this exploration, whether between city and countryside, morality and poetry, or marriage and virginity, resonate throughout this book, in relation to both translations and rewritings of Petrarch in France in this period.

As already noted, this book is divided into two parts, Translations and Rewritings. Translations of an author are particularly interesting for any consideration of the transmission and reception of texts at a given moment in time and place. Translations of Petrarch specifically in nineteenth-century France reveal much about the period and its obsession with Petrarch as with poetry more generally. On the one hand, the translations themselves, whether in prose or verse, provide an exemplary insight into nineteenth-century translation practice. On the other hand, the choice of texts to be translated is illustrative of wider preferences and renown, while translators' prefaces, commentaries, and decisions clearly demonstrate deep-rooted and often idiosyncratic views about Petrarch and his poetry.

In Part I, Chapter 1 reviews the five (or six) complete translations of Petrarch's *Canzoniere* produced in the nineteenth century. Chapter 2 discusses incomplete and partial translations of Petrarch's *Canzoniere*, with particular attention to the poems thereby selected and excluded. Chapters 1 and 2 rely on material and data compiled in Appendix 1. Chapter 2 concludes with a comparison of part of one specific poem in its various translations, namely the first stanza of *RVF* 126, 'Chiare, fresche et dolci acque' ('Clear, fresh, and sweet waters'): these texts are listed in chronological order in Appendix 2. This *canzone* has been chosen because, starting from Voltaire, it is the most popular of Petrarch's poems with translators and readers alike in this period.

Chapter 3 examines two further, distinct sub-sets of translations of Petrarch in nineteenth-century France: the *Triumphi* (*Triumphs*) and the Latin Petrarch. The former is a series of six poems in *terza rima*, a rhyme scheme formulated by Dante in his *Commedia* (*Divine Comedy*); several of the *Triumphi* pertain directly to the love story of Petrarch and Laura. The latter, the Latin Petrarch, comprises a variety of texts including letters, dialogues, and poetry (both epic and eclogues), in turn of a moral, Stoical, religious, and historical nature. Petrarch's Latin works are typically neglected today in favour of his Italian poetry, and it is interesting that this neglect has historical roots traceable back in part to the Romantic obsession with Petrarch as a solitary, vernacular, sonnet-writing poet devoted to love and nature alone. The choice, however limited, of Latin texts by Petrarch to be translated (or more rarely,

---

'importe fort à l'histoire, point à la poésie lyrique' ('matters a great deal to history, and not at all to lyric poetry'): Cochin, 'Le traducteur au lecteur: préface', in *Les Triomphes*, p. x.

[92]   'Per molti Provenzali il culto del Petrarca fu il culto del proprio paese.' Bertoli, *La Fortuna del Petrarca*, p. 23.

[93]   Bertoli, *La Fortuna del Petrarca*, p. 22.

retranslated) reflects a taste, particularly evident during the new philological atten-
tiveness of the later nineteenth century, for a more technical, theological, historical
Middle Ages than is typically suggested by the purportedly timeless and secular
Italian love lyrics bequeathed by Petrarch to posterity, and especially beloved of his
Romantic readers and translators.

Finally, Chapter 4 analyses the specific fate in Avignon of French translations,
often for and around Petrarchan festivals in the city, of texts written by Petrarch
against Avignon, that is, the Latin letters that make up the *Sine nomine* (*Book
Without a Name*), and three sonnets of the *Canzoniere*, *RVF* 136–8. As the final
chapter of Part I reveals, this local adoption of Petrarch by the city of Avignon sits
uneasily alongside Petrarch's own diatribes against the place. In this chapter I also
consider the unusual case of translations of Petrarch's Italian poetry into Provençal
in the second half of the nineteenth century, particularly as a result of the work of
the Félibrige, a group of seven Occitan poets led by the eventual Nobel laureate
Frédéric Mistral.

Part II is devoted to rewritings, particularly in two distinct modes, and is accordingly divided into two larger chapters. The first, Chapter 5, considers the influence of
nineteenth-century French Petrarchism on poetry of the period. I begin by considering certain poems written by translators of Petrarch encountered in Part I and
analyse the ways in which these poems bear witness to the indisputable familiarity
with Petrarch of these translators-turned-poets. I also consider the importance
of the aforementioned Petrarchan anniversaries (in particular, 1874 and 1904) for
the production of poetry inspired by and in praise of Petrarch, whether written by
Petrarch's translators or in response to poetry competitions organized around these
events on specifically Petrarchan themes. The second half of the chapter reviews
Lamartine's enduring and partly genealogical affinity with the medieval poet, before
proceeding to discuss the naming and celebration of Petrarch by Hugo, Alfred de
Musset, and Théophile Gautier in turn. In this chapter Petrarch thus emerges as an
important interlocutor and source of inspiration for certain aspects of nineteenth-
century French poetry, both in and outside the canon. This interest, moreover,
proves to manifest itself in two distinct temporal clusters, the 1830s and the 1870s,
with the first being a sign of a Romantic Petrarch and the second fuelled by the 1874
anniversary celebrations in honour of the poet's death.

In Chapter 6 I analyse the Petrarchan inspiration of particular French novels,
extending Duperray's proposal of the phenomenon of the French Petrarchan
novel (*roman pétrarquiste*) and drawing on the work of Mikhail Bakhtin.[94] More
specifically, I engage in this chapter with Bakhtin's concept of novelization, which
distinguishes between unitary poetic language and novelistic discourse, the latter
characterized by polyphony and even parody. The principal works in question are
Rousseau's *La Nouvelle Héloïse* (1761), Charles-Augustin Sainte-Beuve's *Volupté*
(1834), Balzac's *Le Lys dans la vallée* (1836), Stendhal's *La Chartreuse de Parme*
(1839; *The Charterhouse of Parma*), and George Sand's *Adriani* (1854). The level of

---

[94] Mikhail Bakhtin, *The Dialogic Imagination: Four Essays*, trans. Michael Holquist
(Austin: University of Texas Press, 1981).

engagement with a Petrarchan intertext ranges from direct citation (Rousseau) to partial misinformation (Balzac) and occasional obfuscation of sources (Stendhal), but is consistently underwritten by deliberate, explicit parallels between Petrarch and Laura and the principal lovers in each respective work. Moreover, the parallel between the new beloved and Laura, in all the examples save *Adriani*, is found to be based on the necessary premature death of the male protagonist's love object and muse. Petrarch, for the majority of these novelists, is a proto-Romantic poet of love and death, with the 1830s once more proving to be a crucial decade for nineteenth-century French Petrarchism.

Lastly, the Conclusion is devoted to a discussion of Petrarch and patriotism, informed by the claims for a French Petrarch discussed throughout this book. Here I return to the question of Petrarch's Frenchness, sketched out in this Introduction through quotations from the likes of Sade, Piot, and Cochin. The recurrent question 'Was Petrarch French?' is situated against Petrarch's own assertions of Florentine identity and his choice to receive the laurel crown in Rome rather than Paris. More broadly, then, this book concludes by interrogating the ties between identity, place, home, and homeland, in as well as potentially beyond the specific case of nineteenth-century French Petrarchism.

I
TRANSLATIONS

1

Complete Translations of Petrarch's *Canzoniere*

'THE NINETEENTH CENTURY is doubtless not a very important century for the translation of Petrarch in France': so declared a comprehensive study of translations and translators in nineteenth-century France published in 2012.[1] Such a view requires reconsideration, given the wealth of translations discussed throughout Part I and listed fully, as regards the *Canzoniere* and *Triumphi*, in Appendix 1.[2] There are admittedly only a handful of complete translations into French of Petrarch's *Canzoniere* dating from the long nineteenth century. However, many more incomplete translations, often of isolated poems, were also published in this same period, as detailed in Chapter 2, not to mention translations of Petrarch's *Triumphi* and Latin works, the subject of Chapter 3. Nineteenth-century French translators of Petrarch are divided between a desire for completion (Chapter 1) and the enthrallment of incompletion (Chapters 2 and 3). The latter approach ultimately proves more popular, likely because it is more manageable in practical terms, whilst also giving the translator much freedom in deciding which poems to include. Throughout Part I, I focus on which works and which specific poems by Petrarch translators chose to translate, what version of Petrarch these choices privilege or construct, and what translators' prefaces and other paratextual material reveal about attitudes towards Petrarch's writings during this period.[3] The construction of a nineteenth-century French Petrarch was typically not achieved through a whole-sale importation of the poet's writings into French, but rather through a process of refinement, curation, and selection for a specifically French public.

My analyses in Part I are less concerned with directly comparing original and

---

[1] 'Le XIXe siècle n'est sans doute pas un très grand siècle pour la traduction de Pétrarque en France.' Christine Lombez, 'Poésie', in *Histoire des traductions en langue française: XIXe siècle: 1815–1914*, ed. Yves Chevrel, Lieven D'Hulst, and Christine Lombez (Lagrasse: Éditions Verdier, 2012), pp. 345–442 (p. 378).

[2] The difficulty of locating some of these translations, often published in shortlived journals and ephemera, means that Appendix 1 cannot be definitive or final.

[3] On the preface as a key space for translatorly intervention see Christine Lombez, 'Théories en marge de la pratique: l'art de la préface chez les traducteurs français de poésie au XIXe siècle', in *L'Art de la préface*, ed. Philippe Forest (Nantes: Éditions Cécile Defaut, 2006), pp. 159–75, and *Cent ans de théorie française de la traduction: de Batteux à Littré (1748–1847)*, ed. Lieven D'Hulst (Lille: Presses Universitaires de Lille, 1990), especially pp. 103–72. On paratexts, see Gérard Genette, *Palimpsestes: la littérature au second degré* (Paris: Éditions du Seuil, 1982).

translated text, an approach which typically runs the risk of treating the translation as inferior to or a failed version of the original, that is, as inherently 'defective'.[4] Instead, I privilege translations as worthy of interest in their own right, especially bearing in mind that only rarely were any of these translations published alongside the original texts, meaning that direct comparison of original and translation was typically neither encouraged nor facilitated. Before turning to specific translators and translations, it is useful first to highlight some general editorial problems relating to Petrarch's *Canzoniere* in this period, in particular as regards choice of title and the numbering and order of the work's constituent poems. Such textual uncertainties, if rather dry to recount, were a gift to translators, since they transformed Petrarch's *Canzoniere* into a set of moveable building blocks from which translators could fashion their own, new structures, through processes such as reordering and omission.

Background

Firstly, it is important to remember that while there are a number of titles commonly used in the nineteenth century (and earlier) to refer to Petrarch's principal collection of 366 Italian poems, the one that the poet himself chose was *Rerum vulgarium fragmenta* (*Fragments of Things in the Vernacular*).[5] This title, however, is rarely used by French translators of this period, who prefer less specific titles, such as the generic *Poésies* or *Rimes* (*Poems*), or instead titles that indicate formal features (*Sonnets et/ou canzones*, and so on). Consistently, a vernacular and indeed specifically French title, however vague, is felt to be more appropriate than a potentially alienating, off-putting Latin title. For my part, as is conventional in modern Petrarch criticism, I use the label *Canzoniere* (*Songbook*) as shorthand for the *Rerum vulgarium fragmenta*, and when citing specific numbers of poems these are preceded by the indication *RVF* which refers back to the original Latin title. The question of numeration leads to the second point, that for most of the nineteenth century there is no one, authorially sanctioned, fixed order of these poems. For consistency, I therefore refer to poems according to their numbering in modern editions (with Italian texts drawn from Marco Santagata's authoritative critical edition) when establishing which poems were translated and in what order.[6]

Petrarch's own ordering was only established as the critical norm around the turn of the century, after the independent rediscovery of the partially holograph manuscript of the *Canzoniere* in the Vatican Library (MS Vaticano Latino 3195) in the late 1880s by the French scholar Pierre de Nolhac and a German scholar, Arthur

---

[4]   In Antoine Berman's terms, this judgemental, typically negative approach tends to reveal translation's 'defectivity': Berman, *Pour une critique des traductions: John Donne* (Paris: Gallimard, 1995), p. 41; Berman, *Towards a Translation Criticism: John Donne*, trans. and ed. Françoise Massardier-Kenney (Kent, OH: Kent State University Press, 2009), p. 29.

[5]   See Francisco Rico, '"Rime sparse", "Rerum vulgarium fragmenta": sul titolo e sul primo sonetto del *Canzoniere*', trans. S. Bogliolo, in *Il 'Canzoniere' di Francesco Petrarca: la critica contemporanea*, ed. Gennaro Barbarisi and Claudia Berra (Milan: Edizioni Universitarie di Lettere Economia Diritto, 1992), pp. 117–44.

[6]   Petrarch, *Canzoniere*, ed. Santagata.

Pakscher.[7] This discovery marks a return to manuscript evidence that is typical of the new philological demands of textual accuracy of later nineteenth-century scholars, even if new editions (such as that of Giovanni Mestica) making use of this material were slow to gain the popularity amongst readers and translators required to replace earlier, supposedly superseded versions entirely.[8] Prior to the discoveries of Nolhac and Pakscher, the lack of consensus in the nineteenth century as to the numbering and order of the poems of Petrarch's *Canzoniere* complicates considera-tion of translations in this period. A particular area of frequent divergence from the numbering of modern editions is in the last thirty-one poems of the *Canzoniere*, which Petrarch reordered at a late stage and of which Vat. Lat. 3195 was to be a key, belatedly rediscovered witness.[9] Yet, as we shall see, certain translators also reor-dered and restructured the *Canzoniere* deliberately and without especial concern for authorial approval. The lack of a final version in Petrarch's hand was the cause not merely of confusion, but more especially of an exciting form of freedom from the constraints of authorial control.

One of the most popular Italian editions in this period prior to the recovery of the manuscript recording Petrarch's final (or at least latest) intentions was Antonio Marsand's two-volume *Le rime del Petrarca*, which divided Petrarch's Italian poetry into four distinct sections: sonnets and *canzoni* during Laura's life (*in vita di M. Laura*); sonnets and *canzoni* after Laura's death (*in morte di M. Laura*); *Trionfi* (*Triumphs*) similarly *in vita ed in morte di M. Laura*; and, more surprisingly, sonnets and *canzoni* by Petrarch 'on various topics' (*sopra varj argomenti*).[10] Marsand was himself following the illustrious precedent of Alessandro Vellutello, who had divided the poems of the *Canzoniere* into three parts, during the life of Laura (*in vita di Madonna Laura*), after her death (*in morte di Madonna Laura*), and a third section of 'all those poems written by Petrarch at various times, on other matters, and to other individuals', in addition to the *Triumphi* in a separate, fourth section.[11]

---

[7]   Pierre de Nolhac, *Le Canzoniere autographe de Pétrarque* (Paris: C. Klincksieck, 1886); Arthur Pakscher, *Die Chronologie der Gedichte Petrarcas* (Berlin: Weidmannsche Buchhand-lung, 1887). On Vat. Lat. 3195, see the essays in *Petrarch and the Textual Origins of Interpreta-tion*, ed. Teodolinda Barolini and H. Wayne Storey (Leiden: Brill, 2007).

[8]   *Le rime di Francesco Petrarca: restituite nell'ordine e nella lezione del testo originario sugli autografi col sussidio di altri codici e di stampe e corredate di varianti e note*, ed. Giovanni Mestica (Florence: G. Barbèra, 1896).

[9]   H. Wayne Storey, 'All'interno della poetica grafico-visiva di Petrarca', in Petrarch, *Rerum vulgarium fragmenta, codice Vat. Lat. 3195: commentario all'edizione in fac-simile*, ed. Gino Belloni, Furio Brugnolo, H. Wayne Storey, and Stefano Zamponi (Padua: Editrice Antenore, 2004), pp. 131–71 (pp. 146–7).

[10]   *Le rime del Petrarca: edizione pubblicata per opera e studio dell'ab. Antonio Marsand*, 2 vols (Padua: Nella tipografia del seminario, 1819–20). See the end of Appendix 1 for full details of the composition of this edition.

[11]   'tutti quelli, che in diversi tempi & altri soggetti, & a piu persone da lui furono scritti', Vellutello, *Le volgari opere del Petrarcha*, Sig. A 1. (USTC 847830). On Vellutello, see H. Wayne Storey, 'The Economies of Authority: Bembo, Vellutello, and the Reconstruction of "Authentic Petrarch"', in *'Accessus ad Auctores': Studies in Honor of Christopher Kleinhenz*, ed. Fabian Alfie and Andrea Dini (Tempe: Arizona Center for Medieval and Renaissance Studies, 2011), pp. 493–506, and Storey, 'Canzoniere e petrarchismo: un paradigma di orientamento formale e materiale', in *Il petrarchismo*, ed. Chines, Calitti, and Gigliucci, I, 291–310, as well as

Vellutello's third and Marsand's fourth sections reveal a desire for Petrarch's *Canzoniere* to be more unified and restricted in subject matter than it actually is. In his preface, Marsand makes the bold claim that his aims have been solely 'to render honour and glory to our poet, and to follow diligently, in everything, his intention, as far as it seemed evident to me'.[12] Marsand suggests, even more daringly, that Petrarch would have approved of the fourth section:

> Finally I thought to divide the *Canzoniere* into four parts since, in my opinion, quite reasonably the same was done in some of the early editions, placing, that is, in the final part those compositions which are found scattered here and there in the first and the second part of the *Canzoniere*, and which do not pertain to the poet's love for Laura. I decided to do all these things because I am convinced that he would certainly want them to be done if he were with us.[13]

From this perspective, paraphrasing Roland Barthes, the literal death of the author enables the birth of one particularly interventionist type of reader: the editor.[14]

There are twenty-four poems placed in Marsand's fourth section, with a variety of themes and addressees. Some are moral, such as *RVF* 7 (a criticism of gluttony and laziness) or 232 (against wrath), as well as the anti-Avignon trio of sonnets (*RVF* 136–8) discussed in Chapter 4. Other poems relate to literary study and inspiration (*RVF* 24, 40, 104, 166), with *RVF* 119 a *canzone* on literary glory. In these poems, Petrarch's addressees are often not Laura but select friends and patrons. Of the former, Marsand interprets *RVF* 25 and 26 as in dialogue with Boccaccio; *RVF* 98 addresses Orso dell'Anguillara; *RVF* 120 informs Antonio Beccari da Ferrara that despite rumours Petrarch is not dead; *RVF* 139 reluctantly bids farewell to a friend, possibly Petrarch's brother; *RVF* 92 mourns the death of a poet, now identified as Cino da Pistoia. As regards the latter, Petrarch's patrons, these include, in particular, members of the Colonna family, addressed as 'Glorious Column' (*Gloriosa columna*) by *RVF* 10: *RVF* 58 accompanies gifts to Agapito Colonna; *RVF* 103 is written to Stefano Colonna the Younger after a military victory; *RVF* 322 is a reply to a sonnet from Giacomo Colonna. In other poems, leaders are exhorted to go on crusade (*RVF* 27 and 28), political ideals and projects (perhaps those of Cola di Rienzo) are

---

Belloni, *Laura tra Petrarca e Bembo*, pp. 58–95, and Kennedy, *Authorizing Petrarch*, pp. 45–52 (this last with an appendix listing Vellutello's reordering, pp. 285–8).

[12]   'di rendere onore e gloria al nostro Poeta, e di seguitare studiosamente, in tutto, l'intendimento di lui, tanto quanto parvemi manifesto', Marsand, 'Prefazione', in *Le rime del Petrarca*, ed. Marsand, I, pp. vii–xxiii (p. xix).

[13]   'Finalmente pensai di dividere il Canzoniere in quattro parti, siccome, per mio avviso, ben ragionevolmente fu fatto in alcune delle antiche edizioni, riponendo cioè nell'ultima que' componimenti, che si veggono sparsi qua e là nella prima e nella seconda parte del Canzoniere, e non appartengono agli amori del Poeta verso di Laura. Le quali cose tutte io deliberai di fare, perchè tengo per fermo, ch'ei certamente vorrebbe fatte s'egli fosse con noi.' Marsand, 'Prefazione', in *Le rime del Petrarca*, ed. Marsand, I, p. xxiii.

[14]   To draw on Barthes's famous essay, 'La mort de l'auteur', in *Œuvres complètes*, ed. Éric Marty, new revised edn, 5 vols (Paris: Seuil, 2002), III, 40–5.

encouraged (*RVF* 53), and Petrarch's homeland is celebrated in the famous *canzone* which begins 'My Italy' (*RVF* 128, *Italia mia*).

The difficulty of drawing a line between poems about Laura and poems not about Laura is, however, implied by other poems which are left in the first two sections, but which have affinities with texts moved to the fourth section. *RVF* 102, a sonnet which begins with examples from Caesar and Hannibal (and thereby has strong ties with the following, marginalized sonnet, *RVF* 103, which opens 'Hannibal won', *Vinse Hanibàl*), survives the triage and remains in the first section, presumably because it develops into a record of the poet's own contradictory emotions in the final tercet. Other sonnets complicate Marsand's divisions by discussing Laura and members of the Colonna family in the same breath (such as *RVF* 269, which mourns the deaths of both Laura and Giovanni Colonna). Finally, moral concerns cannot be separated from Petrarch's love for Laura, however much Marsand seems to have wished they might be, and so sonnets such as *RVF* 172, which begins with an invective against envy, remain in the amorous sections. Besides these alterations and discrepancies, Marsand unusually considers *RVF* 91 to be about the death of Laura, and so moves it to the *in morte* section, whereas readers before and after Marsand tend, instead, to interpret this sonnet as about the death of Petrarch's brother's beloved, one cause of Gherardo's monastic retreat to the Chartreuse de Montrieux in 1342.[15]

Marsand's edition is an unusual case of radical reordering and reconceptualization of Petrarch's *Canzoniere* in the nineteenth century, and was to prove popular as a reference edition with many French translators discussed below. Yet even concerning editions of the *Canzoniere* that, unlike Marsand's, remained within Petrarch's original conception of a merely bipartite structure, there were many issues as to titles and point of division.[16] While Petrarch did not give titles to the two halves (which are accordingly typically described in neutral terms in modern editions as *parte prima* and *parte seconda*, first and second parts), thematic interpretations of the division soon after his lifetime led to the assumption that the two halves ought to be understood as, respectively, *in vita* ('in life') and *in morte di Laura* ('after the death of Laura').[17] Connected to this desire to give names to the two halves were concerns over the exact point of transition between poems about Laura's life and poems purportedly written after her death. While Petrarch had his second part start with *RVF* 264, later editors worried that the first poem to address the theme of Laura's death came only several poems later, with the sonnet *RVF* 267, characterized by the insistent cry of 'Alas' (*Oimè*). In particular, the two interceding sonnets, *RVF* 265 (a poem on the constant suffering of love) and 266 (addressed to Giovanni Colonna and asserting allegiance both to this patron and to Laura), posed problems

---

[15] See, for instance, at either end of my time period, Sade, *Mémoires*, II, 64, and Cochin, *Le Frère de Pétrarque*, p. 44.

[16] As discussed more broadly in Teodolinda Barolini, 'Petrarch at the Crossroads of Hermeneutics and Philology: Editorial Lapses, Narrative Impositions, and Wilkins' Doctrine of the Nine Forms of the *Rerum vulgarium fragmenta*', in *Petrarch and the Textual Origins of Interpretation*, pp. 21–44.

[17] See Christoph Niederer, 'La bipartizione *in vita/in morte* del "Canzoniere" di Petrarca', in *Petrarca e i suoi lettori*, ed. Vittorio Caratozzolo and Georges Güntert (Ravenna: Longo, 2000), pp. 19–41.

as they challenged the titular assertion of this section as being 'after Laura's death' (*in morte di Laura*). The solution largely adopted was not to question the validity of the titles attributed to each half, but rather to move these two poems to the first half, *in vita di Laura*, so that the *in morte* section could start, as was deemed more appropriate, with a poem explicitly of mourning and lament, *RVF* 267. As with the titles of the two halves, the decision to start part two with *RVF* 267 was remarkably pervasive, and is present in all nineteenth-century French translations of Petrarch in which a bipartite structure of the *Canzoniere* remains at all operative.

Having reviewed key editorial questions regarding the *Canzoniere*, in particular its title, order, numbering, division, and point of transition between parts, I turn now to analysis of complete translations of Petrarch's *Canzoniere* produced in the nineteenth century. While the remainder of this chapter thus sets out some of the major achievements of nineteenth-century French translators of Petrarch (measuring achievement, for the moment, by completion), the topic will become even more interesting—that is, more fraught and more nuanced—in subsequent chapters which deal with partial (incomplete) translations. For partiality (in both senses of the word) is likely to fascinate more than impartiality and thoroughness, as Petrarch himself knew well.

Complete Translations: An Overview

Of the many French translations of Petrarch's Italian poetry produced in the nineteenth century (and listed in Appendix 1), only five are complete, with a sixth, Hippolyte Godefroy's *Poésies complètes de Francesco Petrarca* (1900; *The Complete Poems of Francis Petrarch*), ostensibly complete though in fact omitting a few poems.[18] In the remainder of this chapter an overview of these complete translations (including Godefroy's) is undertaken, with a particular focus on each translator's motives, where prefatory and other material is available. There will be less analysis of the translation of individual poems in this chapter, save in the final two examples of Brisset and Godefroy, both of which in different ways bring to the fore issues of translation. Instead, a sense of the style and form of these translations can be better gained from examples in subsequent chapters, including translations of the first stanza of *RVF* 126 discussed at the end of Chapter 2 and listed in Appendix 2, as well as further discussion of Ferdinand de Gramont in Chapter 5. In this chapter I am concerned more with the order and structure of these complete translations, as well as with the identity of each translator, where such information is known.[19]

---

[18] Complete French translations of the *Canzoniere* have continued to be surprisingly scarce beyond the nineteenth century: see Georges Barthouil, 'Traductions françaises du *Canzoniere* de Pétrarque', *Cuadernos de filologia italiana*, Extra 12 (2005), 171–85. For an analysis of the composition of Godefroy's translation, see below, with reference to Hippolyte Godefroy, *Poésies complètes de Francesco Petrarca* (Montluçon: Imprimerie A. Herbin, 1900).

[19] On the importance of paying attention to the translator, see Berman, *Pour une critique des traductions*, pp. 73–83 (in English, Berman, *Towards a Translation Criticism*, pp. 57–64). This attention, recommended by Berman, attempts to redress, on a case-by-case basis, what Lawrence Venuti famously described as the 'invisibility' of the translator: Venuti, *The Translator's Invisibility: A History of Translation* (London: Routledge, 1995).

The first complete translations of Petrarch in this period coincidentally fall in the same year, 1842, penned by the comtes Ferdinand de Gramont and Anatole de Montesquiou respectively. These two synchronous translations are symptomatic of the popularity of Petrarch's poetry towards the middle of the nineteenth century in France, in the wake of the craze for poetry inspired by the successes of French Romantic poets in earlier decades.[20] Later in the century two further translations were published, first by Joseph Poulenc in 1865 (with a second edition in 1877) and then by Francisque Reynard (in 1883), both under variations on the title *Rimes de Pétrarque* (*Poems by Petrarch*). Finally, around the turn of the century, in addition to Godefroy's anomalous contribution (1900), Fernand Brisset published a complete translation of the *Canzoniere* across two volumes, the first being *Les Sonnets de Pétrarque à Laure* (1899; *Sonnets from Petrarch to Laura*), and the second *Canzones, triomphes et poésies diverses* (1903; *Canzoni, Triumphs, and Other Poems*).

Of these six translations (including Godefroy), two are in verse (those of Montesquiou and Poulenc) and four in prose (those of Gramont, Reynard, Brisset, and Godefroy). The increasing popularity of prose translation later in the nineteenth century is typical of complete and incomplete translations of Petrarch alike, although a rendition of sonnets into like form was also commonly sought around the same time (see Chapter 2). Significantly, Poulenc's two editions are the only complete translations to provide either a parallel text (in the original version of 1865) or Italian first lines of poems (in the second edition of 1877). The other five translators are seemingly writing for a readership with no knowledge of or interest in Petrarch's original language *per se*, but only in its French incarnation. Notably, this observation unsettles Clive Scott's suggestion that 'One cannot, in fact, imagine an edition of prose translations which is not bilingual', since all four complete prose translations of Petrarch's *Canzoniere* in this period are presented without any form of parallel Italian text.[21] Poulenc's verse translations alone explicitly encourage—in the translator's own words—'comparison with the Italian text' (*la confrontation avec le texte italien*).[22] Three of the five complete translations (excluding Godefroy) follow Marsand's ordering (Poulenc, Reynard, and Brisset), indicating the influence of this edition on French translations of Petrarch throughout the nineteenth century, especially since Gramont, though he does not follow Marsand in structure, continues to use Marsand's edition of the text.[23]

---

[20]   On the Petrarchan inspiration of French Romantic poetry, see Chapter 5.

[21]   Scott, *Translating Baudelaire*, p. 147.

[22]   *Rimes de Pétrarque: traduction complète en vers des sonnets, canzones, sextines, ballades, madrigaux et triomphes, par Joseph Poulenc: deuxième édition, revue et corrigée*, 2 vols (Paris: Librairie des Bibliophiles, 1887), I, p. ix.

[23]   Gramont specifies that he is using the text established by Marsand, as adopted in *Le rime di messer F. Petrarca; le Stanze e l'Orfeo del Poliziano, con note di diversi, per diligenza e studio di Antonio Buttura*, 2 vols (Paris: Baudry, 1830).

The First Complete Nineteenth-Century Translations:
Gramont and Montesquiou

The first complete translation, by Gramont, includes both Petrarch's *Canzoniere* and *Triumphi*, and is divided into three parts: 'Sonnets and *canzoni* composed during the life/after the death of Laura' (*Sonnets et canzones composés du vivant de Laure*; *Sonnets et canzones composés après la mort de Laure*) and *Triumphs* (*Triomphes*).[24] Despite the titles of the first two parts (modelled on Marsand), Gramont necessarily translates the other forms present in Petrarch's *Canzoniere* beyond sonnets and *canzoni* (that is, the rarer *ballate*, *sestine*, and madrigals that complete the collection). The success of Gramont's project is perhaps best indicated by the republication of his translation of Petrarch's *Canzoniere* in 1983 in an accessible paperback format, a feat of modern resurrection which renders Gramont unique amongst other translators of Petrarch in this period.[25] Gramont will also be encountered later in this book as the author of Petrarchan-inspired poetry (see Chapter 5). For the moment it suffices to highlight Gramont's proficiency as a poet, and his academic interest in poetry, which is suggested not so much by his prose translations of Petrarch as by his authorship of various treatises on French versification.[26]

Unusually, Gramont's specific area of expertise lay in the form of the *sestina*, which had a limited revival thanks to his efforts.[27] In *Olim* (1882), Gramont explicitly acknowledged Dante and Petrarch as important precursors as regards the *sestina*, but rightly noted the form to be French rather than Italian in origin (deriving from the twelfth-century troubadour Arnaut Daniel), hence in part Gramont's desire to reinvigorate and reclaim the form in France:

> Dante, Pétrarque, et Camoëns, et Tasse,
> D'autres encor d'une assez haute classe,
> Ont consacré des moments précieux
>   À la sextine.
> Mais c'est chez nous, devers Marseille et Grasse,
> Qu'elle naquit. Durant un long espace
> On la laissa fleurir sous d'autres cieux ;
> Oubli que j'ai réparé de mon mieux,
> Faisant, premier, regrimper le Parnasse

---

[24] Ferdinand de Gramont, *Poésies de Pétrarque: traduction complète: sonnets, canzones, triomphes* (Paris: Paul Masgana, 1842).

[25] Petrarch, *Canzoniere*, trans. Ferdinand de Gramont with preface and notes by Jean-Michel Gardair (Paris: Gallimard, 1983). Gramont's translation is also admired by Bertoli, *La Fortuna del Petrarca*, p. 144, and by Lombez, 'Poésie', in *Histoire des traductions en langue française*, p. 379.

[26] Ferdinand de Gramont, *Les Vers français et leur prosodie* (Paris: J. Hetzel, 1876), and *Sextines précédées de l'histoire de la sextine dans les langues dérivées du latin* (Paris: Alphonse Lemerre, 1872).

[27] The *sestina* as a form contains six stanzas, each of six lines which end with six different words which recur in each stanza through a process of *retrogradatio cruciata*, as well as in a final, three-line *congedo*.

À la sextine.[28]

***

Dante, Petrarch, and Camões, and Tasso,
Others yet still of a fairly high class,
Have consecrated precious moments
  To the *sestina*.
But it is here, in France, around Marseille and Grasse,
That it was born. For a long time
We let it flourish under other skies;
A forgetfulness which I have repaired as best I can,
By being the first to provide help in reclimbing Parnassus
  To the *sestina*.

Gramont's self-restriction to a prose translation is all the more surprising given his fluency in both Italian and French verse, not to mention his verse translation of the Biblical Book of Job.[29] In fact, in a separate study of the *sestina*, Gramont explains that he originally intended to translate Petrarch's *Canzoniere* into verse, but that his publisher had other ideas: 'Thirty or so years ago, or thereabouts, I had undertaken and indeed progressed quite far through a verse translation of Petrarch's *Canzoniere*. It was not completed, the editor, for reasons which had nothing to do with literature, having preferred a translation in prose.'[30] The unspecified motives behind the publisher's interference may be surmised to lie at least in part in the wish to avoid competition with another volume of translations of Petrarch published that same year, in verse, by Anatole de Montesquiou. In the brief 'Notice' preceding his translation, Gramont dismisses earlier French translators of Petrarch either because of their outdated language (in the case of Vasquin Philieul's translation from 1555, or Placide Catanusi's from 1669) or because of the incomplete nature of their translations.[31] Montesquiou, as Gramont's publishers realized, was, however, a more dangerous rival.

For it was not Gramont but Montesquiou who provided the first complete *Canzoniere* in French verse of the nineteenth century, in two volumes in 1842, following the text and ordering of Giosafatte Biagioli's Italian edition from the early 1820s.[32]

---

[28] Gramont, *Olim: sextines et sonnets* (Paris: Paul Ollendorff, 1882), p. 172.

[29] Gramont, *Sonnets* (Paris: Imprimerie d'Amédée Gratiot et Cie, 1840) and *Chant du passé, 1830–1848* (Paris: D. Giraud, 1854), on the which volumes see Chapter 5. For Gramont's Biblical translation, see *Le Livre de Job traduit en vers par le Cte F.-L. de Gramont, suivi du Livre de Ruth, traduit en vers par le Mis A. de Belloy* (Paris: Waille, 1843).

[30] 'Il y a une trentaine d'années environ, j'avais entrepris et même assez avancé une traduction en vers du *Canzoniere* de Pétrarque. Elle ne fut pas achevée, l'éditeur, pour des raisons tout à fait en dehors de la littérature, ayant préféré une traduction en prose.' Gramont, *Sextines*, p. 27.

[31] On this earlier tradition, see Enea Balmas, 'Prime traduzioni del *Canzoniere* nel cinquecento francese', in *Traduzione e tradizione europea del Petrarca: atti del III convegno sui problemi della traduzione letteraria, Monselice, 9 giugno 1974* (Padua: Editrice Antenore, 1975), pp. 37–54.

[32] Anatole de Montesquiou, *Sonnets, canzones, ballades et sextines de Pétrarque traduits*

In his 'Avertissement' ('Foreword') to the first edition, Montesquiou acknowledged Gramont's work but asserted that poetry must be translated into poetry rather than prose (an assertion towards which it seems Gramont would, in fact, have been sympathetic):

> When I started this translation, more than twenty years ago, there was still no complete translation either in verse or in prose; and such a work seemed to me to be a monument demanded by both France and Italy. At the start of this year (1842), M. le comte de Gramont published a complete, literal translation, which almost always has the merit of being scrupulously accurate; but it is in prose, and verse needs to be interpreted by verse: elegance, rhythm, and song then have their correspondence, their echo, from one language to the other. To deprive the text that one wants to render of this assimilation is to serve that text badly.[33]

Montesquiou supplemented his two-volume translation of the *Canzoniere* a year later with a further volume of selections from the Latin Petrarch as well as all six of the *Triumphi*.[34]

Montesquiou's translations of Petrarch are characterized by circumlocution and typically privilege the demands of rhyme over closeness to the original. Yet the lack of facing Italian means that contemporary readers would have been unlikely to have checked Montesquiou's translations pedantically against the original, whether with regard to either form or content. Rather, his translations call for appreciation as independent works with their own, distinct merits. Still, a sonnet added to the front of the second edition (1843), and dedicated to Petrarch, reveals that Montesquiou came under some criticism by his contemporaries for his lack of formal fidelity to Petrarch, in particular his avoidance of the sonnet form:

> Pétrarque, tu sais bien que l'on me fit un tort
> De mètre détourné parfois de mon modèle,
> En donnant à ton œuvre une forme nouvelle,
> En essayant de prendre hors du sonnet l'essor.[35]

***

en vers, 2 vols (Paris: Leroy, 1842); *Rime di F. Petrarca col comento di G. Biagioli*, 2 vols (Paris: Presso l'Editore, 1821).

[33] 'Lorsque je commençai cette traduction, il y a plus de vingt ans, il n'en existait de complète ni en vers, ni en prose ; et une telle œuvre me semblait un monument réclamé par la France et par l'Italie. Au commencement de cette année (1842), M. le comte de Gramont a publié une traduction littérale et complète, qui a presque toujours le mérite d'une scrupuleuse exactitude ; mais elle est en prose, et les vers ont besoin d'être interprétés par des vers : l'élégance, le rythme, le chant ont alors leur correspondance, leur écho d'une langue à l'autre. Priver de cette assimilation le texte qu'on veut rendre, c'est le desservir.' Montesquiou, *Sonnets, canzones, ballades et sextines de Pétrarque*, I, p. v.

[34] Anatole de Montesquiou, *Épîtres, églogues et triomphes de Pétrarque traduits en vers* (Paris: Leroy, 1843). On this volume see Chapter 3.

[35] *Sonnets, canzones, ballades, sextines, traduits en vers par le comte Anatole de Montesquiou*, 2nd edn, 3 vols (Paris: Amyot, 1843), I, unpaginated front matter.

> Petrarch, you know well that I have been accused of wrongdoing
> For having turned away at times from my model,
> By giving your work a new form,
> By trying to expand beyond the sonnet.

By defending himself in a sonnet, Montesquiou in this verse proves his competence, whilst ironically using the form to define the sonnet as easy to produce (*facile*, v. 10) but lacking in grace (*grâce*, v. 8). Yet despite Montesquiou's lack of enthusiasm, it was from the end of this same decade, and increasingly in the second half of the nineteenth century, that French translators such as Emma Mahul and Philibert Le Duc did favour both Petrarch's sonnets and the sonnet form as an ideal mode of translation (see Chapter 2).

Montesquiou later also published translations of Michelangelo's poetry and of a play by Vittorio Alfieri, confirming his credentials as an Italophile, in addition to his own plays and poetry in French.[36] Yet unlike Gramont, whose life was devoted to literature, biographical information on Montesquiou, in contrast, reveals that translation, even supplemented by poetry of one's own, was not typically a full-time job in the nineteenth century. Rather, in the case of Montesquiou the work of translation sat alongside competing commitments and interests, particularly of a military, political persuasion seemingly at odds with the rarefied world of lyric poetry. Born in 1788, Montesquiou served with distinction in Napoleon's army from the age of eighteen, ascending the ranks to eventual aide-de-camp to the Emperor; his devastation at his leader's fall from grace and exile was such, reportedly, that he even sought to accompany Napoleon to Elba.[37] After a brief sojourn in Vienna, where he watched from afar the hopes and repeated disappointment of the Hundred Days, Montesquiou was, nonetheless, able to return to Paris and settle into a new political regime, distinguishing himself to the extent that he was nominated to the *Chambre des Pairs* in 1841 by Louis-Philippe Ier. Then came his translation of Petrarch, the fruit, so Montesquiou's 'Avertissement' records, of more than two decades of quiet rumination in the background to his public life and duties. This brief excursus on Montesquiou's political activities serves as a reminder of the strange connection between Napoleon and Petrarch already encountered in the Introduction in terms of the establishment of the pro-Petrarch Athénée de Vaucluse. In addition to shared loyalties and experiences, Montesquiou's interest in Petrarch may, then, have been partly motivated by Napoleon's approval and promotion of the poet.

Complete Translations of the Later Nineteenth Century

After the coincidentally timed complete translations of the comtes Gramont and Montesquiou, which place Petrarch in a largely Romantic, Parisian, aristocratic sphere, the next complete *Canzoniere* came only in 1865, with Joseph Poulenc's *Rimes*

---

[36] Anatole de Montesquiou, *Myrrha, tragédie d'Alfieri, traduite en vers* (Paris: Amyot, 1856) and *Poésies de Michel-Ange Buonarotti* (Paris: A. Masson, 1875).

[37] Anselme Guy, *Notice historique et littéraire sur M. le comte Anatole de Montesquiou-Fezensac* (Paris: Au Bureau central de la publication, 1847).

de Pétrarque. By this point, interest in Petrarch was coming closer to its provincial, Avignonese roots so memorably celebrated by Sade in his *Mémoires*; Poulenc lived in the south of France, not in Avignon but in Aveyron, though he was present at the 1874 Petrarchan festivities in Avignon.[38] A second edition (not merely a reprint) of Poulenc's translations was published in 1877, also under the general title *Rimes de Pétrarque*. This second edition was published by the Librairie des Bibliophiles, a publishing house founded in 1869 by Damase Jouaust and devoted to the publication of tasteful, carefully curated volumes, including foreign authors and less well-known texts alongside staples of the literary canon.[39]

Interestingly, Poulenc noted in the preface to his first edition from 1865 that he had been advised to publish only selections from Petrarch:

> I have been advised several times to make public only selected extracts from the works of Petrarch; but why would readers not be able to be their own judge and connoisseur of the work in its entirety, by leaving to them the ability to admire what deserves admiration and to pass over what seems less worthy of attention?[40]

This anecdote confirms the scarcity of complete French translations of Petrarch's *Canzoniere* throughout the nineteenth century, and also gives an insight into the motivations behind the desire for textual unity and wholeness, that is, a desire for the reader to be able to decide independently on which poems are of greater or lesser interest. In his preface to the second edition, Poulenc admits that he spent twelve years translating Petrarch before publishing his work, and declares that he was only moved so to do after encouragement from Sainte-Beuve.[41] Unusually, he also explains that his methodology has been one of identification: 'I created a rule for myself that I would identify myself profoundly with the Italian poet, in an attempt to penetrate his most intimate thoughts.'[42] Unlike earlier verse translations (in particular, that of Montesquiou), Poulenc tries to use verse forms that reflect Petrarch's own choices (notably, the decision to translate sonnets into French

---

[38]   Poulenc, as the title page of his translation specifies, was a 'membre de la Société des lettres, sciences et arts de l'Aveyron', and he represented this society at the 1874 festivities in honour of Petrarch held in Avignon and Fontaine-de-Vaucluse: Poulenc, *Rimes de Pétrarque* (1877), I, p. i.

[39]   The same publishing house was also responsible for *Cinquante sonnets et cinq odes de Pétrarque traduits en vers français par Junior Casalis et Ernest de Ginoux* (Paris: Librairie des Bibliophiles, 1887), on which see Chapter 2, as well as many of Petrarch's Latin works translated by Victor Develay and discussed in Chapter 3.

[40]   'On m'a plusieurs fois conseillé de ne livrer à la publicité que des morceaux choisis des œuvres de Pétrarque ; mais pourquoi le lecteur ne serait-il donc lui-même juge et appréciateur de l'œuvre dans son intégrité, en lui laissant la faculté d'admirer ce qui mérite de l'être et de glisser sur ce qui lui paraîtra moins digne de fixer son attention ?' Joseph Poulenc, *Rimes de Pétrarque, traduites en vers, texte en regard*, 4 vols (Paris: A. Lacroix, 1865), I, 7.

[41]   Poulenc, *Rimes de Pétrarque* (1877), I, p. iii.

[42]   'Je me suis fait une loi de m'identifier profondément avec le poëte italien, cherchant à pénétrer sa pensée la plus intime.' Poulenc, *Rimes de Pétrarque* (1877), I, p. vi. Venuti notes in *The Translator's Invisibility*, p. 73, an earlier example of a translator's 'sympathetic identification with the foreign author', in the work of Alexander Fraser Tytler.

sonnets, rather than any looser verse structure), as is more typical of translations of Petrarch's sonnets into French during the second half of the nineteenth century.

Subsequent to Poulenc's two editions, another translation of Petrarch based on Marsand's edition was published by Reynard in 1883, in prose rather than verse.[43] Reynard was an expert in medieval Italian, having translated both Dante's *Commedia* (1877) and Boccaccio's *Decameron* (1879), and with his translation of Petrarch (1883) thereby completing his set of the so-called 'three crowns' (*tre corone*) of Italian literature.[44] Around the same time, Reynard also produced a translation of Ariosto's *Orlando furioso* (1880), confirming both his literary credentials and impressive productivity.[45] After Reynard, a further complete prose translation of the *Canzoniere* was published, by Fernand Brisset in two volumes at the turn of the century; Brisset's translation is, then, the fifth and final complete translation of the *Canzoniere* into French in this time period. At first, Brisset published translations of the majority of Petrarch's sonnets (297 in total, out of a possible 317), restricting himself to this form and omitting poems not directly related to the love story of Petrarch and Laura.[46] The sonnets omitted from this volume are those that also feature in Marsand's fourth section.[47] In a subsequent volume from 1903, Brisset expanded this translation to include other forms (*canzoni, ballate, sestine*, madrigals), as well as the *Triumphi* and a section of 'Diverse subjects' (*Sujets divers*) which contains the twenty sonnets omitted from the 1899 publication.[48] In this manner the 1903 translation complements and completes the initial publication of selected sonnets, and Brisset's source edition of Marsand is confirmed by the four sections into which the second volume is divided: 'To Laura alive', 'To Laura dead', 'The Triumphs', and 'Diverse subjects' (*À Laure vivante, À Laure morte, Les Triomphes*, and *Sujets divers*). Fernand Brisset also published a shorter volume of selected sonnets translated from Petrarch in 1921, as well as a lengthier later volume of new rhythmical translations in 1933.[49]

An unusual feature of the ordering of Brisset's first volume of translations from 1899 is that it ends with *RVF* 91, a sonnet about a beautiful lady (*bella donna*) who has died.[50] As already noted, this sonnet is usually understood as being about

[43] Francisque Reynard, *Les Rimes de François Pétrarque: traduction nouvelle* (Paris: G. Charpentier, 1883).

[44] Dante Alighieri, *La Divine Comédie: traduction nouvelle par Francisque Reynard*, 2 vols (Paris: A. Lemerre, 1877); Giovanni Boccaccio, *Le Décaméron: traduction nouvelle par Francisque Reynard*, 2 vols (Paris: G. Charpentier, 1879).

[45] Ariosto, *Roland furieux: traduction nouvelle par Francisque Reynard*, 4 vols (Paris: A. Lemerre, 1880).

[46] Fernand Brisset *Les Sonnets de Pétrarque à Laure: traduction nouvelle avec introduction et notes* (Paris: Perrin et Cie, 1899).

[47] The sonnets omitted by Brisset in 1899 are, then, *RVF* 7, 10, 24–7, 40, 58, 92, 98, 103–4, 120, 136–9, 166, 232, and 322.

[48] Fernand Brisset, *Canzones, triomphes et poésies diverses: traduction nouvelle avec introduction et notes* (Paris: Perrin et Cie, 1903).

[49] Fernand Brisset, *Sonnets à Laure: traduction* (London: Leopold B. Hill, 1921); Fernand Brisset, *Pétrarque à Laure: les sonnets: traduction nouvelle rythmée* (Paris: Librairie Ancienne J.-A. Quereuil, 1933).

[50] *RVF* 91 is also the concluding sonnet in the translation of Ernest Cabadé, *Les Sonnets*

Petrarch's brother's lady, whose death is seen as a catalyst for Gherardo's retreat to the monastery at Montrieux. This sonnet had been decisively rejected as not relating to Laura in Vellutello's marginalization of it by placing it in his third section.[51] Yet for Marsand this sonnet is instead about Laura, and is placed as the penultimate poem of the *Canzoniere*, directly before *RVF* 366. In translations that follow Marsand's ordering but translate only sonnets (such as Brisset's first translation, and Ernest Cabadé's publication from 1902), *RVF* 91 thus forms an abrupt, new conclusion to the collection. The sonnet stands as a middle ground between mourning and consolation; the death of the lady enables her ascension to Heaven, in a vertical movement of transcendence which the bereaved lover is exhorted to follow. Unlike the austere rejection of Laura in favour of the Virgin Mary in *RVF* 366, this alternative final poem presents earthly and divine love as compatible and sequential, thus offering a more attractive conclusion than the original ending for readers wedded above all to the love story of Petrarch and Laura.

Other notable features of Brisset's translations from the first publication onwards include his willingness to draw attention to the texts as translations. On the one hand, Brisset uses parentheses throughout to mark what he considers to be additions to each text on his part, in a bid to distinguish more clearly the original authorial voice and subsequent translatorly interference. On the other hand, Brisset also embeds the difficulty of translation within his rendition of particular poems. For instance, in *RVF* 286 (vv. 1–6), Petrarch expresses the impossible desire to describe Laura's voice adequately:

> Se quell'aura soave de' sospiri
> ch'i' odo di colei che qui fu mia
> donna, or è in cielo, et anchor par qui sia,
> et viva, et senta, et vada, et ami, et spiri,
>
> ritrar potessi, or che caldi desiri
> movrei parlando!
>
> ***
>
> If that sweet breath of sighs
> which I hear of her who here was my
> lady, now she is in Heaven, and still she seems to be here,
> and to live, and feel, and go, and love, and breathe,
>
> could I portray, then what hot desires
> I would move by speaking!

The verb that Petrarch uses is *ritrar*, meaning 'to portray' or 'depict'. In his translation, Brisset changes the image from one of painting to one aligned with his own specialism, translation.[52] Thus he begins this sonnet 'If I could translate [*traduire*]

de Pétrarque traduits en sonnets français avec une préface de M. de Tréverret (Paris: Alphonse Lemerre, 1902), a volume which has the same ordering as Brisset, *Les Sonnets de Pétrarque à Laure* (1899) and is discussed in Chapter 2.

  51 Kennedy, *Authorizing Petrarch*, p. 288.

  52 On translations which contain and reflect their own metaphors of translation, see

as I feel it the sweetness of the words sighed by she who was my Lady'.[53] Brisset here reaches out sympathetically to the lover's quandary, which is aligned with challenges of translation with which he himself is familiar. Brisset's translation of *RVF* 293 in the same volume similarly features an embedded image of the translator's own art. The first quatrain of this sonnet in Petrarch's original describes how writing poetry is much more difficult after Laura's death:

> S'io avesse pensato che sì care
> fossin le voci de' sospir' miei in rima,
> fatte l'avrei, dal sospirar mio prima,
> in numero più spesse, in stil più rare.

***

> If I had thought that so dear
> would be the sounds of my sighs in rhyme,
> I would have made them, since first I sighed,
> greater in number and rarer in style.

Brisset renders this quatrain as follows:

> Si j'avais pensé que ces traductions poétiques de mes plaintes pussent acquérir une telle valeur, je les aurais faites, dès le premier jour où j'ai soupiré, plus nombreuses comme quantité, plus rares comme style.[54]

***

> If I had thought that these poetic translations of my laments could acquire such value, I would have made them, from the first day that I sighed, more numerous in quantity, rarer in style.

In each case, Brisset inserts into his own translations a reflection of his work as a translator which makes these lines seem particularly apt and personally felt. The reader is reminded that these texts are translations, and the first person of both poems is destabilized and stretched to encompass translator as well as poet. Either Petrarch is already a translator, or the 'sighs' (*RVF* 286) and 'laments' (*RVF* 293) belong as much to Brisset as to Petrarch; both possible interpretations are called into play simultaneously through Brisset's *mise en abyme* of his own art. Particularly in the second example, moreover, Brisset asserts the value (*valeur*) of translation as equal to that of the original poetry.

Amongst these complete translations of Petrarch's *Canzoniere*, Hippolyte Godefroy's translation from 1900 has a peculiar place. It is presented as *Poésies complètes de Francesco Petrarca*, although in reality it omits seven poems in total: *RVF* 55, 59, 63, 99, 149, 314, and 324. These omissions seem accidental rather than deliberate,

Matthew Reynolds, *The Poetry of Translation: From Chaucer & Petrarch to Homer & Logue* (Oxford: Oxford University Press, 2011).

[53] 'Si je pouvais traduire comme je la sens la douceur des paroles soupirées par celle qui fut ma Donna', Brisset, *Les Sonnets de Pétrarque à Laure* (1899), p. 230.

[54] Brisset, *Les Sonnets de Pétrarque à Laure* (1899), p. 237.

since no reason is given for skipping these particular poems, which would normally be included in the main body of the *Canzoniere* even under Marsand's ordering. One possible criterion for exclusion is that the majority of these seven poems are *ballate* (*RVF* 55, 59, 63, 149, and 324), although since Godefroy does translate two other *ballate* (*RVF* 11 and 14) such a decision would seem inconsistent. Moreover, the remaining two poems excluded are both sonnets, making a deliberate exclusion on formal grounds even less likely. The two omitted sonnets are *RVF* 99, a poem declaring the insidiousness of earthly temptations to an unidentified addressee (possibly Petrarch's brother or Giovanni Colonna), and *RVF* 314, a poem which recalls the portents of Laura's death and so bears notable similarities to the sequence of sonnets at the end of the first half of the *Canzoniere*. Godefroy's ordering is the most unpredictable of all the translations studied, which would support the explanation of accidental omission. Most strange about Godefroy's translation is, however, his inclusion of two poems (*RVF* 255 and 308) in both the *in vita* and *in morte* sections, with slightly different renditions in each case (including different titles).[55] The duplication of these two sonnets suggests a lack of attention, since Godefroy did not seem to realize that he had already translated these poems; more positively, however, it also allows an insight into one translator's workshop by revealing competing choices and possible alternatives that have usually been obliterated by the time a translation reaches publication.

RVF 255 is given here first in the original Italian and in English translation of the Italian, and then in Godefroy's two successive translations:

> La sera desiare, odiar l'aurora
> soglion questi tranquilli et lieti amanti;
> a me doppia la sera et doglia et pianti,
> la matina è per me più felice hora:
>
> ché spesso in un momento apron allora
> l'un sole et l'altro quasi duo levanti,
> di beltate et di lume sì sembianti,
> ch'anco il ciel de la terra s'innamora;
>
> come già fece allor che' primi rami
> verdeggiâr, che nel cor radice m'ànno,
> per cui sempre altrui più che me stesso ami.
>
> Così di me due contrarie hore fanno;
> et chi m'acqueta è ben ragion ch'i' brami,
> et tema et odî chi m'adduce affanno.

***

> To desire the evening and hate the dawn
> is the habit of these calm and happy lovers;
> for me evening redoubles my grief and my tears,
> morning is for me the happier time:

---

[55]   For the texts of the two translations of *RVF* 255 see below, and for *RVF* 308 see Godefroy, *Poésies complètes de Francesco Petrarca*, pp. 81–2 and pp. 288–9.

for often in a moment then open
one sun and the other as if two Orients,
so similar in beauty and in light,
so that Heaven again falls in love with Earth;

as it already did when the first branches
that have their roots in my heart were green,
for which I will always love another more than myself.

Thus do two contrary hours affect me;
and it is truly right that I should desire that which calms me,
and fear and hate that which makes me suffer.

***

Le matin est pour lui son heure de choix

Ceux qui désirent le soir et haïssent l'aurore sont toujours en repos et sont d'heureux amants, tandis que pour moi, le soir c'est ma douleur, ce sont mes tourments ! Le matin est pour moi l'heure la plus délicieuse,
Qui souvent, au même instant, ouvre l'un et l'autre soleil, pour ainsi dire deux soleils levants de beauté et d'éclats si semblables, que le ciel a l'air de s'enflammer pour la terre.
Comme il fit alors que ses premiers rameaux, enfonçant dans mon cœur, tout en verdoyant leur premières racines par lesquelles ils me font toujours préférer à moi-même une autre personne.
C'est ainsi que sur moi je vois les deux contraires venir s'exécuter, et il n'y a rien d'étonnant qu'on puisse me voir aspirer vers ce qui vient me tranquilliser et qu'on me voie craindre, qu'on me voie frissonner devant ce qui m'apporte la douleur.[56]

***

Il ne peut avoir de repos, sa passion le dévore toujours

Ceux qui désirent le soir, qui haïssent l'aurore, sont toujours en repos et sont d'heureux amants, tandis que pour moi, le soir c'est ma douleur : c'est mon affliction, ce sont mes tourments !
Le matin est pour moi l'heure la plus délicieuse qui souvent me découvre l'un et l'autre levant. Tous les deux, ils sont si bien semblables de beauté, de lumière, qu'il me semble voir au même instant le ciel se passionner pour la terre.
Lorsque dans le cœur les premiers rameaux commencèrent à verdoyer, que les racines commencèrent à s'enfoncer et me préférer une autre personne à moi-même.
C'est ainsi que sur moi agissent les deux heures contraires que j'appelle le calme, l'espérance, celle que je crains, celle que je hais.[57]

---

[56] Godefroy, *Poésies complètes de Francesco Petrarca*, pp. 233–4.
[57] Godefroy, *Poésies complètes de Francesco Petrarca*, pp. 294–5.

Immediately evident are the contrasting titles given by Godefroy to this poem, and which call for radically different interpretations. The first, 'The morning is for him his favourite hour', presents the sonnet as a happy tale of Petrarch's enjoyment of the start of every new day, ignoring the equal presence of hatred of evening within the poem. The second, in contrast, highlights the poet's unhappiness and inescapable, endless frustration: 'He cannot find any rest, his passion devours him constantly'. These divergent titles are likely motivated not so much by a close reading of the sonnet, twice over, but rather by the wider context of each poem in Godefroy's new ordering. The optimistically-titled version appropriately comes in the *in vita* section, while the pessimistic reframing is justified by its position in the *in morte* half of the *Canzoniere*. From this perspective, Godefroy asserts that there is no rest (*repos*) for Petrarch after Laura's death, even though this sonnet does celebrate morning as an enjoyable time for the poet (as the earlier title acknowledges). In Petrarch's own ordering, this sonnet comes from very late in the first part, at a point of transition when fears over Laura's death are already rife (see, for instance, *RVF* 250–2). Godefroy's confusion highlights the poem's ambiguity as neither wholly *in vita* or *in morte*, but in an interim, uncertain space between the two.

The two translations again diverge significantly in the final tercet. In the original Italian, these lines provide a fitting conclusion to the poem by restating, in a chiasmus, the contrast between morning (*chi m'acqueta*, 'that which calms me') and evening (*chi m'adduce affanno*, 'that which makes me suffer') and the poet's consequent desire for the former and hatred of the latter. Godefroy's first translation renders this contrast clearly and effectively. His second version, however, is much briefer and in this brevity somewhat elides the crucial distinction between the two hours, by losing the important grammatical parallelism on which this distinction is based in the original. These two translations of the same sonnet are likely to undermine the authority of Godefroy's volume, since they make a mockery of the bipartite division (by featuring in both halves) and suggest a worrying memory lapse or lack of care. Yet they also, especially through their titles, reveal the determining relationship between text and macrotext, that is, the *Canzoniere*'s bipartite structure, and unintentionally provide an unparalleled insight into the act of translation as a potentially limitless process of experimentation and rewriting.

Having reviewed the five complete translations of Petrarch's *Canzoniere* in this period (by Gramont, Montesquiou, Poulenc, Reynard, and Brisset, with an account also of the almost complete translation of Godefroy), I would observe that complete translations of Petrarch are slightly more common in the second than the first half of the nineteenth century, and that translating into prose rather than verse also increases in popularity as the century proceeds. The closeness of these results, however, means that these conclusions should be verified through comparison with the situation for incomplete French translations of the *Canzoniere* produced in the nineteenth century, and such translations are, accordingly, the focus of the next chapter. From this perspective, Godefroy's translation of 1900 bridges the gap between a desire for completion and an urge, even if unconscious, to be more selective.

2

Partial Translations of Petrarch's *Canzoniere*

INCOMPLETE TRANSLATIONS OF Petrarch's *Canzoniere* suggest a process of selection and preference that is largely absent from the projects of complete translations of the *Canzoniere* discussed in the previous chapter. Incomplete translations bear witness to choices and decisions made by translators faced with a collection that they do not wish to replicate in its entirety, revealing varying levels of familiarity, preferential treatment, and avoidance. Incomplete translations often also create a new order and narrative which are potentially at odds with the structure desired by the original poet. This type of disorder is particularly visible in translations which do not maintain the *Canzoniere*'s macro-narrative penitential frame, from *RVF* 1 (an introductory sonnet addressed to readers and expressing repentance for past, youthful error) to *RVF* 366 (a *canzone* addressed to the Virgin Mary and a rejection of Laura). Critics have argued about whether the end of the *Canzoniere* represents a true conversion from earthly to divine love or, instead, a desire for conversion that is suspended, interrupted, and incomplete.[1] This type of argument does not seem to have detained French translators of Petrarch, who most often dismantled this penitential frame entirely, either by omitting *RVF* 366 (a common choice), by reordering the poems according to different priorities, or, in extreme cases, by translating only a few sonnets in isolation and entirely out of context. This last example calls into question the broader relationship between incompletion and meaning. In the case of highly selective translations, the burden of distilling the essence of Petrarch is placed on a mere few poems. The choice of appropriate poems for this task is, in such cases, highly charged, but was helped in the nineteenth century by an already more narrow understanding of who Petrarch was and what his poetry represented. Petrarch, for most translators, was and was to remain a love poet and author of sonnets. From this perspective *RVF* 366, a *canzone* ostensibly rejecting both earthly love and Laura explicitly, was predictably unwelcome and all too easily sidelined, while one or two sonnets could, conversely, be celebrated as the essence of his art.

In the following analysis of incomplete translations, I begin with the early examples of late eighteenth-century translators of Petrarch (namely Sade, Nicolas Antoine

---

[1]   See, in particular, Christian Moevs, 'Subjectivity and Conversion in Dante and Petrarch', in *Petrarch and Dante: Anti-Dantism, Metaphysics, Tradition*, ed. Zygmunt G. Barański and Theodore J. Cachey (Notre Dame, IN: University of Notre Dame Press, 2009), pp. 226–59.

Romet, Marianne-Agnès Pillement de Falques, the abbé Roman, and Pierre-Charles Levesque), before proceeding to translators who chose to translate only Petrarch's sonnets (in particular, Emma Mahul and Philibert Le Duc) and the formally more diverse examples of Léonce de Saint-Geniès and Jean-Paul-Louis d'Arrighi. This varied corpus showcases a range of different translation approaches, from the typically freer, more selective attitudes of late eighteenth-century translators to the more frequent commitment of translators in the second half of the nineteenth century to the sonnet form as a viable and obvious choice. Further, through selection and restructuring these translations reveal different Petrarchs according to the preferences of each translator.

I conclude this chapter with a discussion of the most popular (that is, the most frequently translated) poems of the *Canzoniere*, with a particular focus on French translations of *RVF* 126 after Voltaire.[2] These favourite poems help to clarify what French readers and translators of this time found especially attractive about Petrarch, and which parts of his *Canzoniere* they cherished most consistently, in this way revealing much not only about the particular conception of Petrarch in France at this time but also, more generally, about the poetic tastes and concerns shared by these translators.

Late Eighteenth-Century Translators

As already noted in the Introduction, Sade's *Mémoires* were the catalyst for nineteenth-century interest in Petrarch both in France and, less predictably, in England, the latter through Susannah Dobson's abridged English translation of the work.[3] At the outset, Sade relates his decision to retain the poetic aura of Petrarch's texts through verse translation. Justifying this decision, Sade argues that prose translations of poetry render only 'the corpse or the skeleton of a poet' (*le cadavre ou le squelette d'un Poëte*); by analogy, verse form is the flesh and blood of a poet's work and provides the pleasing exterior and covering to the basic underlying structure.[4] A further analogy is soon afterwards employed by Sade, this time no longer in relation to any formal choice, but rather in relation to his translation project more generally. According to this perspective, Sade presents his translations of Petrarch as 'like a bad print of a good painting, and like a poor copy which can only provide a very general idea of the original'.[5] The typical false modesty of *captatio benevolentiae* is no doubt partly in evidence here, but the simile, nonetheless, usefully maps the relationship between translator and august model or original onto that of an art student studiously and dutifully producing copies of a venerable past master. This is a form of the *ut pictura poesis* doctrine amended for the more hierarchical

---

[2]   For the texts of the translations of the first stanza of *RVF* 126 from Voltaire (1756) to Brisset (1903), see Appendix 2.

[3]   On English translations of Petrarch in the second half of the eighteenth century, see François J.-L. Mouret, *Les Traducteurs anglais de Pétrarque 1754–1798* (Paris: Didier, 1976).

[4]   Sade, *Mémoires*, I, p. cvii.

[5]   'comme une mauvaise estampe d'un bon tableau, & comme une foible copie qui ne peut donner qu'une idée très-légere de l'original', Sade, *Mémoires*, I, p. cxi.

relationship traditionally established between translation and original.[6] According to Sade, translating Petrarch is, in short, a form of artful apprenticeship that has fixed, limited parameters.

A further, more complicated choice facing Sade beyond that between prose or verse is that of which poems from Petrarch to translate. The abbé at first expresses his decision to translate 'most of the Italian poems of Petrarch, *canzoni*, sonnets, madrigals, etc.'.[7] As the introductory letters unfold, however, the choices made become more exclusive and restricted, as Sade admits:

> I have left the *sestine* or *ritornelli*, poems of poor taste, where the poet hobbles himself with constraints which oblige him to sacrifice meaning to words and thought to rhyme. I have not thought to translate those of his *canzoni* which are unintelligible, nor certain mysterious sonnets, which Petrarch was pleased to shroud in a darkness impenetrable to all the skill of interpreters. I have done the same with a few sonnets, in which I found wordplay, *concetti*, and outrageous metaphors which would not have been successful in our language. Finally, I have taken the liberty of omitting particular stanzas of certain *canzoni*, and particular quatrains from certain sonnets, where this great poet is unbearable, by the admission even of the best Italian critics; but it is to be acknowledged that such cases are extremely rare.[8]

A key motivation behind Sade's selections is also the desire not to bore (*rebuter*, 'to repel' or 'discourage') readers 'by such a great number of monotonous, weepy verses' (*par un si grand nombre de vers monotones & larmoyans*), since Sade considers the French spirit more attuned to 'pleasure' (*plaisir*) than 'sadness' (*tristesse*), in contrast to his perception of Italian sentimentality.[9] It is this opinion which doubtless motivates Sade's strange self-restriction to the *in vita* poems of the *Canzoniere*. Surprisingly, no poems at all from part two of the *Canzoniere* (the *in morte* section) are translated in the *Mémoires*, as if Laura is of no interest once she has died and as if Petrarch's poems at this point had truly become too tiresomely weepy.

Sade's 'Frenchification' of Petrarch (through both translation into French and

---

[6]   On this particularly eighteenth-century doctrine, see David Marshall, 'Ut pictura poesis', in *The Cambridge History of Literary Criticism*, ed. H. B. Nisbet and Claude Rawson, 9 vols (Cambridge: Cambridge University Press, 1989–2001), IV: *The Eighteenth Century* (1997), 681–99.

[7]   'la plus grande partie des Poésies Italiennes de Pétrarque, Odes, Sonnets, Madrigaux, &c.' Sade, *Mémoires*, I, p. xcvii.

[8]   'J'ai laissé les Sestines ou Ritournelles, Poëmes de mauvais goût, où le Poëte se donne des entraves qui l'obligent de sacrifier le sens aux mots, la pensée à la rime. Je n'ai pas imaginé de traduire des Odes inintelligibles & des Sonnets mystérieux, où il a plu à Pétrarque de s'envelopper de ténèbres, que tout l'art des Interprètes n'a pu percer. J'ai traité de même quelques Sonnets, où j'ai trouvé des jeux de mots, des *concetti* & des métaphores outrées, qui n'auroient pas réussi dans notre Langue. Enfin, j'ai pris la liberté de supprimer quelques stances de Chansons, quelques quatrains de Sonnets, où ce grand Poëte n'est pas supportable, de l'aveu même des meilleurs critiques Italiens ; mais il faut avouer que ces cas-là sont extrêmement rares.' Sade, *Mémoires*, I, pp. cviii–cix.

[9]   Sade, *Mémoires*, I, p. cxii.

the claim of Petrarch's Frenchness, cited in the Introduction) is thus tinged by the awkward awareness that Petrarch's poetry may be irredeemably 'un-French' in its lyrical habits and content, and this awareness is demonstrated not only in the avoidance of poems about death and mourning, but also—as hinted in the passage cited above—in a reluctance to engage fully in Petrarchan wordplay.[10] The author, for instance, soon reveals himself to be uncomfortable with Petrarchan wordplay such as the fragmentation of Laura's name in *RVF* 5, or the polysemy of Laura's name (laurel, breeze, gold, and so on) spread throughout the *Canzoniere*, considering such linguistic tricks or *concetti* (conceits) distasteful to French ears and unworthy of Petrarch. *RVF* 5 is accordingly dismissed as 'childish wordplay on the syllables which make up the name Laure or Laurette which is impossible to render in French and which is very much beneath a genius such as that of Petrarch'.[11] Sade's dislike of *RVF* 5 was to be reiterated more than a century later even more vehemently by Ernest Cabadé, who declared that 'All in all, this sonnet will not add anything to the poet's glory. It is a type of acrostic without great taste'.[12]

Similarly, puns on Laura's name are condemned by Sade with the assumption that 'Petrarch's verses in which Laura is confused at times with the laurel, at others with Daphne herself, will no doubt shock the delicate ears of the wits [*beaux esprits*] of our century'.[13] Mythological identification and onomastic wordplay are, apparently, not highly valued literary exercises in France in the second half of the eighteenth century, at least if Sade's opinion is anything to go by.[14] In this way, many poems lose their original motivation and their polysemy is diminished to merely

---

[10] Sade's view of *sestine* and wordplay as un-French shows a lack of knowledge of literary history, since both—although for Sade highly Petrarchan—in fact have French or rather Occitan origins, in the work of the troubadour Arnaut Daniel. That the *sestina* or *sextine* originated in France was, as we saw in Chapter 1, celebrated by Gramont (*Olim*, p. 172). For the poetic play on *aura* before Petrarch (in particular, in Arnaut), see Contini, 'Préhistoire de l'*aura* de Pétrarque', in *Actes et mémoires du premier congrès international de langue et littérature du Midi de la France* (Avignon: Palais du Roure, 1957), pp. 113–18 (repr. in Contini, *Varianti e altra linguistica*, pp. 193–9).

[11] 'un jeu de mots puerile sur les syllabes qui composent le nom de Laure ou Laurette qu'il est impossible de rendre en François, & qui est bien au-dessous d'un génie tel que celui de Petrarque', Sade, *Mémoires*, I, 177. See also, for a similar opinion, P.-L. Ginguené, *Histoire littéraire de l'Italie*, 14 vols (Paris: Chez Michaud frères, 1811–35), II (1811), 564.

[12] 'Somme toute, ce n'est pas ce sonnet qui ajoutera rien à la gloire du poète. C'est une espèce d'acrostiche sans grande saveur.' Cabadé, *Les Sonnets de Pétrarque*, p. 5. For a translation of *RVF* 5 as, in fact, an acrostic, see *Choix de sonnets de Pétrarque traduits par Madame S. Emma Mahul des comtes Dejean: seconde édition revue, corrigée et augmentée de la traduction de différentes poésies de Pétrarque* (Florence: Héritiers Botta, 1867), p. 125.

[13] 'Les vers de Pétrarque où Laure est confondue tantôt avec le laurier, tantôt avec Daphné elle-même, choqueront sans doutes les oreilles délicates des beaux esprits de notre siecle.' Sade, *Mémoires*, I, 179.

[14] See, nonetheless, on the fundamental myth of Apollo and Daphne in Petrarch: Peter Hainsworth, 'The Myth of Daphne in the *Rerum vulgarium fragmenta*', *Italian Studies*, 34.1 (1979), 28–44, and Marga Cottino-Jones, 'The Myth of Apollo and Daphne in Petrarch's *Canzoniere*: The Dynamics and Literary Function of Transformation', in *Francis Petrarch, Six Centuries Later: A Symposium*, ed. Aldo Scaglione (Chapel Hill: University of North Carolina; Chicago: The Newberry Library, 1975), pp. 152–76.

purported biographical resonance, as the figures of Laura, whether *lauro*, *l'oro*, *l'aura*, or other permutations, are similarly reduced to the univocal denotation of the historical figure of Laure de Sade. Sade's resistance to Petrarchan wordplay was to be shared by the historian Simonde de Sismondi, who himself noted: 'I would rather be reminded of Laura by thought, sentiment, and passion, than by the eternal wordplay of *lauro* (laurel) or *l'aura* (air, the morning breeze).'[15] Even that fervent admirer of Petrarch, Lamartine, expressed some discomfort with 'his sonnets, where he barely disguised the name of Laura under the image a little too transparent and a little too childishly allusive of the laurel (*Lauro*).'[16] Thus, from Sade onwards the typical and omnipresent wordplay of Petrarch's *Canzoniere*, in particular in relation to the name of Laura, was treated with a certain degree of suspicion, resulting both from a consistently biographical reading of Petrarch's poetry and from a belief in the incompatibility of *calembours* and high art.

The task Sade sets himself is to produce, in verse, 'a faithful translation, without being servile' (*une traduction fidele, sans être servile*).[17] Most translators throughout the late eighteenth and nineteenth centuries will similarly assert their fidelity to their chosen texts, although this term fluctuates in meaning depending on by whom it is invoked. As a translator Sade is also openly reflective and self-critical, admitting freely to the reader when his powers of discernment and interpretation are at a loss. One such case is the final tercet of *RVF* 67, of which Sade confesses: 'I have not trans-lated the three last lines of this sonnet, because I have understood nothing in them. Petrarch congratulates himself *on having wet his feet instead of his eyes*; he desires, *that a sweet April come to dry his eyes*. What does that mean?'[18] Here, Sade translates the sonnet's ending literally, but reveals that translation for him is interpretative and enhances meaning, hence he shies away from passages he cannot conceptually analyse even if he can understand what each word denotes. The desire to clarify a difficult text is evident, based on the assumption both that Petrarch and Petrarch in translation ought to be semantically transparent at all times.[19]

While Sade warned from the outset that he would omit incomprehensible passages, at other points he deviates from the parameters which he initially set for

---

[15] 'J'aimerais mieux que la pensée, le sentiment, la passion, me rappelassent Laure, que l'éternel jeu de mots de *lauro* (le laurier), ou *l'aura* (l'air, le souffle du matin).' Simonde de Sismondi, *De la littérature du Midi de l'Europe*, 4 vols (Paris and Strasbourg: Treuttel et Würtz, 1813), I, 408–9.

[16] 'Ses sonnets, où il déguisait à peine le nom de Laure sous l'image un peu trop trans-parente et un peu trop puérilement allusive du laurier (*Lauro*)', Lamartine, *Cours familier de littérature*, VI, 20. On Lamartine and Petrarch, see Chapter 5.

[17] Sade, *Mémoires*, I, p. civ.

[18] 'Je n'ai pas traduit les trois derniers vers de ce Sonnet, parce que je n'y ai rien compris. Petrarque s'applaudit *d'avoir les pieds mouillés au lieu des yeux* ; il desire, *qu'un Avril plus doux vienne sécher ses yeux*. Qu'est-ce que cela veut dire ?' Sade, *Mémoires*, I, 316. The final tercet in Italian is 'Piacemi almen d'aver cangiato stile / dagli occhi a' pie', se del lor esser molli / gli altri asciugasse un più cortese aprile' ('It pleases me at least to have changed style from eyes to feet, if from their being wet a more courteous April might dry the others'), *RVF* 67, vv. 12–14.

[19] The myth of the transparency of translation has been roundly criticized by Venuti, though recognized as historically pervasive, in *The Translator's Invisibility*.

himself. Thus for one sonnet he resorts to a prose rather than a verse translation since, as he confesses, 'I did not dare translate it into verse'.[20] The sonnet in question is *RVF* 31, a poem about a lady's early death and the passage of her soul through the heavenly spheres. On the one hand, Sade's recurrent admissions of failure imbue the author's voice with a certain modest and self-reflective charm. On the other hand, these same admissions bestow on Petrarch the allure of something just out of reach, which is enthralling as well as frustrating.

More strangely, Sade occasionally combines several poems into one translation, arguably recognising Petrarch's habit of repetition and reiteration yet seemingly disregarding poetic nuance and detail in the wish to create one super-Petrarchan poem in French drawing on a number of different poems. Sade resorts to this condensation and mixing in the case of the three *canzoni* on Laura's eyes (*RVF* 71–3), which are translated as one poem in prose without the original Italian, for the following reason:

> I would like to make these known to my readers who cannot understand Italian, but I do not know how to go about doing so. Translating them into French verse is far beyond my strength, and I fear that a translation in prose, though absolutely literal, might weaken the opinion that Italians want us to have of these three graces.
>
> I have undertaken to translate them a little freely, as if a light sketch of them. I have thought it better to merge the three poems into one, without observing scrupulously the order and progress of the author. I have taken the liberty of removing certain repetitions and things which would not work in our language. I do not flatter myself that these liberties will be approved by all.[21]

Once more in this passage, the image of translation as an imperfect copy of a drawing (*une légere esquisse*) returns.

A similar technique is used by Sade for *RVF* 108, 110, and 111 (sonnets about the fleeting but overwhelming presence of Laura, cherished in the poet's memory), as well as for the four sonnets on Laura's glove, which is lost, found, and revered by the poet, only to be reluctantly returned to its owner (*RVF* 199–202). In the latter case, Sade combines self-justification with an attack on the quality of this particular sequence of poems:

---

[20] 'je n'ai pas eu le courage de traduire en vers', Sade, *Mémoires*, 1, 236.

[21] 'Je voudrois les faire connoître à mes Lecteurs qui n'entendent pas l'Italien, mais je ne sçais comment m'y prendre. Les traduire en vers françois, cela est fort au-dessus de mes forces, je crains qu'une traduction en prose, absolument littérale, n'affoiblit l'idée que les Italiens veulent que nous ayons de ces trois graces.

J'ai entrepris d'en faire une traduction un peu libre qui en sera comme une légere esquisse. J'ai cru devoir les fondre toutes les trois en une, sans observer scrupuleusement l'ordre & la marche de l'Auteur. J'ai pris la liberté de retrancher quelques répétitions & des choses qui ne réussiroient pas dans notre langue. Je ne me flatte pas que ces libertés soient approuvées de tout le monde.' Sade, *Mémoires*, 1, 391.

We should be more amazed to witness the most learned man of his century, who was occupied with serious matters (as we will soon see), write four sonnets on such a frivolous subject. [...] Here is the summary of these sonnets: in all my translations, I have never allowed myself so much freedom; I have removed everything that I thought would not be successful in our language. If I dared, I would say that what I have removed does not deserve to be regretted, and is not good even in Italian.[22]

Alongside the original Italian of these four sonnets, Sade places his own sixteen-line French verse summary of the events narrated:

> Un instant a vu naître & finir mon bonheur,
> D'un joli gand, tissu d'or & de soie,
> Le hazard & l'amour m'avoient fait possesseur :
> Rien n'égaloit les transports de ma joie.
> Voulez-vous de ce bien connoître la valeur ?
> Regardez une main plus blanche que l'yvoire,
> De jolis doigts façonnés par l'amour ;
> Ce gand me les cachoit; mais qui pourra le croire ?
> Je n'ai pas su le garder un seul jour.
> Une petite main d'une foiblesse extrême,
> Dans un instant malgré moi l'a repris,
> Pour conserver un objet de ce prix,
> Il falloit fuir, combattre même ;
> Je le sais bien, & j'en rougis ;
> Mais que dis-je ! Il est bientôt pris,
> Ce qu'on dispute à l'objet que l'on aime.

***

> An instant saw my happiness be born and come to an end,
> Of a pretty glove, woven with gold and silk,
> Chance and love had made me the possessor:
> Nothing equalled the transports of my joy.
> Do you want to know the value of this possession?
> Look at a hand whiter than ivory,
> Pretty fingers fashioned by love;
> This glove hid them from me; but who will be able to believe it?
> I did not know how to keep it for one single day.
> A small hand, extremely weak,
> In an instant despite myself retook it,

---

[22] 'On devroit être plus étonné de voir l'homme le plus savant de son siecle, occupé de grandes affaires (comme on le verra bientôt), faire quatre sonnets sur un sujet aussi frivole. [...] Voici le précis de ces sonnets : dans toutes mes traductions, je ne me suis jamais permis tant de liberté ; j'ai retranché tout ce que j'ai cru qui ne réussiroit pas dans notre langue. Si j'osois, je dirois que ce que j'ai retranché, ne mérite pas d'être regretté, & n'est pas bon même en Italien.' Sade, *Mémoires*, II, 88.

> In order to keep an object of such a price,
> It was necessary to flee, to fight even;
> Well do I know it, and I blush at it;
> But what am I saying! It is soon taken,
> That for which we vie with the object that we love.[23]

Of *RVF* 199, Sade omits the extended praise of Laura's hand and glove, retaining the image of ivory but neither that of pearls or roses, and in particular ignoring Petrarch's moral, generalizing commentary on the incident, 'O inconstancy of human things!'[24] This last phrase is perhaps considered inappropriately elevated in tone for the banality and frivolity—in Sade's opinion—of the micro-narrative. *RVF* 200 is entirely absent, since it is only tangential to the tale, and consists in praise of Laura's physical beauty more generally; so, too, is *RVF* 202, which returns to a more general description of the fatal effects of love on the poet.

In contrast, the pivotal *RVF* 201 provides most of the material for Sade's rewriting, including the details that obtaining the glove was the work of chance and love (*Mia ventura et Amor*, *RVF* 201, v. 1), that the possession and renunciation happened the same day (*quel giorno*, v. 5), rendering the poet almost simultaneously rich and poor (*ricco et povero*, v. 6; compare the opening line of Sade's version, where the contrast is between the birth and end of happiness). From *RVF* 201 Sade also gleans the poet's embarrassment (*vergogna*, v. 8) and the feebleness with which he recalls relinquishing the glove to one weaker than him, endowed with 'the strength only of a little angel' (*lo sforzo sol d'un angioletta*, v. 11, with the Italian diminutive transferred, less flatteringly, to the description in Sade of Laura's *petite main d'une foiblesse extrême*). The final couplet of Sade's poem is, however, entirely the abbé's own gloss on the events, namely a lament of the impotence of every lover when faced with the overpowering force of their beloved. Stylistically and thematically, such deliberate confusion (in the etymological sense of *confundere*, to mix together) is a technique of translation peculiar to Sade (and Roman, as discussed below) amongst French translators of Petrarch in the late eighteenth and nineteenth centuries, and is not, perhaps, a method that could survive the increasing demands for clarity and fidelity made on translations in subsequent decades. In contrast to Sade's approach, later translators tend to treat each poem by Petrarch as an inviolable, free-standing, independent text. Yet Sade's honesty in warning his readers about what he has done remains exemplary, and can be lacking in later translators who have less space or inclination for discursive self-analysis and self-justification.

In between the publication of the second (1764) and third (1767) volumes of the *Mémoires*, a short book by Nicolas Antoine Romet afforded a different approach to Petrarch from that taken by Sade.[25] Romet mingled original poetry in the style of Petrarch (a fictional verse letter from Petrarch to Laura) with brief biographical

---

[23] Sade, *Mémoires*, ii, 89–90.

[24] 'O inconstantia de l'umane cose!' *RVF* 199, v. 13.

[25] Nicolas Antoine Romet, *Lettre de Pétrarque à Laure, suivie de remarques sur ce Poëte, & de traduction de quelques-unes de ses plus jolies pièces* (Paris: Sébastien Jorry, 1765). See also Lionello Sozzi, '"Un cœur sensible": Petrarca in Francia nel settecento', in *Dynamique d'une expansion culturelle*, ed. Blanc, pp. 441–9.

information derived from Sade and an 'Essai d'une traduction libre de quelques pièces de Pétrarque' ('Attempt at a free translation of a few poems by Petrarch'). This last section, compared to Sade's encyclopaedic, historical approach, presents slim pickings: only Petrarch's 'most beautiful poems' (*plus jolies pièces*), namely, *RVF* 35, 90, 222, 7, 145, and 126 (in that order), all translated into prose. Of these six, the odd one out is *RVF* 7, a sonnet on gluttony which is typically marginalized or omitted in later selections that are interested only in Petrarch as a love poet.[26] Of the remaining five, *RVF* 145 (a sonnet marking fifteen years of unceasing love for Laura, regardless of changing external circumstances) and 222 (a dialogue sonnet between the lyric subject, who is seeking Laura, and a group of ladies who remember Laura) thrive on typical Petrarchan oxymora but are not especially remarked upon by later French translators. In contrast, *RVF* 35 (a sonnet of solitude and love–melancholy), 90 (in praise of the memory of Laura's hair, face, and walk), and 126 (a celebration of Laura amidst a rural Provençal landscape) remain popular amongst readers and translators throughout the nineteenth century, as we shall see later in this chapter, and arguably retain such a status even in the present day.

A comparably restricted selection of poems from Petrarch is made by the Avignon-born Marianne-Agnès Falques at the start of the next decade, in 1772.[27] Out of a total of only eight sonnets translated, Falques chooses two of the same poems as Romet (*RVF* 7 and 35), in addition to other popular poems including *RVF* 132, which questions the nature of love, and *RVF* 310, in which the poet is out of tune with the return of Spring. The remaining four sonnets translated by Falques are *RVF* 124 (on the mind's reaction to the twin torments of Love and Fortune), 140 (an account of Love's fear of Laura's anger), 226 (a poem of solitude), and 265 (a poem of opposites which ultimately expresses the poet's persistent hope his affections will one day be returned).

Combining the approaches of Sade and Romet is the abbé Roman's *Le Génie de Pétrarque* (1778; *The Genius of Petrarch*), which overtly follows Sade in its historical, biographical information, but like Romet claims to choose Petrarch's 'most beautiful poems' (*plus belles poésies*), rendered in verse imitation 'in order to make known the talent, taste, and manner of this poet'.[28] Roman's translations are far more generous and numerous than the limited selections of either Romet or Falques, though, like Sade, Roman is worried about boring readers with too much material of a monotonous, repetitive nature:

---

[26] In contrast, Zuccato finds that in England *RVF* 7 was 'frequently anthologized' and particularly 'popular in the 1790s': see Zuccato, *Petrarch in Romantic England*, pp. 5 and 108.

[27] Marianne-Agnès Falques, *Nouvelles fables, avec une traduction de quelques sonnets choisis de Pétrarque et une romance* (London: T. R. Delorme, 1772), pp. 41–9.

[28] 'pour faire connoître le talent, le goût & la manière de ce Poëte', abbé Roman, *Le Génie de Pétrarque, ou imitation en vers françois, de ses plus belles poésies, précédée de la Vie de cet Homme célèbre* (Parma and Avignon: Joseph Guichard, 1778; Parma and Paris: Lacombe, 1778), p. vii. On the abbé Roman and Petrarch, see also Yves Giraud, 'Un admirateur de Pétrarque au XVIIIe siècle: les romances de l'abbé Roman', in *Dynamique d'une expansion culturelle*, ed. Blanc, pp. 383–400.

What does Petrarch an injustice is that in his writings falsehood rubs shoulders with truth, and wit with emotion: I have not sought to gloss over this fact. What does Petrarch an even greater injustice is the monotony of his subject matter. I would like to see more taste, variety, nuance, and contrast in his poems. I would get rid of those ballads and *ritornelli* which are often obscure and insipid. I would change the ending of several of his sonnets, which conclude in a manner unworthy of their beginning. I would erase certain cold allegories, hard and forced rhymes, metaphors, turns of phrase, and comparisons which recur too frequently. I would reduce Petrarch to half of himself, and I would have a collection worthy of the greatest poets.[29]

This passage is a bold manifesto in favour of incomplete translations of Petrarch. Rather than bemoaning the inherent lack or insufficiency of such translations, Roman proposes that they are better than what Petrarch originally planned and produced. Further, Roman's practice proves to be even more radical than this already bold statement, since what he offers his readers is in fact more like a quarter than a half of the *Canzoniere*. Included are favourites shared with Romet (*RVF* 7, 35, 90, and 126, but not 145 or 222), major *canzoni* (such as *RVF* 23 and 268, the former known as the *canzone* of the metamorphoses, the latter the first, mournful *canzone* of the second half, after Laura's death), and other popular sonnets (*RVF* 132, on the nature of love, and 311, a poem in which the poet identifies with the nighttime laments of a nightingale). In contrast, notable omissions include *RVF* 5 (which plays on the syllables of Laura's name) and other poems about Apollo or the laurel (such as *RVF* 34 and 197). Such omissions suggest that, again like Sade, Roman is impressed neither by the potential polysemy of Laura's name, nor by mythological imagery more generally. The exclusion of the foundational *RVF* 1 is also surprising and—as with later translators who similarly avoid this poem—suggests both a lack of appreciation of the *Canzoniere* as an authorially ordered text and a wish to downplay religious, penitential elements of the framing narrative.

Indeed, a feature of Roman's selection is a lack of attention to order, as indicated also by this translator's atypical evasion of the common structuring principle of the two halves *in vita* and *in morte*. Instead, Roman's translations from the *Canzoniere* begin with *RVF* 159 and end with *RVF* 360: the first is a sonnet arguing for the unique, celestial beauty of Laura's face, hair, and voice; the second is a *canzone* of complaint between poet and Love in the court of Reason, which ends in suspended judgement. The original penitential framework of the work is thus lost by avoiding both *RVF* 1 and *RVF* 366, as well as other penitential poems such as *RVF* 62, addressed to 'Father

---

[29] 'Ce qui fait tort à Pétrarque, c'est que dans ses Ecrits, le faux est à côté du vrai, l'esprit auprès du sentiment : je ne l'ai point dissimulé. Ce qui lui fait tort encore, c'est la monotonie de son sujet. Je voudrois plus de goût, de variété, de nuances & de contrastes dans ses Poësies. J'en retrancherois ces ballades & ces ritournelles qui sont souvent obscures & insipides. Je changerois la chûte de plusieurs de ses Sonnets, dont la fin n'est pas digne du début. J'effacerois quelques froides allégories, des rimes dures & forcées, des métaphores, des tours de phrase & des comparaisons qui reviennent trop souvent. Je réduirois Pétrarque à la moitié de lui-même, & j'aurois un Recueil digne des plus grands Poëtes.' Roman, *Le Génie de Pétrarque*, p. 297.

of Heaven' (*Padre del ciel*), and *RVF* 364–5, two sonnets of repentance and prayer. This attempt to curb the religious aspects of Petrarch's poetry is consonant with Roman's presentation of Petrarch in the supporting biographical material as an ideal lover rather than as a moralist or historian. It also suggests Roman's taste, at least in literature, for secular, poetic love over any intimations of religious conversion. In this way Petrarch's medieval divided loyalties (between love for lady and love for God) are erased in Roman's selection, in favour of poems about love and about Laura. In these poems, the main source of conflict is no longer the very real (at least for Petrarch) risk of sin leading to eternal damnation, but rather an ongoing and irresolvable quarrel between the poet and the god of love (elucidated in *RVF* 360), combined with the incessant pains of what Roman rather reproachfully describes as Laura's 'system of coquetry' (*système de coquetterie*).[30] This last, Laura as coquette, is very much an eighteenth-century take on the Petrarchan love story; in this interpretation, Petrarch's unconsummated desire can only have lasted so long and through so many poems thanks to the sustenance and stimulation of a coquettish beloved.

An awareness of some sort of order is, nonetheless, present in Roman's occasional conflation of several Italian sonnets into one French poem, following the precedent set by Sade. *RVF* 41 and 42, two mythological sonnets which describe Laura's departure and return, are combined, as are a further four contiguous sonnets of fearful anticipation of Laura's death, under the title 'Premonition' (*Pressentiment*), that is, *RVF* 249–52.[31] A similar quadruple thematic, this time of outright mourning, unites *RVF* 283, 280, 279, and 282, under the heading 'His love outlives Laura'.[32] Also conflated are *RVF* 194 and 113, two sonnets which praise the Vauclusian landscape and address Laura as *l'aura* ('the breeze').[33] Faced with typical Petrarchan repetition, neither Sade nor Roman can resist the temptation on occasion to abridge and reduce, forming one representative Petrarchist French poem out of several Petrarchan sets of theme and variation. This habit of reducing and conflating poems is not continued, however, by nineteenth-century translators of Petrarch who tend, rather, to treat Petrarch's poems as self-contained, separate units. While the solution to undesirable repetition and potential boredom is, for Sade and Roman, sought in a digest, combinatory approach, nineteenth-century translators are more likely to opt for fewer poems, preserved more fully.

In contrast to such abridgement, however, Roman does at times seek a more expansive rendition of Petrarch, allowing himself the freedom of translating sonnets into a looser French verse structure, which can sometimes reach up to thirty-four lines in length as, for instance, in his translation of a sonnet such as *RVF* 230, which is torn between weeping and the consolations of both song (poetry) and pity, the latter represented by the olive, a symbol of peace. The clue to understanding and assessing Roman's contribution to French translations of Petrarch may lie in the titular description 'imitation', which grants the translator much more freedom and inventiveness. Translation as imitation was to decline in popularity throughout the

---

[30]   Roman, *Le Génie de Pétrarque*, p. 57.
[31]   Roman, *Le Génie de Pétrarque*, p. 357 and pp. 409–11.
[32]   'Son amour survit à Laure', Roman, *Le Génie de Pétrarque*, pp. 427–30.
[33]   Roman, *Le Génie de Pétrarque*, pp. 368–9.

nineteenth century, with Gérard de Nerval as early as 1830 famously declaring 'As for imitations, they are no longer wanted, and rightly so.'[34] Yet imitation remained a legitimate option, especially given the 'real terminological uncertainty about the semantic border between notions of imitation and translation [...] throughout the period', and so I have not sought in this volume to distinguish categorically between the two.[35]

Roman's version of Petrarch was to be popular, seeing a reprint in 1786.[36] Roman's popularity perhaps in part lay in the fact that his *Pétrarque* afforded a much abridged version of Sade's historical panorama whilst boasting a comparable level of biographical detail and poetic example. When the Athénée de Vaucluse decided to publish a biography of Petrarch to coincide with the fifth centenary of Petrarch's birth in 1804, they turned to Roman's 'Vie de Pétrarque' ('Life of Petrarch', with minor modifications and corrections), but decided not to include any of Roman's verse translations. In the words of the unnamed editor:

> The Life of Petrarch published in this volume was written by the abbé Roman, whom the Athénée would have sought to add to their ranks, had the author been alive at the time the institution was founded. We have omitted his translation of Petrarch's poems, which is, however, not without elegance, but which has not seemed of a sufficiently general interest. We have smoothed out certain slight blemishes, such as a false date of birth for the Italian poet, and several printing errors, especially regarding Italian words some of which were entirely disfigured. We have removed certain passages which seemed to confuse the progress of the narrative by irrelevant digressions.[37]

The rebuke laid against the Italian quotations may, perhaps, conceal some doubts about the finesse of Roman's comprehension of the language, but a persuasive reason for omitting Roman's translations is more likely to have been their outdated style and character only a few decades after their publication. Indeed, Roman's style

---

[34] 'Quant aux imitations, on n'en veut plus, et on a raison.' Gérard de Nerval, *Poésies allemandes: Klopstock, Goethe, Schiller, Burger: morceaux choisis et traduits* (Paris: Bureau de la Bibliothèque choisie, 1830), p. 3.

[35] 'réelle incertitude terminologique sur le périmètre sémantique des notions d'imitation et de traduction [...] tout au long de la période', Lombez, 'Poésie', in *Histoire des traductions en langue française*, pp. 346–7.

[36] Under the new title *Vie de François Pétrarque, célèbre poëte italien, dont les actions & les écrits sont une des plus singulières époques de l'histoire & de la littérature moderne; suivie d'une imitation en vers François de ses plus belles poésies* (Vaucluse and Paris: J. Cussac, 1786).

[37] 'La Vie de Pétrarque publiée dans ce volume, a été composée par l'abbé Roman, que l'Athénée se serait empressé de s'associer, s'il avait été vivant lors de notre institution. On a supprimé sa traduction des Poésies de Pétrarque, qui n'est cependant pas sans élégance, mais qui n'a point paru d'un intérêt assez général. On a fait disparaître quelques taches légères, telles qu'une fausse date de la naissance du Poète italien, et plusieurs fautes d'impression, surtout pour les mots italiens dont quelques-uns étaient entiérement défigurés. On a supprimé quelques passages qui semblaient embarrasser la marche du récit par des digres- sions qui lui étaient étrangères.' *Vie de Pétrarque, publiée par l'Athénée de Vaucluse; augmentée de la première traduction qui ait paru en Français, de la Lettre adressée à la Postérité par ce Poète célèbre* (Avignon: Mme Vve Seguin, 1804), pp. v–vi.

was criticized soon after its initial publication by Jean-François La Harpe in the following terms:

> Amongst the new publications which never cease to proliferate, we can single out a pamphlet which is entitled the *Genius of Petrarch*, and which contains the life of this poet, and an imitation in French verse of part of his works. This life is too long, this translation is mediocre, the prose is a bit too flowery and the verses too sloppy; nonetheless, not everything in this volume is bad literature; it contains interesting facts and is fairly agreeable to read.[38]

The remaining significant late-eighteenth-century translator of Petrarch, besides Sade, Romet, Falques, and Roman, is Pierre-Charles Levesque, who produced two editions of selected poems of Petrarch translated into French prose in 1774 and 1787 respectively.[39] Levesque's decisions to provide facing Italian texts in full and to translate into prose render his edition perhaps the most faithful of the translations available at that time, at least in terms of content and accessibility of the original. Levesque orders his translations according to form (in the first edition, seven *canzoni*, one *sestina*, twenty-three sonnets, and two *ballate*), which harks back to the manuscript tradition of ordering poems by genre and type.[40] This convention was one with which Petrarch's *Canzoniere* was to break (following in part the example of Dante's *Vita nuova*), but Petrarch's radical attempt to order lyric poetry along narrative rather than formal lines appears to have met with the resistance or miscomprehension of many later translators and editors who strove to reassemble the *Canzoniere* according to their own preferences and beliefs, whether formal or thematic. Within each formal category, however, Levesque does follow the ordering of the *Canzoniere*, and his inclusion of *RVF* 1 (though not *RVF* 366) demonstrates a greater awareness of the work's potential macro-structure than either Roman or Romet. The second edition is presented as 'corrected and expanded' (*corrigée et augmentée*), but the additions are minor; as regards the *Canzoniere* only two poems are added, *RVF* 16 (a sonnet in which the poet's search for Laura is compared to an old man's pilgrimage to Rome to see the Veronica) and *RVF* 135 (another *canzone* of amorous metamorphosis, beginning with the lover as phoenix).[41]

---

[38]   'Parmi les nouveautés qui abondent toujours, on peut distinguer une brochure qui a pour titre le *Génie de Pétrarque*, qui contient la vie de ce poëte, et une imitation en vers français d'une partie de ses ouvrages. Cette vie est trop longue, cette traduction est médiocre, la prose est un peu trop fleurie et les vers trop négligés ; cependant tout ce volume n'est point d'une mauvaise littérature ; il est curieux par les faits et assez agréable à lire.' Jean-François La Harpe, *Correspondance littéraire, adressée à son altesse impériale M.gr le Grand-Duc, aujourd'hui empereur de Russie, et à M. le comte André Schowalow, chambellan de l'impératrice Catherine II, depuis 1774 jusqu'à 1789*, 6 vols (Paris: Migneret, 1801–7), II, 231–2.

[39]   Pierre-Charles Levesque, *Choix des poésies de Pétrarque traduites de l'italien*, 2 vols (Venice and Paris: Valade and Hardouin, 1774) and *Choix des poésies de Pétrarque, traduites de l'Italien: nouvelle édition corrigée et augmentée*, 2 vols (Venice and Paris: Hardouin et Gattey, 1787).

[40]   See Olivia Holmes, *Assembling the Lyric Self: Authorship from Troubadour Song to the Italian Poetry Book* (Minneapolis: University of Minnesota Press, 2000).

[41]   For the text of *RVF* 16, see Chapter 5.

After Levesque's second edition, a significant amount of time elapsed before the next French translation of Petrarch was published. Yet the year 1804 marked the first modern Petrarchan festival in France, organized by the Athénée (later, Académie) de Vaucluse, an organization which was also responsible for subsequent Petrarchan publications and festivities, and which, as already noted, had chosen to publish Roman's *Le Génie de Pétrarque* minus translations in that same *annus mirabilis*. The very early decades of the nineteenth century were not a fertile time for translations of Petrarch, despite the new impetus for reading, studying, and translating him in France created by events both literary (Sade's *Mémoires*) and political (the unification of Avignon with France at the Revolution).

Translators of Sonnets

While these four late eighteenth-century translators tended to select poems from a representative range of the various forms used by Petrarch, on the basis of personal taste as well as likely interest for the reader, the most common rationale for incomplete translations of Petrarch published in the nineteenth century was to translate only sonnets, particularly those about love. Brisset's initial publication of a volume devoted to Petrarch's sonnets in 1899 (discussed in Chapter 1) was, in this respect, not a novel approach to the *Canzoniere*, but rather one which followed in the footsteps of two translators in particular, Philibert Le Duc and Emma Mahul. The translations of the former, Le Duc, were rewarded by a prize at the celebrations for the fifth centenary of Petrarch's death, in 1874.[42] Such celebrations, as explored in Chapter 4, provided new inspiration and incentives for translating Petrarch afresh. Le Duc translates Petrarch's sonnets into regular French sonnets (*sonnets réguliers*), and his commitment to the sonnet form is further suggested by his publication of a didactic anthology of sonnets shortly after his translations of Petrarch.[43] The latter, Mahul, translated all of Petrarch's sonnets in five volumes published between 1847 and 1877, and remained throughout, like Le Duc, faithful to the sonnet form in her translations. In this manner the projects of Mahul and Le Duc represent a compromise between completion and incompletion. These translators have more time for more of Petrarch than earlier translators such as Sade or Roman, yet in other ways they present a less varied Petrarch by choosing to present him as a writer of only one type of poem, the sonnet.

At the start of his translation, Le Duc draws attention to the fact that 'Sonnets, by their number and their artistic value, constitute the most important part of the

---

[42] Le Duc, *Les Sonnets de Pétrarque*, 2 vols (1877–9). It is interesting to note that professionally Le Duc was employed as 'inspecteur des forêts' ('inspector of forests'), with his other publications therefore dealing with matters of landscape and forestry—a not entirely un-Petrarchan occupation, especially if we recall that Petrarch referred to himself at various points as Silvius and Silvanus ('forest dweller', 'lover of forests').

[43] Philibert Le Duc, *Sonnets curieux et sonnets célèbres: étude anthologique & didactique, suivie de sonnets inédits* (Paris: L. Willem; Bourg: Francisque Martin, 1879).

Canzoniere.[44] Yet he balks at their sheer number, and so seeks to break them up into ten supposedly more palatable sections:

> The uninterrupted reading of three hundred and seventeen sonnets, even if they were the best in the world, would not fail to be tiring. In order to alleviate this inconvenience, breaks have been increased by dividing the sonnets into ten sets, and prose has been added to the poetry in the form of a commentary. *A work divided thus will become shorter* (Martial).[45]

This mode of division is unique to Le Duc, and unusual compared with the normatively bipartite model of Petrarch's *Canzoniere* and its translations. This model, if not an exclusive structuring principle, does, nonetheless, also remain at work here, in the overarching sections 'Sonnets written during Laura's life' (*Sonnets composés du vivant de Laure*) and 'Sonnets written after Laura's death' (*Sonnets composés après la mort de Laure*). In Le Duc's publication, French translations of the sonnets appear on the versos, while a commentary that runs continuously within each series or set (*série*) is printed on the rectos. Le Duc explicitly acknowledges that the principal sources for this commentary are not only Sade, but also Ginguené's *Histoire littéraire de l'Italie* (1811–35; *Literary History of Italy*) and Alfred Mézières's *Pétrarque* (1868).[46] Le Duc's commentary often aims to give the original dates and motivations behind each poem, and to create a linear narrative through the lyric collection. Le Duc's juxtaposition of poem and commentary goes far beyond the sparse footnotes or introductory headings typical of most translators. Indeed, his two volumes of Petrarch's sonnets might even be claimed to turn the *Canzoniere* into a sort of *Vita nuova* (*New Life*), Dante's youthful prosimetrum in which poems are surrounded by prose gloss, diary-like narrative, and rudimentary analysis. While Petrarch's innovation lay in producing a lyric sequence without the interspersed prose on which Dante's *Vita nuova* had relied, Le Duc marks the extreme point of a widespread desire to re-embed Petrarch's poetry within a logical, chronological prose narrative, initiated by Sade in his *Mémoires*.[47]

---

[44] 'Les sonnets, par leur nombre et leur valeur artistique, constituent la partie capitale du *Canzoniere*', Le Duc, *Les Sonnets de Pétrarque*, I, p. vi.

[45] 'La lecture suivie de trois cent dix-sept sonnets, fussent-ils les meilleurs du monde, ne laisserait pas que d'être fatigante. Pour obvier à cet inconvénient, les temps d'arrêt ont été multipliés par la division des sonnets en dix séries, et la prose a été mêlée à la poésie au moyen d'un commentaire. *Divisum sic breve fiet opus (Mart.)*.' Le Duc, *Les Sonnets de Pétrarque*, I, p. vii.

[46] On the latter, see Alfred Mézières, *Pétrarque: étude d'après de nouveaux documents* (Paris: Didier, 1868) and Claire Cabaillot, 'Alfred Mézières et la critique du XIXe siècle', in *La Postérité répond à Pétrarque*, pp. 197–207.

[47] See Teodolinda Barolini, 'The Making of a Lyric Sequence: Time and Narrative in Petrarch's *Rerum vulgarium fragmenta*', *Modern Language Notes*, 140.1 (January 1989), 1–38 (repr. in Teodolinda Barolini, *Dante and the Origins of Italian Literary Culture* (New York: Fordham University Press, 2006), pp. 193–223), and, for the influence of Petrarch's innovation on later poets, Roland Greene, *Post-Petrarchism: Origins and Innovations of the Western Lyric Sequence* (Princeton, NJ: Princeton University Press, 1991). For other ramifications of this desire to embed Petrarch within a prose narrative, see Chapter 6 on the 'novelization' of Petrarch.

Besides Le Duc, Emma Mahul published translations of Petrarch's sonnets spread across five editions over a period of thirty years, the last volume being published only two years before her death in 1879, in the same year (1877) as both Poulenc's second edition of Petrarch's complete poems and Le Duc's first volume of Petrarch's sonnets.[48] Mahul is interesting in a number of respects, principally for the longevity and extensiveness of her project, and inevitably as one of very few women translators of Petrarch in this period.[49] Other women translators at that time were typically less ambitious or thorough, often translating only a handful of Petrarch's poems.[50] Mahul's first volume of translations, from 1847, is anonymous, while the next four reveal her authorship. She herself commented on the social and literary expectations that made anonymity initially desirable in the preface to her second volume of translated sonnets: 'It is the only one of our works to have had any success, either because of the celebrity of the author translated, or because it was published anonymously, the book trade encouraging literature of neither amateurs nor women.'[51] Mahul's decision to reveal her name from the second volume onwards was motivated by the desire to affirm the uniform identity of the author of earlier and all subsequent editions, and perhaps also to capitalize on this initial success.

---

[48] [Emma Mahul], *Cent cinquante sonnets et huit morceaux complémentaires traduits des Sonnets de Pétrarque, texte en regard* (Paris: Firmon Didot frères, 1847); Mahul, *Choix de sonnets de Pétrarque* (1867); *Choix de sonnets traduits par madame S. Emma Mahul des comtes Dejean: troisième édition revue, corrigée et augmentée de la traduction de différentes poésies de Pétrarque, etc.* (Paris: Firmin Didot, 1869); *Choix de sonnets traduits de Pétrarque, par madame S. Emma Mahul des comtes Dejean, revue, corrigée et augmentée de la traduction de différentes poésies de Pétrarque* (Paris: Firmin Didot frères, fils et Cie, 1872); *Sonnets inédits traduits de Pétrarque par madame S. Emma Mahul des comtes Dejean, cinquième publication complétant la totalité des sonnets et augmentée de la traduction également inédite de différentes poésies de Pétrarque, etc.* (Rome: Héritiers Botta, 1877).

[49] Duperray, *L'Or des Mots*, pp. 266–7.

[50] Two of Petrarch's sonnets (*RVF* 248 and 302) are translated in *Stances de Messer Angelo Poliziano et poésies extraites de Dante, Pétrarque et Leopardi, traduites de l'italien par Mme la Comtesse de Lalaing* (Brussels: Imprimerie de J. Stienon, 1853), one sonnet (*RVF* 35) in Agathe Baudouin, *Rêveries sur les bords du Cher: poésies* (Paris: Challamel et Cie, 1841), and another sonnet (*RVF* 269) and some extracts in Gabrielle Soumet d'Altenheym, *Les quatre siècles littéraires: récits de l'histoire de la littérature sous Périclès, Auguste, Léon X et Louis XIV, enrichis de fragments des chefs-d'œuvre classiques* (Paris: E. Ducrocq, 1859). See also the translation of *RVF* 279 by Ate Penquer in *Almanach du sonnet: sonnets inédits, publiés avec la collaboration de deux cents Poètes français et des principaux Félibres* (Aix-en-Provence: Vve Remondet-Aubin, 1875), not to mention the various translations of sonnets by Petrarch into Occitan (discussed in Chapter 4) of Roso-Anaïs Roumanille. For further details of all these translations see Appendix 1. The scarcity of female voices in nineteenth-century reappropriations of Petrarch is at odds with both English Petrarchism of a similar period (in particular, as manifested by Charlotte Smith, Anna Seward, and Mary Robinson) and the significant earlier Petrarchan precedent set by female poets writing in Italian (Vittoria Colonna, Gaspara Stampa) or in a foreign language (Pernette du Guillet and Louise Labé in France, Mary Sidney and Mary Wroth in England): see Zuccato, *Petrarch in Romantic England* (especially pp. 52–72 and 77–93) as well as Kennedy, *The Site of Petrarchism*.

[51] 'C'est le seul de nos ouvrages qui ait eu quelque débit, soit à cause de la célébrité de l'auteur traduit, soit parce qu'il était resté anonyme, la librairie n'encourageant ni la littérature d'amateur, ni la littérature féminine.' Mahul, *Choix de sonnets de Pétrarque* (1867), p. 5.

The first edition of 1847 represented for Mahul 'exactly half of a translation of Petrarch's three hundred and seventeen sonnets which we hope, one day, to finish'.[52] Over the four further volumes (from 1867, 1869, 1872, and 1877), Mahul was indeed to translate all of the sonnets of the *Canzoniere*, as well as select other poems by Petrarch along the way. While the first edition retained the facing Italian poems, the later editions were to restrict Italian text to first lines given after descriptive French titles. Mahul consistently divided her translations into the typical bipartite *in vita/ in morte* structure, and started the second half at the customary point of *RVF* 267 (in the third and fourth editions of 1869 and 1872 respectively). Strikingly, Mahul does not translate *RVF* 1 until the last volume (in 1877), preferring instead to start with *RVF* 2 (a sonnet describing Love's attack with bow and arrows on the poet's heart) in all but the second edition, which begins with *RVF* 4 (a sonnet in praise of Laura's birthplace). Combined with the reluctance to translate *RVF* 62 (the sonnet of repentance addressing God the Father which, like *RVF* 1, makes its first appearance in 1877), Mahul until the last moment presents the reader with an amorous Petrarch largely removed from the sphere of religious guilt and penitence. Formally, Mahul strives to retain the sonnet structure in all of her translations, so that the section added after the first edition—'Diverse poems translated from Petrarch' (*Poésies diverses traduites de Pétrarque*)—is no longer a thematic category (as in the editions of Vellutello or Marsand), but rather a space for experimentation, whether in the rendering of sonnets by Petrarch in freer French verse forms, or by the inclusion of a few representative ballads (*RVF* 11, 59, 324), madrigals (*RVF* 52, 54, 106, 121), *sestine* (*RVF* 66, 80, 142, 239, 332), or *canzoni* (*RVF* 28, 71, 126, 127, 268, 359). In this section Mahul stretches her wings and shows her competency in a wider range of forms beyond her chosen specialism, the sonnet. Like Sade and other translators, Mahul's interest in Petrarch was fuelled by living for a time in Avignon, as her husband, Alphonse Mahul, was appointed *préfet de Vaucluse* in 1837.[53] Unusually, however, Mahul also bridged the gap between French and Italian Petrarchism of the period by her subsequent independent travels and residence in Italy, from 1859 onwards, as a consequence of which she was a rare French voice at the celebrations held in Arquà for Petrarch in 1874.[54] Mahul's devotion to Italy and Italian culture is also expressed in a further volume of translations, this time of Sicilian poetry, as well as by her own original poetry on Italian themes.[55]

After Mahul and Le Duc, Ernest Cabadé comes closest to a complete translation of Petrarch's sonnets, in a volume that replicates the structure and contents of Brisset's 1899 *Sonnets*, though likely both are modelled on Marsand's ordering

---

[52] 'l'exacte moitié d'une traduction des trois cent dix-sept sonnets de Pétrarque qu'on espère pouvoir terminer un jour', [Mahul], *Cent cinquante sonnets*, p. 7.

[53] For biographical information see Emma Condorelli, 'Emma Mahul des comtes Dejean, une pétrarquiste oubliée', *Revue des études italiennes*, 31 (1985), 103–11, and Jean-Michel Gardair, 'Encore sur Emma Mahul', *Revue des études italiennes*, 31 (1985), 112–15.

[54] For Mahul's poetic contributions to this centenary, see *Sonnets inédits* (1877), pp. 229–46, and Chapter 5.

[55] Emma Mahul, *Traduction inédite de poëtes siciliens: texte en regard* (Livorno: [n.p.], 1876); Mahul, *Poésies politiques sur les événements de l'Italie* (Turin: Héritiers Botta, 1862).

rather than Cabadé's on Brisset's directly.[56] In Cabadé's volume of translations, the full Italian text is included beneath each French sonnet, as well as brief, often adulatory notes. Cabadé translated 297 out of the 317 sonnets from the *Canzoniere*, and presented them in the usual fashion as 'Sonnets written during Laura's life' and 'Sonnets on Laura's death' (*Les sonnets écrits pendant la vie de Laure; Les sonnets sur la mort de Laure*). The second half begins as is typical with *RVF* 267, although it ends, like Marsand's edition and Brisset's sonnet volume, with *RVF* 91; the twenty sonnets omitted are those also marginalized by Marsand and absent from Brisset's 1899 volume. Cabadé's translations are introduced hyperbolically by Armand-Germain de Tréverret, a professor at Bordeaux, with hopes for the volume's longevity and canonization by posterity:

> Will Cabadé's Petrarch be *our* Petrarch, just as the Bible, translated by Luther, is the *German Bible*? I dare not assert this, for the decisions of the contemporary public and even those of posterity depend upon a thousand mysterious causes; but I am convinced that in manifold places your translation does merit such an honour.[57]

In contrast, one result of exploring translations of Petrarch in nineteenth-century France is the realization that no one translation could claim definitive status amongst the plethora of translations available, and that few (besides Gramont) were to be read and readopted by future generations, save out of historical interest.

Despite these three examples of complete or almost complete translations of Petrarch's sonnets, it was more common for translators to restrict themselves much more in their choices. This self-limitation is true of the first translator of this period to present readers with a volume of sonnets by Petrarch, Camille Esménard in 1830. In his preface, Esménard is aware of his uniqueness in translating Petrarch at this time (during the first decades of the nineteenth century, as noted earlier, French translations of Petrarch remained rare) and suggests that one reason for Petrarch's lack of popularity in France at this point might be the pervasive belief that his poetry is impossible to translate:

> Might not Voltaire and Laharpe have put off a man of talent who would have acquitted himself much better than I, by repeating that Petrarch is impossible to translate? [...] I offer this sketch [*ébauche*] only as an attempt, which, by drawing attention to a famous writer, will be able to gain for him an interpreter whose pen is better trained than mine.[58]

---

[56]   Cabadé, *Les Sonnets de Pétrarque* (1902).

[57]   'Le Pétrarque-Cabadé sera-t-il *notre* Pétrarque, comme la Bible, traduite par Luther, est la *Bible allemande* ? Je n'ose l'affirmer ; car les décisions du public contemporain, et même celles de la postérité, dépendent de milles causes mystérieuses ; mais je suis convaincu que dans maint endroit votre traduction mérite un tel honneur.' Tréverret, 'À M. Ernest Cabadé: lettre pour servir de préface à une traduction en vers des sonnets de Pétrarque', in Cabadé, *Les Sonnets de Pétrarque*, pp. vii–xiii (p. xiii).

[58]   'Voltaire et Laharpe, en répétant qu'il était impossible de traduire Pétrarque, n'auraient-ils pas détourné de ce travail un homme de talent qui s'en serait acquitté beaucoup

This *captatio benevolentiae* is much more modest than the usual prefaces of translators which tend, rather, to denigrate any rival translations and to assert the superiority of the new translation being introduced. Yet later translators have more need to justify their own endeavours, while for Esménard the rarity of such translations is more than sufficient self-validation. Sade's preferred image of translation as an artist's sketch reappears here, though where Sade used the terms *copie* or *esquisse* Esménard uses the word *ébauche*, more properly a preliminary draft or rough outline preparatory to a full, complete painting on the same canvas.[59] Esménard figures the development of translations of Petrarch as a series of canvasses painted by different hands, with his own contribution to this gallery markedly incomplete, and awaiting completion by someone more talented and more experienced.

Esménard's selections follow the accepted ordering of the *Canzoniere* at the time (disregarding Marsand's reorganization), and are divided, as is usual, into two parts, with the second beginning with *RVF* 267. In Esménard's translation, there is a perfect balance between the two sections, as thirty sonnets from each are translated. In practice, however, this means an overprivileging of the second section, which is significantly shorter than the first in its original, complete form.[60] In effect, Petrarch's poetic collection appears perfectly symmetrical, a perhaps more aesthetically pleasing structure (by certain standards—those, for instance, of Esménard) than the asymmetry of the original. Unlike other translations such as those of Mahul or Roman, Esménard's sixty sonnets retain an overarching penitential structure by starting with *RVF* 1 and ending with *RVF* 364, both sonnets of guilt, shame, and remorse. The last line of *RVF* 364, 'for I know my error, and do not excuse it' (*Ch'i' conosco 'l mio fallo, et non lo scuso*), strikes a particularly lucid and poignant note, and is rendered by Esménard as 'I confess my fault and you see my regrets' (*Je confesse ma faute et tu vois mes regrets*), in a direct address to God which also collaterally invokes the reader as witness to and even judge of the poet's suffering.[61] In this final poem, Esménard circles back round to the opening address to the reader (*Voi ch'ascoltate*, 'You who listen') of *RVF* 1.[62]

Esménard's second edition of 1848 is, in general, a more ambitious enterprise: longer, more polemical, and, unusually, including a brief foray into Petrarch's Latin

---

mieux que moi ? [...] Je n'offre cette ébauche que comme un essai, qui, en réveillant l'attention sur un écrivain illustre, pourra lui attirer un interprète dont la plume soit plus exercée que la mienne.' *Choix de sonnets de Pétrarque, traduits en vers par M. Camille Esménard* (Paris: Mme Vve Charles Béchet, 1830), p. 2.

[59] On the uses and differences between the two terms in nineteenth-century discourse, see *Esquisses/Ébauches: Projects and Pre-Texts in Nineteenth-Century French Culture*, ed. Sonya Stephens (New York: Peter Lang, 2007). In the above distinction I draw, in particular, on John House's contribution to this same volume: House, 'Impressionist Painting: *esquisse* or *ébauche*?', in *Esquisses/Ébauches*, pp. 222–9.

[60] In Petrarch's arrangement, the first part consists of 263 poems (*RVF* 1–263) and the second part of only 103 poems (*RVF* 264–366).

[61] Esménard, *Choix de sonnets de Pétrarque* (1830), p. 150.

[62] In Esménard's first volume of translations, this opening address is rendered as 'Vous qui lirez ces vers' ('You who will read these verses'): *Choix de sonnets de Pétrarque* (1830), p. 27.

works.[63] For a start, Esménard is necessarily here much more assertive, French translations of Petrarch having, by this time, become much more common and available, as the complete translations of Gramont and Montesquiou from 1842 testify. Esménard is now openly critical of his precursors beginning with Sade (who, according to Esménard, 'few people read', *peu de personnes lisent*), and arguing that his renewed contribution, despite the complete translations that have been published in the intervening years, will, nonetheless, still contribute to a greater appreciation of Petrarch, who 'is hardly known in France, except by a handful of literary types, save as the hero of Platonic love: perhaps my translation will make him better known'.[64] Esménard's is an unusual voice challenging the dominant and pervasive view of Petrarch as a love poet.

Esménard's later volume is, unlike his first, divided into the customary Marsand-inspired three parts, 'Poems written during Laura's life', 'Poems written after Laura's death', and 'Poems on diverse subjects' (*Poésies composées pendant la vie de Laure, après la mort de Laure*, and *sur divers sujets*). This division (and the notable addition of the third type of poem excluded from the 1830 publication) calls attention to the variety of Petrarch's subject matter beyond Laura and the amorous, although by displacing it to a third section the love story of parts one and two remains intact and undiluted by political, moral, or occasional poetry. Of the *Canzoniere* Esménard translates, in his 1848 publication, 241 poems (out of a possible 366). There is no longer an equal balance between parts one and two, but rather 147 poems in the first and seventy in the second (in addition to part of the *Triumphi* and one eclogue), with a final twenty-four in the third part.[65] Notable omissions include *RVF* 5 (which Sade had already banished as distasteful to a French readership) as well as *RVF* 23, the first *canzone* of the collection, perhaps considered too long and mythological. The typical omission of *RVF* 366 somewhat diminishes the religious turn of the *Canzoniere*'s close, although *RVF* 364, as noted in relation to Esménard's first edition, remains markedly penitential, even if the prayer is addressed not to the Virgin but to God. The omission of *RVF* 366 after the inclusion of other penitential poems such as *RVF* 62 (also addressed to God the Father) is surprising, and in other translators might suggest a possibly anti-Catholic aversion to Petrarch's choice of final intercessor. Yet in the case of Esménard, the fact that he later published a whole volume of French translations of Latin liturgical celebrations of the Blessed Virgin Mary must discount such an assumption.[66]

Esménard's second edition coincided with another translation of Petrarch's poetry, that of an uncle–nephew pairing, Ernest and Edmond Lafond, which also

[63] For details see Chapter 3.

[64] '[Pétrarque] n'est guère connu en France, si ce n'est de quelques littérateurs, que comme le héros de l'amour platonique : peut-être ma traduction le fera-t-elle mieux connaître.' *Poésies de Pétrarque traduites en vers par Camille Esménard du Mazet* (Paris: Au comptoir des imprimeurs-unis, 1848), p. iii. For discussion of Sade see p. iv.

[65] Note that these twenty-four poems are identical to those moved to Marsand's fourth section.

[66] Esménard du Mazet, *Chants à la Sainte Vierge traduits du bréviaire* (Poissy: A. Bouret, 1867).

gave space only to sonnets.[67] Of a possible 317 sonnets, this translation included 192, that is, just over 60% of the total number of sonnets, and just over half of the *Canzoniere* in its entirety. Unlike the small number of sonnets excluded by Marsand (and Brisset and Cabadé in his wake), only twenty in total, the two Lafonds end up excluding 125 in all. They exclude many of the same sonnets as Brisset and Cabadé, although, unusually, they recuperate *RVF* 10 (a sonnet in praise of Stefano Colonna the Elder) and 120 (a sonnet reassuring the poet Antonio da Ferrara that contrary to rumour Petrarch is still alive). Unlike Brisset and Cabadé, Ernest and Edmond Lafond also omit several sonnets with overtly mythological imagery, including *RVF* 34 (a rewriting of the Apollo and Daphne myth), 291 (a reworking of the love story of Tithonus and Aurora), and 321 (in which Laura is figured as a phoenix). Sade, too, had criticized Petrarch for his obsession with myth, and it seems that this mistrust of such Classical language lasted into the nineteenth century, as far as translations of Petrarch were concerned.

Structurally, the selections from Petrarch by Ernest and Edmond Lafond deviate more from the expected order than most of the other translations (Godefroy being, as already discussed, another notable anomaly). Whilst their first half starts with *RVF* 1 and their second half, as is traditional, with *RVF* 267, the choice of endpoints for each are unique to their volume. The Lafond first half ends with *RVF* 250, in which Laura announces her death to the poet in a dream ending "'Do not hope ever to see me again here on Earth'".[68] This choice is no doubt because *RVF* 250 provides the clearest anticipation of Laura's death and therefore acts as an ideal, dramatic point of transition to the second half. The second half ends with *RVF* 351, which describes Laura's contradictory behaviour towards the poet, now with the recognition that it was designed to keep the poet's love within the limits set by religion:

> Ah ! votre alternative eut pour cause et pour but,
> Je le vois à présent, le soin de mon salut
> Qui sans elle et sans vous se perdait en fumée ![69]
>
> ***
>
> Ah! Your inconsistency had for cause and aim,
> I now see, care for my salvation
> Which without it and you would have been lost in smoke!

The Lafond version of the *Canzoniere* is limited by choosing only sonnets, thereby omitting by necessity *RVF* 366, but this placing of *RVF* 351 as the climax of the collection has the deliberate effect of reinstating Laura in Petrarch's affections, in marked opposition to the absent *RVF* 366. The two preceding poems chosen by

---

[67] Ernest and Edmond Lafond, *Dante, Pétrarque, Michel-Ange, Tasse: sonnets choisis traduits en vers et précédés d'une étude sur chaque poëte* (Paris: Comptoir des Imprimeurs-Unis, 1848).

[68] "'N'espère plus me voir désormais ici-bas'" (in the original Italian, "'non sperar di vedermi in terra mai'"). Lafond, *Dante, Pétrarque, Michel-Ange, Tasse*, p. 242; *RVF* 250, v. 14.

[69] Lafond, *Dante, Pétrarque, Michel-Ange, Tasse*, p. 326. The sonnet ends, in the original Italian, 'questo bel variar fu la radice / di mia salute, ch'altramente era ita' ('this beautiful variation was the root of my salvation, which otherwise was gone', vv. 13–14).

the Lafonds are *RVF* 364 and 365, which are each marked as a 'Prayer' (*Prière*) and constitute a rejection of Laura and of earthly love.[70] Both address God and define the will to love what is mortal, that is, Laura, as a vain habit, full of error. Had this version of Petrarch's sonnets ended here, the sequence would be close to the sentiments of *RVF* 366 and Petrarch's original plan. However, the placement of *RVF* 351 as the crowning moment puts Laura back in the picture and undermines the argument that Laura and God are incompatible objects of desire. The translators comment in their heading to *RVF* 351 that 'Now entirely devoted to God, Petrarch could not, however, without being ungrateful forget the one to whom he owes his salvation; thus he addresses himself one last time to her, and recognizes that it is her sweet severity which saved his soul.'[71] This story, achieved through both changes in ordering and the space of translators' comments, is very different from the actual ending of the *Canzoniere*, and in fact much closer to the version narrated in the *Triumphus Mortis*.[72] Commentary and structure are, then, powerful tools of a surreptitious rewriting of Petrarch's love story for an audience unlikely to find a total, ascetic rejection of Laura a satisfying conclusion to so many amorous sonnets.

Later in the century, the translator L. Jehan-Madelaine also published a volume of translations of sonnets by Petrarch, albeit not as many as the Lafond pair.[73] Jehan-Madelaine's fifty-eight sonnets, though formally regular, are characterized by freedom from the original text, both in the sense that no parallel text or first line in Italian is given, making the identification of the originals sometimes tricky, and also in that the translations are overtly presented as a free translation (*traduction libre*). Jehan-Madelaine translates almost exclusively sonnets from part one, and ends his volume with the popular sonnets *RVF* 35 and 90, thus crowning the volume with sonnets about melancholy, Laura's great beauty, and enduring love. Even fewer poems are included in the joint translation of Junior Casalis and Ernest de Ginoux than in Jehan-Madelaine's selections from the same decade.[74] There is still the same emphasis on the sonnet form (with fifty sonnets translated), although this is now expanded to include a selection of typically favourite *odes*, five in total: the ever popular *RVF* 126 (discussed at the end of this chapter); *RVF* 129 (a *canzone* of solitary wandering through hill and vale); the *canzone* of mourning from the start of the *in morte* section, *RVF* 268; two political *canzoni* (the patriotic *RVF* 128 and *RVF* 53). These odes are interspersed amongst the sonnets, although the volume ends with the two political poems together, perhaps with a nod towards the typical

---

[70]   Lafond, *Dante, Pétrarque, Michel-Ange, Tasse*, pp. 324–5.

[71]   'Tout à Dieu maintenant, [Pétrarque] ne pourrait pourtant sans ingratitude oublier celle à qui il doit son salut ; aussi il s'adresse une dernière fois à elle, et reconnaît que c'est sa douce sévérité qui sauva son âme.' Lafond, *Dante, Pétrarque, Michel-Ange, Tasse*, p. 326.

[72]   For a coupling of this dialogue and *RVF* 351 (in Gramont's translation of each) see also Jean Saint-Martin, *La Fontaine de Vaucluse et ses souvenirs: dessins de Bill, Eysséric, Karl, Paul Saïn et Georges Roux* (Paris: Librairie générale de L. Sauvaitre, 1891), pp. 78–83, as well as Chapter 3, below.

[73]   *Sonnets de Pétrarque: traduction libre par L. Jehan-Madelaine: première série* (Paris: Librairie Fischbacher, 1884). I have yet to track down a possible *deuxième série* by the same translator.

[74]   Casalis and Ginoux, *Cinquante sonnets et cinq odes* (1887).

marginalization of such poems by Marsand. Of the fifty sonnets included by Casalis and Ginoux, it is unsurprising to encounter consistently popular sonnets such as *RVF* 35, 90, 302, and 310.

Other Partial Translations

Besides translations of Petrarch's sonnets, other translators followed the early lead of publications such as that of Romet which selected only Petrarch's 'most beautiful poems', comprising both sonnets and other poetic forms. Léonce de Saint-Geniès is the earliest such translator, representing an unusual interest in Petrarch in the first decades of the nineteenth century (specifically, 1816), and including translations into French verse of just over one hundred poems from the *Canzoniere*.[75] Saint-Geniès rightly felt himself to be breaking new ground in choosing to translate Petrarch at this time, and considered this task to be difficult but worthwhile, even long overdue:

> It is only to be marvelled at that, despite his celebrity, no French poet has attempted to translate him, a homage paid to many authors who were less worthy of such an honour. But on further reflection, the reasons which might put someone off from this difficult enterprise become apparent. Petrarch's poems are only a collection of lyric and elegiac verse, and do not offer the interest of an exploit like the great compositions of epic poets; they do not even contain action comparable to that of a romance [*roman*]. All Petrarch has done is explain what he felt, without making a plan, without worrying about inserting variety and contrasts; in this he is very different from erotic poets, who construct their loves as they construct their elegies, and think much more about the public than about their mistress.[76]

This introduction to Petrarch contains both praise and blame; Petrarch's poetic sincerity and spontaneity are admired even as they are identified as a source of the collection's perceived lack of grand design or narrative interest. Saint-Geniès here echoes the traditional hierarchy of genres, by placing epic above lyric poetry.

---

[75] Léonce de Saint-Geniès, *Poésies de Pétrarque, traduites en vers français, suivies de deux poëmes*, 2 vols (Paris: Delaunay and Barrois, 1816). Saint-Geniès's other key publication is poetic and purportedly historical if not Petrarchan: Saint-Geniès, *Balder, fils d'Odin: poëme scandinave en six chants, suivi de notes sur l'histoire, la religion et les mœurs des nations celtiques* (Paris: L'Éditeur, 1824). See also the collaborative prose work by Saint-Geniès and Joseph-Henri de Saur, *Les Aventures de Faust, et sa descente aux enfers*, 3 vols (Paris: Arthus Bertrand, 1825), which claims to be the first French treatment of the tale.

[76] 'On peut seulement s'étonner que, malgré sa célébrité, aucun poète français n'ait tenté de le traduire, hommage accordé à beaucoup d'auteurs qui en étaient moins dignes. Mais en y réfléchissant, on conçoit les motifs qui ont détourné de cette difficile entreprise. Les poésies de Pétrarque ne sont qu'un recueil de vers lyriques et élégiaques, et n'offrent pas l'intérêt d'une action comme les grandes compositions des poètes épiques ; elles n'ont pas même celui d'un roman. Pétrarque n'a fait qu'exprimer ce qu'il éprouvait, sans faire un plan, sans s'occuper d'y mettre de la variété et des contrastes ; bien différent des poètes érotiques, qui composent leurs amours en composant leurs élégies, et pensent au public encore plus qu'à leur maîtresse.' Saint-Geniès, *Poésies de Pétrarque*, I, p. xxiii.

More specifically, this translator also distinguishes Petrarch from action-packed romance as from the work of 'erotic poets' (*poètes érotiques*).[77] As regards the latter, Saint-Geniès likely has Ovid in mind, but excludes Petrarch from this group not because of the purity or chastity of his verse (a more typical reading of Petrarch's poetry in this period), but rather because of Petrarch's apparent aimlessness and self-absorption. These accusations are strange applied to a poet we tend to think of as obsessed with his posterity. These characteristics are not, however, entirely negative or undesirable, since what Petrarch's verse lacks, according to Saint-Geniès, in structure and plot it gains, as already noted, in sincerity and authenticity.

Like Sade, Saint-Geniès additionally accuses Petrarch of lacking 'variety and contrasts' (*de la variété et des contrastes*), and perhaps reorders the *Canzoniere* in his translation in order to compensate for this lack by the new juxtaposition of texts that were originally more distant from each other. In Saint-Geniès's presentation the *Canzoniere*, as anticipated above, appears structure-less and unplanned, for his ordering is extremely disrupted, and also eschews any wider structuring principles, at least explicitly, whether the typical bipartite division of the collection or the potential conversion narrative arc from *RVF* 1 to *RVF* 366. Of the one hundred poems included from the *Canzoniere*, Saint-Geniès incorporates a representative number of all the forms present in the collection, sonnets, madrigals, *canzoni*, and *ballate*.[78] In this manner, Saint-Geniès demonstrates a desire for formal and metrical variety in his selections, again a way of achieving the contrasts which he deemed so desirable, and entirely opposed to subsequent French translators who had more taste for monotony and, as we have seen, typically reduced Petrarch to his sonnets.

Also reminiscent of Sade is Saint-Geniès's evident lack of appetite for the *in morte* poems, although where Sade had entirely avoided poems from this section Saint-Geniès does include eleven of them, all in the second volume of his translation, thereby keeping a certain sense of order and narrative progression from life to death.[79] The final poem of Saint-Geniès's collection (setting aside his addition of two of his own poems at the end of volume two, discussed in Chapter 5) is *RVF* 310, which expresses the poet's continuing grief despite and in contrast to the return of Spring. The latest sonnet from the *Canzoniere* to be included is, however, *RVF* 353, a sonnet which, like *RVF* 311, relates the poet's comparison of his own songs of lament to that of a solitary bird (*Vago augelletto*). In this way the penitential turn of the final series of poems of the *Canzoniere*, culminating in the renunciation of Laura in preference for the Virgin Mary in *RVF* 366, is entirely avoided by Saint-Geniès, adding grist to Costaing's lament, in 1819, only three years later, that *RVF* 366 is

---

[77] The term 'roman' here more likely signifies 'romance' than 'novel', since Saint-Geniès is concerned with situating Petrarch within a typology of poetic forms.

[78] These translations are supplemented by translations of two sonnets addressed to Petrarch and of one *canzone* from Petrarch excluded from the *Canzoniere*, as well as two poems by Saint-Geniès: see Appendix 1 for details.

[79] These *in morte* poems are, in their order from Saint-Geniès's translation, *RVF* 322, 270, 288, 337, 353, 330, 268, 312, 302, 287, and 310.

'a masterpiece of Petrarch's intellect, an eternal monument to his piety and faith, forgotten like his other writings'.[80]

In contrast to Saint-Geniès's verse translation, Arrighi's similarly selective *Odes et sonnets choisis* (1838; *Selected Odes and Sonnets*) over twenty years later show-cases the benefits of prose and anticipates by only a few years Gramont's complete prose translation of 1842.[81] In this publication, Arrighi presents fewer poems than Saint-Geniès (only thirty-nine sonnets and one *canzone*, RVF 268, as well as part of the *Triumphus Temporis*). Oddly, Arrighi only includes ten sonnets from the first part of the *Canzoniere* (all between RVF 1 and 13), with the majority of his selec-tions coming from the second part (thirty poems from RVF 267–353, though not necessarily in sequential order). In this manner, unlike both Sade and Saint-Geniès, Arrighi shows a clear preference for Petrarch's poetry of mourning; this preference for love-in-death is, of course, a typically Romantic trope. Nonetheless, Arrighi still preserves part of the overall structure of the collection and includes the opening sonnets which give the rudimentary details of the start of the poet's love for Laura. Like Saint-Geniès, the last poem of Arrighi's translation is RVF 353, although he does publish a separate translation of RVF 366 first in 1851 and then in 1854.[82] Arrighi's interest in RVF 366 is unusual, since translators, unless aiming for a complete trans-lation, often conveniently excluded this poem from their selections of Petrarch's love poetry, considering the rejection of Laura in favour of the Virgin Mary in the final poem of the *Canzoniere* unfortunate and distasteful. As Guglielmo Gorni has commented: 'It is probable that this final dedication has always been dismissed by readers of the *Canzoniere*, because of the unexpected desertion of the Laurean cult which it marks: such an openly confessional ending is difficult to accept from the founding father of the European lyric tradition.'[83] In the case of incomplete transla-tions of the *Canzoniere*, this dismissal was often literal, banning the poem from the space of the work.

---

[80] 'un chef-d'œuvre de son esprit, un éternel monument de sa piété et de sa foi, oublié comme ses autres écrits', Costaing, *La Muse de Pétrarque*, p. 236.

[81] Jean-Paul-Louis Arrighi, *Odes et sonnets choisis de Pétrarque, traduits en français* (Paris: Impasse du Doyenné, 1838).

[82] Arrighi, *Preghiera di Petrarca alla santissima Vergine/Prière de Pétrarque à la très-sainte Vierge* (Grenoble: Imprimerie de Prudhomme, 1851); Arrighi, *Aspirations de l'âme religieuse: ode à la divine pureté, par Filicaia, en trois langues; suivie de la prière à la très-sainte Vierge, par Pétrarque, en deux langues* (La Côte-Saint-André: Chez le traducteur, 1854), pp. 15–27. For a study of earlier French translations of this *canzone*, see Bruno Donderi, 'The French Renaissance Versions of the Canzone "Vergine Bella"', in *Petrarch: The Self and the World*, ed. Supriya Chaudhuri and Sukanta Chaudhuri (Kolkata: Jadavpur University Press, 2012), pp. 226–40. Part of RVF 366 is also unusually selected for translation by E. J. Delé-cluze, though in the context of a volume on Dante and with a note encouraging comparison between Petrarch's poem and the final *canto* of *Paradiso*: see Delécluze, *Dante Alighieri, ou la poésie amoureuse*, 2 vols (Paris: A. Delahays, 1854), II, 454.

[83] 'È probabile che questa dedica finale sia stata sempre rimossa dal lettore del *Canzo-niere* per l'inopinato abbandono del culto laurano che essa segna indefettibilmente: un esito così scopertamente confessionale si sopporta male nel fondatore della lirica d'arte europea.' Guglielmo Gorni, 'Petrarca Virgini (Lettura della canzone CCCLXVI "Vergine bella")', *Lectura Petrarce*, 7 (1987), 201–18 (p. 212).

While Saint-Geniès's translations remain a rare testimony to interest in Petrarch in French in the first decades of the nineteenth century, Arrighi's work anticipates and participates in the flourishing of translations of Petrarch in the 1840s, a decade which saw the publication of a number of important translations of the poet, including the first modern complete translations of his Italian poetry, by Gramont and Montesquiou, the first volume of Mahul's translations of Petrarch's sonnets, and Esménard's second, more wide-ranging volume of translations from 1848.

Thus far in this chapter we have seen how Petrarch is reworked and reimagined in various ways by all these translators. For eighteenth-century translators such as Sade and Roman, Petrarch is considered too sad and too repetitive, disadvantages remedied by avoiding the *in morte* poems, cutting back the *Canzoniere* significantly, and at times combining poems together. For these translators, a poem is not an inviolable, quasi-sacred unit of meaning, but rather a piece of text ripe for bold amendments and transformation. For Saint-Geniès, Petrarch also lacks variety, again a recurrent motif behind the preference for an incomplete rather than a complete translation of his work, combined once more in Saint-Geniès with further avoidance of the *in morte* poems. However, shifts in taste mean that later in the nineteenth century translators learn to appreciate Petrarch's *in morte* poems more than his *in vita* poems (see, for instance, explicitly in Cabadé), perhaps a result of the Romantic turn. Mournful poetry comes to be in vogue in a way that it was not in the previous century, when Sade expressed the stark view that sadness (*tristesse*) was not only undesirable in poetry but even un-French.[84] Translators also eventually prove to have more stomach for Petrarch's oft-mentioned monotony, as demonstrated by the extensive projects devoted to translating all (or almost all) of his sonnets (Le Duc, Mahul, Cabadé). Restriction to Petrarch's sonnets is also common to less complete projects (such as Esménard's first collection from 1830, or Jehan-Madelaine's 1884 volume). In this manner the variety instilled in Petrarch by a judicious selection of a representative range of all the different poetic forms featured in the *Canzoniere* (particularly in Saint-Geniès's translation) gives way later in the century to interest in Petrarch predominantly and even solely as a sonneteer. Instead of variety later translations seek in Petrarch consistency; monotony is reframed as unity and therefore newly valued.

Despite these changes in attitude, consistent across all these translators is a dislike of Petrarch's recurrent use of mythology and wordplay, manifested in avoidance of the myth of Apollo and Daphne as well as the puns on Laura's name. These translators tend to want to simplify Petrarchan polysemy to one stable meaning that is above all biographical, denoting Petrarch's beloved more directly and straightforwardly. Also shared by these translators is a frequent dismantling of any religious framework of the *Canzoniere*, achieved both by avoiding *RVF* 366 (a common solution) and reordering the poems to create a new and different ending, often focussed on recommitment to love and Laura. In this way Petrarch is presented as a sublime love poet largely freed from any qualms of conscience. Love, in this new collection, is unassailable and irreproachable.

---

[84]   Sade, *Mémoires*, I, p. cxii.

In this way the French Petrarch in this period proves to embody a complex, unstable mix of difference and sameness; some traits come in and out of fashion (and vice versa), while others are remarkably consistent. It is the latter aspect of the French Petrarch that I will explore further in the final part of this chapter, through a focus on just a few poems which were repeatedly selected by translators as the best of Petrarch. These poems include most prominently two sonnets, *RVF* 35 and 302, and a *canzone* highlighted by Voltaire, *RVF* 126, and reveal *in nuce* the type of Petrarch that French translators of this period wanted, above all, to celebrate.

Favourite Poems

Of Petrarch's sonnets singled out most frequently for translation, favourites consistently include *RVF* 35 and *RVF* 302.[85] The first, *RVF* 35 (selected as 'one of Petrarch's most beautiful poems' by Romet as early as 1765) is a sonnet of solitude and slow, amorous wandering with nature as witness to the poet's suffering and Love as sole interlocutor.

RVF 35

Solo et pensoso i più deserti campi
vo mesurando a passi tardi et lenti,
et gli occhi porto per fuggire intenti
ove vestigio human la rena stampi.

Altro schermo non trovo che mi scampi
dal manifesto accorger de le genti,
perché negli atti d'alegrezza spenti
di fuor si legge com'io dentro avampi:

sì ch'io mi credo omai che monti et piagge
et fiumi et selve sappian di che tempre
sia la mia vita, ch'è celata altrui.

Ma pur sì aspre vie né sì selvagge
cercar non so, ch'Amor non venga sempre

---

[85] In addition to translations already discussed, for translations of *RVF* 35, see, for instance, Baudouin, *Rêveries sur les bords du Cher*, pp. 59–62. For translations of *RVF* 302, amongst other sonnets, see: Marc-Antoine Jullien, *La France en 1825, ou mes regrets et mes espérances; discours en vers: seconde édition, suivie de quelques autres poésies détachées du même auteur* (Paris: Chez Antoine-Augustin Renouard, 1825), pp. 26–7; J.-C. Di Negro, *Essais poétiques* (Genoa: Imprimerie des sourds-muets, 1840), p. 76; Philippe Duplessis, *Œuvres posthumes*, 5 vols (Paris: Firmin Didot, 1853), v, 362–73; Lalaing, *Stances*, p. 135; Paul Terris, *Pétrarque: ode qui a obtenu la médaille d'argent de l'académie du Gard aux jeux floraux du centenaire 18–20 juillet 1874* (Carpentras: Chez P. Prière, 1874), p. 14. For a translation of both *RVF* 35 and 302, see Hippolyte Topin, *Études sur la langue italienne, précédées d'un parallèle entre Dante et Klopstock* (Florence: Typographie Galiléienne; Paris: Chez les principaux libraires, 1855), pp. 82–5. Zuccato's investigations of Romantic English Petrarchism also reveal the popularity of *RVF* 35, alongside *RVF* 311 and 353, and with *RVF* 310 a stark favourite: Zuccato, *Petrarch in Romantic England*, p. x.

ragionando con meco, et io co·llui.

***

Alone and pensive the most deserted fields
I go measuring with slow and tardy steps,
and I hold my eyes fixed to flee
wherever human footsteps have marked the sand.

No other screen can I find to save me
from the manifest attention of people,
because in my acts of extinguished happiness
from outside it is legible how I burn inside:

so that I myself believe by now that mountains and shores
and rivers and woods know of what temper
is my life, which is hidden from others.

But still such bitter nor such wild paths
can I not seek, that Love does not come ever
speaking with me, and I with him.

With such themes of solitude amidst nature, the sonnet is understandably attractive for Romantic and post-Romantic translators. Exemplarily, Ginguené admires *RVF* 35 as 'perhaps, in my opinion, the most beautiful and moving of all his sonnets, the one in which he has brought to the highest degree of intimacy the union of those two great sources of interest, bucolic solitude and melancholy'.[86] For Lamartine, too, this poem is 'one of Petrarch's most beautiful sonnets', one which 'expresses more melancholically than has ever been expressed the consonance of the sadness of his spirit [*âme*] with the sadness of the landscape'.[87] *RVF* 35 also contains many typically Petrarchan linguistic features (balanced pairs of adjectives, gerunds, polysyndeton of the natural landscape), making it an ideal and representative choice stylistically as well as thematically.

The second, equally popular sonnet, *RVF* 302, presents an unusual moment of dialogue between the poet and Laura, in which a ghostly Laura professes her love for Petrarch and the desire that they will one day be reunited in Heaven.

RVF 302

Lèvommi il mio penser in parte ov'era
quella ch'io cerco, et non ritrovo, in terra:
ivi, fra lor che 'l terzo cerchio serra,
la rividi più bella e meno altera.

---

[86] 'peut-être, selon moi, le plus beau, le plus touchant [sonnet] de tous les siens, et où il a porté au plus haut point d'intimité l'alliance de ces deux grandes sources d'intérêt, la solitude champêtre et la mélancolie', Ginguené, *Histoire littéraire d'Italie*, II, 507.

[87] 'Un de ses plus beaux sonnets, *Solo et pensoso*, exprime plus mélancoliquemnent qu'on ne le fit jamais cette consonnance de la tristesse de son âme avec la tristesse des lieux.' Lamartine, *Cours familier de littérature*, VI, 27.

Per man mi prese, et disse: – In questa spera
sarai anchor meco, se 'l desir non erra:
i' so' colei che ti die' tanta guerra,
et compie' mia giornata inanzi sera.

Mio ben non cape in intelletto humano:
te solo aspetto, et quel che tanto amasti
e là giuso è rimaso, il mio bel velo. –

Deh, perché tacque et allargò la mano?
Ch'al suon de' detti sì pietosi et casti
poco mancò ch'io non rimasi in cielo.

       ***

My thought lifted me to the place where was
she whom I seek, and do not find, on Earth:
there, amongst those whom the third circle encompasses,
I saw her again more beautiful and less haughty.

She took me by the hand, and said: 'In this sphere
you will be with me once more, if desire does not err:
I am she who gave you such war,
and completed my day before evening.

Human intellect cannot understand my bliss:
I only wait for you, and that which you loved so much
and which has remained down there, my beautiful veil.'

Oh, why did she fall silent and withdraw her hand?
For at the sound of such piteous and modest words,
I very nearly remained in Heaven.

The sonnet is popular because it tells Laura's side of the story, albeit in extremely condensed form, and also because it promises a happy ending for the *Canzoniere* independently of the solution of religious conversion suggested by *RVF* 366. In *RVF* 302, love for Laura is no longer in conflict with love for God, in a way that will be reiterated in the dialogue between the two in the *Triumphus Mortis*, another favourite amongst French translators in this period, as discussed in Chapter 3. Gustave Planche was not alone in considering *RVF* 302 'the most beautiful, serious, and complete [...] of all of Petrarch's sonnets',[88] and his admiration for the *Triumphus Mortis* (cited in due course) is further evidence that *RVF* 302 and the *Triumphus Mortis* were often felt to have important points of resonance. Like *RVF* 35, however, *RVF* 302 is also a poem that is framed by the poet's solitude, in both the first stanza (when Laura is vainly sought on Earth) and the last tercet (when the vision of Laura fades away), making it amenable to interpretations of Petrarch as primarily a

---

[88] 'le plus beau, le plus grave, le plus complet [...] de tous les sonnets de Pétrarque', Gustave Planche, 'Études sur l'art et la poésie en Italie: II. Pétrarque', *Revue des deux mondes*, 18 (1847), 997–1018 (p. 1007).

solitary, melancholy figure. Further, one of the phrases uttered by Laura, "'if desire does not err'" (v. 6), introduces a note of doubt and uncertainty into the scenario, although the sonnet's nineteenth-century French readers such as Planche more typically overlooked this interjection, and instead considered the text a celebration of certain, imminent reunion.

Beyond these two specific poems, Petrarch was consistently revered as the supreme sonneteer. Accordingly, when a journal devoted wholly to sonnets was established in the second half of the nineteenth century, namely the *Almanach du sonnet*, its first issue coincided with the 1874 celebrations surrounding the fifth centenary of Petrarch's death, and both were the projects of the same individual, Léon de Berluc-Pérussis.[89] Moreover, while the inaugural volume of the *Almanach* contained only two sonnets translated from Petrarch (*RVF* 12, a poem expressing the desire to grow old with Laura, and the popular *RVF* 35, cited above), the next two issues were to give more and more space to translations of Petrarch, whether into French or even, on occasion, Occitan (on the latter, see Chapter 4). As we have seen, the obsession with the Petrarchan sonnet led to a marked reduction of the *Canzoniere* not only thematically (along the lines of Marsand's reordering) but also formally. The same obsession is also manifested in the continued commitment to French verse translations of Petrarch throughout the nineteenth century, since the sonnet, in particular, was felt to have a direct French equivalent that could success-fully reproduce the form as well as the contents of the original poems. In a departure from early examples of freer verse translations (Sade, Roman, Montesquiou), later translators of sonnets only (Mahul, Le Duc, Cabadé, and others, with Brisset in 1899 a notable exception) tended to attempt to fit their translations into the tradi-tional mould of regular French sonnets (*sonnets français* or *sonnets réguliers*). In this manner, verse translations of Petrarch remained more popular than prose transla-tions in the second half of the nineteenth century, in contrast to the early precedent set by translators such as Romet and Levesque, and the marginal preponderance of prose translations when it came to complete (or almost complete) translations.

Despite the privileging of Petrarch as a sonnet-monger, Petrarch's *canzoni* were, nonetheless, not wholly neglected in this period. Both La Harpe and Gabrielle Soumet d'Altenheym, for instance, even considered Petrarch's *odes* his best poems.[90] Of the twenty-nine *canzoni* included in the *Canzoniere*, translators often consist-ently returned to a specific handful, which typically included *RVF* 126 and 268 (the latter the first *canzone* of the *in morte* section), as well as two poems of political import, *RVF* 53 and 128. The popularity of this selection of *canzoni* is confirmed by Louis Langlois's *Morceaux choisis* (1852; *Selected Texts*), which includes *RVF* 126,

---

[89]   *Almanach du sonnet*, 3 vols (Aix-en-Provence: Vve Remondet-Aubin, 1874–6).

[90]   La Harpe asserts that 'ses plus belles odes, *Canzoni*, [...] sont, en effet, les chefs-d'œuvre de cet auteur, et ceux de ses ouvrages que les étrangers peuvent goûter davantage' ('his most beautiful odes, *canzoni*, [...] are, in effect, this author's masterpieces, and those of his works which foreigners can most appreciate'): La Harpe, 'Sur une traduction de quelques poésies de Pétrarque', in *Œuvres de La Harpe, de l'Académie française, accompagnée d'une notice sur sa vie et sur ses ouvrages*, 16 vols (Paris: Verdière, 1820–1), xv, 355–67 (p. 357). See also Altenheym, *Les quatre siècles littéraires*, pp. 188–9 ('nous préférons aux sonnets les *canzoni* du même auteur', 'we prefer to the sonnets the *canzoni* of the same author').

268, and 53, alongside *RVF* 270 and a further unidentified *canzone*, as well as by the five *canzoni* translated by Casalis and Ginoux in 1887, namely, *RVF* 53, 126, 128, and 268, alongside the less popular *RVF* 129.[91] *RVF* 268, the first *canzone* after Laura's death, is also privileged as the only *canzone* included in Arrighi's 1838 publication.

Of the non-amorous poems in the *Canzoniere* typically marginalized following the precedent set by Vellutello and Marsand, *RVF* 128 remained ever popular, being frequently selected by translators for independent translation throughout this period, and even hailed as 'Italy's *Marseillaise*' (*la Marseillaise de l'Italie*).[92] Beginning with an apostrophe to 'My Italy' (*Italia mia*), and concluding with an impassioned plea for peace (*pace*, v. 122), in the nineteenth century the poem was seen as particularly relevant both to Italy's journey towards unification, and to the quest of other nations such as France for political stability through strong national unity. One translator of *RVF* 53 made explicit the topicality of Petrarch's political poems, writing in 1859—during the second Italian war of independence, in which Napoleon III was an ally for the Italians against Austria—that:

> The current crisis in Italy gives our work a very particular interest; we like to find in the past these cries of independence and reform which bear witness to the unfailing aspirations of this noble and unhappy land. The energy of the lines which we are going to read will at the same time shed light on the side of Petrarch's talent which is less well known in France.[93]

In contrast to this unusual interest in a political, patriotic Petrarch (markedly at odds with the French and Provençal claims on the poet discussed in the Introduction), the most popular *canzone* of the *Canzoniere* amongst French translators was

---

[91] Louis Langlois, *Morceaux choisis: Catulle, Gallus, Properce, Tibulle, Ovide, Maximien, Pétrarque, et Jean Second; précédés d'une notice biographique sur chacun de ces poètes* (Paris: Leclère fils, 1852), pp. 221–59.

[92] Pierre de Nolhac, 'Préface', in G. Finzi, *Pétrarque: sa vie et son œuvre: traduit avec l'autorisation de l'auteur par Mme Thiérard-Baudrillart* (Paris: Perrin et Cie, 1906), pp. 5–11 (p. 8). For translations of *RVF* 128, see, for instance, J. Michel Berton, *Éleuthérides: poésies* (Paris: Dumont, 1839), pp. 21–7, and A.-F. Villemain, *Cours de littérature française: tableau de la littérature du Moyen Âge en France, en Italie, en Espagne et en Angleterre: nouvelle édition revue, corrigée et augmentée*, 2 vols (Paris: Didier, 1851), II, 29–30. Some lines from *RVF* 128 (vv. 28–30, 81–6) are translated into prose by François-René de Chateaubriand in *Mémoires d'outre-tombe*, ed. Maurice Levaillant and Georges Moulinier, 2 vols (Paris: Gallimard, 1951), I, 480–1. *RVF* 128, in Italian, is also included in several pedagogical manuals published in Paris: see, for instance, P. L. Costantini, *Nuova scelta di poesie italiane, tratte da' più celebri autori antichi e moderni, con brevi notizie sopra la vita e gli scritti di ciascheduno*, 2 vols (Paris: Bossange, 1823), I, 88–90, and Louis Ferri, *Morceaux choisis, en prose et en vers, des classiques italiens publiés avec une introduction, des notices biographiques et des notes en français* (Paris: Hachette, 1868), pp. 272–7.

[93] 'La crise actuelle de l'Italie donne à notre travail un intérêt tout particulier ; on aime à retrouver dans le passé ces cris d'indépendance et de réforme témoignant des constantes aspirations de cette noble et malheureuse contrée. L'énergie des vers qu'on va lire éclairera en même temps le côté le moins connu en France du talent de Pétrarque.' Gustave de Larenaudière, '*Spirto gentil – Noble génie*, canzone de Pétrarque adressée à Cola di Rienzo', *Revue française* (1859), 502–5 (p. 502).

undoubtedly *RVF* 126, which easily holds its own against *RVF* 35 and 302 in terms of popularity and frequency of translation and citation in this period. It is to this poem that the final section of this chapter is devoted.

Translating *RVF* 126 after Voltaire

By sheer number of translations, *RVF* 126 is the most popular of Petrarch's poems with French translators in this period. Despite its exclusion from sonnet-only publications, when translators allowed themselves to include one or two representative *canzoni*, it was to this poem that they returned time and time again. Importantly, there was a good French precedent for such a choice, set by none other than Voltaire, who had translated the first stanza in his *Essai sur les mœurs et l'esprit des nations* (1756).[94] Subsequent French translators often reminded their readers of Voltaire's translation whenever they either attempted the poem themselves or merely mentioned it in passing. Here is the opening stanza (*RVF* 126, vv. 1–13) in Petrarch's Italian and Voltaire's French, both with accompanying English translation:

> Chiare, fresche et dolci acque,
> ove le belle membra
> pose colei che sola a me par donna;
> gentil ramo ove piacque
> (con sospir' mi rimembra)
> a lei di fare al bel fiancho colonna;
> herba et fior' che la gonna
> leggiadra ricoverse
> co l'angelico seno;
> aere sacro, sereno,
> ove Amor co' begli occhi il cor m'aperse:
> date udïenzia insieme
> a le dolenti mie parole extreme.

***

> Clear, fresh, and sweet waters,
> where her beautiful members
> laid she who alone to me seems a lady;
> noble branch where it pleased
> (with sighs I remember)
> her to make a column for her beautiful side;
> grass and flowers that her elegant
> dress covered
> with her angelic breast;
> sacred, serene air,
> where Love with her beautiful eyes opened my heart:
> all hear together
> my sorrowful last words.

---

[94]   Voltaire, *Essai sur les mœurs et l'esprit des nations*, IV, 274.

Claire fontaine, onde amiable, onde pure,
Où la beauté qui consume mon cœur,
Seule beauté qui soit dans la nature,
Des feux du jour évitait la chaleur ;
Arbre heureux, dont le feuillage,
Agité par les zéphyrs
La couvrit de son ombrage,
Qui rappelle mes soupirs,
En rappelant son image ;
Ornements de ces bords, et filles du matin,
Vous dont je suis jaloux, vous moins brillantes qu'elle,
Fleurs qu'elle embellissait quand vous touchiez son sein,
Rossignol dont la voix est moins douce et moins belle,
Air devenu plus pur, adorable séjour.
Immortalisé par ses charmes,
Lieux dangereux et chers, où de ses tendres armes
L'Amour a blessé tous mes sens ;
Écoutez mes derniers accents,
Recevez mes dernières larmes.

***

Clear fountain, amiable water, pure water,
Where the beauty which is consuming my heart,
The only beauty which there is in nature,
From the fires of the day was avoiding the heat;
Happy tree, whose foliage,
Rustled by zephyrs
Covered her with its shade,
Which calls back my sighs,
Remembering her image;
Ornaments of these banks, and daughters of the morning,
You of whom I am jealous, you less brilliant than she,
You flowers which she embellished when you touched her breast,
Nightingale whose voice is less sweet and less beautiful,
Air become purer, adorable sojourn.
Immortalized by her charms,
Places dangerous and dear, where with his tender weapons
Love has hurt all my senses;
Hear my last words,
Receive my last tears.

Despite his singling out of this poem, in general Voltaire expressed a dislike of Petrarch's style and themes. Indeed, one such attack came in the form of an anonymous review of the first volume of Sade's *Mémoires* published in the *Gazette littéraire* on 6 June 1764, in truth more an attack on Petrarch's poetry than on Sade's historical account.[95] Voltaire was one of Sade's first readers and the two were friends, but Voltaire still felt the need to attempt to stem quickly the wave of French Petrarchism that Sade wished to reinvigorate. Voltaire admired Petrarch for his poetic successes so early in the history of literature in the vernacular, but preferred the works of later French writers, or even the Italian Tasso, and ultimately rejected Petrarch for what he perceived as his frivolity:

> It is true that in the fourteenth century Petrarch was the best poet in Europe, and even the only one; but it is no less true that of his little works, almost all of which go on about love, there is not one which can come near to the beautiful sentiments which we find scattered with such profusion in Racine and Quin-ault. I would even dare to assert that we have in our language a prodigious number of songs [*chansons*] which are more delicate and ingenious than those of Petrarch; and we are so rich in this genre that we scornfully refuse to boast about it. [...] Petrarch after all has perhaps no especial merit other than the fact of having written elegantly some trifles without genius at a time when such amusements were highly esteemed because they were very rare.[96]

Voltaire's criticism of Petrarch's Italian poetry here as 'trifles' (*bagatelles*) echoes Petrarch's own classification of his vernacular output as similarly frivolous and trifling, but is harsher both through the addition of the phrase 'without genius' (*sans génie*) and the lack of (perhaps false) modesty as a motivating factor in this assessment.[97]

In this same letter, Voltaire cast aspersions not only on the merits of Petrarch's poetry, but even on the very existence of Laura, a fact which (as charted in the

---

[95]   Voltaire 'Lettre aux Auteurs de la *Gazette littéraire*', in 'Supplément à la *Gazette littéraire de l'Europe*: mercredi 6 juin 1764', *Gazette littéraire de l'Europe. Tome premier. Comprenant les mois de mars, avril & mai 1764* (Paris: De l'Imprimerie de la Gazette de France, aux Galeries du Louvre, 1764), pp. 391–6. Despite the publication of this letter, a footnote from the editors warns that 'nous croyons que l'Auteur juge Pétrarque avec trop de sévérité' ('we believe that the author judges Petrarch too severely'), 'Lettre aux Auteurs de la *Gazette littéraire*', p. 391.

[96]   'Il est vrai que Pétrarque au quatorzième siècle étoit le meilleur Poëte de l'Europe, & même le seul ; mais il n'est pas moins vrai que de ses petits Ouvrages, qui roulent presque tous sur l'amour, il n'y en a pas un qui approche des beautés de sentiment qu'on trouve répandus avec tant de profusion dans Racine & dans Quinault. J'oserais même affirmer que nous avons dans notre langue un nombre prodigieux de chansons plus délicates & plus ingénieuses que celles de Pétrarque ; et nous sommes si riches en ce genre, que nous dédaignons de nous en faire un mérite. [...] Pétrarque après tout n'a peut-être d'autre mérite que d'avoir écrit élégamment des bagatelles sans génie dans un temps où ces amusemens étoient très-estimés parce qu'ils étoient très-rares.' Voltaire, 'Lettre aux Auteurs de la *Gazette littéraire*', pp. 393, 396.

[97]   The Latin terms Petrarch uses to describe his vernacular lyric poetry are equivalent to 'trifles' or 'bagatelles': 'nugae' or 'nugellae'. See, for instance, *Fam.* I, 1, in Petrarch, *Familiarium rerum libri/Le Familiari*, ed. Vittorio Rossi, 4 vols (Florence: G.C. Sansoni, 1933–42), I, 7; *Letters on Familiar Matters: Rerum familiarium libri I–VIII*, trans. Aldo S. Bernardo (Albany, NY: State University of New York Press, 1975), p. 7. Here and subsequently individual letters from this collection are cited with the preceding abbreviation *Fam.*

Introduction) was rarely doubted, at least on paper, throughout the nineteenth century. In Voltaire's words, with reference to a letter of Petrarch which records Giovanni Colonna's suspicion that Laura is merely symbolic or allegorical:

> It matters very little that a pretend or true Laura was the object of so many sonnets; it is rather likely that Laura was what Boileau calls an *Iris in the sky*.[98] A bishop from Lombez, with whom Petrarch stayed for a long time, wrote to him: 'Your Laura is nothing but a phantom of the imagination through which you exercise your muse.' Petrarch replied: 'My father, I am truly in love.' This proves that at that time bishops were called *fathers*, but it does not prove [...] that Petrarch's mistress was indeed called Laura.[99]

Voltaire hoped that his combined criticism of Sade, dislike of Petrarch, and disbelief in Laura would remain anonymous, and wrote accordingly to friends on 22 June 1764:

> I beseech you, my divine angels, to recommend the most profound secrecy to the gentlemen of the *gazette littéraire*. I do not think much of Petrarch's poetry, he is the most fertile genius in the world in the art of always saying the same thing, but it is not for me to topple the abbé Desades's [*sic*] saint from his niche.[100]

Voltaire's dislike of Sade's 'saint' did not, however, prevent French critics from subsequently seeking to highlight similarities between Voltaire and Petrarch, in particular as regards the marriage of philosophical, literary, and political clout in one individual. In 1816, Saint-Geniès proposed that 'We could find in no one else but Voltaire the example of a poet who has received so many marks of esteem from sovereigns, so much homage during his century, and who has, like Petrarch, been

---

[98]   The phrase 'quelque Iris en l'air' ('some Iris in the sky') appears in Boileau, *Œuvres complètes*, ed. Françoise Escal (Paris: Gallimard, 1966), p. 55 ('Satire IX'), and is originally Boileau's mockery of a poem by Charles Perrault ('Élégie à Iris', 'Elegy to Iris'), here appropriated by Voltaire to suggest that Laura, like Iris, exists only in and for poetry.

[99]   'Il importe fort peu qu'une Laure feinte ou véritable ait été l'objet de tant de sonnets ; il est assez vraisemblable que Laure était ce que Boileau appelle une *Iris en l'air*. Un évêque de Lombez, chez qui Pétrarque demeura longtemps, lui écrit : "Votre Laure n'est qu'un fantôme d'imagination sur lequel vous exercez votre muse." Pétrarque lui répond: "Mon père, je suis véritablement amoureux." Cela prouve qu'alors on appelait les évêques *pères*; mais cela ne prouve pas [...] que la maîtresse de Pétrarque s'appelait Laure en effet.' Voltaire, 'Lettre aux Auteurs de la *Gazette littéraire*', p. 396. For the letter by Petrarch to which Voltaire alludes, see Petrarch, *Familiarium rerum libri*, ed. Rossi, I, 94; *Letters on Familiar Matters: Rerum familiarium libri I–VIII*, trans. Bernardo, p. 102 (*Fam.* II, 9).

[100]   'Je vous conjure, mes divins anges, de recommander le plus profond secrêt à mes^rs de la gazette littéraire. Je ne fais pas grand cas des vers de Pétrarque, c'est le génie le plus fécond du monde dans l'art de dire toujours la même chose, mais ce n'est pas à moi à renverser de sa niche le saint de l'abbé Desades [*sic*].' Voltaire, *Correspondence and Related Documents*, ed. Theodore Besterman, 51 vols (Oxford: The Voltaire Foundation, 1968–77), XXVII, 439. See also Clifton Cherpack, 'Voltaire's Criticism of Petrarch', *The Romanic Review*, 46 (1955), 101–7.

present at the spectacle of his own glory.'[101] Variations on this comparison were to recur throughout the century,[102] with Lamartine, moreover, drawing an explicit comparison between Petrarch's coronation in Rome and Voltaire's own crowning on his return to Paris, after a lengthy hiatus in exile, at the Comédie française on 30 March 1778.[103] French readers and critics thus overlooked Voltaire's suspicions about Petrarch and sought to define the two thinkers as kindred spirits in their contribution to both literary and political spheres.

Nor did Voltaire's ambivalence towards Petrarch prevent his translation of *RVF* 126 from standing long afterwards as a bookmark in the *Canzoniere*, drawing generation after generation of readers and translators to this same poem. Critical commentary from the nineteenth century in both French and Italian endorsed the popularity of *RVF* 126, often with Voltaire's earlier appreciation in mind. Francesco De Sanctis hailed the *canzone* as 'the most exquisite thing which ever came from Petrarch's pen', while in a treatise otherwise dedicated to promoting Dante, *RVF* 126 is cited in full by Giosafatte Biagioli in his discussion of the *canzone* and introduced as 'a perfect model of this type of poetry'.[104] Francesco D'Ovidio even expressed coy gratitude to Voltaire for contributing to the celebrity of *RVF* 126, adapting words from Dante's Francesca: 'For the which restoration we Italians must really be grateful to Voltaire, so that we would pray to God for his peace, if to the King of the universe he had not been somewhat averse.'[105] Ginguené, too, cites Voltaire

---

[101] 'On ne pourrait retrouver que dans Voltaire l'exemple d'un poète qui ait reçu autant de marques d'estime des souverains, autant d'hommages de son siècle, et qui ait, comme Pétrarque, assisté au spectacle de sa gloire.' Saint-Geniès, *Poésies de Pétrarque*, I, p. xx.

[102] See Victor Courtet, *Notice sur Pétrarque, avec une pièce inédite de Mirabeau sur la fontaine de Vaucluse* (Paris: Librairie de Charles Gosselin, 1835), p. 62; Villemain, *Cours de littérature française*, II, 8–9; J.-J. Ampère, *La Grèce, Rome et Dante: études littéraires d'après nature* (Paris: Didier, 1848), p. 150; Jules Troubat, 'Pétrarque et Victor Hugo: Livre de M. Mézières – La nouvelle série de la *Légende des siècles* (6 mars 1877)', in *Plume et pinceau: études de littérature et d'art* (Paris: Isidore Liseux, 1878), pp. 93–104 (pp. 96, 98); Henry Cochin, *Le Jubilé de Pétrarque (extrait du 'Correspondant')* (Paris: De Soye et fils, 1904), p. 28.

[103] Lamartine, *Cours familier de littérature*, VI, 44. Lamartine is, however, less convinced by Voltaire's translation of *RVF* 126, though he clearly deems it noteworthy: *ibid.*, p. 54.

[104] Francesco De Sanctis, *Saggio critico sul Petrarca*, ed. by Ettore Bonora (Bari: Gius. Laterza & figli, 1954), p. 173 ('la più squisita cosa che sia uscita dalla penna del Petrarca'); Giosafatte Biagioli, *Traité de la poésie italienne* (Paris: Au magasin de livres italiens, chez Fayolle, 1808), p. 502 ('un modèle parfait de cette espèce de poésie'). Other school textbooks and pedagogical anthologies published in France in the nineteenth and early twentieth centuries also include *RVF* 126 in the original Italian, a further sign of its popularity. See, for instance: Costantini, *Nuova scelta di poesie italiane*, I, 86–7 (following seventeen sonnets and one madrigal from Petrarch, and followed by *RVF* 128, 129, 268, and extracts from the *Triumphi*), or G. Maniani, *Morceaux choisis de classiques italiens précédés d'une introduction historique sur la littérature italienne à l'usage des classes supérieures des lycées: prose et vers* (Paris: Jules Delalain et fils, 1866), pp. 103–5 (where it features along with *RVF* 232).

[105] 'Del qual restauro noi Italiani dobbiamo proprio esser grati al Voltaire, così che pregheremmo Dio per la sua pace, se al Re dell'universo ei non fosse stato alquanto nemico.' Francesco D'Ovidio, *Studii sul Petrarca e sul Tasso* (Rome: Edizioni A.P.E., 1926), p. 3, alluding to lines from Dante's *Commedia* voiced by Francesca addressing Dante–pilgrim in gratitude for his pity: '"se fosse amico il re de l'universo / noi pregheremmo lui de la tua pace"' ('"if the King of the universe were a friend / we would pray to Him for your peace"', *Inferno* V, vv.

and commends the poem as 'One of the most beautiful and most rightly famous of [Petrarch's] *canzoni*, one of the well-known examples of poetry in which there is the greatest number of charming images and magical scenes.'[106]

Voltaire's translation is cited with great frequency by translators and critics in this period, even if opinions range from admiration of Voltaire's taste and style to disapproval of his somewhat lengthy rendition. La Harpe calls *RVF* 126 'this beautiful poem which is so easily imprinted upon one's memory and one's heart', and, with some reservations, admires Voltaire's translation of the first stanza:

> It is evident that the illustrious imitator has added beauties which come from him, to those of the original. It is a genius which leaves its mark on everything that it touches; but if he had translated the entire poem, perhaps he would have reined in this imitation, because the whole poem translated in this manner would have become too long.[107]

Up until the early twentieth century, Voltaire remained a touchstone for this poem, even if by 1933 an underlying suspicion, echoing La Harpe, that Voltaire's translation contained 'little of Petrarch and much of Voltaire' (*peu de Pétrarque et beaucoup de Voltaire*) was also voiced.[108]

In addition to the precedent set by Voltaire, *RVF* 126 was often appreciated by French readers because of its associations with an identifiable, French geographical location, the Fontaine de Vaucluse. In the *Encyclopédie*, Petrarch had been discussed in an article of the same name ('Fontaine de Vaucluse') which included Voltaire's translation (described as 'a free imitation and full of graces') of the opening stanza of *RVF* 126.[109] Voltaire himself introduced his translation in similar terms as 'the start of Petrarch's beautiful ode to the Fontaine de Vaucluse'.[110] After Voltaire, translators almost always gave the *canzone* the title 'À la fontaine de Vaucluse' ('To the Fountain [or Source] of Vaucluse'), highlighting its French credentials and affiliation. In a

---

91–2). Quotations from the *Commedia* are taken from '*La Commedia*' *secondo l'antica vulgata*, ed. Giorgio Petrocchi, rev. edn, 4 vols (Florence, Le Lettere, 1994).

[106] 'L'une des plus belles et plus justement célèbres de ses *canzoni*, l'un des morceaux connus de poésie où il y a le plus d'images délicieuses et de tableaux magiques', Ginguené, *Histoire littéraire*, II, 517.

[107] 'cette belle ode qui se grave si facilement dans la mémoire et dans le cœur'; 'On voit que l'illustre imitateur a joint les beautés qui lui appartiennent, à celles de l'original. C'est le génie qui laisse son empreinte sur tout ce qu'il touche ; mais s'il avait traduit la pièce entière, peut-être aurait-il resserré cette imitation, parce que l'ode traduite dans ce goût serait devenue trop longue.' La Harpe, *Œuvres*, XV, 359, 361.

[108] Augusto De Benedetti, 'Préface', in *Pétrarque à Laure: les sonnets*, trans. Fernand Brisset (Paris: Librairie Ancienne J.-A. Quereuil, 1933), pp. ix–xxiv (p. xvii).

[109] Louis de Jaucourt, 'Vaucluse, fontaine de', in *Encyclopédie, ou dictionnaire raisonné des sciences, des arts et des métiers, par une société de gens de lettres*, ed. Diderot and d'Alembert, 5 vols (Neufchastel: Samuel Faulche; Amsterdam: M. M. Rey, 1751–76, repr. New York: Readex Microprint Corporation, 1969), III, 941 ('imitation libre & pleine de graces'). See also Ana-Maria M'Enesti, 'The Representation of Petrarch in the Eighteenth-Century *Encyclopédie*', *Humanist Studies and the Digital Age*, 1.1 (2011), 136–44.

[110] 'le commencement de sa belle ode à la fontaine de Vaucluse', Voltaire, *Essai sur les mœurs et l'esprit des nations*, IV, 274.

period of Romantic poetic celebration of nature, this poem had a particular potency, seemingly heralded by its auspicious singling out by Voltaire. Appropriately, French critics, readers, and translators also repeatedly highlighted the 'Frenchness' of this *canzone*. For Marc Monnier, it deserved to be compared to key poems of the French nineteenth-century canon; he described it as 'a *canzone* which is Petrarch's "Lake" or "The Sadness of Olympio"', with reference to poems by Lamartine and Hugo respectively.[111] As late as 1928, *RVF* 126 was the only poem from the *Canzoniere* explicitly referenced in Pierre de Nolhac's speech inaugurating the opening of the Musée Pétrarque, and this reference was motivated precisely for its geographical closeness and relevance to a local audience: 'Recall the "clear, fresh, and sweet waters", the very same which flow in our sight.'[112] Only for Sade were the waters, instead, those of the 'fontana della Triade' in Avignon, a further part of his claim for an urban, Avignonese Laura removed from the surrounding countryside.[113]

French translations of the first stanza of *RVF* 126, following Voltaire's example (1756) up until Brisset (1903), are listed in Appendix 2 in chronological order.[114] Perhaps most immediately striking about these translations is the range of languages, not only French but also Mistral's Occitan and even an incursion of Latin via a sixteenth-century translator, in *La Curiosité littéraire* of 1880.[115] Also swiftly evident is the varying length of each translation, ranging from Sade's mere nine lines or the ten lines of Monnier's condensed version to Roman's expansive rendition totalling twenty-four lines. The pervasiveness of Voltaire's influence is indicated by the two translators, Saint-Geniès and Courtet, who, when setting out to translate *RVF* 126, explicitly borrow Voltaire's translation of the opening stanza. The preference for verse over prose translations may also stem in part from the example set by Voltaire, especially given that a number of Voltaire's rhyming pairs crop up in later translations: 'pure' and 'nature' in Sade, Roman, and Esménard; 'charms' (*charmes*) and 'tears' (*larmes*) in Sade and Esménard again, as well as in Langlois.

Focussing on the famous first line, *Chiare, fresche et dolci acque* ('Clear, fresh, and sweet waters'), earlier translators tend to use a wider variety of adjectives than later translators, who more commonly opt for the most literal solution possible, often through recourse to cognate terms. The adjectives *claires*, *fraîches*, and *douces* are thus eventually the favoured solution, in contrast to the earlier assortment (including descriptors such as *pure* or *limpide*). Also interesting in terms of adjectives in this passage is the later phrase 'angelic breast' (*angelico seno*), which is avoided by Sade,

[111] 'une canzone qui est le *Lac* ou la *Tristesse d'Olympio* de Pétrarque', Marc Monnier, *La Renaissance, de Dante à Luther* (Paris: Librairie Firmin-Didot, 1884), p. 106. On Petrarch in Lamartine and Hugo, see Chapter 5.
[112] 'Rappelez-vous les "claires, fraîches et douces eaux", celles même qui coulent sous nos yeux.' Nolhac, *Inauguration de la maison de Pétrarque à Vaucluse*, p. 8.
[113] Sade, *Mémoires*, II, 19 ('Notes').
[114] See also Appendix 2 for bibliographical information.
[115] Frédéric Mistral, 'Traduction provençale de la canzone XI', in *Fêtes littéraires & internationales: cinquième centenaire de la mort de Pétrarque: célébré à Vaucluse et à Avignon le 18, 19 et 20 juillet 1874* (Avignon: Imprimerie administrative Gros frères, 1874), pp. 246–9 (p. 246); Joseph Boulmier, 'La vraie manière de traduire les poètes', in *La Curiosité littéraire et bibliographique: première série* (Paris: Isidore Liseux, 1880), pp. 77–93.

rendered as 'breast of alabaster' (*sein d'albâtte*) by Romet, as 'chaste breast' (*chaste sein*) by Levesque and Langlois, 'pure breast' (*sein pur*) by Ginguené, 'angelic heart' (*cœur angélique*) by Costaing, 'candid breast' (*candide sein*) by Montesquiou, 'pretty breast' (*joli sein*) by Esménard du Mazet, and 'chaste bosom' (*chaste poitrine*) by Brisset. The solution of 'angelic breast' (either *sein angélique* or *angélique sein*) is championed as early as Gramont, in his prose version, as later by Poulenc, Boulmier, Reynard, and Godefroy. Again, later translators seem to tend to take a more literal approach, whereas earlier translators apparently shied away from the boldness of describing Laura as 'angelic', even though it is an adjective that Petrarch had inherited from Dante and the earlier lyric tradition.[116] In this same phrase, even the word 'breast' (*sein*) is avoided by Costaing, appropriately for his version of Laura as a rural virgin in contradistinction to Sade's proclaimed genealogy, as if it is too physical a term, despite its usual metonymical associations in the singular.

A similar problem is posed by the admiration of Laura's 'beautiful limbs' (*belle membra*), which is condensed by Voltaire into 'beauty' (*la beauté*), avoiding any explicit corporeal reference and shifting from a plural to a singular entity. Voltaire's solution was to prove popular, and was followed by Sade, Romet, Levesque, Roman, Montesquiou, and Esménard du Mazet. An even simpler solution was that of Bouvard, who replaced the phrase with Laura's name, thereby reducing the line to its plain denotive function: 'Where Laura appeared to my sight' (*Où Laure apparut à mes yeux*). Later translations, again, were frequently more literal, with *beaux membres* used by Boulmier, Reynard, and Godefroy.

Beyond linguistic details, the poem's opening image often provoked concern amongst translators as to its implications, particularly when taken, in the most literal and biographical of readings, to mean that Petrarch had stumbled across Laura bathing naked in the Sorgue.[117] Such an activity was seen as particularly unbecoming according to those such as Costaing who asserted Laura's chaste virginity (as discussed in the Introduction). Predictably, then, although the verb in the original construction 'waters, / where [*ove*] her beautiful members / laid she [*pose colei*]' may well imply the viewed object's immersion in the water, Costaing opted for a separation of Laura from the water in the translation 'water [...] *next to which* this pure vestal, the only that I have loved, went *to rest* her beautiful person'.[118] The choice of the verb *reposer* ('to rest') reinforces the passivity of Laura in Costaing's version of this scene, and appears in various forms (in addition to the comparable *délasser*, 'to relax') in the translations by Gramont, Boulmier, Brisset, and Romet.

In contrast, Voltaire avoids dealing with the indecorous challenge of *pose* by using the vague periphrasis 'Of the fires of the day avoided the heat' (*Des feux du jour évitait*

---

[116] On the history of this image, see Marco Santagata, *Amate e amanti: figure della lirica amorosa fra Dante e Petrarca* (Bologna: Il Mulino, 1999), pp. 13–61.

[117] For a similar concern amongst Italian commentators on these lines, see Michel David, 'La canzone CXXVI', *Lectura Petrarce*, 8 (1988), 111–61 (pp. 116–18). As for the French readers discussed above, so David notes that Italian readers have interpreted 'ove' as either 'in cui' ('in which') or 'presso alle quali' ('near/next to which').

[118] 'onde [...] *auprès de laquelle* cette pure vestale, la seule que j'ai aimée, allait *reposer* sa belle personne', Costaing, *La Muse de Pétrarque*, p. 200 (my emphasis).

la chaleur), a solution which is imitated by both Sade and Montesquiou.[119] A further popular option was to render the river the subject of the verb, thereby objectifying Laura and again avoiding the challenge of *pose*, although the implication is still that Laura enters the water. Thus the river receives Laura (*as reçu, reçut*) in Levesque, Langlois, and Casalis and Ginoux. In contrast to these examples of languorous passivity on the part of Laura, a more muscular, active image is represented in the choice of the verb *plonger*, 'to dive' or 'plunge', used by Ginguené and Loise (the latter translation seems more generally to be indebted to the former). Later translators such as Poulenc, Mahul, and Chatenet opt, instead, for variants of the verb *baigner*, 'to bathe', seemingly no longer concerned with the propriety of Laura's actions. In this way, Petrarch's Laura became a parallel figure to the Biblical Susanna, whose scene of bathing was popular amongst painters from the Renaissance through to the nineteenth century, and elicited similar debates about the chastity of such an action.[120]

This example shows how details of translation were often motivated by social mores and expectations which typically varied from translator to translator. Other changes also reveal different emphases. Thus the figure of Love (*Amor*) is absent from a handful of translators (Sade, Costaing, and Bouvard), while other translators from Voltaire onwards (Sade, Romet, Roman, and Esménard du Mazet) add to the many features of the typical Provençal landscape highlighted in this stanza the very word 'nature', shifting the emphasis from a Classical to a more modern personification. Finally, some translators tend to be more Petrarchan than Petrarch through their embellishment of this stanza with Petrarchist images and language taken from elsewhere in the *Canzoniere*. A good example of this tendency is Voltaire's addition of the image of a nightingale (perhaps with *RVF* 311 in mind), while Casalis and Ginoux not only describe the breeze as a *zéphyr* ('zephyr' or 'breeze', a term from *RVF* 310) but also highlight that the 'foliage' (*feuillage*) in question is no doubt 'symbolic' (*symbolique*), reminding the reader of the polysemy of the Petrarchan laurel. Similarly, Mahul describes the figure in this poem as composed of 'pure ivory' (*pur ivoire*, drawing on imagery from *RVF* 199), and Mistral adds to his translation the image of dawn, appropriately since one key *senhal* of Laura is Aurora (see, for instance, *RVF* 291).

This type of comparative reading ought to be carried out more thoroughly, with respect to a whole poem as well as several different types of poems. The reader is also encouraged to draw further comparisons between the translations of the opening stanza of *RVF* 126 listed in Appendix 2. For my part, I now turn away from the *Canzoniere* to consider the fates both of Petrarch's other volume of Italian poetry, the *Triumphi*, and of his Latin works in the hands of nineteenth-century French translators. In what ways do these texts confirm or challenge the preferences demonstrated in this chapter as regards incomplete translations of the *Canzoniere*?

---

[119] In Sade we find 'Vient quelquefois rafraîchir ses appas' ('Comes sometimes to refresh her feminine charms'); in Montesquiou, 'Fuyait les ardeurs de l'été' ('Fled the heat of summer').

[120] The story is from the Book of Daniel. As a pictorial theme see, for instance, Alicia Craig Faxon, 'Bath/Bathing', in *Encyclopedia of Comparative Iconography: Themes Depicted in Works of Art*, ed. Helene E. Roberts, 2 vols (Chicago: Fitzroy Dearborn, 1998), I, 109–16 (especially, on the Susanna story, p. 113).

3

Finding Laura in the *Triumphi* and Petrarch's Latin Works

BESIDES THE *CANZONIERE*, Petrarch's other significant poetic work in the vernacular was his six-part *Triumphi*, written in formal imitation of Dante's *Commedia*, that is, borrowing the earlier poet's interlocking tripartite rhyme scheme known as *terza rima*.[1] Each Triumph depicts the victory of a particular abstract concept, although the trappings of chariots and processions fade away as the work proceeds. The *Triumphi* are in ascending order of potency, with Latin titles as follows: the *Triumphus Cupidinis, Triumphus Pudicitie, Triumphus Mortis, Triumphus Fame, Triumphus Temporis*, and the *Triumphus Eternitatis*. Essentially, the poem thus follows a sequence of encounters with and meditations on each concept, namely Love, Chastity, Death, Fame, Time, and Eternity, with each in turn defeating and overturning the former. Moreover, the final triumph is in direct conflict with the close of the *Canzoniere*. The *Canzoniere* concludes in *RVF* 366 with a repudiation of Laura as Medusa (a petrifying, spiritually deadening figure) and an invocation of the Virgin Mary, suggesting the possibility of some sort of conversion on the part of the poet–protagonist at the end of the work from *Eros* to *Caritas*.[2] In contrast, the *Triumphus Eternitatis* reinstates Laura, ending with the whole of Paradise desiring to see Laura's resurrected body.[3] The relationship between the *Canzoniere* and the *Triumphi* can be further refined through attention to late-eighteenth- and nineteenth-century French translators of the *Triumphi*. Again, decisions as to what to include where and under what title reveal more deep-rooted attitudes towards the *Triumphi* deducible from such material.

As with the *Triumphi*, no Latin work by Petrarch comes close to rivalling the number of translations of and from the *Canzoniere* into French produced in the nineteenth century. Moreover, the choice of texts from the Latin works often reflects

---

[1] On the intertextual relationship between the two poets in the *Triumphi*, see Claudio Giunta, 'Memoria di Dante nei *Trionfi*', *Rivista di letteratura italiana*, 11 (1993), 411–52.

[2] See Kenelm Foster, 'Beatrice or Medusa', in *Italian Studies Presented to E. R. Vincent*, ed. C. P. Brand, K. Foster, and U. Limentani (Cambridge: Heffer, 1962), pp. 41–56.

[3] On the theme of resurrection in the *Triumphi*, see Maria Cecilia Bertolani, *Il corpo glorioso: studi sui 'Trionfi' del Petrarca* (Rome: Carocci, 2001) and idem, *Petrarca e la visione dell'eterno* (Bologna: Il Mulino, 2005). More generally on Laura in the poem, see Aldo S. Bernardo, *Petrarch, Laura and the 'Triumphs'* (Albany, NY: State University of New York Press, 1974).

similar motivations to the selections made by translators faced with Petrarch's vernacular poetry. That is, the choice of Latin works, like the decisions made in producing incomplete translations of the *Canzoniere* and/or the *Triumphi*, typically reveals an overriding interest in understanding and presenting Petrarch above all as an autobiographical love poet.

Complete Translations of the *Triumphi*

Perhaps surprisingly, there are marginally more complete translations of the *Triumphi* in this period than there are of the *Canzoniere*: seven of the first, and only five of the latter (six, if Godefroy's intentions rather than actions are taken into consideration). The numbers are similar, however, because many complete translations of the *Canzoniere* also include a translation of the *Triumphi*. Following Marsand's edition, the *Triumphi* are even frequently interpolated into the *Canzoniere*, forming a third section that comes after the main poems *in vita* and *in morte* but before the section of poems considered not to be directly about love or Laura. Such an ordering suggests that the *Triumphi* were seen as an integral part of Petrarch's Italian poetry, within which neither the *Canzoniere* nor the *Triumphi* were considered to form distinct, separate wholes. This interpolation also allows the *Triumphi* to correct the rejection of Laura in *RVF* 366, since the poems about Laura thus end instead with the victorious anticipation of a beautiful, resurrected Laura, at the end of the *Triumphus Eternitatis*. For those translators committed to a complete translation of the *Canzoniere* and who could therefore not simply omit *RVF* 366, the juxtaposition of the *Triumphi* provided an elegant solution, through supersession, to the potential problem of anti-Laura rhetoric that went against Petrarch the archetypal love poet beloved of readers in this period. The first complete, modern, French translation of the *Triumphi* as a self-sufficient, stand-alone text was not to be published until 1923; throughout the nineteenth century, then, the *Triumphi* were always considered inseparable from the *Canzoniere*.[4]

The first complete translation of the *Triumphi* in this period is to be found in Gramont's *Poésies de Pétrarque* of 1842. Here, the *Triumphi* are placed at the end of the volume, after the *Canzoniere*, and translated into prose. Shortly thereafter comes Montesquiou's verse translation of the *Épîtres, églogues et triomphes de Pétrarque* (1843; *Epistles, Eclogues, and Triumphs by Petrarch*), in a separate and subsequent volume to his translation of the *Canzoniere*. By translating all of the *Triumphi* in order and separating them from the *Canzoniere* by a selection of translations from Petrarch's Latin works, Montesquiou had perhaps the best sense of any translator in this period that the *Canzoniere* and the *Triumphi* were two distinct and even perhaps irreconcilable texts. Other translators, in contrast, by including extracts from the *Triumphi* alongside translations from Petrarch's *Canzoniere* (Levesque, Roman), or indeed the whole of the *Triumphi* in Marsand's postulated third section (for instance, Poulenc's translation of 1865), seem to have presumed that the two texts were conterminous and to be conflated because both are in Italian and both discuss

---

[4]   Petrarch, *Les Triomphes*, trans. Cochin (1923).

Laura. This assumption was no doubt encouraged by earlier editions of Petrarch's Italian poetry, which often had simple, generic titles for both the *Canzoniere* and the *Triumphi*, such as *Le volgari opere* (*Vernacular Works*), *Le rime* (*Poems*), or even merely *Il Petrarca* (*Petrarch*).[5]

The later two complete translations by Poulenc (*Rimes de Pétrarque*, 1865 and 1877) and Reynard (*Les Rimes de François Pétrarque*, 1883) follow Marsand's edition and therefore, unlike Montesquiou, place the *Triumphi* as a textual wall between poems from the *Canzoniere* about Laura and poems from the *Canzoniere* on other subjects.[6] Moreover, the *Rimes* of Poulenc and Reynard describe the *Triumphi* in the bipartite terms conventional for the *Canzoniere*, which suggests that for these translators there is even greater continuity between the two works. For both translators, the *Triumphi* are 'Triumphs on the life and death of Laura' (*Les triomphes sur la vie et la mort de Madame Laure*), echoing, of course, Marsand's titular 'Trionfi di Francesco Petrarca in vita ed in morte di madonna Laura'. Such a title is, admittedly, reductive, since of the six *Triumphi* Laura is not even mentioned in two (the *Triumphus Fame* and *Triumphus Temporis*), but it is indicative of the amorous, biographical prism through which Petrarch's works were typically read at this time.

Whilst the translations of Poulenc and Reynard are structurally similar, they are formally distinct, with Poulenc opting to translate into French verse, and Reynard choosing instead the medium of prose. Three further complete prose translations are published, by Ginguené (*Les Œuvres amoureuses de Pétrarque*, 1875, as already noted a modernization of Catanusi's translations of Petrarch), Godefroy (1900), and Brisset (*Canzones, triomphes et poésies diverses*, 1903), in this respect reflecting the trend—already observed as concerns complete translations of the *Canzoniere*—for prose translations to become more common than verse translations in the second half of the nineteenth century.[7] Of the seven complete translations of the *Triumphi* in the nineteenth and very early twentieth centuries, only two are in verse (Montesquiou, Poulenc), with the majority (Gramont, Ginguené, Reynard, Godefroy, and Brisset) in prose, perhaps because of the challenge of replicating the extended *terza rima* form.[8] For Brisset, as for Poulenc and Reynard, the *Triumphi* are appended to the two halves of the *Canzoniere*, before the Marsand-inspired section of 'Diverse subjects' (*Sujets divers*). For Godefroy, the *Triumphi* instead form a third part after the whole of the *Canzoniere*.

[5]   On the question of competing titles, see Kennedy, *Authorizing Petrarch*, p. 1.

[6]   For a later example of such an order, see Ferdinand Bailly, *Pétrarque: nouvelle traduction en vers et dans les formes originales de ses sonnets, canzones, sestines, madrigaux et triomphes*, 2 vols (Paris: Les Éditions Rieder, 1932).

[7]   While this statement holds true for complete translations, in the case of partial translations (as Chapter 2 has demonstrated) verse continued to be popular because of the preponderance of translations of Petrarch's sonnets preserving the sonnet form in the second half of the nineteenth century.

[8]   However, for a French poet who would successfully take on *terza rima*, see the discussion of Gautier in Chapter 5.

Partial Translations of the *Triumphi*

Though there are marginally more complete French translations of the *Triumphi* than of the *Canzoniere* in the long nineteenth century, the relative neglect of the former becomes clearer when selective translations are considered. There are several likely reasons for this neglect. Firstly, the *Triumphi* do not lend themselves as easily or obviously to anthologization as do the shorter poems (particularly the sonnets) of the *Canzoniere*, which work well independently from their original context. Secondly, not all of the six Triumphs are directly about Laura and so were deemed at times less relevant to a portrayal of Petrarch's love. As a consequence, there are very few translations in the nineteenth century which include extracts from the *Triumphi*. Moreover, of those that do, only in some cases are these extracts complete poems, that is, one of the six Triumphs. Instead, in Roman, for instance, we find the start of the *Triumphus Mortis* and a poem amalgamating select passages from both the *Triumphus Fame* and the *Triumphus Temporis*.[9]

Predictably, the favourite parts of the *Triumphi* were those that included Laura and related to love: the *Triumphus Cupidinis*, the *Triumphus Mortis*, and the *Triumphus Eternitatis*. Of these, the *Triumphus Cupidinis* is first translated by Levesque in the first edition of his *Choix des poésies de Pétrarque* (1774; *Selection of Poems by Petrarch*), and also by another translator on its own in 1830.[10] In his second, expanded edition (1787), Levesque adds the *Triumphus Temporis* and the *Triumphus Eternitatis*, as well as twelve lines from the *Triumphus Mortis*.[11] In his 1848 verse translations of the *Poésies de Pétrarque*, Esménard du Mazet includes the *Triumphus Mortis* and the *Triumphus Eternitatis*.

The *Triumphus Mortis* in particular, with its dialogue between the poet and Laura, was to prove an especially popular choice because of its continuity in themes and language with the *Canzoniere*.[12] Indeed, the dialogue displays notable points of similarity to the popular sonnet *RVF* 302 (cited in Chapter 2), in which Laura expresses her desire to be reunited with Petrarch and promises that they will be together in Heaven. In the *Triumphus Mortis* Laura similarly declares her love for the poet, and claims that she hid her feelings while on Earth in order to preserve their reputation and chastity:

> Poi disse sospirando: 'Mai diviso
> da te non fu 'l mio cor, né già mai fia,
> ma temprai la tua fiamma col mio viso;

---

[9]   See Roman, *Le Génie de Pétrarque*, pp. 412–14 and 439–42.

[10]   *Il trionfo d'amore di Petrarca: dedicato al gentiluomo Fr. B. Duppa, da G. C., professore di lingua italiana in Blois* (Blois: Giroud, 1830).

[11]   Levesque, *Choix des poésies de Pétrarque* (1787), II, 174–5.

[12]   See also, on earlier French interest in the *Triumphus Mortis*, Daniel Ménager, 'Le "Triomphe de la mort" dans deux traductions françaises du seizième siècle', in *Dynamique d'une expansion culturelle*, pp. 347–61. The similarity between the second chapter of the *Triumphus Mortis* and the *Canzoniere* has been most recently asserted by Francesca Southerden, 'The Ghost of a Garden: Seeds of Discourse and Desire in Petrarch's *Triumphus Mortis* II', *Le Tre corone: rivista internazionale di studi su Dante, Petrarca, Boccaccio*, 1 (2014), 131–51 (p. 140).

perché a salvar te e me null'altra via
era, e la nostra giovenetta fama;
né per ferza è però madre men pia.
  [...]
  Fur quasi eguali in noi fiamme amorose,
almen poi ch'i' m'avidi del tuo foco;
ma l'un le palesò, l'altro l'ascose.'[13]

***

Then she said sighing: 'Never divided
from you was my heart, nor will it ever be,
but I tempered your flame with my face;
  because there was no other way to save
you and me and our young fame;
nor because of a whip is a mother less loving.
  [...]
  The amorous flames were almost equal in us,
at least once I learnt of your fire;
but the one revealed them, while the other hid them.'

Ginguené considered the *Triumphus Mortis*, while not equal to the *Canzoniere*, at any rate the best of the *Triumphi* ('the best, the most poetic, and the most interesting of them all'), and he even recommended stopping after this poem and ignoring the last three Triumphs altogether.[14] Amable Tastu, similarly, described the *Triumphi* in general as 'very inferior to Petrarch's other works', but with, nonetheless, 'some very beautiful parts, for example the death of Laura'.[15]

Gustave Planche was even more moved by the *Triumphus Mortis*, describing it as 'assuredly one of the most perfect pieces that ever came from Petrarch's pen',[16] and praising in particular what he considered the indisputable sincerity and intimacy of the dialogue with Laura:

We must believe that Petrarch would not have put into Laura's mouth these words suffused with indescribable tenderness, if he had not found in his memories the majority of the thoughts from which this admirable exchange is composed. All his sonnets, all his *canzoni* display such perfect sincerity, he has always shown in the expression of his love such reserve and discretion, he has always given to his laments an accent of such resignation, that doubtless

---

[13] *Triumphus Mortis* II, vv. 88–93, 139–41, cited from Petrarch, *Trionfi, rime estravaganti, codice degli abbozzi*, ed. Pacca and Paolino, pp. 328, 336.

[14] 'le meilleur, le plus poétique et le plus intéressant de tous', Ginguené, *Histoire littéraire de l'Italie*, II, 555.

[15] 'Quoique, en général, ce poëme soit très-inférieur aux autres ouvrages de Pétrarque, il n'en renferme pas moins de très-belles parties, par exemple la mort de Laure.' Amable Tastu, *Tableau de la littérature italienne depuis l'établissement du christianisme jusqu'à nos jours* (Tours: Mame, 1843), p. 82.

[16] 'assurément un des morceaux les plus parfaits qui soient sortis de sa plume', Planche, 'Études sur l'art et la poésie en Italie', p. 1013.

he would have reproached in himself throughout his life, as a profanation, as a sacrilege, an imaginary declaration which his ear had not heard. There is every reason to think that the second chapter of the *Triumph of Death* has at least as much to do with reality as with poetry. If the setting is fictional, the scene must be true.[17]

The same dialogue in the *Triumphus Mortis*, in which Laura retrospectively reveals her love for Petrarch, is also translated by Ernest and Edmond Lafond a year later in their prefatory 'Notice' to their sonnet translations, with the gloss that 'This scene from the *Triumphi* is decisive and convincing; it is, at one and the same time, the argument, the commentary, and the summary of the divine love poem legible in Petrarch's sonnets'.[18] Like Planche, these two translators use this extract to prove that Laura loved Petrarch, but pretended she did not in order to preserve the purity of their love. The same 'Notice', moreover, ends with a citation of the last two lines of the *Triumphi*, which are used to describe Petrarch's state of mind on the point of death:

> He had received, the night before, the last rites of the Church; doubtless, at the moment of death, he thought, for the last time on Earth, of she whom he had loved, and, in the religious hope of being finally reunited with her in Heaven, he remembered these two lines, with which he had concluded his poem *The Triumphs*:
>
> > If it was a joy to see her on Earth,
> > Oh! what joy will it be to see her again in Heaven![19]

Unlike the final question mark in early and modern editions of the *Triumphi*, which seems to cast doubt on whether Petrarch will indeed see Laura again in Heaven, this

---

[17]   'Nous devons croire que Pétrarque n'aurait pas mis dans la bouche de Laure ces paroles empreintes d'une ineffable tendresse, s'il n'eût trouvé dans ses souvenirs la meilleure partie des pensées dont se compose cet admirable entretien. Tous ses sonnets, toutes ses *canzoni* respirent une si parfaite sincérité, il a toujours montré dans l'expression de son amour tant de réserve et de discrétion, il a toujours donné à ses plaintes un accent si résigné, que sans doute il se fût reproché toute sa vie comme une profanation, comme un sacrilége, un aveu imaginaire que son oreille n'eût pas entendu. Il y a tout lieu de penser que le second chapitre du *Triomphe de la Mort* relève au moins aussi directement de la réalité que de la poésie. Si le cadre est une fiction, le tableau doit être vrai.' Planche, 'Études sur l'art et la poésie en Italie', p. 1015. Planche's admiration for *RVF* 302 has already been noted.

[18]   'Cette scène des *Triomphes* est décisive et convaincante ; c'est, à la fois, l'argument, le commentaire et le résumé du divin poëme d'amour que l'on va lire dans les sonnets de Pétrarque.' Lafond, *Dante, Pétrarque, Michel-Ange, Tasse*, pp. 110–11.

[19]   'Il avait reçu, la veille, les dernières consolations de l'Église ; sans doute, au moment de mourir, il pensa, pour la dernière fois sur la terre, à celle qu'il avait aimée, et, dans le religieux espoir de la rejoindre enfin dans le ciel, il se souvint de ces deux vers, par lesquels il avait terminé son poëme des *Triomphes* : Si ce fut un bonheur de la voir sur la terre, / Oh ! que sera-ce donc de la revoir aux cieux !' Lafond, *Dante, Pétrarque, Michel-Ange, Tasse*, p. 130. In the original Italian, 'se fu beato chi la vide in terra, / or che fia dunque a rivederla in cielo?' *Triumphus Eternitatis*, vv. 144–5; *Trionfi, rime estravaganti, codice degli abbozzi*, ed. Pacca and Paolino, p. 538.

version of events is presented as a triumphal certainty, introduced as a 'religious hope' (*religieux espoir*) and crowned with an exclamation mark. In this manner, as in the editorial reordering of Marsand, the *Triumphus Eternitatis* is used to overturn the apparent rejection of Laura at the end of the *Canzoniere* (*RVF* 366).

There is no mention of Laura in the *Triumphus Fame* nor in the *Triumphus Temporis*, and it is therefore unsurprising that both are rarely selected for translation unless as part of a complete rendition of the work. Apart from complete translations, the two appear independently only in a very fragmentary fashion in Roman (*Le Génie de Pétrarque*, 1778), while the *Triumphus Temporis* is translated in Levesque's second edition of 1787 and partially (vv. 109–45) in Arrighi's publications of 1838 and 1851. Also markedly unpopular is the *Triumphus Pudicitie*, with its moral diatribe against human love. Ultimately, for the majority of nineteenth-century French readers and translators of Petrarch it was to prove true (as M.-Th. Laignel would conclude in her assessment of the *Triumphi* from 1926) that 'only the echoes of the *Canzoniere* seem appealing to us in these poems, for Petrarch is only truly himself when he describes his own heart'.[20] The consistent exclusions and preferential treatment of certain of Petrarch's *Triumphi* reflect the types of choices made not only by translators of extracts from the *Canzoniere* (analysed in Chapter 2) but also by translators of Petrarch's Latin works.

Translating Petrarch's Latin Works

As with the *Triumphi*, some parts of Petrarch's Latin works were more readily assimilated than others by nineteenth-century French translators alongside the best of the *Canzoniere*. For a start, the eclogues of the *Bucolicum carmen* that relate directly to the vernacular love story of Petrarch and Laura were accorded particular attention. Montesquiou's selections from the *Bucolicum carmen* (included in his third volume of translations from Petrarch, published in 1843) remained focused on this love story and included only those eclogues which had obvious resonances with the *Canzoniere*, namely Eclogue Three ('The Amorous Shepherd', a dialogue between Stupeus and Daphne, figures who stand for Petrarch and Laura), Eclogue Nine ('Lamentation', about the plague in which Laura died), Eclogue Ten ('The Fallen Laurel', about the death of the laurel/Laura), and Eclogue Eleven ('Galatea', about the grave of Galatea, another figure for Laura). The abbé Costaing de Pusignan had already made a similar selection by translating Eclogues Three, Ten, and Eleven in his *La Muse de Pétrarque* from 1819, and the popularity of the sepulchral eleventh eclogue in particular is confirmed by its inclusion in Esménard's second edition of translations of Petrarch in 1848.[21]

Several of the Latin letters were also early on in the period considered of interest

---

[20] 'seuls les échos du *Canzoniere* nous semblent attachants dans ces poèmes, car Pétrarque n'est vraiment lui-même que lorsqu'il décrit son propre cœur.' M.-Th. Laignel, *La Littérature italienne* (Paris: Armand Colin, 1926), p. 38.

[21] Costaing's reading of the eleventh eclogue as about 'Galas Thea' (and not Galatea) is a key part of his claim for a rural Laura buried not in Avignon but in Galas, near Fontaine-de-Vaucluse. See Costaing, *La Muse de Pétrarque*, pp. 254–80.

from a biographical perspective. Sade was, in this respect, once more a role model given his habit of extensive quotation, in French translation, from Petrarch's letters in his *Mémoires*. Later studies of Petrarch, such Alfred Mézières's *Pétrarque* (1868), tended to continue to follow Sade in viewing the letters as key documentary material providing reliable insight into Petrarch's thoughts, feelings, and friendships. One of the most popular letters, of the hundreds left behind by Petrarch, was the so-called 'Letter to Posterity', which forms the last book of Petrarch's prose letter collection, *Rerum senilium libri (Letters of Old Age)*.[22] This letter is a literary self-portrait reviewing key events in the author's life and addressing future readers, by whom the poet hopes to be remembered. It was an obvious choice for translators wishing to give a potted history of Petrarch, and was often used as an introduction to his Italian poetry. Strikingly, this letter replaced all of Roman's previous translations of Petrarch's Italian poetry in the 1804 anniversary *Vie de Pétrarque* published by the Athénée de Vaucluse.[23] In the same year, Jean Guérin published another translation of the same letter, in his own words 'in order to make Petrarch better known' (*pour mieux faire connoître Pétrarque*).[24] A later translation was also made by Victor Develay, alongside Petrarch's will.[25]

After the 'Letter to Posterity', another popular letter was one from the *Rerum familiarum libri (Letters on Familiar Matters)* which describes Petrarch's ascent of Mont Ventoux with his brother and his providential perusal of a pocket copy of Augustine's *Confessions*.[26] The letter has remained popular because of its introspection and insight into Petrarch's reading habits, religious sensibility, and familial relationships. For nineteenth-century French (and more specifically Avignonese) translators, it had the added attraction of involving a key natural landmark in Provence. This letter is translated by Étienne-Jean Delécluze in 1839, by Pierre

---

[22]   For the Latin text, see Karl Enenkel, 'A Critical Edition of Petrarch's *Epistola Posteritati*', in *Modelling the Individual: Biography and Portrait in the Renaissance, with a Critical Edition of Petrarch's Letter to Posterity*, ed. Karl Enenkel, Betsy de Jong-Crane, and Peter Liebregts (Amsterdam: Rodopi, 1998), pp. 243–81; for an English translation, see *Letters of Old Age/Rerum senilium libri*, trans. Aldo S. Bernardo, Saul Levin, and Reta A. Bernardo, 2 vols (Baltimore: Johns Hopkins University Press, 1992), II, 672–9. On earlier French translations, see Silvia Fabrizio-Costa, 'La prima traduzione francese della *Posteritati*: testo e contesto (1644–1645)', in *Francesco Petrarca, l'opera latina: tradizione e fortuna: atti del XVI Convegno internazionale (Chianciano–Pienza 19–22 luglio 2004)*, ed. Luisa Secchi Tarugi (Florence: Franco Cesati, 2006), pp. 485–502.

[23]   Athénée de Vaucluse, *Vie de Pétrarque*, pp. 299–323. This translation is by François Tissot.

[24]   Jean Guérin, *Pétrarque considéré comme amant, poëte et philosophe* (Avignon: n.p., 1804), p. 66.

[25]   *Épître à la postérité et Testament, traduits du latin par Victor Develay* (Paris: Librairie des Bibliophiles, 1880).

[26]   Petrarch *Familiarium rerum libri*, ed. Rossi, I, 153–61; *Letters on Familiar Matters: Rerum familiarum libri I–VIII*, trans. Bernardo, pp. 172–80. For classic readings of this letter, see Ascoli, 'Petrarch's Middle Age: Memory, Imagination, History, and "The Ascent of Mont Ventoux"', and Robert M. Durling, 'The Ascent of Mt. Ventoux and the Crisis of Allegory', *Italian Quarterly*, 18 (Summer 1974), 7–28.

Leroux in 1842, in a volume curated by François-Joseph Seguin some ten years later, and by Develay in 1880.[27]

Finally, Pompée Mabille, a physician who devoted himself to translation in his spare time, published French translations of certain of Petrarch's prose letters relating to medical matters, which for him evidently held a particular interest.[28] Mabille was also a spokesperson for the merit of Petrarch's letters more broadly:

> Petrarch's incredibly prolific correspondence (more than five hundred letters) is unusual in this respect: that for five centuries it has remained almost entirely unexplored; and yet it is such a rich treasure from which, if mined, all would derive interest and enjoyment, were reading it not difficult in the Latin text, which is disfigured by typographical errors very likely to discourage even the most determined of readers. We have already attempted since 1864 a French translation of one hundred of the letters. We will persevere in this task unceasingly. Will we succeed?[29]

Despite Mabille's hopeful but largely fruitless efforts (at least as regards Petrarch's correspondence), it was Develay (discussed below) who was to make available in French translation sets of Petrarch's letters not limited to those 'To Posterity' and on the ascent of Mont Ventoux. In addition, some of Petrarch's Latin verse epistles (*Epystole*) are included in Montesquiou's third volume of translations from 1843.[30]

---

[27] É.-J. Delécluze, 'Pétrarque au Mont Ventoux', *Revue de Paris* (13 January 1839), 3–11; Pierre Leroux, '*Poésies de Pétrarque, sonnets, canzones, triomphes.* Traduction complète par le comte F.-L. de Gramont', *La Revue indépendante*, 4 (1842), 347–426 (pp. 378–82); F. Seguin, *Pèlerinage au Mont Ventoux par F. Seguin suivi de 'Santo-Croux, douas letro a ma bravo sore touneto' par J. Roumanille avec un appendice relatif au Mont Ventoux, comprenant la lettre de Pétrarque, une notice sur M. Requien, et autres documents divers recueillis par F. S.* (Avignon: Chez F. Seguin aîné, 1852), pp. 71–96; *L'Ascension du Mont Ventoux, traduite pour la première fois par Victor Develay* (Paris: Librairie des Bibliophiles, 1880). See also Gabriel Faure, *Au Ventoux avec Pétrarque, suivi de la Lettre de Pétrarque au P. François Denis, traduite du latin* (Avignon: Aubonel frères, 1928) and Pierre Julian, *Le Pèlerinage littéraire du Mont Ventoux* (Carpentras: Les Éditions du 'Mt Ventoux', 1937).

[28] *Lettre de Pétrarque à Boccace*, trans. Pompée Mabille (Angers: Imprimerie de Lainé frères, 1873); Pompée Mabille, 'Question d'hygiène et de diététique, à propos d'une lettre de Pétrarque', in *Annales de la Société linnéenne du département de Maine-et-Loire*, 11 (1869), 149–71; idem, 'Réponse de Pétrarque à Jean Dondi, célèbre médecin de Padoue', *Annales de la Société linnéenne du département de Maine-et-Loire*, 12 (1870), 203–42.

[29] 'La correspondance de Pétrarque, si volumineuse (plus de cinq cents lettres), offre ceci de particulier : c'est que depuis cinq siècles elle est restée presqu'inexplorée ; et pourtant c'est un riche trésor où tout le monde aurait intérêt et agrément à puiser, si la lecture n'en était difficile dans le texte latin, défiguré qu'il est par des fautes de typographie bien propres à décourager les plus déterminés. Une traduction française, de cent lettres déjà, a été tentée par nous, dès 1864. Nous y persévérons sans relâche. Réussirons-nous ?' Mabille, 'Question d'hygiène et de diététique', p. 171. One product of this perseverance was Mabille, *Pétrarque et l'empereur Charles IV (correspondance)* (Angers: Imprimerie de P. Lachèse et Dolbeau, 1890).

[30] Montesquiou translates into rhyming couplets six of Petrarch's epistles, which are addressed to various friends (including Giacomo Colonna and Boccaccio), are typically of an autobiographical and amorous nature, and several of which are written from Vaucluse. See Montesquiou, *Épîtres, églogues et triomphes*, pp. 1–37.

Like the letters 'To Posterity' and on the ascent of Mont Ventoux, Petrarch's *Secretum* was, too, a relatively popular choice for translation and citation, again because of its overtly autobiographical nature. Ginguené placed the *Secretum* in a long tradition of confession narratives, from Augustine via Montaigne to Rousseau, thereby integrating Petrarch into a hallowed, predominantly French tradition.[31] The full title of this text is *De secreto conflictu curarum mearum* (*On the secret battle of my thoughts*), and the work consists of three dialogues between two characters, Franciscus and Augustinus, in the presence of a silent Lady Truth. Augustinus is modelled on St Augustine (whose *Confessions* no doubt encouraged Petrarch's introspection and meditations on sin), and Franciscus recalls Petrarch's first name, Francesco.[32] The two speakers are above all literary creations, and different facets of Petrarch's complex, tormented personality, although the two nineteenth-century French translators of the *Secretum* in full, Develay and Mabille, both equated these names with their historical personages, calling the speakers *Saint Augustin* and *Pétrarque* respectively. The first book is a discussion of the relationship between happiness and will, the second book analyses Franciscus's sins according to standard medieval classifications, and the third book presents Franciscus as being held back by two 'chains', love of fame and love for Laura, both of which are encapsulated in the laurel tree. As with the *Bucolicum carmen* and the *Triumphi*, the *Secretum* was often primarily of interest for the information it might provide about Laura, including lines (discussed in the Introduction) which provoked much debate as to whether Laura was or was not a virgin.

The novelist, critic, and artist, Delécluze, though remembered more for his translations of Dante, called for a translation of the *Secretum* as early as 1839 and described the text in glowing terms:

> I would advise all those who want to know Petrarch's heart and mind entirely to read his book: *de Contemptu vitae*. In it they will find, in the form of three dialogues between St Augustine and Laura's lover, the most noble and sincere confession that a man can make of the weaknesses of his mind and heart. [...] There have been many commentaries on Petrarch's Italian poetry; but, in my opinion, the complete translation of *Contempt of Life*, to which he also gave the title *his Secret*, would be the best possible addition to such studies. Thus I challenge those who might still persist in believing that the author of the sonnets to Laura was a narrow-minded and cold-hearted individual to read this beautiful and curious work which is too long to be given in full here, and

---

[31] In Ginguené's words, 'Ni Augustin, ni Montaigne, ni même J.-J. Rousseau n'ont découvert plus naïvement leur intérieur, ni fait avec plus de franchise l'aveu de leurs faiblesses' ('Neither Augustine, nor Montaigne, nor even J.-J. Rousseau have revealed more naively their inner life, nor made with more honesty the confession of their weaknesses'), Ginguené, *Histoire littéraire de l'Italie*, II, 451.

[32] See Francesco Tateo, *Dialogo interiore e polemica ideologica nel 'Secretum' del Petrarca* (Florence: Le Monnier, 1965) as well as *Petrarca e Agostino*, ed. Roberto Cardini and Donatella Coppini (Rome: Bulzoni, 2004).

whose parts are all so strongly interlinked that it is impossible to extract any one in isolation.[33]

Despite Delécluze's warm endorsement, which sought to remedy the kind of criticism ultimately levelled at Petrarch by Voltaire, no translation was immediately forthcoming. Instead, non-Latinate French readers had to wait for Develay's complete translation of 1879, an accomplishment which was repeated by Mabille soon afterwards (1886), in a perhaps unhelpful distraction from his incomplete project of translating Petrarch's Latin letters.[34] Besides promoting Petrarch's *Secretum*, Delécluze was also one of the first to wish to prove more generally that Petrarch was not merely 'a skilful arranger of madrigals, whose every verse revolves around one or two thoughts of love':[35]

I wanted to destroy the prejudice or, to put it better, the false ideas which we have entertained for so long in France concerning the moral character and the whole of Petrarch's writings. I wanted to demonstrate that this poet, who immortalized himself by the superiority and angelic purity of his Italian poetry, is no less remarkable for the generous instincts of his soul and the prodigious breadth of his mind and knowledge. [...] It was this which made me commit to making Petrarch's work written in Latin prose better known.[36]

Notwithstanding the unusual example of Delécluze's enthusiasm for Petrarch's Latin works, writers and translators in the earlier part of the nineteenth century were mostly happy to consider Petrarch's Latin works only insofar as they were relevant to Petrarch's love for Laura, meaning that Petrarch's many other writings

[33] 'Je conseillerai à ceux qui veulent connaître entièrement le cœur et l'esprit de Pétrarque, de lire son livre : *de Contemptu vitae*. Ils y trouveront sous la forme de trois dialogues entre saint Augustin et l'amant de Laure, la plus noble et la plus sincère confession qu'un homme puisse faire des faiblesses de son esprit et de son cœur. [...] On a fait bien des commentaires sur les poésies italiennes de cet homme ; mais, à mon sens, la traduction complète du *Mépris de la vie*, qu'il a intitulée aussi *son Secret*, serait le meilleur que l'on pût y ajouter. J'engage donc ceux qui persisteraient encore à croire que l'auteur des sonnets de Laure était un esprit restreint et avait le cœur froid, à lire ce bel et curieux ouvrage trop long pour être donné en entier ici, et dont toutes les parties sont si fortement enchaînées qu'on ne peut en extraire aucune.' Delécluze, 'Pétrarque au Mont-Ventoux', pp. 3–4.

[34] Develay, *Mon secret* (1879); Pompée Mabille, *Pétrarque philosophe et confessionniste* (Angers: A. Burdin, 1880), pp. 9–32 (a translation of the prologue and book one); Mabille, *Mon secret* (1886). See also Daniela Costa, 'La ricezione francese del *Secretum*', in *Francesco Petrarca, l'opera latina*, ed. Secchi Tarugi, pp. 477–84.

[35] 'un habile arrangeur de madrigaux, faisant pivoter tous ses vers sur une ou deux pensées d'amour', Delécluze, 'Vie de F. Pétrarque écrite par lui-même', *Revue de Paris* (17 March 1839), 5–15 (p. 3).

[36] 'J'avais à cœur de détruire le préjugé ou pour mieux dire les idées fausses que l'on entretient depuis si long-temps en France sur le caractère moral et l'ensemble des écrits de Pétrarque. Je voulais démontrer que ce poète, qui s'est rendu immortel par l'élévation et l'angélique pureté de ses vers italiens, n'est pas moins remarquable encore par les instincts généreux de son âme et par la prodigieuse étendue de son esprit et de ses connaissances. [...] C'est ce qui m'a engagé à faire connaître les œuvres de Pétrarque, écrites en prose latine.' Delécluze, 'Vie de F. Pétrarque', p. 1.

in Latin not about Laura had to wait until later in the century for attention. At this later point, burgeoning interest in Petrarch as a Latin historian and moralist rather than a vernacular love poet coincided with the turn to philology and a return to the original manuscripts themselves. In this respect, Pierre de Nolhac led the way, being responsible not only for bringing the autograph manuscript of the *Canzoniere* in the Vatican Library to light in the 1880s, but also for studies of Petrarch's Latin works such as the *De viris illustribus* (*On Illustrious Men*), which underpinned his magisterial *Pétrarque et l'humanisme*.[37] The French scholar Cochin subsequently followed in Nolhac's footsteps, with studies of Petrarch's letters as well as a French prose translation of Petrarch's penitential psalms, with a preface by Nolhac, published in 1929.[38] Yet even this late, as with the 'Letter to Posterity' or the *Secretum*, Cochin admires the penitential psalms for their autobiographical qualities: 'Petrarch has left no document more direct, more personal, or more vibrant as regards his self and the history of his soul than his Penitential Psalms. [...] [I]f the Psalms were written in the vernacular rather than in Latin, they would be famous.'[39] In this manner, even well into the twentieth century, Petrarch's Latin works are promoted as masterpieces of sincerity and self-reflection even as they are criticized for their Latin garb. Latin is recognized by Cochin as an enduring barrier to the popularity of this part of Petrarch's *œuvre*, and translation into French is presented as one way of overcoming this linguistic hurdle, as the most prominent and prolific nineteenth-century translator of Petrarch's Latin works, Victor Develay, had already realized.

The Work of Victor Develay

Though scholars such as Nolhac and Cochin played a vital role in renewing interest in Petrarch's Latin achievements, it was an earlier translator, Victor Develay, a Paris-based scholar and librarian, who was principally responsible for bringing Petrarch's Latin works back into a French spotlight in the second half of the nineteenth century.[40] As already noted, Develay translated the most popular of Petrarch's Latin works such as the *Secretum*, the 'Letter to Posterity' (the latter alongside Petrarch's last will and testament), and the letter on the ascent of Mont

---

[37]   Pierre de Nolhac, 'Le *De viris illustribus* de Pétrarque', *Notices et extraits des manuscrits de la Bibliothèque nationale et autres bibliothèques*, 34.1 (1891), 61–148, and idem, *Pétrarque et l'humanisme*.

[38]   See Henry Cochin, *Un ami de Pétrarque: lettres de Francesco Nelli à Pétrarque* (Paris: Honoré Champion, 1892); idem, 'Les "Epistolae metricae" de Pétrarque: remarques sur le texte et la chronologie', *Giornale storico della letteratura italiana*, 74 (1919), 1–40; Henry Cochin, *Les Psaumes pénitentiaux publiés d'après le manuscrit de la bibliothèque de Lucerne*, *préface de Pierre de Nolhac* (Paris: L. Rouart et fils, [1929]), the latter text having already been translated by Develay, *Psaumes pénitentiaux* (Paris: Librairie des Bibliophiles, 1880). As noted above, Cochin also published a translation of the *Triumphi* in 1923.

[39]   'Pétrarque ne nous a pas laissé sur lui-même, sur l'histoire de son âme de document plus direct, plus personnel, plus vivant que ses Psaumes Pénitentiaux. [...] [S]i les Psaumes étaient écrits en vulgaire plutôt qu'en latin, ils seraient célèbres.' Cochin, *Les Psaumes pénitentiaux*, p. 9.

[40]   For biographical information see Étienne Wolff, 'Victor Develay, les études néo-latines et Pétrarque', *Latomus*, 58.1 (January–March 1999), 172–8.

Ventoux, as well as Petrarch's rewriting of the penitential psalms (later retranslated by Cochin).[41] Develay was also responsible for the first complete French translation of the *Bucolicum carmen*.[42] His real contribution was, however, to the forgotten and neglected Latin works: Petrarch's letters beyond the two obvious choices; the epic poem *Africa*; the treatise on moral philosophy *De remediis utriusque fortune* (*Remedies for Fortune Fair and Foul*). As regards the former, Develay tended to group the letters according to either theme or, most commonly, addressee. French geography is a pervasive unifying factor for the *Lettres de Vaucluse* (*Letters from Vaucluse*), although Petrarch's uncomplimentary writing about Avignon is also, unusually, acknowledged by Develay in his translation of the nineteen letters that form the *Sine nomine*.[43] Develay also grouped together a number of letters relating to books and book-collecting.[44] In terms of addressee, Develay published translations of letters written by Petrarch to Cola di Rienzo, to his brother Gherardo, and to Boccaccio, with these last supplemented by a translation of Petrarch's translation from Italian into Latin of the last story of Boccaccio's *Decameron*.[45]

Beyond this unusual breadth of interest in Petrarch's letters, Develay also forged new ground in his translations from and of Petrarch's Latin epic *Africa*, in the face of widespread French criticism of this work throughout the nineteenth century. The poem is named *Africa* because it is set in Africa, at the time of the Second Punic War, a war between Africa and Italy, or more properly between the Carthaginian Empire on the one hand and the Roman Republic on the other. This war brought face to face two great warriors, Hannibal and Scipio (to give the latter his fuller appellation, Publius Cornelius Scipio Africanus, also known as Scipio the Elder). Scipio might for us be a forgotten hero, but in the medieval period in particular he remained a paradigm of virtue, military prowess, loyalty, patriotism, and stoicism. He crops up in Dante's writings, as well as elsewhere in Petrarch's corpus, with the

---

[41]   *Mon secret*; *Epître à la postérité et Testament*; *L'Ascension du Mont Ventoux*; *Psaumes pénitentiaux*. On Petrarch's will, see also 'Testament de Pétrarque', in Gabriel Peignot, *Choix de testaments anciens et modernes, remarquables par leur importance, leur singularité, ou leur bizarrerie; avec des détails historique et des notes*, 2 vols (Paris: Renouard; Dijon: Victor Lagier, 1829), I, 56–65.

[42]   *Églogues, traduites pour la première fois par Victor Develay*, 2 vols (Paris: Librairie des Bibliophiles, 1891).

[43]   *Lettres de Vaucluse, traduites du latin pour la première fois par Victor Develay* (Paris: E. Flammarion, 1899); *Lettres sans titre, traduites pour la première fois par Victor Develay*, 2 vols (Paris: Librairie des Bibliophiles, 1885). On this last work, see Chapter 4.

[44]   Develay, 'Lettres de Pétrarque sur l'amour des livres', *Bulletin du bibliophile et du bibliothécaire: revue mensuelle publiée par Léon Techener* (1879), 1–21, 153–79, and 405–29; *Bulletin du bibliophile et du bibliothécaire* (1880), 305–20 and 529–37; *Bulletin du bibliophile et du bibliothécaire* (1881), 48–53, 207–19, 289–95, 385–8, and 481–93.

[45]   *Lettres à Rienzi, traduites pour la première fois par Victor Develay* (Paris: Librairie des Bibliophiles, 1885); *Lettres de Pétrarque à son frère, traduites pour la première fois par Victor Develay*, 2 vols (Paris: Librairie des Bibliophiles, 1884); *Lettres de François Pétrarque à Jean Boccace, traduites du latin pour la première fois par Victor Develay* (Paris: E. Flammarion, 1891); *Grisélidis, conte traduit du latin par Victor Develay* (Paris: Librairie des Bibliophiles, 1872). The Griselda story forms letter three of book seventeen of the *Seniles*. See also Develay, 'Pétrarque épistolier', *Le Carnet historique et littéraire: revue mensuelle*, 10 (November 1901), 211–25; *Le Carnet historique et littéraire*, 11 (January 1902), 81–93.

Africa being entirely devoted to his great feats.[46] With this work Petrarch sought to revive the genre of the Classical epic and to follow in the footsteps of Homer and Virgil, and it was for the *Africa*, albeit incomplete (and destined so to remain), that Petrarch received the laurel crown in Rome on 8 April 1341.[47] Chapter 5 and the Conclusion discuss French authors such as Musset and Gautier who rewrote and reinterpreted this key event in the life of Petrarch, in particular by disassociating the *Africa* from the coronation. For the present, it suffices to cite a handful of nineteenth-century French writers who are representative of a wider antipathy towards the *Africa* at the time.

Perhaps most damningly, Sismondi described the work as 'tiring to the ear, bloated in style, lacking in interest, so boring as to render it impossible to read'.[48] Roman had early on dismissed it as a 'Latin poem that nobody reads',[49] while Stendhal was to reiterate in 1818 that 'Petrarch, the great Petrarch himself, wrote in Latin and nobody reads his *Africa*'.[50] Sainte-Beuve, too, was of a similar opinion, commenting acerbically that 'Four or five of Petrarch's sonnets make me forget entirely whether he finished his *Africa* or not.'[51] The *Africa*, geographically, historically, linguistically, and thematically, was rejected by many readers at this time as too far from the amorous Provençal world of Laura and the vernacular *Canzoniere*. French writers such as Théodore Pierre also lamented that Petrarch had not turned his hand to an epic in Italian rather than Latin:

> If, instead of producing Latin poems, such as his *Africa*, which today is no longer read, he had continued to devote himself to Italian poetry, his homeland might perhaps count in its records of literary achievements one more epic poem, and the language of his nation would have benefited likewise.[52]

---

[46] See Robert Hollander and Albert L. Rossi, 'Dante's Republican Treasury', *Dante Studies*, 104 (1986), 59–82, and Aldo S. Bernardo, *Petrarch, Scipio and the 'Africa': The Birth of Humanism's Dream* (Baltimore: Johns Hopkins Press, 1962).

[47] For the speech Petrarch made on this occasion, see: in Latin, *Collatio laureationis*, in *Opere latine di Francesco Petrarca*, ed. Antonietta Bufano with Basile Aracri and Clara Kraus Reggiani, 2 vols (Turin: Unione tipografico-editrice, 1975), II, 1255–83; in English, E. H. Wilkins, *Studies in the Life and Works of Petrarch* (Cambridge, MA: The Mediaeval Academy of America, 1955), pp. 300–13; in French, Victor Develay, 'Pétrarque au capitole', *Le Livre: revue du monde littéraire: archives des Écrits de ce temps: bibliographie rétrospective*, 6 (1885), 278–88.

[48] 'fatigant à l'oreille, enflé dans le style, dépourvu d'intérêt, ennuyeux enfin de manière à ne pouvoir être lu', Sismondi, *De la littérature du Midi de l'Europe*, I, 421–2.

[49] 'Poëme latin que personne ne lit', Roman, *Le Génie de Pétrarque*, p. 255.

[50] 'Pétrarque, le grand Pétrarque lui-même, a écrit en latin et personne ne lit son *Africa*.' *Journal littéraire*, ed. Victor Del Litto, cited from Stendhal, *Œuvres complètes*, ed. Victor Del Litto and Ernest Abravanel, new edn, 50 vols (Geneva: Edito-Service S. A., 1968–74), XXXV (1970), 73.

[51] 'Quatre ou cinq des sonnets de Pétrarque me font parfaitement oublier s'il a terminé ou non son *Afrique*.' Sainte-Beuve, *Œuvres: Premiers lundis, Portraits littéraires, Portraits des femmes*, ed. Maxime Leroy, 2 vols (Paris: Gallimard, 1949–51), II, 254.

[52] 'Si, au lieu de produire des poèmes latins, tels que son *Afrique*, qu'on ne lit plus aujourd'hui, il avait continué de s'adonner aux poésies italiennes, sa patrie pourrait peut-être compter dans ses annales littéraires, un poème épique de plus et le langage de sa nation aurait

A similar regret that Petrarch had not written the *Africa* in Italian rather than in Latin was later expressed by Nolhac: 'This poem full of beauty that is dead to us, written in Italian, would have competed with *The Divine Comedy*.'[53] In this manner both Pierre and Nolhac seem to overlook the epic tendencies of Petrarch's *Triumphi*, which though written in Italian and in *terza rima*, had, nonetheless, ultimately failed to rival the popularity and appeal of Dante's *Commedia*.

Despite the general lack of appreciation of the *Africa*, Develay, undeterred, set about translating the text, initially by rescuing from it the apparently most palatable and interesting portion, namely the narrative of the tragic love story of Massinissa and Sophonisba (Book V of the *Africa*).[54] This story bears some situational similarities with the famous tale of adultery and murder of Paolo and Francesca from the fifth canto of Dante's *Inferno*, and indeed Develay's decision to excerpt this passage is mirrored, and perhaps inspired, by the existence of translations of *Inferno* V alone and out of context in this century.[55] The presentation of *Inferno* V by itself tends to ennoble the two lovers by removing them from the moral judgement associated with their location in Hell, but no such alleviation of tension or guilt is possible where the story of Massinissa and Sophonisba is concerned. When the king of Carthage, Syphax, is defeated, Scipio's friend and ally Massinissa (king of Numidia) moves in to take possession of the city and imprison Syphax, and at the same time falls in love with Syphax's wife Sophonisba and marries her. While this amorous interlude provides narrative relief from the detailed descriptions of military stratagems, it comes to a tragic end as Scipio urges Massinissa to give up this guilty, politically dangerous, and distracting love. Massinissa's sole function, in the end, seems to be to reveal Scipio's moral principles by way of contrast. While Massinissa is associated with love, lust, passion, foreignness, weakness, and betrayal, Scipio is on the side of virtue, duty, friendship, control of one's emotions, Rome, and piety to family and fatherland. Inspired by Scipio's exhortations and reproaches, Massinissa regretfully sends Sophonisba a poisoned chalice from which she willingly drinks and passes to the Underworld. While the initial decision to translate this episode by itself suggests a desire to contribute first and foremost to the image of Petrarch as love poet,

---

profité d'autant.' Théodore Pierre, *Abrégé de l'histoire de Pétrarque* (Vaucluse: Maria Brun; Avignon: Seguin frères, 1879), p. 46.

[53] 'Ce poème plein de beautés mortes pour nous, écrit en italien, eût rivalisé avec *La Divine Comédie*.' Pierre de Nolhac, 'L'Année de Pétrarque', p. 7.

[54] *Sophonisbe, épisode du poème de 'l'Afrique', traduit pour la première fois par Victor Develay* (Paris: Librairie des Bibliophiles, 1880). On this episode, see Johannes Bartuschat, 'Sofonisba e Massinissa. Dall'*Africa* e dal *De viris* ai *Trionfi*', in *Petrarca e i suoi lettori*, pp. 110–41, and Bernardo, *Petrarch, Scipio and the 'Africa'*.

[55] See Francesca Bugliani-Knox, '"Galeotto fu il libro e chi lo scrisse": Nineteenth-Century English Translations, Interpretations and Reworkings of Dante's Paolo and Francesca', *Dante Studies*, 115 (1997), 221–50; Deirdre O'Grady, 'Francesca da Rimini from Romanticism to Decadence', in *Dante Metamorphoses: Episodes in a Literary Afterlife*, ed. Eric C. Haywood (Dublin: Four Courts Press, 2003), pp. 221–39; Nick Havely, 'Francesca Observed: Painting and Illustration, c. 1790–1840', in *Dante on View: The Reception of Dante in the Visual and Performing Arts*, ed. Antonella Braida and Luisa Calè (Aldershot: Ashgate, 2007), pp. 95–107.

Develay subsequently translated the whole of the *Africa*, no doubt aided by work on critical editions of the poem such as that published by Léonce Pingaud in 1872.[56]

Develay's eventual comprehensiveness when it came to the *Africa* was not, however, to be mirrored in his approach to some of Petrarch's other lengthy Latin works. The *De remediis utriusque fortune*, for instance, reached only the stage of excerpts in Develay's corpus. This work is a series of dialogues between abstract personifications, the Stoical voice of Reason (*Ratio*) versus irrational emotions, namely Sorrow (*Dolor*), Joy (*Gaudium*), Hope or Desire (*Spes sive Cupiditas*), and Fear (*Metus*). Of this work, Develay translated only two chapters, one on love and another on books.[57] Perhaps because of the existence of earlier French translations of the *De remediis*, Develay did not seek to produce a complete translation of the work which, unlike the majority of his publications, would not therefore have been able to be labelled 'translated for the first time' (*traduit pour la première fois*).[58] The *De remediis* was also often at this time, like the *Africa*, dismissed as arid and unreadable, with Ginguené, for instance, describing its dialogues as 'dry and lacking in skill' (*secs et dépourvus de l'art*) and as capable of producing only 'tiredness and boredom' (*de la fatigue et de l'ennui*).[59] Later critics expressed little more affection for the work, with Cochin complaining 'There is nothing more drily Scholastic than the method of exposition chosen by the author, and nothing more tedious, I dare say, than his enormous work.'[60] Similarly, even though Charles Dejob unusually recognized the work as 'One of his most important in terms of its scope and the intellect which shines through at many points', he concluded that the work 'makes one smile at the ingenuity of its composition' and dismissed its 'two interminable series of dialogues'.[61]

In spite of the wide-ranging nature of Develay's forays into Petrarch's Latin works (not to mention his other extensive translation projects including the works of Erasmus), a significant number of Petrarch's Latin works remained untranslated for

---

[56] *L'Afrique, poème épique, traduit du latin pour la première fois par Victor Develay*, 5 vols (Paris: Librairie des Bibliophiles, 1882); Léonce Pingaud, *De poemate F. Petrarchae cui titulus est Africa, Thesim facultati litterarum parisiensi* (Paris: Ernest Thorin, 1872).

[57] *Des amours charmantes, traduit du latin par Victor Develay* (Paris: Librairie des Bibliophiles, 1883) and *De l'abondance des livres et de la réputation des écrivains, traduit du latin par Victor Develay* (Paris: Librairie des Bibliophiles, 1883).

[58] See Léopold Delisle, *Anciennes traductions françaises du traité de Pétrarque 'Sur les remèdes de l'une et l'autre fortune'* (Paris: Imprimerie nationale, 1891); Nicholas Mann, 'La fortune de Pétrarque en France: recherches sur le *De remediis*', *Studi francesi*, 37 (1969), 1–15; Romana Brovia, *Itinerari del petrarchismo latino: tradizione e ricezione del 'De remediis utriusque fortune' in Francia e in Borgogna (secc. XIV–XVI)* (Alessandria: Edizioni dell'Orso, 2013) and idem, 'Du nouveau sur la fortune du *De remediis* en France (XIVe–XVIe siècles)', in *La Postérité répond à Pétrarque*, pp. 87–110.

[59] Ginguené, *Histoire littéraire de l'Italie*, II, 446, 448.

[60] 'Rien de plus sèchement scolastique que le procédé d'exposition choisi par l'auteur, et rien de plus fastidieux, j'ose dire, que son énorme ouvrage.' Cochin, *Le Jubilé de Pétrarque*, p. 15.

[61] 'Un de ses plus importants par la dimension, par l'esprit même qui y brille en beaucoup d'endroits', 'fait sourire par l'ingénuité de la composition', 'deux interminables séries de dialogues', Charles Dejob, 'Le "Secretum" de Pétrarque', *Bulletin italien*, 3.1 (1903), 261–80 (p. 267).

a French readership at the end of the nineteenth century. These included Petrarch's invectives, in one of which Chateaubriand had, unusually, expressed a passing interest (alongside the *Secretum*):

> Petrarch is better known for his *canzoni* than for his treatises *de Contemptu Mundi; de sua ipsa et aliorum ignorantia*, although this last work is worth more than the majority of his sonnets. But Laura and Vaucluse are sweet names, and men are more easily entranced by the heart than by the head.[62]

This view was, however, atypical, with Ginguené's judgement of the *Invectives* particularly harsh and no doubt more influential: 'Many of his works have happily been lost. There remains one in particular far too long, which we cannot but regret that it has not encountered the same fate as the others. Its title is *Invectives* which is entirely apt.'[63] Other major Latin works by Petrarch which remained untranslated in this period included moral and religious treatises, such as the *De vita solitaria* (*On the Solitary Life*) and the *De otio religioso* (*On Religious Leisure*), as well as historical prose writings including the *Rerum memorandarum libri* (*Books of Things to be Remembered*) and the *De viris illustribus*, despite Nolhac's work on the latter.[64]

To conclude, interest in Petrarch's Latin works in this period was—aside from the more thorough and wide-ranging commitment of Develay—predominantly focused on texts of an autobiographical nature, especially those with explicit reference to Laura, such as the *Secretum* and specific eclogues from the *Bucolicum carmen*. Such preferences match the favourite parts of the *Triumphi* (that is, the *Triumphus Mortis*), confirming that the French Petrarch of the nineteenth century is, above all, the amorous poet of Laura's life and death. In order to uphold this view of Petrarch, certain texts had to be excluded or suppressed from his *œuvre*. These texts included not only particular works in Latin discussed in this chapter, but also three sonnets of the *Canzoniere* (*RVF* 136–8) which, in their harsh critique of Avignon, sat uneasily with French and Avignonese enthusiasm for a poet considered, as shown in the

---

[62] '[Pétrarque] est plus connu par ses Canzones que par ses Traités *de Contemptu Mundi; de sua ipsa et aliorum ignorantia*, quoique ce dernier ouvrage vale mieux que la plupart de ses sonnets. Mais Laure, Vaucluse, sont de doux noms, et les hommes se prennent plus aisément par le cœur que par la tête.' Chateaubriand, *Essai historique, politique, et moral, sur les révolutions, anciennes et modernes* (London: Henri Colburn, 1815), p. 344. The invective in question is a response to four friends who accused Petrarch of not knowing Aristotle, to which Petrarch responded by assenting to this charge of ignorance. See William J. Kennedy, 'The Economy of Invective and a Man in the Middle: *De sui ipsius et multorum ignorantia*', in *Petrarch: A Critical Guide to the Complete Works*, pp. 263–73.

[63] 'Plusieurs de ses pièces sont heureusement perdues. Il en reste une beaucoup trop longue, qu'on est réduit à regretter qui n'ait pas eu le sort des autres. Elle porte le titre d'*Invectives* qu'elle ne justifie que trop.' Ginguené, *Histoire littéraire de l'Italie*, II, 396.

[64] A lone voice in favour of the *De vita solitaria* in nineteenth-century France seems to have been Sainte-Beuve, who borrowed a passage from Petrarch's work as one of two epigraphs to *Les Consolations: poésies* (Paris: U. Canel, 1830): I return to Sainte-Beuve in Chapter 6. See, in contrast, on earlier French interest in this work, François Rouget, 'La fortune du *De vita solitaria* de Pétrarque dans la littérature française de la Renaissance: Peletier, Ronsard, Pibrac et Montaigne', in *Francesco Petrarca, l'opera latina*, pp. 461–76.

Introduction, to be quintessentially French and Provençal. It is to a discussion of these sonnets, alongside the Latin letters against Avignon (the *Sine nomine*), that the final chapter of Part I is devoted.

4

Petrarch and Avignon:
The Fate of the *Sine nomine* and *RVF* 136–8

A S WE HAVE seen in the Introduction, late eighteenth- and nineteenth-century
French readers and translators of Petrarch sought to highlight his association with France, and with Avignon and the surrounding countryside in
particular. In this chapter, further manifestations of this locally motivated interest
in Petrarch are explored in relation to celebrations of Petrarch held in Avignon
and Fontaine-de-Vaucluse at key moments throughout the nineteenth century.
These celebrations of Petrarch and Avignon had a fatal, often thinly veiled flaw:
Petrarch's own dislike of Avignon, which I have heretofore, much like most French
nineteenth-century readers of Petrarch, set deliberately to one side. This dislike is
most intensely expressed in three sonnets in the *Canzoniere*, *RVF* 136–8, as well
as in a collection of nineteen Latin letters, enigmatically entitled the *Sine nomine*
(*Without Name*). The various ways in which French translators deal with these two
sets of texts forms the second part of this chapter. The first part of this chapter sets
the festal stage over which these two sets of texts stubbornly and intermittently cast
their awkward shadows.

Petrarchan Festivities in Nineteenth-Century Avignon

Nineteenth-century Avignon was a key 'site of Petrarchism' and a vital 'Petrarchan
place'.[1] From the days of the Avignon papacy until the French Revolution, Avignon
had remained a papal annexe governed by the Vatican. At the French Revolution,
after a series of revolts and not inconsiderable local and papal resistance, Avignon
was officially recognized as part of France by the Assemblée nationale on 14
September 1791. When Avignon became part of the French Republic, both therefore had a newly vested interest in recovering Avignon's medieval past as French,
and the ensuing acts of recuperation were expressed in part through a variety of
Petrarch-inspired celebrations, often around key anniversary dates, beginning with
1804, peaking in 1874, and continuing into the early twentieth century with 1904.

The first anniversary celebrations dedicated to Petrarch and organized in
Avignon were those of 1804, Petrarch's five hundredth birthday, although the poet's

---

[1]   For these terms in their original contexts, see Kennedy, *The Site of Petrarchism* and
Trapp, 'Petrarchan Places'.

various homes in Arezzo, Fontaine-de-Vaucluse, and Arquà (some more historically verifiable than others) had long been important sites of literary pilgrimage
and devotion.[2] The 1804 festivities were modest affairs compared to later events,
although they were an early success for the only recently established Avignon-based
institution responsible for promoting Petrarch throughout the nineteenth century,
the Athénée de Vaucluse, later rebranded the Académie de Vaucluse.[3] This same
Athénée, as already noted in Chapter 2, republished Roman's *Vie de Pétrarque* to
mark the 1804 anniversary. On this occasion, the celebrations of Petrarch were also
seen as an opportunity to contribute to praise of Napoleon, fittingly since Napoleon
had himself founded the Athénée as a means of consolidating culturally the French
integration of Avignon.[4]

Other celebrations followed in the footsteps of those of 1804, with 1874 a
particularly important date marking five centuries since Petrarch's death, and
1904 returning to birthday festivities. Both these celebrations were opulent public
events with banquets, fireworks, and toasts, but they also had a more serious side,
in the commissioning and encouragement of translations of Petrarch and of critical
studies and biographies of the poet. As Cochin observed after the 1904 celebrations,
'festivals in all countries around the world have their habitually banal aspects', but
they do have a saving grace: 'There is, in effect, one fortunate consequence of these
centennial festivals that our age has adopted the habit of instituting in honour of
great men of the past: they are the starting point for excellent periods of work.'[5]
The earlier 1874 festivities were particularly committed to both translation and new
writing, with competitions held for translations of any poem by Petrarch, as well as
original poetry inspired by Petrarchan themes (Laura's eyes, Petrarch in Vaucluse,
and so on).[6]

Interestingly, on the occasion of the 1874 celebrations, these compositions
could be submitted in either French or Occitan. In the latter case, the model was
the Occitan of the Félibrige, a group of seven poets who had come together in the
1850s to promote Occitan as a modern literary language.[7] Mistral, in particular, was
closely involved in the Petrarchan celebrations of 1874, offering toasts to Petrarch
and Laura in Occitan, as well as reading aloud his own translation into Occitan of
the famous *RVF* 126.[8] In a review of the 1874 festivities, one critic noted that:

---

[2]   See Hendrix, 'The Early Modern Invention of Literary Tourism' and 'From Early
Modern to Romantic Literary Tourism'.

[3]   For documents pertaining to this institution's foundation, see *Mémoires de l'Athénée
de Vaucluse* (1804).

[4]   Hendrix, 'Petrarch 1804–1904', p. 121. See also the Introduction, above.

[5]   'les fêtes en tous pays du monde ont leurs usuelles banalités', 'C'est là, en effet,
l'heureuse conséquence des fêtes séculaires que notre temps a pris coutume d'instituer en
l'honneur des grands hommes du passé : elles sont le point de départ de belles périodes de
travail.' Cochin, *Le Jubilé de Pétrarque*, pp. 6, 7.

[6]   See Chapter 5.

[7]   On the associated topic of Dante and the Félibrige, see James W. Thomas, 'Dante
and the Provençal Renaissance', in *Dante in France*, ed. Russell Goulbourne, Claire Honess,
and Matthew Treherne (= *La Parola del testo: rivista internazionale di letteratura italiana e
comparata*, 17.1–2 (2013)), pp. 71–83.

[8]   On the involvement of the Félibrige, see Alphonse V. Roche, 'Petrarch and the

The name of Petrarch must have reminded the Félibres of glorious memories of the past. The heirs of the troubadours of old, in their endeavours to revive the admirable language of the thirteenth century, could hope that along with Laura's lover, the Provençal language, too, was going to emerge from the grave and regain definitively, in solemn, national gatherings, its great place in the sun. It was impossible, moreover, not to associate with the gentle, fine, and delicate bard of sonnets, that other contemporary poet, more daring in scope, both of whom were inspired by the same sun and by emotions as keenly felt and as refined.[9]

The modern poet alluded to here is Mistral himself, who later in the same review is described as 'our Provençal Homer' (*notre Homère provençal*).[10] The Petrarchan festivities became more generally a celebration of Provençal poetry, with a particular focus on the work of the Félibrige headed by Mistral.

Beyond affinities sensed between Mistral and Petrarch, perhaps the most striking manifestation of such a local adoption of Petrarch as belonging by rights to the south of France and continuous with the tradition of the troubadours was the translation of a sonnet by Petrarch (*RVF* 333) purportedly into the Provençal of Petrarch's day (*Prouvençau dóu tèms de Petrarco*), during the 1874 festivities. I give the sonnet first in Italian and in English translation:

> Ite, rime dolenti, al duro sasso
> che 'l mio caro thesoro in terra asconde,
> ivi chiamate chi dal ciel risponde,
> benché 'l mortal sia in loco oscuro et basso.
>
> Ditele ch'i' son già di viver lasso,
> del navigar per queste horribili onde;
> ma ricogliendo le sue sparte fronde,
> dietro le vo pur così passo passo,
>
> sol di lei ragionando viva et morta,
> anzi pur viva, et or fatta immortale,
> a ciò che 'l mondo la conosca et ame.

Felibres', *Italica*, 30.1 (March 1953), 1–18, and Francesca Zantedeschi, 'Petrarch 1874: Pan-National Celebrations and Provençal Regionalism', in *Commemorating Writers in Nineteenth-Century Europe*, ed. Leerssen and Rigney, pp. 134–51. For the opening stanza of Mistral's translation of *RVF* 126, see Appendix 2.

    [9] 'Le nom de Pétrarque devait rappeler aux félibres les glorieux souvenirs du passé. Les héritiers des anciens troubadours, s'efforçant de ressusciter l'admirable langue du XIIIe siècle, pouvaient espérer qu'à côté de l'amant de Laure, la langue provençale allait sortir de la tombe et reconquérir définitivement, dans des assises nationales et solennelles, sa grande place au soleil. Il était impossible de ne pas associer, d'autre part, au chantre doux, fin et délicat des Sonnets, cet autre poëte contemporain, au vol plus hardi, qu'ont inspiré le même soleil et des sentiments aussi vifs et aussi élevés.' Paul Glaize, 'Le centenaire de Pétrarque', *Revue des langues romanes: publiée par la société pour l'étude des langues romanes*, 6 (July and October 1874), 278–91 (p. 278).

    [10] Glaize, 'Le centenaire de Pétrarque', p. 286.

Piacciale al mio passar esser accorta,
chè presso omai; siami a l'incontro, et quale
ella è nel cielo a sé mi tiri et chiame.

***

Go, sorrowful rhymes, to the hard stone
that hides my dear treasure in earth,
there call to the one who from Heaven answers,
although what is mortal of her is in a place that is dark and low.

Tell her that I am already tired of life,
of navigating these horrendous waves;
but that gathering up her scattered leaves,
I still follow behind her one step at a time,

only speaking of her alive and dead,
rather still alive, and now become immortal,
so that the world may know and love her.

May it please her to be attentive to my passing,
which is by now near; may she meet me, and what
she is in Heaven may she draw and call me to her.

***

Complansa, vai deves la peira dura
Que dins la terra escond mon car tresor,
Clam l'arma qu'es en celestial lugor
Entre tant qu'es sos cors en tomba escura.

Di li que ja ma vida trop mi dura,
De las ondas iradas ai paor,
Mas membratz de son pretz e sa valor
De la segui pas apres pas ai cura.

O viva o morta a lei cug solamens ;
Ar inmortal viéu perdurablemens,
Vuelh que lo munz e la conosca e l'ame,

Plassi li m'estre cortes quand morrai,
Venga m'encontra, que non tardarai,
En cel am elha mi tire e mi clame.[11]

The same poem was also rendered soon afterwards by the same translator into
French, as follows:

Allez, mes vers plaintifs, jusqu'à la roche dure
Qui dans la terre, hélas ! cache mon cher trésor ;

---

[11]   Marc, 'Planh', in *Fête séculaire et internationale de Pétrarque célébrée en Provence
1874*, ed. Berluc-Pérussis and Guillibert, p. 183.

Tandis que vers le ciel son âme a pris l'essor,
Son corps est enfermé dans une tombe obscure.

Dites-lui que, lassé du tourment que j'endure
Des flots qui contre moi se soulèvent encor,
Je n'ai d'autre souci que d'arriver au port
En marchant pas à pas sur sa trace si pure.

Vive ou morte, immortelle au céleste séjour,
Je ne parle que d'elle, y songeant nuit et jour,
Pour que le monde entier la connaisse et qu'il l'aime.

Qu'elle me soit en aide à l'heure où je mourrai ;
Qu'elle accoure vers moi quand vers elle j'irai ;
Qu'elle m'appelle au ciel et m'y guide elle-même.[12]

The translation of Petrarch's poetry into the Provençal of Petrarch's day realizes fully the desire to portray Petrarch as belonging to a medieval French tradition, specifically one stemming from Provence.

Besides Marc's medievalizing attempt, modern Occitan translations of Petrarch can be found in several published accounts of the Petrarch celebrations of 1874.[13] A further venue for such translations was the already mentioned, short-lived *Almanach du sonnet*, which was published in three instalments between 1874 and 1876 and included translations of Petrarch into both French and Provençal.[14] The 1904 celebrations of the sixth centenary of Petrarch's birth continued to have a Provençal flavour, with Mistral once more present and giving a speech in honour of Petrarch, Laura, and the Provençal language in that same language. In this speech, Mistral even proposed 'Our language... Is it not the one that Petrarch spoke to the beautiful Laura?', with the choice of present tense and opening first-person plural possessive adjective in this rhetorical question stressing the continuity between Petrarch's language and that of the Félibrige.[15] There were also prizes awarded to poems in French and Provençal on Petrarchan themes, following the model of the 1874 celebrations.[16]

---

[12] *Almanach du sonnet* (1875), p. 202.
[13] See, in particular, *Fêtes littéraires & internationales* and *Fête séculaire et internationale de Pétrarque*, ed. Berluc-Pérussis and Guillibert. The former volume contains prizewinning translations into Provençal of *RVF* 194 (by Roso-Anaïs Roumanille), *RVF* 164 (by V. Lieutaud), and *RVF* 272 (by Anfos Tavan), as well as Mistral's translation of *RVF* 126: *Fêtes littéraires & internationales*, pp. 176–9 and 246–9. The latter volume contains a translation of *RVF* 280 by Mistral, as well as Marc's translation of *RVF* 333, cited above (*Fête séculaire et internationale de Pétrarque*, pp. 184, 183).
[14] *Almanach du sonnet* (1875), p. 185 (a translation of *RVF* 346 by Roso-Anaïs Roumanille) and pp. 191–2 (Mistral's translation of *RVF* 281). The third *Almanach du sonnet* (1876), p. 178, includes Roso-Anaïs Roumanille's translation of *RVF* 194.
[15] 'Nosto lengo... N'es-ti pas elo que Petrarco parlavo emé la bello Lauro?' Académie de Vaucluse, *Sixième centenaire de la naissance de Pétrarque*, p. 21. I thank Louise Esher for help with this quotation. The postulation that Petrarch could speak Provençal was reasserted by Wilkins, *The Life of Petrarch*, p. 3; see the Conclusion for further discussion of this point.
[16] On these anniversary competitions, see Chapter 5.

This kind of reiterated, Provençal and Avignonese enthusiasm for all things Petrarch-related was, however, in a way fundamentally flawed, as it was predicated upon ignoring Petrarch's actual hatred of Avignon for its usurping of Rome's rightful place as home of the papacy. Ever since the arrival of the papacy in Avignon in 1309, led by the French pope Clement V, Petrarch had longed for its return to Rome, though this desired homecoming was to take place only after his death.[17] In spite of the years Petrarch spent in Provence and which are celebrated so fondly by nineteenth-century French readers, writers, and translators, Petrarch's love for what he called 'My Italy' (*Italia mia*, the opening words of *RVF* 128) was unwavering, and as a result he wrote a number of texts that attacked Avignon aggressively: the *Sine nomine* and *RVF* 136–8. These writings were particularly problematic for French readers and translators of Petrarch, as they challenged the cosy view of Petrarch and Avignon as happily united throughout history, and translators accordingly developed a variety of ways of dismissing and diminishing these texts, as explored below.

This misunderstanding at the heart of Petrarch's relations with Avignon was revealed by a lone voice following the 1874 festivities: Eugène Roulleaux.[18] Roulleaux took it upon himself to challenge the organizers of and participants in the celebrations of the purportedly reciprocal love of Avignon and Petrarch. Roulleaux bemoaned the involvement of the Félibrige in the festivities, seeing their participation as a sign of self-absorbed regionalism and unhelpful anti-French sentiment. More generally, he also complained of the inflated prices around the time of the festival, which suggested to him that the celebrations were mere money-making activities for local shops, hotels, and restaurants, not to mention local pickpockets, rather than suitable offerings on the altar of poetry. From the start, Roulleaux placed himself against the French (and specifically Provençal) adoption of Petrarch, asking both 'Why not leave Petrarch to Italy?' and 'What is, then, the value of this festival?'[19] Roulleaux then sought to expose the festival as feeding off people's appetite for food rather than poetry: 'Tables laden with pitchers of beer and powdery cakes impede the way, besieged by a crowd which is more eager for refreshments than for literature.'[20] The Félibrige came under attack for their seemingly petty 'Provençal pride' (*amour-propre provençal*), and Roulleaux composed a sonnet ostensibly in their honour which concluded with a complaint of the indigestion that ensued from the unavoidable sound of 'so many Provençal verses' (*tant de*

---

[17]   In Chateaubriand's narrative, Petrarch is, nonetheless, responsible for this return: 'C'est à Pétrarque que nous devons le retour du souverain pontife au Vatican' ('It is to Petrarch that we owe the return of the supreme pontiff to the Vatican'), cited from Chateaubriand, *Mémoires d'outre-tombe*, I, 481.

[18]   Eugène Roulleaux, *Pétrarque et les fêtes du centenaire à Vaucluse et à Avignon (18, 19 et 20 juillet 1874)* (Bourg: Imprimerie P. Comte-Milliet, 1875), also highlighted in Duperray, 'Le pétrarquisme en Provence'.

[19]   'Pourquoi alors ne pas laisser Pétrarque à l'Italie ?', 'Quelle est donc la valeur de cette fête [...] ?' Roulleaux, *Pétrarque et les fêtes du centenaire*, pp. 9, 13.

[20]   'Des tables couvertes de cruchons de bière et de gâteaux poudreux encombrent la voie, investies d'une foule plus avide de rafraîchissements que de littérature.' Roulleaux, *Pétrarque et les fêtes du centenaire*, p. 12.

vers provençaux) during the festivities.[21] Unlike Cochin's appreciation of centennial festivals as the productive catalyst for renewed critical investigation, cited above, Roulleaux dismissed the supposed academic value of the celebrations, asserting that 'you don't do history with enthusiasm'.[22]

Finally, Roulleaux translated into prose *RVF* 136, the first of the three anti-Avignon sonnets, with an introduction of his own which insistently asserts Petrarch's Italianness against French and more local adoptive claims:

> People of Avignon, you decorate your public monuments with the bust of the Italian Petrarch; you place under his invocation the streets and boulevards of your city; here is how the Italian Petrarch treated your city, at that point in time which you rightly consider to be the most glorious of your history; here is how he loved France, how he acknowledged the hospitality of your ancestors, what sort of prelude he offered to your hymns of brotherhood, how he made himself worthy of your gratitude and admiration. M. Nigra did not tell you this, and many of you are ignorant in this matter. M. Scipion Doncieux and the Félibres, those faithful and eloquent guardians of Provence, have covered the accents of their ungrateful guest with magnanimous forgetfulness; but the calm and slow hour of justice leads us to the memory of the outrages which issued from an Italian mouth.[23]

It is difficult to gauge the impact of Roulleaux's pamphlet, since it, like the anti-Avignon sonnets it sought to unveil, was apparently met with a similar silence of 'magnanimous forgetfulness'. One crucial exception is Paul Terris's report of the proceedings, which summarized Roulleaux's work acerbically in the following manner: 'We will leave to M. Roulleaux the satisfaction of having poured out in 47 pages in octavo his pitiful grudge against the South.'[24] Terris thus dismisses Roulleaux as a biased voice, misappropriating the Petrarchan celebrations as an excuse to vent wider anti-Provençal invective. Yet this example importantly suggests, albeit through negation and rebuttal, that Roulleaux's pamphlet did not pass entirely

---

[21]   Roulleaux, *Pétrarque et les fêtes du centenaire*, pp. 33, 41.

[22]   'On ne fait pas de l'histoire avec de l'enthousiasme.' Roulleaux, *Pétrarque et les fêtes du centenaire*, p. 31.

[23]   'Avignonnais, vous décorez vos monuments publics du buste de l'italien Pétrarque ; vous placez sous son invocation les rues et les boulevards de votre cité ; voici comment l'italien Pétrarque traitait votre cité, à cette époque que vous considérez justement comme la plus glorieuse de votre histoire ; voici comment il aimait la France, comme il reconnais-sait l'hospitalité de vos aïeux, comme il préludait à vos cantiques de confraternité, comme il se rendait digne de votre gratitude et de votre admiration. M. Nigra ne vous l'a pas dit, et beaucoup d'entre vous l'ignorent. M. Scipion Doncieux et les félibres, ces fidèles et éloquents gardiens de l'honneur de la Provence, ont couvert les accents de son hôte ingrat d'un magnanime oubli ; mais l'heure calme et lente de la justice nous ramène au souvenir des outrages sortis d'une bouche italienne.' Roulleaux, *Pétrarque et les fêtes du centenaire*, p. 42.

[24]   'Nous laisserons à M. Roulleaux la satisfaction d'avoir épanché en 47 pages in-8ᵉ, sa petite rancune contre le Midi.' Paul Terris, *Le Centenaire de Pétrarque: rapport présenté à la Société littéraire d'Apt dans la Séance du 20 septembre 1874* (Apt: Typographie et lithographie J. S. Jean, 1876), p. vi.

unnoticed by the more adulatory voices at such festivities.[25] Roulleaux remains a unique but important witness to a desire to return to a less hagiographic under-standing of the lived relationship between Petrarch and Avignon. Other French translators, as the remainder of this chapter explores, were, however, to seek alter-native solutions to the problem of the Avignon sonnets in contrast to Roulleaux's mode and model of direct, deliberately polemical confrontation.

Petrarch's Anti-Avignon Texts

Before exploring in depth the responses of nineteenth-century French critics and translators to Petrarch's anti-Avignon sonnets, beyond the example of Roulleaux, it is first helpful to give the texts of the sonnets, and also to discuss the contents of the associated Latin letter collection, the *Sine nomine*. The Italian texts (with English translation) of the three anti-Avignon sonnets are given below:

> #### RVF 136
>
> Fiamma dal ciel su le tue treccie piova,
> malvagia, che dal fiume et da le ghiande
> per l'altrui impoverir se' ricca et grande,
> poi che di mal oprar tanto ti giova;
>
> nido di tradimenti, in cui si cova
> quanto mal per lo mondo oggi si spande,
> de vin serva, di lecti et di vivande,
> in cui Luxuria fa l'ultima prova.
>
> Per le camere tue fanciulle et vecchi
> vanno trescando, et Belzebub in mezzo
> co' mantici et col foco et co li specchi.
>
> Già non fostù nudrita in piume al rezzo,
> ma nuda al vento, et scalza fra gli stecchi:
> or vivi sì ch'a Dio ne venga il lezzo.
>
> *** * ***
>
> May heavenly fire rain down on your tresses,
> O evil one, who from the river and from acorns
> by the impoverishment of others are rich and great,
> since you so much enjoy doing evil;
>
> nest of betrayals, in which is nursed
> all evil which today spreads through the world,

---

[25] See also the brief discussion of Roulleaux (in part salvaged because of Roulleaux's admiration of Le Duc's translation) in Le Duc, *Les Sonnets de Pétrarque*, II, 356–8 and 362–4, for further evidence of the text's circulation. Le Duc seems at least to have shared Roulleaux's antipathy towards the number of Provençal verses and speeches recited during the three-day festivities.

a slave to wine, bed, and victuals,
in whom immoderate desire [*Luxuria*] makes its ultimate test.

Through your chambers young girls and old men
go cavorting, and Beelzebub in their midst
with bellows and fire and mirrors.

Before you were not raised on feather pillows in the shade,
but naked to the wind, and barefoot amongst thorns:
now you live so that to God may reach the stench.

RVF 137

L'avara Babilonia à colmo il sacco
d'ira di Dio, e di vitii empii et rei,
tanto che scoppia, ed à fatti suoi dèi
non Giove et Palla, ma Venere et Bacco.

Aspectando ragion mi struggo et fiacco;
ma pur novo soldan veggio per lei,
lo qual farà, non già quand'io vorrei,
sol una sede, et quella fia in Baldacco.

Gl'idoli suoi sarranno in terra sparsi,
et le torre superbe, al ciel nemiche,
e i suoi torrer' di for come dentro arsi.

Anime belle et di virtute amiche
terranno il mondo; et poi vedrem lui farsi
aurëo tutto, et pien de l'opre antiche.

***

Avaricious Babylon has fully filled the sack
with God's anger, and with evil and wicked vices,
so that it is overflowing, and has made her gods
not Jove and Pallas, but Venus and Bacchus.

Waiting for justice I pine and tire;
but still a new sultan do I see for her,
who will make, not as soon as I would like,
only one seat, and that will be in Baghdad.

Her idols will be scattered on the Earth,
and her proud towers, to Heaven inimical,
and those who dwell in these towers from outside as inside burnt.

Beautiful souls and friends of virtue
will occupy the world; and then we will see it become
all golden, and full of ancient deeds.

RVF 138

Fontana di dolore, albergo d'ira,
scola d'errori et templo d'eresia,
già Roma, or Babilonia falsa et ria,
per cui tanto si piange et si sospira;

o fucina d'inganni, o pregion dira,
ove 'l ben more, e 'l mal si nutre et cria,
di vivi inferno, un gran miracol fia
se Cristo teco alfine non s'adira.

Fondata in casta et humil povertate,
contra' tuoi fondatori alzi le corna,
putta sfacciata: et dove ài posto spene?

negli adulteri tuoi? ne le mal nate
richezze tante? Or Constantin non torna,
ma tolga il mondo tristo che 'l sostene.

***

Fountain of suffering, dwelling-place of anger,
school of errors, and temple of heresy,
once Rome, now false, guilty Babylon,
for whom there is much weeping and sighing;

O hotbed of deceits, O dire prison,
where good dies, and evil is nourished and born,
for the living, Hell; it will be a great miracle
if Christ in the end does not get angry with you.

Founded in chaste and humble poverty,
against your founders you raise your horns,
brazen prostitute: and where have you put your hope?

In your adulterers? In your many ill-born
riches? Now Constantine is not coming back,
but may the sad world which sustains him take you away.

In these three sonnets, the Avignon papacy is consistently criticized for a wide range of sins including avarice, heresy, lust, and gluttony. Petrarch's language, though perhaps unexpected in a love poet, taps into a well-established poetic tradition of vituperation.[26] Nonetheless, these sonnets were at various points deemed so controversial as to be placed on the papal *Index librorum prohibitorum* (*Index*

---

[26]　Emilio Pasquini, 'Il mito polemico di Avignone nei poeti italiani del trecento', in *Aspetti culturali della società italiana nel periodo del papato Avignonese: 15–18 ottobre 1978* (Todi: L'Accademia tudertina, 1981), pp. 257–309; Fabian Alfie, 'Old Lady Avignon: Petrarch's *Rerum vulgarium fragmenta* 136 and the topos of *Vituperium in vetulam*', *Italian Culture*, 30.2 (September 2012), 100–9; Franco Suitner, 'L'invettiva antiavignonese del Petrarca e la poesia infamante medievale', *Studi petrarcheschi*, n.s., 2 (1985), 201–10.

of Banned Books) which was first published in 1559 and finally abolished in 1966. Such a placement is a striking instance of misreading; Rome apparently saw the sonnets as unacceptable attacks on the very institution of the papacy rather than on its temporary residence in Avignon. *RVF* 136–8 were put on the Index in its first incarnation after the Council of Trent, along with the *Sine nomine*.[27] For this reason, many sixteenth- and seventeenth-century editions of Petrarch have these sonnets crossed out or defaced. As we shall see, the French nineteenth-century habit of omitting these sonnets is a more civilized version of the same impulse to hide and repress. Petrarch's attack on the papacy led to his adoption by some sixteenth-century proto-Protestant commentators such as Fausto da Longiano, Antonio Brucioli, and Lodovico Castelvetro.[28] Nineteenth-century translators, in contrast, seem rarely to have been motivated by religious affiliations, but rather by local geographical interest, so that these three sonnets became unpopular for civic and patriotic rather than ecclesiastical reasons.

The three sonnets are akin in language and sentiment to the *Sine nomine*, their partners in prohibition, so much so that it has even been asserted that 'the sonnets against Avignon can be almost entirely reconstructed using the thoughts and phrases of the letters of the *Sine nomine*'.[29] In both the letters and the sonnets, Avignon is consistently presented as a new Babylon, in contrast to the sacredness of Jerusalem/ Rome, drawing on Scriptural analogies, especially from Psalm 136 which begins 'Upon the rivers of Babylon, there we sat and wept: when we remembered Sion'.[30] The defeat of Jerusalem by Babylon and the consequent exile of the Jewish people is mirrored for Petrarch in the papacy's abandonment of Rome and preferment of Avignon. Such imagery provides a stark contrast to the celebration of the Fontaine de Vaucluse of *RVF* 126, especially since the rivers around Avignon are subsequently denigrated in the letters of the *Sine nomine* in no uncertain terms:

---

[27] In 1559 and 1564 we find banned both *Alcuni importanti luoghi tradotti fuor delle epistole latine di Francesco Petrarca, con 3. sonetti suoi* and *Sonetti: Dell'empia Babilonia, Fiamma del ciel, Fontana di dolore, L'Avara Babilonia*: see *Thesaurus de la littérature interdite au XVIe siècle: auteurs, ouvrages, éditions avec addenda et corrigenda*, ed. J. M. de Bujanda (Geneva: Librairie Droz; Sherbrooke: Centre d'Études de la Renaissance, 1996), p. 317. Later on, the nineteenth-century volume *Epistole di Francesco Petrarca*, ed. Ferdinando Ranalli (Milan: Per Giovanni Silvestri, 1836) was also added: *Index librorum prohibitorum 1600–1966*, ed. J. M. de Bujanda (Montreal: Médiaspaul, 2002), pp. 701, 740. I thank David Hook for drawing my attention to these catalogues.

[28] For discussion of these commentators see Kennedy, *The Site of Petrarchism* and *Authorizing Petrarch*.

[29] 'I sonetti contro Avignone si posson quasi ricostruir per intero con pensieri e locuzioni delle lettere *Sine titulo*.' G.A. Cesareo, *Su le 'poesie volgari' del Petrarca: nuove ricerche* (Rocca S. Casciano: Licinio Cappelli, 1898), p. 96. See also, on the *Sine nomine*, Ronald L. Martinez, 'The Book Without a Name: Petrarch's Open Secret', in *Petrarch: A Critical Guide to the Complete Works*, pp. 291–9, and Francesca Southerden, 'Between Autobiography and Apocalypse: The Double Subject of Polemic in Petrarch's *Liber sine nomine* and *Rerum vulgarium fragmenta*', in *Polemic: Language as Violence in Medieval and Early Modern Discourse*, ed. Almut Suerbaum, George Southcombe, and Benjamin Thompson (Farnham: Ashgate, 2015), pp. 17–42.

[30] 'Super flumina Babylonis illic sedimus et flevimus cum recordaremur Sion.' Quotations (and Psalm numbering) are taken from the Vulgate and the Douay-Rheims translation.

Durance indeed! So you are called in the vernacular, from the harshness of your wines—or Ruance, as some writers refer to you, from the verb 'to rush'. Oh swift, destructive river, the inhabitants along your banks are no kinder than your rapids and rough bed, and rush into every kind of crime with just as much fury. Oh you streams so shamelessly proud, so irreverent and faithless: you river Sorgue, sucking in what is not your own and swelling up proudly against your lord; you Rhone, gnawing at everything! Is this the way you recognize the Tiber? Is this the way you honour your master?[31]

Another letter describes the Rhone as a river of hell, comparable to Cocytus or Acheron,[32] and accordingly Avignon is dubbed as 'that "living hell"' (*ille viventium infernus*),[33] in the words of *RVF* 138 'for the living, Hell' (*di vivi inferno*).[34] As in the sonnets, Avignon is indicted hyperbolically for every possible sin: greed, avarice, opulence, sloth, and so on. Nineteenth-century French translations of the *Sine nomine*, given their scarcity, will first be considered, while the remainder of the chapter will address French translations of *RVF* 136–8.

Reactions to the Latin Letters

In truth, the letters of the *Sine nomine* are more often referred to and suppressed than translated in this period. The abbé de Sade, in his *Mémoires*, set a good precedent for avoiding the *Sine nomine*, which was unwelcome evidence of Petrarch's dislike of Avignon in volumes that otherwise sought to prove Laura's Avignonese identity and to celebrate Avignon's illustrious history. Sade justified his omission of these letters by arguing that the French language was too chaste to cope with such imagery and his French readers too delicate: 'The chastity of our language cannot tolerate details of a certain nature, and my pen refuses to draw images which are capable of alarming the modesty of whoever will perhaps make the effort to read these memoirs.'[35] One wonders, however, whether Sade's warning might on occasion have had the opposite effect, by intriguing readers and stimulating them to track down the texts that he had so coyly omitted.

Having excluded the letters (and the sonnets, considered in due course) on behalf of a fragile readership, Sade does, nonetheless, seek partially to justify Petrarch's

---

[31] 'O vere Durantia, ut vulgus appellat: durities antium, sive ut quidam scriptores vocant, Ruentia: a ruendo diceris, preceps fluvius damnosusque, cuius accole nichil undis et alveo mitiores et ipsi tanto impetu in quodlibet scelus ruunt. O impudenter elati, o irreverentes et indevoti amnes! O non tua sorbens, et tumide in dominum surgens Sorga! O Rodanus rodens omnia! Sic Tyberim recognoscitis? Sic dominum honoratis?' Francesco Petrarca, *Sine nomine: lettere polemiche e politiche*, ed. Ugo Dotti (Bari: Laterza, 1974), p. 20; Norman P. Zacour, *Petrarch's 'Book Without a Name': A Translation of the 'Liber sine nomine'* (Toronto: The Pontifical Institute of Mediaeval Studies, 1973), pp. 37–8.

[32] Petrarch, *Sine nomine*, p. 68; Zacour, *Petrarch's 'Book Without a Name'*, pp. 58–9.

[33] Petrarch, *Sine nomine*, p. 96; Zacour, *Petrarch's 'Book Without a Name'*, p. 68.

[34] *RVF* 138, v. 7.

[35] 'La chasteté de notre langue ne souffre pas des détails d'une certaine nature, & ma plume se refuse à tracer des images capables d'allarmer la pudeur de quelques personnes qui prendront peut-être la peine de lire ces mémoires.' Sade, *Mémoires*, I, 71.

unsavoury language, for instance by suggesting that Petrarch's anger and disgust were no doubt aimed more at foreigners residing in Avignon at the time than at the good people of Avignon themselves: 'It is essential to observe for the honour of the Avignonese people, that these keenly loaded traits, and which provoke such horror, had less to do with the original citizens of the city than with the greedy foreigners, whom fortune had drawn to the city from far and wide.'[36] Sade also stresses that eighteenth-century Avignon must be presumed to be a very different place from its medieval incarnation:

> Those who see Avignon today find it hard to recognize this city from the portrait of it painted by Petrarch, and they blame his mood for the majority of the traits which make up this portrait. It is true that its expressions are exaggerated, and seem to be coloured by the bile of an ill-tempered poet; but it must also be admitted that when Petrarch arrived in Avignon, this city was very different from how it is today. [...] If we could be transported to the century in which he lived, perhaps we would find that he was not so very wrong, and we would be more inclined to forgive him for having painted in such black colours a city which is proud to have raised him in her bosom, and to have been the theatre of a chaste passion, which inspired in him such beautiful poetry.[37]

The tension between Petrarch's anti-Avignon sentiment and Avignon's subsequent pro-Petrarch stance is deftly negotiated by Sade, who tempers mild criticism of Petrarch for using such uncharitable language with a degree of sympathy for the difficulties faced by Petrarch in the no doubt barbaric times and places in which he lived, when Avignon was at the mercy of uncivilized foreigners (including, no doubt, a good number of Italians). Yet in the second volume Sade finally wonders whether the presumed unkindness of Laura's husband might not be the real reason for Petrarch's antipathy towards Avignon, thereby reducing an attack motivated by matters of international political and ecclesiastical import to petty domestic troubles and the strained dynamics of a classic love triangle: 'I do not doubt but that the harsh and unfair behaviour of Laura's husband was largely responsible for the aversion that our poet felt towards time spent in Avignon and for the contempt which he manifests for the inhabitants of this city.'[38] These various excuses all, importantly,

---

[36] 'Il est essentiel d'observer pour l'honneur des Avignonois, que ces traits si chargés, & qui font tant d'horreur, portoient moins sur les Citoyens originaires de cette ville, que sur les étrangers avides, que la fortune y avoit attirés de toutes parts.' Sade, *Mémoires*, I, 27.

[37] 'Ceux, qui voient Avignon à présent, ont bien de la peine à reconnoître cette ville, au portrait qu'en fait Pétrarque, & mettent sur le compte de son humeur la plûpart des traits qui le composent. Il est vrai que les expressions en sont exagérées, & paroissent teintes de la bile d'un Poëte de mauvaise humeur ; mais il faut convenir aussi, que lorsque Pétrarque arriva à Avignon, cette ville étoit bien différente de ce qu'elle est aujourd'hui. [...] Si on pouvoit se transporter dans le siecle où il vivoit, peut-être trouveroit-on qu'il n'avoit pas tant de tort, & on seroit plus porté à lui pardonner d'avoir peint avec de si noires couleurs une ville, qui fait gloire de l'avoir élevé dans son sein, & d'avoir été le théâtre d'une passion honnête, qui lui a inspiré de si beaux vers.' Sade, *Mémoires*, I, 27–9.

[38] 'Je ne doute pas que ces procédés durs & injustes du mari de Laure n'influassent

occupy the space left by choosing not to cite from or translate the original, potentially inflammatory texts.

Although Sade's amorous explanation was to be less popular amongst translators, another explanation proffered was that Petrarch had had less social or political
success in Avignon than he might have desired. Levesque, for one, suggested that
Petrarch's criticism of Avignon was unfair and motivated by resentment: 'This same
city of Avignon, against which he railed incessantly, [...] would perhaps have been
less displeasing to him, if he had found recognition and fortune there.'[39] This suggestion was even subsequently reiterated by Cochin, who argued that 'Petrarch's anger
had a personal reason, and he personally had cause for complaint', citing the cause
as a benefice which Petrarch wanted and did not obtain.[40] There was certainly more
evidence for such a slight than for unfriendliness on the part of the fictitious figure
of Laura's husband, even if both explanations were similarly convenient ways of
refusing to consider Petrarch's criticisms of Avignon as at all legitimate or objective.

While Sade sought to make excuses for Petrarch and exonerate Avignon, J.-B.
Christophe's treatment of the *Sine nomine* and its author in his *Histoire de la papauté
pendant le XIVe siècle* (1853; *History of the Papacy during the Fourteenth Century*) was
much harsher, not only rejecting the letters as unfair and untrue but also attacking
Petrarch quite vehemently for daring to write such slanderous comments:

> Several of these letters contain, in relation to the morals of the papal court
> of Avignon, declamatory language which has been used by enemies of the
> Church to criticize her. But too much authority is generally granted to these
> diatribes, which are not an expression of fact. No doubt, in a court made up
> of grand lords, there must indeed have been certain worldly temptations,
> tastes, and splendours which were not always in keeping with ecclesiastical
> simplicity; but was it for a canon such as Petrarch, whose life was no different
> from that of secular priests, to set himself up as court censor? How seriously
> should we take a moralizer who did not blush to advertise publically his
> passion for a woman? I am wary of a reformer who is himself in need of
> reform. Besides, despite his great genius, the poet had a bitter, disconsolate,
> jealous personality, which made him often unfair; and it seems that, lacking in
> confidence in the truth of his accusations, he feared to take responsibility for
> them, because they are almost all contained in the collection of letters which
> are untitled.[41]

beaucoup sur l'aversion que notre Poëte avoit pour le séjour d'Avignon & sur le mepris qu'il
témoigne pour les habitans de cette ville.' Sade, *Mémoires*, II, 481.

[39] 'Cette même ville d'Avignon, contre laquelle il déclamoit sans cesse, [...] lui auroit
moins déplu peut-être, s'il y avoit trouvé les honneurs & la fortune.' 'Vie de Pétrarque', in
Levesque, *Choix des poésies de Pétrarque* (1774), I, 11–35 (pp. 16–17).

[40] 'Il y a aux colères de Pétrarque une raison personnelle, et il a eu personnellement à
se plaindre.' Henry Cochin, 'Les récents progrès des Études Petrarquesques: Arnaldo Foresti',
Études italiennes, 8 (1926), 85–104 and 140–70 (p. 98). For more recent discussion of the
evidence that Petrarch might have been disappointed not to have been made a cardinal, see
Wilkins, *Studies in the Life and Works of Petrarch*, pp. 63–80.

[41] 'Plusieurs de ces lettres renferment, sur les mœurs de la cour romaine d'Avignon,
des déclamations dont les ennemis de l'Église se sont servis pour la décrier. Mais on accorde

Stendhal's account of the letters in *Mémoires d'un touriste* (1838; *Memoirs of a Tourist*), in an entry marked Avignon, instead more sympathetically challenged the clarity and coherence of Petrarch's argument:

> The astute and powerful men who made up the court of Avignon had no need to obstruct or to conceal their passions: for in that century, there were passions. Which, in my eyes, is ample justification for instances of cruelty and injustice.
>
> What is more, they were still far from the days of Luther and Voltaire.
>
> I recalled those Latin letters of Petrarch in which he talks openly about what went on in the palace in Avignon during the heyday of that court. There is nothing more curious, but the Latin is obscure. It must be admitted that it is a matter of actions which are very different from those which occupied Rome in the time of Cicero, whose style Petrarch imitated as best he could.
>
> In these letters we see an intellectual man, advanced in years and adorned with great dignity, who, in order to complete the seduction of a young girl aged fourteen, dons a red hat. Unfortunately, nothing is less clear or precise than the Latin language, to which I hear learned men respond that I am an ignoramus. Perhaps both sides are right, but I have an advantage, that of not being paid to have the opinions that I write.
>
> Petrarch is often indignant in Latin, but what is he indignant about?[42]

---

généralement trop de valeur à ces diatribes, qui n'articulent aucun fait. Sans doute, dans une cour composée de grands seigneurs, il devait bien y avoir quelques allures mondaines, des goûts et un faste qui n'étaient pas toujours conformes à la simplicité ecclésiastique ; mais était-ce à un chanoine comme Pétrarque, dont la vie ne différait pas de celle des séculiers, à s'en établir le censeur ? Quel cas doit-on faire d'un moraliste qui ne rougissait pas d'afficher publiquement sa passion pour une femme ? Je me défie d'un réformateur qui a lui-même besoin de réforme. D'ailleurs, malgré son beau génie, le poëte avait un caractère aigre, chagrin, jaloux, qui le rendait souvent injuste ; et il semble que, peu confiant dans la vérité de ses accusations, il ait craint d'en prendre la responsabilité, car elles sont presque toutes renfermées dans le recueil des lettres qui sont sans titres.' J.-B. Christophe, *Histoire de la papauté pendant le XIVe siècle avec des notes et des pièces justificatives*, 2 vols (Paris: Librairie de L. Maison, 1853), II, 436.

[42] 'Les hommes adroits et puissants qui composaient la cour d'Avignon n'avaient aucun besoin de gêner ou de dissimuler leurs passions : car dans ce siècle-là, on avait des passions. Ce qui, à mes yeux, est une grande justification pour les cruautés et les injustices.

De plus, on était bien loin encore des temps de Luther et de Voltaire.

Je me suis rappelé ces lettres latines de Pétrarque où il parle à cœur ouvert de ce qui se passait dans le palais d'Avignon aux temps brillants de cette cour. Rien de plus curieux ; mais le latin est obscur. Il faut convenir qu'il s'agit d'actions fort différentes de celles qui occupaient Rome du temps de Cicéron, dont Pétrarque copie le style tant qu'il peut.

Nous voyons dans ces lettres un homme d'esprit fort âgé et revêtu d'une éminente dignité, qui, pour achever de séduire une jeune fille de quatorze ans, se met sur la tête une barrette rouge. Malheureusement, rien n'est moins clair et précis que la langue latine, à quoi j'entends les savants répondre que je suis un ignorant. Peut-être avons-nous raison des deux côtés ; mais j'ai un avantage, je ne suis pas payé pour avoir les opinions que j'écris.

Pétrarque s'indigne beaucoup en latin ; mais de quoi s'indigne-t-il ?' *Mémoires d'un touriste*, in Stendhal, *Œuvres complètes*, XV (1968), 294–5. Note that the 'homme d'esprit' here is not Petrarch but a cardinal.

In *Promenades dans Rome* (1829; *Walks in Rome*), Stendhal had, nonetheless, already indicated these letters as worthwhile reading material. In a condensed three-stage argument, Stendhal first criticized an eighteenth-century French travel writer, Jérôme de La Lande, for avoiding these letters entirely, then reiterated that the letters lack clarity, and finally reported his own enjoyment of their perusal:

> The historical part of Lalande's voyage is filled with Jesuitical falsifying. He is very careful, for instance, not to talk about the letters which Petrarch wrote about the papal court. Unfortunately Petrarch wants to show off his elegant Latin style, and often becomes vague and obscure. Some nice memoirs could be written with these letters; we read several of them, on our return, in the lovely copy in-folio of Petrarch's *œuvres*.[43]

Obscurity is a consistent theme in Stendhal's assessment of the *Sine nomine* as of Petrarch's Latin works more generally, as the following comment from *Histoire de la peinture en Italie* (1817; *History of Painting in Italy*) also bears witness: 'If Petrarch had never written songs [*chansons*, i.e. vernacular lyric poetry], he would undoubtedly have been only an obscure pedant.'[44]

A later reference to the *Sine nomine* in *Promenades dans Rome* repeats Stendhal's endorsement of the interest and importance of the letters, all the while reiterating that they frustratingly lack precise information: 'Petrarch, an eyewitness, has described in many letters the morals of this court of Avignon; I recommend them to the reader. Unfortunately, Petrarch, alike in every respect to an author of the nineteenth century, wants to write nobly and is afraid of degrading himself by providing details.'[45] In this manner, Petrarch is a recurrent presence in Stendhal's travels to both Avignon and Rome; indeed, these travels are, in both *Mémoires d'un touriste* and *Promenades dans Rome*, mapped out according to memories of Petrarch's vituperation of Avignon, a city which continues to haunt Stendhal's experience in Rome through the connections provided by the papacy as well as Petrarch. Stendhal is well aware that he is walking in Petrarch's footsteps, and chooses the *Sine nomine* as a strange sort of out-of-date, polemical guidebook to his travels.

While Stendhal's is thus an unusual (and admittedly ambivalent) voice in favour

---

[43] 'La partie historique du voyage de Lalande est remplie de falsifications jésuitiques. Il se garde bien, par exemple, de parler des lettres que Pétrarque a écrites sur la cour des papes. Malheureusement Pétrarque veut faire du beau style latin, et devient souvent vague et obscur. On écrirait de plaisants mémoires avec ces lettres ; nous en avons lu plusieurs, en rentrant, dans le bel exemplaire in-folio des *Œuvres* de Pétrarque.' *Promenades dans Rome*, in Stendhal, *Voyages en Italie*, ed. Victor Del Litto (Paris: Gallimard, 1973), pp. 593–1189 (p. 676), with reference to Jérôme de La Lande, *Voyage d'un François en Italie fait dans les années 1765 & 1766*, 8 vols (Venice and Paris: Chez Desaint, 1769).

[44] 'Si Pétrarque n'eût jamais fait de chansons, il ne serait qu'un pédant obscur, sans doute.' *Histoire de la peinture en Italie*, ed. Paul Arbelet, in Stendhal, *Œuvres complètes*, XXVI (1969), 101.

[45] 'Pétrarque, témoin oculaire, a décrit dans plusieurs lettres les mœurs de cette cour d'Avignon ; je les recommande au lecteur. Malheureusement, Pétrarque, semblable en tout à un auteur du XIXe siècle, veut écrire noblement et craint de s'avilir en donnant les détails.' Stendhal, *Promenades dans Rome*, p. 939.

of the *Sine nomine*, Delécluze, whose enthusiasm for Petrarch's Latin works was noted in the previous chapter, is unique amongst French readers of Petrarch in recommending unreservedly the work as a sign of Petrarch's moral integrity:

> If you want to judge at once the horror which evil inspired in him and how boldly he strove against it, read his *Letters without a name* aimed at the excesses of the papal court at Avignon, and you will see that vice has never more energetically made virtue wail.[46]

The *Sine nomine* was eventually translated by Victor Develay in 1885, though he too expressed some reservations about the text, and attributed Petrarch's dislike of Avignon to Italian patriotism rather than to the reality of life and morals in Avignon at the time:

> Let us be careful not to take these regrettable exaggerations literally, and above all not to associate ourselves with a hatred inspired less by religious scruples and more by a sense of the greatness of our country. Let us never forget that the unforgivable crime of the Avignon popes, in the eyes of jealous Italy, was that of being French and of loving France.[47]

Extracts also later appeared in Gaston Broche's *Sur Pétrarque* (1913; *On Petrarch*), with the author like Develay before him attributing Petrarch's dislike principally to pro-Italian patriotism: 'what he hated about Avignon was above all that she was Rome's rival, at once a sign and a cause of Italy's decadence'.[48] In this manner both Develay and Broche undermine Petrarch's credibility by suggesting his proto-nationalist bias in this matter.[49]

Broche's essay begins as follows: 'It is generally known that Petrarch did not like Avignon. What is less well known are the reasons for his dislike and to what extremes he carried it.'[50] Besides the question of rivalry broached above, Broche attributes Petrarch's dislike of Avignon firstly to a more general disgust with city

---

[46] 'Si l'on veut juger tout à la fois de l'horreur que lui inspirait le mal et de la hardiesse avec laquelle il le combattait, qu'on lise ses *Lettres sans titre* dirigées contre les excès de la cour des papes à Avignon, et l'on verra que le vice n'a jamais fait gémir plus énergiquement la vertu.' Delécluze, 'Vie de F. Pétrarque', p. 2.

[47] 'Gardons-nous donc de prendre à la lettre ces exagérations regrettables, et surtout de nous associer à une haine inspirée moins par des scrupules religieux que par le pressentiment de la grandeur de notre pays. N'oublions jamais que le crime irrémissible des papes d'Avignon, aux yeux de la jalouse Italie, ce fut d'être Français et d'aimer la France.' Develay, *Lettres sans titre* (1885), I, 12.

[48] 'ce qu'il détesta dans Avignon ce fut par dessus tout la rivale de Rome, à la fois signe et cause de la décadence de l'Italie', Gaston Broche, *Sur Pétrarque: ses imprécautions contre Avignon* (Avignon: Imprimerie Rullière frères, 1913), p. 8.

[49] Ginguené similarly attributes Petrarch's dislike of Avignon to his 'amour pour la patrie' ('love for his homeland'), *Histoire littéraire d'Italie*, II, 551. For a discussion of Petrarch's *patrie*, see the Conclusion.

[50] 'On sait généralement que Pétrarque n'a pas aimé Avignon. On sait moins bien quels ont été les mobiles de son aversion et à quelle extrémité il l'a portée.' Broche, *Sur Pétrarque*, p. 3.

life, particularly its noisy, crowded nature: 'It was not Avignon which he fled: it was the city.'[51] Only secondly is the papal court given as another reason for Petrarch's animosity. Yet Broche continues to defend Avignon against charges of corruption uniquely inherent to the city itself:

> In the reasons which we have just developed, there was in any case hardly anything which applied in particular to Avignon. Noise and loose morals were not any more characteristic of Avignon than of any other large city at the time and especially Italian cities. As for the atmosphere of the papal court, it would have been the same, more or less, elsewhere than in Avignon.[52]

Not only are other Italian cities explicitly implicated in Petrarch's rejection of city life, but Rome is implicitly invoked (the possible 'elsewhere', *ailleurs*, of the papal court). Oddly, Broche's conclusion even presents Petrarch's letters as ultimately to Avignon's credit: 'They are also strangely honourable for Avignon: they constitute the most resounding witness to the importance of the role that the French Papacy and Avignon played at that time in the history of Europe.'[53]

In this way, across the nineteenth century the fate of the *Sine nomine* moved between the opposite poles of suppression (Sade) and recommendation (Delécluze), the latter albeit also alongside an acknowledgement of the difficulty of comprehension (Stendhal), to eventual complete translation (by Develay). Throughout, the text remained a thorn in the side of French readers of Petrarch who sought to understand, and often at the same time to diminish, the motives behind Petrarch's antipathy towards Avignon.

Reactions to the Anti-Avignon Sonnets

If the *Sine nomine* posed problems for French readers at various Petrarchan moments in the nineteenth century, the three anti-Avignon sonnets were even more troublesome as they were much less easy to ignore. Part of Petrarch's popular *Canzoniere*, these *sonnets maudits* had by necessity to be included when translators set out to produce complete translations of the Italian Petrarch. Even so, French translators typically adopted one of three different ways of smoothing over the anti-Avignonese sentiment of these sonnets: avoidance, marginalization, and paratextual reinterpretation.

Avoidance, in the case of partial translations, was the simplest of these three options; in this case, translators could happily omit the three sonnets as extraneous

---

[51] 'Ce n'était pas Avignon qu'il fuyait : c'était la ville.' Broche, *Sur Pétrarque*, p. 5.
[52] 'Dans les mobiles que nous venons de développer, il n'y avait d'ailleurs à peu près rien qui s'appliquât particulièrement à Avignon. Le bruit, les mœurs faciles, ne caractérisaient pas plus Avignon que toute autre grande ville du temps et surtout que les villes italiennes. Quant à l'atmosphère de la cour papale elle eût été la même, à peu de chose près, ailleurs qu'à Avignon.' Broche, *Sur Pétrarque*, p. 8.
[53] 'Elles sont aussi singulièrement honorables pour Avignon : elles constituent le plus éclatant témoignage de l'importance du rôle que la Papauté française et Avignon jouèrent alors dans l'histoire de l'Europe.' Broche, *Sur Pétrarque*, p. 22.

to the main theme, the love story of Petrarch and Laura, with no need for any further comment or even mention of their existence. The sonnets are in this manner omitted by translators such as Ernest and Edmond Lafond (1848), Casalis and Ginoux (1887), Brisset (in his 1899 publication), and Cabadé (1902).[54] As always, what is excluded is as revealing as what is included. Unusually, *RVF* 136–8 are not, however, omitted from Roman's selections of Petrarch's 'most beautiful poems', although this translator does amalgamate them into a single poem, on the model of Sade's conflation of several poems into one.[55]

Marginalization was the second most popular option, and had good historical precedents. In fact, Petrarch's separation of the *Sine nomine* from his other letter collections (the *Letters on Familiar Matters* and *Letters of Old Age*) was a form of willing, deliberate marginalization, as Petrarch explained in a prefatory note:

> I refer to some letters written to friends on different matters and at various times. I have assembled them in a single collection so that they would not, being scattered as they were, sully the whole body of my correspondence and make it hateful to the enemies of truth; and so that whoever wants to read them may know where to find them, and whoever doesn't may know what to avoid. Then, too, if anyone decides that they should be obliterated or suppressed, he can the more easily destroy them as a unit without wrecking the entire collection. I quite deliberately planned it this way, not only for the reader but also for myself.[56]

The reasons given for such marginalization and separation—ease of identification, ease of suppression, even ease of destruction—uncannily anticipate the fate of the Avignon sonnets in the hands of early editors and papal censors. The urge to select and compartmentalize, discussed in terms of editorial practices in Chapter 1 and in terms of translators' preferences in Chapter 2, proves to be already at work in Petrarch's own treatment of his *Sine nomine*. This same treatment destabilizes the distinction established between complete and incomplete texts, since Petrarch's presentation of the *Sine nomine* is paradoxically of a work that is as whole and unified as it is partial and selective.

Marginalization also, importantly, had the authoritative earlier backing of Vellutello and Marsand. As discussed in Chapter 1, the former instituted the division of

---

[54]   Omission is also the solution adopted by later translators of a selected Petrarch such as Marie-Anne Glomeau, *De l'Amour et de la Mort (Sonnets choisis), traduction litté-rale conforme aux commentaires de Léopardi* (Paris: Maurice Glomeau, 1920) and Jacques Langlois, *Les Sonnets amoureux de Pétrarque: traduits en sonnets français avec le texte italien en regard: précédés d'un résumé de la vie du poète et du récit de son amour pour Laure* (Paris: Éditions Marc Artus, 1936).

[55]   Roman, *Le Génie de Pétrarque* (1778), p. 319.

[56]   'Epistolas scilicet aliquot, diversis ex causis variisque temporibus ad amicos scriptas, quas unum in locum ideo conieci ne, ut erant sparse, totum epistolarum corpus aspergerent ac veri hostibus odiosum facerent, et ut qui has legere voluerit, sciat ubi eas querat; qui nolu-erit, intelligat quid declinet; si quis autem eradendas abiciendasque censuerit, possit facilius partem unam sine totius operis deformitate convellere. Qua in re et lectori consultum volui et michi.' Petrarch, *Sine nomine*, p. 4; Zacour, *Petrarch's 'Book Without a Name'*, pp. 27–8.

the *Canzoniere* into not two but three parts, through the creation of an additional, third section for poems not ostensibly about Laura in life or in death. Here, predictably, Vellutello placed *RVF* 136–8. In the early nineteenth century, Marsand adopted and adapted Vellutello's concept, structuring his own edition in four parts (because of his interpolation of the *Triumphi* before Vellutello's third section of the *Canzoniere*), with the fourth part 'on various topics' (*sopra varj argomenti*) including the Avignon sonnets. As already noted, Marsand's ordering was followed by a significant proportion of the translators of Petrarch's *Canzoniere* in full (that is, Poulenc, Reynard, and Brisset). Esménard, having omitted the Avignon sonnets from his 1830 volume, subsequently included them in the new third section which he added to his 1848 publication, under a title clearly indebted to the editions of Vellutello and Marsand: 'Poems on various topics' (*Poésies sur divers sujets*), not to be confused with Esménard's own *Poésies diverses* which he had chosen to append to the 1830 volume. In this way, the anti-Avignon sonnets, though included in the translation, could be set to one side as irrelevant to the story of Petrarch's love for Laura.

Finally, in addition to omission and marginalization, a third solution was to reinterpret the three sonnets through the strategic use of paratexts, a key space of intervention and manipulation for translators desirous of explaining and elucidating their choices and interpretations. The most common paratext surrounding nineteenth-century French translations of the Avignon sonnets was a note reminding readers that they had been censured. Here, as ever, Sade's *Mémoires* were an important source of information, Sade having refused to translate *RVF* 136–8 first because of their language and secondly because of this censorship: 'Our language, more chaste than Italian, would not tolerate a literal version of these sonnets: moreover, there are three sonnets in particular which have been condemned by the Roman court, which means that they are not to be found in most editions of Petrarch's *Canzoniere*.'[57] Rather than simple omission, this type of commentary acts as a replacement for and avoidance of translation, with the paratext entirely assuming the place of the absent text. Using the Index as a foil, Sade's avowed respect for Rome neatly protects Avignon from defamation.

More common, though, than Sade's replacement of text with commentary is the positioning of paratexts as a warning note alongside the texts themselves. Following in Sade's footsteps, some nineteenth-century French translators who included these sonnets, such as Mahul and Le Duc, added a footnote stating that these three sonnets had been censured. Mahul first translated *RVF* 137, noting in a title that it formed part of the 'Invectives against the court of Avignon' (*Invectives contre la cour d'Avignon*), and added to the poem a footnote commenting that 'This sonnet has been censured as well as sonnets CV and CVII', *RVF* 136 and 138.[58] Notes at the back of the same volume undermine the translation, however, with Mahul admitting 'We

---

[57] 'Notre langue, plus chaste que l'Italienne, ne souffriroit pas une version littérale de ces sonnets : d'ailleurs, il y en a trois qui ont été condamnés par la Cour de Rome, ce qui fait qu'on ne les trouve pas dans la plus grande partie des éditions du *Chansonnier* de Pétrarque.' Sade, *Mémoires*, II, 96.

[58] 'Ce sonnet a été censuré ainsi que les sonnets CV et CVII', [Mahul], *Cent cinquante sonnets*, pp. 116–17.

have followed for the second quatrain the prose translation of M. de Gramont, not having understood by ourselves the meaning. [...] The meaning of the fourth verse escapes us entirely.'[59] In the fourth edition, Mahul once more included her translation of *RVF* 137 and similar paratextual apparatus, but with the addition to the notes 'Let us be content, without battling with ambiguities, with the passages where vice is blamed in this sonnet, without specifying to whom this vice ought to be attributed directly or indirectly.'[60] Here, Mahul takes up a position of bafflement and resignation similar to Stendhal's question, cited above, in relation to the *Sine nomine*: 'Petrarch is often indignant in Latin, but what is he indignant about?'[61]

In Mahul's fifth and final edition the other two poems, *RVF* 136 and 138, are included as a final concession to the translator's commitment to translating all of Petrarch's sonnets. Mahul warns readers at the start of the volume that 'this new choice will inevitably put forward in order to complete our work certain sonnets of a somewhat delicate or insalubrious nature, which our youth at first and then the reserve of our sex had made us set to one side.'[62] The Avignon sonnets are prime culprits amongst these sonnets, which Mahul soon after notes she will not comment on for fear of drawing further attention to them: 'As for the insalubrious sonnets we will be forgiven for not explaining them in our notes.'[63] Mahul steps back from the uncertain and unsatisfactory note to *RVF* 137 included in earlier editions, and accordingly there are no explanatory notes or commentary on these sonnets in the fifth edition, save a reiteration of the information that 'The original sonnet and three others from the same period of the poet's life have been censured.'[64] In her choice of title to these sonnets, moreover, Mahul introduces a further note of ambiguity in the final edition, since while *RVF* 137 had previously been introduced as 'Invectives against the court of Avignon', *RVF* 136 now appears with the heading 'Invective against the court of Avignon or against a feminine type',[65] with *RVF* 138 marked 'Same subject' (*Même sujet*), harking back to earlier explanations of the sonnets as possibly

---

[59] 'Nous avons suivi pour le second quatrain la traduction en prose de M. de Gramont, n'ayant pas compris par nous-mêmes le sens. [...] Le sens du quatrième vers nous échappe entièrement.' [Mahul], *Cent cinquante sonnets*, p. 369.

[60] 'Contentons-nous, sans batailler avec les équivoques, des passages où le vice est blâmé dans ce sonnet, sans spécifier à qui on doit l'attribuer directement ou indirectement.' Mahul, *Choix de sonnets* (1872), pp. 267–8.

[61] 'Pétrarque s'indigne beaucoup en latin ; mais de quoi s'indigne-t-il ?' *Mémoires d'un touriste*, in Stendhal, *Œuvres complètes*, xv (1968), 295.

[62] 'ce nouveau choix offrira forcément pour parachever notre travail certains sonnets un peu épineux ou un peu scabreux, que notre jeunesse d'abord puis la retenue de notre sexe nous avaient fait écarter', Mahul, *Sonnets inédits* (1877), p. 5.

[63] 'Quant aux sonnets scabreux on nous dispensera de les élucider dans nos notes.' Mahul, *Sonnets inédits* (1877), p. 6.

[64] 'Le sonnet original et les trois autres de la même période de la vie du poëte ont été censurés.' Mahul, *Sonnets inédits* (1877), p. 169. The fourth sonnet of this group is *RVF* 114, which begins 'De l'empia Babilonia' ('From wicked Babylon') and bears evident affinities with *RVF* 136–8, even if it was typically considered as distinct from the three juxtaposed sonnets and was, tellingly, placed by Marsand in the first rather than the fourth section of his edition.

[65] 'Invective contre la cour d'Avignon ou contre un type féminin', Mahul, *Sonnets inédits* (1877), p. 49.

against a woman rather than the papal court.[66] From this perspective the sonnets are half-stripped of their potential incendiary content for the city of Avignon, by introducing as equally possible a more personal, individual explanation.

Like Mahul, Le Duc is forced to include the Avignon sonnets as he, too, is committed to a complete translation of Petrarch's sonnets, and he similarly uses paratextual space to warn readers that these sonnets have been censured. Le Duc introduces *RVF* 136–8 as 'three sonnets put on the Index', and subsequently clarifies:

> It is in the Index published in 1563, following the Council of Trent, that can be found indicated a collection, malignantly composed of all that which Petrarch has written against the papal court, including these three sonnets. This collection, entitled *Some important passages translated from the Latin epistles of M. Francesco Petrarca, etc., with three of his sonnets*, is no longer on the list of banned books. The *Index of Banned Books*, published in Naples in 1862, makes no mention of it.[67]

Le Duc seems to feel justified in translating the banned sonnets since he cannot find them in a recent edition of the Index. Unlike Mahul's latest edition, the headings given by Le Duc to the three sonnets leave no doubt as to their content and unity of theme: 'Invectives against Avignon and the papal court', with the next two marked 'Same subject' (*Même sujet*).[68]

Headings and titles given to these sonnets could, however, as the example of Mahul has already suggested, present an ideal opportunity for reinterpretation. The most common headings were those derived from Marsand, which presented *RVF* 136 as 'He denounces the scandals caused at that time by the Court at Avignon', *RVF* 137 as 'He predicts to Rome the coming of a great person, who will make her return to her ancient virtue', and *RVF* 138 as 'He attributes the evils of the Roman Court to the donations made to it by Constantine'.[69] These titles were often lifted wholesale in translations.[70] In them, the slippage from Avignon to Rome is crowned by the final, ambiguous specification of the Roman court, which might refer to either city. The geographical ambiguity of Marsand's interpretative titles was to prove particularly

---

[66]   On the thesis that these sonnets might be about a woman see, for instance, Jean de Nostredame, *Vies des plus célèbres poètes provençaux: nouvelle édition*, ed. Camille Chabaneau and Joseph Anglade (Paris: Honoré Champion, 1913), p. 125.

[67]   'trois sonnets mis à l'index', 'C'est dans l'index publié en 1563, à la suite du concile de Trente, que se trouve désigné un recueil, composé malignement de tout ce que Pétrarque a écrit contre la cour pontificale, y compris ces trois sonnets. Ce recueil, intitulé *Alcuni importanti luoghi tradetti* [sic] *fuor delle epistole latine di M. Francesco Petrarcha, etc., con tre sonnetti suoi*, n'est plus au nombre des livres prohibés. *L'Index librorum prohibitorum*, publié à Naples en 1862, n'en fait nulle mention.' Le Duc, *Les Sonnets de Pétrarque*, I, 229, 233.

[68]   'Invectives contre Avignon et la cour pontificale', Le Duc, *Les Sonnets de Pétrarque*, I, 228, 230, 234.

[69]   'Inveisce contro gli scandali, che recava a que' tempi la Corte di Avignone', 'Predice a Roma la venuta di un gran personaggio, che la ritornerà all'antica virtù', 'Attribuisce le reità della Corte di Roma alle donazioni fattele da Costantino', Marsand, *Le rime del Petrarca*, II, 272–4.

[70]   For instance in Reynard, *Les Rimes de François Pétrarque*, pp. 354–6.

fertile for French translators, as it played on confusion (later reiterated by Stendhal and Mahul) as to who was implicated in and by the invective of these sonnets, even suggesting a potential substitute scapegoat for Avignon. For instance, Montesquiou's choice of titles reveals a similar confusion that leads, in the third of the three sonnets, to a renunciation of interpretation. Although the first sonnet is explicitly identified as 'Against the Court of Rome which at that time was resident in Avignon' and the second is described in similar terms to Marsand ('The poet promises to Rome the imminent arrival of a liberator who will return her to the golden age'), the third is labelled merely, without further elucidation, 'Babylon will be punished', as if Montesquiou has by the final sonnet of the set renounced any attempt at identification.[71] This renunciation is further suggested by the comparative shortness of Montesquiou's translation of *RVF* 138, which runs to only ten lines, in contrast to the expansiveness (twenty-two lines) of his translation of *RVF* 136.

This type of confusion opens a space for the eventual identification of the target of these sonnets as not Avignon at all but rather Rome, a conclusion reached by four nineteenth-century French translators of Petrarch, seemingly independently one from the other. The first translator to do so is Saint-Geniès, who translates only one of the three sonnets, *RVF* 138. Though Saint-Geniès includes no paratexts to this poem (whether title or footnote), his version is startlingly and explicitly anti-Rome:

> Temple de l'hérésie, école de l'erreur,
> Où président l'orgueil, la fourbe et la fureur,
> Où des tyrans sacrés les humains sont victimes,
> Mes yeux sont las de voir tes palais et tes crimes.
> Rome, enfer des vivans, puisse un dieu punisseur
> Délivrer les humains de ton joug oppresseur !
> Jadis l'humble vertu fit ta grandeur naissante ;
> Aujourd'hui je te vois avilie et puissante.
> Puisses-tu perdre, en proie à tes profanateurs,
> Cet empire conquis par tes saints fondateurs !
> Périsse et la tiare et la pourpre adultère
> De tes tyrans voués au mépris de la terre,
> Et tout l'or sacrilége amassé dans ton sein !
> Non, ce n'est point assez qu'un nouveau Constantin
> Transporte loin de toi la majesté suprême
> Et ravisse à ton front son dernier diadème :
> Il faut, il faut encor que des gouffres ouverts
> Engloutissent tes murs pour venger l'univers.[72]

***

> Temple of heresy, school of error,
> Where pride, dishonesty, and fury reign,

---

[71] 'Contre la cour de Rome qui résidait alors à Avignon', 'Le poète promet à Rome la prochaine arrivée d'un libérateur qui doit lui rendre l'âge d'or', 'Babylone sera punie', Montesquiou, *Sonnets, canzones, ballades et sextines de Pétrarque*, I, 240–2.

[72] Saint-Geniès, *Poésies de Pétrarque* (1816), I, 180.

Where humans are the victims of sacred tyrants,
My eyes are tired of seeing your palaces and your crimes.
Rome, Hell of the living, may a punishing god
Deliver mankind from your oppressive yoke!
Formerly humble virtue made your nascent greatness;
Now I see you degraded and powerful.
May you lose, in the grip of your profaners
This empire won by your founding saints!
Let perish both the tiara and the purple adultery
Of your tyrants devoted to disregard of the Earth,
And all the sacrilegious gold hoarded in your breast!
No, it is not enough that a new Constantine
Carries far from you the supreme majesty
And steals from your forehead its last diadem:
It is necessary, it is still necessary that open abysses
Engulf your walls to avenge the universe.

This eighteen-line poem entirely transforms Petrarch's sonnet into an attack on Rome, where it had originally been an attack on the papal court in Avignon. The crux of misunderstanding is *RVF* 138, v. 3, 'once Rome, now false and guilty Babylon' (*già Roma, or Babilonia falsa et ria*). Through omission of the second term (Babylon/Avignon) in this comparison as well as the temporal contrast between past and present, Saint-Geniès reads the whole poem as an attack on Rome. This attack is, moreover, voiced in the strongest of terms, since the translator brings together 'Rome, Hell of the living' (*Rome, enfer des vivans*), conjoining phrases which in the original had been lines apart (*Roma*, v. 3; *di vivi inferno*, v. 7). The translation continues by transforming the tale of the Church's original poverty (*RVF* 138, v. 9) into praise of the Roman Empire's virtuous foundations, in contrast to its decline and fall into decadence. Finally, where the original denied the return of Constantine (v. 13), Saint-Geniès's 'new Constantine' (*nouveau Constantin*) is responsible for the transfer of the papacy from Rome to Avignon. This transfer is lamented in Saint-Geniès's translation as Rome's loss of its 'supreme majesty' (*majesté suprême*) and 'its last diadem' (*son dernier diadème*), but the responsibility seems to lie with Rome's corruption rather than with Avignon, which gets off scot-free.

Unlike this rather stark and singular example, the further three instances of nineteenth-century French translators who interpret these sonnets as against Rome include all three sonnets in their reinterpretation, and carry out this reinterpretation through paratextual apparatus rather than through translation alone. Firstly, in Gramont's translation from 1842 the sonnets are given the simple explanatory heading 'Invectives against Rome' (*Invectives contre Rome*), while a footnote adds the information, already present in Sade, that 'This sonnet and the two following have been censured by the holy Inquisition.'[73] Secondly, in his translation from 1900

---

[73] 'Ce sonnet et les deux suivants ont été censurés par la sainte Inquisition.' Gramont, *Poésies de Pétrarque*, p. 104. The other two sonnets are marked 'Même sujet' ('Same subject'), p. 105.

Godefroy similarly introduces *RVF* 136 with the title 'Against Rome' (*Contre Rome*), noting before the next two sonnets 'Same subject' (*Même sujet*).[74] Finally, Fernand Brisset in his edition of 1903 adds to each sonnet the epigraph 'To Rome' (*À Rome*), and also appends a simple, one-word footnote to the opening phrase of *RVF* 137 (in his translation, *L'avide Babylone*): 'Rome'.[75] Surely Brisset protests too much, coupling as he does here the task of translation with critical commentary in order to insinuate a new, highly un-Petrarchan meaning behind these sonnets, in flagrant contradiction of Petrarch's professed and constant love of Rome.

In conclusion, the fate of the *Sine nomine* and the anti-Avignon sonnets in the hands of French translators demonstrates that nineteenth-century French Petrarchism is not an easy commodification of past culture, but rather a site of controversy and conflict. Festivals organized in Avignon sought to honour the memory of Petrarch and to claim him as a local poet of international importance. Yet translators attempting to produce a French Petrarch had somehow to come to terms with the uncomfortable truth about Petrarch's own attitude towards Avignon. Through omission, marginalization, and paratextual control, the latter at times enabling starkly un-Petrarchan reinterpretation, French translators proposed varying solutions to the problem of the anti-Avignon letters and sonnets. Thus the city that Petrarch had decried was still able to claim the poet for its own.

---

[74] Godefroy, *Poésies complètes de Francesco Petrarca*, pp. 133–4.
[75] Brisset, *Canzones, triomphes, et poésies diverses*, pp. 316–18.

II
REWRITINGS

5
Petrarch in Poetry

THIS CHAPTER ARGUES for the Petrarchan inspiration of a number of nineteenth-century French poets, both canonical and less well-known. In the latter camp, we encounter several translators discussed in Part I, who were also poets in their own right. The question here is whether their experience of translating Petrarch might have discernibly influenced their own poetry, and in what ways. This question is the subject of the first part of this chapter ('Translators as Poets'), while the second part—'Anniversary Celebrations and Poetry Competitions'—treats the allied topic of poems written for the Petrarchan centenary festivities which span this century (in particular, those of 1874 and 1904). These anniversary poems were at times written by some of the same translators of Petrarch, as well as being the product of poetry competitions with Petrarchan themes.

The second half of this chapter is devoted to the Petrarchan inspiration of canonical French poets, beginning with Lamartine, whence a distinctively Romantic Petrarch emerges.[1] As already noted in the Introduction, Lamartine had a special relationship with Petrarch, both genealogical—via his mother and the abbé de Sade's family tree—and intellectual, leading him to write passionately about Petrarch in his *Cours familier de littérature* (1856–69).[2] Lamartine's affinity with Petrarch extended, as I demonstrate in this chapter, to his activity as a poet, with a number of his poems having been written in the margins of various editions of Petrarch which he owned (hence the title of this section, 'In the Margins'). The final part of this chapter, 'In the Canon', continues the exploration of a canonical Petrarch, by considering the attitudes towards Petrarch expressed in the poetry and prose of Victor Hugo, Alfred de Musset, and Théophile Gautier. In particular, the latter two share a fascination with Petrarch's coronation on the Capitol, inspired by Louis Boulanger's depiction of this same scene in *Le Triomphe de Pétrarque* (*The Triumph of Petrarch*), a large-scale painting commissioned by the marquis de Custine and exhibited at the Paris Salon

---

[1] That Petrarch is an overlooked figure in European-wide Romanticism has been persuasively argued by Hoffmeister, 'The Petrarchan Mode in European Romanticism', with brief suggestion of French examples (Lamartine, Hugo, Musset, Baudelaire) pp. 102–4.

[2] Lamartine's lectures on Petrarch were also subsequently republished posthumously, alongside those on Dante and Tasso, under the title *Trois Poètes italiens* (Paris: A. Lemerre, 1893), although I cite from the text as it appears in Lamartine, *Cours familier de littérature*, VI (1858), 1–155.

of 1836.[3] Despite Hugo's eventual preference for Dante, all three poets, along with Lamartine, confirm and consolidate Petrarch's place in French Romanticism. As for the later part of the nineteenth century, it is primarily up to Petrarch's translators, in combination with the organizers of the 1874 and 1904 celebrations held in Avignon, to perpetuate this newly re-established French poetic Petrarchan tradition.

Translators as Poets

An interesting fact regarding nineteenth-century French translations of Petrarch, and which largely fell outside the scope of Part I, is that these same volumes at times included poems by the translator. Beyond prefatory or dedicatory poems, the end of the volume was the prime location for such texts. Accordingly, the second and final volume of Saint-Geniès's *Poésies de Pétrarque* (1816) concludes with two long poems by the translator, entitled 'Le Rossignol' ('The Nightingale') and 'Le Lis' ('The Lily').[4] Similarly, Camille Esménard's first volume of translations from 1830 concludes with a section of other poems (*Poésies diverses*), comprising six poems by the translator himself.[5] The final volume of Emma Mahul's five-volume series of Petrarch's complete sonnets also ends with a short section devoted to the translator's own poetry, written for the fifth centenary of Petrarch's death, in 1874.[6]

In contrast, for other translators the balance was much more towards poetry than translation. Thus in certain volumes a handful of poems, often sonnets, by Petrarch are included in volumes otherwise dedicated to the author's own poetry. Representative in this regard are publications such as Bouvard's *Fables nouvelles et poésies diverses* (1835; *New Fables and Diverse Poems*), which contains translations of only four poems by Petrarch. Similarly composite are Berton's *Éleuthérides* (1839; *Daughters of Freedom*) and Baudouin's *Rêveries sur les bords du Cher* (1841; *Dreams by the Banks of the River Cher*), each of which contains only one poem translated from Petrarch (in the former, *RVF* 128; in the latter, *RVF* 35), drowning in a sea of original poems by the same poet–translator.

Finally, some translators such as Gramont and Montesquiou separated their activities as poets and as translators into distinct, independent publications. Gramont published his complete volume of prose translations of Petrarch's Italian poetry in 1842, but—as already noted in Part I—devoted the later years of his writing career both to didactic books on French poetry (in particular, the *sestina*) and to his own poetic efforts.[7] Gramont had entered the world of publishing in 1840 with a volume of sonnets, only two years before his translation of Petrarch, and subsequently published two further significant volumes of his own poetry, *Chant du*

---

[3]   The whereabouts of this painting is now, unfortunately, unknown. On Boulanger, see, for a start, Aristide Marie, *Le Peintre poète Louis Boulanger* (Paris: H. Floury, 1925).

[4]   Saint-Geniès, *Poésies de Pétrarque*, ii, 165–85.

[5]   Esménard, *Choix de sonnets de Pétrarque* (1830), pp. 155–92.

[6]   'Ve centenaire de Pétrarque: Vaucluse et Arquà: poésies par Madame Emma Mahul des comtes Dejean: membre honoraire de l'Académie d'Arezzo et de diverses académies d'Italie et de Sicile: seconde édition', in Mahul, *Sonnets inédits traduits de Pétrarque* (1877), pp. 229–46.

[7]   Gramont, *Les Vers français et leur prosodie* and *Sextines*.

passé (1854; *Song of the Past*) and *Olim* (1882; *Formerly*), not to mention other works including poetry for children.[8] As for Montesquiou, his poetic career included volumes of poetry before and alongside his verse translation of Petrarch (published, like Gramont's, in 1842), as well as two long poems, one Biblical (on Moses) and the other Classical (on Hercules).[9]

This recurrent juxtaposition of poetry and translation, whether in a single volume or across different volumes authored by the same hand, calls into question any clear distinction between poetry and translation. Instead, these two activities are seen to be complementary and to overlap, so much so that the distinction between translation and creative writing becomes unstable, and ultimately tenable only with difficulty.[10] This is a conclusion towards which previous chapters have moved, and which is confirmed in the first half of the present chapter. Amongst this plethora of poet–translators, this section will begin with discussion of one of the two poems included by Saint-Geniès at the end of his *Poésies de Pétrarque*, before focussing on the poetry of Gramont.

The first of the two poems by Saint-Geniès, 'Le Rossignol', tells the story of a musical competition between the eponymous nightingale and Linus, brother of Orpheus and 'a favourite of the god of harmony'.[11] The competition is set against a pastoral, idyllic backdrop of rivers, birds, and laurels, and is presented as a struggle between human art (Linus) and nature (the nightingale). The winner is, naturally, the nightingale, yet the poem ends with the nightingale's victory over Linus being swiftly followed by the bird's own death. In this way the poem adopts a Petrarchan setting, shares Petrarch's interest in Ovid's *Metamorphoses*, and concludes in a tragic fashion appropriate to the tenor of the second part of the *Canzoniere* in particular.[12] At the end of the poem, Saint-Geniès describes how Linus buries the nightingale in his lute. The song of both man and bird has been silenced, in a manner reminiscent of the end of *RVF* 292 (not translated by Saint-Geniès): 'my lyre turned to tears'.[13]

Importantly, the nightingale is a Petrarchan figure with illustrious Classical forebears. As well as featuring in the story of Tereus and Philomela from Ovid's *Metamorphoses*, it reaches Petrarch via Virgil's *Georgics*, where the bird is a point of comparison for Orpheus's own laments. Importantly, the poem with which Saint-Geniès's translations of Petrarch concludes is *RVF* 310, a sonnet about the return of

---

[8]   Gramont, *Les Bébés: vignettes par Oscar Pletsch* (Paris: Hetzel, 1861).

[9]   Montesquiou *Poésies*, 2 vols (Paris: F. Didot, 1820–1), *Chants divers*, 2 vols (Paris: Amyot, 1843), *Moïse: poëme en vingt-quatre chants*, 2 vols (Paris: Amyot, 1850), *Hercule, poème épique*, 2 vols (Paris: A. Lemerre, 1873).

[10]   See, similarly, Clive Scott, *Translating Baudelaire*, p. 252, for the assertion that 'Translation is an integral part of creative writing, as the work of poets enough will testify.'

[11]   'un favori du dieu de l'harmonie', Saint-Geniès, *Poésies de Pétrarque*, II, 166 ('Le Rossignol', v. 17).

[12]   On Petrarch and Ovid, see Lynn Enterline, 'Embodied Voices: Petrarch Reading (Himself Reading) Ovid', in *Desire in the Renaissance: Psychoanalysis and Literature*, ed. Valeria Finucci and Regina Schwartz (Princeton, NJ: Princeton University Press, 1994), pp. 120–45.

[13]   'la cetera mia rivolta in pianto', *RVF* 292, v. 14. The line in Petrarch is a borrowing from Job 30.31, 'versa est in luctum cithara mea'.

Spring in which nature is presented under a mythological guise, including Zephyrus (the west wind), Procne (a swallow), and Philomela (the nightingale) herself.[14] Saint-Geniès does not translate the next poem of Petrarch's *Canzoniere*, although this poem—*RVF* 311—overtly continues the nightingale theme in its opening line 'That nightingale, which so sweetly weeps' (*Quel rosignuol, che sì soave piagne*). In this manner Saint-Geniès's own long poem about a nightingale takes the place of a sonnet by Petrarch about the same bird. There may be little discernible formal influence of Petrarch on Saint-Geniès's 190-line poem largely in rhyming couplets, but there is an obvious thematic continuity that renders Saint-Geniès's own poetry an appropriate extension of his activity as a translator. That the same is less true for Saint-Geniès's second poem, which explores the lily (or fleur-de-lys) as a symbol of France, only highlights further the role of 'Le Rossignol' as a poem of transition from Petrarchan poetry to other concerns.

Saint-Geniès's *Poésies de Pétrarque* both drew attention to Petrarch at an unusually early point in the nineteenth century and set a precedent encouraging later translators to append their own poetry to their translations. In contrast, for the other poet–translator I will consider in this section, Ferdinand de Gramont, poetry bore volume-shaped fruits which were published as entirely separate enterprises from the author's work as a translator, although this poetry was, even more than Saint-Geniès's, demonstrably influenced by that same experience of translating Petrarch. As already stated, Gramont's first publication was a volume of sonnets from 1840, at a point when he must already have been hard at work on his complete translation, into prose, of Petrarch's *Canzoniere* and *Triumphi*. As discussed in Chapter 1, Gramont renounced his desire to produce a verse translation of Petrarch's Italian poetry in response to pressures from his publisher, who was likely worried about competition from Montesquiou's verse translation of Petrarch published in the same year. Gramont's literary debut as a sonneteer suggests the reluctance with which this renunciation of verse must have been made.

Posterity has not been particularly kind to Gramont, who in his day moved in eminent literary circles and was, perhaps most notably, a friend and collaborator of Balzac; Balzac's *La Muse du département* (1843; *The Muse of the Department*) is, for instance, dedicated to Gramont. Gramont is now principally remembered as a translator of Petrarch, thanks in large part to the republication of his translation of Petrarch's *Canzoniere* by Gallimard in 1983. In his lifetime, however, his poetry was much more widely appreciated, as his presence in a number of poetry anthologies from the nineteenth century attests.[15] Théodore de Banville acclaimed Gramont as 'one of our most learned and sensitive poets', and especially admired his rediscovery

---

[14] For Saint-Geniès's translation of *RVF* 310, see *Poésies de Pétrarque*, II, 144–7 (including facing Italian).

[15] See, for instance, *Souvenirs poétiques de l'école romantique, 1825 à 1840: précédés d'une notice biographique sur chacun des auteurs*, ed. Édouard Fournier (Paris: Laplace, 1886), pp. 172–5, which contains four sonnets and a *sestina* by Gramont and, in the short biographical paragraph preceding the poems, recalls Gramont's translation of Petrarch as the inspiration for his interest in the form of the *sestina*.

of the French *sestina* or *sextine*.[16] Charles Asselineau similarly praised Gramont as 'the only contemporary poet, and perhaps the first French poet, who has dared to tackle the difficulties of the *sestina*'.[17] That the form of the *sestina* likely originated in France with Arnaut Daniel was still at that time typically overshadowed by its better known early Italian adoption by Dante and Petrarch. Gramont's promotion of the potential of the *sestina* as a rich poetic form is one clear indication of the Petrarchan inspiration of his own poetry.

Gramont's first volume of poetry, a collection of sonnets published is 1840, is dedicated to his friend and fellow author Auguste de Belloy. It is structured in three parts, each consisting of fifty sonnets, plus two introductory sonnets (one proeminal, the other dedicatory) and two concluding sonnets (an 'Epilogue' and an 'Adieu', the last a farewell, albeit temporary, to the sonnet form). In general, the sonnets in Gramont's first collection are populated by flowers, nymphs, and nightingales, likely deriving from a broader lyric tradition than Petrarch (although, as we have seen with Saint-Geniès, the nightingale is not without Petrarchan precedent). Closer to Petrarch in theme are darker poems about time passing and about repentance, as well as sonnets of an overtly religious nature, for instance one sonnet addressing the Virgin Mary, a mutual interlocutor for both Gramont and Petrarch.[18] In such poems Gramont shares with Petrarch a distrust of earthly beauty, love, and sensuality. One sonnet accordingly exhorts the volume's dedicatee 'Friend, let us be wary of all love of things', and asserts that 'Eternity alone should have our sighs'.[19] The penultimate sonnet, 'Epilogue', also suggests the volume's formal indebtedness to Petrarch, despite its reduction to sonnets alone, since Gramont's concluding address to the reader—'You who will read one day these detached rhymes [*rimes détachées*]'—has evident echoes of the *Canzoniere*'s own proeminal apostrophe, 'You who listen in scattered rhymes' (*Voi ch'ascoltate in rime sparse*).[20]

---

[16] 'un de nos poètes les plus savants et les plus délicats', Théodore de Banville, cited in *Anthologie des poètes français du XIXème siècle*, 2 vols (Paris: Alphonse Lemerre, 1887–8), I, 348. This anthology (pp. 348–50) contains, of Gramont, one *sestina* (entitled 'La Clairière', 'The Clearing') and one sonnet (entitled 'Sur le siècle actuel', 'On the present century', and which is also one of the four sonnets included in *Souvenirs poétiques de l'école romantique*, ed. Fournier, pp. 172–3. See also Banville, *Petit traité de poésie française* (Paris: Librairie de l'Écho de la Sorbonne, 1872), pp. 204–13 (with the same quotation in praise of Gramont, p. 204), for discussion and analysis of the form of the *sextine*, based on an example by Gramont.

[17] 'Il est le seul des poètes contemporains, et peut-être est-il le premier des poètes français, qui ait osé s'attaquer aux difficultés de la sextine.' Charles Asselineau, cited in *Les Poëtes français: recueil des chefs-d'œuvre de la poésie française depuis les origines jusqu'à nos jours, avec une notice littéraire sur chaque poëte*, ed. Eugène Crépet, 4 vols (Paris: Librairie de L. Hachette, 1861–3), IV, 723. For a similar statement to those of Banville and Asselineau, see also Théophile Gautier, *Histoire du romantisme suivie de Notices romantiques et d'une Étude sur la poésie française 1830–1868* (Paris: Charpentier et Cie, 1874), p. 500: 'M. de Gramont est le seul poëte français qui ait pu réussir la *Sextine*, ce tour de force qu'on croirait impossible dans notre langue' ('M. de Gramont is the only French poet who has been able to succeed with the *Sextine*, that *tour de force* which would seem impossible in our language').

[18] For this last, see Gramont, *Sonnets*, p. 128.

[19] 'Ami, défions-nous de tout amour des choses', 'seule, l'Éternité / Doit avoir nos soupirs', Gramont, *Sonnets*, p. 126 (Sonnet XVI of Part Three, vv. 1, 10–11).

[20] 'Vous qui lirez un jour ces rimes détachées', Gramont, *Sonnets*, p. 161. Gramont's

Petrarch is, moreover, named explicitly at a number of points in Gramont's *Sonnets*, bringing the Petrarchan inspiration of the volume intermittently to the fore. The first of such instances links Petrarch to his lyric forebear Dante, in an attack on wilful misreaders of their life and works:

> De Pétrarque et de Dante ils profanent les traits !
> Ils nous font de leur vie un vulgaire poëme !
> Et Laure, et Béatrix ne seraient, ô blasphème !
> Que de mortels flambeaux et de rares attraits.[21]

> ***

> Of Petrarch and of Dante they profane the features!
> They make for us of their lives a vulgar poem!
> And Laura and Beatrice would be, O blasphemy!
> But mortal flames with rare appeal.

In an unusual rejection of curiosity about the historical reality of Laura (as discussed in the Introduction, typically a key unifying factor of nineteenth-century French Petrarchism), Gramont instead proposes in this poem that Laura and Beatrice were not real women for their respective poets but rather symbols of poetry: 'Under these enticing names by which the crowd is amused, / Both of you sought only to invoke the eternal Muse.'[22] This bold claim is one from which, by the time of the preface to his *Poésies de Pétrarque*, Gramont has, however, backed down, perhaps for fear of angering the more literal-minded factions of his desired readership. The preface to his translation therefore returns to familiar notions of sincerity and veracity as crucial criteria against which poetry must be judged; from such a perspective, Gramont newly pledges his belief in the living reality of Petrarch's Laura, despite expressing no firm opinion as to her precise historical identity.[23]

A later reference to Laura and Beatrice in the *Sonnets* volume bemoans the lack of such a guide for the modern poet, returning to a similar point as the earlier sonnet that modernity has killed off poetic mysticism and allegory: 'It is over, the age of amorous symbols'.[24] Yet it is in the other two references to Petrarch that Gramont reveals the extent of his intimacy with the *Canzoniere* at that time. In the first, Sonnet XXVII of Part Three, Gramont admires Petrarch's 'ideal love' (*amour idéal*) for Laura, which has survived the vicissitudes of time.[25] This sonnet recalls both *RVF* 12, with which it shares praise of a love impervious to change even as the poet's hair turns white, and *RVF* 291, from which it borrows the figure of Laura as Aurora to the poet's aging Tithonus. Connecting the two sonnets in the original Italian,

---

own translation of the opening line of *RVF* 1 is 'Vous qui écoutez, aux rimes que j'ai répandues' ('You who listen, to the rhymes which I have scattered'), Gramont, *Poésies de Pétrarque*, p. 3.

[21]   Gramont, *Sonnets*, p. 135 (vv. 1–4).

[22]   'Sous ces noms scintillants dont la foule s'amuse, / Vous n'imploriez tous deux que l'éternelle Muse.' Gramont, *Sonnets*, p. 135 (vv. 9–10).

[23]   Gramont, *Poésies de Pétrarque*, pp. ii–iv.

[24]   'Il est passé, le temps des amoureux symboles', Gramont, *Sonnets*, p. 138 (v. 1).

[25]   Gramont, *Sonnets*, p. 137 (v. 12).

beyond the obvious theme of old age, are verbs of pallor: *scolorir* and *mi discoloro*.[26] This language seems to resurface in the opening image of Gramont's own sonnet, which describes Petrarch as 'at the age when all pales [*se décolore*]'.[27] That Gramont's own translation of *RVF* 291 also draws attention to Petrarch's aged, pale face (*visage décoloré*) supports the connection drawn between these poems.[28]

Even more striking, however, is Gramont's retelling of another Petrarchan sonnet of old age, *RVF* 16, in Sonnet XXXII of Part Three. Petrarch devotes three quarters of *RVF* 16 to the narrative of an old man who leaves behind his loyal, affectionate little family in order to set out on a pilgrimage to Rome to see, before he dies, the Veronica (the veil on which Christ's suffering face was imprinted on the way to Calvary). In the final tercet, Petrarch draws a strange and unsettling parallel between his own quest for Laura's face, and the earlier pilgrim's desire to see the face of Christ.[29] Gramont retells this story in the *Sonnets* volume, beginning with a clear declaration of the tale's paternity: 'Petrarch has told us the story of an old man'.[30] This sonnet, alongside Gramont's translation of *RVF* 16 from his complete translation of 1842, provides the interesting comparative perspective of a prose and a verse version of the same story by the same author, albeit told from two different angles. It also gives us a glimpse of what a verse translation of Petrarch might have looked like in Gramont's hands. Here are the texts, first in Petrarch's original and Gramont's translation from his *Poésies de Pétrarque* (glossed in English), and then his rewriting of the same poem in *Sonnets*:

RVF 16

Movesi il vecchierel canuto et bianco
del dolce loco ov'à sua età fornita
et da la famigliuola sbigottita
che vede il caro padre venir manco;

indi trahendo poi l'antiquo fianco
per l'extreme giornate di sua vita,
quanto più pò, col buon voler s'aita,
rotto dagli anni, et dal camino stanco;

et viene a Roma, seguendo 'l desio,
per mirar la sembianza di Colui
ch'ancor lassù nel ciel vedere spera:

---

[26]   *RVF* 12, v. 7 and *RVF* 291, v. 3.

[27]   'Lorsque Pétrarque, à l'âge où tout se décolore', Gramont, *Sonnets*, p. 137 (v. 1).

[28]   Gramont, *Poésies de Pétrarque*, p. 199.

[29]   For readings of *RVF* 16, see Enrico Fenzi, 'Note petrarchesche: R.V.F. XVI, *Movesi il vecchierel*', *Italianistica*, 25.1 (1996), 43–62, and Giorgio Bàrberi Squarotti, 'Il vecchio Romeo: Petrarca, 16', *Critica letteraria*, 22.1 (1994), 43–52.

[30]   'Pétrarque nous a dit l'histoire d'un vieillard', Gramont, *Sonnets*, p. 142 (v. 1). Note that a later version of this sonnet published in Gramont, *Chant du passé*, p. 126, has a different first line: 'Pétrarque nous a fait le tableau d'un vieillard' ('Petrarch has painted for us the picture of an old man').

così, lasso, talor vo cerchand'io,
donna, quanto è possibile, in altrui
la disiata vostra forma vera.

Gramont's translation (1842)

Il s'en va, le pauvre vieillard chauve et blanc, loin du doux lieu où s'est accompli son âge, loin de la tendre famille qui se désole en se voyant abandonnée de son bien-aimé père.

Puis de là, traînant ses flancs antiques, à travers les dernières journées de sa vie, autant qu'il le peut, il s'aide de sa bonne volonté, tout rompu des ans et lassé du voyage.

Et il arrive à Rome, conduit par son désir, pour y contempler l'image de Celui qu'il espère revoir encore dans le ciel.

Hélas ! ainsi parfois, Madame, je vais m'efforçant, autant qu'il est possible, de retrouver en autrui l'image fidèle de votre beauté désirée.[31]

***

Off he goes, the poor old man, bald and white, far from the sweet place where he has filled his years, far from the tender family which is distraught at finding itself abandoned by its beloved father.

Then from thence, dragging his ancient body through the last days of his life, as much as he can, he helps himself with good will, all broken by the years and exhausted by the journey.

And he reaches Rome, led by his desire, there to gaze upon the image of He whom he still hopes to see in Heaven.

Alas, thus at times, Lady, I go searching, as far as possible, to find in others the faithful image of your desired beauty.

Gramont's rewriting (1840)

Pétrarque nous a dit l'histoire d'un vieillard
    Qui, de l'âge sentant venir le dernier terme,
    Rassembla ses enfants ; et là, tranquille et ferme,
    Des biens et des conseils fit à chacun sa part ;
Puis il leur dit adieu, prend son bâton et part.
    De la douce famille et de l'antique ferme
    Il s'éloigne, et son cœur dans son désir s'enferme ;
    Il se hâte, craignant qu'il ne soit déjà tard.
Quand le blanc pèlerin fut à Rome la sainte,
    Il mourut, en voyant l'image de Celui
    Qu'il allait retrouver dans la céleste enceinte.

---

[31]   Gramont, *Poésies de Pétrarque*, p. 11.

Ô Poésie ! ainsi, repoussant toute plainte,
 Je m'achemine au but d'où ton éclair m'a lui.
 Que la Mort jusque-là suspende ton atteinte ![32]

                    ***

Petrarch has told us the story of an old man
 Who, sensing the approach of the last stage of old age,
 Gathered his children; and there, calm and firm,
 To each he gave their share of goods and advice;
Then he bids them farewell, takes up his stick, and departs.
 From the sweet family and the old homestead
 He moves away, and his heart's desire is resolved;
 He hurries, fearing that it might already be too late.
When the white-haired pilgrim was at Rome the holy,
 He died, whilst gazing on the image of Him
 Who he was going to join in the heavenly city.
O Poetry! thus, rejecting all complaint,
 I move towards the goal from whence your brightness has shone
    on me.
 May Death until then suspend your accomplishment!

Gramont's rewriting of this sonnet is notable for its elaboration on and divergence from the invoked Petrarchan exemplar. While the pilgrim at the start of Petrarch's sonnet is already in motion (*Movesi il vecchierel*), Gramont pauses to imagine a fit and proper leave-taking of the *paterfamilias* in particular from his children, to whom he imparts support of both a financial and a moral nature. Also markedly different are Petrarch's and Gramont's treatments of the pilgrim's experience in Rome. Petrarch leaves off his story as the pilgrim arrives dramatically in Rome at the start of the sestet (*et viene a Roma*); we assume that the pilgrim's journey is successfully completed, although his encounter with the Veronica is not described in the sonnet. Gramont, in contrast, renders explicit what Petrarch had left unsaid, not only by describing the pilgrim's sight of the Veronica, but also by making this moment and the pilgrim's death one and the same, granting the tale ideal closure. The stories of both authors then coalesce in the pilgrim's soon to be fulfilled desire of joining Christ in Heaven, only to diverge once more in the final tercet.

In the original Italian, this tercet suggests the poet's doomed quest for other women (the enigmatic *altrui*) who might remind him of Laura's beauty. Yet the relationship between these others and Laura proves, despite the comparative structure of the sonnet, to be entirely unlike the absolute likeness and even real presence embodied by the Veronica as by Christ. Gramont's rewriting is, if possible, even stranger, for it does away with the original characters (Petrarch's lyric subject, Laura, other women), substituting in their stead a new relationship between a first-person voice that emerges for the first time in the final lines of the sonnet and invokes, as its own Veronica, poetry (*Ô Poésie !*). The replacement of Laura with poetry fits

---

[32]   Gramont, *Sonnets*, p. 142.

Gramont's earlier interest in a symbolic reading of Laura and Beatrice, but means that the parallelism of the original sonnet breaks down even further, since the turn to poetry has no comparable other (*autrui*). In Petrarch's sonnet, the analogy whereby the Veronica is to Christ as other women are to Laura was already strained and unworkable. In Gramont's rewriting, the second term has entirely lost any comparable duality. Rather, what holds Gramont's new sonnet together is the theme of desire that connects and motivates both pilgrim and poet, regardless of the object of their respective quests. This desire encompasses the wish for a timely death at and not before the longed for goal, whether that goal be the Veronica or poetry.

Gramont's second volume of poetry, *Chant du passé*, is once more dedicated to Belloy, and even includes a sonnet by this friend, alongside Gramont's response.[33] Many poems from the *Sonnets* volume are reprinted in the earlier part of *Chant du passé*. The later volume is, however, much more formally and linguistically adventurous than Gramont's first book of poetry. In *Chant du passé*, Gramont experiments not only with his signature form, the *sestina*, but also with poems in *terza rima*, the latter likely inspired by his translation of Petrarch's *Triumphi*, itself, as already noted, indebted to Dante's invention of the rhyme scheme in his *Commedia*.[34] Gramont also reconfirms his credentials as an Italophile, firstly by including a number of sonnets in Italian in the collection, and secondly by exhorting his readers:

> Si vous voulez chercher des modèles suprêmes,
> Ne lisez point Ronsard et nos autres anciens,
> Mais épelez Pétrarque et les Italiens.[35]

***

> If you want to find the best models,
> Do not read Ronsard and our other ancient authors,
> But call for Petrarch and the Italian poets.

In a moment of anti-nationalistic generosity, Gramont here becomes a spokesperson for the Italian literary tradition, at the forefront of which he places Petrarch. Yet despite this pro-Italian injunction, another linguistic innovation of *Chant du passé* is the inclusion of a set of poems written in pseudo-sixteenth-century French, suggesting that the French literary tradition cannot be entirely ignored by Gramont in favour of Italian sources.[36]

With his second volume of poems Gramont marks his own transition from youth to middle age. The flowers of his youth—commemorated in his first volume of poetry, simply titled *Sonnets*—are now distant memories, accessible only in moments of intense introspection, as one sonnet addressing 'Flowers, pleasure of springtime' (*Fleurs, plaisir du printemps*) laments:

---

[33] Gramont, *Chant du passé*, p. 233.

[34] For *sestine*, see Gramont, *Chant du passé*, pp. 63–4, 111–12, 135–6, 187–8. For poems in *terza rima*, see Gramont, *Chant du passé*, pp. 65–70, 198–200, and 213–16.

[35] Gramont, *Chant du passé*, p. 242 (Sonnet CCLXXVII, vv. 1–3). For sonnets in Italian, see Gramont, *Chant du passé*, pp. 162, 172–3, 185, 203–4, 229.

[36] Gramont, *Chant du passé*, pp. 15–20.

> Vous ne me semblez plus que des images blêmes,
> Sans puissance, sans vie, et l'ombre de vous-mêmes :
> Pour vous revoir il faut que je ferme les yeux.[37]

***

> You seem to be no more than pale images,
> Without power, without life, and the shadow of yourselves:
> In order to see you again I have to close my eyes.

Accompanying this withdrawal from nature is a stark rejection of earthly love as inherently mortal and unreliable, a lesson that is—as Gramont well knows—intensely Dantean and Petrarchan. Indeed, in *Chant du passé* the death of the beloved is, following the explicit example of these two medieval poets, presented as a release from sensual temptation and as a means of access to a purer love:

> On l'a dit, et plus d'un le doit redire encore :
> Heureux celui qui met ses amours au tombeau,
> Et qui, dans le cercueil, pour jamais voit enclore
> Tout ce qu'à ses regards la terre offrit de beau !
>
> Heureux, dans leur exil, Dante et l'amante de Laure ![38]

***

> It's been said before, and more than one ought to say it again:
> Happy he who puts his loves in the grave,
> And who, in the coffin, sees forever enclosed
> All that the Earth offered to his sight that was beautiful!
>
> Happy, in their exile, Dante and Laura's lover!

The personal relevance of this moral lesson is confirmed in the contiguous sonnet, in which Gramont relates the death and burial of his own beloved. Gramont begins this sonnet by boasting of the chastity of his love:

> Dans les plis du linceul j'ai mis ma bien-aimée,
> Ô mort, et dans ton sein je viens la déposer
> Vierge, et sans que ma lèvre ait, d'un chaste baiser,
> Effleuré seulement sa tempe inanimée.[39]

***

> In the folds of a funeral shroud I have laid my beloved,
> O death, and in your breast I have come to place her
> Virgin, and without my lips having even with a chaste kiss
> Touched her inanimate forehead.

The sonnet concludes describing the transformation, through death, of the beloved from a mortal flower into an immortal star:

---

[37] Gramont, *Chant du passé*, p. 177 (Sonnet CCI, vv. 12–14).
[38] Gramont, *Chant du passé*, p. 202 (Sonnet CCXXXVIII, vv. 1–5).
[39] Gramont, *Chant du passé*, p. 203 (Sonnet CCXXXIX, vv. 1–4).

> Désormais envolée aux campagnes d'azur,
> La fleur que je suivais m'ouvre, splendide étoile,
> Vers l'éternel amour un chemin toujours sûr.[40]

***

> Henceforth flown away to celestial pastures,
> The flower that I followed opens to me, splendid star,
> Towards the eternal love a path always certain.

In this way, the dead lady becomes a heavenly guide, placed within an illustrious poetic lineage.

Appropriately, then, the religious themes foreshadowed in Gramont's *Sonnets* are given centre stage in *Chant du passé*, and amongst these themes Gramont demonstrates a particular predilection for the Virgin Mary as object and addressee of his poetry. In a parallel movement to that of Petrarch rejecting Laura in favour of Mary in *RVF* 366, Gramont declares at the end of one sonnet that from now on there will be room for only one lady in his heart:

> Désormais, je le dis sans regret ni courroux,
> Pour ma voix, ma pensée, et mes yeux, et mon âme,
> Ô Marie, il n'est plus d'autre dame que vous.[41]

***

> Henceforth (I declare it with neither regret nor anger)
> For my voice, my thought, and my eyes, and my soul,
> O Mary, there is no other lady than you.

Unusually, then, Gramont's poetry is Petrarchan not because of its borrowing from a lyric repertory to describe the experience of earthly love and to celebrate the mortal beauty of a particular lady, but rather because of its engagement with religious themes and ideals mediated and inspired by Petrarch's own poetry. Gramont, we can surmise, is one of very few nineteenth-century French readers of Petrarch truly to have appreciated the turn to the Virgin Mary at the end of the *Canzoniere*. This appreciation becomes even clearer if we consider Gramont's final collection of poetry, *Olim*, where we find yet another poem which addresses Mary directly. In this poem, in fact a *sestina*, each stanza begins with invocation of the Virgin (*Vierge*), followed by the intensifier *très* ('very') and an adjective: holy, pure, glorious, good, just, and powerful.[42] This structure seems almost liturgical in its repetitive nature, but it is just as certainly inspired by Petrarch's own poem to the Virgin Mary, *RVF* 366, the first six stanzas of which each also begin with an address to the Virgin defined by a sequence of specific adjectives of praise: beautiful, wise, pure, holy, unique in the world, and bright.[43]

---

[40]   Gramont, *Chants du passé*, p. 203 (Sonnet CCXXXIX, vv. 12–14).

[41]   Gramont, *Chant du passé*, p. 232 (Sonnet CCLXII, vv. 12–14). For other poems to the Virgin Mary in the same volume, see also pp. 211–12.

[42]   'sainte', 'pure', 'glorieuse', 'bonne', 'juste', 'puissante', Gramont, *Olim*, pp. 162–4.

[43]   'bella', 'saggia', 'pura', 'santa', 'sola al mondo', 'chiara', *RVF* 366, vv. 1, 14, 27, 40, 53, 66.

Besides this *sestina* inspired by the language and structure of *RVF* 366, Gramont's third and last collection of poetry, *Olim*, bears only scattered, intermittent marks of discernibly Petrarchan influence, although in a sonnet in Italian published in this collection Gramont does present himself as 'an obscure priest' (*scuro sacerdote*) of the 'prophet' (*vate*) who is Petrarch.[44] Dedicated this time to the memory of his friend, *Olim* is composed principally of sonnets and *sestine*, including several of each in Italian.[45] Its title, as Gramont explains late on in the collection, signifies *Autrefois* ('in the past', 'formerly').[46] Appropriately, memory has a key role to play in much of this poetry, particularly in terms of nostalgia for a lost past (specifically, Gramont's birthplace Jersey), perhaps rendered newly compelling by the death of his mother.[47] Celebration of the past also inevitably results in strident criticism of a modern France that is seen to be in the thrall of scientific materialism and woefully alienated from Catholic values and beliefs. As one sonnet sarcastically reports, in a clear allusion to the ideas of Darwin, 'Science has spoken, man is but a brute / Who by selection is descended from the Barbary macaque.'[48]

Petrarchan aspects of the poems of *Olim* include the aforementioned *sestina* to the Virgin Mary, a sonnet in Italian addressed to Petrarch, and the volume's final poem which—as already noted in Chapter 1—is in praise of the *sestina* and names Petrarch amongst the form's illustrious devotees.[49] Beyond these three texts, Gramont's third collection also contains a sonnet which, if not as direct a rewriting of *RVF* 16 as in *Sonnets*, still calls out to a Petrarchan intertext in its opening lines:

> De penser en penser, de désir en désir,
> De crainte en espérance et d'espérance en crainte,
> Ainsi passe la vie en entier presque éteinte
> Qu'on ne sait même pas ce qu'on voudrait choisir.[50]

***

> From thought to thought, from desire to desire,
> From fear to hope and from hope to fear,
> Thus the whole of life passes by almost extinguished
> So that we do not even know what we would like to choose.

This sonnet begins as a literal translation of the start of *RVF* 129, *Di pensier in pensier* ('From thought to thought'), identical to the opening of Gramont's prose translation of this *canzone* from 1842.[51] Yet instead of proceeding to a spatialization of this restlessness as in the *canzone* by Petrarch (which continues *di monte in monte*, 'from

---

[44] Gramont, *Olim*, p. 169.

[45] For two *sestine* in Italian, see Gramont, *Olim*, pp. 82–4 and 166–8, and for sonnets in Italian, pp. 85–90 as well as p. 169.

[46] Gramont, *Olim*, p. 138 (Sonnet 91, v. 14).

[47] On Jersey, see Gramont, *Olim*, p. 58, and on the death of his mother pp. 109–10.

[48] 'La science a parlé, l'homme n'est qu'une brute / Qui par sélection procède du magot.' Gramont, *Olim*, p. 131 (Sonnet 87, vv. 1–2).

[49] See Gramont, *Olim*, pp. 171–2 (a poem entitled 'Post-scripta').

[50] Gramont, *Olim*, p. 80 (Sonnet 51, vv. 1–4).

[51] 'De penser en penser', Gramont, *Poésies de Pétrarque*, p. 97.

mountain to mountain'),[52] Gramont remains in an emotional limbo that in line two becomes a chiastic impasse and later in the sonnet is developed into an impossible, and classically Petrarchan, dilemma between virtue and pleasure. Still, for all these resonant moments, *Olim* does not come near to the sustained dialogue with Petrarch that we find in *Sonnets* or in *Chant du passé*, when Gramont was at the peak of his activities as a reader and translator of Petrarch.

Reading Gramont's own poetry is a salutary reminder that poetry and translation are not separate, hermetically sealed activities, but rather mutually formative and overlapping endeavours. This conclusion is one likely to have been borne out by consideration of the poetry of other translators of Petrarch, but it is particularly evident in the case of Gramont whose own poetry is particularly accomplished and a project of considerable longevity and uniformity. Other poet–translators such as Le Duc and Mahul will be encountered in the next section, which is devoted to a discussion of poetry written for and around anniversary celebrations of Petrarch's birth and death across the nineteenth century.

Anniversary Celebrations and Poetry Competitions

As already established in Part I, anniversary dates—1804, 1874, and 1904—were key catalysts for renewed interest in Petrarch throughout the nineteenth century. This interest manifested itself not only in further scholarship and new translations of Petrarch, as previous chapters have charted, but also in poetry dedicated to Petrarch and often written in response to poetry competitions linked to these same anniversary festivities, in particular those of 1874 and 1904. This section will first consider some of the poetry written on and for such occasions by two translators of Petrarch, Mahul and Le Duc, before focussing on the poetry competitions organized both in 1874 and 1904 on particular Petrarchan themes.

Atypically, I begin not in Avignon but in Arquà, with a sonnet in French written and recited by the translator Mahul on the occasion of the 1874 festivities held in the hilltop village that could boast both Petrarch's last home and his tomb.[53] This sonnet is of particular interest because, like Gramont's varied treatment of *RVF* 16, it once more straddles any ostensible divide between the co-extensive activities of translation and rewriting, in this instance by taking as its explicit source of inspiration a sonnet by Petrarch: *RVF* 333, itself originally addressed to Laura's grave.

RVF 333

> Ite, rime dolenti, al duro sasso
> che 'l mio caro thesoro in terra asconde,
> ivi chiamate chi dal ciel risponde,
> benché 'l mortal sia in loco oscuro et basso.

---

[52] 'de montagne, en montagne', Gramont, *Poésies de Pétrarque*, p. 97.

[53] 'Sonnet récité à Arquà devant la tombe de Pétrarque dans la cérémonie du centenaire le 18 juillet 1874 par Madame Emma Mahul des comtes Dejean, traductrice de Pétrarque: imitation du sonnet *Ite rime dolenti al duro sasso* appropriée à la tombe du Poëte', in Mahul, *Sonnets inédits traduits de Pétrarque* (1877), p. 231.

Ditele ch'i' son già di viver lasso,
del navigar per queste horribili onde;
ma ricogliendo le sue sparte fronde,
dietro le vo pur così passo passo,

sol di lei ragionando viva et morta,
anzi pur viva, et or fatta immortale,
a ciò che 'l mondo la conosca et ame.

Piacciale al mio passar esser accorta,
chè presso omai; siami a l'incontro, et quale
ella è nel cielo a sé mi tiri et chiame.

Mahul's rewriting

Allez, rimes de deuil, à cette dure pierre
Qui cache mon trésor dans une avare terre,
Appelez en pleurant qui vous répond du ciel
Bien qu'en ces lieux obscurs soit son voile mortel.

Dites-lui, dites-lui que je me désespère
Et suis las d'affronter les vents et l'onde amère,
Mais que pour recueillir son feuillage immortel
Je reviens sur ses pas dans mon exil cruel.

De *lui seul trépassé* repaîssant ma pensée...
Trépassé... Non ! là-haut sa gloire est commencée,
Le monde va par moi le connaître et l'aimer.

Qu'*il* me soit favorable au moment du passage
Si prochain désormais ; que sa voix m'encourage ;
Ah ! puisse-t-*il* vers moi descendre et me nommer ![54]

***

Go, poems of grief, to that hard stone
That hides my treasure in an avaricious earth,
Call whilst crying to the one who replies to you from Heaven
Although in these dark places is *his* mortal veil.

Tell *him*, tell *him* that I am desperate
And tired of facing the winds and the bitter waves,
But that in order to gather up *his* immortal foliage
I have retraced my steps in my cruel exile.

[54] Mahul, *Sonnets inédits traduits de Pétrarque* (1877), p. 231 (emphases in the original). Note that in my English translation the regendering of the addressee has been necessary earlier and more frequently than in Mahul's rewriting because of the lack of similar neutrality of *lui* (the third-person indirect object pronoun of line five) and, more problematically for such a reworking in English, because of the agreement of the possessive pronoun in English with the subject rather than the object. For an English translation of *RVF* 333, see Chapter 4.

On *him alone passed away* feasting my thoughts...
Passed away... No! Up there *his* glory has begun,
The world through me is going to know and love *him*.

May *he* be favourable to me at the point of passage
Which is by now so close; may *his* voice encourage me;
Oh! May *he* descend towards me and call out my name.

Mahul's reworking is largely identical to her earlier translation of *RVF* 333, which is included in three of her four previous volumes of translations of Petrarch's sonnets.[55] The only deviations are marked by the translator herself in the new version in italics, and are all to be found in the sestet; the majority involve a change in pronoun since the poem's addressee is no longer Laura but Petrarch, although the first two lines of the sestet have also been amended.[56] This newly minted sonnet works beautifully as a translator's manifesto, for not only does the translator speak to the silent, deceased poet, in the place and with the words of that same poet, but the promise of line eleven boldly emphasizes the role of translation in ensuring the poet's posterity: 'The world through me [that is, through translation] is going to know and love *him*.'

On the one hand, Mahul herself steps back a little from such a claim, by failing to inscribe her own gender into the new version of the sonnet. Despite the liberties taken with subject pronouns in the sestet in order to make space for Petrarch, Mahul (at a minimum, for metrical reasons) does not add to the adjective *las* ('tired') in line six the obligatory feminine ending which would solidify the identification between translator and first-person speaker. From this perspective, the *je* of the new poem both is Mahul (she, after all, is both author and reciter of the text) and is not Mahul, but rather stands for a more generalized, male (neutral) figure come to pay homage to Petrarch. On the other hand, however, Mahul is no wallflower in this poem. The *je* is figured as motivated by the desire 'to gather up *his* [Petrarch's] immortal foliage' (*recueillir son feuillage immortel*, v. 7), with the implications that this poem records, in part, a quest for the laurel crown and coronation. This is the crown which Petrarch has dropped (either through death or on the ascent of his spirit to Heaven) and which his translator promises to pick up, thereby suggesting that translation, too, is deserving of laureation. The poem ends with the translator's desire to be named (v. 8) by Petrarch, a further attempt to secure glory and approval from the subject of the poem's eulogy through a process of election and filiation.

Further complications arise in this rewriting in terms of the interaction between geography and language. The original Italian sonnet is addressed to Laura's grave, a 'hard stone' (*duro sasso*, v. 1) located vaguely 'in earth' (*in terra*, v. 2) and 'in a

---

[55]   For Mahul's translation of *RVF* 333, see Mahul, *Choix de sonnets de Pétrarque* (1867), p. 103, and *Choix de sonnets* (1869), p. 143. An earlier version of the same sonnet can also be found in [Mahul], *Cent cinquante sonnets*, p. 301, with the main difference from the later translation being that the first version (from 1847) begins 'Allez, vers douloureux', rather than 'Allez, rimes de deuil' (as in both the 1867 and 1869 versions).

[56]   In Mahul's original translation (in all three published versions), these lines read, instead, 'D'*Elle* seule parlant, vivante ou trépassée, / —Vivante... Eh ! quoi ? là-haut sa gloire est commencée' ('Of *Her* alone speaking, living or dead, / —Living... Yes indeed! Up there her glory has begun').

dark and low place' (*in loco oscuro et basso*, v. 4). As charted in the Introduction, Laura's place of burial was a key piece of evidence in the *querelle* over the identity and marital status of Petrarch's beloved, though little practical information can be gleaned from this sonnet. In Mahul's rewriting, these spatial indications are intensified, firstly with the added adjective *avare* ('an avaricious earth', v. 2), a phrase which Mahul transplants from the opening line of *RVF* 300, an earlier sonnet also about Laura's grave.[57] Secondly, Mahul turns the phrase *loco oscuro et basso* into a plural reinforced by a deictic demonstrative adjective: 'these dark places' (*ces lieux obscurs*). These changes have an odd effect in a sonnet explicitly designed to celebrate Petrarch's tomb at Arquà, since they suggest that his gravesite is neither as noble nor as desirable as might have been expected. Through its French rewriting, the original resentment expressed by the Italian poet towards the ground that encloses his deceased French beloved is transformed into the expression by a French translator, representing her nation at these Italian celebrations, of jealousy towards Arquà for keeping the treasure (*trésor*, v. 2) of Petrarch's body from Avignon. On closer consideration, Arquà emerges, in this new sonnet, as avaricious (*avare*) and obscure (*obscur*), insults which are further complemented by the translator's lament of her own 'cruel exile' (*mon exil cruel*, v. 8), the exile of a French speaker in northern Italy.

While Mahul remained, despite these subtle complications, an honoured guest in Arquà, the 1874 celebrations in Avignon brought to prominence another translator of Petrarch's sonnets: Philibert Le Duc. Le Duc's two-volume translation of the three hundred and seventeen sonnets of the *Canzoniere* (*Les Sonnets de Pétrarque*, 1877–9) was a direct outcome of the warm reception that his work as a translator of Petrarch had had back in 1874. Like Mahul, Le Duc's final volume of translations also includes an appendix of poems written in honour of the same Petrarchan anniversary.[58] Of particular interest among Le Duc's own poetry featured in this appendix is a sonnet which reflects on Petrarch's dislike of Avignon, a topic already explored in Chapter 4. Introducing this sonnet, Le Duc explains that he wrote it out a fragile desire for reconciliation between Petrarch and Avignon: 'It seemed to me that the shade of the poet must have regretted his invectives when he saw with what enthusiasm his memory was honoured.'[59] The sonnet is dedicated to Berluc-Pérussis, organizer of the 1874 festivities and founder of the *Almanach du sonnet*, has the title 'Posthumous regret' (*Regret posthume*), and is dated Avignon, 19 July 1874, that is, from the heart of the celebrations:

> Pays des esprits vifs et du bleu firmament,
> Sois bénie à jamais, poétique Provence !

---

[57]   See *RVF* 300, v. 1: 'Quanta invidia io ti porto, avara terra' ('How much envy I bear towards you, avaricious earth'). This line is translated by Mahul as 'Combien je te l'envie, ô terre, avare terre !' in the first volume of her translations of Petrarch's sonnets: [Mahul], *Cent cinquante sonnets* (1847), p. 267. The adjective 'avara' also appears at the start of *RVF* 137 ('L'avara Babilonia', 'Avaricious Babylon').

[58]   'Appendice: Fêtes de Vaucluse et d'Avignon: Sonnets à Pétrarque et à Laure', in Le Duc, *Les Sonnets de Pétrarque*, II, 351–82.

[59]   'Il me sembla que l'ombre du poëte devait regretter ses invectives en voyant avec quel enthousiasme sa mémoire était honorée.' Le Duc, *Les Sonnets de Pétrarque*, II, 360.

Cinq siècles ont passé, le sixième s'avance
Depuis qu'ici l'amour fut chanté chastement.

Et tu fêtes encor le platonique amant !
À l'envi chaque muse apporte sa chevance,
Et des flots de sonnets, comme l'eau de Jouvence,
Rajeunissent sa gloire et son couronnement.

Pourtant le doux Pétrarque avec d'acerbes rimes
De Babylone un jour t'a reproché les crimes,
Et trois fois t'a maudite, ô papale cité !

Ah ! qu'il regretterait ses paroles blessantes,
S'il voyait à présent tant d'âmes frémissantes,
Fières de rendre hommage à sa célébrité ![60]

***

Land of lively minds and a blue firmament,
Be forever blessed, poetic Provence!
Five centuries have passed, and the sixth is underway
Since here love was chastely sung.

And still you celebrate the Platonic lover!
Again and again every muse brings her offerings,
And from the floods of sonnets, like the water of Jouvence,
His glory and coronation are renewed.

Yet gentle Petrarch with bitter rhymes
Of the crimes of Babylon did once reproach you,
And three times did curse you, O papal city!

Oh! How he would regret his hurtful words,
If could see today so many trembling souls,
Proud to offer homage to his celebrity!

In this way, poetry is a further tool in the wider project of dismantling and defusing the tensions of the three anti-Avignon sonnets of the *Canzoniere*, already charted in Chapter 4.

After giving space to his own memories of and poetic response to the festivities, Le Duc devotes the remainder of the appendix to sonnets about Petrarch and Laura written on the occasion of the anniversary by poets other than himself, nineteen in French and the final two in Italian and Provençal respectively.[61] Constant among these sonnets is a celebration of Vaucluse and the Provençal landscape, as well as an idealization of Petrarch's love and Laura's beauty. Here, then, is a much more familiar and even stereotypical poetic image of Petrarch than previously encountered, for

[60] Le Duc, *Les Sonnets de Pétrarque*, II, 361.
[61] 'Sonnets à Pétrarque et à Laure', in Le Duc, *Les Sonnets de Pétrarque*, II, 365–82.

instance, in the poetry of Gramont. Unsurprisingly, these sonnets repeatedly assert the French claim on Petrarch, as the following sonnet attests:

> De saint Pierre le Rhône avait reçu la barque,
> Et les papes français se faisaient provençaux,
> Lorsqu'un vendredi saint tu vis Laure, ô Pétrarque ;
> Cinq siècles ont, depuis, passé sur vos tombeaux.
>
> Trop loin d'elle, tu dors sur la colline d'Arque ;
> Vaucluse te rappelle au milieu de ses eaux ;
> Les sonneurs de sonnets t'y nomment leur monarque,
> Viens compter tes sujets dans ces chanteurs nouveaux.
>
> Au bruit de nos concerts, dont elle semble fière,
> Ta dame, secouant son antique poussière,
> Se lève du cercueil que lui garde Avignon.
>
> Triomphe du sonnet qui la rend immortelle !
> La voici, grâce aux vers qui célèbrent son nom,
> Vieille de cinq cents ans, mais toujours jeune et belle.[62]

∗∗∗

> Of Saint Peter the Rhône had received the ship,
> And the French popes were making themselves Provençal,
> When one Good Friday you saw Laura, O Petrarch;
> Five centuries have, since, passed over your graves.
>
> Too far from her, you sleep on the hill of Arquà;
> Vaucluse is calling you back in the middle of her waters;
> There the sonnet-ringers name you their monarch,
> Come count your subjects in these new singers.
>
> At the sound of our concerts, of which she seems proud,
> Your lady, shaking off the ancient dust,
> Gets up from the grave which Avignon has kept for her.
>
> Triumph of the sonnet which makes her beautiful!
> There she is, thanks to the verses which celebrate her name,
> Five hundred years old, but still young and beautiful.

In this poem, Edmond Lafond vocalizes explicitly the competing claims of Arquà and Avignon on Petrarch, claims which we have already found to be implicit in Mahul's French version of *RVF* 333. In Lafond's sonnet, the poet's death and entombment in Italy are portrayed not as some sort of homecoming (even if Arquà was not,

---

[62] Lafond, 'Le centenaire de Pétrarque', in Le Duc, *Les Sonnets de Pétrarque*, II, 375–6. This sonnet, as Le Duc records in a footnote, was awarded third prize and a silver medal under the category 'Sonnet about Petrarch' (*Sonnet sur Pétrarque*). Its author is comte Lafond, that is Edmond Lafond, author with his uncle Ernest of the volume of translations including Petrarch discussed in Chapter 2: *Dante, Pétrarque, Michel-Ange, Tasse* (1848).

after all, Florence), but rather as a culpable abandonment of and estrangement from Petrarch's French ties, amongst which most potently, of course, Laura. Giving full credence to the identity of Laura promulgated first by Maurice Scève (who claimed to have found Laura's grave in a church in Avignon in 1533) and later by the abbé de Sade (who consolidated the Avignonese identity of Laura), Lafond posits Laura's gravesite in opposition to Petrarch's and, in so doing, reinforces the association between Avignon and Petrarch, so vital to the anniversary celebrations. Finally, these same celebrations are depicted in this sonnet as a form of resuscitation or resurrection from the dead, a powerful image of the new life which the festivities sought to bestow on both Petrarch and his ever beautiful muse. Poetry is a potent elixir for eternal youth.

Further poetry written for the 1874 festivities can be found, along with the festival programme and many speeches, in two commemorative volumes published as a record of the events.[63] This poetry was solicited by the organizers in either French, Provençal, or Italian, and included, as well as an open category, the following two strands: poems in honour of Clémence Isaure; poems about either Petrarch's garden or respect for small birds.[64] The first topic celebrates a mythical lady from Toulouse credited with founding the city's own ancient, annual poetry competition, the *Jeux floraux*. This addressee may seem a strange and un-Petrarchan choice, perhaps even suggesting that Laura had a rival in the hearts of her Provençal admirers, even at celebrations at least partly in her honour. Much of the motivation behind such a choice must, however, have been the desire not only to celebrate, once more, local culture and history, but also to grant the poetry competition itself a certain legitimacy and grandeur that it might otherwise have lacked, being in truth newly instituted and without the illustrious tradition of Toulouse's *Jeux*. Besides, Clémence is invoked by one of the winning entries in a manner designed precisely to dispel fears that she might prove a rival to Laura: 'O Laura, O Beatrice, sisters of Isaure and of the angels'.[65] All three famous, ancient beloveds are thus invoked as harmonious, divine patrons of poetry.

The second theme of the competition invokes two pastoral but quite diverse topics: as noted above, Petrarch's garden, and respect for small birds. The latter is, rather like the choice of Clémence Isaure, somewhat unexpected, though it may stem either from sonnets in which Petrarch himself addresses a bird (for instance *RVF* 353, which begins *Vago augelletto che cantando vai*, 'Wandering little bird who goes singing') or, more generally, from poems which feature birdsong—and *augelletti* specifically—as part of an idyllic, lyric landscape.[66] The former topic, however, anchors Petrarch firmly to a local, Provençal landscape, and celebrates his French

---

[63] *Fêtes littéraires & internationales; Fête séculaire et internationale*, ed. Berluc-Perussis and Guillibert.

[64] For the poems in honour of Clémence Isaure, see *Fêtes littéraires & internationales*, pp. 202–18, and for those in the second category (*le Jardin de Pétrarque, et Respect aux petits oiseaux*), see pp. 224–32.

[65] 'Ô Laure, ô Béatrix, sœurs d'Isaure et des anges'. This line appears in a poem 'À Clémence Isaure' by d'Audeville which was joint third in this particular category (*Fêtes littéraires & internationales*, pp. 213–18, with the quotation on p. 217).

[66] See, for example, *RVF* 239, v. 3; 280, v. 10; 310, v. 12.

roots both literally and metaphorically, since one of the attractions of a pilgrimage to the source of the Sorgue was the possibility of communing with the very laurel trees (or descendants thereof) that Petrarch himself had reputedly planted with his own hands out of love for Laura.[67]

The already noted linguistic variety of the competition criteria promised a coming together of three distinct languages and literary traditions, namely French, Italian, and Provençal, with the last, in particular, a result and sign of the intense involvement of the Félibrige, led by Mistral, at these festivities. In practice, however, it is reported that no poems in Italian were judged worthy of any prizes, although from the tone of this information it is difficult to tell whether this omission marks a pointed refusal to participate in the French proceedings on the part of the Italian jury, or was, alternatively, an engineered and anticipated consequence of the inherently pro-Provençal set up: 'The Royal Accademia della Crusca, charged with judging the 173 pieces submitted to the competition, has decided, following the report which it has had the honour of presenting to the literary committee, that none of these pieces seemed in its opinion worthy of being awarded a prize.'[68] Between the French and Provençal poetry, there was, in contrast, almost parity quantitatively, in terms of prizes, although commentators naturally made different value judgements as to the quality of the poems in each language. For Roulleaux, as cited in Chapter 4, the sound of 'so many Provençal verses' (*tant de vers provençaux*) provoked indigestion,[69] whereas, of a decidedly antithetical opinion, the pro-Félibrige Paul Glaize recorded that 'the French poetry had in general, in the competition, borne a marked inferiority compared to the inspired Provençal submissions [*des inspirations provençales*]'.[70] Less partisan but wholly damning is, moreover, a much later assessment of the 1874 festivities from Alphonse Roche, who declared—rather ungenerously—that 'nothing of particular interest on Petrarch and his works was said or written on this occasion'.[71] Regardless of such criticisms, however, the assessment of Auguste Laforêt at the time remains useful and perspicacious:

> The result of this enthusiasm was a total of one thousand and seventy pieces: sonnets in French, Italian, and Provençal, odes in the same languages, translations, pieces of various genres.
>   Undoubtedly, quantity and quality are not the same thing:
>   *Sunt bona, sunt quaedam mediocria, sunt....*[72]

---

[67] For discussion of Petrarch as gardener see 'Excursus II: Pétrarque jardinier', in Nolhac, *Pétrarque et l'humanisme*, ii, 259–68.

[68] 'L'Académie royale de la Crusca, chargée de juger les 173 pièces envoyées au concours, a décidé, suivant le rapport qu'elle a fait l'honneur d'adresser au Comité littéraire, qu'aucune de ces pièces ne lui paraissait digne d'être couronnée.' *Fêtes littéraires & internationales*, p. 233.

[69] Roulleaux, *Pétrarque et les fêtes du centenaire*, p. 41.

[70] 'La poésie française avait gardé en général, dans le concours, une infériorité marquée vis-à-vis des inspirations provençales', Glaize, 'Le centenaire de Pétrarque', p. 280.

[71] Roche, 'Petrarch and the Felibres', p. 5.

[72] This line in Latin is the beginning of an epigram from Martial which reads in full 'Sunt bona, sunt quaedam mediocria, sunt mala plura quae legis hic: aliter non fit, Avite,

But, in the present circumstance, quantity, by itself, is meaningful, wide-reaching, and valuable.[73]

Unlike the rather idiosyncratic topics of the 1874 poetry competition, the competition held on the occasion of the next significant Petrarchan anniversary, six hundred years since the poet's birth, was conceived along much more canonical lines. For the 1904 celebrations, individuals were invited to submit poems of no longer than 150 lines, in either French or Provençal, in response to the following, eminently Petrarchan themes:

> Laura's eyes: what they inspire and what they say. (Petrarch wrote on the song of the eyes three poems which Italians call the Three Sisters or the Three Graces. The abbé de Sade has translated them.)
> Petrarch's garden and the symbolic laurel.
> Petrarch's dream (Vision of the death of Laura).
> Petrarch at the Capitol.
> Ode to the Fontaine de Vaucluse.[74]

The second suggested topic, Petrarch's garden, obviously reiterates one of the three themes from the 1874 competition, albeit with the clarification, left implicit in the earlier guidelines, that this garden should not only include a laurel, but that this laurel ought to be symbolic, thereby pointing towards the laurel's inevitable associations with both Laura and poetry. The remaining topics, meanwhile, are even more deeply rooted in Petrarch's life and works, with the former most evident in the subject of 'Petrarch at the Capitol', that is, the poet's coronation on the Capitoline Hill in Rome in 1341 (an event that, later in this chapter, we will find already discussed by Musset and transposed into poetry by Gautier). The first suggested subject matter, Laura's eyes, is explicitly connected to a set of three well-known poems from Petrarch's *Canzoniere*: *RVF* 71–3. Surprisingly, Sade's translation is still the sole point of reference here, 140 years after its publication (in volume one of his *Mémoires*), despite the many French translations of Petrarch's *Canzoniere* published in the intervening decades. Indeed, the reference to Sade is even more surprising if

---

liber' ('There are good things that you read here, and some indifferent, and more bad. Not otherwise, Avitus, is a book made'). Martial, *Epigrams*, trans. D. R. Shackleton Bailey, 3 vols (Cambridge, MA: Harvard University Press, 1993), I, 52, 53.

[73] 'Le résultat de cet empressement a été un total de mille et soixante-dix pièces : sonnets français, italiens, provençaux, odes dans les même langues, traductions, pièces de divers genres. Sans doute, quantité et qualité ne sont pas une même chose : *Sunt bona, sunt quaedam mediocria, sunt....* Mais, dans la circonstance actuelle, la quantité, par elle seule, a une signification, une portée, une valeur.' Auguste Laforêt, 'Cinquième centenaire de Pétrarque: fêtes de Vaucluse–Avignon les 18, 19, et 20 juillet 1874', in *Revue de Marseille et de Provence fondée et publiée au profit des pauvres*, 20.7 (July 1874), 361–76 (pp. 362–3).

[74] 'Les yeux de Laure : ce qu'ils inspirent et ce qu'ils disent. (Pétrarque a composé sur la chanson des yeux trois poésies que les Italiens appellent les Trois Sœurs ou les Trois Grâces. L'abbé de Sade les a traduites.) / Le jardin de Pétrarque et le laurier symbolique. / Le songe de Pétrarque (Vision de la mort de Laure). / Pétrarque au capitole. / Ode à la Fontaine de Vaucluse.' Académie de Vaucluse, *Sixième centenaire de la naissance de Pétrarque*, p. 9.

we recall that—as discussed in Chapter 2—his translation of 'the Three Graces' is, in fact, an amalgamation of the three texts into one super-poem. From this perspective, the organizers' wish to direct potential competitors to Sade's potted version of the three *canzoni* is perplexing, to say the least, and bespeaks the undimmed importance and authority that Sade's *Mémoires* continued to wield amongst French Petrarchists even into the twentieth century.

In addition to the explicit reference to *RVF* 71–3, and indeed to a specific translation thereof, other poems from the *Canzoniere* are also alluded to in the remaining chosen themes, 'Petrarch's dream' and 'Ode to the Fontaine de Vaucluse'. The latter is strongly reminiscent of *RVF* 126, a *canzone* which, as we have seen, was often retitled in French translation *À la fontaine de Vaucluse*, and was popularized by Voltaire. The former, 'Petrarch's dream', qualified parenthetically as a 'Vision of the death of Laura', recalls, instead, a number of different texts: *RVF* 250, the sonnet in which Laura appears to the poet in a dream and warns him not to expect to see her alive on Earth again; *RVF* 302, cited in Chapter 2 as a favourite amongst translators, in which the poet is visited by Laura's spirit again in a dream and reassured that he will one day be with her in Heaven; and the *Triumphus Mortis*, with which *RVF* 302 was often connected, and in which the poet has a vision, in yet another dream, of Laura's death. The choice of themes for the 1904 poetry competition thus reflects, much more directly and closely than the 1874 competition, poems from the *Canzoniere* towards which French translators throughout the previous century had already manifested a marked predilection. The 1904 competition thereby seems to require greater textual knowledge of Petrarch's poetry (even in translation, with a special recommendation of Sade) than had the earlier competition.

Amongst the prize-winning poems in Provençal, first prize was awarded to a poem on the theme of 'Petrarch at the Capitol', by one François Favier of Avignon.[75] In contrast, no first prize was awarded for any poem in French, although there were joint second, third, and fourth winners in this category.[76] In this manner, celebration of the Provençal language and local culture continued to be a driving force for the festivities, even if the initial fervour of the Félibrige that had animated the 1874 events and activities had somewhat died down. In 1904, moreover, poems in Italian were no longer solicited, no doubt an inevitable consequence of the Accademia della Crusca's already noted refusal to participate or collaborate on the occasion of the earlier anniversary celebrations of 1874.

These poetry competitions might, ultimately, seem like provincial affairs intent on bringing to light local, amateur poets. However, one crucial exception from early in the nineteenth century suggests the surprising reach and potential of these competitions. This exception is a mere two lines of poetry, easy to overlook had they not been from the pen of Lamartine. Lamartine first expressed his intention to write something in praise of Petrarch in a letter to his friend Aymon de Virieu dated Mâcon, 30 September 1810:

[75] Académie de Vaucluse, *Sixième centenaire de la naissance de Pétrarque*, pp. 36–9.
[76] 'Poésie française / Pas de premier prix.' Académie de Vaucluse, *Sixième centenaire de la naissance de Pétrarque*, p. 111.

I receive at the present time the gazettes, and I have read in them that the Athénée de Vaucluse is proposing a eulogy for Petrarch or a poem in his honour which must not be longer than two hundred lines. The prize is a medal worth 300 francs. The work must be submitted by the first of May. Send me, I beg you, a note of your own devising on Petrarch, his life, his *works*, his good points [*qualités*], etc. I want to take part, and I don't know much at all about him except his Laura and his sonnets. You should enter as well; what do you think, and what would you advise me, poetry or prose?[77]

Later that same year, on 12 December, Lamartine wrote again to share with the same friend the meagre two lines that he had thus far managed, and to reiterate his appeal for help:

> Sur les bords que Vaucluse arrose,
> Beaux lieux qu'ont illustrés de touchants souvenirs !

> On the banks that Vaucluse waters,
> Beautiful places which have illustrated touching memories!

You see that I have started my piece for the Athénée d'Avignon. Where is yours? Mine is stuck at these two lines; for two months I have hardly known what to say. I'm not sufficiently Italian to be able to read fluently the works by Petrarch about which it is necessary that I should speak as an expert. Help me then with some notes, and I will continue. Is it not a shame to stop on such a beautiful path?[78]

Perhaps Virieu knew no more about Petrarch than Lamartine, or Lamartine got distracted by other projects. Either way, Lamartine's writer's block in this regard, not to mention his false start seemingly confusing Vaucluse with the Sorgue, was to prove insurmountable, leaving us with only tantalizing crumbs of how this poem might eventually have developed, and depriving nineteenth-century Petrarchan poetry competitions of their most prestigious participant.

---

[77] 'Je reçois en ce moment les gazettes, et j'y lis que l'Athénée de Vaucluse propose un éloge en prose de Pétrarque ou un poème en son honneur qui ne doit pas passer deux cents vers. Le prix est une médaille de 300 fr. L'ouvrage doit être remis le premier de mai. Envoie-moi, je t'en prie, une notice de ta façon sur Pétrarque, sa vie, ses *ouvrages*, ses qualités, etc. J'ai envie de concourir, et je ne sais pas grand-chose de lui que sa Laure et ses sonnets. Tu devrais concourir aussi ; qu'en dis-tu, et que me conseilles-tu, vers ou prose ?' *Correspondance d'Alphonse de Lamartine: deuxième série (1807–1829)*, ed. Christian Croisille and Marie-Renée Morin, 5 vols (Paris: Honoré Champion, 2004–7), I, 255.

[78] 'Tu vois que j'ai commencé ma pièce pour l'Athénée d'Avignon. Où en est la tienne ? La mienne en reste à ces deux vers ; depuis deux mois je ne sais trop que dire. Je ne suis pas assez italien pour lire couramment les ouvrages de Pétrarque dont il faut bien que je parle en connaisseur. Aide-moi donc de quelques notes, et je continuerai. N'est-il pas dommage de s'arrêter en si beau chemin ?' *Correspondance d'Alphonse de Lamartine: deuxième série*, I, 259–60. The two lines are also reprinted in Lamartine, *Œuvres poétiques*, ed. Marius-François Guyard (Paris: Gallimard, 1963), p. 1636, with the title 'Éloge de Pétrarque'.

In the Margins: The Case of Lamartine

As cited in the epigraph to the Introduction, it was Lamartine who declared that 'The nineteenth century needed its own Petrarch.' In truth, this statement was made in a letter to Évariste Boulay-Paty dated 8 August 1851 and beginning 'My dear Petrarch'; in this context, the quotation originally read, more fully 'The nineteenth century needed its own Petrarch. You are he.'[79] Thus, Lamartine's point was not merely that every century wants its own Petrarch (both its own version of Petrarch and a new poet who can equal Petrarch), but rather that this desire had, in his opinion, been fulfilled by none other than Boulay-Paty, author, most memorably, of *Sonnets de la vie humaine* (1852; *Sonnets on Human Life*), as well as of a translation of a sonnet by Petrarch admired and adopted by Lamartine.[80] Nonetheless, Lamartine's comment might equally be turned back on himself, for his own *Méditations poétiques* (1820; *Poetic Meditations*) have often been considered a highly Petrarchan celebration of nature, solitude, memory, and grief.[81] That Lamartine wants us to read his poetry in this light is, moreover, suggested by the explicit comparison he himself establishes in the poem 'À Elvire' between his eponymous muse and Petrarch's Laura, in terms of the power of poetry to immortalize the names of both lover and beloved; 'Vaucluse has retained the cherished name of Laura', Lamartine notes, just as he hopes that, through his own poetry, Elvire will live forever.[82]

At the end of the previous section, we noted that at the end of 1810 Lamartine had declared himself to be 'not sufficiently Italian' (*pas assez italien*) to understand Petrarch's *Canzoniere* in the original. In fairness to Lamartine, it ought also to be recalled that, at that early point in the nineteenth century, there were few options (save Sade) for French readers such as Lamartine other than braving Petrarch in the original Italian. By late March 1813, however, this is a challenge in which Lamartine has gained considerable confidence, as a later letter to Virieu attests:

> I am reading Petrarch's sonnets, which I hardly understood at all in Italy and which I used to find poor. Now I understand them as if they were in French [*comme du français*], I do not know why, and I find delightful things in them. There is a time for everything, and such and such a disposition of soul or spirit leads us to find a man or a book either repugnant or enjoyable.[83]

---

[79] 'Mon cher Pétrarque', 'Il fallait au 19ème siècle son Pétrarque. Vous l'êtes.' *Correspondance d'Alphonse de Lamartine (1830–1867)*, VI, 232.

[80] Lamartine cites in full Boulay-Paty's verse translation of *RVF* 301 in his *Cours familier de littérature*, VI, 78–9. In his own right Boulay-Baty published first *Sonnets* (Paris: H. Féret, 1851), then a new edition under the amended title the following year: *Sonnets de la vie humaine* (Paris: Firmin Didot frères, 1852).

[81] See, for instance, Jacqueline Bloncourt-Herselin, *Lamartine et l'Italie* (Paris: Le Cerf-Volant, 1970), pp. 36–9, and Charles Dédéyan, *Lamartine et la Toscane* (Moncalieri: Centro interuniversitario di ricerche sul 'Viaggio in Italia'; Geneva: Slatkine, 1981), pp. 112–15. This subject remains, nonetheless, one that would be worth further exploration.

[82] 'Vaucluse a retenu le nom chéri de Laure', Lamartine, *Œuvres poétiques*, p. 12.

[83] 'Je lis des sonnets de Pétrarque, que je n'entendais guère en Italie et que je trouvais mauvais. Je les entends maintenant comme du français, je ne sais pourquoi, et j'y trouve des choses ravissantes. Il y a un temps pour tout, et telle ou telle disposition de l'âme ou de l'esprit

Undoubtedly, Lamartine's travels in Italy between July 1811 and April 1812 must have been a key contributing factor in his improved linguistic fluency, even if—as he records here—his time abroad did not, at first, endear him to Petrarch. From 1813 onwards, however, his appreciation of Petrarch was only to increase, while his confidence in Italian must have continued to be bolstered by subsequent diplomatic appointments in Italy, particularly in Florence, where he was resident between October 1825 and August 1828. This newfound love of Petrarch is audible throughout Lamartine's published work from the early success of the *Méditations poétiques* to his much later, financially motivated *Cours familier de littérature*. This last was circulated in monthly instalments from March 1856 up to the year of his death (1869), and its thirty-first and thirty-second chapters (*entretiens*), published in 1858, are dedicated to Petrarch's life and works.[84] Lamartine has made marked progress since his inability to formulate more than two lines in honour of Petrarch back in 1810. From his position as an ignorant student of Petrarch begging help from a friend, Lamartine has become an educator with ambitions for a wide and varied readership via subscription.

In this section, I will first consider the image of Petrarch painted by Lamartine in the two chapters of the *Cours familier* dedicated to the medieval poet, before discussing some of the poems that Lamartine wrote in the margins of his own copies of Petrarch's Italian poetry. Lamartine certainly had an essential role to play in establishing Petrarch as a source of inspiration for French Romanticism, one consequence of which was the recurrent naming of Petrarch 'In the Canon' (see the following section of this chapter), by poets such as Hugo, Musset, and Gautier. Yet the phrase 'In the Margins' conveys one key aspect of Lamartine's engagement with Petrarch, the later poet's habit of writing in the actual margins and on blank pages of his copies of Petrarch, a practice which Hugo was also to imitate and repeat in his own poem 'Écrit sur la première page d'un Pétrarque' ('Written on the first page of a Petrarch'), discussed in due course.

Lamartine begins his written lectures on Petrarch distinguishing between two types of love, 'sensual love and love between souls', and firmly places Petrarch as a 'psalmist' of the latter category.[85] The Petrarch that emerges from Lamartine's lessons is a Platonic, spiritual, devoted, and devotional figure. Purity and pureness are key concepts throughout the two chapters, and are applied in turn to Petrarch, to his poetry, to Laura, and to their love. Accordingly, Lamartine asserts that 'Laura for Petrarch is not a woman, but rather an incarnation of beauty, in which he adores the divinity of love.'[86] Yet there is never any doubt in Lamartine's mind that Laura was certainly also a woman, and more specifically his very own maternal ancestor

---

nous donne de la répugnance ou du goût pour un homme ou pour un livre.' *Correspondance d'Alphonse de Lamartine: deuxième série*, I, 409 (letter begun on 27 March 1813 and continued on 28 March).

[84]   Lamartine, 'Vie et œuvres de Pétrarque', in *Cours familier de littérature*, VI, 1–155.

[85]   'l'amour des sens et l'amour des âmes', 'psalmiste de l'amour des âmes', Lamartine, *Cours familier de littérature*, VI, 1, 3. On Petrarch in the *Cours familier*, see also Duperray, *L'Or des mots*, pp. 133–43.

[86]   'Laure pour lui n'est pas une femme, c'est une incarnation du beau, dans laquelle il adore la divinité de l'amour.' Lamartine, *Cours familier de littérature*, VI, 3.

via the genealogy established by the abbé de Sade, as already noted in the Introduction.[87] It is likely that Sade's *Mémoires* provided much of the material for Lamartine's own brief history of Petrarch's life.

Beyond the bare, purported facts of this life, Lamartine litters his text with fervent admiration for the medieval poet and his vernacular poetry, again in stark contrast to his own writer's block back in 1810 when faced with the comparable task of writing a piece, in either verse or prose, in honour of Petrarch. Over half a century later, Lamartine is newly eloquent and impassioned, declaring, for instance, that 'As for me, I consider Petrarch, without any possible comparison, as the most perfect poet of the soul of all times and all countries, since the death of the gentle Virgil.'[88] For Lamartine, Petrarch's *Canzoniere* truly provides an unparalleled linguistic repertory of human emotion, being replete, for him, with verses which are deemed so true and absolute as to function as 'proverbs of love and grief'.[89] Even more explicitly, Lamartine concludes his discussion of Petrarch in the *Cours familier* by suggesting that Petrarch's poems, in particular his sonnets, are an ideal companion through life's trials and tribulations: 'The sonnets of the poet of Vaucluse are a manual which should be carried in one's heart and in one's memory like a confidant or a consoler through all the vicissitudes of human attachments.'[90]

For Lamartine himself, it seems that Petrarch was, furthermore, an author that he carried not only in his heart and mind but also in his pocket.[91] Of the two editions of Petrarch's Italian poetry definitively known to have been in Lamartine's possession, one is a pocket edition from 1809–10 (perhaps purchased around the time he was seeking to learn more about Petrarch for the Athénée de Vaucluse's poetry competition), and both contain marginal annotations that testify to Lamartine's active use of these volumes.[92] Lamartine's marginalia do not, however, fit the usual purpose of this form (typically, the reader's space to comment, highlight, query, and respond to the published text); instead, he frequently adopts margins and blank pages in his copies of Petrarch as places for the elaboration and recording of his own poetry.

For evidence, we can turn first to Lamartine's own accounts of the gestation of parts of his poetry. Thus, in a letter to Antoine de Latour dated 22 November 1835,

---

[87]   Lamartine, *Cours familier de littérature*, vi, 14.

[88]   'Quant à moi, je considère Pétrarque, sans aucune comparaison possible, comme le plus parfait poëte de l'âme de tous les temps et de tous les pays, depuis la mort du doux Virgile.' *Cours familier de littérature*, vi, 4.

[89]   'les proverbes de l'amour et de la douleur', Lamartine, *Cours familier de littérature*, vi, 4.

[90]   'Les sonnets du poëte de Vaucluse sont un manuel qu'il faut porter sur son cœur ou dans sa mémoire comme un confident ou un consolateur dans toutes les vicissitudes des attachements humains.' Lamartine, *Cours familier de littérature*, vi, 155.

[91]   As Maurice Toesca remarks in *Lamartine ou l'amour de la vie* (Paris: Albin Michel, 1969), p. 222, Lamartine always carried a pocket copy of Petrarch with him ('il en porte toujours un petit exemplaire sur lui').

[92]   For details of the various editions, see Henri Guillemin, *Le Jocelyn de Lamartine: étude historique et critique avec des documents inédits* (Paris: Boivin et Cie, 1936), p. 600, n. 2, as well as Léon Séché, *Études d'histoire romantique: Lamartine de 1816 à 1830: Elvire et les 'Méditations' (documents inédits), avec le portrait d'Elvire en héliogravure* (Paris: Société de Mercure de France, 1906), p. 167, n. 2.

Lamartine records that 'For two months I have been immersed in pure and juvenile poetry. This morning I just finished copying out to be printed eight or nine thousand verses lost in the pages of an album or in the margins of a folio edition of Petrarch. It's poetry from when I was sixteen.'[93] What this anecdote suggests, in combination with evidence cited earlier, is that the young Lamartine (if we accept his own dating as sincere and not hyperbolic) owned a copy of Petrarch which he did not, or could not read. For by the age of twenty, when he was considering submitting a poem in praise of Petrarch to the competition organized by the Athénée de Vaucluse, the insurmountable barrier to this task was Lamartine's lack of knowledge of both Petrarch and Italian. Instead, aged sixteen (by his own account), Lamartine's folio edition of Petrarch seems, strangely, to have served as writing rather than reading material. At this stage, writing in the margins of Petrarch appears to be fortuitous, opportunistic, and without any of the dialogue with the main text that might have been expected, save for Lamartine's already mentioned inability, at this young age, to engage with the Italian language.

This habit of writing in the margins proves to remain a consistent feature of Lamartine's at first limited interaction with Petrarch, even at a point when he has become fluent in Italian. Thus Lamartine's own commentary to 'Hymne du matin' ('Morning Hymn'), from the collection *Harmonies poétiques et religieuses* (1830; *Poetic and Religious Harmonies*), much of which was written during the years he spent in Florence, relates a strange tale not only of writing in the margins, but of further desecration of the book:

> This *Harmonie* was written at *Montenero*, like the preceding one, during a stop of an entire day under the green oaks of this beautiful coast. It was written down on the blank pages of a lovely quarto of *Petrarch* which I often used to carry with me. At the point that I was tearing out these pages, they were taken from me by the violent evening wind which comes from Limona, and which blows in gusts out to sea. They whirled around for a moment above me, and fell back down a thousand feet away under the hollow of the coastline. I thought that they had been swallowed up by the waves. I regretted them for a moment, then I returned to collect my horse from the *locanda*, and thought no more of it.
>
> The next day, a pretty, half-naked child, the daughter of a poor shellfish harvester from the outskirts of Livorno, brought them to me, all of them soaked with saltwater. She told me that her father had found them floating on the foam on the coast below *Montenero*; that he had got the Capuchins at the convent to read them; that the monks, being unable to understand this language, had said that the papers should be taken to the Frenchman, at Villa Palmieri. I thanked the little girl; I gave her for her father as many Italian coins [*écus*] as there were pages, and for her a red-striped cotton dress, a blouse, and

---

[93] 'Je suis depuis deux mois dans la poésie pure et juvénile. Je viens ce matin d'achever pour l'impression la copie de huit ou neuf mille vers perdus sur des pages d'album ou sur des marges de Pétrarque in-folio. C'est ma poésie de seize ans.' *Correspondance d'Alphonse de Lamartine (1830–1867)*, II, 375.

some slippers. She went away delighted and her hands full of figs, believing no doubt that she had brought me a treasure. Alas! It was only some leaves snatched from the sea breeze, and released to the winds of time![94]

While Lamartine here succeeds in portraying himself and his poetry as at one with, and even almost indistinguishable from, the natural, Tuscan landscape, this vignette also calls into question, once more, the use Lamartine makes of Petrarch. The torn pages scattered to the wind evoke a Virgilian precedent, that of the Sybil from the third book of the *Aeneid*, thus elevating Lamartine's poetry to tragic heights.[95] They also, however, represent a strange insouciance towards the volume from which these pages are extracted. In this tale, we learn, on the one hand, that Lamartine, as a budding Petrarchist, often carried a copy of Petrarch with him at this point in his life; on the other hand, however, we also discover that his attitude towards this volume was at times surprisingly pragmatic, irreverent, and even destructive.[96]

The folio rather than quarto edition of Petrarch also makes an appearance three decades later in Lamartine's narrative of the gestation of 'La Vigne et la Maison' ('The Vineyard and the House'), a late poem once more written hastily amidst the delights of rural life, this time at harvest (October 1856) in the village where Lamartine was born:

During the last days of the autumn which has just come to an end, I went alone to watch the October grape-harvest, in the little village in the Mâcon region where I was born. Whilst the groups of joyous grape pickers answered each other from one hill to the other with those lengthy cries of joy which are

[94] 'Cette Harmonie fut écrite à *Montenero*, comme la précédente, pendant une halte de toute une journée sous les chênes verts de ce beau cap. Elle fut notée sur les feuilles blanches d'une belle édition in-quarto de *Pétrarque* que je portais souvent avec moi. Au moment où je détachais ces feuilles, elles me furent enlevées par le vent violent du soir qui s'élève de Limone, et qui souffle par rafale à la mer. Elles tourbillonnèrent un moment au-dessus de moi, et retombèrent à mille pieds sous la concavité du cap. Je les crus englouties par les lames. Je les regrettai un moment, puis je retournai prendre mon cheval à la *locanda*, et je n'y pensai plus.

Le surlendemain, une jolie enfant à demi nue, fille d'un pauvre ramasseur de coquillages des faubourgs de Livourne, me les rapporta, toutes trempées de l'eau salée. Elle me dit que son père les avait trouvées surnageant sur l'écume au bas du cap de *Montenero* ; qu'il les avait fait lire aux capucins du couvent ; que les capucins, ne comprenant pas cette langue, avaient dit qu'il fallait reporter ces papiers au Français, à la villa Palmieri. Je remerciai la petite fille ; je lui donnai pour son père autant d'écus italiens qu'il y avait de pages, et pour elle une robe de cotonnade rayée de rouge, une chemise et des souliers. Elle s'en alla joyeuse et les mains pleines de figues, croyant sans doute qu'elle m'avait rapporté un trésor. Hélas ! ce n'était que des feuilles arrachées au vent de mer, et rejetées au vent du temps !' 'Commentaire de la troisième harmonie', in *Harmonies poétiques et religieuses*, cited from Lamartine, *Œuvres complètes* (Paris: Chez l'auteur, 1860–6), II (1860), 263–4.

[95] See Virgil, *Eclogues, Georgics, Aeneid 1–6*, trans. H. Rushton Fairclough, rev. G. P. Goold (Cambridge, MA: Harvard University Press, 1999), pp. 402–3 (*Aeneid* III, vv. 445–52).

[96] For Roger Pearson, this action is, however, likely motivated by a sense of humility, that is, the sense that Lamartine's own poem is 'unworthy to remain in manuscript juxtaposition with the real treasures of Petrarch'. See Pearson, *Unacknowledged Legislators: The Poet as Lawgiver in Post-Revolutionary France: Chateaubriand–Staël–Lamartine–Hugo–Vigny* (Oxford: Oxford University Press, 2016), p. 345.

man's thanksgiving to the furrow which provides him with food and drink, whilst the stony village paths were ringing out under the groaning of the wheels which were carrying, at the slow pace of the oxen crowned with vine shoots, the red bunches to the presses, I lay down on the grass, in the shadow of my father's house, looking at the closed windows, and I thought about days gone by.

It was thus that this song rose from my heart to my lips, and that I wrote its stanzas in pencil in the margins of an old *folio edition of Petrarch*, whence I have copied them in order to give them here to my readers.[97]

This narrative presents a typical Romantic set-up, from the melancholy of autumn and remembrance of childhood and times past to the emphasis on solitary communion with nature and the depiction of poetry as a spontaneous outpouring of emotions inspired by the natural surroundings and by private meditation. Yet once the more detail of Petrarch as essential companion and recipient of Lamartine's verses emerges, grounding the supposedly spur-of-the-moment poem in a more literary framework. Indeed, here more than in the two previous examples (the 'thousands' of lines of teenage poetry and 'Hymne du matin'), Petrarch seems to have served not merely as handy notepaper, but more properly as a source of inspiration. That this should be the case is, moreover, likely given the late dating of this poem, which thus precedes by only a year or two Lamartine's prose paean to Petrarch in subsequent issues of the *Cours familier*, discussed above.

For a start, the poem's form—as elucidated in its subtitle, 'dialogue between my soul and myself' (*dialogue entre mon âme et moi*)—recalls sonnets from Petrarch's *Canzoniere* which are similarly structured according to the lyric subject's interrogation of his soul:

> – Che fai, alma? che pensi? avrem mai pace?
>   (*RVF* 150, v. 1)
>
> ***
>
> 'What are you doing, soul? What are you thinking? Will we ever
>   have peace?'

---

[97] 'Dans les derniers jours de l'automne qui vient de finir, j'allai assister seul aux vendanges d'octobre, dans le petit village du Mâconnais où je suis né. Pendant que les bandes de joyeux vendangeurs se répondaient d'une colline à l'autre par ces cris de joie prolongés qui sont les actions de grâce de l'homme au sillon qui le nourrit ou qui l'abreuve, pendant que les sentiers rocailleux du village retentissaient sous le gémissement des roues qui rapportaient, au pas lents des bœufs couronnés de sarments en feuilles, les grappes rouges aux pressoirs, je me couchai sur l'herbe, à l'ombre de la maison de mon père, en regardant les fenêtres fermées, et je pensai aux jours d'autrefois.

Ce fut ainsi que ce chant me monta du cœur aux lèvres, et que j'en écrivis les strophes au crayon sur les marges d'un vieux *Pétrarque in-folio*, où je les reprends pour les donner ici aux lecteurs.' Lamartine, *Cours familier de littérature*, III, 163–4. For the poem in question, 'La Vigne et la Maison: psalmodies de l'âme: dialogue entre mon âme et moi', see Lamartine, *Cours familier de littérature*, III, 165–88, as well as Lamartine, *Œuvres poétiques*, pp. 1484–94 (it is from the latter edition that the poem is subsequently cited).

Che fai? che pensi? che pur dietro guardi
nel tempo, che tornar non pote omai?
Anima sconsolata, che pur vai
giugnendo legne al foco ove tu ardi?
>   (*RVF* 273, vv. 1–4)

***

What are you doing? What are you thinking? Why are you
>   looking back
to a time, that by now can never return?
Disconsolate soul, why do you go
adding wood to the fire in which you burn?

Lamartine's poem begins, similarly, with 'Myself' (*Moi*) addressing his soul (*L'Âme*) as follows: 'What a burden weighs you down, O my soul! / On this old bed of days dishelleved by boredom [*ennui*].'[98] In the first two stanzas, the voice of *Moi* subsequently touches on themes of aging, the passing of time, and the irreversible distance from childhood ('At a distance in flight my youth retreats'),[99] all of which invoke Petrarchan *topoi* of mortality, the fleetingness of life, and the reliance of poetry on the consolations of memory.

The two speakers then engage in a discussion of the value of evening (a typical figure for old age) and of poetry. The soul at first somewhat acerbically declares his allegiance to songs of mourning alone: 'As for songs I only listen to those funereal stanzas / That the priest sobs while leading a coffin.'[100] In contrast, the lyric subject insists that there is a certain type of beauty, expressed in increasingly oxymoronic Petrarchan phrases ('sad charms', 'bitter sweetness')[101] in the descent into night/death, as well as in the exploration of memory, even if this last is met by a stark reminder of loss, in the empty house and the village depopulated of familiar faces:

Rien n'a changé là que le temps ;
Des lieux où notre œil se promène,
Rien n'a fui que les habitants.[102]

***

Nothing has changed there except time;
Of the places where our eyes wander,
Nothing has fled except the inhabitants.

The return to the abandoned childhood home, now home only to spiders and nesting swallows, serves as a reminder of the poet's distance from his childhood and

---

[98] 'Quel fardeau te pèse, ô mon âme ! / Sur ce vieux lit des jours par l'ennui retourné.' Lamartine, *Œuvres poétiques*, p. 1484.

[99] 'Dans un lointain qui fuit ma jeunesse recule', Lamartine, *Œuvres poétiques*, p. 1484.

[100] 'Je n'écoute des chants que ces strophes funèbres / Que sanglote le prêtre en menant un cercueil.' Lamartine, *Œuvres poétiques*, p. 1485.

[101] 'tristes charmes', 'l'amère douceur', Lamartine, *Œuvres poétiques*, p. 1485.

[102] Lamartine, *Œuvres poétiques*, p. 1486.

of cherished family members long since dead. Departed female beauty and youth are remembered in a line that owes much to the famous opening line of *RVF* 90: 'Their blond hair, scattered to the mountain wind'.[103] Unlike the prose commentary, which celebrated the joy of the grape pickers, the hustle and bustle of harvest time, and the abundance of nature, the resultant poem focuses almost exclusively on the house and its departed family, and on the poetic associations of autumn with old age rather than harvest.[104]

Ultimately, then, while its form, *incipit*, and certain themes and turns of phrase are traceable back to Petrarch's *Canzoniere*, 'La Vigne et la Maison' eventually departs from any Petrarchan model in its intensely personal meditation on the distance from childhood and the loss of family, inspired by a return to a specific place. Yet we find the same Petrarchan distinction between the poet's self and soul, combined with further meditation on the solitude resulting from multiple bereavements, in an untitled quatrain from the first page of one of Lamartine's copies of Petrarch:[105]

> Hélas, sur tant d'objets autrefois égarée
> Toute mon âme aimante en moi-même est rentrée !
> Les êtres que j'aimais, où j'avais répandu
> Ce cœur qui débordait, hélas, me l'ont rendu ![106]

***

> Alas, on so many objects once lost
> All my loving soul has returned to myself!
> The beings whom I loved, in whom I had poured out
> This heart which was overflowing, alas, have returned it to me!

The privileging of this stanza as an epigraph to Petrarch's Italian poetry additionally suggests the at least partial indebtedness of 'La Vigne et la Maison' to Lamartine's reading of Petrarch.

No doubt, these three dramatic stories about the conception and development of his poetry must be treated with a degree of suspicion, particularly Lamartine's claims to have written the poems down in a moment of spontaneity and inspiration, and to have copied them out for a wider public without any changes or need

---

[103] 'Leurs blonds cheveux, épars au vent de la montagne', Lamartine, *Œuvres poétiques*, p. 1489. Compare to *RVF* 90, v. 1: 'Erano i capei d'oro a l'aura sparsi' (Her blond hair was scattered to the wind [*a l'aura*, to Laura/herself]).

[104] On the theme of the childhood home more broadly in Lamartine, see Olivier Catel, 'Terre natale et maison onirique: l'expression et la commémoration de soi', in *Lamartine: autobiographie, mémoires, fiction de soi*, ed. Nicolas Courtinat (Clermont-Ferrand: Presses Universitaires Blaise-Pascal, 2009), pp. 63–73.

[105] This copy is reported as an edition of Petrarch's *Opera omnia*, and is likely to be the folio rather than the quarto. See Lamartine, *Œuvres poétiques*, p. 1960.

[106] Lamartine, *Œuvres poétiques*, p. 1793. These lines were first published in 1840 by Ernest Falconnet in *Alphonse de Lamartine: études biographiques, littéraires et politiques* (Paris: Furne et Cie, 1840), p. 68 (introduced as 'ces vers que vous-même avez écrits à la première page de votre Pétrarque', 'these verses which you yourself wrote on the first page of your Petrarch').

for reworking.[107] Yet Lamartine's deliberate and repeated association of his own creative output with Petrarch begs the following questions: why would Lamartine have wanted so insistently to present his copies of Petrarch as a prime space for poetic self-expression? Why would he have embedded his narratives of the germination of his own poetry into a wider Petrarchist discourse? Put simply, several motives are likely. Firstly, Lamartine evidently wanted to encourage comparison of himself with Petrarch, for instance on the grounds that both are poets of nature, solitude, and melancholy. Secondly, Lamartine must have wished to highlight that he was for some years inseparable from his own volumes of Petrarch, even when on various outdoor excursions. This second motive both helps to confirm Lamartine's credentials as a fervent Petrarchist and, more broadly, tempers the narrative of spontaneous self-expression inspired by nature with the unignorable presence of a very literary, prestigious volume of lyric poetry at the moment of poetic genesis. Moreover, although Lamartine seems to have begun by using his copies of Petrarch as convenient notebooks, with little ostensible regard to the original content, there was, as we have seen, in later cases a greater permeability and exchange of language, ideas, and style from text to margin. The fruits of such an interaction are already evident in 'La Vigne et la Maison', and are even starker in the final example from Lamartine, 'Le Retour'.

'Le Retour' was composed at Brugg in Switzerland during the summer of 1824 on the blank pages of the second volume of an edition of Petrarch's Italian poetry belonging to Lamartine, and was first published in a volume entitled *Épîtres* in 1825, in and amongst three verse letters addressed to Victor Hugo, Amédée de Parseval, and Casimir Delavigne respectively.[108] It is a compelling rewriting of a sonnet from the second half of the *Canzoniere*, *RVF* 301. In his introduction to *RVF* 301 in the 'Entretiens' dedicated to Petrarch, Lamartine relates that he had formerly tried to translate this poem 'but without being able to contend with the impalpability of Petrarch's ethereal verses'.[109] In the *Cours familier de littérature*, Lamartine therefore defers to Boulay-Paty's translation of the sonnet, which he considers superior to his own earlier attempt.[110] Yet Lamartine's discussion of *RVF* 301 also, once more, highlights both his personal involvement in Petrarch's poetry and his wish to establish grounds for comparison between the medieval poet and his own *œuvre*:

---

[107] See Pearson, *Unacknowledged Legislators*, p. 344 on Lamartine's repeated narrative of the spontaneous poetic act as an 'artful reconstruction' designed to guarantee the authenticity of poetic inspiration.

[108] Lamartine, *Œuvres poétiques*, p. 1838, reports that one of two sources of this poem is in the 'Musée Carnavalet : sur les pages blanches à la fin du t. II du petit Pétrarque de Lamartine (*Rime di Petrarca*, Londra, 1810)'. In addition to 'Le Retour', a draft of 'Paysage' (Lamartine, *Œuvres poétiques*, p. 495) was also written in this same copy of Petrarch, as noted in Lamartine, *Œuvres poétiques*, p. 1861. For the first publication of 'Le Retour', see Lamartine, *Épîtres* (Paris: Urbain Canel, 1825), pp. 19–22.

[109] 'mais sans pouvoir lutter avec l'impalpabilité des vers éthérés de Pétrarque', Lamartine, *Cours familier de littérature*, vi, 78.

[110] For Boulay-Paty's translation, see Lamartine, *Cours familier de littérature*, vi, 78–9.

They are the same emotions and almost the same images which I myself expressed in a larger and infinitely less perfect form than that of Petrarch, by writing the elegiac ode entitled *the Lake*, of which a few stanzas have remained in the memory and in the heart of my time. But, alas! It is neither the language nor the verse of the poet of Vaucluse![III]

Lamartine is caught, exemplarily, between a desire to identify himself and his poetry with Petrarch and a feeling of his own unworthiness.

Setting aside such expressions of modesty and mature self-criticism, let us consider Lamartine's rewriting of *RVF* 301, preceded by the original Italian sonnet, and with both accompanied by English translations:

RVF 301

Valle che de' lamenti miei se' piena,
fiume che spesso del mio pianger cresci,
fere selvestre, vaghi augelli et pesci,
che l'una et l'altra verde riva affrena,

aria de' miei sospir' calda et serena,
dolce sentier che sì amaro riesci,
colle che mi piacesti, or mi rincresci,
ov'anchor per usanza Amor mi mena:

ben riconosco in voi l'usate forme,
non, lasso, in me, che da sì lieta vita
son fatto albergo d'infinita doglia.

Quinci vedea 'l mio bene; et per queste orme
torno a vedere ond'al ciel nuda è gita,
lasciando in terra la sua bella spoglia.

                        ***

Valley which are full of my laments,
river which often from my weeping increases,
sylvan beasts, wandering birds, and fish,
which the one and the other green bank contain,

air with my sighs warm and serene,
sweet path which turns so bitter,
hill which used to please me, and now saddens me,
where still out of habit Love leads me:

well do I recognize in you the habitual forms,

[III] 'Ce sont les mêmes sentiments et presque les mêmes images que j'ai exprimés moi-même dans une forme plus large et infiniment moins parfaite que celle de Pétrarque, en écrivant l'ode élégiaque intitulée *le Lac*, dont quelques strophes sont restées dans la mémoire et dans le cœur de mon temps. Mais, hélas ! ce n'est ni la langue ni le vers du poëte de Vaucluse !' Lamartine, *Cours familier de littérature*, VI, 79.

not, alas, in myself, who from such a happy life
am become a dwelling place of infinite grief.

From there I used to see my good; and in these footsteps
I return to see whence to Heaven naked she went,
leaving on the Earth her beautiful body.

Lamartine's rewriting: 'Le Retour' ('The Return')

Vallon, rempli de mes accords,
Ruisseau, dont mes pleurs troublaient l'onde,
Prés, colline, forêt profonde,
Oiseaux qui chantiez sur ses bords !

Zéphir, qu'embaumait son haleine,
Sentiers, où sa main, tant de fois,
M'entraînait à l'ombre des bois,
Où l'habitude me ramène !

Ce temps n'est plus ! mon œil glacé,
Qui vous cherche à travers ses larmes,
À vos bords, jadis pleins de charmes,
Redemande en vain le passé !

La terre est pourtant aussi belle,
Le ciel aussi pur que jamais !
Ah ! je le vois; ce que j'aimais,
Ce n'était pas vous, c'était elle ![112]

***

Valley, filled with my harmonies,
Stream, whose flow was disrupted by my tears,
Meadows, hill, dense forest,
Birds who sing on its banks!

Zephyr, which her breath embalmed,
Paths, where her hand, so many times,
Led me to the shadow of the woods,
Where habit brings me back!

That time is no longer! My icy eyes,
Which search for you through their tears,
At your banks, formerly full of charms,
Vainly asks for the past again!

Yet the earth is still as beautiful,
The sky as pure as ever!

---

[112] Cited from Lamartine, *Œuvres poétiques*, p. 281.

> Ah! I understand; what I loved
> Was not you, it was she!

Lamartine's version begins by closely replicating the opening structure of *RVF* 301, with the repeated apostrophe to various parts of the natural landscape, from the valley, the river, and singing birds to the warm breeze (*aria* in the original). As is frequent with such rewritings (for instance, Voltaire's rendition of the first stanza of *RVF* 126, discussed at the end of Chapter 2), this last is over-translated with a Petrarchan word not in *RVF* 301, although it is present at the start of *RVF* 310: 'Zephyr' [*Zéphir*].

It is in the second half of 'Le Retour', however, that Lamartine deviates more extensively from *RVF* 301. In particular, Laura's absence from the landscape through reason of death is downplayed by Lamartine, whose poem lacks both the dramatic statement 'I am become a dwelling place of infinite grief' and the concluding lines which distinguish between Laura's soul, now in Heaven, and her body, still on Earth.[113] Instead, Lamartine's poem develops into a critique of the landscape despite the initial appreciation of its riches, again more like *RVF* 310, which concludes that because of Laura's death, nature, even in springtime, is for the poet 'a desert' (*un deserto*, v. 14). Lamartine's final point, in 'Le Retour', is that it is not the landscape which has changed, but rather his own emotions, as a result of being now deprived of Laura's company (the only oblique allusion to her death). Material in support of such a statement can be found in *RVF* 301, in particular in vv. 9–10, 'well do I recognize in you the habitual forms, / not, alas, in myself' [*ben riconosco in voi l'usate forme, / non, lasso, in me*], i.e. nature is the same, but the poet has changed. Yet the conclusion of *RVF* 301 (vv. 13–14) reveals that in truth nature, too, has changed, since Laura's death has transformed both earth (where her body is buried) and sky (where her soul has ascended).

More generally, Lamartine's poem clearly diverges from the sonnet form of the original, being instead composed of four quatrains of *rimes embrassées* (ABBA). As found in Chapters 1 and 2, verse translations of Petrarch were typically freer in the earlier part of the century (Montesquiou being a striking example), with a preference for replicating the sonnet form emerging later, with such translators as Mahul and Le Duc. In line with this observation, the sonnet form, for all Lamartine's avowed Petrarchism, was not one for which he was ever to evince much interest on his own account; the rediscovery of the sonnet in France was, instead, to be the task of the next generation of poets, led by Sainte-Beuve, and of which we will see one example by Musset later in this chapter.[114] Paradoxically, however, despite the subsequent popularity of the sonnet form amongst later nineteenth-century French poets and their readers, Lamartine's fervour for and familiarity with Petrarch was never subsequently to be equalled. Other poets after Lamartine, as the final section of this

---

[113]   'son fatto albergo d'infinita doglia', *RVF* 301, v. 11.

[114]   On the rediscovery of the sonnet form in nineteenth-century France, see David Scott, *Sonnet Theory and Sonnet Practice in Nineteenth-Century France: Sonnets on the Sonnet* (Hull: University of Hull Publications, 1977) and Max Jasinski, *Histoire du sonnet en France: thèse présentée à la Faculté des Lettres de Paris* (Douai: Imprimerie H. Brugère, A. Dalsheimer et Cie, 1903), especially pp. 195–200 on the role of Sainte-Beuve in this rediscovery.

chapter will chart, would go on to cite Petrarch in their poetry, without necessarily wanting either to be Petrarch or to incarnate in more than a fleeting fashion the values of Petrarchan love, poetry, and love poetry so warmly lauded by Lamartine.

In the Canon: Hugo, Musset, Gautier

In the final section of this chapter, I consider three different poets who chose, at a certain point in their career, to write at least one poem explicitly about Petrarch, and who, in so doing, registered Petrarch indelibly in the canon of nineteenth-century French Romantic poetry. The presence of Petrarch in the canon complements the discussion, in the first half of this chapter, of less well-known poems written by French translators of Petrarch. In this way, interest in Petrarch proves to run like a thread throughout French poetry of the nineteenth century, both in and out of the canon, at times deep-rooted, at others at a more superficial, though still noteworthy, level.

Hugo's engagement with Petrarch, like his contemporary and fellow Romantic poet, Lamartine, emerges most prominently in a bibliographically marginal fashion in a poem entitled 'Écrit sur la première page d'un Pétrarque' ('Written on the first page of a Petrarch'). This poem is dated 14 October 1835, and is part of a wider French passion for Petrarch in this decade, as also manifested by Musset and Gautier (see below), and by three Petrarchan novels of the same period discussed in the next chapter: Sainte-Beuve's *Volupté* (1834), Balzac's *Le Lys dans la vallée* (1836), and Stendhal's *La Chartreuse de Parme* (1839). As seen in Chapter 1, this French Romantic fervour for Petrarch culminates in the first two complete French nineteenth-century translations of Petrarch's Italian poetry, both published in 1842, by Gramont and Montesquiou respectively.

Hugo's contribution to this trend is a poem that celebrates Petrarch through an emphasis on the enjoyment he derives from reading the medieval poet:

'Écrit sur la première page d'un Pétrarque'

> Quand d'une aube d'amour mon âme se colore,
> Quand je sens ma pensée, ô chaste amant de Laure,
> Loin du souffle glacé d'un vulgaire moqueur,
> Éclore feuille à feuille au plus profond du cœur,
> Je prends ton livre saint qu'un feu céleste embrase,
> Où si souvent murmure à côté de l'extase
> La résignation au sourire fatal,
> Ton beau livre, où l'on voit, comme un flot de cristal
> Qui sur un sable d'or coule à sa fantaisie,
> Tant d'amour ruisseler sur tant de poésie !
> Je viens à ta fontaine, ô maître ! et je relis
> Tes vers mystérieux par la grâce amollis,
> Doux trésor, fleur d'amour qui, dans les bois recluse,
> Laisse après cinq cents ans son odeur à Vaucluse !
> Et tandis que je lis, rêvant, presque priant,
> Celui qui me verrait me verrait souriant,

Car, loin des bruits du monde et des sombres orgies,
Tes pudiques chansons, tes nobles élégies,
Vierges au doux profil, sœurs au regard d'azur,
Passent devant mes yeux, portant sur leur front pur,
Dans les sonnets sculptés, comme dans des amphores,
Ton beau style, étoilé de fraîches métaphores ![115]

***

'Written on the first page of a Petrarch'

When by a dawn of love my soul is embellished,
When I feel my thought, O chaste lover of Laura,
Far from the icy breath of a vulgar mocker,
Blossoming leaf by leaf in the depths of my heart,
I take your holy book which a celestial fire enflames,
Where so often murmurs next to ecstasy
Resignation with a fatal smile,
Your beautiful book, where we see, like a crystalline wave
Which over golden sand flows wherever it wishes [*à sa fantaisie*],
So much love streaming over so much poetry!
I come to your spring, O master! and I reread
Your mysterious verses softened by grace,
Sweet treasure, flower of love which, sequestered in the woods,
Leaves after five hundred years its fragrance at Vaucluse!
And while I read, dreaming, almost praying,
Anyone who saw me would find me smiling,
For, far from the world's noises and dreadful debauchery,
Your modest songs, your noble elegies,
Virgins with a pleasing profile, sisters with an azure gaze,
Pass before my eyes, bearing on their pure foreheads,
In sculpted sonnets, as if in amphorae,
Your beautiful style, starred with fresh metaphors!

The image of Petrarch depicted in this poem is that of a celestial, chaste, modest, noble poet, broadly comparable to Lamartine's pure, Platonic Petrarch. Hugo's Petrarch is solitary, wood-dwelling, and aristocratic, at a distance from any dangerous, unsympathetic readers (such as the *vulgaire moqueur*), as well as from the corruption of society more broadly. Once more, Petrarch is anchored in French soil, with the image of a flower that continues to fill Vaucluse with its perfume five centuries on. The source (*fontaine*) mentioned in this poem is not only that of the Sorgue, a classic site of Petrarchan pilgrimage, but also Petrarch's poetry, following as the reference does a series of water-based images that have fused together love and poetry (*comme un flot ... / Qui ... coule; ruisseler*). This fluid imagery is

---

[115]   Victor Hugo, *Œuvres poétiques*, ed. Pierre Albouy, 2 vols (Paris: Gallimard, 1964–7), I, 903.

counterbalanced towards the end of the poem in the theme of poetry as ancient container (*amphores*), which complements the analogy between sonnet and sculpture, designed to flatter Petrarch's compositional skills. Nonetheless, the emphasis is still very much on movement: the personified poems pass before Hugo's eyes, the amphorae are likely to contain precious liquid, and the whole poem concludes in a movement of transcendence from forehead (*front pur*) to amphorae to metaphorical stars. As in the polysemy of Laura's name for Petrarch, which invokes both a woman and the laurel (that is, poetry), so here Petrarch's poems are figured by Hugo as statuesque virgins. In this vision, women are poems (both *chanson* and *élégie* are gendered as female), as well as bearers of poetry and figures to whom poetry is attached.

Finally, in addition to rendering homage to Petrarch and his poetry (the latter reduced, as is typical, to the sonnet form), Hugo also offers himself in this poem as an ideal reader of Petrarch. This ideal reader is one whose soul is familiar with love and whose thoughts are profound, heartfelt, and undistracted by worldly cares. For this reader, reading is a source of pleasure (visible smiles), but also a more ethereal, spiritual experience, akin to dreaming and even to prayer. Above all, this reader is a rereader (*je relis / Tes vers*); Petrarch's poetry requires commitment, meditation, loyalty, and familiarity. By placing this poem as an epigraph to his copy of Petrarch, this text acts in turn as an appreciation of the author, as an anticipation of the volume's contents, as a record of a reading experience, and as a brief, elliptical user's guide. Hugo's reading of Petrarch begins as a solitary exercise, but soon calls for witnesses, readers not only of Petrarch, but of Hugo reading Petrarch (*Celui qui me verrait*). In this way the mediated nature of many nineteenth-century French readings of Petrarch (reliant upon and guided by authors such as Sade, Lamartine, or Hugo himself) is figured within the poem.

A later poem by Hugo, dated July 1843, and placed at the beginning of Book Three of *Les Contemplations*, acts as a sort of companion piece to this poem, bearing as it does the analogous title 'Écrit sur un exemplaire de la *Divina Commedia*' ('Written on a copy of the *Divine Comedy*').[116] This shorter text (only fourteen lines long in *rimes plates*, AABB etc.) relates a fleeting encounter between the poet and Dante, during which Dante explains, in a speech occupying nine lines of the poem, how he climbed the ladder of being from mountain to oak to lion, before becoming—as the final line of the poem reveals—a man named Dante.[117] This admittedly odd conceit portrays Dante as an eternal creature of metamorphosis, with intimate knowledge not only of nature and the animal kingdom, but, eventually, of mankind too. Although this poem has little to do with the plot, structure, or style of the *Divine Comedy*, it does stand as a marker in *Les Contemplations* of Hugo's fondness for the

---

[116] For a discussion and summary of the many references to Dante in Hugo's work, see Pitwood, *Dante and the French Romantics*, pp. 174–208 and 287–96, and Luigi Foscolo Benedetto, 'Victor Hugo e Dante', *Lettere italiane*, 20.1 (1968), 40–55. More broadly, see also Patricia A. Ward, *The Medievalism of Victor Hugo* (University Park: Pennsylvania State University Press, 1975).

[117] "Maintenant, je suis homme, et je m'appelle Dante". Hugo, *Œuvres poétiques*, II, 568.

apparently immortal Dante. This fondness, moreover, eventually eclipses Petrarch entirely in Hugo's heart and mind, despite the laudatory poem written on a copy of Petrarch. Ultimately, then, Hugo turns out not to be such an ideal reader of Petrarch after all.

The eventual limits to Hugo's interest in Petrarch are delineated especially starkly in a letter which he sent politely declining the invitation to attend and participate in the 1874 celebrations organized in Avignon in honour of Petrarch. The letter begins apologetically, but also with a determined emphasis on Hugo's own detachment from the festivities, which he wishes to watch from a safe distance:

> I am sorry to be absent from you. I would have been proud to welcome, in all your names, these brothers, these generous Italians, who are coming to celebrate Petrarch in the country of Voltaire. But from afar I will observe, filled with emotion, your solemnities. They will capture the attention of the civilized world. Petrarch, who was the glory [*auréole*] of a dark century, loses none of his brightness in this high noon of progress which we name the nineteenth century.[118]

Many reasons might be adduced for Hugo's absence, from the expected and the forgivable (old age, illness, the difficulty of the journey) to more revealing and ideologically inclined motives (resistance both to the regionalism of the festivities and even to Petrarch himself). Evidence of the latter emerges, forcibly and somewhat surprisingly, later in the same letter, as Hugo proves unable to resist clarifying his position, even at the risk of offending his obviously Petrarch-enthused addressee (Jean Saint-Martin, *conseiller général de Vaucluse*, writing on behalf of the festival's organizing committee):

> Petrarch is one those rare examples of a happy poet. He was understood in his lifetime, a privilege granted neither to Homer, nor to Aeschylus, nor to Shakespeare. He was never slandered, booed, or stoned. Petrarch had on this Earth every splendour, the respect of popes, the enthusiasm of the masses, showers of flowers on his way through the streets, the golden laurel on his forehead like an emperor, the Capitol like a god. Let's speak the truth with virility: he lacks unhappiness. I prefer to his purple robe the staff of the wandering Dante. Petrarch lacks that indefinable hint of tragedy [*cet on ne sait quoi de tragique*] which adds to the grandeur of poets a black crown, and which has always marked the highest summit of genius. In glory Petrarch is surpassed by Dante, and triumph by exile.[119]

---

[118] 'Je regrette d'être absent du milieu de vous. J'eusse été fier de souhaiter, en votre nom à tous, la bien-venue à ces frères, à ces généreux italiens, qui viennent fêter Pétrarque dans le pays de Voltaire. Mais de loin j'assisterai, ému, à vos solennités. Elles fixeront l'attention du monde civilisé. Pétrarque, qui a été l'auréole d'un siècle ténébreux, ne perd rien de sa clarté dans ce plein midi du progrès qu'on nomme le dix-neuvième siècle.' Hugo, 'Le centenaire de Pétrarque', p. 319.

[119] 'Pétrarque est un des rares exemples du poëte heureux. Il fut compris de son vivant, privilège que n'eurent ni Homère, ni Eschyle, ni Shakespeare. Il n'a été ni calomnié, ni hué, ni

In his differentiation of Dante and Petrarch, Hugo fails to recognize that Petrarch, too, was a poet in exile, and also gives Petrarch no credit for the language of mourning that overflows in the *Canzoniere*, especially the second half. Doubt is thereby cast on the extent of Hugo's familiarity with either Petrarch's life or his works, while this disclosure of a marked preference for Dante over Petrarch makes his turning down of the invitation to participate in the 1874 Petrarchan celebrations perhaps a blessing in disguise.

Hugo's comparison of Dante and Petrarch, much to the detriment of the latter, is in stark contrast to Lamartine's own discussion of the two poets in his *Cours familier de littérature*, where, predictably, Petrarch has the upper hand:

> Italy has excessively preferred to him her Dante, that sublime but primitive [*sauvage*] genius, with the disorderly proportions of a dream of Patmos; greatness is more striking than perfection in peoples who are born or reborn to literature: Dante is a product of a still barbaric Middle Ages; Petrarch of the most refined antiquity, though both of them are, nonetheless, Christian.[120]

Thus, while Hugo does—like Lamartine, though less prolifically—write a poem on a copy of Petrarch, his attitude towards Petrarch is, ultimately, one of suspicion and a distinct lack of appreciation, in striking contradistinction to that of Lamartine. The existential opposition between Dante and Petrarch, whether formulated by Hugo or Lamartine, and despite the shifting terms of the debate, is, nevertheless, one which has largely remained both divisive and operative to this day.[121]

Like Hugo, Musset's interest in Petrarch is inseparable from a broader fascination with medieval Italian poetry, in which Dante inevitably has a prominent place.[122] It is also, like Hugo's 'Écrit sur la première page d'un Pétrarque', indicative of a wider French obsession with Petrarch in the 1830s. Most memorably, Petrarch graces the pages of Musset's novella *Le Fils de Titien* from 1838, as a foil to the tale's Italian,

---

lapidé. Pétrarque a eu sur cette terre toutes les splendeurs, le respect des papes, l'enthousiasme des peuples, les pluies de fleurs sur son passage dans les rues, le laurier d'or au front comme un empereur, le Capitole comme un dieu. Disons virilement la vérité, le malheur lui manque. Je préfère à cette robe de pourpre le bâton d'Alighieri errant. Il manque à Pétrarque cet on ne sait quoi de tragique qui ajoute à la grandeur des poëtes une cime noire, et qui a toujours marqué le plus haut sommet du génie. Dans la gloire Pétrarque est dépassé par Dante, et le triomphe par l'exil.' Hugo, 'Le centenaire de Pétrarque', p. 320.

[120] 'L'Italie lui a trop préféré son Dante, génie sublime mais sauvage, aux proportions désordonnés d'un rêve de Pathmos ; la grandeur frappe plus que la perfection les peuples qui naissent ou qui renaissent à la littérature : Dante émane du moyen âge encore barbare ; Pétrarque de l'antiquité la plus raffinée, mais tous les deux cependant sont chrétiens.' Lamartine, *Cours familier de littérature*, VI, 4. On Lamartine's limited knowledge and appreciation of Dante, see also Pitwood, *Dante and the French Romantics*, pp. 145–64.

[121] See, for instance, the following edited volume which similarly positions Petrarch as against Dante: *Petrarch and Dante: Anti-Dantism, Metaphysics, Tradition*, ed. Barański and Cachey.

[122] See Valentina Ponzetto, 'Musset et les écrivains italiens du Moyen Âge et de la Renaissance', in *Poétique de Musset*, ed. Sylvain Ledda, Frank Lestringant, and Gisèle Séginger (Mont-Saint-Aignan: Presses universitaires de Rouen et du Havre, 2013), pp. 29–52, and, on Dante and Musset, Pitwood, *Dante and the French Romantics*, pp. 209–17.

amorous hero, Pippo, the eponymous son of Titian. At a certain point in this text, the mandolin-playing protagonist seeks to write a sonnet to his mysterious bene-factor, revealed as the young, rich, and beautiful widow Béatrice Loredano. Pippo eventually manages to compose a poem to this lady in a moment of inspiration:

> Sans réfléchir et sans s'arrêter, il écrivit à la hâte un sonnet, dont voici à peu près la traduction :

> Lorsque j'ai lu Pétrarque étant encore enfant,
> J'ai souhaité d'avoir quelque gloire en partage.
> Il aimait en poète et chantait en amant ;
> De la langue des dieux lui seul sut faire usage.

> Lui seul eut le secret de saisir au passage
> Les battements du cœur qui durent un moment,
> Et, riche d'un sourire, il en gravait l'image
> Du bout d'un stylet d'or sur un pur diamant.

> O vous qui m'adressez une parole amie,
> Qui l'écriviez hier, et l'oublierez demain,
> Souvenez-vous de moi qui vous en remercie.

> J'ai le cœur de Pétrarque et n'ai pas son génie.
> Je ne puis ici-bas que donner en chemin
> Ma main à qui m'appelle, à qui m'aime ma vie.[123]

***

Without reflecting and without pausing, he wrote in haste a sonnet, of which here is more or less the translation:

> When I read Petrarch when I was still a child,
> I wished to have some share of his glory.
> He loved as a poet and sang as a lover;
> Only he knew how to make use of the language of the gods.

> He alone knew the secret of grasping as it happened
> The beating of the heart which lasted a moment,
> And, inspired by a smile, he would carve its image
> On a pure diamond with the tip of a golden stylus.

> O you who have addressed to me a friendly word,
> Who wrote it yesterday, and will forget it tomorrow,
> Remember me who thanks you for it.

> I have the heart of Petrarch but do not have his genius.

---

[123] Alfred de Musset, *Le Fils de Titien*, in *Œuvres complètes en prose*, ed. Maurice Allem (Paris: Gallimard, 1951), pp. 428–69 (p. 441). The same sonnet is also reproduced in Musset, *Poésies complètes*, ed. Maurice Allem (Paris: Gallimard, 1957), pp. 384–5 (dated 3 May 1838).

I can only here on Earth offer on the way
My hand to whoever calls me, and to whoever loves me my life.

Here, the Petrarchan sonnet sits uneasily amidst a tale of gambling, love, and intrigue in sixteenth-century Venice. Musset's *vignette* of the art of the sonnet demonstrates a nonchalant attitude towards the writing of poetry, which—at least in Pippo's eyes—is deemed to be necessarily unpremeditated and unselfconscious, the product of an absence of thought or pause (*Sans réfléchir et sans s'arrêter*), as if in a parody of Lamartinian poiesis.[124] Ultimately, Pippo's ability to spout sonnets when in love does not reveal any especial talent, but rather is as stereotypically and picturesquely Italian as his talent for the mandolin. Moreover, the passage reveals an equally flippant attitude towards the work of translation, which is present only as a fiction that gestures towards the story's supposed Italian setting and characters and is subject to a similarly haphazard approach: 'here is more or less the translation' (*voici à peu près la traduction*). Finally, the line 'I have the heart of Petrarch but do not have his genius' (*J'ai le cœur de Pétrarque et n'ai pas son génie*) posits Petrarch as a model whom it is both desirable and impossible to imitate.

That Musset, perhaps more even than Pippo, did have a heart like Petrarch's is further suggested by an anecdote from his biography which records that his brief and unsuccessful courtship of one Laure Mélesville in early 1843 was carried out in an overtly Petrarchan manner. Musset apparently sent to Mlle Mélesville a portrait of the first meeting between Petrarch and Laura, with his own traits imposed on the poet and Laura's features inspired by his new Laure.[125] Accompanying this portrait (the work of Musset's friend Chenavard) was Musset's own translation of the first quatrain of *RVF* 61:

> Bénis soient le moment, et l'heure, et la journée,
> Et le temps et les lieux, et le mois de l'année,
> Et la place chérie où, dans mon triste cœur,
> Pénétra de ses yeux la charmante douceur ![126]

***

> Blessed be the moment, the hour, and the day,
> And the time and the place, and the month of the year,
> And the dear place where my sad heart was pierced
> By the charming sweetness of her eyes!

No sooner was this missive dispatched to the Mélesville household than Musset

---

[124] On the image of creativity in *Le Fils de Titien* more broadly, see Henry F. Majewski, *Paradigm and Parody: Images of Creativity in French Romanticism: Vigny, Hugo, Balzac, Gautier, Musset* (Charlottesville, VA: University Press of Virginia, 1989), pp. 137–43.

[125] Paul de Musset, *Biographie de Alfred de Musset, sa vie et ses œuvres*, 4th edn (Paris: G. Charpentier, 1877), pp. 364–5. This story is also retold in Ponzetto, 'Musset et les écrivains italiens', pp. 41–2.

[126] Musset, 'À Mademoiselle Mélesville', in *Poésies complètes*, p. 544. In the original Italian these lines read 'Benedetto sia 'l giorno, e 'l mese, et l'anno, / et la stagione, e 'l tempo, et l'ora, e 'l punto, / e 'l bel paese, e 'l loco ov'io fui giunto / da' duo begli occhi che legato m'ànno' (*RVF* 61, vv. 1–4).

learnt, belatedly, that the object of his Petrarchan affections was already betrothed to another. In finding himself in a situation of impossible, thwarted love, Musset assumed more of the Petrarchan mantle than he had anticipated.

The final reference to Petrarch by Musset which I will consider here provides a connection to the interest of Gautier too in the poet. This connection is the French painter Louis Boulanger's *Triomphe de Pétrarque* from 1836, which inspired Gautier's long poem of the same name (discussed below) as well as the following reflection from Musset:

> What a beautiful subject, in any case, and what a day! That man, dressed in a purple robe, carried on a triumphal chariot, surrounded by the elite of the nobility, by poets, scholars, and warriors, processing through the middle of the city, on a carpet of rose petals, followed by a choir of young girls and preceded by Reverie, applauded, celebrated, admired by all, and what had he then done to obtain so much glory? He had loved and sung his mistress. It was not him who was being crowned and led to the Capitol, it was grief and love. Conquerors have had many trophies; the sword has triumphed a hundred times, love only once. Petrarch is the first of the poets. What happened on the day in that great heart thus rewarded? What was he looking at from the height of that chariot? Alas, his Laura was no more; he hid perhaps a tear, and repeated to himself quietly: *Beati gli occhi che la vider viva* ('Blessed the eyes which saw her alive')![127]

This passage is quite a startling misreading of the dating and significance of Petrarch's crowning with the laurel in April 1341 on the Capitoline Hill. The invitation to receive the laurel crown was in truth based on the reputation of Petrarch's unfinished Latin epic *Africa*. Moreover, if the poet had been thinking of Laura during the ceremony, he can hardly have been mourning her death, which was not to occur, by Petrarch's account, until later in the same decade, in 1348. Yet these misreadings are highly revealing for the construction of a French Romantic Petrarch. The triumph of this Petrarch is no longer that of Latinity or learning; indeed, as Chapter 3 has found, the *Africa* was markedly unpopular with nineteenth-century French readers and translators. Instead, this triumph marks—in the words of Musset—the coronation of that irresistible partnership, grief and love (*la douleur et l'amour*). For, as the

---

[127] 'Quel beau sujet, du reste, et quelle journée ! Cet homme, vêtu d'une robe de pourpre, traîné sur un char triomphal, entouré de l'élite de la noblesse, des poètes, des savants, des guerriers, marchant au milieu d'une ville, sur un tapis de roses effeuillées, suivi d'un chœur de jeunes filles et précédé par la Rêverie, applaudi, fêté, admiré de tous, et qu'avait-il donc fait pour tant de gloire ? Il avait aimé et chanté sa maîtresse. Ce n'était pas lui qu'on couronnait et qu'on menait au Capitole, c'étaient la douleur et l'amour. Les conquérants ont eu bien des trophées ; l'épée a triomphé cent fois, l'amour une seule. Pétrarque est le premier des poètes. Que se passa-t-il ce jour-là dans ce grand cœur ainsi récompensé ? Que regardait-il du haut de ce char ? Hélas ! sa Laura n'était plus ; il cachait peut-être une larme, et il se répétait tout bas : *Beati gli occhi che la vider viva* !' Musset, 'Salon de 1836', in *Œuvres complètes en prose*, ed. Allem, pp. 969–97 (pp. 992–3). The Italian quotation comes from *RVF* 309 (v. 14).

Muse instructs the Poet in Musset's 'Nuit d'octobre' (1837; 'October Night'), beauty and poetry are ultimately inseparable from the experience of suffering:

> Aimerais-tu les fleurs, les prés et la verdure,
> Les sonnets de Pétrarque et le chant des oiseaux,
> Michel-Ange et les arts, Shakspeare et la nature,
> Si tu n'y retrouvais quelques anciens sanglots ?[128]

***

> Would you love flowers, meadows, and greenery,
> The sonnets of Petrarch and the song of birds,
> Michelangelo and the arts, Shakespeare and nature,
> If you did not find in them some ancient sobs?

The same painting analysed by Musset (and now lost) was also the catalyst for Gautier's 'Le Triomphe de Pétrarque', dedicated to Boulanger, the painter of the eponymous work.[129] Writing to Gautier, Boulanger himself referred to this text as 'your beautiful translation [*traduction*] of *Petrarch*', a useful reminder of the breadth of meaning accorded to the concept of translation in this period.[130] Gautier's long poem represents an unusual experimentation in *terza rima*, suggesting the poet's familiarity with Dante (the originator of this distinctive verse form) as well as with Petrarch's *Triumphi*, which adopts the same rhyme scheme.[131] Indeed, Gautier's poem functions as a sort of appendix to the latter work, imagining as it does a seventh triumph, that of Petrarch himself, in addition to the six triumphs depicted in Petrarch's poem, those of Love, Chastity, Death, Fame, Time, and Eternity. Gautier's poem was first published in *Ariel: journal du monde élégant* on 30 April 1836, thereby adding a further voice to the French Romantic Petrarchan chorus.[132] The majority

---

[128]   Musset, *Poésies complètes*, p. 326.

[129]   This poem is discussed briefly by Henry F. Majewski in *Transposing Art into Texts in French Romantic Literature* (Chapel Hill: North Carolina Studies in the Romance Languages and Literatures, 2002), pp. 23–5, with the conclusion to this same book a further consideration of the art of Boulanger (pp. 103–7). See also, more generally, the essays collected in *Théophile Gautier: l'art et l'artiste: actes du colloque international*, 2 vols (Montpellier: La Société Théophile Gautier, 1982), Robert Snell, *Théophile Gautier: A Romantic Critic of the Visual Arts* (Oxford: Clarendon Press, 1982), and David Scott, *Pictorialist Poetics: Poetry and the Visual Arts in Nineteenth-Century France* (Cambridge: Cambridge University Press, 1988). I cite the poem from the following edition: 'Le Triomphe de Pétrarque: à Louis Boulanger', in Gautier, *Œuvres poétiques complètes*, ed. Michel Brix (Paris: Bartillat, 2004), pp. 203–8.

[130]   'Votre belle traduction de *Pétrarque*'. Letter dated 10 November 1837 and cited from Marie, *Le Peintre poète Louis Boulanger*, p. 63.

[131]   Banville particularly admires Gautier's use of *terza rima*, writing in his *Petit traité de poésie française*, p. 152, that 'Pour les *Terza Rima*, le poëte qu'il faut lire et étudier toujours, c'est Théophile Gautier, maître et seigneur absolu de ce rythme, qu'il a poussé à la dernière perfection' ('For poems in *Terza Rima*, the poet to read and study always, is Théophile Gautier, master and absolute lord of this rhythm, which he has stretched to the highest degree of perfection').

[132]   Gautier subsequently added a further twenty-one lines to the opening of the poem; see Gautier, 'Le Triomphe de Pétrarque', pp. 203–4. I ignore these additional tercets in my analysis as not being directly related to the painting, but rather a much more Dantean tale of

of the poem is a detailed description of Boulanger's painting, which emerges as a busy, chaotic, opulent *tableau*. At its centre, of course, is Petrarch, surrounded by Classical (the Muses, the Graces) and allegorical figures (*la rêverie et l'inspiration*), as well as by mortals from all walks of life:

> Rien n'y manque… Seigneurs blasonnés et superbes,
> Prêtres, marchands, soldats, professeurs, écoliers,
> Les vieillards tout chenus, et les pages imberbes.[133]

> ***

> Nothing is lacking…Proud, emblazoned lords,
> Priests, merchants, soldiers, teachers, pupils,
> White-haired old men, and smooth-faced pages.

The initial setting of the poem is Gautier's silent, awestruck encounter with Boulanger's painting (here, the painter is addressed directly):

> Je demeurai longtemps sans pouvoir te parler,
> Plongeant mes yeux ravis au fond de ta peinture
> Qu'un rayon de soleil faisait étinceler.[134]

> ***

> I remained for a long time unable to talk to you,
> Immersing my delighted eyes deep within your painting
> Which a ray of sunlight was causing to glitter.

As the poem progresses, however, the original mediation of the painting falls away, through the image of resurrection. This image is appropriate to the Easter Sunday setting of Petrarch's coronation and also underpins the shift in the ecphrasis from static, past description to living, present performance:

> Ô miracle de l'art ! ô puissance du beau !
> Je sentais dans mon cœur se redresser mon âme
> Comme au troisième jour le Christ dans son tombeau.[135]

> ***

> O miracle of art! O power of beauty!
> In my heart I felt my soul uplifted
> Like Christ from his tomb on the third day.

After this point, Petrarch, rather than Boulanger, becomes the principal addressee, and is hailed, Christologically, as 'living and returned to us!'.[136] Subsequently, Gautier describes the scene not as he might a painting, but rather as if it were actually

---

being lost in a dark wood on the threshold of Purgatory (*sic*) without one's Beatrice. Gautier's reading of Dante is discussed in Pitwood, *Dante and the French Romantics*, pp. 219–25.

[133] Gautier, 'Le Triomphe de Pétrarque', p. 206.
[134] Gautier, 'Le Triomphe de Pétrarque', p. 204.
[135] Gautier, 'Le Triomphe de Pétrarque', p. 205.
[136] 'vivante et revenue à nous !' Gautier, 'Le Triomphe de Pétrarque', p. 205 (the feminine agreement here refers back to Petrarch as a 'Figure').

unfolding before his very eyes, partly in homage to the vividness of Boulanger's depiction and partly as a result of the fervour of his own imagination.

Gautier complements his lively description of the procession with a discussion of the significance of the coronation, which, for him, lies in its celebration of peace rather than war:

> Tu viens du Capitole où César est monté,
> Cependant tu n'as pas, ô bon François Pétrarque,
> Mis pour ceinture au monde un fleuve ensanglanté.[137]
>
>   ***
>
> You come from the Capitol where Caesar ascended,
> Yet you have not, O good Francis Petrarch,
> Given the world a bloody river as a belt.

In emphasizing Petrarch's 'peaceful and calm' nature and calling, Gautier shifts territory from Italy to France, moving away both from Rome (the site of the coronation) and from the wider political turmoil ('Italy in flames').[138] Stressing that Petrarch was not involved in the latter, Gautier depicts the poet by way of contrast in the familiar, French location of the Fontaine de Vaucluse:

> Loin des cités, l'auberge et l'atelier des crimes,
> Tu regardes, couché sous les grands lauriers verts,
> Des Alpes tout là-bas bleuir les hautes cimes ;
>
> Et, penchant tes doux yeux sur la source aux flots clairs
> Où flotte un blanc reflet de la robe de Laure,
> Avec les rossignols tu gazouilles des vers.[139]
>
>   ***
>
> Far from cities, residence and workshop of crime,
> You watch, lying under great green laurels,
> The high peaks of the Alps far over there turning blue;
>
> And, turning your sweet eyes to the spring with clear waters
> Where a white reflection of Laura's dress shimmers,
> With the nightingales you warble verses.

These lines adopt well-worn Petrarchan images, alluding as they do both to the *incipit* of RVF 126 (with the mention of 'the spring with clear waters', *la source aux flots clairs*) and to classic symbols of poetry such as the laurel and the song of nightingales. In this way, Gautier inserts not only Laura (as Musset had done) but also the Provençal landscape into a scene that is otherwise predominantly Roman, masculine, and Latinate. Moreover, an earlier reference to Laura in the poem suggests that Musset's chronology of the coronation as postdating Laura's death was shared by Gautier, since Gautier, too, has the triumphant Petrarch thinking about his beloved

---

[137] Gautier, 'Le Triomphe de Pétrarque', p. 206.
[138] 'pacifique et serein', 'l'Italie en feu', Gautier, 'Le Triomphe de Pétrarque', p. 207.
[139] Gautier, 'Le Triomphe de Pétrarque', p. 207.

'blonde mistress' whom his 'eyes seem to seek in the liquid blue', that is, in a heavenwards gaze suggesting Laura's demise.[140] Both Musset and Gautier accordingly invest the coronation with a patina of sadness, and bring Laura to the fore in a scene in which she would otherwise risk being forgotten or overlooked.

Finally, Gautier concludes 'Le Triomphe de Pétrarque' with an introduction of a further, third addressee: future poets (himself included?) whom he exhorts to follow in Petrarch's footsteps so that, one day, a 'great painter' (*grand peintre*) might, in an 'enormous painting' (*immense toile*), depict them, too, crowned with laurel leaves and carried on a triumphal chariot.[141] Gautier's poem thus progresses from his encounter with Boulanger's painting recounted in the past historic, and a description of Petrarch's coronation in the present, to, finally, addressing upcoming poets in the future tense. In this manner, Gautier circles back round to the theme of painting, returning to Boulanger (the initial and titular addressee of the poem) with the flattering implication that he is a great painter of the present, whom great painters of the future will be pleased to imitate.

This chapter has explored the presence of Petrarch in French poetry throughout the nineteenth century, both in and out of the canon. In this analysis the celebration of Petrarch in French verse turns out to be clustered around the 1830s (whence emerges a distinctively French Romantic Petrarch), as well as around key anniversary dates (in particular, 1874 and 1904), though of greater longevity in the writings of Lamartine. This exploration has been far from exhaustive, and might fruitfully be continued, particularly in broader terms concerning the possible influence of the French Romantic obsession with Petrarch on the subsequent popularity of the French sonnet amongst later nineteenth-century French poets.[142] After all, as Jacques Roubaud has provocatively asserted, '*Every sonnet is a sonnet by Petrarch*'.[143] Such an exploration is all the more enticing if we recall that Paul Verlaine's 'À la louange de Laure et de Pétrarque' ('In Praise of Laura and Petrarch'), first published in the early 1880s, is really a sonnet in praise of the sonnet and of illustrious sonneteers (Shakespeare, Ronsard) not limited to Petrarch.[144] A further line of enquiry, lying beyond the remit of the present book, would be to trace the continued importance of

---

[140] 'Tes yeux semblent chercher dans le fluide azur / [...] ta maîtresse blonde', Gautier, 'Le Triomphe de Pétrarque', p. 205.

[141] Gautier, 'Le Triomphe de Pétrarque', p. 208.

[142] For some work in this direction, see Elliott Forsyth, 'Baudelaire and the Petrarchan Tradition', *Australian Journal of French Studies* 16 (1979), 187–97, and also Sandra L. Bermann, *The Sonnet Over Time: A Study in the Sonnets of Petrarch, Shakespeare and Baudelaire* (Chapel Hill, NC: University of North Carolina Press, 1988). It is also important that one early exponent of the sonnet in nineteenth-century France, Sainte-Beuve, was familiar with both Petrarch and the early history of French Petrarchism: see Sainte-Beuve, *Tableau historique et critique de la poésie française et du théâtre français au seizième siècle* (Paris: Sautelet et Compagnie, 1828).

[143] '*Tous les sonnets sont des sonnets de Pétrarque*', Jacques Roubaud, *La Fleur inverse: essai sur l'art formel des troubadours* (Paris: Éditions Ramsay, 1986), p. 344 (emphasis in the original).

[144] For this text, see Paul Verlaine, *Œuvres poétiques complètes*, ed. Yves-Gérard Le Dantec and rev. Jacques Borel (Paris: Gallimard, 1962), p. 320. See also, more generally, Scott,

Petrarch in much more recent French poetry, including that of René Char, Philippe Jaccottet, and Yves Bonnefoy, as well as Roubaud.

I will conclude the present chapter, however, by turning for a final piece of evidence of the Petrarchan obsession of nineteenth-century French poetry not to another poem but rather to a novel, Balzac's *Illusions perdues* (*Lost Illusions*), first published in three parts between 1837 and 1843. This work depicts the trials and tribulations of a provincial poet who goes to Paris to seek his fortune and literary glory, and instead encounters poverty and snobbery and is lured into journalism. Lucien Chardon, or Lucien de Rubempré, to give him his assumed, more noble, maternal name, desires to enter into literature and to become a writer. His offerings in this vein are twofold: a collection of sonnets entitled *Les Marguerites* (*Daisies*); a historical novel by the name of *L'Archer de Charles IX* (*The Archer of Charles IX*). Lucien introduces his manuscript of the former to the journalist Étienne Lousteau as follows:

> 'The sonnet, *monsieur*, is one of the most difficult works of poetry. This little poem has generally been abandoned. Nobody in France has been able to rival Petrarch, whose language, infinitely more flexible than ours, allows mental gymnastics [*jeux de pensées*] rejected by our *positivism* (forgive me this word). It therefore seemed to me original to start with a collection of sonnets. Victor Hugo has taken the ode, Canalis is committed to fugitive poetry, Béranger monopolizes the Song [*Chanson*], Casimir Delavigne has cornered Tragedy and Lamartine the Meditation.'[145]

In this *compte rendu* of French contemporary poets and their preferred poetic forms, Lucien clears a space for a French sonneteer which he himself hopes soon to occupy to general public acclaim. Lucien's opening poetic manifesto both places Petrarch as an unparalleled master of the sonnet and encourages competition from French writers (himself, in particular) which has heretofore been either lacking or without success. Following Lucien's example, Lousteau later presents Lucien's *Marguerites* to the bookseller Dauriat as '"a collection of sonnets to embarrass Petrarch"'.[146] Towards the end of the novel, Lucien will indeed be proclaimed, if only by a local newspaper back in Angoulême, as '"a rival of Petrarch!!!"' (punctuation in the original).[147]

The parallel between Lucien and Petrarch is also the source of the following Petrarchan pun made by Dauriat on the subject of Lucien's poetry collection:

Sonnet Theory and Sonnet Practice in Nineteenth-Century France, with discussion of Verlaine pp. 69–77.

[145] '"Le sonnet, monsieur, est une des œuvres les plus difficiles de la poésie. Ce petit poème a été généralement abandonné. Personne en France n'a pu rivaliser Pétrarque, dont la langue, infiniment plus souple que la nôtre, admet des jeux de pensée repoussés par notre *positivisme* (pardonnez-moi ce mot). Il m'a donc paru original de débuter par un recueil de sonnets. Victor Hugo a pris l'ode, Canalis donne dans la poésie fugitive, Béranger monopolise la Chanson, Casimir Delavigne accapare la Tragédie et Lamartine la Méditation.'" Balzac, *Illusions perdues*, ed. Roland Chollet, in *La Comédie humaine*, ed. Castex, v (1977), 1–732 (p. 337).

[146] '"Un recueil de sonnets à faire honte à Pétrarque"', Balzac, *Illusions perdues*, p. 369.

[147] '"un rival de Pétrarque !!!"', Balzac, *Illusions perdues*, p. 649.

'And our sonnets!' cried Michel Chrestien, 'will they not earn us the triumph of Petrarch?'

'Gold [*L'or*] (Laure) already has something to do with it', replied Dauriat whose pun excited universal appreciation.[148]

In the hands of Dauriat, the typical Petrarchan pun on Laura's name, criticized by many French readers and translators at this time (beginning with Sade, as noted in Chapter 2), produces a debased version of Petrarch's beloved. For Petrarch, the sonic association between Laura and gold (*l'oro*, in French Laure/*l'or*) was a symbol of preciousness, beauty, and luxury, denoting in particular her golden hair. In contrast, for Dauriat this gold is, simply, the money he hopes to make from the sales of Lucien's book. In the seamy world of nineteenth-century publishers and booksellers depicted in *Illusions perdues*, Petrarch's muse is reduced to an object more of financial than rarefied aesthetic value.

The treatment of Petrarch in Balzac's novel reflects, in a somewhat parodic light, the popularity of the medieval poet, and in particular his sonnets, at the height of French Romanticism. That Lucien desires to be a second, French Petrarch and Dauriat can perform a Petrarchan play on words which his audience is expected to recognize suggests how widespread and familiar was the myth of the poet at this time. Balzac's *Illusions perdues* acts as an ideal bridge leading from the topic of the present chapter, 'Petrarch in Poetry', to that of Chapter 6, 'The Novelization of Petrarch'. In the final chapter, novelistic parody will emerge, as already in Balzac's *Illusions perdues*, as one possible consequence of the introduction of Petrarch into the nineteenth-century French novel.

---

[148] '— Et nos sonnets ! dit Michel Chrestien, ne nous vaudraient-ils pas le triomphe de Pétrarque ?
— L'or (Laure) y est déjà pour quelque chose, dit Dauriat dont le calembour excita des acclamations générales.' Balzac, *Illusions perdues*, p. 474.

6

The Novelization of Petrarch

T HIS CHAPTER DRAWS on and develops the discovery, in the Introduction,
of prose texts that tell stories about Petrarch's life, and in particular about
Petrarch's love for a specific historical individual named Laura. While these
texts were typically works of criticism, history, and biography, in this chapter the
texts under discussion are, instead, novels.[1] Here, the Petrarchan novel is considered to pursue to its logical limit the desire of both critics and certain translators
to embed the *Canzoniere* into a prose narrative, that is, to a point where prose
has all but pushed poetry out of the picture entirely. Petrarchan novels represent
a surprising product of nineteenth-century French Petrarchism, in contrast to
the formally contiguous influence of Petrarch on French poetry delineated in the
previous chapter. The increasing popularity of the novel in nineteenth-century
France, conjoined with Romantic medievalism, enables a true transformation of
Petrarch from poetry to prose.[2]

Reading Petrarch's *Canzoniere* explicitly as a novel perhaps begins with the
German poet, critic, and philosopher Friedrich Schlegel, who asserted that 'Petrarch's poems are classical fragments of a novel.'[3] This comment adopts Petrarch as an
avatar of the new (and admittedly ill-defined) genre of the novel, even as it acknowledges the discontinuous, fragmentary, and therefore rather un-novelistic form of
Petrarch's aptly named *Rerum vulgarium fragmenta*. In the middle of the century,
Ernest and Edmond Lafond reiterated and developed this statement, praising
Petrarch's novelistic insight into human emotions: 'His *Canzoniere* is the true source
of the modern novel, which has taken as its aim the metaphysical analysis of love
in its battle with duty.'[4] Such novelistic readings of Petrarch's poetry went hand-in-
hand with the sporadic transformation of Petrarch's story into material for a novel,

---

[1] For a work that spans these categories, being a blend of history, biography, and
novelization, see Stéphanie-Félicité de Genlis, *Pétrarque et Laure*, 2 vols (Paris: Chez l'éditeur
des œuvres de Mme de Genlis, 1819), to which I will return briefly in the Conclusion for its
narrative of Petrarch's coronation.

[2] On the medieval inspiration of the French nineteenth-century novel more generally, see *La Fabrique du Moyen Âge*, ed. Bernard-Griffiths, Glaudes, and Vibert, pp. 753–921.

[3] 'Petrarcha's Gedichte sind classische Fragmente eines Romans', Friedrich Schlegel,
Literary Notebooks 1797–1801, ed. Hans Eichner (London: The Athlone Press, 1957), p. 50 (no.
353). See also Diana Behler, *The Theory of the Novel in Early German Romanticism* (Bern:
Peter Lang, 1978).

[4] 'Son *Canzoniere* est la véritable source du roman moderne, qui a pris pour but

a process to which a number of seminal French novels of the late eighteenth and the first half of the nineteenth centuries are, in various ways, committed. In 1902, Henri Hauvette exhorted readers of Petrarch to beware of 'seeking in the *Canzoniere* what it does not contain, by which I mean analysis of the female heart or even a romantic novel [*un roman d'amour*]'.[5] This warning, however, came far too late.

Theoretical Framework

Two theoretical models are at work in this chapter, stemming from Mikhail Bakhtin and Ève Duperray respectively. From the former I borrow the titular term 'novelization' which, for Bakhtin, describes how in a period of intense novel-writing, such as the nineteenth century, other forms often take on various attributes of the novel (with, for instance, poetry becoming novelized, that is, perhaps more narrative or plot-based). This type of novelization is at work in Schlegel's reading of Petrarch, cited above, though novelization is a mode not only of reading but also of writing. The novel in this sense is not a strictly defined genre but rather a fluctuating and trespassing force in and across many different forms of writing. Crucially, Bakhtin places the novel in a much wider and older history than it is often granted. On the one hand, Bakhtin explicitly evokes Petrarch as a possible avatar in his suggestion that in 'Augustine and Petrarch we can detect the embryonic beginnings of the *Prüfungs-* and *Bildungsroman*'.[6] On the other hand, he argues that the novel is not an isolated form, but rather is placed and places itself in a productive, disruptive, and often parodic dialogue with other pre-existing, better established genres:

> In an era when the novel reigns supreme, almost all the remaining genres are to a greater or lesser extent 'novelized': drama (for example Ibsen, Hauptmann, the whole of Naturalist drama), epic poetry (for example, *Childe Harold* and especially Byron's *Don Juan*), even lyric poetry (as an extreme example, Heine's lyrical verse). Those genres that stubbornly preserve their old canonic nature begin to appear stylized. In general any strict adherence to a genre begins to feel like a stylization, a stylization taken to the point of parody, despite the artistic intent of the author. In an environment where the novel is the dominant genre, the conventional languages of strictly canonical genres begin to sound in new ways, which are quite different from the ways they sounded in those eras when the novel was *not* included in 'high' literature.[7]

Bakhtin's observations chime with theories of the novel from the early nineteenth century, which often stressed the universality of the novel as a new form invading

---

l'analyse métaphysique de l'amour dans sa lutte avec le devoir.' Lafond, *Dante, Pétrarque, Michel-Ange, Tasse*, p. 112.

[5]   'Soyons prudents et gardons-nous à notre tour de chercher dans le *Canzoniere* ce qui n'y est pas, je veux dire l'analyse d'un cœur de femme ou même un roman d'amour.' Henri Hauvette, 'Laure de Noves?', *Bulletin italien*, 2 (1902), 15–22 (p. 22).

[6]   Bakhtin, *The Dialogic Imagination*, p. 350.

[7]   Bakhtin, *The Dialogic Imagination*, pp. 5–6.

and encompassing all other forms.[8] Yet specific to Bakhtin's formulation are the concepts of dialogism, polyphony, and especially parody, which are guiding features of the novels discussed in this chapter.

Bakhtin further distinguishes between poetic and novelistic writing, defining the former as unitary, singular, and closed, in direct contrast to the dialogism, heteroglossia, plurality, and openness of the latter:

> The language in a poetic work realizes itself as something about which there can be no doubt, something that cannot be disputed, something all-encompassing. [...] The language of the poetic genre is a unitary and singular Ptolemaic world outside of which nothing else exists and nothing else is needed. [...]
>
> The world of poetry, no matter how many contradictions and insoluble conflicts the poet develops within it, is always illumined by one unitary and indisputable discourse. Contradictions, conflicts and doubts remain in the object, in thoughts, in living experiences—in short, in the subject matter—but they do not enter into the language itself. In poetry, even discourse about doubts must be cast in a discourse that cannot be doubted.[9]

This description of poetry, though open to debate and refutation, to a certain extent seems apt in the case of Petrarch's *Canzoniere*, which clearly embodies a tension between content (the poet's 'contradictions, conflicts and doubts', to borrow Bakhtin's phrase) and form (the melodious, smooth, highly structured and polished style of the poems themselves).[10] The description also begs questions including what happens to poetic language when it becomes novelized and how Petrarch's poetic language can survive importation (by deformation or transformation) into the novel, and yet still remain recognizable. Since the novel, in Bakhtin's view, necessarily tends towards dialogism, polyphony, and parody, the novelization of Petrarch's monologic, monophonic poetic language must necessitate a sea change.[11]

It is particularly telling, as detailed below, that parody or its potential (a defining characteristic of Bakhtinian novelization) emerge as a key feature of the

---

[8]   See, for instance, Marguerite Iknayan, *The Idea of the Novel in France: The Critical Reaction, 1815–1848* (Geneva: Droz, 1961), p. 114.

[9]   Bakhtin, *The Dialogic Imagination*, p. 286.

[10]   Nonetheless, Bakhtin's polarized model of poetic versus novelistic discourse has been usefully criticized as overly reductive and as ignoring the often rich dialogism of poetry. Redressing this balance are essays in *Dialogism and Lyric Self-Fashioning: Bakhtin and the Voices of a Genre*, ed. Jacob Blevins (Selinsgrove, PA: Susquehanna University Press, 2008) and *Poetry and Dialogism: Hearing Over*, ed. Mara Scanlon and Chad Engbers (Basingstoke: Palgrave Macmillan, 2014), as well as Jahan Ramazani, *Poetry and Its Others: News, Prayer, Song, and the Dialogue of Genres* (Chicago: University of Chicago Press, 2013), especially pp. 1–62 devoted to the proposal of 'A Dialogic Poetics'.

[11]   The classic albeit contentious argument for Petrarch's monolingualism is made, in contrast to Dante's plurilingualism, by Contini, 'Preliminari sulla lingua del Petrarca [1951]', in idem, *Varianti e altra linguistica*, pp. 169–92. It is notable that French translators seem to share this view of Petrarch, by consistently complaining of the repetitiveness and lack of variety of his poetry (see, for instance, Sade and Saint-Geniès, discussed in Chapter 2).

nineteenth-century French Petrarchan novel, particularly in the later examples that I consider. While Bakhtin recognizes that 'there never was a single strictly straightforward genre [...] that did not have its own parodying and travestying double, its own comic-ironic *contre-partie*',[12] his specific connection between novelization and parody is persuasive, particularly if we recall, following Linda Hutcheon, the etymological meaning of parody (*parodia*) as both 'counter-' and 'beside-song':

> The prefix *para* has two meanings, only one of which is usually mentioned— that of 'counter' or 'against'. Thus parody becomes an opposition or contrast between texts. [...] However, *para* in Greek can also mean 'beside', and therefore there is a suggestion of an accord or intimacy instead of a contrast.[13]

The second meaning, in particular, allows Hutcheon to propose an understanding of parody as potentially constructive and respectful, rather than a necessarily aggressive, critical stance towards the parodied text or author. In the case of the nineteenth-century French Petrarchan novel, parody exists both against and alongside song (poetry), suggesting a possible 'accord or intimacy' (Hutcheon's phrase) with the original—Petrarch's *Canzoniere*—thereby invoked, however hazily or intermittently.

The second theoretical model underpinning this chapter is the work of Ève Duperray, whose identification and description of the phenomenon of the Petrarchist or Petrarchan novel (*le roman pétrarquiste*) has laid the groundwork for the present chapter's discussion and analysis of key examples of nineteenth-century French Petrarchan novels.[14] Duperray has highlighted a tendency for particular French novels to use Petrarch as a source of inspiration through 'reference to the mythical fable, the patronage of Petrarch and his *Canzoniere*, finally a Petrarchan conception of love'.[15] As regards the last, René Girard's theory of desire as typically mimetic or mediated (including by literary models) is also germane.[16] I follow Duperray both in considering Rousseau's *Julie, ou la Nouvelle Héloïse* (1761) as a foundational Petrarchan novel for the French literary tradition and in taking as the upper limit of this phenomenon George Sand's *Adriani* (1853).[17] In between these two novels, I explore, in order of date of publication, three further apposite examples: Sainte-Beuve's *Volupté* (1834), Balzac's *Le Lys dans la vallée* (1836), and Stendhal's *La*

[12]   Bakhtin, *The Dialogic Imagination*, p. 53.

[13]   Linda Hutcheon, *A Theory of Parody: The Teachings of Twentieth-Century Art Forms* (New York and London: Methuen, 1985), p. 32.

[14]   Duperray, *L'Or des mots*, pp. 109–23; Duperray, 'Le mythe littéraire de Vaucluse dans le roman pétrarquiste de *L'Astrée* (1607–1628) à *Adriani* (1853)'.

[15]   'la référence à la fable mythique, le patronage de Pétrarque et de son *Canzoniere*, enfin la conception pétrarquiste de l'amour', Duperray, *L'Or des mots*, p. 110.

[16]   René Girard, *Mensonge romantique et vérité romanesque* (Paris: Bernard Grasset, 1961).

[17]   See Duperray, *L'Or des mots*, pp. 110–13, 116–22. See also, on Rousseau's novel as particularly Petrarchan, Montoya, *Medievalist Enlightenment*, pp. 169–71, and Jürgen Stackelberg, 'Du paysage de l'amour au paysage de l'âme: Rousseau et Pétrarque', in *Vérité et littérature au XVIIIe siècle: mélanges rassemblés en l'honneur de Raymond Trousson*, ed. Paul Aron et al. (Paris: Champion, 2001), pp. 265–70.

Chartreuse de Parme (1839).[18] By choosing to analyse novels by canonical authors of the period, I hope to confirm the centrality of Petrarchism as a thread running through nineteenth-century French culture, a thread which I have already followed and attempted to untangle in relation to the spheres of translation and poetry.

Rousseau's *Julie, ou la Nouvelle Héloïse* (1761)

Rousseau's epistolary novel *Julie, ou la Nouvelle Héloïse* set a paradigm for French Petrarchan novels just as Voltaire's translation of *RVF* 126 acted as a bookmark for subsequent French translations of Petrarch.[19] Moreover, just as critics often sought to identify more general links between Voltaire and Petrarch in terms of literary and political prestige, so readers proposed parallels between Rousseau and Petrarch, most prominently with regard to a shared love of solitude, nature, and introspection, and a habit of autobiographical, confessional writing. Marc Monnier was far from unique in proclaiming, in the second half of the nineteenth century, that 'Petrarch appears to us today like a medieval Jean-Jacques'.[20] For Pierre Leroux, in a review of Gramont's complete translation of Petrarch's *Canzoniere* and *Triumphi* from 1842, the situation was similarly unambiguous: 'Rousseau was, in almost all matters, a successor [*continuateur*] of Petrarch'.[21]

Petrarch is explicitly present in *La Nouvelle Héloïse* through nine citations, from the novel's epigraph to a late reference in its sixth and final part.[22] These quotations in Italian imply a linguistic fluency not only on the part of the lovers, but also on the part of Rousseau's readership, which was to be incredibly numerous and enthusiastic.[23] Rousseau did, however, translate his quotations into French for a later edition of *La Nouvelle Héloïse*, the Édition Duchesne of 1764, thus making a limited and fragmentary but nonetheless interesting contribution to the vogue for translating Petrarch instigated more memorably and influentially by Voltaire.[24] Petrarch is initially cited within *La Nouvelle Héloïse* for his perceived applicability to

[18] These last two are also signalled as relevant texts in Duperray, *L'Or des mots*, pp. 113–16.

[19] On Voltaire, see the end of Chapter 2. All quotations from Rousseau's novel are from the following edition: *Julie, ou la Nouvelle Héloïse*, in Jean-Jacques Rousseau, *Œuvres complètes*, ed. Bernard Gagnebin and Marcel Raymond, 5 vols (Paris: Gallimard, 1959–95), II (1961), 1–793, with notes pp. 1333–829; and English translations my own.

[20] 'Pétrarque nous apparaît aujourd'hui comme un Jean-Jacques du moyen âge', Monnier, *La Renaissance, de Dante à Luther*, p. 111.

[21] 'Rousseau fut, presque en tout, un continuateur de Pétrarque', Leroux, 'Poésies de Pétrarque', p. 423.

[22] Rousseau, *La Nouvelle Héloïse*, p. 1339; Duperray, *L'Or des mots*, p. 111.

[23] Saint-Preux notes in an early letter to Julie her knowledge and love of Italian: *La Nouvelle Héloïse*, p. 60. As for the readership of Rousseau's novel, it included at least one key figure from the previous chapter, Lamartine, one of whose earliest quotations from Petrarch, in Italian, can be found in a letter singing the praises of Rousseau's *La Nouvelle Héloïse*. See *Correspondance d'Alphonse de Lamartine: deuxième série*, I, 199, in a letter once more addressed to Aymon de Virieu, and dated 11 March [1810?].

[24] Subsequent quotations in this section cite from Petrarch's poetry precisely as it appears in Rousseau's novel, with English translations, as usual, my own.

emotional situations experienced by the two protagonists, Julie and her anonymous lover, later baptized Saint-Preux. The latter, complaining of Julie's coldness towards him in private, invokes the following lines by Petrarch:

> E poi ch'amor di me vi fece accorta
> Fur i biondi capelli allor velati,
> E l'amoroso sguardo in se raccolto.[25]

> ***

> And once Love made you aware of me
> Your blonde hair was at that moment veiled,
> And your amorous gaze kept to itself.

In this manner, the relationship between Julie and Saint-Preux is inscribed under a Petrarchan sign which codifies both the lady's withdrawal and the lover's reproaches. Less explicitly, their love is also introduced through a wider Petrarchan vocabulary of fault, pity, desires, hope, torment, and sighs, and is typically considered to be an irresistible evil (*mal*) and a fatal poison, with the lover torn incessantly and irreconcilably between passion and virtue.[26]

Beyond the sphere of love, Petrarch is explicitly cited in *La Nouvelle Héloïse* for his love of the countryside and appreciation of the natural world, one expression of which Saint-Preux adopts in his admiration of the Haut-Valais:

> Qui non palazzi, non teatro o loggia,
> Ma'n lor vece un' abete, un faggio, un pino
> Trà l'erba verde e 'l bel monte vicino
> Levan di terra al Ciel nostr' intelletto.[27]

> ***

> Here not palaces, neither theatre nor loggia,
> But in their place a fir, a beech, a pine
> Between the green grass and the beautiful mountain nearby
> They lift from Earth to Heaven our mind.

Julie similarly borrows from Petrarch when describing the peaceful, isolated, rustic landscape near the source of the Vevaise, to which Saint-Preux again responds in like vein.[28] In this manner, Petrarch is a shared language of love and love of nature for both lovers; unusually, Julie is an active participant rather than merely a passive

---

[25] *La Nouvelle Héloïse*, p. 35, citing from *RVF* 11, vv. 8–10.

[26] Words such as 'faute', 'pitié', 'désirs', 'espoir', 'tourment', and 'soupirs' can all be found in the very first letter of the collection, Saint-Preux's declaration of love to Julie: *La Nouvelle Héloïse*, pp. 32–4.

[27] *La Nouvelle Héloïse*, p. 79, citing from *RVF* 10, vv. 5–7, 9 (thus eliding line 8 entirely). On these lines see also Virginia E. Swain, 'Le sublime et le grotesque: la lettre du Valais et la théorie esthétique de Rousseau', in *L'Amour dans 'La Nouvelle Héloïse': texte et intertexte: Actes du Colloque de Genève (10–11–12 juin 1999)*, ed. Jacques Berchtold and François Rosset (Geneva: Droz, 2002) (= *Annales de la société Jean-Jacques Rousseau*, 44 (2002)), pp. 101–18 (pp. 111–13).

[28] *La Nouvelle Héloïse*, pp. 113, 116; *RVF* 323, vv. 40–1, and *RVF* 142, vv. 7–8.

object in this game of Petrarchan citation. Thus Julie adopts lines from Petrarch about Laura's omnipresence in the landscape and applies them to Saint-Preux, taking advantage of the common omission of the subject pronoun in Italian:

Je suis environnée de tes vestiges, et je ne saurois fixer les yeux sur les objets qui m'entourent, sans te voir autour de moi.

> Qui cantò dolcemente, e qui s'assise:
> Qui si rivolse, e qui ritenne il passo;
> Qui co' begli occhi mi trafise il core:
> Qui disse una parola, e qui sorrise.[29]

***

I am surrounded by your traces, and I would not know how to gaze on the objects which encircle me, without seeing you all around me.

> Here he sang sweetly, and here he sat:
> Here he turned, and here he stayed his step;
> Here with his beautiful eyes he pierced my heart:
> Here he said a word, and here he smiled.

Julie boldly assumes the voice of the poet–lover of the *Canzoniere*, establishing a parallel between her male beloved Saint-Preux and Petrarch's Laura.[30] Julie's cousin (later Mme d'Orbe) importantly proves her similarity to the two lovers in terms of education and sensibility by also participating in this habit of drawing Petrarchan parallels, though in her case these parallels are drawn along more traditional lines: she describes Saint-Preux as a weeping lover, rather than as an absent, desired Laura.[31]

Of the nine quotations from Petrarch in *La Nouvelle Héloïse*, four come in the first of the six parts (not including the title page), thereby suggesting that Petrarch is a foundational presence in the narrative which nonetheless becomes less pronounced and more scattered as the novel progresses. This pattern is appropriate since Petrarch is most relevant to the description of the burgeoning love between Julie and Saint-Preux, while later situations diverge from the Petrarchan model. Yet despite these explicit citations, Petrarch vies throughout the novel for importance with other Italian poets (in particular, Metastasio and Tasso), as well as the titular intertext of the letters of Abelard and Heloise.[32] Moreover, in contrast to such explicit points of reference, Saint-Preux also attempts to free Julie from any literary

---

[29]   *La Nouvelle Héloïse*, p. 236, citing from *RVF* 112, vv. 9–12. As in my English translation, Rousseau's translation into French of these lines uses 'il' ('he') explicitly and consistently: 'C'est ici qu'il chanta' ('It is here that he sang'), and so on: *La Nouvelle Héloïse*, p. 1480.

[30]   See also *La Nouvelle Héloïse*, p. 222, where Julie cites from *RVF* 215, v. 3.

[31]   *La Nouvelle Héloïse*, p. 411; *RVF* 243, vv. 10–11.

[32]   See Laure Challandes, 'D'Abélard à Julie: un héritage renversé' and Jacques Domenech, 'Saint-Preux et Julie lecteurs du Tasse: connivence érotique et spiritualité amoureuse dans *La Nouvelle Héloïse* (Quand Rousseau "se fait un rempart du Tasse" dans *La Nouvelle Héloïse*)', both in *L'Amour dans 'La Nouvelle Héloïse'*, pp. 55–80 and 119–47 respectively.

comparisons, by describing her repeatedly as 'incomparable',[33] by asserting both that 'there is only one Julie in the world' and that 'There will never be but one Julie in the world',[34] and by asking 'Who else but Julie has ever loved, thought, spoken, acted, written like her?'[35] Assertions of Julie's uniqueness contradict the literary models of desire evoked by *La Nouvelle Héloïse* from its very title and epigraph.

Julie's marriage to M. de Wolmar after the death of her mother and at the behest of her father marks an end to the predominantly Petrarchan mode of the narrative of the love of Julie and Saint-Preux. After Julie's marriage and Saint-Preux's return from his distant travels, Saint-Preux's letters, now often sent to his friend Édouard Bomston, are less amorous and more often devoted to lengthy descriptions of life at Clarens, touching on practical matters such as how ideally to run a household, treat servants, design a garden, or bring up children. These letters continue the pattern of observation established by Saint-Preux's letters to Julie from Paris, and also elaborate on the distinction between corrupt city life (Paris) and peaceful rustic living (the Swiss countryside), which may owe something to Petrarch's critique of Avignon and love of rural life at Vaucluse. Petrarchan love, nonetheless, is absent from most of these discussions, except as a powerful, dangerous, and threatening force in the memories of Julie and Saint-Preux, in particular as these memories relate to specific places. Emblematically, when they visit Meillerie together they are both moved to discover Saint-Preux's earlier amorous annotations:

> I led her to the rock and showed her her initials etched in a thousand places, and several verses from Petrarch and Tasso relating to the situation that I was in as I drew them. On seeing them again myself after such a long time, I felt how the presence of objects can bring back powerfully the violent emotions by which we had been troubled close to them.[36]

Petrarchan love, tinged with an Ariostan twist (the inscription of initials and poetry on rock, and the madness such texts may provoke), is here a potent and fondly remembered model from the past which at times lurks dangerously close to the present.

Rousseau's novel seems to move gradually away from Petrarchan love, providing a clear model of conversion from love to virtue which is only hazily perceived and desired rather than enacted at the end of the *Canzoniere* and even then only after the death of the beloved rather than in relation to her marriage to another. Julie's death at the end of *La Nouvelle Héloïse* is a belated Petrarchan move which retrospectively

---

[33]   *La Nouvelle Héloïse*, pp. 73, 106, 607.

[34]   'il n'y a qu'une Julie au monde', 'Il n'y aura jamais qu'une Julie au monde', *La Nouvelle Héloïse*, pp. 198, 532.

[35]   'Quelle autre que Julie a jamais aimé, pensé, parlé, agi, écrit comme elle ?' *La Nouvelle Héloïse*, p. 244.

[36]   'Je la conduisis vers le rocher et lui montrai son chiffre gravé dans mille endroits, et plusieurs vers du Pétrarque et du Tasse relatifs à la situation où j'étois en les traçant. En les revoyant moi-même après si longtems, j'éprouvai combien la présence des objets peut ranimer puissamment les sentimens violens dont on fut agité près d'eux.' *La Nouvelle Héloïse*, p. 519.

explains the relevance of the Petrarchan epigraph chosen for the whole novel: 'The world did not know her, while it had her: / I knew her, who am left here to cry.'[37] Yet Saint-Preux's tears are silent; with Julie's death the novel comes to an end, cutting short any expressions of grief. There is no comparable second, *post-mortem* part in *La Nouvelle Héloïse* as there is in the *Canzoniere*. Instead, any indulgence in a Petrarchan language of bereavement is evaded by bringing the novel to a close with the death of the beloved lady. In a moment of weakness, Saint-Preux had already anticipated Julie's death in Petrarchan terms:

> If only she were dead! I dared to cry to myself in a transport of rage; yes, I would be less unhappy: I would dare to give myself over to my sorrows; I would embrace without remorse her cold tomb, my regrets would be worthy of her; I would say: she hears my cries, she sees my tears, my laments move her, she approves and receives my pure devotion... But she lives; she is happy!... she lives, and her life is my death, and her happiness is my torment, and Heaven after having torn her from me, takes from me even the sweetness of missing her![38]

In this passage, the 'cold tomb' echoes poems such as *RVF* 333, in which the poet addresses Laura's stony grave.[39] More generally, Saint-Preux here seems to recognize that the poet of the *Canzoniere* paradoxically becomes closer to Laura after her death, when she visits him in dreams and reassures him of her love and their eventual union (as recorded most memorably in *RVF* 302 and in the *Triumphus Mortis*). However, when Julie does die, this type of anticipated Petrarchan relationship with the deceased beloved who is mourned on Earth and invoked in Heaven is not fulfilled as the letters cease.

The conclusion of *La Nouvelle Héloïse* is further un-Petrarchan in its presentation of the possibility of a happy marriage for Saint-Preux after Julie's death. Julie herself desires and proposes that Saint-Preux marry her cousin Claire, though this marriage is resisted by both parties as a degrading form of infidelity, and is further repugnant to Claire because of her vow to remain forever unmarried after the death of her first husband. Julie's suggestion that Claire might be 'another Julie' (*une autre Julie*), a second Julie, is unthinkable to Saint-Preux and Claire who are equally devoted to Julie's uniqueness.[40] Saint-Preux's refusal of this proposed marriage

---

[37] 'Non la conobbe il mondo, mentre l'ebbe: / Conobill'io ch'a pianger qui rimasi.' *La Nouvelle Héloïse*, p. 3, citing from *RVF* 338, vv. 12–13. See also, on the epigraph as anticipating the conclusion of the novel and in the voice of Saint-Preux, Yannick Séité, *Du livre au lire: 'La Nouvelle Héloïse', roman des lumières* (Paris: Honoré Champion, 2002), pp. 189–98.

[38] 'Que n'est-elle morte ! osai-je m'écrier dans un transport de rage ; oui, je serois moins malheureux : j'oserois me livrer à mes douleurs ; j'embrasserois sans remords sa froide tombe, mes regrets seroient dignes d'elle ; je dirois : elle entend mes cris, elle voit mes pleurs, mes gémissemens la touchent, elle approuve et reçoit mon pur hommage... Mais elle vit ; elle est heureuse !... elle vit, et sa vie est ma mort, et son bonheur est mon supplice, et le Ciel après me l'avoir arrachée, m'ôte jusqu'à la douceur de la regretter !' *La Nouvelle Héloïse*, p. 615.

[39] For the text of this poem, see Chapter 4; the same poem is also rewritten by Mahul, as discussed in Chapter 5.

[40] *La Nouvelle Héloïse*, p. 741.

appropriately returns to Petrarch in order to reassert eternal fidelity through a recognition that there can be no future without the beloved: 'My time is completed in the middle of my years'.[41] Strikingly, this quotation comes from the turning point of the *Canzoniere*, late in the first half and in anticipation of Laura's death (the theme of the second half), but is appropriated by Rousseau close to the end of his novel, highlighting the impossibility and apparent undesirability of a *post-mortem* narrative as far as *La Nouvelle Héloïse* is concerned. Besides the uncertainty of any future marriage between Saint-Preux and Claire, Julie's desire (which is much more likely to be fulfilled) for Saint-Preux to comfort her husband and to educate her children remains equally un-Petrarchan in its eventual integration of the lover into the family of the beloved.

To conclude, Rousseau engages with Petrarch in *La Nouvelle Héloïse* in two distinct ways. Firstly and most strikingly, Rousseau demonstrates his intimate first-hand familiarity with Petrarch's *Canzoniere* in the original language. No other French novelist in the following century will cite so frequently or so extensively from Petrarch's poetry; instead, in later novels the presence of Petrarch is often reduced to more general parallels and invocations rather than specific quotations in Italian. Thus *La Nouvelle Héloïse* is literally a '*Canzoniere* put into prose' (*mis en prose*), in the sense that it presents fragments of Petrarch's poetic work inserted into (set in, placed within) a wider prose narrative, in the manner of a *prosimetrum*, albeit a *prosimetrum* which overwhelmingly privileges prose over poetry.[42] The novelization of Petrarch in *La Nouvelle Héloïse* is, unusually, neither at the expense of the *Canzoniere*'s original language (Italian) or form (poetry), making Rousseau one of the most faithful and sensitive of the French novelists who turn to Petrarch for inspiration.

Secondly, Rousseau exemplifies a willingness to play with the Petrarchan model, imitating the *Canzoniere* sporadically rather than slavishly, as it suits the wider narrative. Crucially, the novelization of Petrarch is from the outset a transformative process, and in Rousseau this process involves most prominently both the granting of a voice to the female beloved, Julie, unlike the typically silent, distant Laura, and a lack of interest in imitating or reproducing the poetic narrative of solitary mourning from the second part of the *Canzoniere*. While later novelists will often disregard the former, the latter is a marked feature of subsequent nineteenth-century French Petrarchan novels, and bears similarities with the abbé de Sade's decision, discussed in Chapter 2, not to translate any poems from the second part of the *Canzoniere*, since he fears boring his French readers 'by such a great number of monotonous, weepy verses'.[43] Mourning, it seems, is peculiarly unsuited to the French language and to prose, at least according to the standards of the 1760s, the decade in which both Rousseau's *La Nouvelle Héloïse* and Sade's *Mémoires* were published.

---

[41] 'È fornito 'l mio tempo a mezzo gli anni', *La Nouvelle Héloïse*, p. 677, citing from *RVF* 254, v. 14.

[42] Denis de Rougemont, *L'Amour et l'Occident* (Paris: Plon, 1939), p. 206.

[43] 'par un si grand nombre de vers monotones & larmoyans', Sade, *Mémoires*, I, p. cxii.

Sainte-Beuve's *Volupté* (1834)

The next significant French Petrarchan novel to be discussed is by an author whose engagement with the history of lyric poetry and the medieval Italian poetic tradition merits further investigation. This author, Sainte-Beuve, has already been mentioned in this book, albeit only in passing. The first reference, in Chapter 1, related Sainte-Beuve's encouragement of Poulenc in his translation project. Two further references, in Chapter 3, demonstrated Sainte-Beuve's varying attitude towards Petrarch's Latin works. While, on the one hand, Sainte-Beuve expressed a distinct lack of interest in the *Africa*, on the other hand he did unusually choose an extract from Petrarch's *De vita solitaria* as an epigraph to his own poetry collection *Les Consolations*. Finally, Sainte-Beuve's rediscovery and promotion of the sonnet form, thanks in large part to his work on sixteenth-century French Petrarchan poetry, was also suggested at the end of Chapter 5 to raise the possibility of a wider Petrarchan influence on the popularity of the sonnet form in France over the course of the nineteenth century. Indeed, in one of his own sonnets, entitled 'L'Amant antiquaire' ('The Antiquarian Lover'), Sainte-Beuve hailed Petrarch encouragingly as 'master of all of us in poetry'.[44] In this chapter, however, Sainte-Beuve's work as a novelist is discussed particularly in the light of one of Petrarch's own works in prose, the *Secretum*.

Sainte-Beuve's *Volupté* consists of a series of letters from a priest exhorting a friend to pursue a better life and to free himself from their shared titular vice of *volupté*, the quest for sensual pleasure. The fictive author of the letters, Amaury, presents his tale as an exemplary one of conversion, from which it is hoped that the addressed friend will take due warning and mend his ways. This trajectory from youthful error to a life of religious devotion resembles that signalled in the opening sonnet of the *Canzoniere*, in which the poet expresses his distance from his 'first youthful error / when I was in part another man from what I am'.[45] Amaury's conversion, however, seems far more successful and complete than Petrarch's; as modern critics have consistently noted, the phrase 'in part' (*in parte*) casts doubt on the narrative of conversion invoked in the first sonnet of the *Canzoniere*, since it presents this conversion from the outset as partial and therefore failed.[46] The same desire for and possibility of conversion is also a theme that is at the heart of Petrarch's *Secretum*.[47] Indeed, in addition to echoes of the *Canzoniere*, Amaury's stance as moral adviser with his own imperfect past mirrors the role of Augustinus in the *Secretum*, although the interlocutor (Amaury's addressee) is, in Sainte-Beuve's set-up, silent unlike the very vocal, stubborn, and sinful Franciscus of the *Secretum*. Instead, Amaury assumes the roles of both Franciscus (in terms of his past) and Augustinus (in terms of his present), and the dialogue form of Petrarch's *Secretum* is obscured in Sainte-Beuve's

---

[44] 'Pétrarque, notre maître à tous en poésie', Sainte-Beuve, *Livre d'amour* (Paris: A. Durel, 1904), p. 137 ('L'Amant antiquaire', v. 4).

[45] 'in sul mio primo giovenile errore / quand'era in parte altr'uom da quel ch'i' sono', *RVF* 1, vv. 3–4.

[46] On the *Canzoniere* as a tale of failed conversion, see Moevs, 'Subjectivity and Conversion in Dante and Petrarch'.

[47] For a brief introduction to the *Secretum* and discussion of its nineteenth-century French translations, see Chapter 3.

Volupté by the one-sidedness of the letter exchange. Amaury initially adopts the position of Franciscus, enamoured of women and earthly glory, but tempers this with a teleological narrative that ends with a renunciation of selfish, earthly cravings of the sort desired by Augustinus for Franciscus.

Sainte-Beuve's *Volupté* begins with Amaury's memories of his rural childhood and adolescence far from temptation in the years shortly after the Revolution. Amaury remembers these initial years fondly as having been devoted wholly to pious study and devotion to Classical languages and literature, although he—like Augustine in the *Confessions*—also recognizes that key Classical texts (in particular, Virgil) may act as incitements to *volupté* and as a distraction not only from God but also from oneself.[48] Amaury then records how he initially became involved with the seventeen-year-old Mademoiselle de Liniers (Amélie), who at that time was living with her grandparents at the old farm of La Gastine after the death of both her parents in swift succession. Forays further abroad lead Amaury to the château de Couaën where he forges a lifelong friendship with the marquis de Couaën and a complicated friendship with the marquis's wife, Madame de Couaën (née Lucy O'Neilly). A third female temptation comes in the form of Madame R., when for political reasons the Couaën family, to which Amaury is devoted, are forced to spend significant amounts of time in Paris. Wracked with indecision and guilt at his successive infidelities, Amaury regrets abandoning each lady in turn and continually contaminating his love with sensual desires. Amaury ultimately finds peace and resolution through religious conversion and embarking on a life of ordained ministry, during which one of his first duties is to hear Madame de Couaën's confession and give her the last rites, in a touching moment of reconciliation.

That Petrarch is an important intertext in this story is explicitly signalled in *Volupté*:

> One day, Laura's lover, the learned and melodious Petrarch, during a week of pious retreat, thought he saw enter the great Augustine, his revered patron saint, who spoke to him. And the great Saint, after having reassured the trembling man of faith, began to interrogate him, and he examined his life as an attentive teacher, and on every part of that life he gave his advice: honours, studies, poetry, and glory, in turn, were considered, and, when he got to Laura, he cut her off. But Petrarch, who had yielded to all the Saint's decisions, at this point reacted vociferously full of pain, and on his knees begged he who had wept over Dido to leave him his thoughts of Laura.[49]

---

[48] On Augustine's youthful reading of Virgil, see Augustine, *Confessions*, trans. William Watts, 2 vols (Cambridge, MA: Harvard University Press, 1912), I, 38–43 (Book One, Chapter XIII).

[49] 'Un jour, l'amant de Laure, le docte et mélodieux Pétrarque, dans une semaine de retraite pieuse, crut voir entrer le grand Augustin, son patron révéré, qui lui parla. Et le grand Saint, après avoir rassuré le fidèle tremblant, se mit à l'interroger, et il examinait cette vie en directeur attentif, et il y portait dans chaque partie son conseil : les honneurs, l'étude, la poésie et la gloire, tour à tour, y passèrent, et, lorsqu'il arriva à Laure, il la retrancha. Mais Pétrarque, qui s'était incliné à chaque décision du Saint, se récria ici plein de douleur, et supplia à genoux

This passage indicates that Sainte-Beuve has in mind in *Volupté* Petrarch's *Secretum* more any other of Petrarch's works, even the *Canzoniere*. Accordingly, *Volupté* has even been dubbed 'Sainte-Beuve's *Secretum*'.[50] Sainte-Beuve's choice is unusual given the typical reduction of Petrarch at this time to a poet of Italian love sonnets, and it allows Sainte-Beuve to harness Petrarch's confessional, introspective prose as a model for the modern novel. Sainte-Beuve's *Volupté* is thus an interesting reminder that there are works by Petrarch in prose that writers can take as their model, rather than the purely poetic example of the *Canzoniere* which is otherwise more typically the focal point of the French Petrarchan novel (as, for instance, the example of Rousseau's *La Nouvelle Héloïse* has already shown).

The Petrarchan influence on Sainte-Beuve's novel may, moreover, be audible from the work's very title, *Volupté*, a vice which is glossed within the text as 'monotonous tiredness' and 'melancholy of a guilty source'.[51] This vice is strikingly akin to the sin of *acedia* or *aegritudo* discussed in Book Two of Petrarch's *Secretum*.[52] Other aspects of *Volupté* similarly resonate with the *Secretum*, although they also belong to a much wider tradition of both lyric and religious imagery. In the third book of the *Secretum*, Augustinus accuses Franciscus of being bound by two chains, love and glory, and these chains, which appear in *Volupté* precisely as 'heavy chains' (*lourdes chaînes*), similarly bind Amaury in the form of ceaseless desire for amorous satisfaction and political, military success.[53] This image is compounded by further characterization in *Volupté* of love not only as chains but according to a sequence of further Petrarchan tropes: love as a wound or illness; love as the cause of moral shipwreck leading the lover far from God who is harbour and port; love as a labyrinth.[54] As regards the last image, Paris, in particular, is characterized as a labyrinth of sin and temptation, in terms that also recall Dante's *Inferno* V: the capital is described as 'a whirling labyrinth like that of the lustful damned'.[55] Other Petrarchan themes in *Volupté* include precisely this contrast between sinful city versus peaceful countryside, incarnated

celui qui avait pleuré sur Didon de lui laisser l'idée de Laure.' Sainte-Beuve, *Volupté*, ed. André Guyaux (Paris: Gallimard, 1986), p. 74. All subsequent quotations are from this same edition.

[50] 'Il *Secretum* del Sainte-Beuve'. Bertoli, *La Fortuna del Petrarca*, p. 132.

[51] 'fatigue monotone', 'une mélancolie de source coupable', *Volupté*, pp. 34 and 149.

[52] For more evidence from Sainte-Beuve's novel that *volupté* is *acedia*, see Patrick Labarthe, 'Expérience intimiste et politique dans *Volupté*', in *La Pensée du paradoxe: approches du romantisme: hommage à Michel Crouzet*, ed. Fabienne Bercegol and Didier Philippot (Paris: Presses de l'université de Paris-Sorbonne, 2006), pp. 107–40 (pp. 130–2). For discussion of Petrarchan *acedia*, see Jennifer Rushworth, *Discourses of Mourning in Dante, Petrarch, and Proust* (Oxford: Oxford University Press, 2016), in particular Ch. 2 and the bibliography therein.

[53] *Volupté*, p. 34.

[54] For love as a wound ('blessure'), see *Volupté*, p. 86, and as a shipwreck ('naufrage'), *Volupté*, pp. 34 and 113. God is 'the indestructible port in the midst of storms' ('l'impérissable port au sein des tempêtes') in *Volupté*, p. 217. The Petrarchan theme of shipwreck is especially evident in RVF 189, on which sonnet see Michelangelo Picone, 'Il sonetto CLXXXIX', *Lectura Petrarce*, 9 (1989), 151–77, and Cachey, 'From Shipwreck to Port: RVF 189 and the Making of the *Canzoniere*', *Modern Language Notes*, 120 (2005), 30–49.

[55] 'un labyrinthe tournoyant comme celui des damnés luxurieux', *Volupté*, p. 112. On Dante and Sainte-Beuve, see Pitwood, *Dante and the French Romantics*, pp. 239–50. On love as a labyrinth in the *Canzoniere*, see RVF 211, v. 14.

for Petrarch in Avignon and Vaucluse respectively. Further, for post-conversion Amaury as for Petrarch, the only virtuous, admirable, habitable city is Rome. As Amaury recalls, 'This city of meditation, of continuity, of eternal memory, suited me above all; I needed this immense cloister, this slow and permanent celebration, and the calm of holy tombs. It is Rome where one can best, after all shipwreck, soothe the last floods of one's heart.'[56] Here Roman Catholicism atypically trumps the often nationalistic construction of a French Petrarch.

More generally, themes of repentance, guilt, memory, tears, and sighs in *Volupté* may be attributable to Petrarchan inspiration, while the conflict between earthly and divine love is a constant in both Sainte-Beuve's novel and Petrarch's writings. Within this conflict, however, Amaury hopes that pure love for a virtuous lady can lead to God, inspired by the example of Dante's Beatrice and a particular, Platonizing interpretation of Petrarch's Laura and his love for the same. For this reason, the rejection of Laura advocated by Augustinus in the *Secretum* (as in the final poem of the *Canzoniere*) is considered by Amaury to be unnecessarily harsh:

> And why also, O the most tender of doctors, O the most irrefutable of Fathers, if it is permitted for me to ask it humbly, why did you not leave her to him? Is it then absolutely forbidden to love in thought a choice being, when the more we love, the more we feel ourselves ready to believe, to suffer, and to pray; when the more we pray and the more we raise ourselves up, the more we feel an appetite to love this being? What's wrong especially when this unique being is already dead and rapt [*ravie*], when she is already to be found in relation to us on the other side of Time, with God?[57]

This defence of Laura as leading to God is closer to the solution of the *Triumphi* than that of the *Canzoniere*, although, as we have seen, sonnets such as *RVF* 302 do also approximate this resolution of Laura in Heaven.

Nonetheless, in certain respects *Volupté* is distinctly un-Petrarchan, both in terms of its cast of characters and its structure. For a start, Laura is presented as the unique object of the poet's affections, whereas Amaury becomes involved with three different ladies, even if there is a hierarchy with Madame de Couaën indisputably his foremost attachment.[58] Furthermore, Amaury's trajectory from human to divine

---

[56] 'Cette cité de méditation, de continuité, de souvenir éternel, m'allait avant tout ; j'avais besoin de ce cloître immense, de cette célébration lente et permanente, et du calme des saints tombeaux.' *Volupté*, p. 385. For Petrarch's love of Rome, see, for instance, *Fam.* II, 9: *Familiarium rerum libri*, ed. Rossi, I, 96–7; *Letters on Familiar Matters: Rerum familiarium libri I–VIII*, trans. Bernardo, p. 104. Petrarch's choice to receive the laurel crown in Rome rather than Paris is discussed in the Conclusion.

[57] 'Et pourquoi aussi, ô le plus tendre des docteurs, ô le plus irréfragable des Pères, s'il m'est permis de le demander humblement, pourquoi ne la lui laissais-tu pas ? Est-il donc absolument interdit d'aimer en idée une créature de choix, quand plus on l'aime, plus on se sent disposé à croire, à souffrir et à prier ; quand plus on prie et l'on s'élève, plus on se sent en goût de l'aimer ? Qu'y a-t-il surtout quand cette créature unique est déjà morte et ravie, quand elle se trouve déjà par rapport à nous sur l'autre rive du Temps, du côté de Dieu ?' *Volupté*, pp. 74–5.

[58] On hints of Petrarchan infidelity, see, however, Justin Steinberg, 'Dante *Estravagante*,

love culminating in his admission to the priesthood is far more decisive and final than any conversion achieved by Petrarch. Not only does *RVF* 1, as noted above, present a partial conversion, but the *Secretum* itself, the closest model for *Volupté*, culminates in an impasse. Franciscus recognizes the truth of Augustinus's advice, but delays acting on it until an indeterminate point in the future, so that Augustinus is forced, against his better judgement, to 'let things carry on like this, since they cannot be otherwise'.[59] The relationship between loss and conversion is also different in Sainte-Beuve and Petrarch. Importantly, Madame de Couaën's death comes after Amaury's conversion at the end of the text, so that her death signals the endpoint of the narrative and is not a factor in Amaury's decision to become a priest. Laura's death is discussed but still in the future in the *Secretum*, so that this text narrates neither bereavement nor conversion. However, in the *Canzoniere* Laura's death is at the heart of the collection, but still does not lead to any decisive conversion, despite the prayer to the Virgin Mary that constitutes the final poem of the *Canzoniere*. Amaury's conversion both in terms of its success and its timing is strikingly at odds with these Petrarchan models.

It is also notable that the defence of Petrarch's love for Laura in *Volupté* is tempered by implicit criticism of some of the circumstances surrounding this love, particularly Petrarch's *innamoramento* in church on Good Friday, a detail that, as related in the Introduction, was rejected by Costaing as being so shocking as to be incredible and therefore impossible. Amaury accepts the potentially beatific nature of human love but warns precisely against allowing love for a lady to obscure love for God, particularly on a day such as Good Friday:

> I am not one of those, you know, who would take away every Beatrice from in front of the steps of a mortal pilgrim. But remember, my friend, never to abuse the heart which would have given itself to you, and to make of this cult of a chosen being but a translucent and more tangible form of divine Love. If one Good Friday evening, in a church at the railings of the Tomb which we adore, you find yourself by chance on your knees not far from her, if, after the first exchange of glances, you then abstain from all further glances, out of devotion to the terrible Sepulchre, oh! how you will then feel that you have never loved her more than in these sublime moments![60]

The turning away from the lady recommended here seems to take Petrarch to task

---

Petrarca *Disperso*, and the Spectre of the other Woman', in *Petrarch and Dante: Anti-Dantism, Metaphysics, Tradition*, pp. 263–89.

[59] Petrarch, *My Secret Book*, trans. Nichols, p. 93. For the original Latin, see *Secretum*, ed. Carrara, p. 214 ('Sed sic eat, quando aliter esse non potest').

[60] 'Je ne suis pas de ceux, vous le savez, qui retrancheraient toute Béatrix de devant les pas du pèlerin mortel. Mais souvenez-vous mon ami, de ne jamais abuser du cœur qui se serait donné à vous, de ne faire de ce culte d'une créature choisie qu'une forme translucide et plus saisissable du divin Amour. Si quelque soir de Vendredi-Saint, dans une église à la grille du Tombeau qu'on adore, vous vous trouvez par hasard à genoux non loin d'elle, si, après le premier regard échangé, vous vous abstenez ensuite de tout regard nouveau, par piété pour le Sépulcre redoutable, oh ! comme vous sentirez alors que vous ne l'avez jamais mieux aimée qu'en ces sublimes moments !' *Volupté*, p. 296.

for the circumstances of his first sight of Laura (related in *RVF* 3), a situation for which the poet, too, expresses some guilt. The conflict between the laurel (Laura, earthly glory, poetry) and the wood of the Cross is particularly evident in *RVF* 62, which commemorates both the first sight of Laura, eleven years on, and Good Friday.

Moreover, the Petrarchan intertext forms but one example within a network of literary references around which characters and situations are constructed in *Volupté*. For instance, the marquis's wife Lucy is ultimately modelled explicitly neither on Laura nor on Beatrice (even though 'the names of Beatrice and Laura' are recorded in passing),[61] but rather on St Lucy, who appears in Dante as 'Lucy, enemy of all cruelty', a line from *Inferno* which is cited in the original Italian twice in *Volupté* in relation to Madame de Couaën, first by Amaury and later by the marquis.[62] The second occurrence is endowed with particular weight since it then stands as the marquis's final, posthumous understanding of his wife's life and character. Along-side Petrarch, the presence of Dante becomes more and more insistent, even though Amaury's vision of Dante is markedly revisionist, for instance suggesting a new area in the Afterlife for the punishment of youthful *volupté*, 'in the circles of Hell, not far from the area of the lukewarm, or perhaps at the bottom of the ramps of Purgatory, a plain not described, the only place that Dante and his divine guide did not visit'.[63] This uncertainty about the precise location of the voluptuous sinners has wider implications for an understanding of *volupté*, whether a mortal sin leading to Hell (though the lukewarm are outside Hell) or a capital vice that is revocable and permits entry to Purgatory.

Besides the identification with St Lucy, Madame de Couaën is compared to St Augustine's mother, 'Saint Monica in her house at Ostia',[64] while Amaury draws attention to 'the striking relationship of the situations and suffering with ours' in Barbara Juliane von Krüdener's epistolary novel *Valérie* (1804).[65] Amaury also feels himself to be closer to Chateaubriand's René or to Goethe's Werther than to either Petrarch or Dante,[66] while Madame R. shares her first name (Herminie) with the unloved Erminia from Tasso's *Gerusalemme liberata* (*Jerusalem Delivered*), a coincidence upon which Amaury reflects.[67] Within these various patterns of literarily inflected desire, Petrarch is only one possible, though privileged model amongst a plethora of explicitly invoked literary avatars. Sainte-Beuve's novelistic engagement with Petrarch remains, nonetheless, remarkable in particular for its atypical foray into Petrarch's Latin works.

---

[61] 'les noms de Béatrix et de Laure', *Volupté*, p. 231.

[62] 'Lucia, nimica di ciascun crudele'. *Inferno*, II, v. 100. See *Volupté*, pp. 106 and 382.

[63] 'dans les cercles d'Enfer, non loin de la région des tièdes, ou peut-être au bas des rampes du Purgatoire, une plaine non décrite, seul endroit que Dante et son divin guide n'aient pas visité', *Volupté*, p. 280.

[64] 'Sainte Monique en sa maison d'Ostie', *Volupté*, p. 232.

[65] 'le rapport frappant des situations et des souffrances avec les nôtres', *Volupté*, p. 284. See Barbara Juliane von Krüdener, *Valérie, ou Lettres de Gustave de Linar à Ernest de G...*, 2 vols (Paris: Henrichs, 1804).

[66] *Volupté*, pp. 178, 207.

[67] *Volupté*, p. 248.

Balzac's *Le Lys dans la vallée* (1836)

The third case study, Balzac's *Le Lys dans la vallée*, is in dialogue not only with Petrarch but also with the preceding two novels, *La Nouvelle Héloïse* and *Volupté*. In this way the French Petrarchan novel undergoes a layering effect, whereby Petrarch is mediated by earlier novelists, with Rousseau remaining a particularly foundational model. The three novels are also connected formally, as they are all epistolary in nature. This structuring device is more evident in *La Nouvelle Héloïse*, with its multiple correspondents, than in the later two novels, which rely on one voice either entirely (*Volupté*) or almost entirely (*Le Lys dans la vallée* concludes with a short, sarcastic reply from the novel's addressee). These three epistolary novels act as a transition point between the fragmentation and discontinuity of Petrarch's 'scattered rhymes' (*rime sparse*, RVF 1, v. 1) and the narrative prose of our final two examples, Stendhal's *La Chartreuse de Parme* and Sand's *Adriani* (which is not to say that letters and letter-writing are entirely absent from these last two). A developed Petrarchan analysis of *Le Lys dans la vallée* has hitherto been lacking, perhaps because the extent of Balzac's knowledge of Petrarch remains in question.[68] In *Le Lys dans la vallée*, absent are the explicit quotations from Petrarch of Rousseau's *La Nouvelle Héloïse*; instead, the story of Petrarch and Laura is referenced primarily through invocation of their names, as in Sainte-Beuve's *Volupté*. More troublingly, Petrarch is erroneously described in Balzac's novel as a Venetian poet, thereby casting further doubt on Balzac's familiarity with him.[69]

The story of *Le Lys dans la vallée* is an elaboration of a situation similar to that narrated in *La Nouvelle Héloïse* and most especially in *Volupté*, that is, a situation in which a young man (Félix de Vandenesse) falls in love with a married woman (Mme de Mortsauf, whom Félix addresses as Henriette) who becomes a sort of Platonic guardian angel figure and dies at the end of the novel.[70] This love for a married woman entails an inevitable intimacy with Henriette's husband, who, however, is depicted as a figure of selfish, hypochondriacal, brutal madness, unlike the genuine friendship between lover and husband in the two novels of Rousseau and Sainte-Beuve. Like Julie, Mme de Mortsauf is depicted as particularly devoted to her children, Jacques and Madeleine; in a letter from beyond the grave, Mme de Mortsauf repeats her desire that Félix might watch over her remaining family and even one day

[68] The critical neglect of the Petrarchan aspects of Balzac's *Le Lys dans la vallée* is lamented, for instance, by Robert O. J. Van Nuffel, 'Note e rassegne: per la fortuna del Petrarca in Francia', *Studi petrarcheschi*, 6 (1956), 225–31 (p. 230). Balzac's *Le Lys dans la vallée* is also discussed briefly in Duperray, *L'Or des mots*, pp. 113–15.

[69] See Balzac, *Le Lys*, p. 1081; Balzac, *The Lily*, p. 186.

[70] On the connections between these three novels and their authors, see: Robert J. Niess, 'Sainte-Beuve and Balzac: *Volupté* and *Le Lys dans la vallée*', *Kentucky Romance Quarterly*, 20.1 (1973), 113–24; Patrick Labarthe, 'Balzac et Sainte-Beuve, ou de l'inimitié créatrice', *L'Année balzacienne*, 9 (2008), 7–23; Raymond Trousson, *Balzac, disciple et juge de Jean-Jacques Rousseau* (Geneva: Librairie Droz, 1983); Jacques Borel, *'Le Lys dans la vallée' et les sources profondes de la création balzacienne* (Paris: Librairie José Corti, 1961); Nancy K. Miller, '"Tristes Triangles": *Le Lys dans la vallée* and Its Intertext', in *Pre-text, Text, Context: Essays on Nineteenth-Century French Literature*, ed. Robert L. Mitchell (Columbus: Ohio State University Press, 1980), pp. 66–77.

marry her daughter Madeleine. As in *La Nouvelle Héloïse*, in the projected marriage between Claire and Saint-Preux, this suggestion reveals the generosity and apparent lack of jealousy of the beloved lady, but is unlikely ever to be fulfilled because of the loyalty felt in particular by the female relation (whether cousin or daughter) to their departed relative. Moreover, Félix is at times closer to Amaury than to Saint-Preux, in that he remains spiritually devoted to the original lady (Mme de Mortsauf), while becoming involved with another woman, the Lancastrian Lady Dudley (Arabelle). This involvement is suggested to be the cause of Mme de Mortsauf's death, from jealousy and a broken heart. The novel's *dénouement* thus casts a strange shadow of guilt over Félix that is absent from the male protagonists of *La Nouvelle Héloïse* or *Volupté*, and this guilt is further increased by the context of the narration, which is that of a long letter to a third lady, Natalie de Manerville. Félix's differences from Amaury and Saint-Preux are only underscored further by the fact that at one point he did contemplate following in both their footsteps, combining the twin destinies of priest and tutor: "'I will enter a seminary, I will leave it a priest, and I will bring up Jacques.'"[71] Félix's addressee, Natalie, undermines the protagonist's supposedly Petrarchan fidelity, even though Natalie ultimately forestalls any further, immediate infidelity by rejecting his advances because of his impossible obsession with the past, in a letter with which *Le Lys dans la vallée* comes to a close.

Petrarch and Laura are explicitly invoked on several occasions in *Le Lys dans la vallée*. The first instance is particularly interesting for the question it poses which is of relevance to much nineteenth-century interest in Petrarch: "'Can Petrarch's Laura be again renewed?'"[72] This question is voiced by Mme de Mortsauf as she tries to explain what she wants her relationship with Félix to be like: intimate, friendly, selfless, unique, pure, and chaste, after the manner of Petrarch's love for Laura. Yet Mme de Mortsauf's immediate answer is "'I was mistaken. God does not will it.'"[73] In this way the Petrarchan model is denied at the same moment that it is introduced. In contrast, Félix is more optimistic and self-important; he aims not only to equal but even to surpass the Petrarchan model, as the second explicit reference makes clear: 'I had no other ambition than to love Henriette better than Petrarch loved Laura.'[74] Given Félix's later infidelities, particularly after Henriette's death, this wish is subsequently revealed to be ill-founded and unfulfilled.

The third reference to Petrarch in *Le Lys dans la vallée* is Félix's recommitment to this Petrarchan love. Mme de Mortsauf tells Félix she wants to be his "'star'" and "'sanctuary'", to which Félix replies "'You shall be my religion and my light, you shall be all!'"[75] Félix then notes in his narrative commentary on this exchange that 'From that day, [...] she became what Beatrice was to the Florentine poet, the

---

[71] "'Je vais entrer dans un séminaire, j'en sortirai prêtre, et j'élèverai Jacques.'" *Le Lys*, p. 1041; *The Lily*, p. 121.

[72] "'La Laure de Pétrarque peut-elle se recommencer ?'" *Le Lys*, p. 1035; *The Lily*, p. 110.

[73] "'Je me suis trompée, Dieu ne le veut pas.'" *Le Lys*, p. 1035; *The Lily*, p. 110.

[74] 'Je n'avais d'autre ambition que celle d'aimer Henriette, mieux que Pétrarque n'aimait Laure.' *Le Lys*, p. 1045; *The Lily*, p. 127.

[75] "'Je veux être l'étoile et le sanctuaire'", "'Vous serez ma religion et ma lumière, vous serez tout'", *Le Lys*, p. 1081; *The Lily*, p. 185.

spotless Laura to the Venetian poet.[76] As already noted, the purported Venetian identity of Petrarch is rather strange, although the description of Laure as spotless (*sans tache*) is typical of idealizing, Platonic readings of Petrarch's supremely chaste beloved. Mme de Mortsauf is represented as similarly spotless given her frequent associations with the colour white, which indicates her own chastity and virginity. Her husband even calls her Blanche (Henriette is the name used only in the past by her aunt and later by Félix) and complains at a certain point that '"She is virgin at my expense"', a phrase which reassures Félix greatly.[77] Thus after Henriette's death, Félix is able to dismantle conceptually the marriage between M. and Mme de Mortsauf, convincing himself that 'The souls of these two beings had been no more united than their bodies', thereby discrediting this union in order to magnify by way of contrast his own, superior 'fraternal marriage' with Henriette.[78] In this way, the *querelle* between Laura as virgin and Laura as mother, outlined in the Introduction, is resolved in Balzac's imagining of a female character, Henriette/Blanche, who is both a mother and a virgin, on the model not only of Petrarch's Laura (in Balzac's reading) but also of the Virgin Mary (as discussed below).

At times Félix strives to emulate Henriette's virginal whiteness, again as a result of explicitly Petrarchan inspiration:

> She was a figure so religiously adored, that I resolved to stand without stain in the presence of my secret divinity, and ideally reclothed myself in the white robe of the Levites, thus imitating Petrarch, who never presented himself before Laura de Noves but dressed entirely in white.[79]

Yet Félix's love is more commonly red than white ('as a red-hot iron',[80] suffused with passion as both desire and suffering), and even the white Mme de Mortsauf is not immune to physical desire, as her death-bed fury and *post-mortem* letter remembering Félix's first and only embrace suggest.[81] Nonetheless, Mme de Mort-sauf remains a paradigm of purity, provoking both admiration and frustration in Félix. Félix thus reflects on Mme de Mortsauf's chastity in terms of an opposition between Petrarch's chaste Laura and Dante's adulterous Francesca from *Inferno* V of the *Commedia*: 'Most assuredly she loved, as Laura de Noves loved Petrarch, not as

---

[76]   'Dès ce jour [...] elle devint ce qu'était la Béatrix du poète florentin, la Laure sans tache du poète vénitien.' *Le Lys*, p. 1081; *The Lily*, pp. 185–6.

[77]   '"Elle est vierge à mes dépens."' *Le Lys*, p. 1072; *The Lily*, p. 172.

[78]   'Les âmes de ces deux êtres ne s'étaient pas plus mariées que leurs corps', 'fraternel mariage'. *Le Lys*, pp. 1213, 1048; *The Lily*, pp. 397, 132.

[79]   'Elle fut une figure si religieusement adorée que je résolus de rester sans souillure en présence de ma divinité secrète, et me revêtis idéalement de la robe blanche des lévites, imitant ainsi Pétrarque qui ne se présenta jamais devant Laure de Noves qu'entièrement habillé de blanc.' *Le Lys*, p. 1083; *The Lily*, p. 189.

[80]   'comme un fer rouge', *Le Lys*, p. 1048; *The Lily*, p. 132.

[81]   In this sense, Mme de Mortsauf is a red as well as a white lily, as remarked by Pierre Laforgue, *L'Œdipe romantique: le jeune homme, le désir et l'histoire en 1830* (Grenoble: ELLUG, 2002), p. 183.

Francesca da Rimini loved Paolo: an awful discovery for whomsoever should dream of the union of both these loves!'[82]

This contrast between Laura and Francesca is reflected in Félix's passion for both the chaste, French Henriette and the sensual, English Lady Dudley, and is part of a wider series of antitheses which structure the work in a Petrarchan fashion.[83] As in Petrarch's *Canzoniere*, so in *Le Lys dans la vallée* the narrative is constructed around sets of paired oppositions, which revolve around the essential conflict of Earth versus Heaven and extend in general to a conflict between Eros and Caritas ('a carnal love and a divine love', *amour charnel* versus *amour divin*), thus ultimately complicating and enriching the impossible choice of love object.[84] Félix concludes: 'So I was the dupe of the two irreconcilable passions [...]. I loved an angel and a devil.'[85] This sense of irreconcilability is repeated by Mme de Mortsauf: "'I see now that heaven and earth are incompatible."'[86] Emblematically, her dying enacts a final 'struggle between the body and soul' which further stresses these opposing forces.[87] As discussed below, Félix's quest for a conciliatory union of these oppositions embodied by a third woman, Natalie, turns out to be equally impossible. The contrast established between Henriette and Lady Dudley along national as well as more specifically regional lines (French vs. English; *Tourangelle*, from Touraine, vs. Lancastrian) shifts the interest in nationality from a 'Venetian' Petrarch to the lady, or rather ladies, in question, with a particular form of Englishness usurping Italianness as a novelistic theme in the case of *Le Lys*.

Besides specific references to Petrarch and Laura and an investment in oppositions between human love and love divine, Félix and Henriette may be considered to reflect other aspects of their predecessors. In particular, Mme de Mortsauf takes on a number of characteristics associated with Petrarch's Laura as with the beloved lady of much of the early Italian lyric tradition. Mme de Mortsauf is considered to be not only angelic, in the manner of the typical medieval angelic lady (*donna-angelo*) of Guinizzelli or Dante, but saintly, and ultimately even comparable to the Virgin Mary. As regards the latter, Mme de Mortsauf's most frequent association with the Virgin Mary is through the symbol of the white lily, a sign of purity and virginity.[88] Even more explicitly, Mme de Mortsauf wants Félix to love her "'As a

---

[82] 'Certes, elle aimait comme Laure de Noves aimait Pétrarque, et non comme Francesca da Rimini aimait Paolo : affreuse découverte pour qui rêvait l'union de ces deux sortes d'amour !' *Le Lys*, p. 1127; *The Lily*, p. 260. The published translation actually writes 'Paola'.

[83] Heinz Weinmann, 'Bachelard et l'analyse du roman: structure des thèmes et des images dans *Le Lys dans la vallée* de Balzac', *Revue des sciences humaines*, 157 (1975), 122–41 (p. 128).

[84] *Le Lys*, p. 1146; *The Lily*, p. 289.

[85] 'J'étais donc le jouet de deux passions inconciliables [...]. J'aimais un ange et un démon.' *Le Lys*, p. 1183; *The Lily*, p. 349.

[86] "'Je comprends aujourd'hui que le ciel et la terre sont incompatibles."' *Le Lys*, p. 1168; *The Lily*, p. 324.

[87] 'lutte du corps et de l'âme', *Le Lys*, p. 1196; *The Lily*, pp. 369–70.

[88] See Jean Gaudon, 'Le Rouge et le blanc: notes sur *Le Lys dans la vallée*', in *Balzac and the Nineteenth Century: Studies in French Literature Presented to Herbert J. Hunt by Pupils, Colleagues, and Friends*, ed. D. G. Charlton, J. Gaudon, and Anthony R. Pugh (Leicester:

Virgin Mary'".[89] Finally, as Mme de Mortsauf is dying the Angelus bell rings out, further reinforcing her links with Virgin Mary: 'This night the *Ave Maria* seemed to us a salutation from Heaven.'[90] In fact, that Mme de Mortsauf might be both Laura and the Virgin Mary ultimately suggests, like the description of Petrarch as Venetian, a lack of familiarity with the *Canzoniere*, which ends with a poem addressed to the Virgin Mary and which rejects love for Laura as sinful and irreconcilable (*RVF* 366). Since this *canzone* was, however, often omitted from selected translations of Petrarch, Balzac's view of Laura and Mary as conterminous can more easily be understood.[91] Moreover, Mme de Mortsauf as a mother, if not a virgin mother, does reflect the Laura of both the *Canzoniere* (where after death she appears to the poet in the loving guise of both mother and lover, *madre* and *amante*) and the commentary tradition, in particular the abbé de Sade's family history (which Balzac adopts by calling Laura 'Laure de Noves').[92]

Besides these similarities, Mme de Mortsauf, like Julie and Mme de Couaën before her, is most like Laura in the simple fact of her death, even if this death marks the division of Petrarch's *Canzoniere* into two halves, but is typically the final event of these novels. While, as already noted, there seems to be little taste amongst French novelists for a narrative of mourning much beyond the death of the beloved, it remains true for the most part (though not in the example of George Sand's *Adriani*, discussed below) that to be like Laura, one must sooner or later die.[93] After her death, Mme de Mortsauf's letter from the grave functions in a similar way to the popular dialogue between Laura and Petrarch from the *Triumphus Mortis*. After death, both Petrarch's Laura and Mme de Mortsauf disclose their love but state that they hid this love during their life in order to preserve their chastity.

Finally, the figure of Mme de Mortsauf, while modelled on Petrarch's Laura, also shares more general medieval characteristics, which relate to both chivalry and medieval Christianity broadly conceived. As regards the former, Henriette is, in Félix's words, '"the Lady in whose hands glitters the crown promised to the victors in the tourney"', a phrase which situates her in a medieval world of chivalric romance and courtly love.[94] In the same vein, Mme de Mortsauf wants to be loved '"Chivalrously"' by Félix, thereby invoking medieval precedent in order to justify her demand for obedience and love-vassalage.[95] This demand is consonant with Félix's own behaviour, which he himself justifies from the outset according to chivalric codes, asserting, for instance, that his quest for Mme de Mortsauf's dwelling entails

---

Leicester University Press, 1972), pp. 71–8 (p. 73). In contrast, Laforgue remarks that the lily is also a royal emblem: Laforgue, *L'Œdipe romantique*, p. 178.

[89]   '"Comme une vierge Marie"', *Le Lys*, p. 1112; *The Lily*, p. 236.

[90]   'Ce soir, l'*Ave Maria* nous parut une salutation du ciel.' *Le Lys*, p. 1207; *The Lily*, pp. 387–8.

[91]   See Chapter 2.

[92]   For Laura as mother and lover see *RVF* 285, v. 9.

[93]   For a feminist critique of this situation, see Elisabeth Bronfen, *Over Her Dead Body: Death, Femininity and the Aesthetic* (Manchester: Manchester University Press, 1992).

[94]   '"la Dame aux mains de laquelle reluit la couronne promise aux vainqueurs du tournoi"', *Le Lys*, p. 1028; *The Lily*, p. 98.

[95]   '— Chevaleresquement', *Le Lys*, p. 1112; *The Lily*, p. 236.

'an indescribable chivalry'.[96] While the wish to *recommencer* (to repeat or restart; in the translation, 'renew') Petrarch's Laura remains doubtful as to outcome,[97] Félix's love is more assertively considered to be a way of reliving medieval chivalry: 'My passion [...] revived [*recommençait*] the Middle Ages and recalled chivalry'.[98] As regards the wider frame of medieval Christianity with which the novel seems to be imbued in its stringent conflict between body and soul and ideal suppression of earthly desires, one possible source has been noted to be the mysticism of the philosopher (the *philosophe inconnu*, Unknown Philosopher, according to his typical pseudonym) Louis-Claude de Saint-Martin.[99] Félix's own account of the influence of Saint-Martin links the movement to putatively medieval origins: 'Active prayer and pure love are the elements of this faith which departs from the Catholicism of the Roman Church to return to the Christianity of the Early Church'.[100]

If Mme de Mortsauf is like Laura in her death and voice beyond the grave, as well as in her devotion to Catholic ideals of chastity and motherhood, whether Félix ought to be considered in any way analogous to Petrarch is less certain. On the one hand, Balzac is at pains to present Félix as a poetic individual, even if his self-expression is typically through the medium of often ill-advised letters and meaningfully chosen and arranged flowers rather than actual poetry. This last talent, fluency in the language of flowers, is presented by Félix as a noble task of 'poetic work' (*œuvre poétique*) on which he accordingly embarks 'not so much as a botanist as a poet'.[101] The resultant bouquets are, as a result, described as a 'poem of luminous flowers', indeed as many 'poems of flowers'.[102] Yet on the other hand, Mme de Mortsauf's most Laura-like moment, her death, also marks Félix's failure to assume the absolute fidelity required of a Petrarchan lover. Even during Mme de Mortsauf's lifetime, Félix's affair with Lady Dudley marks an extended moment of weakness and disloyalty more comparable, perhaps, to Amaury's competing affection for Madame R. than to the invoked Petrarchan model.

Félix's infidelity is further underscored by the fact that the whole novel is presented as a letter written to a third lady, Natalie. Paradoxically, the specific motive behind the Petrarchan narrative of love and loss thus undermines the Petrarchan myth through seeking a replacement love object. If, as Peter Brooks argues, Félix may be presumed to be abandoned at the end of the narrative in a melancholic space consumed by regret and guilt for the irreplaceable dead beloved, this isolation is thanks not to any newly discovered constancy but is, instead, a result of Natalie's

---

[96] 'je ne sais quoi de chevaleresque', *Le Lys*, p. 986; *The Lily*, p. 31.

[97] *Le Lys*, p. 1035; *The Lily*, p. 110.

[98] 'Ma passion [...] recommençait le Moyen Âge et rappelait la chevalerie.' *Le Lys*, p. 1139; *The Lily*, p. 280.

[99] On this subject, see Robert Amadou, 'Balzac et Saint-Martin', *L'Année balzacienne* (1965), 35–60.

[100] 'La prière active et l'amour pur sont les éléments de cette foi qui sort du catholicisme de l'Église romaine pour rentrer dans la christianisme de l'Église primitive.' *Le Lys*, p. 1010; *The Lily*, p. 70.

[101] 'moins en botaniste qu'en poète', *Le Lys*, p. 1054; *The Lily*, p. 142.

[102] 'poème de fleurs lumineuses', 'poèmes de fleurs', *Le Lys*, pp. 1057, 1139; *The Lily*, pp. 147, 279.

rejection of his advances in no uncertain terms in a letter with which the narrative concludes.[103] Given these infidelities, Félix's Petrarchan claim concerning Mme de Mortsauf, 'Ah, I loved her dead, as much as I loved her living', is shown to be unreliable, unless this phrase is taken in an ironic fashion to mean that just as Félix betrayed Mme de Mortsauf for Lady Dudley while she was alive, so after her death he will love her while continuing to be unfaithful.[104]

If Félix fails in the amorous sphere to be a second Petrarch, he may, nonetheless, be more like Petrarch in his involvement with key political figures of the day, most notably Louis XVIII. Yet Petrarchan love is ultimately presented as incompatible with politics in this novel, since, as Félix admits, 'I did not know what the privy council was; I knew nothing about politics or public affairs; I had no other ambition than to love Henriette better than Petrarch loved Laura'.[105] This lack of interest in politics is later reiterated, and shared by Mme de Mortsauf: 'When I came down for dinner, I was told of the disasters of Waterloo, Napoleon's flight, the march of the allies upon Paris and the probable return of the Bourbons. These events were everything to the count, to us they were nothing'.[106]

In addition to Petrarchan characterization, however much Félix falls short of the ideal model, *Le Lys dans la vallée* presents a Petrarchan landscape which is in certain aspects reminiscent of the idyllic natural scene depicted in *RVF* 126 and translated so frequently by nineteenth-century French translators from Voltaire onwards. This valley may be far from Provence (it is specifically located in Touraine and traversed by the river Indre), but it, too, is composed of fountains, streams, rocky outcrops, solitary walks, wooded glades, and amorous sentiments, accompanied by the song of nightingales. The valley is also a site with which the lady is inextricably associated. Indeed, while the whole landscape of Vaucluse reminds Petrarch of Laura (and often of her present absence), Henriette in devotion to her husband never leaves the valley. In this way Balzac's valley literalizes the meaning of Vaucluse (in Latin, *vallis clausa*, closed valley). The passing of the seasons further enhances the morbid associations of the valley, in a typical association of spring with new love and autumn with death:

---

[103] See Peter Brooks, 'Virtue-tripping: Notes on *Le Lys dans la vallée*', *Yale French Studies*, 50 (1974), 150–62. Persistent readers can, however, encounter Félix married in Balzac, *Une fille d'Ève*, ed. Roger Pierrot, in *La Comédie humaine*, ed. Castex, 11 (1976), 245–383.

[104] 'Ah ! je l'aimais morte, autant que je l'aimais vivante.' *Le Lys*, p. 1211; *The Lily*, p. 394.

[105] 'J'ignorais ce qu'était le conseil privé ; je ne connaissais rien à la politique ni aux choses du monde ; je n'avais d'autre ambition que celle d'aimer Henriette, mieux que Pétrarque n'aimait Laure.' *Le Lys*, p. 1045; *The Lily*, p. 127.

[106] 'Quand je descendis pour dîner, j'appris les désastres de Waterloo, la fuite de Napoléon, la marche des alliés sur Paris et le retour probable des Bourbons. Ces événements étaient tout pour le comte, ils ne furent rien pour nous.' *Le Lys*, p. 1100; *The Lily*, p. 215. That *Le Lys* is, however, like *Volupté* a political novel is the thesis of Laforgue, *L'Œdipe romantique*, pp. 125–43 (on *Volupté*) and pp. 177–96 (on *Le Lys*). See also Owen Heathcote, 'Balzac's "mal d'archive"? "Lieux de mémoire" in *Le Lys dans la vallée*', in *Mapping Memory in Nineteenth-Century French Literature and Culture*, ed. Susan Harrow and Andrew Watts (Amsterdam: Rodopi, 2012), pp. 193–207. Gaston Bachelard, in contrast, criticizes the inclusion of Louis VIII's court in *Le Lys*: Bachelard, *La Poétique de la rêverie* (Paris: Presses Universitaires de France, 1960), p. 64.

If you want to see nature in the beauty and purity of a betrothed, go there on a spring day; if you want to soothe the bleeding wounds of your heart, return there during the last days of autumn; there, in springtime, Love flutters his wings in mid-air; there, in autumn, one thinks of those who are no more.[107]

Félix's retrospective narration here anticipates Mme de Mortsauf's death in October, an event which is in harmony with the typical associations of autumn with decline and mortality. Yet Mme de Mortsauf is far from a passive element of the landscape; instead, her relationship to nature is practical, concrete, and enterprising in a way which is more reminiscent of Rousseau's Julie than Petrarch's Laura, even if Mme de Mortsauf's interests are predominantly agricultural in contrast both to Julie's horticultural endeavours and Félix's habitual, floral poetry.

Finally, in contrast to Mme de Mortsauf's enclosure in this natural space, Félix's frequent movement between Touraine and Paris reflects Petrarch's journeying between Vaucluse (a place of love, writing, intimacy, and solitude) and the corrupt papal court of Avignon. Just as in Sainte-Beuve's *Volupté* Paris had been presented as a labyrinth of sinful lust, so in *Le Lys dans la vallée* the capital is depicted as 'as dangerous a sea to pure affection as to the innocence of conscience'.[108] This nautical imagery reflects the wider Petrarchan theme which resurfaces in *Le Lys*, that of the danger of shipwreck, where shipwreck functions as a symbol for both political and amorous turmoil. In *Le Lys dans la vallée*, the French Revolution is recalled as 'the great wreck which closed the XVIIIth century',[109] while Mme de Mortsauf's death is for Félix a 'great wreck' (*grand naufrage*) in which the proposed marriage with her daughter Madeleine appears all too briefly as a safe haven or 'island' (*île*).[110]

The preceding examples have demonstrated how *Le Lys dans la vallée* can to a certain extent be defined as Petrarchan in terms of explicit comparisons, characterization, and setting. Yet the novel ultimately undoes its own Petrarchan aura through its form and structure, which point towards dialogism, irony, and parody. These techniques are, for Bakhtin, as noted at the start of this chapter, typical of novelistic discourse and inevitably undermine any attempt at reproducing unitary, monologic, poetic language. In *Le Lys dans la vallée* the dialogic aspect is particularly prominent, since the whole work is, as already noted, a letter to a third lady who responds in the final four pages to the preceding two-hundred page narrative. For Félix, Natalie represents the promise of reconciliation and synthesis; she appears to him to be an ideal replacement love object whom he hopes will be an adequate substitute for both Mme de Mortsauf and Lady Dudley. Félix congratulates himself, it turns out prematurely, on his find: 'blessed is he who can find the two in one;

---

[107] 'Si vous voulez voir la nature belle et vierge comme une fiancée, allez là par un jour de printemps ; si vous voulez calmer les plaies saignantes de votre cœur, revenez-y par les derniers jours de l'automne ; au printemps, l'amour y bat des ailes à plein ciel, en automne on y songe à ceux qui ne sont plus.' *Le Lys*, pp. 987–8; *The Lily*, p. 34.

[108] 'une mer aussi dangereuse aux chastes amours qu'à la pureté des consciences', *Le Lys*, p. 1107; *The Lily*, p. 226.

[109] 'le grand naufrage qui termina le dix-huitième siècle', *Le Lys*, p. 1002; *The Lily*, p. 57.

[110] *Le Lys*, p. 1221; *The Lily*, p. 409.

blessed, Natalie, is the man whom you love!'[111] In the end, this hope is as doomed as the desire to unite Petrarch's Laura and Dante's Francesca, since Félix's hopes for Natalie are overturned by Natalie's own perspective on the events narrated. Natalie refuses to participate in Félix's complicated games of role-play, informing him in her response that 'Your project is impracticable. To be both Madame de Mortsauf and Lady Dudley,—why, my friend, is not that trying to unite fire and water?'[112] Natalie's written refusal of Félix drastically undermines the preceding tale and along with it Félix's ability to judge other people and to control events unfolding around him.

What is particularly interesting about Natalie's letter is the way in which it turns Félix's words against him, playing on the ambivalence of quotation which can slide all too easily into parody. Most strikingly, Mme de Mortsauf's virginal, Marian attributes are mocked by Natalie in her descriptions of Félix's beloved as 'the Virgin of Clochegourde' and 'your Saint Henriette'.[113] Nor is Félix safe from Natalie's attack: his medievalist pretentions are derided in her reference to his initially intriguing but ultimately tiresome 'air of the Knight of the Rueful Countenance'.[114] More subtly, small changes in quotation can have strong reverberations. In this manner Félix's opening attempt at honesty and self-awareness—'yes, my life is overshadowed by a phantom'—is not only rejected by Natalie but also transformed into a plural, implying Félix's several infidelities and multiple griefs: 'I do not care for fighting phantoms', Natalie declares.[115] As Richard Bales has discussed, this epistolary structure creates a distancing effect: 'we are never being addressed directly: someone else is, and although we can liberally plunder the text, we must always remain at a certain distance from it.'[116] This distance creates a space for analysis, suspicion, and resistance on the part of the reader, so that, like Madeleine, Lady Dudley, and Natalie, we, too, can choose to reject Félix's tale of persuasion and self-justification.

Yet Natalie's dissenting voice serves not only to provide welcome ironic distance from Félix's tale, but also, paradoxically, may protect Félix's story at the very moment that it appears to be attacking it. Natalie's voice reassures any reader frustrated by the main love story that resistance and wide-ranging suspicion are possible, even desirable, yet in so doing potential criticisms from the reader are thereby ushered into a clearly marked path already sanctioned within the novel. It is in this respect that Victor Brombert has described the late addition of Natalie and her final letter as paradoxically setting in motion 'an ironic protection'.[117] Crucially, moreover, Félix's

---

[111] 'heureux qui peut trouver les deux en une seule ; heureux, Natalie, l'homme que vous aimez !', *Le Lys*, p. 1184; *The Lily*, p. 350.

[112] 'Votre programme est inexécutable. Être à la fois Mme de Mortsauf et lady Dudley, mais, mon ami, n'est-ce pas vouloir réunir l'eau et le feu ?' *Le Lys*, p. 1228; *The Lily*, p. 420. On this polarity of fire and water, see Weinmann, 'Bachelard et l'analyse du roman: structure des thèmes et des images dans *Le Lys dans la vallée* de Balzac'.

[113] 'la Vierge de Clochegourde', 'votre sainte Henriette', *Le Lys*, p. 1226; *The Lily*, p. 418.

[114] 'air de chevalier de la Triste Figure', *Le Lys*, p. 1228; *The Lily*, p. 420.

[115] 'oui, ma vie est dominée par un fantôme', *Le Lys*, p. 970; *The Lily*, p. 5. Contrast to 'je ne me soucie pas de combattre des fantômes', *Le Lys*, p. 1226; *The Lily*, p. 418.

[116] Richard Bales, *Persuasion in the French Personal Novel: Studies of Chateaubriand, Constant, Balzac, Nerval, and Fromentin* (Birmingham, AL: Summa Publications, 1997), p. 58.

[117] Victor Brombert, *The Hidden Reader: Stendhal, Balzac, Hugo, Baudelaire, Flaubert*

direct addresses to Natalie throughout the tale mean that the reader is constantly reminded of the dialogic nature of the narrative and its ostensible *raison d'être* within the novel's economy, in anticipation of the voice of suspicion and resistance that will be revealed explicitly only at the novel's close.[118]

The most extreme form of this distancing from the original tale that this narrative frame enacts is Natalie's exhortation of Félix not to repeat his tale since it will be unpalatable to contemporary society and particularly any other women readers he may later wish to seduce. Natalie consequently instructs Félix to 'take care that you do not renew [*recommencer*] such confidences, which expose your disenchantment, discourage love and drive a woman to diffidence of herself'.[119] Not only can Petrarch's Laura not relive (*recommencer*) in Mme de Mortsauf (and certainly not in Natalie), but Félix's Petrarchan tale is here similarly itself forbidden to be repeated and reiterated. Natalie concludes: 'If you are desirous of remaining in society, of enjoying the acquaintance of women, carefully hide from them all that you have told me.'[120] According to Natalie, Félix's tale of attempted Petrarchan love is no longer socially acceptable, and will struggle to find a sympathetic audience. Yet Natalie's warning thus echoes in a specular fashion key themes of *RVF* 1, in particular the love story as fodder for damaging society gossip: 'But well do I see now how I was for a long time the talk of the town'.[121] Also redolent of *RVF* 1 is the male protagonist's experience of shame (*mi vergogno*, v. 11; *vergogna*, v. 12) and the need for repentance ('*l pentérsi*, v. 13), though in *Le Lys* it is up to Natalie rather than the protagonist's conscience to point to these sentiments as appropriate and necessary. In a strange inversion, Balzac's novel not only elides the *in morte* part of the *Canzoniere* but also ends where Petrarch's poetry began, with embarrassment and a recantation, if complex and partial, of the amorous tale. The strangeness of the placement of *RVF* 1, a retrospective injunction not to love and perhaps even not to read, at the start of the *Canzoniere*, is highlighted by Balzac's placement of a similar text at the end of *Le Lys*.

In Balzac's novel what, then, survives of Petrarch? Is it possible to redo (*recommencer*) Petrarch in novel form? In *Le Lys dans la vallée*, the novelization of Petrarch comes at the cost of opening the tale up to ridicule, rejection, and eventual silencing, albeit in a manner reminiscent of the proeminal sonnet of the *Canzoniere*. The dialogic form of the novel, by subjecting the poetic, unitary, monologic Petrarchan situation to analysis (both examination and undoing), ultimately renders the tale untenable in prose form. Yet, as Leo Bersani highlights, in Balzac's failure to repeat Petrarch and Laura lies the originality and success of the novel:

(Cambridge, MA: Harvard University Press, 1988), p. 24.

[118] See Lucienne Frappier-Mazur, 'Le régime de l'aveu dans *Le Lys dans la vallée*: formes et fonctions de l'aveu écrit', *Revue des sciences humaines*, 175 (1979), 8–16.

[119] 'gardez-vous de recommencer de pareilles confidences qui mettent à nu votre désenchantement, qui découragent l'amour et forcent une femme à douter d'elle-même', *Le Lys*, p. 1227; *The Lily*, p. 418.

[120] 'Si vous tenez à rester dans le monde, à jouir du commerce des femmes, cachez-leur avec soin tout ce que vous m'avez dit.' *Le Lys*, p. 1229; *The Lily*, p. 421.

[121] 'Ma ben veggio or sì come al popol tutto / favola fui gran tempo', *RVF* 1, vv. 9–10. I thank David Bowe for this observation.

Le Lys is a tragedy of a failure of coincidence, that is, of the unbridgeable gap between this work of fiction and other fictional models. It may seem peculiar to speak of what is, after all, Balzac's originality as a failure, but his very fidelity to his own imagination seals Henriette's doom. Nothing would serve her love better and Balzac's work more poorly than the success of Félix's appeals to medieval heroes and heroines.[122]

In this way Balzac's *Le Lys dans la vallée* points away from the endorsement of Petrarchan love in Rousseau's *La Nouvelle Héloïse* and *Volupté* (despite his debts to these two novels), and towards a more problematic, resistant, difficult relationship to Petrarch staged by later Petrarchan novels such as Stendhal's *La Chartreuse de Parme* and George Sand's *Adriani*.

Stendhal's *La Chartreuse de Parme* (1839)

Stendhal's interest in Petrarch is unusually consistent, if typically fleeting, throughout his varied writings, more so than is the case for the previous three authors considered thus far.[123] The medieval poet makes it onto a list of 'Works to look at. / Works of first importance.' compiled by Stendhal in his *Journal littéraire* in 1803, alongside Homer, Ariosto, Dante, Virgil, and others.[124] Moreover, as already traced in Chapter 4, Stendhal was a rare, if somewhat ambivalent, proponent of Petrarch's collection of Latin letters against Avignon (the *Sine nomine*). He was also unusually aware of the gap between Petrarch's self-valuation as a Latinist and posterity's celebration of his Italian poetry, and even anticipated and identified with such a discrepancy for his own part: 'I am accustomed to seem the opposite of what I am. I consider and have always considered my works as lottery tickets. I only expect to be reprinted in 1900. Petrarch counted on his Latin poem the *Africa* and gave hardly any thought to his sonnets.'[125]

Despite this unusual awareness of Petrarch's Latin writings, Stendhal's tastes as regards Petrarch were, nonetheless, also canonical, with both *RVF* 1 and 302 singled out as favourite sonnets. Of the former, Stendhal comments on visiting Pavia (on 16 December 1816):

---

[122] Leo Bersani, *Balzac to Beckett: Center and Circumference in French Fiction* (New York: Oxford University Press, 1970), p. 66.

[123] For a summary of references across Stendhal's corpus, see Carlo Cordié, *Ricerche stendhaliane* (Naples: Morano Editore, 1967), pp. 451–99.

[124] 'Ouvrages à voir. / Ouvrages de première importance.' *Journal littéraire*, in Stendhal, *Œuvres complètes*, XXXIII, 104. Petrarch is here listed as Petrarca, with no indication of specific works that Stendhal might have had in mind. Petrarch also figures in a similar list of 'Auteurs que je puis lire' ('Authors that I can read') in *Journal littéraire*, in Stendhal, *Œuvres complètes*, XXXIII, 95. On the related topic of Stendhal and Dante, see Pitwood, *Dante and the French Romantics*, pp. 127–43.

[125] 'Je suis accoutumé à paraître le contraire de ce que je suis. Je regarde et j'ai toujours regardé mes ouvrages comme des billets à la loterie. Je n'estime que d'être réimprimé en 1900. Pétrarque comptait sur son poème latin de l'*Africa* et ne songeait guère à ses sonnets.' Stendhal, *Souvenirs d'égotisme*, in *Œuvres intimes*, ed. Victor Del Litto, 2 vols (Paris: Gallimard, 1981–2), II, 425–521 (p. 474).

These young people all know Petrarch by heart, and at least half of them write sonnets. They are seduced by the passionate sensibility that the Platonic and metaphysical pathos of Petrarch does not always hide. One of these young people recited to me, by himself, the most beautiful sonnet in the world, the first of Petrarch's collection.[126]

Similarly, in *Promenades dans Rome*, Stendhal praises and cites in full in Italian *RVF* 302, arguing that it is untranslatable (even though, as charted in Chapter 2, this sonnet was one of the most frequently translated into French of Petrarch's poems throughout the nineteenth century):

> *17 June 1828.* – Will the great pleasure that the most beautiful sonnet by Petrarch gave us this evening be a sufficient excuse to put it here? The unexpected sight of a new painting by Raphaël would not have moved us more. The Italian language is so bold in the expression of passions, and so little spoilt by the subtleties of the court of Louis XV, that I dare not attempt a translation of this piece. Italians, for their part, will berate me for having quoted verses which everyone knows by heart.[127]

Stendhal's praise of these two sonnets is, in contrast, tempered by his hyperbolic expression of antipathy for much of the remainder of the *Canzoniere*:

> Petrarch counted on his great Latin poem the *Africa* in order to see continue in posterity the immense glory which he enjoyed during his lifetime, and he is immortalized like La Fontaine for thirty divine sonnets, hidden in a collection which contains two hundred mediocre sonnets and as many more which are incomprehensible.[128]

Like many of the translators discussed in Chapter 2, Stendhal had time only for a selected, abridged Petrarch.

The focus in this section will be on *La Chartreuse de Parme*, although Stendhal's

---

[126] 'Ces jeunes gens savent tout Pétrarque par cœur, la moitié au moins fait des sonnets. Ils sont séduit par la sensibilité passionnée que le pathos platonique et métaphysique de Pétrarque ne cache pas toujours. Un de ces jeunes gens m'a récité, de lui-même, le plus beau sonnet du monde, le premier du recueil de Pétrarque.' 'Rome, Naples et Florence (1826)', in Stendhal, *Voyages en Italie*, ed. Del Litto, pp. 285–592 (p. 383).

[127] '17 juin 1828. – L'extrême plaisir que nous a fait ce soir le plus beau sonnet de Pétrarque me sera-t-il une excuse suffisante pour le placer ici ? La vue imprévue d'un nouveau tableau de Raphaël ne nous eût pas émus davantage. La langue italienne est si hardie dans l'expression des passions, et si peu gâtée par les délicatesses de la cour de Louis XV, que je n'ose essayer la traduction de ce morceau. Les Italiens me reprocheront, de leur côté, d'avoir cité des vers que tous savent par cœur.' 'Promenades dans Rome', in Stendhal, *Voyages en Italie*, ed. Del Litto, pp. 880–1.

[128] 'Pétrarque comptait sur son grand poème latin de l'*Afrique* pour voir continuer dans la postérité la gloire immense dont il jouissait de son vivant, et il est immortalisé comme La Fontaine pour trente sonnets divins, cachés dans un recueil qui en compte deux cents de médiocres et autant d'inintelligibles.' 'La Comédie est impossible en 1836', in Stendhal, *Œuvres complètes*, XLVI (1972), 265–78 (p. 269).

De l'amour (1822; *On Love*) should additionally be signalled for its demonstration of familiarity with key texts on medieval love (not only Petrarch, but also Dante, the troubadours, and Andreas Capellanus).[129] Stendhal's interest in Petrarch must also be situated in relation to his love of Italy, which for Stendhal was an ideal and idyllic place of music, opera, poetry, and passion.[130] As we have seen, French writers such as Sade and Lamartine tended to claim an affinity with Petrarch through genealogical descent from his French beloved, Laure de Sade. Stendhal, in contrast, identified as Italian via his maternal line, claiming 'Through my mother whom I resemble I am perhaps of Italian blood.'[131] Italy was, as a consequence, what Roland Barthes has described as a 'motherland' (*matrie*) for Stendhal.[132] As Michel Crouzet has pointed out, the Italy of the Romantics typically represented 'less a journey in space than a return to a past time, to "medieval" or "baroque" sources'.[133] It is this medieval prototype in *La Chartreuse* which I wish in particular to highlight, through a focus on the presence of Petrarch and Petrarchan poetry in the novel, in contrast to the more typical acknowledgement of the importance of the atmosphere of Renaissance Italy and the romance epics of Ariosto and Tasso. While the latter are undeniably important parodic reference points for the battle scenes at the start of the novel, the Petrarchan archetype becomes more and more important as the novel returns to Parma and delves into the more lyric matters of the heart.[134]

In contrast to the French claims for Petrarch, which typically stressed the poet's upbringing and years spent in Carpentras, Avignon, and Vaucluse, the Italianate Stendhal adds a new geographical association to the plethora of competing Petrarchan sites: Parma. *La Chartreuse de Parme* alludes to Petrarch's connections to this eponymous city, in particular his residence there at various times during the 1340s. Petrarch bought a house near the church of Santo Stefano which he occupied

[129] On this text, see Cordié, *Ricerche stendhaliane*, p. 461; Pierrette Pavet-Jörg, 'Les erreurs amoureuses. La poétique pétrarquiste et la poétique du ridicule dans *De l'amour*', in *La Pensée du paradoxe*, ed. Bercegol and Philippot, pp. 249–70; Pietro Paolo Trompeo, *Incontri di Stendhal* (Naples: Edizioni scientifiche italiane, 1963), pp. 33–48; Muriel Augry-Merlino, 'Pétrarque, Stendhal et la souveraineté féminine', in *Dynamique d'une expansion culturelle*, pp. 457–64; Fabienne Gégou, 'Stendhal et l'amour en "Provence" au Moyen Âge', *Stendhal Club*, 72 (15 juillet 1976), 316–26.

[130] In these attributes, Stendhal's Italy resembles the foundational Romantic image of Italy presented by Germaine de Staël in *Corinne, ou, l'Italie* (1807); see Robert Casillo, *The Empire of Stereotypes: Germaine de Staël and the Idea of Italy* (New York: Palgrave Macmillan, 2006) and Michel Crouzet, *Stendhal et l'italianité: essai de mythologie romantique* (Paris: Librairie José Corti, 1982).

[131] 'Par ma mère à laquelle je ressemble je suis peut-être de sang italien.' Stendhal, *Vie de Henry Brulard*, in *Œuvres intimes*, ed. Del Litto, II, 523–963 (p. 887). On Italian, then, as Stendhal's mother tongue, see Philippe Berthier, *Stendhal et la Sainte Famille* (Geneva: Droz, 1983), p. 176.

[132] 'On échoue toujours à parler de ce qu'on aime', in Barthes, *Œuvres complètes*, V, 906–14 (p. 907).

[133] 'moins comme un voyage dans l'espace qu'un retour dans le temps passé, vers les sources "médiévales" ou "baroques"', Crouzet, *Stendhal et l'italianité*, p. 1.

[134] See Béatrice Didier, *Stendhal ou la dictée du bonheur: paroles, échos et écritures dans 'La Chartreuse de Parme'* (Paris: Klincksieck, 2002), p. 34, for the similar observation that references to Petrarch increase towards the end of the novel.

intermittently during this decade whilst working on various literary projects and consolidating his relationship with the Carrara family in Padua.[135] In this manner the association of Petrarch with Vaucluse and/or Avignon delineated in the Introduction is usurped and replaced with a new site, that of Parma, which points ultimately to Petrarch's nomadic lifestyle and to the complexity of his geographical affiliations.[136] In *La Chartreuse*, the prince Ranuce-Ernest V expresses his wish to give the duchesse the '*palazzetto* of San Giovanni, which once belonged to Petrarch, or so they say at least'.[137] A similarly Petrarchan residence is in turn offered to Fabrice by the comte as a desirable site of poetic retreat:

> 'The Duchessa and I have at our disposal, as you know, Petrarch's old house on that fine slope in the middle of the forest, near the Po; if ever you are weary of the little mischief-makings of envy, it has occurred to me that you might be the successor of Petrarch, whose fame will enhance your own.'[138]

The prince, the duchesse, and the comte are clearly proud of these Petrarchan connections, and are eager to use them to bolster both the value of their real estate and their own prestige. The comte goes further in hoping that the spiritual affinity offered by historical, geographical proximity might add to Fabrice's reputation and inspire him to be 'the successor of Petrarch'. The question of whether Fabrice del Dongo, the protagonist of *La Chartreuse*, can fulfil this hope of being a second Petrarch is the focus of the remainder of this section.

La Chartreuse de Parme tells the story of a young nobleman who is likely illegitimate and is shunned by his older brother and official father the marquis del Dongo, and so is brought up largely by his doting mother and aunt. His aunt, in particular, the sister of the marquis, plays a particularly important role in Fabrice's development as in the novel as a whole. The first part of the book focuses on Fabrice's journey to France to fight for Napoleon; this section proceeds as a debunking of myths about chivalry and the glamour and nobility of warfare. At first, Fabrice is inspired by epic sentiments: 'He saw arise between [the soldiers] and himself that noble friendship of the heroes of Tasso and Ariosto.'[139] However,

---

[135] On this period in Petrarch's life, see Ugo Dotti, *Petrarca a Parma* (Reggio Emilia: Edizioni Diabasis, 2006).

[136] This point is developed in the Conclusion.

[137] '*palazzeto* [*sic*] de San Giovanni, que jadis appartint à Pétrarque, du moins on le dit'. *La Chartreuse de Parme*, in Stendhal, *Œuvres romanesques complètes*, ed. Yves Ansel, Philippe Berthier, Xavier Bourdenet, and Serge Linkès, 3 vols (Paris: Gallimard, 2005–14), III, 137–597 (p. 515); Stendhal, *The Charterhouse of Parma*, trans. C. K. Scott Moncrieff, 2 vols (London: Chatto & Windus, 1926), II, 214. All subsequent quotations are from this same edition and Moncrieff's translation, abbreviated respectively to *La Chartreuse* and *The Charterhouse*.

[138] 'La duchesse et moi nous disposons, comme vous le savez, de l'ancienne maison de Pétrarque sur cette belle colline au milieu de la forêt, aux environs du Pô : si jamais vous êtes las des petits mauvais procédés de l'envie, j'ai pensé que vous pourriez être le successeur de Pétrarque, dont le renom augmentera le vôtre.' *La Chartreuse*, p. 563; *The Charterhouse*, II, 279.

[139] 'Il voyait entre eux [les soldats] et lui cette noble amitié des héros du Tasse et de l'Arioste.' *La Chartreuse*, p. 184; *The Charterhouse*, I, 59.

when his horse is unceremoniously stolen by those he thought were on his side, Fabrice is forced to reconsider his preconceptions: 'He abandoned one by one all those beautiful dreams of a chivalrous and sublime friendship, like that of the heroes of the *Gerusalemme Liberata*.'[140] He soon concludes: 'So war was no longer that noble and universal uplifting of souls athirst for glory which he had imagined it to be from Napoleon's proclamations!'[141] Fabrice's experience of war is marked by incomprehension and chaos; his principal question remains whether he was actually at the Battle of Waterloo (the nondescript field is difficult to identify) and, therefore, whether or not he can proudly claim to have engaged in combat for Napoleon. Fabrice thus begins as a parody of a chivalric hero caught up in a parody of an epic battle.[142]

On his return home after Napoleon's defeat, Fabrice finds himself subject to perse-cution given the suspected political motives behind his absence. As a consequence he is sent off first to Romagnan, where he attempts to be as conformist as possible, and then to Naples, where he studies theology with a view to rising through the ranks of the Church. During this time Fabrice's aunt's liaison with the comte Mosca at the court of Parma means that there are high hopes of Fabrice continuing a family tradition and becoming an archbishop, especially since the duchesse's increasingly intense feelings for Fabrice make him her overriding concern. Fabrice himself engages in a series of half-hearted courtships of various ladies, but feels himself to be incapable of true love. Up to this point there is no reference to Petrarch, although references to the sonnet form are present from the opening page with its mention of 'the printing of sonnets upon handkerchiefs of rose-coloured taffeta whenever the marriage occurred of a young lady belonging to some rich or noble family'.[143] This detail imparts local colour to the novel, placing it squarely in a feminine and Italianate sphere (which is also that of the powerlessness and triviality of life under Austrian rule), into which Napoleon's masculine, French army erupts.[144] These sonnets anticipate, albeit bathetically and dismissively, the importance that sonnet-writing will later assume in the novel.[145]

A key turning point in the plot comes when Fabrice kills the actor Giletti, from a variety of confused motives: Giletti challenges Fabrice out of rivalry over the actress Marietta, whereas Fabrice is really prompted in the heat of the moment more by

---

[140] 'Il se défaisait un à un tous ses beaux rêves d'amitié chevaleresque et sublime, comme celle des héros de la *Jérusalem délivrée*.' *La Chartreuse*, p. 186; *The Charterhouse*, I, 61.

[141] 'La guerre n'était donc plus ce noble et commun élan d'âmes amantes de la gloire qu'il s'était figuré d'après les proclamations de Napoléon !' *La Chartreuse*, pp. 186–7; *The Char-terhouse*, I, 62.

[142] See Marvin J. Ward, 'Fabrice del Dongo et Perceval le Gallois: intertextualité?', *Stendhal Club*, 119 (15 April 1988), 209–22, and John West-Sooby, 'Quête et mythe: Fabrice del Dongo et le *Conte du Graal*', *L'Année Stendhal*, 1 (1997), 117–30.

[143] 'imprimer des sonnets sur de petits mouchoirs de taffetas rose quand arrivait le mariage d'une jeune fille appartenant à quelque famille noble ou riche', *La Chartreuse*, p. 143; *The Charterhouse*, I, 3.

[144] On a wider tension in the novel between French and Italian traits, see Roger Pearson, *Stendhal's Violin: A Novelist and his Reader* (Oxford: Clarendon Press, 1988), pp. 203–54.

[145] On this point, see Ann Jefferson, *Reading Realism in Stendhal* (Cambridge: Cambridge University Press, 1988), p. 211.

fearful anger that he has been disfigured in the initial attack. Fabrice escapes and reaches Bologna, but is eventually caught and imprisoned in the dreaded Farnese Tower (*tour Farnèse*) outside Parma. Fabrice's connections with the duchesse mean that he has become a political pawn in a more complex power game with ramifications at court far beyond those of an apparent *crime passionnel*. It is in prison that Fabrice falls in love for the first and only time, with Clélia Conti, the daughter of the prison warden. It is here, also, that references to Petrarch begin to emerge at key moments in the narrative of the developing relationship between Fabrice and Clélia. As Balzac first commented, prison is experienced by Fabrice as a Petrarchan idyll: 'This terrifying abode is a Vaucluse: he makes love there to Clelia, he is happy there.'[146] Fabrice's experience of love in prison acts as a literalization of the image of love as a prison common to Petrarch and the troubadours.[147] In this way Petrarch replaces Tasso and Ariosto, against a background of a culture primarily of sonnet production and recitation, whether of an amorous or a satirical nature. Chivalry is even partially reinstated, though this form of chivalry is now predominantly of an amorous rather than a military persuasion; Fabrice's escape from prison is marked by prayers to God and thoughts of Clélia 'like a hero of the days of chivalry'.[148]

Unlike Tasso or Ariosto, Petrarch seems largely safe from parody in *La Chartreuse*, at least as far as the relationship of Fabrice and Clélia is concerned. Yet before falling in love with Clélia, Fabrice in disguise had already tried his hand at a Petrarchan style, in a sonnet to the actress Fausta of which a brief summary is provided: 'Inspired by the colour of his wig, which was that of the flames that were devouring his heart, he composed a sonnet which Fausta thought charming.'[149] This situation is markedly un-Petrarchan, since typically a sonnet by Petrarch might be expected to admire the beloved's golden hair, and certainly not to dwell on the lover's crop of fake red hair.[150] Also comic in tone is the sonnet Fabrice plans to write relating his fear of passport control having just killed Giletti: '"I am not lacking in courage

---

[146] 'Cet épouvantable séjour est une Vaucluse : il y fait l'amour avec Clélia, il y est heureux.' Balzac, 'Études sur M. Beyle (Frédéric Stendalh [*sic*]), *Revue parisienne*, 25 septembre 1840', cited from Stendhal, *Œuvres romanesques complètes*, ed. Ansel, Berthier, Bourdenet, and Linkès, III, 619–58 (p. 639); Balzac, 'A Study of M. Beyle', in Stendhal, *The Charterhouse of Parma*, trans. Scott Moncrieff, I, pp. vii–lxxiii (p. xlii).

[147] See Sarga Moussa, 'La tradition de l'amour courtois dans *De l'amour* et dans *La Chartreuse de Parme* de Stendhal', *Romantisme*, 91 (1996), 53–65; Michel Crouzet, *Le Roman stendhalien: 'La Chartreuse de Parme'* (Orléans: Paradigme, 1996), pp. 19–54; Victor Brombert, *La Prison romantique: essai sur l'imaginaire* (Paris: Librairie José Corti, 1975), pp. 67–92. On love as a prison in Petrarch, see, for instance, *RVF* 89, which presents the god of love as a gaoler and love as a prison (*pregione*, v. 1) with yoke and chains (*il giogo et le catene*, v. 10), all of which are sweeter (*più dolci*, v. 11) than freedom for the lovesick poet, just as Clélia makes prison an idyll for Fabrice, and even preferable to Heaven (as discussed below).

[148] 'comme un héros des temps de chevalerie', *La Chartreuse*, p. 489; *The Charterhouse*, II, 180.

[149] 'À propos de la couleur de ces cheveux, qui était celle des flammes qui brûlaient son cœur, il fit un sonnet que la Fausta trouva charmant.' *La Chartreuse*, pp. 340–1; *The Charterhouse*, I, 270–1.

[150] On this disguise as part of a wider sequence of disguises and masks in *La Chartreuse*, see Jefferson, *Reading Realism in Stendhal*, pp. 192–8.

to face actors, but clerks with brass jewelry send me out of my mind; I shall make a humorous sonnet out of that to amuse the Duchessa.'"[151]

Subsequently, however, Fabrice puts his poetic talent to more Petrarchan use in addressing Clélia in the margins of his copy of the works of St Jerome:

> That fine idea: *To die near what one loves!* expressed in a hundred different fashions, was followed by a sonnet in which one saw that this soul, parted, after atrocious torments, from the frail body in which it had dwelt for three-and-twenty years, urged by that instinct for happiness natural to everything that has once existed, would not mount to heaven to mingle with the choirs of angels as soon as it should be free, and should the dread Judgment grant it pardon for its sins; but that, more fortunate after death than it had been in life, it would go a little way from the prison, where for so long it had groaned, to unite itself with all that it had loved in this world. And 'So', said the last line of the sonnet, 'I should find my earthly paradise'.[152]

This fictive sonnet contains echoes of medieval philosophy, such as the separation of body and soul, the concept of natural happiness, and a suggestion of some sort of purgatorial experience that may result in forgiveness and freedom for the separated soul at the Day of Judgement. Yet Heaven is ultimately rejected by the wilful soul, for whom the ties with Earth are still overpowering. Thus, while in *RVF* 302 (a sonnet explicitly admired by Stendhal) the poet's thoughts ascend from Earth to Heaven in search of his glorious lady, who promises that he will join her there one day, Fabrice's sonnet traces a movement of descent back to the hallowed sites of his earthly love, in the vicinity of the prison tower.

Besides producing his own Petrarchan sonnets, Fabrice adopts a sonnet by Petrarch in order to communicate with Clélia, charging the duchesse Sanseverina's coach driver, Ludovic, 'to convey to Clelia Conti a handkerchief on which was printed a sonnet of Petrarch. It is true that a word was altered in this sonnet.'[153] These lines are intriguing, since they suggest that Stendhal had a specific sonnet by Petrarch in mind, even though no further clues are given as to which poem precisely. For Cordié, the most obvious suggestion is the replacement of Laura's

---

[151] 'Je ne manque pas de courage entre les comédiens, mais les commis ornés de bijoux de cuivre me mettent hors de moi ; avec cette idée je ferai un sonnet comique pour la duchesse.' *La Chartreuse*, p. 315; *The Charterhouse*, I, 236.

[152] 'Cette belle idée: *Mourir près de ce qu'on aime !* exprimée de cent façons différentes, était suivie d'un sonnet où l'on voyait que l'âme séparée, après des tourments atroces, de ce corps fragile qu'elle avait habité pendant vingt-trois ans, poussée par cet instinct de bonheur naturel à tout ce qui exista une fois, ne remonterait pas au ciel se mêler aux chœurs des anges aussitôt qu'elle serait libre et dans le cas où le jugement terrible lui accorderait le pardon de ses péchés ; mais que, plus heureuse après la mort qu'elle n'avait été durant la vie, elle irait à quelques pas de la prison, où si longtemps elle avait gémi, se réunir à tout ce qu'elle avait aimé au monde. Et ainsi, disait le dernier vers du sonnet, j'aurai trouvé mon paradis sur la terre.' *La Chartreuse*, p. 500; *The Charterhouse*, II, 194.

[153] 'faire parvenir à Clélia Conti un mouchoir de soie sur lequel était imprimé un sonnet de Pétrarque. Il est vrai qu'un mot était changé à ce sonnet.' *La Chartreuse*, p. 505; *The Charterhouse*, II, 201.

name with Clélia's in the famous opening line of *RVF* 90: 'Erano i capei d'oro a *l'aura/Clélia* sparsi' ('The golden hair was scattered in the breeze [*l'aura*]/Clélia').[154] Of course, since the name Clélia lacks the polysemy of Laura, such a substitution would, even if a romantic gesture on the part of Fabrice, render the opening of the sonnet relatively meaningless. More persuasive, if resting on equally slim evidence, is the suggestion that the sonnet in question is *RVF* 242, 'Mira quel colle, o stanco mio cor vago' ('Look at that hill, O my tired, wandering heart'), with the noun *colle* replaced by *torre* (tower), creating a pertinent reference to memories of the prison tower close to the beloved.[155]

Either solution is, however, forced to ignore the later details supplied about this sonnet, which throw even more uncertainty rather than clarity on the problem. A later reference to this same poem muddies the waters further, by invoking lines written not, as advertised, by Petrarch, but rather by the eighteenth-century poet and librettist Pietro Metastasio:

> He approached her and repeated, in an undertone and as though he were speaking to himself, two lines from that sonnet of Petrarch which he had sent her from Lake Maggiore, printed on a silk handkerchief: 'What was not my happiness when common people believed me to be unhappy, and now how my fate has changed!'
>
> 'No, he has not forgotten me,' Clelia told herself with a transport of joy. 'That fine soul is not inconstant!'
>
> > *No, you will never see me change,*
> > *Beautiful eyes which taught me to love.*
>
> Clelia ventured to repeat to herself these lines of Petrarch.[156]

These lines are cited in the original by Rousseau in *La Nouvelle Héloïse*, and Paul Veyne is no doubt correct in identifying Rousseau as Stendhal's source:[157]

> Nò, non vedrete mai
> Cambiar gl' affetti miei,

[154] Cordié, *Ricerche stendhaliane*, p. 474.

[155] For this suggestion see Élisabeth Edl and Wolfgang Matz, 'Un sonnet de Pétrarque dans *La Chartreuse de Parme*', *L'Année stendhalienne*, 7 (2008), 379–84.

[156] 'Il s'approcha d'elle et prononça, à demi-voix et comme se parlant à soi-même, deux vers de ce sonnet de Pétrarque, qu'il lui avait envoyé du lac Majeur, imprimé sur un mouchoir de soie : "Quel n'était pas mon bonheur quand le vulgaire me croyait malheureux, et maintenant que mon sort est changé !"
Non, il ne m'a point oubliée, se dit Clélia avec un transport de joie. Cette belle âme n'est point inconstante !
Non, vous ne me verrez jamais changer, / Beaux yeux qui m'avez appris à aimer.
Clélia osa se répéter à elle-même ces deux vers de Pétrarque.' *La Chartreuse*, p. 569; *The Charterhouse*, II, 286–7. I diverge from the English translation here, since in this passage Moncrieff inserts two lines in Italian from *RVF* 332, vv. 36–7, and three further lines, also in Italian, from *RVF* 195, vv. 12–14, likely in an attempt to correct Stendhal's falsely attributed quotation.

[157] Paul Veyne, 'Parme et Modène: un premier jet de la *Chartreuse*', *Annales de la faculté des lettres d'Aix*, 38 (1964), 161–6.

Bei lumi onde imparai
A sospirar d'amor.[158]

***

No, you will never see
My affections change,
Beautiful eyes [literally, lights] whence I learnt
To sigh with love.

Stendhal's narrator thus makes two false claims about these lines, namely that they are by Petrarch, and that they come from a sonnet, whereas in fact the source is Metastasio's libretto for *Ciro riconosciuto* (1736; *Cyrus Recognized*). Since the source is not explicitly given in Rousseau, it may be that Stendhal simply assumed the quotation came from Petrarch, taking into account the many quotations from Petrarch in *La Nouvelle Héloïse* charted earlier in this chapter.[159] Another, more cunning explanation would be that the reader is meant to recognize the mistake and impute it to the potential ignorance of Fabrice and Clélia in poetic matters.[160] Either way, the earlier problem of what word is changed by Fabrice does not become any clearer. Instead, the difficulty of identifying the original points to the obscuring of Petrarch through a combination of translation and novelization. As encountered in Part I, poems can be difficult to identify if they are given solely in French, enabling the translation to stand alone independent from any comparison with the original. Here, the novelization of Petrarch creates spurious attributions that make any quest for sources somewhat otiose. While Petrarch is deliberately invoked in *La Chartreuse de Parme* in order to ennoble the love story of Fabrice and Clélia, references to actual poems by Petrarch remain deliberately vague. In this way, Stendhal's own prose eclipses any putative Italian poetic model. Although Fabrice, like the youthful Italians encountered by Stendhal in Pavia, proves his passionate, Italian nature by spouting (pseudo-)Petrarchan sonnets to his beloved, the French prose narrative translation of such sentiments complicates the identification and restricts the possible meanings of this poetry.

Fabrice and Clélia are also far from the only poetic souls in *La Chartreuse*. Almost every character can seemingly tap into a poetic vein when it might be deemed advantageous so to do. Ludovic, a friend in distress for Fabrice, is a self-professed '"poet in the *lingua volgare*"', although his sonnets are judged by Fabrice as 'not worth the trouble of putting them on paper'.[161] Some of the prisoners even write sonnets to celebrate Fabio Conti's recovery from the poisoning incident, though here, as elsewhere, such poems are more often alluded to than cited in *La*

---

[158] Rousseau, *La Nouvelle Héloïse*, p. 106.

[159] Rousseau himself also on occasion confused Metastasio and Petrarch, for instance attributing lines from *RVF* 11 to Metastasio in the Duchesne edition (Rousseau, *La Nouvelle Héloïse*, p. 1365), a further reason for confusion on the part of Stendhal.

[160] For Ann Jefferson, this misattribution is due to Stendhal's 'characteristic carelessness': Jefferson, *Reading Realism in Stendhal*, p. 227; see also p. 109, for a discussion of the comparable false attributions of epigraphs rife in *Le Rouge et le Noir*.

[161] '"poète en *langue vulgaire*"', 'ne val[ant] pas la peine d'être écrits', *La Chartreuse*, pp. 316, 321; *The Charterhouse*, I, 237, 244.

Chartreuse.[162] Against this backdrop of frequent sonnet-making, the poet Ferrante Palla is allegedly the most memorable and accomplished. He is introduced early on in the novel by comte Mosca to comtesse Pietranera (the future Sanseverina) as "'a lunatic of our country but also something of a genius'", in short a poet who "'has written a couple of hundred lines in his time which are like nothing in the world; [...] as fine as Dante'".[163] The duchesse eventually meets Ferrante Palla, who becomes her accomplice in wreaking revenge on the prince who had imprisoned and threatened to kill Fabrice. The duchesse is thus eventually able to decide for herself that Ferrante is indeed a poetic genius: 'he recited to her one of his sonnets which seemed to her equal if not superior to any of the finest work written in Italy in the last two centuries.'[164] While the comte's immediate comparison is to Dante, there are traces of a Petrarchan lineage in Ferrante Palla, not least in the initials he shares with Francesco Petrarca. Again, Balzac was one of the first to sense this lineage, describing Ferrante Palla as 'a lover after the style of Petrarch of the Duchessa Sanseverina'.[165] Yet Ferrante is certainly a parodied alter ego: reputed to be mad; forced to steal to cover publishing costs and the upkeep of his five children; willing to commit murder at the request of his beloved.

Nonetheless, Ferrante's poetry remains free from tarnish, and takes on political tones that Stendhal, given his appreciation of Petrarch's diatribes against Avignon, might well have thought appropriate to a Petrarchan figure. Fabrice is exhorted to flee prison by 'a magnificent sonnet' written 'in an exquisite hand', undoubtedly that of Ferrante.[166] After Fabrice's escape, Ferrante writes a further, celebratory sonnet that achieves immediate popularity: 'On the evening of the following day, the whole of Parma was repeating a sublime sonnet. It was Fabrizio's monologue as he let himself slide down the cord, and passed judgment on the different incidents of his life.'[167] In this manner Fabrice is more commonly the object of Petrarchan poetry than himself a true 'successor of Petrarch'. Fabrice remains a self-absorbed reader, recipient, and citer of Petrarch and Petrarchan poetry, rather than a poet in his own right. As Ann Jefferson comments:

> One of the most striking features of this recourse to the arts on the part of the lovers is that, rather than creating their own work, they almost always use the arts of others. Love is not an inspiration for artistic expression, but

[162] *La Chartreuse*, p. 486; *The Charterhouse*, II, 175.

[163] "'un fou de notre pays, mais quelque peu homme de génie'", "'a fait deux cents vers en sa vie, dont rien n'approche ; [...] aussi beau que le Dante'", *La Chartreuse*, p. 239; *The Charterhouse*, I, 131.

[164] 'Il lui récita un de ses sonnets qui lui sembla égal ou supérieur à tout ce qu'on a fait de plus beau en Italie depuis deux siècles.' *La Chartreuse*, p. 475; *The Charterhouse*, II, 160.

[165] 'amant à la Pétrarque de la duchesse de Sanseverina', Balzac, 'Études sur M. Beyle', p. 643; Balzac, 'A Study of M. Beyle', p. xlviii.

[166] 'd'une petite écriture fine un sonnet magnifique', *La Chartreuse*, p. 466; *The Charterhouse*, II, 148.

[167] 'Le surlendemain soir, tout Parme répétait un sonnet sublime. C'était le monologue de Fabrice se laissant glisser le long de la corde, et jugeant les divers incidents de sa vie.' *La Chartreuse*, p. 504; *The Charterhouse*, II, 199.

the precondition of artistic response; and the lovers are readers much more than they are writers when it comes to the strictly literary use of language in the novel.[168]

Finally, *La Chartreuse de Parme* shares with *La Nouvelle Héloïse*, *Volupté*, and *Le Lys dans la vallée* the fact that the death of the beloved brings the narrative to a more or less abrupt end. Once more, there is no Petrarchan, second *post-mortem* half to the narrative, though the task of being a second Laura still necessitates a premature death, a fate to which Clélia, like Julie, Mme de Couaën, and Mme de Mortsauf before her, inevitably succumbs. At the end of the *Chartreuse*, having been implicated through deceit in the death of their son and consequently of a heart-broken Clélia, Fabrice is left to ponder his possible guilt and to hope for reunion with his beloved in the afterlife: 'he hoped to meet Clelia again in a better world, but he had too much intelligence not to feel that he had first to atone for many faults'.[169] In the *Triumphus Mortis*, Petrarch is warned by Laura that this reunion is still distant: '"I believe that you will be on earth without me for a long time."'[170] In contrast, Fabrice's death follows shortly after the death of Clélia, although whether the lovers are reunited (as promised by the example of the *Triumphi*) lies beyond the purview of Stendhal's narrative. Unlike the successful turn to religion of Amaury in *Volupté*, Fabrice's life in the titular charterhouse is short and inconsequential. Ultimately, Fabrice's Petrarchan devotion to Clélia, so different to the fickleness of Balzac's Félix, meets a strangely tragic and silent end. After the demise of the beloved, the Petrarchan myth, as in the novels of Rousseau, Sainte-Beuve, and Balzac, proves to be unsustainable. In the final example of this chapter, however, the same myth collapses not as a result of tragedy, but rather as a consequence of a wholly un-Petrarchan happy ending.

Sand's *Adriani* (1854)

The late eighteenth- and early nineteenth-century French novelization of Petrarch culminates, as already suggested by Duperray, in the demystification of Petrarchan geography and poetry in George Sand's *Adriani*.[171] This novel reworks the Petrarchan tale in an odd retelling in which Laure (Madame de Monteluz, née Mademoiselle Laure de Larnac) is a widow with whom an Italian tenor named Adriani falls in love. Such a retelling begs questions already encountered in the preceding analysis of earlier incarnations of the French Petrarchan novel. How far can the story of Petrarch and Laura be transformed and still remain recognizable? What are the

---

[168] Ann Jefferson, *Stendhal, 'La Chartreuse de Parme'* (London: Grant & Cutler, 2003), p. 78. See, nonetheless, on the lovers' non-literary systems of writing, Peter Brooks, 'L'invention de l'écriture (et du langage) dans *La Chartreuse de Parme*', *Stendhal Club*, 78 (1978), 183–90.

[169] 'il espérait retrouver Clélia dans un meilleur monde, mais il avait trop d'esprit pour ne pas sentir qu'il avait beaucoup à réparer', *La Chartreuse*, p. 597; *The Charterhouse*, II, 324.

[170] '"Al creder mio, / tu starai in terra senza me gran tempo."' *Triumphus Mortis II*, vv. 189–90, cited from Petrarch, *Trionfi, rime estravaganti, codice degli abbozzi*, p. 346.

[171] See Duperray, *L'Or des mots*, pp. 116–22.

remaining elements that render the story still noticeably Petrarchan? Moreover, as with the earlier texts discussed in this chapter, so, too, Sand's familiarity with Petrarch is mediated by the example of previous Petrarchan novels. As much is suggested by two facts in particular: firstly, Sand's praise of Sainte-Beuve's *Volupté* as 'the most beautiful novel which exists in our modern literature';[172] secondly, Sand's tour of Avignon in the company of Stendhal.[173]

In *Adriani*, the story of Petrarch and Laura is invoked explicitly by the bestowing on the novel's principal female character of the name Laure. This connection is confirmed through geographical associations; the novel's heroine is 'she who was called the *new Laura of Vaucluse*'.[174] When Laure's maid Antoinette Muiron describes Laure's Provençal connections to Adriani, a reference to Petrarch is thus inevitable; though Laure is originally from Languedoc, Toinette explains that '"for a long time, the Larnac family had been settled in Provence, in the vicinity of Vaucluse. A beautiful country, *monsieur*! The loves of Petrarch!"'[175] Laure's association with Vaucluse becomes important in *Adriani* when she is followed there by the eponymous protagonist, a narrative move which acts as a geographical reminder of the novel's Petrarchan backdrop. Adriani's manservant Comtois proudly writes to his wife '"Nothing more astonished than me at the sight of the water sung by Monsieur Petrarch."'[176] For Adriani, Petrarch provides a useful justification for visiting Vaucluse: 'He had the best excuse in the world for finding himself in a place which attracts all travellers by the beauty of the surrounding area, the closeness of the famous fountain, and the memories of the great poet.'[177] Yet once there, so obsessed with Laure is Adriani that, unlike Comtois, he fails to grant the hallowed waters any attention whatsoever: 'Adriani had, however, passed in front of the source without bestowing on it one single glance.'[178]

Adriani's failure to go on the customary literary pilgrimage signals a certain degree of disengagement with his supposed avatar which the rest of the novel rather confirms. Laure is, surprisingly, both a reminder of and a distraction from the Petrarchan model. Adriani's only brush with Petrarch in Vaucluse is his choice of accommodation, 'l'Hôtel de *Pétrarque*', an appellation which anticipates Eugène Roulleaux's criticism of Petrarchan anniversary festivities (discussed in Chapter 4)

---

[172] 'le plus beau roman qui existe dans notre littérature moderne.' George Sand, *Correspondance*, ed. Georges Lubin, 26 vols (Paris: Éditions Garnier Frères, 1964–95), II, 709.

[173] George Sand, *Histoire de ma vie*, 10 vols (Saint-Cyr-sur-Loire: Christian Pirot, 1993–2003), IX, 143.

[174] 'celle qu'on appelait la *nouvelle Laure de Vaucluse*', George Sand, *Adriani* (Paris: Éditions France-Empire, 1980), p. 137 (emphasis in the original). All subsequent quotations are to this same edition.

[175] '"Depuis longtemps, les Larnac étaient fixés en Provence, du côté de Vaucluse. Un beau pays, monsieur ! les amours de Pétrarque !"' *Adriani*, p. 35.

[176] '"Rien de plus étonné que moi à la vue de cette eau chantée par M. Pétrarque !"' *Adriani*, p. 139.

[177] 'Il avait le meilleur prétexte du monde pour se trouver dans un lieu qui attire tous les voyageurs par la beauté des sites environnants, le voisinage de la célèbre fontaine et les souvenirs du grand poète.' *Adriani*, p. 136.

[178] 'Adriani avait pourtant passé devant la source sans lui accorder un regard.' *Adriani*, p. 140.

as simple money-making schemes for local businesses and canny residents.[179] As we shall see, the connection between money and art is a key theme of *Adriani*. From such evidence, Duperray sees *Adriani* as a bathetic *terminus ad quem* for the French Petrarchan novel, arguing that 'George Sand [...] puts the literary myth of Vaucluse, popularized and inevitably diminished in beauty, within everyone's reach.'[180] From this perspective, it is no coincidence that the democratic accessibility of the myth to the whole of society, including Comtois, means that those of more elitist, artistic leanings (such as the eponymous protagonist) no longer evince any genuine interest or emotional interaction with the tale.

Aspects of Sand's Laure do, nonetheless, recall her Petrarchan namesake, even if in other respects she is far removed from her medieval model. For a start, Adriani's first dreams of Laure are marked by Petrarchan ambiguity ('At times it was an angel from Heaven, at times a fairy, a supernatural being or a monster'), reminiscent of the portrayal of Laura in the *Canzoniere* as 'an angel', 'a thing incredible', and a 'beautiful wild creature'.[181] Specifically Petrarchan wordplay may also be at work in associations with Laure and Aurora (she is 'the beautiful sad one at sunrise';[182] George Sand's real first name was, incidentally, Aurore) as well as in 'the halo [*l'auréole*] of purity' which surrounds Laure in Adriani's eyes.[183] Laure is 'the Muse of the Renaissance' and 'a poem to thrill the soul, and not a being to stir the senses'.[184] She is also, when Adriani first meets her, a ghostly figure, and the implicit example of Petrarch should surely have warned Adriani against belief in 'the impossibility of falling in love with a ghost'.[185]

Yet Laure does not die in *Adriani*, nor is she the passive object of others' poetry. Instead, despite some points of resonance, Laure, like Adriani, deviates from the model ascribed by Petrarch's *Canzoniere* in a number of ways. Most prominently, Laure herself is bereaved, rather than being the object of another's mourning. At the start of the novel, three years on, Laure is still mourning the death of her cousin and husband Octave, killed in a hunting accident only six months into their marriage. As the novel progresses, Laure's mourning for an apparently irreplaceable, ideal husband is, however, revealed to be tinged with guilt and regret at the truth that their marriage was not that happy. Laure eventually admits to herself and to Adriani that her love for Octave was rooted in fantasies stemming from memories of childhood attachment, and that the reality of their marriage was, in contrast, disappointing. All the glorious fidelity to a deceased beloved of Dante or Petrarch is thus deflated by Laure's declaration that '"It is awful to love someone who is

---

[179] *Adriani*, p. 139.

[180] 'George Sand [...] met à la portée de tous le mythe littéraire de Vaucluse, vulgarisé et inévitablement enlaidi.' Duperray, *L'Or des mots*, p. 119.

[181] 'tantôt c'était un ange du ciel, tantôt une péri, une fée ou un monstre', *Adriani*, p. 26. Compare to Petrarch's Laura as 'un'angioletta' (*RVF* 201, v. 11), 'cosa incredibil' (*RVF* 160, v. 2), and a 'fera bella' (*RVF* 23, v. 149).

[182] 'la belle désolée au soleil levant', *Adriani*, p. 48.

[183] 'l'auréole de pureté', *Adriani*, p. 48.

[184] 'la Muse de la Renaissance', 'un poème pour ravir l'âme, et non un être pour émouvoir les sens', *Adriani*, pp. 51, 52.

[185] 'l'impossibilité de devenir amoureux d'un fantôme', *Adriani*, p. 79.

dead!'"[186] *Adriani* is a tale committed to conciliatory distance from the past, to hope in the future, and to the living rather than the dead. For these reasons the novel is hopelessly un-Petrarchan. Faced with Laure's own ambivalent grief, doubt is cast on the absoluteness and purity of Petrarch's mourning for his Laura. Laure's acknowledgment of the complexity of her grief and her willingness to move beyond it to a new life with Adriani also contrast with the turn from grief (*douleur*) to religious devotion embodied by Octave's mother, along a path similar to that envisaged if not undertaken by the poet in the final, penitential poems of the *Canzoniere*.[187]

Besides these discrepancies between Petrarch's Laura and Sand's Laure, the Petrarchan intertext in *Adriani*, as for instance in *Volupté*, also jostles with other literary references, rather than being placed on a pedestal as the novel's only or principal archetype. In the case of *Adriani*, the most significant of these references involves Shakespeare's *Othello* in its operatic reworking by Rossini and his librettist Francesco Berio: *Otello, ossia il Moro di Venezia* (1816; *Othello, or the Moor of Venice*). In *Adriani*, this reworking oddly speaks more of Dante than of Shakespeare, since the specific song cited in Sand's novel sets lines from *Inferno* V. The song's first appearance is when the celebrated Italian tenor Adriani (travelling *incognito* under his family name d'Argères) hears Laure singing 'the admirable air of the gondolier in *Otello*: *Nessun maggior dolore, etc.* "There is no greater pain than to remember happy time in misery"'.[188] Adriani later returns to sing this song back to Laure several times, so that this aria becomes the 'national anthem of their love' (to borrow a phrase from Proust).[189] However, Laure is as distanced from Dante's Francesca as she is from Petrarch's Laura, since their situations are, again, markedly different. Francesca speaks these lines to Dante–pilgrim in the presence of her beloved Paolo, and the '"happy time"' is presumably that of the joys of earthly love in contrast to the present, eternal sufferings of Hell. For Laure, unlike the adulterous, damned Francesca, this song becomes instead a prelude to a loving future consecrated through marriage. In this respect, the song's function in *Adriani* seems to be to bestow a melancholic, Italianate atmosphere on the first meetings between Laure and Adriani and to highlight their mutual bond through music, regardless of the original context from which the

---

[186] "'Aimer un être mort, c'est affreux !'" *Adriani*, p. 90.

[187] See *Adriani*, p. 56.

[188] 'l'air admirable du gondolier dans *Otello* : *Nessun maggior dolore, etc.* "Il n'est pas de plus grande douleur que de se rappeler le temps heureux dans l'infortune."' *Adriani*, p. 25. The citation from Dante is from *Inferno* V, vv. 121–3: "'Nessun maggior dolore / che ricordarsi del tempo felice / ne la miseria'".

[189] 'l'air national de leur amour', Marcel Proust, *À la recherche du temps perdu*, ed. Jean-Yves Tadié, 4 vols (Paris: Gallimard, 1987–9), I, 215. On music in George Sand, see David A. Powell, *While the Music Lasts: The Representation of Music in the Works of George Sand* (Lewisburg: Bucknell University Press; London: Associated University Presses, 2001) and Thérèse Marix-Spire, *Les Romantiques et la musique: le cas George Sand 1804–1838* (Paris: Nouvelles Éditions latines, 1954). George Sand attended a performance of Rossini's *Otello* with Maria Malibran as Desdemona in January 1831 in Paris, as noted in Sand, *Correspondance*, I, 789, and in Annarosa Poli, 'George Sand et l'opéra italien', in *Présences de l'Italie dans l'œuvre de George Sand* (Moncalieri: Centro interuniversitario di ricerche sul 'Viaggio in Italia', 2004), pp. 113–47 (p. 118).

text is drawn.[190] The comparison of Laure with Desdemona is a constant in *Adriani* because of this musical, operatic connection; she is 'like a dreamy Desdemona' and even, in Adriani's thoughts, 'my Desdemona', even though the story of Shakespeare's Desdemona lacks any especial relevance to her plight, and indeed might be deemed potentially detrimental to the lovers because of its narrative of jealousy and violence.[191]

The above discussion accounts for the presence of a number of models both literary and musical in *Adriani*, not limited to Petrarch. However, in order to understand the novel and its at times polemical relationship to Petrarch's poetry more fully, it is useful to return at this juncture to Bakhtin's concept of novelization. Sand's *Adriani* confirms many of Bakhtin's observations about novelization and novelistic discourse, including a tendency towards self-criticism and parody, the incorporation of extra-literary elements, and the presentation of a polyphony of narrative voices and points of view. The extra-literary elements of *Adriani* are no doubt the most obvious; the novel proceeds through a third-person narrative that connects and comments on a mixture of letters—some even unfinished and unsent—as well as often comical entries from Comtois's journal. This typical recourse to extra-literary genres represents, for Bakhtin, the novel's all-encompassing heterogeneity and destabilizing of any strict literary canon. The presence of a multitude of witnesses to the events also enables a plurality of voices to be heard, and this plurality is strengthened through large parts of *Adriani* being devoted to the almost theatrical transcription of dialogue between characters, whether between Toinette and Adriani, Adriani and Laure, or Laure and her mother-in-law.[192] As Shira Malkin observes, 'In this novel Sand orchestrates her authorial voice in a polyphony of perspectives and literary styles', creating a hybrid text.[193]

In turn, this polyphony perhaps inevitably leads to self-criticism and parody, since characters from different social strata comment, often critically, on each other's actions. Most frequent in this regard are the suspicions about Adriani voiced by his manservant Comtois. Comtois also often assesses his surroundings with an unfavourable eye. Although he enjoys the prestige of Vaucluse, he typically casts aspersions on the countryside around Mauzères, even though this, too, is composed of Petrarchan elements:

> The region we are in is extremely ugly. The sort of place you lose your shoes.
> It is a desert where there is nothing but rocks, woods, water which falls from

---

[190] In Rossini's *Otello*, the song, instead, is a last moment of nostalgia for Desdemona which induces her to sing her own swan song (the 'willow song') before she is unjustly murdered by her husband.

[191] 'comme une Desdemona rêveuse', 'ma Desdemona', *Adriani*, pp. 48, 64.

[192] Simone Vierne, 'George Sand et le dialogue: d'une forme à une philosophie', in *George Sand, l'écriture du roman: actes du XIe colloque international George Sand*, ed. Jeanne Goldin (Montréal: Département d'Études françaises, Université de Montréal, 1996) (= *Paragraphes*, 12 (1996)), pp. 133–41 (repr. in Simone Vierne, *George Sand, la femme qui écrivait la nuit* (Clermont-Ferrand: Presses Universitaires Blaise Pascal, 2004), pp. 247–58).

[193] 'Dans ce roman Sand orchestre sa voix d'auteur en une polyphonie de perspectives et de styles littéraires.' Shira Malkin, 'Tableau et coup de théâtre: le pathétique dans *Adriani*', *Études littéraires*, 35.2–3 (2003), 107–22 (p. 111).

rocks, and not a soul to talk to, because a sort of dialect is prevalent in this area, and the locals are entirely uncivilized.[194]

Adriani's friend Baron West expresses a similar dislike of rural life that again makes a mockery of the geography beloved by Petrarch: 'I am not cut out for this bourgeois, rustic lifestyle. I was mistaken in thinking that the solitude and sun of the Midi would be good for me. Me, I'm a plant from the North, and I feel like a foreigner here.'[195] Moreover, as we have already noted, Adriani himself fails to notice Petrarch's famous source, signalling definitively a rejection of Vaucluse and its past, poetic associations despite the author's own pleasure in visiting these Petrarchan haunts.[196]

In addition, *Adriani* dramatizes a conflict between poetry and prose that also tends towards a parody of either genre and further distances itself from its Petrarchan predecessor, the *Canzoniere*. Although (Bakhtin might say, because) it is itself a novel, parts of *Adriani* express ambivalence about novelistic projects. On the one hand, Laure's personal history is described as a novel ('all the novel [*roman*] of the sad one');[197] on the other hand, this same history is superior to novelistic discourse according to Toinette, who remembers Laure's letters to Octave as '"so childish, so chaste, and so tender! There isn't a novel in which I have ever seen the like."'[198] Even more worrying are moments in *Adriani* which proclaim its incompatibility with the novelistic tradition, for instance in the following characterization of Laure: 'Laure de Larnac was like nothing less than what we understand, in general, to be the character of a heroine in a novel. She was not at all novelistic [*romanesque*].'[199] As cited above, Laure is, instead, 'a poem' (*un poème*).[200]

Nonetheless, poetry, too, comes under fire in *Adriani*, particularly through Adriani's friends Daniel and Baron West. The first, a violinist, was once in love with Laure and is remembered by Adriani as '"a true Petrarch, minus the sonnets"'.[201] This description is undeniably strange, and suggests that the cult of Petrarch has moved away from the already reductive view of him as a sonneteer towards an even more extreme view of Petrarch as solely a famous lover from history. In Adriani's phrase, Petrarch functions merely to denote a celebrated individual faithful to his beloved; from this perspective, the 'true Petrarch' is a lover rather than a poet. Furthermore, the fact that Daniel is not even constant in his affections for Laure, eventually

---

[194] 'Le pays où nous sommes est fort vilain. On y perd ses chaussures. C'est un désert où il n'y a que des rochers, des bois, des eaux qui tombent des rochers, et pas une âme à qui parler, car il règne dans le pays une espèce de patois, et les gens sont tout à fait sauvages.' *Adriani*, p. 23.

[195] 'Je ne suis pas fait pour cette vie bourgeoise et rustique. Je me suis trompé quand j'ai cru que la solitude et le soleil du Midi me seraient favorables. Je suis une plante du Nord, moi, et je me sens étranger ici.' *Adriani*, p. 193.

[196] Sand, *Histoire de ma vie*, x, 235.

[197] 'tout le roman de la *désolée*', *Adriani*, p. 32 (emphasis in the original).

[198] '"si enfant, si honnêtes et si tendres ! Il n'y a pas de roman où j'en aie jamais trouvé de pareilles."' *Adriani*, p. 38.

[199] 'Laure de Larnac n'était rien moins que ce qu'on entend, en général, par une nature d'héroïne de roman. Elle n'était nullement romanesque.' *Adriani*, p. 121.

[200] *Adriani*, p. 52.

[201] '"un vrai Pétrarque, moins les sonnets"', *Adriani*, p. 45.

marrying his laundrywoman (as the reader learns in the sentence directly preceding the comparison to Petrarch), underlines the inappropriateness of the reference to Petrarch. This reincarnation of Petrarch in a man who loves a lady called Laure but marries his laundrywoman is a stark sign of how far novelization takes Petrarch from his poetic origins. Novels, unlike Petrarchan lyric poetry, can have happy, if unexpected or bathetic endings.

Within Sand's novel, the story of Daniel acts as a mirror to that of Laure. Like Daniel, Laure eventually leaves behind the idol glimpsed from afar (Laure for Daniel, Octave for Laure) and accepts a misalliance with the paid operatic tenor Adriani that is, at least for Laure's family and especially for her mother-in-law, perhaps as shocking as Daniel's marriage to his laundrywoman. Moreover, Laure's love for Octave can even be said to parody certain aspects of medieval courtly love. Firstly, their love for one other is based on sight followed by enforced absence, during which time Laure constructs an ideal image of Octave that the real man cannot but disappoint. Secondly, Octave's obsession with going out hunting every day suggests a lifestyle reminiscent of the aristocratic hero of medieval romance. That Octave is only happy outdoors spells doom for the domestic intimacy envisioned by Laure. Laure's courtly, medievalist marriage to Octave is a failure and ends in death, in contrast to her happy, bourgeois marriage with Adriani, from which ensues new life in the form of a daughter named Adrienne. Adriani succeeds by being unlike both the courtly Octave and the Petrarchan though unpoetic Daniel.

Even more acutely than Daniel, Baron West represents the failure of poetry in *Adriani*. At one point, the baron dreams about writing a collection of poems called *La Lyre d'Adriani* (*Adriani's Lyre*), which he wants Adriani to set to music and hopes would be an artistic triumph for them both. Adriani, however, refuses to participate, in part because he feels that 'his soul would be imprisoned in this case carved and bejewelled by the hands of the baron'.[202] Adriani views the proposed poetic collection as beautiful and precious but also hard, artificial, and even claustrophobic, a view of poetry which recalls images from the *Canzoniere* of verse as constructed with precious jewels and a form of containment or enclosure.[203] Adriani is happy to be a modern Petrarch who sings and is even paid for singing, but is unwilling to be the object of another's poetry.

Further devastating for the cause of poetry, the end of the novel contrasts the impecunious life of the poet with the lucrative life of the musician. Baron West declares that '"Poetry is a ruinous taste!"' and laments that poetry relies on self-publishing and so leads to bankruptcy: '"My poems are read, but so rarely bought, that I had to take on all the publication costs, which have never come back to me."'[204] Here we have echoes of the concerns over the money to be made from publishing

---

[202] 'Son âme serait emprisonnée dans cet étui ciselé et diamanté par les mains du baron.' *Adriani*, p. 115.

[203] In *RVF* 155, for instance, Love writes on the poet's diamantine heart ('mi scrisse entro un diamante in mezzo 'l core', v. 11). Poetry as enclosure is particularly present in the recurrent phrase 'chiudere in versi' ('enclose in verses'): *RVF* 29, v. 50; *RVF* 95, v. 1.

[204] '"La poésie est un goût ruineux !"', '"Mes poèmes sont lus, mais si peu achetées, qu'il m'a fallu faire tous les frais de publication, lesquels ne me sont jamais rentrés."' *Adriani*, p. 184.

Petrarchan poetry already expressed in Balzac's *Illusions perdues*, in particular through the pun on *Laure/l'or* (Laura/gold).[205] In Sand's novel, music offers Adriani a means of earning a decent wage and paying off all his debts, in stark contrast not only to the baron's experience of poetry but also to the character Descombes's experience of painting (in the novel Descombes dies by his own hand after disastrous investments). In a hierarchy of the arts according to financial reward, music easily outstrips both poetry and painting.

In *Adriani*, the theme of money is omnipresent and un-Petrarchan, unless viewed from the perspective of the bookseller Dauriat's revisionist mockery of Petrarch. Questions of how much people earn, how much they might inherit, how investments are doing, or what purchasing power different characters have are constant concerns.[206] Yet in Sand's novel money is cleared of any especial taint of immorality, since Adriani's decision to sell his musical talents as both a singer and a composer, though it shocks the conventional values of the marquise de Monteluz, pays off not only financially but also personally: 'Far from diminishing his talent and exhausting his spirit, the theatre had developed in him new abilities.'[207] Adriani's three years on stage become a necessary corollary to Laure's three years of widowhood; each rite of passage brings with it an experience of sacrifice, suffering, and self-abnegation that is educative and redemptive. Poetry, in contrast, offers no such fruits within the parameters of Sand's novel.

Baron West's failure to become a poet in his own right leads him to seek refuge and success in the task of poetic translation:

> The baron had written some epic poems which would never have drawn him out of obscurity if he had not fortunately decided to translate into verse some Greek masterpieces. A consummate Hellenist, gifted with ease in producing harmonious verse, he had a true talent for dressing the thought of others in a noble fashion. For his own part, he had few ideas, and form cannot cover emptiness without ceasing to be form altogether. Form is then like a splendid garment, limply hanging off a stake.
>
> The success of his translations had almost upset the baron. He smiled at the compliments, but inside he was humiliated. He still yearned to shine by himself.[208]

This passage provides an interesting new perspective on the study of translations

---

[205] See the end of Chapter 5.

[206] See Duperray, *L'Or des mots*, p. 121.

[207] 'Loin d'amoindrir son talent et d'épuiser son âme, le théâtre avait développé en lui des facultés nouvelles.' *Adriani*, p. 223.

[208] 'Le baron avait fait des poèmes épiques qui ne l'eussent jamais tiré de l'obscurité s'il ne se fût heureusement avisé de traduire en vers quelques chefs-d'œuvre grecs. Grand helléniste, doué du vers facile et harmonieux, il avait un talent réel pour habiller noblement la pensée d'autrui. Pour son propre compte, il avait peu d'idées, et la forme ne peut couvrir le vide sans cesser d'être forme elle-même. Elle est alors comme un vêtement splendide, flasque et pendant sur un échalas.

Le succès de ses traductions avait presque affligé le baron. Il souriait aux éloges, mais il était humilié intérieurement. Il aspirait toujours à briller par lui-même.' *Adriani*, p. 113.

and translators with which this volume began, since it points to a fracture between poetry and translation. While these two activities were found in the previous chapter to be often complementary, the baron's dissatisfaction with translation highlights how this reciprocity may not always be as harmonious as at first apparent. The baron's assumption that translation is inferior to poetry and the purview of those who have no ideas of their own is an unfortunate, uncomfortable afterthought to the earlier part of this study. *Adriani* may parody both Petrarch in particular and poetry in general, but its approach to translation is even less kind.

Bakhtin's claim that '*European novel prose is born and shaped in the process of a free (that is, reformulating) translation of others' works*' proves true for key French novels of the late eighteenth- and nineteenth-century literary canon, each of which reworks, in different ways, the love story of Petrarch and Laura.[209] In this reworking, the poetic model is transformed through its exposure to a process of novelization. Early exponents of the French Petrarchan novel such as Rousseau had already taken the bold step of amputating the *Canzoniere* severely, by ignoring the second part. Subsequent novelists would not only imitate Rousseau (and indeed Sade) in this decision, but would also subject the story to a dialogic, polyphonic treatment, one consequence of which is, according to Bakhtin, parody. Ultimately, the transformation of Petrarch into prose results in novelistic parody that is already present in Balzac's *Le Lys dans la vallée* (through Félix's un-Petrarchan infidelities and Natalie's debunking of the tale), becomes more intrusive in Stendhal's *La Chartreuse de Parme* (in particular in the figure of Ferrante Palla), and culminates in Sand's *Adriani*. This last brings the Petrarchan mode of the French novel to an end by envisaging a happy, middle-class ending that goes entirely against the Petrarchan example of unfulfilled love-in-death.

Three of the novels discussed in this chapter are clustered in the 1830s: Sainte-Beuve's *Volupté*, Balzac's *Le Lys dans la vallée*, and Stendhal's *La Chartreuse de Parme*. This confluence suggests that the novelization of Petrarch, like the Petrarchan poetry of Hugo, Musset, and Gautier studied in the previous chapter, is principally a Romantic concern. The novelization of Petrarch, like French Petrarchan poetry, thus largely coincides with the first flourishing of French translations of Petrarch. As charted in Part I, the 1830s and 1840s were key decades for French translations of Petrarch, counting not only the first two complete translations of Petrarch's *Canzoniere*, by Gramont and Montesquiou (in 1842), but also other significant publications such as Esménard's two volumes of translations (from 1830 and 1848 respectively), and the first of Emma Mahul's five volumes of the complete sonnets of Petrarch (dating from 1847). The Romantic vogue for Petrarchan poetry and novels, as well as translations of Petrarch, was no doubt mutually invigorating and supportive, and the readership of all three—poetry, prose, translation—is likely to have overlapped, especially at a time when medievalism more broadly was fashionable across the arts.

By way of conclusion to this consideration of various French Petrarchan novels, I want to dwell for a further moment on the notion of parody, introduced at the start

---

[209] Bakhtin, *The Dialogic Imagination*, p. 378 (emphasis in the original).

of this chapter as a key element of Bakhtinian novelization. Drawing on Gérard Genette, the novelization of Petrarch can be described as doubly transformative, not only in the sense of a change in form (the transition from verse to prose), but also because, for Genette, parody is itself a type of transformation.[210] For Hutcheon, similarly, parody is not merely destructive but also potentially constructive, as encapsulated in the ambivalence of the prefix *para* in parody, which means both 'against' and 'beside' (as cited earlier). It is particularly in the latter sense that parody, as Hutcheon writes, can suggest 'an accord or intimacy'.[211]

Moreover, Hutcheon's question 'Is parody in the eye of the beholder?' serves as a further reminder that parody relies on a shared code and common cultural aware-ness—a form of intimacy—between writer and reader.[212] Correspondingly, what must be stressed in general terms about the novelization of Petrarch is the frequent expectation that a Petrarchan aura, however contorted, will be recognizable to readers and that the namedropping of Petrarch will trigger associations, however riddled with clichés. As Simon Dentith reminds readers in his introductory study, 'One of the features of parody is that it depends for its effect upon recognition of the parodied original, or at least, upon some knowledge of the style or discourse to which allusion is being made.'[213] This expectation of recognition is further proof of the importance of Petrarch in nineteenth-century French culture, particularly in the first half of the century, and no doubt suggests the success of the translations and biographies (analysed in earlier chapters) at promulgating Petrarch to a wide French reading public around this time.

Like Hutcheon, Arthur Quiller-Couch expressed well already in 1912 that parody is often a result of reverence rather than of ridicule:

> Now, the first thing to be said about Parody is that it plays with the gods: its fun is taken with Poetry, which all good men admit to be a beautiful and adorable thing, and some would have to be a holy thing. It follows then that Parody must be delicate ground, off which the profane and vulgar should be carefully warned. A deeply religious man may indulge a smile at this or that in his religion; as a truly devout lover may rally his mistress on her foibles, since for him they make her the more enchanting. [...] So, or almost so, should it be with the parodist. He must be friends with the gods, and worthy of their company, before taking these pleasant liberties with them.[214]

From this perspective, the novelization of Petrarch undertaken by Rousseau, Sainte-Beuve, Balzac, Stendhal, and Sand remains, even when it tends towards parody, an expression of friendship, and even of love.

---

[210] See Genette, *Palimpsestes*, pp. 39–40, where Genette distinguishes between parody as transformation and pastiche as imitation.

[211] Hutcheon, *A Theory of Parody*, p. 32.

[212] Hutcheon, *A Theory of Parody*, p. 84.

[213] Simon Dentith, *Parody* (London and New York: Routledge, 2000), p. 39.

[214] Arthur Quiller-Couch, 'Foreword on the Gentle Art', in *Parodies and Imitations Old and New*, ed. J. A. Stanley Adam and Bernard C. White (London: Hutchinson & Co., 1912), pp. v–xvi (p. vi). This passage is also cited in Dentith, *Parody*, p. 24.

Conclusion: Petrarch and Patriotism

W AS PETRARCH FRENCH? This controversial question has been at the heart of this book. In the Introduction, I drew on passages from Piot and Cochin, at either end of the nineteenth century, to the effect that Petrarch was French through his upbringing, education, residence, and love for Laura. The same point had already been made earlier and more forcibly by the abbé de Sade in his *Mémoires pour la vie de François Pétrarque*, first in the polemical prefatory letter to his Italian readers (also cited in the Introduction) and more generally in his claim for the Avignonese—and indeed specifically Sadean—identity of Petrarch's beloved, Laure de Sade, née de Noves. In Part I, Petrarch's Frenchness was found to have been further asserted and promoted in the translation into French of his Italian poetry as well as carefully chosen parts of his Latin works across the nineteenth century, with the 1840s and 1870s particularly productive periods. Here the question concerned not only the Frenchness of Petrarch, but more especially which parts of Petrarch's corpus had to be ignored or privileged in order to support this identification. In contrast, Chapter 4 also acknowledged the regional claims on Petrarch, which posed a more local counter-narrative to the nationalistic story of a French Petrarch. Such local claims often boasted of Petrarch's connections with Avignon and Vaucluse particularly around key Petrarchan anniversary dates (1804, 1874, 1904), and were most explicitly expressed in the act of translating Petrarch not into French, but rather into Provençal, an act in which the Provençal group of poets known as the Félibrige were especially implicated.

In Part II, we saw how nineteenth-century French Petrarchism was manifested not only in the act of translation but also in two different modes of rewriting, poetry and prose. The former uncovered translators as poets in their own rights, interrogated the motivations for the production of Petrarchan poetry around particular anniversary dates, and traced Petrarch as a touchstone for Lamartine and as a figure of more transitory but still keen attention for Hugo, Musset, and Gautier. The latter, finally, followed Petrarch as a key influence on the French novel from Rousseau's *La Nouvelle Héloïse* to Sand's *Adriani*. This survey of Petrarchan influence across nineteenth-century French literary culture is far from exhaustive, and could, moreover, fruitfully be extended to other forms of cultural response and appropriation, in particular to include areas absent from the present study such as music, sculpture, and the visual arts.[1]

---

[1]   On the French reception of Petrarch in the visual arts, see Duperray, *L'Or des mots*,

Nonetheless, instead of seeking to account, imperfectly, for other areas of nineteenth-century French transformations beyond the literary, this Conclusion is devoted to a consideration of Petrarch and patriotism, under the aegis of this century-long specifically French devotion to the medieval poet. I will approach the general question of the nineteenth-century French adoption of Petrarch and, consequently, Petrarch's putatively French identity by beginning with an interrogation of different definitions of nationality, and of the various criteria on which such definitions are based. I will continue by considering in what ways Petrarch's choice to be crowned not in Paris but in Rome constitutes a further, though crucially not insurmountable challenge to the construction of a French Petrarch. A final section will argue that *patria*, for Petrarch, is inherently performative, and therefore unstable.[2]

Nationality and Identity

Let us begin with the supposition, itself not uncontentious, that identity and community might be based on a shared language.[3] In the case of a French or more properly Provençal Petrarch, this shared language is postulated as a historical fact of which we have no written trace, but the truth of which is beyond doubt. As cited in Chapter 4, Mistral's rhetorical question 'Our language… is it not the one that Petrarch spoke to the beautiful Laura?' assumed that, given the real existence of Laura and her intimacy with Petrarch, the two lovers must have communicated with each other in medieval Occitan.[4] Yet Mistral's assumption cannot be entirely

---

pp. 283–326, and idem, *Galeria d'une triade mythique: Pétrarque, Laure, Vaucluse* (Fontaine-de-Vaucluse: Musée Pétrarque, 1995). See also, on Petrarchan iconography more generally, J. B. Trapp, 'Petrarch's Laura: The Portraiture of an Imaginary Beloved', *Journal of the Warburg and Courtauld Institutes*, 64 (2001), 55–192, and Victor Masséna, prince d'Essling, and Eugène Müntz, *Pétrarque: ses études d'art, son influence sur les artistes, ses portraits et ceux de Laure, l'illustration de ses écrits* (Paris: Gazette des Beaux-Arts, 1902). On the topic of Petrarch and nineteenth-century music, particularly deserving of mention is Hippolyte Duprat's *Pétrarque: opéra en cinq actes*, with libretto by Duprat and Frédéric Dharmenon, and which was premiered at the Grand-Théâtre de Marseille on 19 April 1873. See also Marie-Thérèse Bouquet-Boyer, 'Franz Liszt: les sonnets de Pétrarque pour piano', in *Dynamique d'une expansion culturelle*, ed. Blanc, pp. 575–9.

   [2] Here I draw on the seminal study of performative language, J. L. Austin's *How to Do Things with Words: The William James Lectures delivered at Harvard University in 1955* (Oxford: Clarendon Press, 1962). In Austin's own words, 'The term "performative" […] indicates that the issuing of the utterance is the performing of an action' (*How to Do Things with Words*, p. 6). My argument also develops Judith Butler's now classic argument about the performativity of identity, though while her focus is on gender identity mine is on national identity: Butler, *Gender Trouble: Feminism and the Subversion of Identity* (New York: Routledge, 1990).

   [3] This connection between national identity and the vernacular has been traced back to Dante: see, for instance, V. H. Galbraith, 'Nationality and Language in Medieval England', *Transactions of the Royal Historical Society*, 23 (1941), 113–28. In what follows I am largely sidestepping vexed issues about the relevance of theories of the nation, nationality, nationalism, or national identity to the Middle Ages, since my interest lies more in claims made by either Petrarch himself or his modern nineteenth-century French readers.

   [4] Words from Mistral cited in Académie de Vaucluse, *Sixième centenaire de la*

discounted as culturally motivated moonlighting, since the eminent American scholar and biographer of Petrarch, E. H. Wilkins, made a similar suggestion as to Petrarch's linguistic competencies, albeit without the intrusion of Laura. According to Wilkins, 'Most of the children's talk that Francesco heard outdoors in Carpentras must have been in Provençal: it is accordingly very probable that he was soon able to understand and to speak the language.'[5] Besides such assumptions, the postulation of a shared language is also potentially achieved through translation, most strikingly in Marc's translation of *RVF* 333 into the 'Provençal of Petrarch's day' (*Prouvençau dóu tèms de Petrarco*).[6] This last project provides, in theory, a glimpse of what Petrarch's works would have looked and sounded like had he chosen Provençal as his medium, and a similar form of local appropriation is evident in the comparable project of translating Petrarch into the (admittedly modern) Provençal promoted by the Félibrige. Under such guises, Petrarch truly emerges as 'a poet of Provence'.[7]

There are two principal problems with this grounding of identity in language. The first is that such a connection is undermined by historical examples which demonstrate much weaker ties between nationality and language. M. J. Toswell, for example, notes that 'In the Middle Ages, language did not have an indelible connection to nationhood, or even to the potentiality of nationhood', citing as a case in point the French-speaking Angevin kings of England.[8] In contrast, from a nineteenth-century French perspective a shared language is, nonetheless, considered a vital part of a stable and unified nation, with, accordingly, one of the first acts of the First Republic being to commission a review of languages spoken across France and to insist on linguistic unity and the superiority of French as a national language.[9]

The second problem is specific to the cultivation of a French Petrarch, and lies in Petrarch's decision, setting aside his Latin corpus, to write vernacular poetry not in Occitan but in an elevated, literary, rarefied, Florentine form of Italian.[10] If identity is revealed by language, there is much more evidence for a Florentine

---

naissance de Pétrarque, p. 21: 'Nosto lengo... N'es-ti pas elo que Petrarco parlavo emé la bello Lauro?'.

[5]   Wilkins, *The Life of Petrarch*, p. 3.

[6]   Marc, 'Planh', in *Fête séculaire et internationale de Pétrarque célébrée en Provence 1874*, ed. Berluc-Pérussis and Guillibert, p. 183; for the text of this sonnet, see Chapter 4.

[7]   The phrase is from Paden, 'Petrarch as a Poet of Provence'.

[8]   See M. J. Toswell, 'Lingua', in *Medievalisms: Key Critical Terms*, ed. Emery and Utz, pp. 117–24 (p. 120).

[9]   See Ferdinand Brunot, *Histoire de la langue française des origines à nos jours*, 13 vols (Paris: Librairie Armand Colin, 1967–8), IX (*La Révolution et l'Empire*). See also René Balibar and Dominique Laporte, *Le Français national: politique et pratiques de la langue nationale sous la Révolution française* (Paris: Hachette, 1974) and Michel de Certeau, Dominique Julia, and Jacques Revel, *Une Politique de la langue: la Révolution française et les patois: l'enquête de Grégoire* (Paris: Gallimard, 1975).

[10]   This linguistic question has been formulated more extensively in relation to Dante: see Tore Janson, *Speak: A Short History of Languages* (Oxford: Oxford University Press, 2002), especially pp. 108–28 where Janson addresses the question 'Did Dante Write in Italian?'. See also Giulio Lepschy, 'Mother Tongues in the Middle Ages', in *Dante's Plurilingualism: Authority, Knowledge, Subjectivity*, ed. Sara Fortuna, Manuele Gragnolati, and Jürgen Trabant (London: Legenda, 2010), pp. 16–23, where Janson's work is also referenced.

than a Provençal Petrarch, if only because the former survives in writing unlike the latter, oral language of the playground (Wilkins) or of conversations with Laura (Mistral). Indeed Petrarch's Laura, when she does speak (for instance, in *RVF* 302 or in the *Triumphus Mortis*), seems not to speak in Occitan, but rather to share Petrarch's Italian poetic vernacular as far as is recorded in Petrarch's own writings. Yet Petrarch's choice of Florentine as his language and, by extension, his identity is far from obvious or straightforward. Instead, Petrarch's choice bespeaks, in the words of Gianfranco Contini, a 'transcendental Florentineness' (*Fiorentinità* [...] *trascendentale*) that is constituted not by birth or residency, but solely by a language which transcends its roots in a specific place and which is, strangely for a vernacular, experienced chiefly as written rather than as spoken.[11] As Santagata records, this self-proclaimed Florentine in fact spent only a few days in the city:

> To Florence he only makes two brief visits, each of a few days, during the outward and return legs of the pilgrimage undertaken to Rome on the occasion of the Jubilee in 1350. [...] Petrarch likes to sign himself 'Florentine' and likes to recall his origins 'by the banks of the Arno' (*RVF* 366, 82), but he is a Florentine who almost did not step foot in his city.[12]

Further, Petrarch even refused Boccaccio's invitation to take up a post at Florence's recently established university, thereby flouting his one chance to return to this city where he had never lived.[13]

Yet the Tuscan Boccaccio remained, in spite of this refusal, committed to cultivating Petrarch's Florentineness, for instance in the very title of his biography, in Latin, of his friend and fellow poet: *De vita et moribus Domini Francisci Petracchi de Florentia secundum Iohannem Bochacii de Certaldo* (*On the Life and Customs of Francis Petrarch of Florence, according to Giovanni Boccaccio of Certaldo*).[14] At the start of this same text, Boccaccio also asserts, rather vaguely, that Petrarch was raised by the Muses in Florence:

> He was born in Arezzo on 20th day of July of Sir Petracco and his mother Letta, when four years had already passed from the happy beginning of the thirteenth Christian century; but it was later in Florence, the most prosperous

---

[11]   Contini, 'Preliminari sulla lingua del Petrarca [1951]', in *Varianti e altra linguistica*, p. 175.

[12]   'A Firenze fa solo due rapide soste, di pochi giorni ciascuna, durante l'andata e il ritorno del pellegrinaggio compiuto a Roma in occasione del Giubileo del 1350. [...] Petrarca ama firmarsi "florentinus" e ama ricordare le sue origini "in su la riva d'Arno" (*RVF* 366, 82), ma è un fiorentino che quasi non ha messo piede nella sua città.' Santagata, 'Introduzione', in Petrarch, *Canzoniere*, ed. Santagata, pp. xix–ci (pp. xxviii–xxix).

[13]   This failed attempt to persuade Petrarch to take up residence in Florence is narrated in Wilkins, *The Life of Petrarch*, pp. 99–102.

[14]   For the Latin text of the biography, see 'Vite di Petrarca, Pier Damiani e Livio', ed. Renata Fabbri, in Boccaccio, *Tutte le opere*, ed. Vittore Branca, 10 vols in 11 (Milan: Arnoldo Mondadori, 1964–98), v.1 (1992), 898–911.

of Tuscan cities, where his parents were originally from and where they had long lived with great fortune, that, I believe, he was raised by the Muses.[15]

In this statement Boccaccio reveals both an unease with the lack of time spent by Petrarch in Florence and a desire to affirm that Petrarch's poetic skills are due to specifically Florentine Muses. In this interpretation Petrarch's formative years of education and upbringing are shifted from Provence to Florence, more in line with the desire of the biographer than the evidence of history.[16] That we tend to think of Petrarch as Florentine is, then, testimony both to the enduring power of Petrarch's self-portrait and to the Florentine reception of readers of Petrarch such as Boccaccio and, later, the likes of Pietro Bembo.

For despite the above assertion by Boccaccio, Petrarch's only tangible connection to Florence was his choice to write poetry in a form of Florentine that was inflected not so much by lived, oral experience of the language as by the literary activities of reading and writing from afar.[17] In other words, Petrarch's Florentine-ness is based on an elective affinity rather than on biographical or historical fact. In this respect, it can be said of Petrarch as Barbara Cassin has recently claimed for Hannah Arendt, namely that one's homeland (*patrie*) might be not geographical but linguistic. Drawing on the example of Arendt, a German-speaking exile in America, Cassin advocates the possibility of having 'for homeland one's language, for one's only homeland even', and reiterates: 'It is one's mother tongue, and not the land of one's fathers, which constitutes one's homeland.'[18] From this perspective, having neither been born nor ever lived in Florence is not a barrier to Petrarch's Florentine identity: all that matters is language.

Language thus proves, particularly in the case of Petrarch, to be a problematic and contested site and expression of identity, which allows for a French Petrarch only in the afterlife of reception, whether in the form of translation or rewriting. Yet other theories of nationality may allow greater space and scope for Petrarch's

---

[15] I cite the English translation from Jason M. Houston, *Building a Monument to Dante: Boccaccio as Dantista* (Toronto: University of Toronto Press, 2010), p. 58, with Latin text from Boccaccio, 'Vite di Petrarca, Pier Damiani e Livio', p. 898: 'Hic aput Aritium XII kalendas augusti ex ser Petracco patre, Letta vero matre natus est post tamen christianorum iubileum XIII anno IIII; sed postmodum aput Florentiam, opulentissimam Etrurie civitatem, ex qua parentes eiusdem longis fuerant retro temporibus oriundi in copiosa fortuna, a Musarum, ut puto, fuit uberibus educatus.'

[16] As Houston comments on this passage, 'Boccaccio marks his own biographical contribution to Petrarch's putative Florentine citizenship by inserting the phrase "ut puto" ["I believe"] into the biographical narrative that recasts Petrarch's origins as Florentine.' Houston, *Building a Monument to Dante*, p. 58.

[17] The key figure responsible for establishing Florentine as a literary language being, of course, Dante, with whom Petrarch had a notoriously fraught relationship. See, for a start, the essays collected in *Petrarch and Dante: Anti-Dantism, Metaphysics, Tradition*, ed. Barański and Cachey.

[18] 'Avoir pour patrie sa langue, pour seule patrie même', 'C'est la langue maternelle, et non pas la terre de ses pères, qui constitue sa patrie.' Barbara Cassin, *La Nostalgie: quand donc est-on chez soi? Ulysse, Énée, Arendt* (Paris: Librairie Arthème Fayard/Pluriel, 2015), pp. 21, 86.

postulated Frenchness. Let us consider the five criteria proposed by David Miller in a book devoted to the subject:

1. 'National communities are constituted by belief: nations exist when their members recognize one another as compatriots, and believe that they share characteristics of the relevant kind.'

2. 'Nationality [...] is an identity that embodies historical continuity. Nations stretch backwards into the past, and indeed in most cases their origins are conveniently lost in the mists of time.'

3. 'National identity [...] is an active identity. Nations are communities that do things together, take decisions, achieve results, and so forth.'

4. 'A national identity [...] connects a group of people to a particular geographical place [...]. A nation [...] must have a homeland.'

5. 'A national identity requires that the people who share it should have something in common, a set of characteristics that in the past was often referred to as a "national character", but which I prefer to describe as a common public culture. [...] There must be a sense that the people belong together by virtue of the characteristics that they share.'[19]

From the perspective of criteria 2 and 4 in particular, there is a more compelling case for Petrarch's French identity, since the poet is undeniably strongly connected to a particular geographical place (Avignon and Vaucluse), and there is some form of historical continuity through the bloodline (though not Petrarch's directly) stretching back to Laure de Sade, née de Noves. This genealogy is, as we have seen, affirmed and celebrated by first Sade and then Lamartine, and is an important aspect of the cultivation of a French Petrarch, which relies on the assumption that, put somewhat crudely, you are what you love, at least in part. Yet the first criterion once more casts doubt on Petrarch's Frenchness, given Petrarch's clear lack of belief in or assent to such an idea, manifested both in his insistent self-identification as Florentine (noted above) and in his antipathy towards Avignon (discussed in Chapter 4). Here, the question is: is nationality something one can choose for oneself (as Petrarch chose Florence), or which others can choose on our behalf (as the French chose Petrarch)? For Miller, the former is necessarily the case, since identity relies fundamentally, according to his analysis, on belief and mutual recognition.[20] The latter, however, is the premise of Petrarch's nineteenth-century French readers and translators. Nineteenth-century Avignon recognized Petrarch as a compatriot; the sentiment was not, however, reciprocal. Does this invalidate the French claim on Petrarch? By Miller's account, undoubtedly; but not necessarily, according to Petrarch's nineteenth-century French—and often specifically Avignonese—readers.

---

[19]   David Miller, *On Nationality* (Oxford: Clarendon Press, 1995), pp. 22–5.

[20]   See, for a similar argument, Ernest Gellner, *Nations and Nationalism* (Oxford: Basil Blackwell, 1983), p. 7: 'Two men are of the same nation if and only if they *recognize* each other as belonging to the same nation.'

As Cochin declared in 1903, 'Petrarch belongs a little to France, whatever he might have said or thought himself'.[21]

While Miller's criteria throw further doubt on the possibility and even the ethics of French claims on Petrarch, they are also useful as a way of understanding the identity-building motivations behind nineteenth-century Avignon's Petrarchan activities. Miller's third criterion includes the stipulation 'Nations are communities that do things together', and one of the things that the French did together across the nineteenth century was celebrate Petrarch's life and read and translate his works. Similarly, the fifth criterion insists on 'a common public culture' in which, in the case of Avignon, Petrarch and Petrarchism clearly have a significant role to play. In this respect, the Petrarchan anniversaries, discussed in particular in Chapters 4 and 5, once more prove to be a crucial activity serving the dual purposes of promoting Petrarch and Avignon and relying on a strong community spirit. Avignon's incorporation into France at the Revolution, and its relative proximity to Italy, meant that the 1804 celebrations benefited from Napoleonic patronage. Yet the 1874 celebrations, as charted in Chapter 4, betrayed a more local focus and impetus. In this way, the French Petrarch of the later nineteenth century proves to be not so much a product of burgeoning nationalism as of regionalism, a force resistant to nation-building yet susceptible to similar criteria and constraints as those proposed for nationality by Miller.

Miller's criteria can be usefully compared to and supplemented by theories of nationality from the nineteenth century, most notably Ernest Renan's lecture on 'Qu'est-ce qu'une nation?' ('What is a nation?') given at the Sorbonne on 11 March 1882. In particular, while Miller's third and fifth criteria are based on a common culture and shared activities, Renan's analysis highlights that what nations do together is not merely remember but also, importantly, forget: 'the essence of a nation is that all individuals have many things in common, and also that they have forgotten many things'.[22] That commemoration and culture always involve an unstable dialectic of memory and *oubli* is a key facet of medievalism, which has strikingly selective hearing when it comes to listening to the past. Moreover, as regards Petrarch in particular Renan's comment is especially applicable to the 'magnanimous forgetting' (*magnanime oubli*) of the poet's antipathy towards Avignon by the Avignonese; this *oubli* is a force that binds Avignonese readers and translators of Petrarch together, particularly around Petrarchan anniversary dates.[23]

---

[21] 'Pétrarque appartient un peu à la France, quoi qu'il ait pu en dire et en penser lui-même', Cochin, *Le Frère de Pétrarque*, p. 1.

[22] 'l'essence d'une nation est que tous les individus aient beaucoup de choses en commun, et aussi que tous aient oublié bien des choses', Ernest Renan, *Qu'est-ce qu'une nation? Conférence faite en Sorbonne, le 11 mars 1882*, 2nd edn (Paris: Calmann Lévy Éditeur, 1882), p. 9; Renan, 'What is a nation?', trans. Martin Thom, in *Nation and Narration*, ed. Homi K. Bhabha (Abingdon: Routledge, 1990), pp. 8–22 (p. 11). Note, however, that Renan's theory of nationhood is complex, and also rejects language, for instance, as a basis for national identity.

[23] The phrase, laden with irony, is from Roulleaux, *Pétrarque et les fêtes du centenaire*, p. 42, discussed in Chapter 4.

Petrarch's Coronation

A final piece of evidence to be considered in response to the question of Petrarch's Frenchness is his coronation. This key event in the life of Petrarch allowed the poet to revive and connect to a hallowed tradition, whilst also assuring his place in posterity.[24] It took place on Easter Sunday (8 April) in the year 1341, on the Capitoline Hill in Rome, a site imbued with history and suiting Petrarch's reverence for the Eternal City and the great men of its past. This location was the result not of chance or external circumstances but rather of choice. Petrarch received two separate letters on the same day, 1 September 1340, inviting him to receive the laurel crown both in Rome and in Paris, as the following account of the matter to his friend and patron Giovanni Colonna summarizes:

> I find myself at a difficult crossroads, and do not know the best path to take. It is an extraordinary but brief story. On this very day, almost at the third hour, a letter was delivered to me from the Senate, in which I was in a most vigorous and persuasive manner invited to receive the poetic laureate at Rome. On the same day at about the tenth hour a messenger came to me with a letter from an illustrious man, Robert, the chancellor of the University of Paris, a fellow citizen of mine and well acquainted with my activities. He, with the most delightful reasons, urges me to go to Paris. I ask you, who could ever have guessed that anything like this could possibly have happened among these cliffs?[25]

Petrarch ultimately chose Rome, on the advice of Giovanni Colonna (*Fam.* IV, 5) but also because of his own love for the imperial city and its Classical heritage. In a letter to Giovanni Colonna's brother Giacomo (*Fam.* IV, 6), Petrarch justified his decision as follows:

---

[24]   On the coronation, see Wilkins, *The Life of Petrarch*, pp. 24–9, and Wilkins, *The Making of the 'Canzoniere' and Other Petrarchan Studies*, pp. 9–69, as well as J. B. Trapp, 'The Poet Laureate: Rome, *Renovatio* and *Translatio Imperii*', in *Rome in the Renaissance: The City and the Myth: Papers of the Thirteenth Annual Conference of the Center for Medieval & Early Renaissance Studies*, ed. P. A. Ramsey (Binghamton, NY: Medieval & Renaissance Texts & Studies, 1982), pp. 93–130. Petrarch composed a speech in Latin on the occasion of his coronation: for the text in Latin, see *Collatio laureationis*, in *Opere latine di Francesco Petrarca*, ed. Bufano with Aracri and Reggiani, II, 1255–83; for an English translation, see Wilkins, *Studies in the Life and Works of Petrarch*, pp. 300–13; for this text's first translation into French, Develay, 'Pétrarque au capitole'. Petrarch's speech is discussed in Dennis Looney, 'The Beginnings of Humanistic Oratory: Petrarch's *Coronation Oration*', in *Petrarch: A Critical Guide to the Complete Works*, ed. Kirkham and Maggi, pp. 131–40.

[25]   'Ancipiti in bivio sum, nec quo potissimum vertar scio. Mira quidem sed brevis historia est. Hodierno die, hora ferme tertia, litere Senatus michi reddite sunt, in quibus obnixe admodum et multis persuasionibus ad percipiendam lauream poeticam Romam vocor. Eodem hoc ipso die circa horam decimam super eadem re ab illustri viro Roberto, Studii parisiensis cancellario, concive meo michique et rebus meis amicissimo, nuntius cum literis ad me venit: ille me exquisitissimis rationibus ut eam Parisius hortatur. Quis unquam, oro te, eventurum tale aliquid hos inter scopulos divinasset?' English translation from *Letters on Familiar Matters: Rerum familiarium libri I–VIII*, trans. Bernardo, p. 188; Latin text from *Familiarium rerum libri*, ed. Rossi, I, 167–8 (*Fam.* IV, 4).

And when I in my insignificance was eagerly implored by two of the greatest
cities, Rome and Paris, one the capital of the world and queen of cities, the
other the mother of the studies of our time, after careful consideration and
thanks primarily to your great brother who above all others served as my
advisor and counselor, I determined finally to receive it nowhere else than in
Rome on the ashes of ancient poets and in their dwelling.[26]

As this letter suggests, the choice of Rome was not for Petrarch either easy or inevitable; indeed he seems largely to place the burden of responsibility for the decision
on Giovanni Colonna's shoulders. In contrast to his antipathy for Avignon, Petrarch
here clearly expresses admiration for Paris, even if the French city is forced to cede
to the greater claims of imperial and ecclesiastical Rome, 'the capital of the world'.
Further, the earlier letter to Giovanni asking for advice already destabilizes any stark
dichotomy between the two places, by noting that the invitation from Paris comes
from a 'fellow citizen' (*concive*), the Florentine Roberto de' Barbi, Chancellor of the
University at that time. The two invitations cannot, then, be immediately contrasted
neatly along proto-nationalistic lines.

Nonetheless, in the 'Letter to Posterity' Petrarch reiterates this tale of two cities
and two letters in more polemical terms as a competition: 'there came to me on the
same day, strange to say, a letter from the Senate of the city of Rome and from the
Chancellor of the University of Paris, vying to invite me, one to Rome and one to
Paris, to receive the laurel crown of poetry'.[27] As Giuseppe Mazzotta highlights in
his gloss on these lines, the choice, in this subsequent account, has become more
polarized and has been more explicitly invested with symbolic meaning:

The image of the 'competition' between the University of Paris and the Roman
Senate, which stand for modernity and antiquity in the historical paradigm
of the *translatio studii*, certainly conveys Petrarch's sense of playfulness and
surprise at the honor bestowed on him by competing power structures. The
image has another side: it stages the domain of culture as a confrontation of
conflicting forces and interests. The value of the poet, to put it simply, depends
on the desires of the competing institutions.[28]

The initial account is framed as a 'crossroads' (*bivium*), an image which is at least in

---

[26] 'Quamque, cum me tantillum certatim due maxime urbes exposcerent, Roma atque
Parisius, altera mundi caput et urbium regina, nutrix altera nostri temporis studiorum, post
varias deliberationes ad extremum non alibi quam Rome super cineribus antiquorum vatum
inque illorum sede percipere, ingenti ante alios frate tuo suasore et consultore, disposui.'
Letters on Familiar Matters: Rerum familiarium libri I–VIII, trans. Bernardo, p. 192; *Familiarium rerum libri*, ed. Rossi, I, 170–1.

[27] 'dictu mirabile—uno die et ab urbe Romana senatus et de Parisius cancellarii studii
ad me litere pervenerunt, certatim me ille Romam, iste Parisius ad percipiendam lauream
poeticam evocantes', 'Sen. XVIII, 1 (To Posterity)', in Petrarch, *Letters of Old Age*, trans.
Bernardo, Levin, and Bernardo, II, 676; Enenkel, 'A Critical Edition of Petrarch's *Epistola
Posteritati*', p. 272.

[28] Giuseppe Mazzotta, *The Worlds of Petrarch* (Durham, NC: Duke University Press,
1993), p. 190.

part literal: only some roads lead to Rome, while others point to Paris. The two cities are in different, even opposite directions. The later account, that of the 'Letter to Posterity', rereads this originally more neutral, geographical image of spatial opposition under the much stronger, more aggressive heading of 'competition' (through the adverb *certatim*). From this perspective, Rome is the winner and Paris the loser, a narrative which, like Petrarch's antipathy towards Avignon, poses a challenge to those responsible for constructing a nineteenth-century French Petrarch.

In Chapter 4, three main ways of overcoming or undermining Petrarch's anti-Avignon sentiment were traced in the response of nineteenth-century French translators to the three anti-Avignon sonnets (*RVF* 136–8): omission, marginalization, and paratextual reinterpretation. Petrarch's rejection of Paris, through his declining of the Parisian invitation, appeared to be a further instance of anti-French sentiment, and called for similarly special treatment by later French readers. This treatment typically involved neither omission nor marginalization, since the event of the coronation was far too well-known and central an episode in Petrarch's life simply to be either ignored or sidelined.[29] Yet the third solution found for the anti-Avignon sonnets, reinterpretation, did prove to be a similarly essential tool in nineteenth-century French readings of Petrarch's coronation. Moreover, this solution was accompanied by a further means of resolution, that is, the possibility of repeating or reliving the event, with new, changed parameters. The most extreme reinterpretation of the anti-Avignon sonnets meant postulating the three poems as anti-Rome, in the translations of Saint-Geniès, Gramont, Brisset, and Godefroy (see Chapter 4). In contrast, French reinterpretations of Petrarch's coronation could not be anti-Rome, since Rome had been the indisputably glorious site of the ceremony. They could, however, still stake out a particular French claim on or connection to the event.

In Chapter 5, Petrarch's coronation was discovered to have been reread by both Musset and Gautier in response to the now lost painting by Louis Boulanger of *Le Triomphe de Pétrarque*. Both poets, reflecting on Boulanger's work, read the coronation in a Romantic light as a celebration of love and death, by situating the public event in relation to the death of Laura. In this way, an event that was originally a celebration of Petrarch's Latin writing, rested on the reputation of the unfinished Latin epic *Africa*, and preceded Laura's death by seven years, was reinvested with significance for Petrarch as a melancholy love poet in the vernacular.[30] This ahistorical rereading had, however, to a certain extent been encouraged by Petrarch himself, in lines from the *Triumphi* which already reinterpret the coronation in a personal light as a celebration of love, Laura, and memory:

---

[29]   As noted in the volume of proceedings from the 1874 Avignon festivities, 'l'option de Pétrarque n'est ignorée de personne : elle s'explique suffisamment par son puissant amour pour la Patrie' ('Petrarch's choice is not ignored by anyone; it is sufficiently explained by his fervent love for his Homeland'). *Fête séculaire et internationale de Pétrarque*, ed. Berluc-Pérussis and Guillibert, p. 7.

[30]   In contrast, from a historical perspective Wilkins asserts that 'it is unthinkable that either Petrarch or his influential friends should have considered that his Italian lyrics constituted even a partial basis for coronation'. Wilkins, *The Making of the 'Canzoniere' and Other Petrarchan Studies*, p. 34.

[C]olsi 'l glorïoso ramo
onde forse anzi tempo ornai le tempie
in memoria di quella ch'io tanto amo.

***

I gathered the glorious branch
with which perhaps too soon I adorned my temples
in memory of she whom I love so much.[31]

Although according to Petrarch's own dating Laura died on 6 April 1348, the phrase 'in memory of' (*in memoria di*) already implies the possibility of a *post-mortem* dynamic. More straightforwardly, these lines provide ample justification for the connection made by writers such as Musset and Gautier between the coronation and Laura, beyond the pun on the laurel (*lauro*) and laurel crown (*laurea*) contained within Laura's very name.

Even more radically, earlier in the nineteenth century a purportedly historical novel, Madame de Genlis's *Pétrarque et Laure* (1819), found a way to bring Laura into the coronation not merely through imagining Petrarch's melancholy thoughts of her (as already in Petrarch's *Triumphi* and later in Musset and Gautier), but rather by suggesting that a still living and recently widowed Laura had travelled to Rome to witness the ceremony:

His triumph lacked only the presence of Laura; he said silently to himself that all of Europe having known for six months that he was to be crowned in Rome, it was not impossible that Laura would have made this long journey in secret, in order to witness the triumph of he whom she loved, and who owed one of his crowns to his passion for her![32]

Once more, the coronation is connected to Petrarch's love poetry rather than to his Latin writings. It seems certain, for these writers, that Petrarch owes the laurel crown to Laura. Moreover, if Laura is an added spectator in Madame de Genlis's account, the crowd in Gautier's poetic narrative, inspired by Boulanger, has been even more strangely transformed into a French audience for the event. Gautier's poem was a way of reliving the coronation, not only through his own poetic ecphrasis, as discussed in Chapter 5, but also through his very presence in the painting. Gautier modelled as one of the spectators in Boulanger's work, so that the depicted scene was transplanted from Roman crowds to a circle of French contemporaries.[33]

---

[31] *Triumphus Cupidinis IV*, vv. 79–81, in Petrarch, *Trionfi, rime estravaganti, codice degli abbozzi*, p. 202.

[32] 'Il ne manquoit à son triomphe que la présence de Laure; il se dit intérieurement que toute l'Europe sachant depuis six mois qu'il devoit être couronné à Rome, il n'étoit pas impossible que Laure eût fait ce grand voyage secrètement, pour être témoin du triomphe de celui qu'elle aimoit, et qui devoit une de ses couronnes à sa passion pour elle !' Stéphanie-Félicité de Genlis, *Pétrarque et Laure*, 2 vols (Paris: Chez l'éditeur des œuvres de Mme de Genlis, 1819), II, 167–8.

[33] Marie, *Le Peintre poète Louis Boulanger*, p. 62.

Belatedly, Boulanger succeeded, through his painting, in bringing Petrarch's coronation to Paris.

Two earlier coronations in Paris were also read as re-enactments of Petrarch's Roman triumph, thus presenting two very different French figures as successors and even rivals to Petrarch's fame. The first was Voltaire's return to Paris in 1778, which Lamartine explicitly compared to Petrarch's coronation.[34] The second was Napoleon's coronation as Emperor of the French, first with a laurel wreath and then with the newly minted crown of Charlemagne, on 2 December 1804 in Notre Dame de Paris, the same year that marked five hundred years since Petrarch's birth.[35] That this numerological coincidence would not have escaped Napoleon's attention is evident from his founding of the Athénée de Vaucluse in 1801 (as noted in the Introduction), at a time when, as we have seen, claiming Avignon as newly French (after centuries as a papal annexe) relied on claiming Petrarch as French, and went hand in hand with broader imperial designs on Italy. Napoleon's wish to transform the Italian and Avignonese Petrarch into a French citizen stands as a first step and as a microcosm for his political and military desires to annexe Italy to the new French Empire. Napoleon's identification with the poet is further suggested by the pomp of his own coronation, the connection between the two being not only the Petrarchan year of 1804, but also the significance of the laurel crown, apt—in Dante's words—'to celebrate the triumph of either Caesar or poet' (*per triünfare o cesare o poeta*).[36]

The revival of this Petrarchan ceremony also found its way into novelistic discourse of the early nineteenth century, in particular in Book Two of Germaine de Staël's *Corinne ou l'Italie* (1807), devoted to the narrative of Corinne at the Capitol (*Corinne au Capitole*). This work was foundational for French Romantic perceptions of Italy as a country of passion and art.[37] Like Rousseau's *Nouvelle Héloïse*, Staël's novel advertised its Petrarchan affiliation from the title page onwards, through the citation, in Italian, of the following lines from a sonnet by Petrarch: 'the beautiful country that the Apennines divide and the sea and the Alps surround will hear it'.[38] Corinne's coronation is explicitly placed in relation to a Petrarchan tradition by its introduction as 'this ceremony consecrated by the names of Petrarch and Tasso'.[39]

Against these successors of Petrarch, crowned either in Paris (Voltaire, Napoleon) or in Rome (Corinne), nineteenth-century French readers of Petrarch also sought to repeat the coronation of Petrarch himself on French soil. One form such

---

[34]   Lamartine, *Cours familier de littérature*, VI, 44.

[35]   On Rome as an inspiration for Napoleon more generally, see also Diana Rowell, *Paris: The 'New Rome' of Napoleon I* (London: Bloomsbury Academic, 2012).

[36]   Dante, *Paradiso* I, v. 29.

[37]   See, for instance, Casillo, *The Empire of Stereotypes*.

[38]   'udrallo il bel paese / ch'Appennin parte, e 'l mar circonda et l'Alpe' (*RVF* 146, vv. 13–14). The direct object in this quotation is Laura's name, as is clear from the lines in context but not from the epigraph alone. On Rousseau's *Nouvelle Héloïse* see Chapter 6.

[39]   Germaine de Staël, *Corinne ou l'Italie*, ed. Simone Balayé (Paris: Gallimard, 1985), p. 49: 'cette cérémonie consacrée par les noms de Pétrarque et du Tasse'. On the coronation of Corinne as a deliberate bestowal of Petrarchan glory on a female poet, see Zuccato, *Petrarch in Romantic England*, pp. 144–6. Staël would not, of course, have endorsed Napoleon's appropriation of Petrarch to his pro-imperial cause.

repetition took was, as we have seen, artistic: Boulanger's painting of the event, celebrated by Musset in prose and by Gautier in verse. In addition, anniversary celebrations allowed for the event to be repeated in an even more overt form, through the crowning of a bust of Petrarch during the anniversary celebrations held in 1874 in Avignon. In one record of these festivities, this moment is situated as a means of compensation for the failed coronation in Paris during Petrarch's lifetime: 'The crown offered by France in 1341 has in any case not wilted over five centuries; it had, on 18 July 1874, to be solemnly placed on his bust.'[40] According to this account, the French coronation of Petrarch was not permanently rendered impossible by Petrarch's rejection of the initial invitation from Paris, but merely postponed and rescheduled to take place in Avignon in the second half of the nineteenth century. The new, Avignonese location sidesteps the Rome/Paris rivalry of the initial invitation, whilst also fuelling a new rivalry, one between Paris (whose invitation Petrarch had, after all, turned down) and Avignon.

A final means of rooting Petrarch's coronation in French locations, despite Rome having been its actual site, was offered by a text which has emerged frequently in this book as one of the prime catalysts for nineteenth-century French Petrarchism: the abbé de Sade's *Mémoires*. In this work, the final reason proposed in favour of Petrarch's Frenchness was that 'it is here that he conceived the epic poem to which he owes his crown.'[41] From this perspective, the coronation in Rome proves to be a ceremony celebrating Petrarch's arguably French achievements. Unusually, in the case of Sade though not of later French readers (including Musset and Gautier, but also Stendhal and Sainte-Beuve), Petrarch's Frenchness is tied in part to his Latin epic poem the *Africa*.[42] Yet the *Africa* is a text that was to remain incomplete not only at the time of but even after Petrarch's coronation; it was 'conceived' (*conçu*), as Sade recounts, at Vaucluse, but finished neither there nor elsewhere. In this respect, Petrarch's coronation turns out to be an even more complex and problematic event, since it is haunted by a fear of failure and incompletion. This fear is, for instance, implicitly recorded in the admission, in the passage cited above from the *Triumphus Cupidinis*, that the coronation was perhaps premature (*anzi tempo*, 'too soon').[43] As Wilkins comments, 'the invitations to be crowned were extended on the basis of faith rather than of performance. The faith was justified—but not by the *Africa*.'[44]

Moreover, while nineteenth-century French readers tended to approach Petrarch's coronation with the attitude that it did not preclude Petrarch from being considered French, despite the missed opportunity of a ceremony in Paris, Thomas M.

---

[40] 'La couronne offerte par la France en 1341 ne s'est d'ailleurs point flétrie pendant cinq siècles ; elle devait, le 18 juillet 1874, être solennellement posée sur son buste.' *Fête séculaire et internationale de Pétrarque*, ed. by Berluc-Pérussis and Guillibert, p. 7.

[41] 'c'est là qu'il a conçu ce Poëme épique auquel il doit la couronne', Sade, *Mémoires*, I, p. lxxi.

[42] See Chapter 3 for discussion of the frosty reception of Petrarch's *Africa* in nineteenth-century France, and Chapter 5 for the obscuring of any connection between the *Africa* and Petrarch's coronation in the discussions of Musset and Gautier concerning this event.

[43] *Triumphus Cupidinis IV*, v. 80, in Petrarch, *Trionfi, rime estravaganti, codice degli abbozzi*, p. 202.

[44] Wilkins, *The Making of the 'Canzoniere' and Other Petrarchan Studies*, p. 35.

Greene inversely casts doubt on what the actual ceremony in Rome achieved: 'The references to this coronation scattered endlessly through Petrarch's œuvre cannot be explained simply as self-advertisements; they make better sense as obsessive returns to a source of insecure reinforcement. Did the laureate truly become a Roman that day on the Capitoline?'[45] In theory, the coronation did make Petrarch Roman, the final award in the *privilegium* (diploma) bestowed on him that day being Roman citizenship.[46] In practice, however, as I discuss below, it is not certain that language alone is capable of such a transformation. Instead, Greene's question remains unanswerable and points to the instability of the significance of the Roman coronation even before French readers start to invent means to redress the un-French choice which the event seems, on some level, to represent. Greene highlights a risk that the coronation may have been un-transformative for Petrarch, and, more generally, calls into question the ways in which identity and self-identity are legitimately defined and formed.

Petrarch's *Patria*

Let us return, then, enriched by this discussion of the significance of Petrarch's coronation, to the question of Petrarch's *patria*, his fatherland or homeland. A number of contenders for this title can be identified, beyond the generic, polarized claimants, France and Italy. Indeed, since neither country was a unified nation in Petrarch's day, more local sites doubtless deserve independent consideration. On the Italian side, the following are especially notable contenders: Arezzo, Petrarch's actual birthplace; Florence, Petrarch's chosen, if distant, spiritual home; Rome, the site of the coronation; Arquà, Petrarch's last residence and gravesite. As regards the last, it is notable that in one of the dialogues towards the end of the *De remediis utriusque fortune*, Reason suggests that the grave, regardless of location, is one's 'true homeland' (*verior patria*):

> Wherever you die, there will be your true homeland, for sure. It will hold you much longer than any other, nor let you depart, and keep you forever clasped to its bosom as its very own inhabitant. Learn to like it. It will accept you as its citizen although you were born somewhere else.[47]

---

[45] 'Petrarch *Viator*', in Thomas M. Greene, *The Vulnerable Text: Essays on Renaissance Literature* (New York: Columbia University Press, 1986), pp. 18–45 (p. 30).

[46] See Wilkins, *The Life of Petrarch*, p. 28, and Wilkins, *The Making of the 'Canzoniere' and Other Petrarchan Studies*, p. 56. In the latter Wilkins cites from the *privilegium* the lines 'Insuper eundem Franciscum petrarcham [...] civem romanum facimus pronunciamus' ('Above all the same Francis Petrarch [...] we make and pronounce Roman citizen').

[47] 'Ubi moreris, illa demum verior patria tua est, illa te diutius possidebit, nec vagari sinet, et proprium perpetuumque incolam sinu amplexa constringet; disce hanc terram pati, que te ortum alibi transformabit in se.' 'Death Away from Home', in *Petrarch's Remedies for Fortune Fair and Foul: A Modern English Translation of 'De remediis utriusque fortune', with a Commentary*, ed. and trans. Conrad H. Rawski, 5 vols (Bloomington: Indiana University Press, 1991), III, 317–21 (p. 318); 'De moriente extra patriam', in *Les remèdes aux deux fortunes/De remediis utriusque fortune (1354–1366)*, ed. and trans. Christophe Carraud, 2 vols (Grenoble: Millon, 2002), I, 1104–13 (p. 1104).

Petrarch recognizes here the possibility of what the French philosopher Jacques Derrida has described as 'cultural belonging, *by death* [...], by sepulture', belonging through burial rather than the traditional location of identity in birth and birthplace.[48] From this perspective, the following list of possible gravesites enumerated in Petrarch's *Testamentum* (*Testament*, dated 4 April 1370) reveals an uncertainty and anxiety about identity and belonging that continue to plague him even in the last years of his life: Padua, Arquà, Venice, Milan, Pavia, Rome, and Parma, or, finally, any 'church in the neighbourhood of the place of my death'.[49] With this last detail Petrarch renounces as impossible the attempt to anticipate where he will die, suggesting an expected continuation of his nomadic lifestyle up until death. At the same time, however, the wish for a certain place of burial, evident in the *Testamentum*, demonstrates a continued concern with identity and belonging, and the possibility that death may provide some resolution to this concern. The importance of belonging through place of death and burial is further suggested by the lament that Petrarch is buried far from Avignon and from Laura in poems cited in Chapter 5.

Against all these diverse Italian locations stand the compelling claims of the various French sites with which Petrarch is associated: Carpentras, where he was brought up; Montpellier, where he studied; Avignon, which, however, was to become Italian through its papal ties, incurring Petrarch's wrath; and, above all, Vaucluse and the source of the Sorgue. While Chapter 4 has considered how Petrarch's anti-Avignon writings make him a complicated figure for French and specifically Avignonese appropriation, it remains nonetheless true that for Petrarch as a young man, Avignon was in some sense home. In the 'Letter to Posterity', having noted his studies in law first at Montpellier and then at Bologna, cut short by the death of his parents, Petrarch continues: 'So at the age of twenty-two I returned home [*domum*]. I call home that place of exile, Avignon, where I had been since my later child-hood, for habit is like a second nature.'[50] In hindsight, Petrarch recognizes Avignon paradoxically as both home and exile, and admits that home can be forged by habit rather than by any more exalted sentiments. Recently orphaned and with reservations about Avignon, Petrarch's homecoming aged twenty-two after university is a matter of reluctant inevitability, but still, for all that, a homecoming.

In contrast, Petrarch's affection for the solitary, natural idyll of Vaucluse is as fervent as his hatred of Avignon, and is a key element in most claims for a French Petrarch. The love Petrarch felt for Vaucluse was even sufficient to challenge his

---

[48] 'l'appartenance culturelle *par la mort*', 'par la sépulture', Jacques Derrida, *Monolingualism of the Other; or, The Prosthesis of Origin*, trans. Patrick Mensah (Stanford: Stanford University Press, 1998), p. 13; Derrida, *Le Monolinguisme de l'autre, ou la prothèse d'origine* (Paris: Galilée, 1996), p. 30. The traditional importance of birth in determining identity and citizenship is evident in the very etymology of the word 'nation' (*natio*), from *nāscī* ('to be born'), noted, for instance, in the *OED* entry on 'nation'.

[49] 'in quacumque alia ecclesia, que vicinior fuerit loco mortis', *Petrarch's Testament*, ed. and trans. Theodor E. Mommsen (Ithaca, NY: Cornell University Press, 1957), pp. 74, 75.

[50] 'Itaque secundum et vigesimum annum agens domum redii. Domum voco Avinionense illud exilium, ubi ab infantie mee fine fueram: habet enim consuetudo proximam vim nature.' Petrarch, '*Sen.* XVIII, 1 (To Posterity)', in Petrarch, *Letters of Old Age*, p. 675; Enenkel, 'A Critical Edition of Petrarch's *Epistola Posteritati*', p. 266.

attachment to Italy, the country which he famously invoked passionately as his own at the start of *RVF* 128. In one letter praising his house and gardens at Vaucluse, Petrarch declared: 'Briefly, I do not believe that there can be such a place anywhere else, and—if I must confess a childish weakness—I only regret that it is not in Italy.'[51] Later in the same letter, Petrarch contemplated taking up permanent residence at Vaucluse, despite the attraction of Italy and the repulsiveness of Avignon:

> Perhaps I could live here for the rest of my life, if Italy were not so far away and Avignon so near. Why should I hide my double weakness? Love of Italy charms and lures me; and hatred of Avignon, and of the stench of it that sickens all the world, stings and embitters me.[52]

In an epigram sent to Philippe de Cabassoles in Spring 1351, Petrarch further declared: 'No place in the whole world is dearer to me than the Vale Enclosed, and none more favorable for my toils.'[53]

Most strikingly, in a letter to Zanobi da Strada dated 22 February 1353, Petrarch even embraced Vaucluse explicitly as his chosen *patria*, writing that 'For the present I have made this my Rome, my Athens, and my fatherland [*patriam*].'[54] This statement collapses distinctions between Frenchness and Italianness, including the competition between Rome and Paris leading up to Petrarch's coronation, by suggesting that *patria* is a matter of the heart and that affection can radically transform one's experience of place and space. While Avignon was home through force of habit, Vaucluse is elected as *patria* through strength of emotional attachment. Strangely, *patria* here proves to be a mobile concept for Petrarch, and something that is not inherited at birth, but rather grown into and chosen later in life. Vaucluse as *patria* is, moreover, suggested to be a potentially transient and temporary phenomenon, since it is introduced by the temporal indication of 'For the present' (*interea*, 'meanwhile'). There is, then, the likelihood that instead of being a fixed, immutable identity, one's *patria*, according to Petrarch, may be more pragmatic and impermanent. Finally, with Miller's criteria for nationality once more in mind, it is notable that in Petrarch's proposal of Vaucluse as *patria*, there is a distinct lack of community spirit or sense of collectivity. Instead, this Petrarchan *patria* is all about

---

[51] 'In summa vix situ simile aliquid reor habeat orbis terrarum, et si femineam levitatem fateri oportet, tale quicquam esse extra Italiam indignor.' *Fam.* XIII, 8, 13–14. English translation from *Petrarch at Vaucluse: Letters in Verse and Prose*, trans. E. H. Wilkins (Chicago: University of Chicago Press, 1958), p. 122; Latin text from Petrarch, *Familiarium rerum libri*, ed. Rossi, III, 86. These lines are also cited by Lamartine, *Cours familier de littérature*, VI, 35.

[52] 'Possem forsan hic vivere nisi vel tam procul Italia vel tam prope esset Avinio. Quid enim dissimulem geminam animi mollitiem? illius me amor mulcet ac vellicat, huius me odium pungit et asperat odorque gravissimus toti mundo pestifer.' *Fam.* XIII, 8, 16. Cited from *Petrarch at Vaucluse*, trans. Wilkins, p. 123, and Petrarch, *Familiarium rerum libri*, ed. Rossi, III, 87. See also Lamartine, *Cours familier de littérature*, VI, 36.

[53] 'Valle locus Clausa toto michi nullus in orbe / gratior aut studiis aptior ora meis.' Latin and English translation cited from *Petrarch at Vaucluse*, trans. Wilkins, p. 80.

[54] 'Interea equidem hic michi Romam, hic Athenas, hic patriam ipsam mente constituo.' *Fam.* XV, 3, 14, cited from: *Petrarch at Vaucluse*, trans. Wilkins, p. 178; *Familiarium rerum libri*, ed. Rossi, III, 139.

a beautiful landscape, interesting books, and private study; Vaucluse is a *patria* for one, complemented by visits from friends and the discreet companionship of 'a dog and two servants', in that order.[55]

These competing French and Italian sites render the question of Petrarch's *patria* complex and inevitably open-ended, since by his own idiosyncratic definition one's *patria* is, unusually, a result of choice and liable to change. For a French perspective on this issue, we can return to the comments of Sade and Piot cited in the Introduction, both of whom suggest that education and love are more important than assignation of identity according to place either of birth or death. As Sade suggests, 'It is necessary, then, to consider now whether a man of letters does not belong more to the country where he was brought up, formed, and educated, and where he composed his best works, than to the earth where he received life and from whence he departed the same.'[56] Similarly, Piot explicitly proposes a new definition of *patria* to accommodate Petrarch as French: 'If homeland [*la patrie*] means above all the places where the mind is formed and the heart cultivated, Petrarch belongs to no one but us.'[57] Both Sade and Piot are motivated by nationalistic sentiment in wishing to claim Petrarch as French, yet they raise important and unsettling questions about belonging and identity, including questioning why so much meaning is attributed to place of birth rather than, for instance, place of upbringing or education.

It is tempting to conclude in a mood of reconciliation between the Italian Petrarch and the French Petrarch, either by suggesting that it is possible to have more than one *patria* or, widening the scope, by pitching Petrarch as European. The former is the less polemical stance occasionally adopted by French writers: for instance the assertion, during the 1874 festivities, that 'Our beautiful Provence' is 'this second homeland of the great Italian poet'.[58] From this perspective, the French Petrarch is not mutually exclusive or incompatible with his Italian *alter ego*. Yet this approach is more harmonious and conciliatory than that adopted by Sade and Piot, for whom, in contrast, the assertion of Petrarch's Frenchness is predicated upon the denial of his Italianness.

According to the latter alternative, the French and Italian Petrarchs can be subsumed into a larger whole, the European Petrarch. This view is one that was already circulating at the beginning of the nineteenth century, with Friedrich Schlegel, for instance, suggesting that 'Petrarch's poetry [is] not Italian, but rather generally European.'[59] Harald Hendrix has more recently suggested three principal

[55]   'ubi cum cane unico et duobus tantum servis habito', *Fam.* XIII, 8 to Francesco Nelli, cited from *Petrarch at Vaucluse*, trans. Wilkins, p. 122; Petrarch, *Familiarium rerum libri*, ed. Rossi, III, 86.

[56]   'Il s'agit à présent de sçavoir, si un homme de Lettres n'appartient pas plus au Pays où il a été élevé, formé, instruit, où il a composé ses meilleurs Ouvrages, qu'à la terre où il a reçu & quitté la vie.' Sade, *Mémoires*, I, p. lxxi.

[57]   'Si la patrie est sur-tout aux lieux où l'esprit se forma, où se développa le cœur, Pétrarque n'est pas à d'autres qu'à nous.' Piot, 'Proposition', in *Mémoires de l'Athénée de Vaucluse* (1804), pp. 105–6.

[58]   *Fêtes littéraires & internationales*, p. 15.

[59]   'Petrarcha's Lyrik nicht Italiänisch sondern allgemein Europäisch', Schlegel, *Literary Notebooks 1797–1801*, p. 40 (no. 239).

reasons in support of the assertion that Petrarch is a European rather than a national figure: his nomadic life, his prolific works in the common language of Latin, and, finally, his European-wide reception, which means that even his Italian poetry transcends national borders.[60] In this respect Petrarch's coronation might, too, be read not as a competition between countries, but rather as a sign of the poet's European appeal and fame already in his lifetime, at a relatively young age. Yet there is something radical and even persuasive about the nineteenth-century proposal of an exclusively French Petrarch which resists being smoothed over in either of these ways.

From this Conclusion, two key aspects of Petrarchan identity emerge: its rootedness in local more than national space; its fluidity rather than fixity. As regards the former, it is important that Petrarch considers Vaucluse to be his *patria* and not Avignon or France (understood broadly by Petrarch as Gaul). Extrapolating this connection to a national level in claims for a French Petrarch would be irresistible to many nineteenth-century French readers, conditioned as they were by living in a period of particularly intense nation-formation and burgeoning nationalism. Yet the regionalism of the specifically Avignonese and Provençal adoption of Petrarch, particularly in the later nineteenth century through the involvement of the Félibrige, was to keep alive this local tradition, initiated by Petrarch himself. As regards the latter point, the fluidity of identity in Petrarch's conception, Petrarch's theory of *patria* might best be summed up as performative, in that it is reliant on language and context-dependent. Illustrative in this regard is the *privilegium* bestowed on Petrarch at the coronation, and which asserted Petrarch's Roman citizenship; this example not only implies that language can create citizenship, but also reveals the power of self-identification, since the *privilegium* is believed to have been largely the work of Petrarch himself.[61] For Petrarch, *patria* is once more something one can, even must, choose for oneself.

Yet the performativity of Petrarch's *patria* also creates problems in terms of unreliability, inconsistency, and the possibility of failure (what Austin would call 'infelicity'). As Greene has suggested, Petrarch's repeated, boastful assertions of his post-coronation Roman identity likely bespeak anxiety and disappointment (in Greene's phrase, 'insecure reinforcement') more than conviction.[62] Thus, for instance, when Petrarch declares in one of his invectives 'In fact, I am Italian by birth, and glory in being a Roman citizen', the boldness of this statement may mask a dread of self-delusion, and the fear that this certain identity lasts only the time taken for these words to be inscribed or read.[63] This example also reveals that

---

[60] Hendrix, 'Petrarch 1804–1904', p. 117.

[61] See Wilkins, *The Making of the 'Canzoniere' and Other Petrarchan Studies*, p. 60 ('All things considered, it seems probable that Petrarch brought to Rome something like a draft or outline of the *Privilegium*, prepared wholly or chiefly by himself'). Trapp similarly comments that 'The *privilegium* awarded to Petrarch on that high occasion was almost certainly drafted by himself' (Trapp, 'Rome, *Renovatio* and *Translatio imperii*', p. 105).

[62] See Greene, *The Vulnerable Text*, p. 30, as cited earlier.

[63] 'Sum vero Italus natione, et Romanus civis esse glorior'. 'Invectiva contra eum qui maledixit Italie (Invective Against a Detractor of Italy)', in Petrarch, *Invectives*, ed. and trans. David Marsh (Cambridge, MA: Harvard University Press, 2003), pp. 364–475 (pp. 402, 403).

patria, even if ideally solitary for Petrarch, is often an almost aggressive gesture directed at others of a different, competing identity. In this case, defining himself as Roman is particularly polemical in an invective addressed to a Frenchman (*Gallus*). Further, coupling this statement with Petrarch's affectionate adoption of Vaucluse as his *patria* and 'his Rome', cited above, reveals an irreconcilable rift in his thoughts on self-identity. For Petrarch, *patria* is hopelessly—but also excitingly and inventively—contingent on time, place, language, and even addressee.

Petrarch is, then, peculiarly open to adoption at points of nation-building and the formation of national culture, because of his contradictory, protean, and nomadic nature. As a consequence, his afterlives, in markedly different ways, span many centuries and many countries. The transformations of Petrarch in nineteenth-century France are one vital fragment in that wider picture to which future readers of Petrarch, the world over, will forever add their piece.

Appendix 1

A Chronological Survey of Translations of Petrarch's Italian Poetry (the *Canzoniere* and *Triumphi*) between 1764 and 1903 in France

These translations are listed in date order, with RVF numbering following that of modern editions, specifically the reference edition: Petrarch, Canzoniere, *ed. Marco Santagata, 4th edn (Milan: Arnoldo Mondadori, 2010). Also included at the end of Appendix 1 is the listing of the order of poems in Antonio Marsand's influential edition,* Le rime del Petrarca, *2 vols (Padua: Nella tipografia del seminario, 1819–20).*

1764–7. abbé de Sade, *Mémoires pour la vie de François Pétrarque, tirés de ses œuvres et des auteurs contemporains, avec des notes ou dissertations, & les pieces justificatives,* 3 vols (Amsterdam: Arskée & Mercus).

Includes many translations from Petrarch's Italian poetry into French verse often with Italian in parallel columns and French prose paraphrases of sonnets identified in the margins by number, as well as French prose translations from various Latin letters. The poems translated are, in order, as they appear interspersed throughout the prose narrative of volumes one and two (but not three): *RVF* 1, 211 (partial), 54 (partial), 181, 144, 159, 2–3, 62 (partial), 10, 6, 34, 148 (partial), 12–13, 8 (partial), 9, 7, 15–16, 176–7, 103, 98, 35–6, 32, 31, 33, 27–8, 53, 39, 47–9, 59, 63, 56–7, 64, 54–5, 65, 68, 67 (partial), 82–3, 89, 85, 84, 96–7, 71–3 (amalgamated into one), 77–8, 81, 109, 108, 110–12, 90, 213, 91, 115–16, 199–202 (also in one), 114, 259, 118, 128, 194, 113, 126, 125, 123, 180, 209, 266, 129, 139, 208, 140–1, 147, 240, 134, 132, 155–8 (in one), 238, 143, 150, 153, 168–70, 183, 172, 174, 184, 218, 231, 233, 203, 206, 229–30 (230 partial), 231+230+174 (in one), 212, 216–17, 221, 234–5, 225, 257, 249+250 (in one), 253, 250–2+254 (in one), 160, 192, 263, 154, 262, 261, 167, 222, 45–6, 100, 219+255 (in one), two sonnets not in the *Canzoniere*,[1] 162, and 247.

---

[1] The two sonnets not in the *Canzoniere* begin in Italian 'Siccome il padre del folle Fetonte' ('Since the father of the mad Phaethon') and 'La bella Aurora' ('The beautiful Aurora/ Dawn'); the first is by Petrarch while the second is Sennuccio del Bene's response: see Francesco Petrarca, *Trionfi, rime estravaganti, codice degli abbozzi,* ed. Vinicio Pacca and Laura Paolino (Milan: Arnoldo Mondadori, 1996), p. 688.

1765. Nicolas Antoine Romet, *Lettre de Pétrarque à Laure, suivie de remarques sur ce Poëte, & de traduction de quelques-unes de ses plus jolies pièces* (Paris: Sébastien Jorry).

Fictional letter (pp. 9–26) from Petrarch to Laura in rhyming verse, followed by 'Remarques sur le Pétrarque' (pp. 27–9) and 'Essai d'une traduction libre de quelques pièces de Pétrarque' (pp. 30–40). These translations are in French prose with no facing Italian although the first few words of the first line of each poem are given. The poems Romet selects are *RVF* 35, 90, 222, 7, 145, and 126.

1772. *Nouvelles fables, avec une traduction de quelques sonnets choisis de Pétrarque et une romance* 'par l'auteur d'*Abbassaï*, & de la *Guerre des Bêtes*' [i.e. Marianne-Agnès Falques] (London: T. R. Delorme).

'Sonnets de Pétrarque' (pp. 41–9) includes the following eight sonnets translated into French verse without Italian text/first line: *RVF* 132, 140, 7, 124, 226, 265, 310, 35. This section is followed by a sonnet translated from Tasso, and a further section of 'Imitations de plusieurs passages de Pétrarque' (pp. 51–5) in the form of 'Stances' and an ode.

1774. Pierre-Charles Levesque, *Choix des poésies de Pétrarque traduites de l'italien* (Venice and Paris: Valade and Hardouin).

French prose with facing Italian. Includes a 'Vie de Pétrarque' (pp. 11–35). Levesque translates seven *canzoni* (*RVF* 50, 53, 73, 126–7, 268, 270), one sestina (*RVF* 22), twenty-three sonnets (*RVF* 1, 3, 7, 12, 102, 108, 112, 132, 134, 144–5, 153, 159, 162, 164, 170, 176, 180, 192, 205, 219, 223, 310), two *ballate* (*RVF* 106 and 121), and the *Triumphus Cupidinis*. At the end is a section entitled 'Frammenti scelti' (Selected fragments), composed of extracts from the *Canzoniere* (*RVF* 66, vv. 1–6 and vv. 13–24; *RVF* 125, vv. 40–78; *RVF* 129, vv. 40–52; *RVF* 237, vv. 25–36; *RVF* 264, vv. 55–72). For a second, enlarged edition, see 1787.

1778. abbé Roman, *Le Génie de Pétrarque, ou imitation en vers françois, de ses plus belles poésies, précédée de la Vie de cet Homme célèbre, dont les actions & les Écrits sont une des plus singulières époques de l'Histoire & de la Littérature moderne* (Parma and Avignon: Joseph Guichard; Parma and Paris: Lacombe).

'Vie de François Pétrarque' (pp. 1–288), 'Lettre à un professeur d'éloquence' (pp. 289–98), 'Poésies imitées de Pétrarque' (pp. 299–442), and 'Remarques sur quelques passages de la vie de Pétrarque' (pp. 443–68). Verse translations (described by Roman as 'imitations') of many poems (eighty-nine Italian poems from the *Canzoniere*, although some of them are amalgamated so the number of French poems is slightly less) of which only the first line in Italian is provided: in order, *RVF* 159, 140, 13, 9, 7 (accompanied by a poem by Giustina Levi-Perotti, 'Io vorrei pur drizzar queste mie piume'), 23, 208, 103, 35–6, 33, 28, 136–8 (in one), 53, 50, 147, 17, 93, 37, 135, 131, 89, 85, 97, 71–3, 154, 78, 123, 129, 149, 90, 213, 41–2 (in one), 199, 201, 200, 259, 257, 128, 194+113 (in one), 126, 125, 180, 156–7 (in one), 121, 172, 174, 203, 206, 230, 22, 202, 52, 19, 146, 132, 192, 181, 220, 261, 196, 14, 127, 249–52 (in one), an abbreviated rendition of *Triumphus Mortis I* (pp. 412–14), 311, 268, 292, 290, 270, 300, 359, 283+280+279+282 (in one), 278, 293, 360, 'Le triomphe de la renommée et du temps' (an amalgamation of passages from both the *Triumphus Fame* and the *Triumphus Temporis*, pp. 439–42).

1786. Jean-Joseph-Thérèse Roman, *Vie de François Pétrarque, célèbre poëte italien, dont les actions & les écrits sont une des plus singulières époques de l'histoire & de la littérature moderne; suivie d'une imitation en vers François de ses plus belles poésies* (Vaucluse and Paris: J. Cussac).

  Reprint of 1778 edition.

1787. *Choix des poésies de Pétrarque, traduites de l'Italien par M. Levesque: nouvelle édition corrigée et augmentée*, 2 vols (Venice and Paris: Hardouin et Gattey).

  Prose translation with facing Italian, ordered by form (*canzoni, sestine, ballate*, and sonnets). Volume one contains the same selections from the *Canzoniere* as in the 1774 edition, with the addition of two poems: *RVF* 135 and *RVF* 16. Volume two contains the same 'Frammenti scelti/Fragmens choisis' (pp. 160–73), except that the *Triumphus Temporis* and *Triumphus Eternitatis* are now translated in full after the *Triumphus Cupidinis*, as well as *Triumphus Mortis* II, vv. 79–90 (pp. 174–5). There is an additional section at the end (pp. 183–203) which is a translation with facing Italian of 'Amore fuggitivo' ('Fugitive love') by Torquato Tasso. A selection of Levesque's translations (*RVF* 132, 126, 112, 144, 310, and 7) also appear in Jean Guérin, *Pétrarque considéré comme amant, poëte et philosophe* (Avignon: [n.p.], 1804), p. 131 and pp. 138–43.

1811. Pierre-Louis Ginguené, *Histoire littéraire d'Italie*, 14 vols (Paris: Michaud frères, 1811–35), II, 486–566 ('Chapitre XIV: Poésies italiennes de Pétrarque, ou son CANZONIERE. De la Poésie érotique chez les anciens Grecs et Latins: Ovide, Properce, Tibulle. Éléments dont se composa la Poésie érotique de Pétrarque; caractère de cette poésie, ses beautés, ses défauts. Poésies lyriques de Pétrarque sur d'autres sujets que l'Amour').

  Verse translation of *RVF* 35 (p. 508), prose translation of *RVF* 126 (pp. 519–21), verse translation of *RVF* 129 (pp. 521–23), prose translation of extracts from *RVF* 71–3 (pp. 523–9), prose translations of *RVF* 279, 301, 310, and 302 (pp. 536–9), and 136–8 (pp. 551–3).

1813. J. C. L. Simonde de Sismondi, *De la littérature du Midi de l'Europe*, 4 vols (Paris and Strasbourg: Treuttel et Würtz), I, 386–425 ('Chapitre X: Influence du Dante sur son siècle; Pétrarque').

  Translations of *RVF* 1 (p. 404), 16, 19, 90, 292, 320 (pp. 410–16) and part of 28 (pp. 418–20). The Italian texts are given in footnotes, and all but *RVF* 90 are translated into prose.

1816. *Poésies de Pétrarque, traduites en vers français, suivies de deux poëmes*, by M. Léonce de Saint-Geniès, 2 vols (Paris: Delaunay and Barrois).

  Verse translation with facing Italian. Volume one contains: 'Notice sur la vie et les ouvrages de Pétrarque' (pp. i–xxiv), followed by *RVF* 1, 3, 55, 160, 220, 11, 44, 38, 126, 144, 146, 213, 90, 41, 159, a sonnet from Giustina Levi-Perotti to Petrarch ('Io vorrei pur drizzar queste mie piume'), 7, 128, 112, 238, 10, 162, 125, 14, 102, 9, 13, 8, 23, 141, 64, 205, 227, 50, 34, 148, 134, 132, 129, 35, 24, 52, 192, 203, 127, 176–7, 139, 172, 106, 121, 174, 253, a canzone by Petrarch excluded from the *Canzoniere*,[2] 21, 45, 135, 114, 138, 70, 145, 117. Volume two contains: *RVF* 53, 60, 71–3, 247, 154, 12, 158, 206, 179, 119, a sonnet from Giacomo Colonna to Petrarch ('Se le parti del corpo mio distrutte'), 322, 259, 67, 93, 37, 194, 149, 111, 116, 245, 56, 48, 61, 115, 222, 196, 123, 27, 270, 288, 337, 353, 330, 268, 312, 302, 287, and 310. The two poems by Saint-Geniès included at the end of volume two are 'Le rossignol' ('The Nightingale', pp. 165–72) and 'Le lis' ('The Lily', pp. 173–85).

1819. abbé Costaing de Pusignan (conservateur des musées de la ville d'Avignon), *La Muse de Pétrarque dans les collines de Vaucluse, ou Laure des Baux, sa solitude et son tombeau dans le vallon de Galas* (Paris: Chez Rapet; Avignon: Chez Bonnet fils).

Translations from Petrarch's *Canzoniere*, *Triumphi*, and *Bucolicum carmen* integrated into the prose narrative, mainly translated into prose although occasionally into verse, and often not complete translations of poems but only extracts. Some Italian text in footnotes. Includes Eclogues 3, 10, 11, parts of the *Triumphus Mortis*, and the last four lines of the *Triumphus Eternitatis* (pp. 179–80 of Pusignan), as well as, in order, *RVF* 325, 190, 3, 209, 96, 113–14, 261–3, 148, 160–2, 197, 116, 192, 100, 10, 206, 249–50, 234, 323, 126, 303–6, 308–11, 280–3, 333, 313, 320, 312, 338, 334, 271, 77–8, 259, 1.

1821. *Les Souvenirs poétiques, ou recueil de poésies de M. F. D. L. P.* [de La Pommeraye] (Paris: Chez Eymery).

'Préface' pp. v–xiii. Section at end of 'Sonnets de Pétrarque' (pp. 169–93): *RVF* 7, 159, 310, 311, 291, 283, 282, 292, 281, 301, 353, and 330. The sonnets are translated into verse, preserving the sonnet form, with facing Italian. They are dated between 1813 (*RVF* 7) and 1818 (*RVF* 330), the others being ascribed to 1817. See also the second edition of 1825.

1825. Marc-Antoine Jullien, *La France en 1825, ou mes regrets et mes espérances; discours en vers: seconde édition, suivie de quelques autres poésies détachées du même auteur* (Paris: Chez Antoine-Augustin Renouard).

Contains a French verse translation in rhyming couplets of *RVF* 302, pp. 26–7, entitled 'La vision'. The first five lines in Italian are given at the start.

1825. *Souvenirs poétiques et satiriques de M. F. de La Pommeraye, deuxième édition* (Paris: Chez C. J. Trouvé).

Section at the end entitled 'Traductions et imitations' (pp. 56–107). With translations from Tasso, Metastasio, and Virgil (the first three eclogues), and a section on 'Sonnets de Pétrarque' (pp. 64–78): *RVF* 7, 159, 229, 310, 311, 291, 283, 282, 292, 281, 301, 353, 330, 346, and 293 (fifteen sonnets in total). Three sonnets are thus added

---

[2]   'Quel ch'à nostra natura in se più degno' ('That which our nature has in itself most worthy'); see, for the Italian text, *Trionfi, rime estravaganti, codice degli abbozzi*, ed. Pacca and Paolino, pp. 739–42.

compared to the first edition: *RVF* 229, 346, and 293. The translations preserve the sonnet form as in the earlier edition, although the facing Italian has now been reduced to first lines in Italian.

1829. *Le Kaléidoscope, journal de la littérature, des mœurs et des théâtres; rédigé par M. J. Arago* (11 avril), 257–8.
A translation of *RVF* 310 which is presented as a 'traduction libre' ('free translation') and whose translator is enigmatically identified as 'R.'.

1830. Camille Esménard, *Choix de sonnets de Pétrarque, traduits en vers* (Paris: Mme Vve Charles Béchet).
Divided into two halves 'pendant la vie' and 'après la mort de Laure'. Sixty sonnets translated into French verse retaining the sonnet form, with Italian first line included after a French descriptive title of each poem. Part One: *RVF* 1, 3, 12, 15–16, 35, 61, 82, 85, 87, 90, 111–12, 132, 134, 141, 156, 181, 187, 208, 213, 218, 220, 224, 226, 231, 240, 245, 261, 249. Part Two: *RVF* 267, 272–3, 278–9, 281, 285, 291–2, 299, 301–2, 305, 310–11, 315, 328, 333, 335, 338, 342–3, 346, 348–9, 361–2, 354, 353, 364. The translator chooses to have an equal balance between the two parts (as thirty sonnets are included in each section). See 1848 for an enlarged edition. The volume ends with 'Poésies diverses' ('Other poems', pp. 155–92) which are original poems by the translator, as well as a section of 'Notes' (pp. 193–222).

1830. *Il trionfo d'amore di Petrarca: dedicato al gentiluomo Fr. B. Duppa, da G. C., professore di lingua italiana in Blois* (Blois: Giroud, 1830).
This translation of the *Triumphus Cupidinis* is in French prose with facing Italian.

1835. A.-P.-A. Bouvard, *Fables nouvelles et poésies diverses* (Auxerre: Imprimerie de Gallot-Fournier).
Includes a section of 'Chants et sonnets traduits de Pétrarque' (pp. 177–91), consisting of translations in French rhyming verse of the following four poems: *RVF* 50, 126, 68, and 311. Italian first lines only are provided.

1835. Victor Courtet, *Notice sur Pétrarque, avec une pièce inédite de Mirabeau sur la fontaine de Vaucluse* (Paris: Librairie de Charles Gosselin).
As indicated in the title, this volume includes Mirabeau's 'La fontaine de Vaucluse' (pp. 15–19). Translations from Petrarch into French prose, preceded by the original Italian text, are the following: *RVF* 3 (pp. 31–2), 53 (pp. 41–7), and 126 (with the first stanza given in Voltaire's verse translation, and the remainder in prose, pp. 67–74). The last page advertises a forthcoming volume by the same author entitled *Poésies de Pétrarque traduites en français (texte en regard) avec notes et dissertations critiques*, though this does not appear to have survived.

1837. Antony Deschamps, *Poésies: traduction de Dante Alighieri: les dernières paroles* (Brussels: E. Laurent).
Section on 'Traductions de Pétrarque' dedicated to M. De Lécluze (*sic*), pp. 217–23. Verse translation with no Italian text or first line. Translation of *RVF* 133, presented

as an 'Imitation libre' (p. 219). Also includes *RVF* 61 and 121 (pp. 220-1), an uniden-tifiable madrigal (p. 221),[3] *RVF* 180, 346, and 272 (pp. 221-3).

1838. Jean-Paul-Louis d'Arrighi, *Odes et sonnets choisis de Pétrarque, traduits en français* (Paris: Impasse du Doyenné).

Of Petrarch's sonnets, Arrighi translates *RVF* 1-6, 8-9, 12-13, 267, 269, 273-5, 278, 282, 284, 283, 285, 289, 291, 317, 353, 299, 311, 302-3, 310, 300, 305-6, 308-9, 312-14, 320, 316, followed by *RVF* 268 and the *Triumphus Temporis*, vv. 109-45 (pp. 88-101). All the poems are translated into French prose with facing Italian. Ends with a verse translation of 'La libertà di Nice' by Metastasio (pp. 100-7). See also the reprint of 1851.

1839. J. Michel Berton, *Éleuthérides: poésies* (Paris: Dumont).

Volume consists of a mixture of translations and original poetry, including (pp. 21-7) a translation of *RVF* 128, dated 1821 and entitled 'Ode XVI de Pétrarque: sur les malheurs de l'Italie' ('on the misfortunes of Italy'), in rhyming verse with no accompanying Italian.

1840. J.-C. Di Negro, *Essais poétiques* (Genoa: Imprimerie des sourds-muets).

Includes translations of five sonnets by Petrarch into French verse with facing Italian, pp. 76-84: in order, *RVF* 302, 267, 90, 311, 3.

1841. Agathe Baudouin, *Rêveries sur les bords du Cher: poésies* (Paris: Challamel et Cie).

Includes a translation of *RVF* 35 (pp. 59-62) in French verse retaining the sonnet form but no accompanying Italian.

1842. le comte Ferdinand L. de Gramont, *Poésies de Pétrarque: traduction complète: sonnets, canzones, triomphes* (Paris: Paul Masgana).

Volume begins with a 'Notice' (pp. i-x) about Petrarch's life and works, and is then divided into 'Sonnets et canzones composés du vivant de Laure' (pp. 3-179), 'Sonnets et canzones composés après la mort de Laure' (pp. 181-251), and 'Triom-phes' (pp. 255-314). Translated into French prose with restrained footnotes and no facing Italian or Italian first lines. Complete translation, as the title indicates. In the first half ('du vivant de Laure'), poems are in the usual order of modern editions (such as Santagata's) except that *RVF* 121 precedes *RVF* 120 (p. 87), i.e. *RVF* 1-119, 121, 120, 122-266. The second half ('après la mort de Laure') starts at *RVF* 267, and follows the usual modern numbering from *RVF* 267 up to *RVF* 336, at which point

---

    [3]   The text of this reads as follows: 'Voir marcher par le ciel flamboyantes étoiles, / Sur la tranquille mer, vaisseaux aux blanches voiles, / Dans les prés verdoyans, beaux chevaliers armés / Et timides chevreuils sous les bois embaumés ; / Danser parmi les fleurs et les claires fontaines, / Dames aux blonds cheveux, à la taille de reines, / Sont choses qui déjà ne me disent plus rien, / Tant elle a su, partant pour les rives lointaines, / Emporter, Dieu du ciel ! mon cœur avec le sien.'

the poems in order of appearance are: *RVF* 350, 355, 337–49, 356–65, 351–2, 354, 353, 366.

1842. Anatole de Montesquiou, *Sonnets, canzones, ballades et sextines de Pétrarque traduits en vers*, 2 vols (Paris: Leroy).

No Italian (either facing Italian or indication of original first lines). In verse but using loose forms (often not replicating sonnet structure for instance). Complete translation. Volume one contains 'Avertissement' (pp. v–viii), and translations of *RVF* 1–13, 15, 14, 16–160. Volume two contains *RVF* 161–336, 350, 355, 337–49, 356–65, 351–2, 354, 353, 366. There is no indication of the usual bipartite division 'in vita'/'in morte'. A second edition of 1843 adds two introductory sonnets to the first volume ('Dédicace. Sonnet' and 'À Pétrarque. Sonnet') but omits the 'Avertissement'.

1843. Anatole de Montesquiou, *Épîtres, églogues et triomphes de Pétrarque traduits en vers* (Paris: Leroy).

Presented as volume three of the 1842 publication. The epistles ('Épîtres', pp. 1–37) are in rhyming verse (a selection of six verse letters from the *Epystole*). Of the *Bucolicum carmen*, Montesquiou translates 'Daphné', 'L'épidémie', 'Le laurier', and 'Galatée' (i.e Eclogues 3, 9, 10, and 11, pp. 39–87). All the *Triumphi* are included in translation (pp. 90–176). The Latin texts of the '*Epistolae*' (pp. 177–204) and the Eclogues (pp. 205–44) translated are to be found at the end of the volume, as well as brief explanatory endnotes (chiefly about historical, Classical, or mythological figures featured in the texts, pp. 247–266). As with the *Canzoniere* (1842), the Italian text of the *Triumphi* is not provided.

1847. [Emma Mahul], *Cent cinquante sonnets et huit morceaux complémentaires traduits des Sonnets de Pétrarque, texte en regard* (Paris: Firmon Didot frères).

Presented as half of the sonnets of the *Canzoniere*. Anonymous translation although by Emma Mahul (see other dates for four subsequent volumes: 1867, 1869, 1872, 1877). Verse translations with facing Italian. Contains: 'Sonnets composés du vivant de Laure' (pp. 8–235), namely *RVF* 2–4, 6–10, 12–13, 21, 24, 27, 31, 33–4, 38, 40–1, 43–4, 47–9, 56, 58, 64, 68, 77–8, 82, 84, 87, 90–3, 96, 99, 100, 108–9, 111–15, 123–4, 130–3, 137, 139, 141, 151, 153–4, 159–60, 162, 164–5, 167–70, 172, 176–7, 180, 184, 186–7, 189–90, 193, 196, 199–202, 205, 208, 212–13, 215, 217–20, 222, 224–5, 229–31, 233, 238, 242–3, 245–9, 253, 261–3, followed by 'Sonnets composés après la mort de Laure' (pp. 237–333), consisting of *RVF* 269, 272, 278–80, 285–7, 291–3, 296–7, 299, 300, 302–3, 305, 309–10, 312–16, 320–1, 326–7, 330, 333–4, 336, 355, 339, 346, 347, 349, 357, 361, 363–4, 351–2, 354, and 353. At the end of the volume can be found a section of variants (pp. 335–44) and notes (pp. 345–96). Most of the translations preserve the sonnet form, although eight do not (hence the title's indication of 'huit morceaux complémentaires', eight complementary compositions).

1848. Camille Esménard du Mazet, *Poésies de Pétrarque traduites en vers* (Paris: Comptoir des imprimeurs-unis).

No facing Italian, no longer limited to only sonnets (as in Esménard's 1830 publication). Volume divided into 'Première partie: Poésies composées pendant la vie de

Laure' (pp. 21–194), 'Deuxième partie: Poésies composées après la mort de Laure' (pp. 195–322), and 'Troisième partie: Poésies sur divers sujets' (pp. 323–66). Part One: 1, 3–4, 8–9, 11–16, 19–22, 32–3, 35–6, 39, 41–2, 44–5, 48–52, 54–7, 59, 61–4, 67–9, 73–4, 78, 80, 82–5, 87–90, 99–102, 106–8, 110–18, 121–3, 126–7, 129, 132, 134, 140–1, 144, 146–7, 149, 153–4, 156–7, 159–62, 164–5, 167, 169–70, 174, 176, 179–81, 183, 185, 187, 189–92, 196, 199, 201, 265, 203, 205, 208–9, 266, 211–13, 216, 218–20, 222–8, 231, 233–4, 240, 242, 245, 247–8, 253, 259, 261–3, 249–51. Part Two: 267–73, 275, 278–81, 285, 287–93, 297–305, 307–12, 315, 317–18, 320–1, 324–5, 328–9, 331–3, 335–6, 350, 355, 338–43, 346–9, 356, 358, 361–2, 365, 351, 354, 353, then the *Triumphus Mortis*, *Triumphus Eternitatis*, *Galatea* (Eclogue Eleven), plus *RVF* 364 as an 'Epilogue'. Part Three: *RVF* 7, 10, 24–8, 40, 53, 58, 92, 98, 103–4, 119–20, 128, 136–9, 166, 232, 322.

1848. Ernest and Edmond Lafond, *Dante, Pétrarque, Michel-Ange, Tasse: sonnets choisis traduits en vers et précédés d'une étude sur chaque poëte* (Paris: Comptoir des Imprimeurs-Unis).

Translations of a selection of sonnets retaining the sonnet form. The earlier part of the volume on Dante includes a translation of the *Vita nuova*. On Petrarch, see pp. 91–326, which contains a 'Notice' (pp. 91–130) including a prose translation of an extract from the *Triumphus Mortis* (pp. 110–111) as well as a translation of the note in Petrarch's copy of Virgil (pp. 123–4). The translated sonnets are divided into 'Sonnets composés pendant la vie de Laure' (pp. 131–242; one hundred and ten sonnets included) and 'Sonnets composés après la mort de Laure' (pp. 243–326, eighty-two sonnets). No Italian text/title is provided, but a French heading is given to each sonnet. The *in vita* section contains *RVF* 1, 3–5, 8–10, 12–13, 15–16, 33, 32, 36, 35, 56, 61–2, 64, 68, 74, 77–8, 81–2, 85, 91, 99–100, 108–9, 111, 114–16, 120, 123, 132–3, 140, 143, 145–6, 150, 153–7, 159–60, 162–5, 167, 169–71, 174–6, 179–81, 183, 188, 190–2, 194, 196, 199, 201, 203–4, 213, 205, 208, 212, 215, 217–19, 220, 222–7, 229, 234, 236, 238, 240, 244, 259, 245, 261, 248, 246, 265, 256, 253, 257, 258, 249, 254, 250. The section *in morte* includes *RVF* 267, 269, 271–5, 277–90, 292, 294–309, 354, 310–20, 326–30, 339, 333–6, 350, 355, 337, 340, 342–3, 341, 344–7, 349, 356–8, 352, 361–5, 351. The end of the volume contains musical settings by A. Bessems of two sonnets by Petrarch, *RVF* 335 and 76.

1848. Alphonse Chapellon, *Souvenirs* (Odessa: [n. p.]).

Contains a translation of *RVF* 61, retaining the sonnet form (pp. 91–2), with the Italian first line indicated as an epigraph and the given French title 'Pétrarque à Laure: sonnet' ('Petrarch to Laura: sonnet').

1851. Jean-Paul-Louis d'Arrighi, *Odes et sonnets choisis de Pétrarque, traduits en français* (Paris: T. Mayer).

A reprint of the 1838 volume.

1851. Jean-Paul-Louis d'Arrighi, *Preghiera di Petrarca alla santissima Vergine/Prière de Pétrarque à la très-sainte Vierge, traduite de l'italien* (Grenoble: Imprimerie de Prudhomme).

Translation of *RVF* 366 into French prose with facing Italian. No prefatory material or notes.

1851. Abel-François Villemain, *Cours de littérature française: tableau de la littérature du Moyen Âge en France, en Italie, en Espagne et en Angleterre: nouvelle édition revue, corrigée et augmentée*, 2 vols (Paris: Didier).

'Treizième leçon' (II, 1–31) discusses Petrarch, and includes a prose translation of *RVF* 1, vv. 1–8 (p. 26, with accompanying Italian text), and a prose translation of *RVF* 128 (pp. 29–30, of which only the first line in Italian is given).

1852. Louis Langlois, *Morceaux choisis: Catulle, Gallus, Properce, Tibulle, Ovide, Maximien, Pétrarque, et Jean Second; précédés d'une notice biographique sur chacun de ces poètes* (Paris: Leclère fils).

Section on Petrarch (pp. 221–59) includes 'Notice sur Pétrarque (François)' (pp. 223–40), and translations of five *canzoni*: *RVF* 126, an unidentified poem,[4] 268, 270, and 53 (pp. 241–59). All five are translated into French verse with no facing Italian or first line.

1853. Mme la comtesse de Lalaing, *Stances de Messer Angelo Poliziano et poésies extraites de Dante, Pétrarque et Leopardi, traduites de l'italien* (Brussels: Imprimerie de J. Stienon).

Contains only two sonnets by Petrarch, with parallel text (*RVF* 248 and 302), translated into prose, pp. 132–5.

1853. Philippe Duplessis, *Œuvres posthumes, imprimées en exécution de son testament*, 5 vols (Paris: Firmin Didot).

Volume 5 contains a section of 'Sonetti di Petrarca/Sonnets de Pétrarque' (pp. 362–73), translations of six sonnets by Petrarch into French verse with facing Italian, namely *RVF* 302, 311, 263, 254, 62, and 248.

1854. Jean-Paul-Louis d'Arrighi, *Aspirations de l'âme religieuse: ode à la divine pureté, par Filicaia, en trois langues* [Italian, Latin, French]; *suivie de la prière à la très-sainte Vierge, par Pétrarque, en deux langues* [Italian, French] (La côte-Saint-André: Chez le traducteur).

Translation of *RVF* 366 into French prose with facing Italian, pp. 15–27, as in the 1851 publication.

1854. É.-J. Delécluze, *Dante Alighieri ou de la poésie amoureuse*, 2 vols (Paris: Adolphe Delahays).

Section on 'Sonnets et chansons de F. Pétrarque', II, 444–55, which includes prose

---

[4] This *canzone* begins in French 'Insensé ! quelle était ma funeste imprudence' (pp. 244–7) and is noted in the *Cornell University Library Catalogue of the Petrarch Collection bequeathed by Willard Fiske*, ed. Mary Fowler (London: Oxford University Press, 1916) as 'not easy to identify' (p. 167). I have done no better.

translations (with footnoted Italian texts) of *RVF* 35, 282, 302, 129, and the end of *RVF* 366 (vv. 118–37).

1855. Hippolyte Topin, *Études sur la langue italienne, précédées d'un parallèle entre Dante et Klopstock* (Florence: Typographie Galiléienne; Paris: Chez les principaux libraires).

As well as translations from Dante's *Commedia*, this pamphlet includes a section of 'Sonetti del Petrarca' in French verse with facing Italian (pp. 82–5): *RVF* 3, 35, and 302.

1859. Gabrielle Soumet d'Altenheym, *Les quatre siècles littéraires: récits de l'histoire de la littérature sous Périclès, Auguste, Léon X et Louis XIV, enrichis de fragments des chefs-d'œuvre classiques* (Paris: E. Ducrocq).

Includes a French prose translation of *RVF* 269 (p. 194), and an extract in French prose from the *Triumphus Eternitatis* (vv. 1–24, and 49–63). On Petrarch see pp. 188–95.

1859. Gustave de Larenaudière, '*Spirto gentil* – *Noble génie*, canzone de Pétrarque adressée à Cola di Rienzo', *Revue française*, 502–5.

A French verse translation of *RVF* 53, without facing Italian.

1860. Auguste Brizeux, *Œuvres complètes: précédées d'une notice par Saint-René Tail-landier*, 2 vols (Paris: Michel Lévy frères), II, 405–6.

French verse translation of *RVF* 54, with no facing Italian/first line given. The poem is introduced as a 'Canzone (de Pétrarque)', even though it is actually a madrigal.

1862. Antoine Péricaud l'aîné, 'Quelques remarques sur le VIIe sonnet de Pétrarque et sur une traduction anonyme de Pétrone', in *Curiosités littéraires: Pétrarque & Pétrone; Louis Sygée & Nicolas Chorier* (Lyon: Imprimerie d'Aimé Vingtrinier).

Reproduces verse (sonnet) translations of Giustina Levi-Perotti's sonnet to Petrarch, and Petrarch's reply (*RVF* 7) by Paul Saint-Olive (pp. 13–14) and Roman (pp. 15–16), an anonymous translation of the two sonnets into Latin (pp. 16–17), Beauverie's rendition of *RVF* 7 (p. 14), and three seventeenth-century imitations of sonnets by Petrarch by Chalvet (*RVF* 265, 163, 132; pp. 3–6).

1865. Joseph Poulenc, *Rimes de Pétrarque, traduites en vers, texte en regard*, 4 vols (Paris: A. Lacroix).

In verse. Includes a preface (pp. 4–12, dated February 1865), and an introductory French translation of the 'Letter to Posterity' from Marsand's Italian translation, pp. 13–35. Poulenc translates the *Triumphi*, IV, 2–211, and divides the *Canzoniere* into three parts, to produce: 'Première partie: Sonnets et canzones sur la vie de Laure' (volumes one and two), 'Deuxième partie: Sonnets et canzones sur la mort de Laure' (volume three), and a fourth volume including both 'Troisième partie: Triomphes sur la vie et la mort de Laure' and 'Quatrième partie: Sonnets et canzones sur des sujets divers'. Poulenc is following Marsand's ordering (see below for details).

1867. Emma Mahul, *Choix de sonnets de Pétrarque: seconde édition revue, corrigée et augmentée de la traduction de différentes poésies de Pétrarque* (Florence: Héritiers Botta).

Volume comprises an 'Avertissement de la présente édition' (pp. 5–9), sonnets [in vita] (pp. 11–82), 'Sonnets composés après la mort de la belle Laure' (pp. 83–114), 'Poésies diverses traduites de Pétrarque' (pp. 115–55), variants and corrections (pp. 157–63), notes (pp. 165–74), 'Citations de commentateurs italiens, commentaires de la traductrice et notes biographiques' (pp. 175–241), 'Sonnets de la première édition non réimprimés dans celle-ci' (pp. 241–7), 'Table alphabétique des sonnets traduits dans ce recueil' (pp. 249–52), and a 'Table des poésies diverses traduites de Pétrarque' (pp. 252–3). Poems have headings in French, followed by Italian title in brackets, then French text. The poems translated are, in the first part: *RVF* 4, 8, 10, 12–13, 31, 40–4, 48, 51, 64–5, 68, 75, 77, 90, 92, 111, 113, 116–17, 123–4, 132–3, 137, 139–40, 148, 153–4, 159, 162, 164, 167, 169, 180, 183, 185–9, 192–3, 196, 199–202, 208, 211, 213, 215, 218, 220, 222, 224–5, 227–8, 242–5, 248, 250, 253, 259. The second part contains: *RVF* 269, 275, 278–80, 282, 285, 292–3, 302, 306, 311–12, 314–15, 320, 326, 330, 333, 355, 337, 344–6, 356–7, 361, 363, 365, 352. The section 'Poésies diverses' is different in form rather than subject matter, both in that Mahul translates sonnets into looser forms, and in that she includes other types of poems by Petrarch: *RVF* 5, 11, 39, 54, 66, 91, 121, 127, 142, 156–7, 176, 268, 316, 324, 347.

1869. Emma Mahul, *Choix de sonnets: troisième édition revue, corrigée et augmentée de la traduction de différentes poésies de Pétrarque, etc.* (Paris: Firmin Didot).

Third edition, as indicated. 'Avertissement de la présente édition' (pp. 5–8); [*in vita*, pp. 11–108] *RVF* 2, 6–7, 10, 16–17, 19–20, 33–5, 38, 43, 45–7, 56, 58, 60–1, 64, 75–8, 81, 84, 87, 90, 92, 96, 99, 101, 108, 110, 112, 114–17, 120, 123, 130, 132, 137, 139, 145, 153–4, 159–60, 163–5, 167–70, 175, 177, 179, 184, 188–9, 192–4, 198–200, 202, 205, 208–9, 212–13, 215, 219–25, 228, 232, 238, 241, 243, 247, 249, 251, 253, 257, 259, 261, 265–6; 'Sonnets composés après la mort de la belle Laure' (pp. 109–59), *RVF* 267, 269, 272–3, 275, 278–9, 282, 285–6, 289, 291, 293–4, 296, 299–303, 305–6, 308–10, 312–13, 315, 321, 326–7, 330, 333, 336, 350, 355, 340–2, 344, 346, 356–8, 361–2, 351–2, 354; 'Poésies diverses traduites de Pétrarque' (pp. 161–208), *RVF* 5, 52, 54, 66, 91, 121, 127, 142, 156–7, 172, 176, 255, 263, 268, 287, 316, 324, 347, 353; variants and corrections (pp. 209–18); notes (pp. 219–30); 'Citations de commentateurs italiens, commentaires de la traductrice, et notes biographiques' (pp. 231–342). No facing Italian text although the first line in Italian is given.

1872. Emma Mahul, *Choix de sonnets traduits de Pétrarque, revue, corrigée et augmentée de la traduction de différentes poésies de Pétrarque* (Paris: Firmin Didot frères, fils et Cie).

Fourth edition. Contains: 'Sonnets composés du vivant de Laure' (pp. 11–108), *RVF* 2, 6–7, 10, 16–17, 19–20, 33–5, 38, 43, 45–7, 56, 58, 60–1, 64, 75–8, 81, 84, 87, 90, 92, 96, 99, 101, 108, 110, 112, 114–17, 120, 123, 130, 132, 137, 139, 145, 153–4, 159–60, 163–5, 167–70, 175, 177, 179, 184, 188–9, 192–4, 198–200, 202, 205, 208–9, 212–13, 215, 219–25, 228, 232, 238, 241, 243, 247, 249, 251, 253, 257, 259, 261, 265–6; 'Sonnets composés après la mort de la belle Laure' (pp. 109–59), *RVF* 267, 269, 272–3, 275, 278–9, 282,

285–6, 289, 291, 293–4, 296, 299–303, 305–6, 308–10, 312–13, 315, 321, 326–7, 330, 333, 336, 350, 355, 340–2, 344, 346, 356–8, 361–2, 351–2, 354; 'Poésies diverses traduites de Pétrarque' including *RVF* 5, 11, 54, 66, 91, 121, 127, 142, 156–7, 172, 176, 255, 263, 268, 287, 316, 324, 347, and 353. The volume closes with the same format of apparatus as in the previous volume (1869). Again, no facing Italian text although the first line in Italian is given.

1874. *Fêtes littéraires & internationales: Cinquième centenaire de la mort de Pétrarque: Célébré à Vaucluse et à Avignon le 18, 19 et 20 juillet 1874*, ed. Léon Berluc-Pérussis and Hippolyte Guillibert (Avignon: Imprimerie administrative Gros frères).

Contains translations into Provençal of *RVF* 194 (by Roso-Anaïs Roumanille, p. 176), 164 (by V. Lieutaud, pp. 177–87), 272 (by Anfos Tavan, pp. 178–9), and 126 (by Frédéric Mistral, pp. 246–9) as well as translations into French of *RVF* 364 (by Philibert Le Duc), 310, 278, 333, and 300, these last four translated by d'Audeville (pp. 198–201).

1874. Auguste Laforêt, 'Cinquième centenaire de Pétrarque: fêtes de Vaucluse-Avignon les 18, 19, et 20 juillet 1874', *Revue de Marseille et de Provence fondée et publiée au profit des pauvres*, 20.7 (July 1874), 361–76.

Contains original poetry about Petrarch, discussion of the festivities, and also two translations, p. 370: of *RVF* 132 (by Charles Bessat) and *RVF* 181 (by Camille Allary).

1874. *Almanach du sonnet pour 1874: Sonnets inédits, publiés avec le concours de 150 Sonnettistes* (Aix: Vve Remondet-Aubin).

Includes a sonnet 'Imité de Pétrarque' (*RVF* 12) by Comte Xavier de la Canorgue (pp. 142–3), and a French translation of *RVF* 35 by comte Siméon (pp. 143–4).

1875. *Almanach du sonnet: Sonnets inédits, publiés avec la collaboration de deux cents Poètes français et des principaux Félibres* (Aix-en-Provence: Vve Remondet-Aubin).

Includes translations into Provençal of *RVF* 346 (by Roso-Anaïs Roumanille, p. 185) and 281 (by Frédéric Mistral, pp. 191–2), as well as a section devoted to French translations of Petrarch (pp. 198–203) consisting of *RVF* 279 (by Ate Penquer), part of 366 (by Charles Baret into a single sonnet, based on stanza four), 1 (by A. Boursault), 320 (by Louis Guibert), 35 (by P. Jonain), 333 (by A. Marc), 226 (by Edmond Py), and 177 (by Joséphin Soulary).

1875. *Fête séculaire et internationale de Pétrarque célébrée en Provence 1874: procès-verbaux & vers inédits* (Aix-en-Provence: Vve Remondet-Aubin).

Includes translations into Provençal of *RVF* 333 by A. Marc and of *RVF* 280 by Frédéric Mistral.

1875. *Armana prouvençau pèr lou bèl an de diéu 1875 adouba e publica de la man de Felibre: an vint-e-unen dóu Felibrige* (Avignon: Encò de Roumanille).

Includes translations by Roso-Anaïs Roumanille of *RVF* 194 (pp. 36–7) and of *RVF* 164 by V. Lieutaud (p. 77).

1875. *Revue des langues romanes: publiée par la Société pour l'Étude des langues romanes*, 7 (January–April–July 1875).

Includes a section of 'Poésies couronnées au centenaire de Pétrarque', pp. 385–402, with a mixture of original poetry about Petrarch and some translations, namely, Roso-Anaïs Roumanille's translation of *RVF* 194 (pp. 393–4), V. Lieutaud's translation of *RVF* 164 (p. 394), Alphonse Tavan's translation of *RVF* 272 (pp. 394–5), and A. Mir's translation of *RVF* 302 (p. 395).

1875. Pierre-Louis Ginguené, *Les Œuvres amoureuses de Pétrarque: sonnets–triomphes, traduites en français avec le texte en regard et précédées d'une notice sur la vie de Pétrarque* (Paris: Garnier frères).

This translation is in prose and is a republication, with modernized spelling, of Placide Catanusi's translation of Petrarch, *Les Œuvres amoureuses de Pétrarque traduites en françois avec l'Italien à costé par le sieur Placide Catanusi* (Paris: Chez Estienne Loyson, 1669). The ordering and selection of Ginguené's own *Les Œuvres amoureuses de Pétrarque* is identical to Catanusi. Includes all of the *Triumphi* ('Les Triomphes de Pétrarque', pp. 199–393) but only a selection of the *Canzoniere*, 'Sonnets de Pétrarque' (pp. 1–197), comprising ninety-seven sonnets and one madrigal (*RVF* 121): *RVF* 1, 3, 12, 21, 36, 208, 108, 85, 132, 134, 151, 199, 220, 168, 176, 141, 203, 255, 223, 265, 216, 170, 212, 163, 93, 82, 311, 10, 97, 123, 2, 153, 205, 95, 180, 253, 351, 215, 164, 193, 310, 159, 187, 226, 121, 49, 13, 35, 65, 90, 219, 224, 19, 39, 69, 101, 240, 192, 162, 152, 145, 243, 147, 64, 184, 154, 107, 44, 260, 112, 75, 102, 183, 130, 144, 9, 124, 230, 229, 113, 133, 160, 227, 211, 213, 218, 209, 195, 252, 174, 283, 273, 300, 338, 303, 269, 291–2.

1875. Eugène Roulleaux, *Pétrarque et les fêtes du centenaire à Vaucluse et à Avignon (18, 19 et 20 juillet 1874)* (Bourg: Imprimerie P. Comte-Milliet).

Includes a French prose translation of *RVF* 136, p. 42.

1876. *Almanach du sonnet: sonnets inédits publiés avec la collaboration de deux cents Poètes français et des principaux Félibres* (Aix-en-Provence: Vve Remondet-Aubin).

Again includes a section devoted to French translations of Petrarch (pp. 167–74) consisting of *RVF* 1 (by Ate Penquer), 278 (by d'Audeville), 302 (by Alphonse Baudouin), 32 (by Charles Bessat), 164 (by Pierre Feuillade), 279 (by Henri Guillemot), 302 (by Jean Lescossois), 90 (by Lucien Paté), 208 (by Joséphin Soulary), 253 (by Charles Soullier), and 338 (by Arsène Thévenot), as well as a Provençal translation of *RVF* 194 by Roso-Anaïs Roumanille (p. 178).

1877. Emma Mahul, *Sonnets inédits traduits de Pétrarque, cinquième publication complétant la totalité des sonnets et augmentée de la traduction également inédite de différentes poésies de Pétrarque, etc.* (Rome: Héritiers Botta).

The final volume completing Mahul's project of translating all of Petrarch's sonnets. Composed of: 'Avertissement de la présente publication' (pp. 5–8); *RVF* 1, 3, 9, 15, 18, 21, 24–7, 32, 36, 49, 57, 62, 67, 69, 74, 79, 82–3, 85–6, 88–9, 93–5, 97–8, 100, 102–4, 107, 109, 118, 122, 131, 134, 136, 138, 141, 143–4, 146–7, 150–2, 155, 158, 161, 166, 171, 173–4, 176, 178, 181–2, 190–1, 195, 197, 203–4, 210, 216–17, 226, 234–6, 240, 246, 252, 254, 256, 258, 260, 262; sonnets 'Après la mort de la belle Laure', *RVF* 271, 274,

276–7, 281, 283–4, 288, 290, 295, 297–8, 304, 307, 317–19, 322, 328–9, 334–5, 338–9, 343, 348–9, 364; 'Poésies diverses traduites de Pétrarque' (pp. 119–58), *RVF* 28, 52, 59, 71, 80, 106, 126, 229–31, 233, 239, 332, 359; 'Variantes et corrections' (pp. 159–66); 'Notes' (pp. 167–78); 'Citations de commentateurs italiens, commentaires de la traductrice et notes biographiques' (pp. 179–208); 'Appendice de sonnets des précédentes éditions avec corrections nécessaires par la traductrice' (pp. 209–20), *RVF* 7, 33, 68, 163, 192, 232, 249, 251, 253, 312, 337, 'Beltà di donna' (translation of sonnet by Guido Cavalcanti); 'Sonnets originaux et inédits de la traductrice rélatifs aux études pétrarquistes' (pp. 221–39); 'Ve centenaire de Pétrarque: Vaucluse et Arquà: poésies par madame Emma Mahul: seconde édition' (pp. 229–46).

1877. Joseph Poulenc, *Rimes de Pétrarque: traduction complète en vers des sonnets, canzones, sextines, ballades, madrigaux et triomphes: deuxième édition, revue et corrigée*, 2 vols (Paris: Librairie des bibliophiles).

Volume one contains 'Préface' (pp. iii–ix), 'Notice sur Pétrarque par lui-même: extraite de ses œuvres latines et traduite en italien par M. le professeur Marsand' (in French, pp. 1–12, plus gloss pp. 12–14), 'Première partie: sonnets et canzones pendant la vie de Laure' (pp. 15–317). Volume two contains 'Deuxième partie: sonnets et canzones après la mort de Laure' (pp. 1–131), 'Troisième partie: Triomphes sur la vie et la mort de Laure' (pp. 133–239), 'Quatrième partie: sonnets et canzones sur des sujets divers' (pp. 241–84), and an unnumbered section at the end entitled 'Poésies recueillies à l'occasion du cinquième centenaire de Pétrarque à Avignon', which includes a sonnet by Arsène Houssaye, a poem by Auguste Barbier, and a translation of sonnet *RVF* 280 into Occitan by Frédéric Mistral. This edition no longer includes facing Italian texts, although it does supply the first line of each poem.

1877. F. A. de La Rochefoucauld, *Poésies intimes* (Paris: Didier et Cie).

Includes a section at the end on 'Sonnets traduits de Pétrarque' (pp. 293–9), all of which are translated into French sonnet form. Five sonnets are translated: *RVF* 19, 219, 90, 311, and 303.

1877, 1879. Philibert Le Duc, *Les Sonnets de Pétrarque: traduction complète en sonnets réguliers, avec introduction et commentaire: ouvrage couronné aux fêtes littéraires de Vaucluse et d'Avignon à l'occasion du cinquième centenaire de Pétrarque*, 2 vols (Paris: Leon Willem).

In verse ('sonnets réguliers', regular sonnets), with Italian first-lines but not full original texts. Only the sonnets from the *Canzoniere*, but all 317 of them. Volume one contains 'Préface' (pp. v–x), 'À Pétrarque: sonnet' (p. xi), 'Introduction' (pp. xiii–xlii), and then 'Sonnets composés du vivant de Laure', divided as follows: 'Première série' (pp. 3–53), *RVF* 1–13, 15–21, 24–7 (note that in the 'Première série' Le Duc includes *RVF* 11, the first ballad of the collection); 'Deuxième série' (pp. 55–121), *RVF* 31–6, 38–49, 51, 56–8, 60–2, 64–5, 67–9, 74–5; 'Troisième série' (pp. 123–205), *RVF* 76–9, 81–104, 107–18; 'Quatrième série' (pp. 207–69), *RVF* 120, 122–4, 130–4, 136–41, 143–8, 150–8; 'Cinquième série' (pp. 271–337), *RVF* 159–90. Volume two contains: 'Sixième série' (pp. 3–69), *RVF* 191–205, 208–13, 215–25; 'Septième série' (pp. 71–149), *RVF* 226–36, 238, 240–63, 265–6; then 'Sonnets composés après la mort de Laure', including 'Huitième série' (pp. 153–215), *RVF* 267, 269, 271–98; 'Neuvième série' (pp. 217–79), *RVF* 299–322, 326–30, 333; and 'Dixième série' (pp. 281–343), *RVF* 334–6, 350, 355, 337–49, 356–8, 361–5, 351–2, 354, 353. At the end of volume two there is also a 'Note finale: Arquà, le tombeau et la maison de Pétrarque' (pp. 344–50) and an 'Appendice: Fêtes de Vaucluse et d'Avignon: Sonnets à Pétrarque et à Laure' (pp. 351–82).

1878. Charles Soullier, *Mes Sansonnets: précédés de l'historique du sonnet et de la critique des sonnets célèbres, de diverses pièces de littérature très-curieuses, entre autres le 'Tableau de la vie', ouvrage rare et épuisé* (Paris: Chez l'auteur).

Includes verse (sonnet) translations of the following of Petrarch's sonnets, without Italian text/first line: *RVF* 199, 201, 90, 253, 281, and 279.

1880. *La Curiosité littéraire et bibliographique: première série* (Paris: Isidore Liseux).

Includes a translation of *RVF* 126 into French by Joseph Boulmier with facing Italian ('À la fontaine de Vaucluse', pp. 82–7, in Joseph Boulmier, 'La vraie manière de traduire les poètes', pp. 77–93) and a sixteenth-century Latin imitation of the same by Marc-Antoine Flaminio ('De Delia', pp. 86–93), which Boulmier also translates into French.

1883. Francisque Reynard, *Les Rimes de François Pétrarque: traduction nouvelle* (Paris: G. Charpentier).

Prose translation, no facing Italian. Collection divided into 'Première partie: Sonnets et canzones pendant la vie de Madame Laure' (pp. 1–182), 'Deuxième partie: Sonnets et canzones après la mort de Madame Laure' (pp. 183–261), 'Troisième partie: Les triomphes sur la vie et la mort de Madame Laure' (pp. 262–334), and 'Quatrième partie: Sonnets et canzones sur des sujets variés' (pp. 335–58). Reynard, like others before him (including Poulenc) is following the order of Marsand's edition (detailed below).

1883. F. Bertrand, *Laure et Pétrarque: la Fontaine de Vaucluse: rencontre dans les solitudes qui dominent Vaucluse* (Avignon: Librairie H. Chassing).

Prose translation of *RVF* 156, p. 20.

1884. L. Jehan-Madelaine, *Sonnets de Pétrarque: traduction libre: première série* (Paris: Librairie Fischbacher).

In verse (retaining the sonnet form). A selection of fifty-eight sonnets. No Italian text or first lines. Begins with a dedicatory sonnet by Jehan-Madelaine to Madame Marie Édouard Lenoir, her response (also in sonnet form), and two further sonnets (Robert Bengesco, 'À M. L. Jehan-Madelaine en le félicitant de ses traductions de Pétrarque', 'To M. L. Jehan-Madelaine congratulating him on his translations of Petrarch'; comte Urbain de Botzari, 'Au poète L. Jehan-Madelaine qui a dédié à Mme Marie Édouard Lenoir des sonnets traduits de Pétrarque', 'To the poet L. Jehan-Madelaine who has dedicated to Mme Marie Édouard Lenoir some sonnets translated from Petrarch'). The sonnets translated are *RVF* 1, 213, 164, 75, 227, 159, 203, 123, 168, 19, 220, 49, 85, 162, 36, 193, 310, 144, 9, 95, 183, 209, 13, 199, 211, 130, 219,

195, 229–30, 145, 7, 351, 12, 102, 132, 134, 153, 170, 176, 160, 44, 260, 205, 180, 151, 265, 224, 243, 124, 174, 133, 163, 192, 3, 2, 35, 90.

1884. Marc Monnier, *La Renaissance, de Dante à Luther* (Paris: Librairie Firmin-Didot).

'Chapitre II. Pétrarque et Boccace' (pp. 81–147) contains the first stanza of *RVF* 126 and *RVF* 61, 62, and 302 (pp. 106–10), all translated into French verse with the Italian text in footnotes.

1886. François Vallon, *Écrin de poésies anglaises, allemandes, italiennes et espagnoles* (Paris: Alphonse Lemerre).

Contains a translation of *RVF* 279 into French verse, pp. 61–2, which is given the title 'Pétrarque et Laure' and lacks either facing Italian or an Italian first line.

1887. Junior Casalis and Ernest de Ginoux, *Cinquante sonnets et cinq odes de Pétrarque traduits en vers français* (Paris: Librairie des Bibliophiles).

Volume begins with 'Préface', pp. 1–16 (by Ernest de Ginoux) and 'Mémoires de Pétrarque' (pp. 17–31, a French prose version of the 'Letter to Posterity'), followed by verse translations of the following poems with facing Italian: 1–3, 12–13, 15–16, 21, 32–3, 35, 49, 61–2, 68, 85, 90, 102, 108–9, 126, 129, 112, 132, 145, 159–62, 140, 164–5, 192, 196, 201–2, 208, 220, 222, 248–9, 268, 272, 299–302, 305, 310, 312, 320, 339, 365, 128, 53. The five 'odes' (*canzoni*) are thus *RVF* 126, 129, 268, 128, and 53.

1891. Jean Saint-Martin, *La Fontaine de Vaucluse et ses souvenirs: dessins de Bill, Eysséric, Karl, Paul Saïn et Georges Roux* (Paris: Librairie générale de L. Sauvaitre).

Contains chapters on 'Pétrarque' (pp. 39–57), 'Laure et Pétrarque' (pp. 59–96), and 'Pétrarque à Vaucluse' (pp. 97–143), with this last including the dialogue between Petrarch and Laura in the *Triumphus Mortis* (in Gramont's French prose translation, pp. 78–82) and *RVF* 351 (also in Gramont's translation, p. 83). A final section on 'Fragments littéraires: sonnets de Pétrarque' (pp. 171–93) includes verse translations of *RVF* 61, 346, 272 (by Antony Deschamps), and 301 (by Boulay-Paty), amongst other poetic tributes to Petrarch.

1892. Gustave Chatenet, *Études sur les poètes italiens Dante, Pétrarque, Alfieri et Foscolo et sur le poète sicilien Giovanni Meli, avec la traduction en vers français des plus belles parties de leurs œuvres* (Paris: Librairie Fischbacher).

Includes a brief life of Petrarch (pp. 73–85), a brief study of his works (pp. 86–92), a 'Choix de sonnets (traduction de Pétrarque)', pp. 93–9 (seven in total, in rhyming verse: *RVF* 281, 288, 302, 310, 338, 348, and 353), and 'À la fontaine de Vaucluse', pp. 100–2 (i.e. *RVF* 126).

1893. Alphonse de Lamartine, *Trois Poètes italiens: Dante – Pétrarque – Le Tasse* (Paris: Alphonse Lemerre).

Extracts from the *Cours familier de littérature* (with the section on Petrarch dating from 1858). On Petrarch, see pp. 97–218, which includes: complete prose translations of *RVF* 1, 3, 159, 35, 250, 279, 282, 302, 310, 312, 320, 333, 340, 362, 352; partial prose translations of *RVF* 3, 62, 10, 123, 129, 150, 275, 291, 278, 311, 306, 309, 249, 314; and a complete verse translation by Boulay-Paty of *RVF* 301.

1895. Ferdinand Loise, *Histoire de la poésie mise en rapport avec la civilisation en Italie depuis les origines jusqu'à nos jours* (Bruxelles: Alfred Castaigne; Paris: Thorin & fils, A. Fontemoing).

Includes a prose translation of *RVF* 279, 302, and 126, as well as a verse translation by Boulay-Paty of *RVF* 301 (pp. 136–42).

1899. Fernand Brisset, *Les Sonnets de Pétrarque à Laure: traduction nouvelle avec introduction et notes* (Paris: Perrin et Cie).

Includes 297 sonnets translated into prose and divided into 'À Laure vivante' (pp. 1–209, 207 sonnets) and 'À Laure morte' (pp. 211–304, 90 sonnets), plus 'Préface' (pp. vii–xxiii). No Italian texts or first lines provided. 'À Laure vivante' contains *RVF* 1–6, 8–9, 12–13, 15–21, 31–6, 38–9, 41–9, 51, 56–7, 60–2, 64–5, 67–9, 74–9, 81–90, 93–7, 99–102, 107–18, 122–4, 130–4, 140–1, 143–8, 150–65, 167–205, 208–13, 215–31, 233–6, 238, 240–63, 265–6. 'À Laure morte' contains *RVF* 267, 269, 271–321, 326–30, 333–6, 350, 355, 337–49, 356–8, 361–5, 351–2, 354, 353, 91. See 1903 for Brisset's completion of his translations of Petrarch, including the twenty sonnets omitted from the 1899 volume.

1900. Hippolyte Godefroy, *Poésies complètes de Francesco Petrarca, traduction nouvelle: sonnets, canzones, sestines, triomphes* (Montluçon: A. Herbin).

'Introduction' (pp. iii–x); 'Sonnets – canzones – sestines: première partie: pendant la vie de Madame Laure' (pp. 1–246); 'Sonnets – canzones – sestines: deuxième partie: après la mort de Madame Laure' (pp. 247–345); 'Troisième partie: triomphes' (pp. 347–428). Translated into French prose with no Italian text/Italian first line but brief French headings. 'Sonnets – canzones – sestines: première partie: pendant la vie de Madame Laure': *RVF* 1–6, 23, 22, 9–10, 8, 7, 12–13, 15–21, 24–7, 31–6, 38–44, 28, 30, 29, 45–7, 37, 50, 48–9, 51–2, 54, 11, 14, 58, 57, 60–1, 53, 70, 62, 64–5, 67–8, 71–3, 106, 121, 69, 74–5, 66, 308, 76–9, 83–4, 81–2, 85–8, 80, 89–98, 100–4, 107–9, 105, 119, 110–18, 120, 122–3, 125, 124, 130–2, 126, 133–4, 153, 127, 136–8, 128–9, 135, 139–41, 143–8, 150–2, 154–204, 206, 205, 208–13, 215–28, 142, 214, 229–35, 207, 238, 236, 240–3, 237, 239, 244–55, 264, 256–63, 265, 266. 'Sonnets – canzones – sestines: deuxième partie: après la mort de Madame Laure': *RVF* 267, 269, 271, 268, 272–82, 270, 283–93, 323, 325, 294–9, 331, 300, 301, 308–10, 304–7, 302–3, 255, 311–13, 315–21, 326, 322, 327–30, 333–4, 332, 335–6, 350, 355, 337–49, 356–8, 361–3, 359, 364–5, 351–2, 360, 354, 353, 366. 'Troisième partie: triomphes'. Godefroy's translation is not complete, despite its claims, since it omits *RVF* 55, 59, 63, 99, 149, 314, and 324. Also strange is the translating of *RVF* 255 and 308 twice, in both parts one and two.

1900. Marc Legrand, translation into French sonnet form of *RVF* 292 (*Le Figaro*, 29 January, p. 5).

1902. Ernest Cabadé, *Les Sonnets de Pétrarque traduits en sonnets français avec une préface de M. de Tréverret, professeur de littératures étrangères à la Faculté des*

Lettres de Bordeaux, et un portrait authentique de Pétrarque (trouvé à la Bibliothèque nationale par M. Pierre de Nolhac) (Paris: Alphonse Lemerre).

Contains 'À M. Ernest Cabadé: lettre pour servir de préface à une traduction en vers des sonnets de Pétrarque' by M. de Tréverret ('Letter to serve as a preface to a translation in verse of Petrarch's sonnets', pp. vii–xiii), followed by 'Les sonnets écrits pendant la vie de Laure' ('Sonnets written during Laura's life', pp. 1–207) and 'Les sonnets sur la mort de Laure' ('Sonnets on Laura's death', pp. 209–300). Cabadé's structure and choice of poems are identical to Brisset's 1899 volume (see above).

1903. Fernand Brisset, *Canzones, triomphes et poésies diverses: traduction nouvelle avec introduction et notes* (Paris: Perrin et Cie).

As the title indicates, this volume goes beyond the sonnets of the *Canzoniere* and also includes the *Triumphi* and a section entitled 'Sujets divers'. Brisset continues to translate into prose and to omit both the original Italian text and Italian first-lines. 'Préface' (pp. ix–xxiv), 'À Laure vivante' (pp. 1–100), *RVF* 11, 14, 22–3, 29–30, 37, 50, 52, 54–5, 59, 63, 66, 70–3, 80, 105–6, 121, 125–7, 129, 135, 142, 149, 206–7, 214, 237, 239, 264; 'À Laure morte' (pp. 101–44), *RVF* 268, 270, 323–5, 331–2, 359–60, 366; 'Les Triomphes' (pp. 145–277); 'Sujets divers' (pp. 279–323), *RVF* 7, 10, 24–8, 40, 53, 58, 92, 98, 103–4, 11–20, 128, 136–9, 166, 232, 322. This volume completes Brisset's earlier volume of 1899.

Composition of Marsand's *Le rime del Petrarca*

The ordering of the popular *Le rime del Petrarca: edizione pubblicata per opera e studio dell'ab. Antonio Marsand, p. professore nella r. università di Padova: come poi sia stata da lui formata, illustrata, ed adornata, è manifesto per la seguente sua prefazione*, 2 vols (Padua: Nella tipografia del seminario, 1819–20) is as follows: 'Prefazione' (I, pp. vii–xxiii) 'Memorie della vita di Francesco Petrarca ch'egli stesso ne lasciò scritte nelle opere sue latine' ('Memoirs of the life of Francis Petrarch which he himself left written in his Latin works'), I, pp. xxxv–lix; 'Parte prima: sonetti e canzoni di Francesco Petrarca in vita di madonna Laura' ('First part: sonnets and *canzoni* of Francis Petrarch during the life of madonna Laura', I, 1–322), *RVF* 1–6, 8–9, 11–23, 29–39, 41–52, 54–7, 59–90, 93–7, 99–102, 105–18, 121–7, 129–35, 140–65, 167–231, 233–66; 'Parte seconda: sonetti e canzoni di Francesco Petrarca in morte di madonna Laura' ('Part two: sonnets and *canzoni* of Francis Petrarch after the death of madonna Laura', II, 1–135), *RVF* 267–321, 323–36, 350, 355, 337–49, 356–65, 351–2, 354, 353, 91, 366; 'Parte terza: trionfi di Francesco Petrarca in vita ed in morte di madonna Laura' ('Part three: triumphs of Francis Petrarch during the life and after the death of madonna Laura', II, 137–234); 'Parte quarta: sonetti e canzoni di Francesco Petrarca sopra varj argomenti' ('Part four: sonnets and *canzoni* of Francis Petrarch on various topics', II, 235–78), *RVF* 7, 10, 24–8, 40, 53, 58, 92, 98, 103–4, 119–20, 128, 136–9, 166, 232, 322.

Appendix 2

Translations of the Opening Stanza of *RVF* 126 from Voltaire (1756) to Brisset (1903)

Chiare, fresche et dolci acque,
ove le belle membra
pose colei che sola a me par donna;
gentil ramo ove piacque
(con sospir' mi rimembra)
a lei di fare al bel fiancho colonna;
herba et fior' che la gonna
leggiadra ricoverse
co l'angelico seno;
aere sacro, sereno,
ove Amor co' begli occhi il cor m'aperse:
date udïenzia insieme
a le dolenti mie parole extreme.

Voltaire (1756)

Claire fontaine, onde amiable, onde pure,
Où la beauté qui consume mon cœur,
Seule beauté qui soit dans la nature,
Des feux du jour évitait la chaleur ;
Arbre heureux, dont le feuillage,
Agité par les zéphyrs
La couvrit de son ombrage,
Qui rappelle mes soupirs,
En rappelant son image ;
Ornements de ces bords, et filles du matin,
Vous dont je suis jaloux, vous moins brillantes qu'elle,
Fleurs qu'elle embellissait quand vous touchiez son sein,
Rossignol dont la voix est moins douce et moins belle,
Air devenu plus pur, adorable séjour.
Immortalisé par ses charmes,

Lieux dangereux et chers, où de ses tendres armes
L'Amour a blessé tous mes sens ;
Écoutez mes derniers accents,
Recevez mes dernières larmes.[1]

Sade (1764)

Onde fraiche, limpide & pure,
Où la beauté dont je cherche les pas,
Seule beauté qui soit dans la nature,
Vient quelquefois rafraîchir ses appas !
Fleurs qui touchez son sein, qui formez sa parure !
Arbres heureux qui lui servez d'appui !
Séjour embelli par ses charmes !
Pour la derniere fois je vous parle aujourd'hui ;
Ecoutez mes soupirs, & recevez mes larmes.[2]

Romet (1765)

Onde claire, Bords aimables & chéris où la seule Beauté que je trouve dans la Nature vint souvent se délasser ; tendre arbrisseau, qui lui servis d'appui, quand elle venoit se reposer sous ton ombrage (avec quelle émotion je m'en souviens encore !) herbes fraîches ; brillantes fleurs, qui couvriez sa robbe & son sein d'albâtte ; air pur & sacré ; lieu cher, où l'Amour a frappé mes sens ; entendez tous mes derniers accens, recevez tous mes derniers pleurs.[3]

Levesque (1774/1787)

Clair & tranquille ruisseau, qui, dans tes ondes pures, as reçu la beauté qui m'est chere, toi dont les flots heureux ont caressé ses membres délicats ; rameau fortuné, qui lui prêtas un appui, (je me le rappelle encore en soupirant) tendre verdure, jeunes fleurs, qui avez paré ses vêtemens, qui avez baisé son chaste sein ; air serein, air sacré pour moi ; séjour charmant, où l'amour, où deux beaux yeux ont blessé mon cœur ; écoutez ma voix plaintive, recevez mes derniers accens.[4]

Roman (1778)

Heureux ruisseau, qui reçois dans ton sein,
   Qui baignes, de ton onde pure,
   La Beauté qui, dans la Nature,
A seule, sur mon cœur, l'empire souverain !

[1]   Voltaire, *Essai sur les mœurs et l'esprit des nations*, IV, 274.
[2]   Sade, *Mémoires*, II, 208.
[3]   Romet, *Lettre de Pétrarque à Laure*, p. 36.
[4]   Levesque, *Choix des poésies de Pétrarque* (1787), I, 89, 91.

Beaux arbres de ce verd bocage,
Dont la tige soutient ses membres délicats ;
Rameaux qui la couvrez de votre épais feuillage ;
   Gazon, qui naissez sous ses pas ;
   Fleurs, écloses sur ce rivage,
Qui touchez son beau sein, malgré mes yeux jaloux ;
Vous, le simple ornament de sa robe éclatante,
   Qui voyez Laure plus brillante,
   Plus belle & plus fraîche que vous ;
   Zéphyrs que sa bouche respire ;
   Bord solitaire, où je soupire,
Témoin de mes plaisirs, comme de ma douleur ;
   Cher asyle, lieux pleins de charmes,
   Vous, qui rappellez à mon cœur
   Le souvenir de ses alarmes,
   Et l'image de son bonheur ;
Vous, qui, dans deux beaux yeux, vîtes briller la flamme,
   Que l'Amour lance dans mon ame,
   Ecoutez mes tendres adieux,
   Et recevez mes derniers vœux.[5]

Ginguené (1811)

Claires, fraîches et douces ondes, où celle qui me paraît la seule femme qui soit sur la terre, a plongé ses membres délicats ; heureux rameau (je me le rappelle en soupirant), dont il lui plut de se faire un appui ; herbes et fleurs que sa robe élégante renferma dans son sein pur comme celui des anges, air serein et sacré, où planait l'amour quand il ouvrit mon cœur d'un trait de ses beaux yeux, écoutez tous ensemble mes plaintifs et derniers accents.[6]

Saint-Geniès (1816)

   Claire fontaine, onde amiable, onde pure,
Où la beauté qui consume mon cœur,
Seule beauté qui soit dans la nature,
Des feux du jour évitait la chaleur ;
   Arbre heureux, dont le feuillage
   Agité par les zéphyrs
   La couvrit de son ombrage,
   Qui rappelle mes soupirs
   En rappelant son image ;
Ornemens de ces bords, et filles du matin,

---

[5]   Roman, *Le Génie de Pétrarque*, pp. 370–1.
[6]   Ginguené, *Histoire littéraire d'Italie*, II, 519.

Vous, dont je suis jaloux, vous, moins brillantes qu'elle,
Fleurs, qu'elle embellissait quand vous touchiez son sein,
Rossignols, dont la voix est moins douce et moins belle,
Air devenu plus pur ; adorable séjour,
    Immortalisé par ses charmes ;
Lieux dangereux et chers, où de ses tendres armes
    L'amour a blessé tous mes sens,
    Ecoutez mes derniers accens,
    Recevez mes dernières larmes.[7]

Costaing (1819)

Onde pure, onde douce et fraîche, auprès de laquelle cette pure vestale, la seule que j'ai aimée, allait reposer sa belle personne ! Heureux rameau de cet arbre, qui vous plaisiez à lui faire une colonne d'ombrage (je m'en souviens ici avec douleur) ; fleurs et feuilles, qui la recouvrant de votre ombre, retombiez sur les vêtemens de ce cœur angélique ! air sacré et serein, où la beauté avec des yeux purs, trouva l'issue de mon affection, donnez tous ensemble audience à ma plainte, à mes dernières paroles dolentes.[8]

Bouvard (1835)

Ondes fraîches, claire fontaine,
Où Laure apparut à mes yeux ;
Rameau, dont la tige incertaine
Lui fit un appui gracieux ;
Fleurs, gazon, mousse bocagère,
Duvet des champs, où ses genoux,
Son beau sein, sa taille légère
Se dérobaient à l'œil jaloux ;
Air consacré par son haleine,
Où partirent les traits qui m'ont percé le cœur ;
Vous tous, sensibles à ma peine,
De mes derniers accens écoutez la douleur.[9]

---

[7]   Saint-Geniès explicitly uses Voltaire's translation of the first stanza, noting in a footnote that 'Cette traduction de la première strophe est de Voltaire et se trouve dans son *Histoire générale*. On ne s'est pas permis de refaire le travail d'un si grand maître' ('This translation of the first stanza is from Voltaire, and can be found in his *Histoire générale*. We did not allow ourselves to redo the work of such a great master'), Saint-Geniès, *Poésies de Pétrarque*, I, 17. The stanza is recopied above in order to show minor punctuation and spelling changes in Saint-Geniès's version.

[8]   Costaing, *La Muse de Pétrarque*, p. 200.

[9]   A.-P.-A. Bouvard, *Fables nouvelles et poésies diverses* (Auxerre: Imprimerie de Gallot-Fournier, 1835), pp. 183–4.

Courtet (1835)

Claire fontaine, onde aimable, onde pure,
Où la beauté qui consume mon cœur,
Seule beauté qui soit dans la nature,
Des feux du jour évitait la chaleur !
Arbre heureux, dont le feuillage,
    Agité par les zéphirs,
  La couvrit de son ombrage
  Qui rappelle mes désirs,
  En rappelant son image !
Ornements de ces bords, et filles du matin,
Vous, dont je suis jaloux, vous, moins brillantes qu'elle,
Fleurs, qu'elle embellissait quand vous touchiez son sein,
Rossignol dont la voix est moins douce et moins belle;
Air devenu plus pur, adorable séjour.
    Immortalisé par ses charmes,
Lieux dangereux et chers, où de ses tendres armes
  L'amour a blessé tous mes sens,
  Ecoutez mes derniers accens,
  Recevez mes dernières larmes.[10]

Gramont (1842)

Claires, fraîches et douces ondes où reposa son beau corps, celle qui seule me paraît
une dame ; arbre gracieux, dont elle se plut (le souvenir m'en fait soupirer) à faire
une colonne pour son beau flanc ; herbe et fleurs qu'a recouvertes la robe charmante
ainsi que le sein angélique ; air sacré et serein dans lequel Amour et les beaux yeux
m'ont ouvert le cœur ; prêtez ensemble attention à mes gémissantes paroles qui
seront les dernières.[11]

Montesquiou (1842)

Onde fraîche, douce, limpide,
Où le type de la beauté
Avec une grâce timide
Fuyait les ardeurs de l'été,
Rameau cher à ma souvenance,
Et qu'en soupirant je revois,
Pour la soutenir, quelquefois
Vous lui prêtiez votre assistance.
Gentilles fleurs au prompt déclin,

---

[10]   Voltaire's translation of the first stanza, borrowed by Courtet, *Notice sur Pétrarque*,
pp. 70–1.
[11]   Gramont, *Poésies de Pétrarque*, p. 91.

A la gloire trop passagère,
Que couvraient sa robe légère
Et son jeune et candide sein,
Air serein pur et délectable,
Où l'Amour éclaira mon cœur,
Donnez un accueil favorable
Aux derniers chants de ma douleur.[12]

Esménard du Mazet (1848)

Limpide rivière, onde pure
Où j'ai vu, dans tes flots d'argent,
La Beauté qui de la Nature
Est pour moi l'unique ornement ;
Heureuse branche où de la dame
Qui seule règne sur mon âme
S'est appuyé le corps divin ;
Charmant gazon, fleurs éphémères
Qui touchiez ses robes légères
Et parfumiez son joli sein ;
Air dangereux et plein de charmes,
Doux lieux où de ses tendres armes
L'Amour a déchiré mon cœur,
Recevez mes dernières larmes,
Ecoutez encor ma douleur.[13]

Langlois (1852)

　Tranquille et frais ruisseau, qui, dans ton onde pure,
As reçu mon amante avec un doux murmure ;
　　Toi, dont les flots silencieux
Caressaient mollement ses membres gracieux ;
Trop fortuné rameau qui soutins sa faiblesse,
Arbre où vint s'appuyer sa taille enchanteresse,
Je m'en souviens encor, vous me rendiez jaloux ;
Je voulais lui prêter un appui comme vous !
Vert gazon, jeunes fleurs, dès l'aube matinale,
Vous qui veniez parer sa robe virginale,
Qui baisiez chaque jour son blanc et chaste sein ;
Air qu'elle m'envoyait plus pur et plus serein,
Réduit mystérieux où posèrent ses charmes,
FONTAINE, où ses beaux yeux ont fait couler mes larmes,

---

[12]　Montesquiou, *Sonnets, canzones, ballades et sextines de Pétrarque*, I, 205–6.
[13]　Esménard, *Poésies de Pétrarque* (1848), p. 109.

Où l'amour a blessé mon cœur et tous mes sens,
Daigne écouter ma voix et mes derniers accents.[14]

Poulenc (1865)

Claires, fraîches, douces eaux,
Où baigna ses traits si beaux
La dame que je dis de son sexe la reine ;
Charmant rameau qu'en la plaine
(En soupirant il m'en souvient)
Elle daigna donner à son corps pour soutien
Fleurs brillantes, herbes vertes,
Que sa robe a recouvertes
Avec l'angélique sein ;
Air immortel, air serein
Où par ses deux beaux yeux l'Amour causa ma flamme
Venez donc tous en essaim
Écouter les accents bien plaintifs de mon âme.[15]

Mistral (1874)

Aigo claro e fresqueto
Ounte si poulit mèmbre
Pausè ma Damo, aquelo que me raubo ;
Tu que prenguè, branqueto,
(Souspirous me remèmbre),
Pèr s'apiela, courouso coume l'Aubo ;
Erbo e flour que sa raubo
E soun sen curbiguèron ;
Aire sant, aire linde,
Ounte soun divin brinde
E si bèus iue lou cor me durbiguèron,
Ensèn prestas l'ausido
A mi plagum, à ma debalausido.[16]

Mahul (1877)

Claires, fraîches, douces eaux
Où baigne ce pur ivoire ;
Bel arbre aux épais rameaux
Que m'offre encor ma mémoire

---

[14]   Langlois, *Morceaux choisis*, p. 241.
[15]   Poulenc, *Rimes de Pétrarque* (1865), I, 329. See below, Poulenc (1877), for the stanza as it appears in the second edition.
[16]   Frédéric Mistral, 'Traduction provençale de la canzone XI', p. 246.

Alors qu'à ses flancs si beaux
Tu prêtais ton appui, riche et ferme colonne,
Offrant à son front pur un digne couronne,
    Versant tes fleurs sur le sein
De celle qu'ici-bas seule j'appelle Dame ;
Herbe qu'elle a foulée, air consacré, serein
        Où l'Amour par la flamme
    De ses beaux yeux m'ouvrit le cœur,
    Ensemble donnez audience
    A ces paroles que d'avance
Je nomme les derniers témoins de ma douleur ![17]

Poulenc (1877)

    Claires, fraîches, douces eaux
    Où baigna ses traits si beaux
Celle qui de son sexe est l'unique merveille,
    Belle tige et sans pareille
    (Le cœur triste, il m'en souvient)
Qu'elle daigna donner à son corps pour soutien,
    Fleurs brillantes, herbe verte,
    Qui sa robe avez couverte
    Et son angélique sein ;
    Air immortel, air serein
Où par ses deux beaux yeux l'amour causa ma flamme,
    Écoutez tous en essaim,
Écoutez les accents bien plaintifs de mon âme.[18]

Boulmier (1880)

Claires ondes, fraîches et douces,
Où reposa ses beaux membres
Celle qui, seule, à moi, semble une dame ;
Gentil rameau, dont il lui plut
(Avec soupir m'en revient la remembrance)
De faire à son beau flanc une colonne ;
Herbe et fleurs, que recouvrirent
Une toilette élégante,
Un sein angélique,
Air sacré, air serein,
Où Amour, s'aidant de beaux yeux, m'ouvrit le cœur ;

---

[17] Mahul, *Sonnets inédits traduits de Pétrarque* (1877), p. 138.
[18] Poulenc, *Rimes de Pétrarque* (1877), I, 158.

Donnez audience ensemble
A mes dolentes paroles, les dernières !![19]

O fons Melioli sacer,	O fontaine sacrée de Méliole,
Lympha splendide vitrea,	Onde brillamment cristalline,
In quo virgineum mea	Où vint un jour ma Délie
Lavit Delia corpus;	Baigner son beau corps ;
Tuque lenibus enitens	Et toi, arbre en fleurs,
Arbor florida ramulis,	Dressant ta douce ramée,
Qua latus niveum, et caput	Où elle appuya son flanc de neige
Fulsit illa decorum;	Et sa tête charmante ;
Et vos, prata recentia,	Et vous, prairies du renouveau,
Quae vestem nitidam, et sinum	Qui, à sa robe élégante, à son sein
Fovistis tenerum uvida	Délicat, avez fait un joyeux nid
Laeti graminis herba;	De votre humide gazon ;
Vosque, aurae liquidi aetheris,	Vous enfin, brises du limpide azur,
Nostri consciae amoris, ad-	Confidentes de ma peine amoureuse,
este, dum queror, atque vos	Venez recueillir mes plaintes
Suprema alloquor hora.	Et mon adjuration suprême.[20]

Reynard (1883)

Claires, fraîches et douces eaux, sur les bords desquelles celle que j'ai seule pour Dame a reposé ses beaux membres ; arbres gracieux où elle se plaisait—je me le rappelle en soupirant—à appuyer son beau flanc ; herbes et fleurs que sa robe légère a couvertes en même temps que son sein angélique ; air serein et béni où Amour m'ouvrit le cœur avec ses beaux yeux, écoutez tous mes douloureuses dernières paroles.[21]

Monnier (1884)

   Claires, fraîches et douces ondes
      Où flotta le corps gracieux
De celle qui me charme avec ses tresses blondes
      Et qui seule est femme à mes yeux ;
Rameau qui lui servis d'appui, fleurs embaumées
      Qu'elle a dans sa robe enfermées,
Air serein et sacré, solitude où je sens

---

[19] Joseph Boulmier, 'La vraie manière de traduire les poètes', p. 83.
[20] Boulmier, 'La vraie manière de traduire les poètes', pp. 86–7. This is a translation, by Boulmier, of a sixteenth-century Latin imitation of *RVF* 126 by Marc-Antoine Flaminio.
[21] Reynard, *Les Rimes de François Pétrarque*, p. 86.

Encore ses beaux yeux ouvrir mon cœur qui tremble,
Écoutez, écoutez ensemble
Mes plaintifs et derniers accents ![22]

Casalis and Ginoux (1887)

Claire, fraîche, douce fontaine,
Dont l'azur reçut l'inhumaine,
Qui seule a la vertu d'être belle à mes yeux !
Arbre au symbolique feuillage
(Que de soupirs dans cette image !),
Qui ployas tes rameaux sous son flanc gracieux !
Fleurs, gazon, qui gardez l'empreinte
Reçue en une douce étreinte,
Lorsque son sein vous fit fléchir !
Pure atmosphère, frais zéphyr,
Témoins du premier feu dont j'ai senti l'atteinte,
Écoutez, après cet aveu,
Et ma dernière plainte et mon suprême vœu ![23]

Chatenet (1892)

Eau claire, fraîche et bienfaisante
Où la dame, unique à mes yeux,
Baignait ses membres gracieux ;
Gentil rameau sur qui sa main charmante,
Je tressaille à ce souvenir,
Se plaisait à se soutenir ;
Gazon fleuri sur lequel s'étendirent
Sa jupe et son beau sein ; air pur où sans retour
Ses yeux adorables ouvrirent
L'accès de mon cœur à l'amour ;
Soyez tous attentifs à ma plainte dernière.[24]

Loise (1895)

Claires, fraîches et douces ondes, où celle qui est l'unique femme, à mes yeux, a
plongé ses membres délicats ; heureux rameau (je me le rappelle en soupirant), dont
elle voulut faire à son beau corps un appui ; herbes et fleurs que sa robe élégante
renferma dans son sein d'une angélique pureté, air serein et sacré, où l'amour ouvrit

---

[22]   Monnier, *La Renaissance, de Dante à Luther*, pp. 106–7.
[23]   Casalis and Ginoux, *Cinquante sonnets et cinq odes de Pétrarque*, p. 81.
[24]   Gustave Chatenet, *Études sur les poètes italiens Dante, Pétrarque, Alfieri et Foscolo et sur le poète sicilien Giovanni Meli, avec la traduction en vers français des plus belles parties de leurs œuvres* (Paris: Librairie Fischbacher, 1892), p. 100.

mon cœur par de beaux yeux, écoutez tous ensemble mes plaintifs et derniers accents.[25]

Godefroy (1900)

Claires, fraîches et douces ondes où elle étendit ses beaux membres celle qui seule a pour moi l'aspect d'une dame ; Heureux rameau, que toujours je me rappelle avec un soupir, dont elle se fit pour son beau flanc une colonne, herbe et fleur qu'a recouvert la robe gracieuse qui recouvrait aussi son sein angélique ; Air sacré et serein au milieu duquel Amour et les beaux yeux qui m'ont blessé le cœur, prêtez l'oreille ensemble à mes douloureuses paroles qui seront les dernières.[26]

Brisset (1903)

Ondes limpides, fraîches et pures, près desquelles s'est reposé le beau corps de la seule femme qui existe pour moi ; charmant arbuste au tronc duquel—je soupire en y pensant—elle aimait à s'appuyer ; herbes et fleurs qu'ont recouvertes ses vêtements gracieux et sa chaste poitrine ; air calme et béni où ses beaux yeux ouvrirent mon cœur à l'amour, écoutez tous ensemble mes tristes et suprêmes paroles.[27]

[25] Loise, *Histoire de la poésie*, p. 141.
[26] Godefroy, *Poésies complètes de Francesco Petrarca*, p. 125.
[27] Brisset, *Canzones, triomphes et poésies diverses*, p. 63.

Bibliography

The Bibliography is divided into three sections: Works by Petrarch; Other Primary Texts; Secondary Works. The first section includes details of translations of Petrarch's works, organized alphabetically by name of translator for ease of reference; original editions are similarly, in this section only, ordered under name of editor.

Works by Petrarch

Arrighi, Jean-Paul-Louis d', trans., *Aspirations de l'âme religieuse: ode à la divine pureté, par Filicaia, en trois langues; suivie de la prière à la très-sainte Vierge, par Pétrarque, en deux langues* (La Côte-Saint-André: Chez le traducteur, 1854).

—— *Odes et sonnets choisis de Pétrarque, traduits en français* (Paris: Impasse du Doyenné, 1838).

—— *Preghiera di Petrarca alla santissima Vergine/Prière de Pétrarque à la très-sainte Vierge, traduite de l'italien* (Grenoble: Imprimerie de Prudhomme, 1851).

Bailly, Ferdinand, trans., *Pétrarque: nouvelle traduction en vers et dans les formes originales de ses sonnets, canzones, sestines, madrigaux et triomphes*, 2 vols (Paris: Les Éditions Rieder, 1932).

Bergin, Thomas G., ed. and trans., *Bucolicum carmen* (New Haven, CT: Yale University Press, 1974).

Bernardo, Aldo S., trans., *Letters on Familiar Matters: Rerum familiarium libri I–VIII* (Albany: State University of New York Press, 1975).

——, Saul Levin, and Reta A. Bernardo, trans, *Letters of Old Age/Rerum senilium libri*, 2 vols (Baltimore: Johns Hopkins University Press, 1992).

Biagioli, G., ed., *Rime di F. Petrarca col comento*, 2 vols (Paris: Presso l'Editore, 1821).

Brisset, Fernand, trans., *Canzones, triomphes et poésies diverses: traduction nouvelle avec introduction et notes* (Paris: Perrin et Cie, 1903).

—— *Pétrarque à Laure: les sonnets: traduction nouvelle rythmée* (Paris: Librairie Ancienne J.-A. Quereuil, 1933).

—— *Sonnets à Laure* (London: Leopold B. Hill, 1921).

—— *Les Sonnets de Pétrarque à Laure: traduction nouvelle avec introduction et notes* (Paris: Perrin et Cie, 1899).

Bufano, Antonietta, with Basile Aracri and Clara Klaus Reggiani, eds, *Opere latine di Francesco Petrarca*, 2 vols (Turin: Unione tipografico-editrice, 1975).

Buttura, Antonio, ed., *Le rime di messer F. Petrarca; le Stanze e l'Orfeo del Poliziano, con note di diversi*, 2 vols (Paris: Baudry, 1830).

C[...]., G[...]., trans., *Il trionfo d'amore di Petrarca: dedicato al gentiluomo Fr. B. Duppa, da G. C., professore di lingua italiana in Blois* (Blois: Giroud, 1830).

Cabadé, Ernest, trans., *Les Sonnets de Pétrarque traduits en sonnets français avec une préface de M. de Tréverret, professeur de littératures étrangères à la Faculté des Lettres de Bordeaux, et un portrait authentique de Pétrarque (trouvé à la Bibliothèque nationale par M. Pierre de Nolhac)* (Paris: Alphonse Lemerre, 1902).

Carrara, Enrico, ed., *Secretum* [*De secreto conflictu curarum mearum*], in *Prose* (Milan and Naples: Riccardo Ricciardi, 1955), pp. 22–215.

Carraud, Christophe, ed. and trans., *Les remèdes aux deux fortunes/De remediis utriusque fortune (1354–1366)*, 2 vols (Grenoble: Millon, 2002).

Casalis, Junior, and Ernest de Ginoux, trans., *Cinquante sonnets et cinq odes de Pétrarque traduits en vers français* (Paris: Librairie des Bibliophiles, 1887).

Catanusi, Placide, trans., *Les Œuvres amoureuses de Petrarque traduites en François avec l'Italien à costé* (Paris: Chez Estienne Loyson, 1669).

Cochin, Henry, ed. and trans., *Un ami de Pétrarque: lettres de Francesco Nelli à Pétrarque, publiées d'après le Manuscrit de la Bibliothèque nationale, avec une introduction et des notes* (Paris: Honoré Champion, 1892).

—— *Les Psaumes pénitentiaux publiés d'après le manuscrit de la bibliothèque de Lucerne, préface de Pierre de Nolhac* (Paris: L. Rouart et fils, [1929]).

—— *Les Triomphes, ornés de vignettes gravées sur bois par Alfred Latour* (Paris: Léon Pichon, 1923).

De contemptu mundi, colloquiorum liber quem Secretum suum inscripsit; De VII. psalmi poenitentiales (Bern: Ioannes le Preux, 1604), bound with *De vita solitaria* (Bern: Ioannes le Preux, 1605): Bodleian Toynbee 1885.

Delécluze, É.-J., 'François Pétrarque, "De l'art de bien gouverner un état, dédié à Fr. Carrara prince de Padoue"', *Revue de Paris*, 60 (1838), 108–20.

—— 'Pétrarque au Mont Ventoux', *Revue de Paris* (13 January 1839), 3–11.

—— 'Vie de F. Pétrarque écrite par lui-même', *Revue de Paris* (17 March 1839), 5–15.

Develay, Victor, *L'Afrique, poème épique, traduit du latin pour la première fois*, 5 vols (Paris: Librairie des Bibliophiles, 1882).

—— 'L'amour des livres (chapitre inédit de Pétrarque)', *Le Livre: revue du monde littéraire: archives des Écrits de ce temps: bibliographie rétrospective*, 4 (1883), 196–200.

—— *L'Ascension du Mont Ventoux, traduite pour la première fois* (Paris: Librairie des Bibliophiles, 1880).

—— *De l'abondance des livres et de la réputation des écrivains, traduit du latin* (Paris: Librairie des Bibliophiles, 1883).

—— *Des amours charmantes, traduit du latin* (Paris: Librairie des Bibliophiles, 1883).

—— *Églogues, traduites pour la première fois*, 2 vols (Paris: Librairie des Bibliophiles, 1891).

—— *Épître à la postérité et Testament, traduits du latin* (Paris: Librairie des Bibliophiles, 1880).

—— *Grisélidis, conte traduit du latin* (Paris: Librairie des Bibliophiles, 1872).

—— *Lettres à Rienzi, traduites pour la première fois* (Paris: Librairie des Bibliophiles, 1885).

—— *Lettres de François Pétrarque à Jean Boccace, traduites du latin pour la première fois* (Paris: E. Flammarion, 1891).

—— *Lettres de Pétrarque à son frère, traduites pour la première fois*, 2 vols (Paris: Librairie des Bibliophiles, 1884).

—— 'Lettres de Pétrarque sur l'amour des livres', *Bulletin du bibliophile et du bibliothécaire: revue mensuelle publiée par Léon Techener* (1879), 1–21, 153–79, and 405–29; *Bulletin du bibliophile et du bibliothécaire* (1880), 305–20 and 529–37; *Bulletin du bibliophile et du bibliothécaire* (1881), 48–53, 207–19, 289–95, 385–8, and 481–93.

—— *Lettres de Vaucluse, traduites du latin pour la première fois* (Paris: E. Flammarion, 1899).

—— *Lettres sans titre, traduites pour la première fois*, 2 vols (Paris: Librairie des Bibliophiles, 1885).

—— *Mon secret, ou du conflit de mes passions, traduit pour la première fois*, 3 vols (Paris: Librairie des Bibliophiles, 1879).

—— 'Pétrarque au capitole', *Le Livre: revue du monde littéraire: archives des Écrits de ce temps: bibliographie rétrospective*, 6 (1885), 278–88.

—— 'Pétrarque épistolier', *Le Carnet historique et littéraire: revue mensuelle*, 10 (November 1901), 211–25; *Le Carnet historique et littéraire*, 11 (January 1902), 81–93.

—— *Psaumes pénitentiaux* (Paris: Librairie des Bibliophiles, 1880).

—— *Sophonisbe, épisode du poème de 'l'Afrique', traduit pour la première fois* (Paris: Librairie des Bibliophiles, 1880).

Dotti, Ugo, ed., *Sine nomine: lettere polemiche e politiche* (Bari: Laterza, 1974).

Enenkel, Karl, ed., 'A Critical Edition of Petrarch's *Epistola Posteritati*', in *Modelling the Individual: Biography and Portrait in the Renaissance, with a Critical Edition of Petrarch's Letter to Posterity*, ed. Karl Enenkel, Betsy de Jong-Crane, and Peter Liebregts (Amsterdam: Rodopi, 1998), pp. 243–81.

Esménard (du Mazet), Camille, trans., *Choix de sonnets de Pétrarque, traduits en vers* (Paris: Mme Vve Charles Béchet, 1830).

—— *Poésies de Pétrarque traduites en vers* (Paris: Au comptoir des imprimeurs-unis, 1848).

Ginguené, Pierre-Louis, trans., *Les Œuvres amoureuses de Pétrarque: sonnets–triomphes, traduites en français avec le texte en regard et précédées d'une notice sur la vie de Pétrarque* (Paris: Garnier frères, 1875).

Glomeau, Marie-Anne, trans., *De l'Amour et de la Mort (Sonnets choisis), traduction littérale conforme aux commentaires de Léopardi* (Paris: Maurice Glomeau, 1920).

Godefroy, Hippolyte, trans., *Poésies complètes de Francesco Petrarca* (Montluçon: Imprimerie A. Herbin, 1900).

Gramont, Ferdinand de, trans., *Canzoniere*, with preface and notes by Jean-Michel Gardair (Paris: Gallimard, 1983).

—— *Poésies de Pétrarque: traduction complète: sonnets, canzones, triomphes* (Paris: Paul Masgana, 1842).

Jehan-Madelaine, L., trans., *Sonnets de Pétrarque: traduction libre: première série* (Paris: Librairie Fischbacher, 1884).

Lafond, Ernest and Edmond Lafond, trans., *Dante, Pétrarque, Michel-Ange, Tasse: sonnets choisis traduits en vers et précédés d'une étude sur chaque poëte* (Paris: Comptoir des Imprimeurs-Unis, 1848).

Lalaing, Marie-Henriette, trans., *Stances de Messer Angelo Poliziano et poésies extraites de Dante, Pétrarque et Leopardi, traduites de l'italien* (Brussels: Imprimerie de J. Stienon, 1853).

Langlois, Jacques, trans., *Les Sonnets amoureux de Pétrarque: traduits en sonnets français avec le texte italien en regard: précédés d'un résumé de la vie du poète et du récit de son amour pour Laure* (Paris: Éditions Marc Artus, 1936).

Larenaudière, Gustave de, trans., '*Spirto gentil – Noble génie*, canzone de Pétrarque adressée à Cola di Rienzo', *Revue française* (1859), 502–5.

Le Duc, Philibert, trans., *Les Sonnets de Pétrarque: traduction complète en sonnets réguliers, avec introduction et commentaire*, 2 vols (Paris: Leon Willem, 1877–9).

Levesque, Pierre-Charles, trans., *Choix des poésies de Pétrarque traduites de l'italien*, 2 vols (Venice and Paris: Valade and Hardouin, 1774).

—— *Choix des poésies de Pétrarque, traduites de l'Italien: nouvelle édition corrigée et augmentée*, 2 vols (Venice and Paris: Hardouin et Gattey, 1787).

Mabille, Pompée, trans., *Lettre de Pétrarque à Boccace* (Angers: Imprimerie de Lainé frères, 1873).

—— *Mon secret, ou du mépris du monde: confessions de Pétrarque translaté du latin en quasi français* (Angers: Imprimerie P. Lachèse et Dolbeau, 1886).

—— *Pétrarque et l'empereur Charles IV (correspondance)* (Angers: Imprimerie de P. Lachèse et Dolbeau, 1890).

—— *Pétrarque philosophe et confessionniste* (Angers: A. Burdin, 1880).

—— 'Question d'hygiène et de diététique, à propos d'une lettre de Pétrarque', in *Annales de la Société linnéenne du département de Maine-et-Loire*, 11 (1869), 149–71.

—— 'Réponse de Pétrarque à Jean Dondi, célèbre médecin de Padoue', *Annales de la Société linnéenne du département de Maine-et-Loire*, 12 (1870), 203–42.

Mahul, Emma, trans., *Cent cinquante sonnets et huit morceaux complémentaires traduits des Sonnets de Pétrarque, texte en regard* (Paris: Firmon Didot frères, 1847).

—— *Choix de sonnets de Pétrarque: seconde édition revue, corrigée et augmentée de la traduction de différentes poésies de Pétrarque* (Florence: Chez les Héritiers Botta, 1867).

—— *Choix de sonnets traduits de Pétrarque, revue, corrigée et augmentée de la traduction de différentes poésies de Pétrarque* (Paris: Firmin Didot frères, fils et Cie, 1872).

—— *Choix de sonnets: troisième édition revue, corrigée et augmentée de la traduction de différentes poésies de Pétrarque, etc.* (Paris: Firmin Didot, 1869).

—— *Sonnets inédits traduits de Pétrarque, cinquième publication complétant la totalité des sonnets et augmentée de la traduction également inédite de différentes poésies de Pétrarque, etc.* (Rome: Héritiers Botta, 1877).

Marsand, Antonio, ed., *Le rime del Petrarca*, 2 vols (Padua: Nella tipografia del seminario, 1819–20).

Marsh, David, ed. and trans., *Invectives* (Cambridge, MA: Harvard University Press, 2003).

Mestica, Giovanni, ed., *Le rime di Francesco Petrarca: restituite nell'ordine e nella lezione del testo originario sugli autografi col sussidio di altri codici e di stampe e corredate di varianti e note* (Florence: G. Barbèra, 1896).

Mistral, Frédéric, 'Traduction provençale de la canzone XI', in *Fêtes littéraires & internationales: cinquième centenaire de la mort de Pétrarque: célébré à Vaucluse et à Avignon le 18, 19 et 20 juillet 1874* (Avignon: Imprimerie administrative Gros frères, 1874), pp. 246–9.

Mommsen, Theodor E., ed. and trans., *Petrarch's Testament* (Ithaca, NY: Cornell University Press, 1957).

Montesquiou, Anatole de, trans., *Épîtres, églogues et triomphes de Pétrarque traduits en vers* (Paris: Leroy, 1843).

—— *Sonnets, canzones, ballades et sextines de Pétrarque traduits en vers*, 2 vols (Paris: Leroy, 1842).

—— *Sonnets, canzones, ballades, sextines, traduits en vers*, 2nd edn, 3 vols (Paris: Amyot, 1843).

Nichols, J. G., trans., *My Secret Book* (London: Hesperus Press, 2002).

Pacca, Vinicio, and Laura Paolino, eds, *Trionfi, rime estravaganti, codice degli abbozzi* (Milan: Arnoldo Mondadori, 1996).

Peignot, Gabriel, 'Testament de Pétrarque', in *Choix de testaments anciens et modernes, remarquables par leur importance, leur singularité, ou leur bizarrerie; avec des détails historique et des notes*, 2 vols (Paris: Renouard; Dijon: Victor Lagier, 1829), I, 56–65.

Philieul, Vasquin, trans., *Toutes les euvres vulgaires de Françoys Pétrarque, contenans quatre Livres de M.D. Laure d'Avignon sa maistresse: jadis par luy composez en langage Thuscan, & mis en François: avecques briefz Sommaires ou Argumens requis pour plus facile intelligence du tout* (Avignon: De l'Imprimerie de Barthelemy Bonhomme, 1555).

Pingaud, Léonce, *De poemate F. Petrarchae cui titulus est Africa, Thesim facultati litterarum parisiensi* (Paris: Ernest Thorin, 1872).

Poulenc, Joseph, trans., *Rimes de Pétrarque: traduction complète en vers des sonnets, canzones, sextines, ballades, madrigaux et triomphes: deuxième édition, revue et corrigée*, 2 vols (Paris: Librairie des Bibliophiles, 1887).

—— *Rimes de Pétrarque, traduites en vers, texte en regard*, 4 vols (Paris: A. Lacroix, 1865).

Ranalli, Ferdinando, ed., *Epistole di Francesco Petrarca* (Milan: Per Giovanni Silvestri, 1836).

Rawski, Conrad H., ed., *Petrarch's Remedies for Fortune Fair and Foul: A Modern English Translation of 'De remediis utriusque fortune', with a Commentary*, 5 vols (Bloomington: Indiana University Press, 1991).

Reynard, Francisque, trans., *Les Rimes de François Pétrarque: traduction nouvelle* (Paris: G. Charpentier, 1883).

Romet, Nicolas Antoine, trans., *Lettre de Pétrarque à Laure, suivie de remarques sur ce Poëte, & de traduction de quelques-unes de ses plus jolies pièces* (Paris: Sébastien Jorry, 1765).

Rossi, Vittorio, ed., *Familiarum rerum libri/Le Familiari*, 4 vols (Florence: G. C. Sansoni, 1933–42).

Saint-Geniès, Léonce de, trans., *Poésies de Pétrarque, traduites en vers français, suivies de deux poëmes*, 2 vols (Paris: Delaunay and Barrois, 1816).

Santagata, Marco, ed., *Canzoniere*, 4th edn (Milan: Arnoldo Mondadori, 2010).

Vellutello, Alessandro, ed., *Le volgari opere del Petrarcha con la espositione di Alessandro Vellutello da Lucca* (Venice: Giovanni Antonio et Fratelli da Sabbio, 1525).

Wilkins, E. H., ed. and trans., *Petrarch at Vaucluse: Letters in Verse and Prose* (Chicago: University of Chicago Press, 1958).

Zacour, Norman P., trans., *Petrarch's 'Book Without a Name': A Translation of the 'Liber sine nomine'* (Toronto: The Pontifical Institute of Mediaeval Studies, 1973).

Other Primary Texts

Académie de Vaucluse, *Sixième centenaire de la naissance de Pétrarque célébré à Vaucluse et Avignon les 16, 17, et 18 juillet 1904* (Avignon: François Seguin, 1904).

Alighieri, Dante, '*La Commedia' secondo l'antica vulgata*, ed. Giorgio Petrocchi, rev. edn, 4 vols (Florence, Le Lettere, 1994).

—— *La Divine Comédie: traduction nouvelle par Francisque Reynard*, 2 vols (Paris: A. Lemerre, 1877).

—— *Œuvres: la Divine Comédie, traduction d'A. Brizeux; la Vie nouvelle, traduction d'É.-J. Deléscluze* (Paris: Charpentier, 1847).

—— *Vita nova*, trans. Henry Cochin (Paris: Bibliothèque de l'Occident, 1905).

Almanach du sonnet, 3 vols (Aix-en-Provence: Vve Remondet-Aubin, 1874–6).

Altenheym, Gabrielle Soumet d', *Les quatre siècles littéraires: récits de l'histoire de la littérature sous Périclès, Auguste, Léon X et Louis XIV, enrichis de fragments des chefs-d'œuvre classiques* (Paris: E. Ducrocq, 1859).

Ampère, J.-J., *La Grèce, Rome et Dante: études littéraires d'après nature* (Paris: Didier, 1848).

Arago, Jacques, ed., *Le Kaléidoscope, journal de la littérature, des mœurs et des théâtres* (11 avril 1829).

Ariosto, Ludovico, *Roland furieux: traduction nouvelle par Francisque Reynard*, 4 vols (Paris: A. Lemerre, 1880).

Athénée de Vaucluse, *Mémoires de l'Athénée de Vaucluse, contenant le compte rendu des travaux de cette Société depuis son institution, et le recueil des ouvrages en prose et en vers, lus à sa séance publique* (Avignon: De l'Imprimerie d'Alph. Berenguier, An XII/1804).

—— *Vie de Pétrarque; augmentée de la première traduction qui ait paru en Français, de la Lettre adressée à la Postérité par ce Poète célèbre: avec la liste des Souscripteurs qui ont concouru à lui faire ériger un Monument à Vaucluse, le jour séculaire de sa naissance, 20 Juillet 1804, 1er Thermidor an 12* (Avignon: Mme Vve Seguin, 1804).

Audibert, Armand, *Les Amours de Pétrarque et de Laure à la Fontaine de Vaucluse* (Toulon: G. Mouton, 1924).

Augustine, Saint, *Confessions*, trans. William Watts, 2 vols (Cambridge, MA: Harvard University Press, 1912).

Austin, J. L., *How to Do Things with Words: The William James Lectures delivered at Harvard University in 1955* (Oxford: Clarendon Press, 1962).

Balzac, Honoré de, 'Études sur M. Beyle (Frédéric Stendalh [*sic*]), *Revue parisienne*, 25 septembre 1840', in Stendhal, *Œuvres romanesques complètes*, ed. Yves Ansel, Philippe Berthier, Xavier Bourdenet, and Serge Linkès, 3 vols (Paris: Gallimard, 2005-14), III, 619-58.

—— *Une fille d'Ève*, ed. Roger Pierrot, in *La Comédie humaine*, ed. Pierre-Georges Castex, 12 vols (Paris: Gallimard, 1976-81), II (1976), 245-383.

—— *Illusions perdues*, ed. Roland Chollet, in *La Comédie humaine*, ed. Pierre-Georges Castex, 12 vols (Paris: Gallimard, 1976-81), V (1977), 1-732.

—— *The Lily in the Valley* (London: The Caxton Publishing Company, 1897).

—— *Le Lys dans la vallée*, ed. Jean-Hervé Donnard, in *La Comédie humaine*, ed. Pierre-Georges Castex, 12 vols (Paris: Gallimard, 1976-81), IX (1978), 873-1229.

—— 'A Study of M. Beyle', in Stendhal, *The Charterhouse of Parma*, trans. C. K. Scott Moncrieff, 2 vols (London: Chatto & Windus, 1926), I, pp. vii-lxxiii.

Banville, Théodore de, *Petit traité de poésie française* (Paris: Librairie de l'Écho de la Sorbonne, 1872).

Barthes, Roland, *Œuvres complètes*, ed. Éric Marty, new revised edn, 5 vols (Paris: Seuil, 2002), in particular 'La mort de l'auteur' (III, 40-5) and 'On échoue toujours à parler de ce qu'on aime' (V, 906-14).

Bartholoni, Jean, *Le Roman de Pétrarque et de Laure (1327-1348)* (Paris: Albert Messein, 1927).

Baudouin, Agathe, *Rêveries sur les bords du Cher: poésies* (Paris: Challamel et Cie, 1841).

Benjamin, Walter, 'On Language as Such and on the Language of Man', trans. Edmund Jephcott, in *Selected Writings*, ed. Marcus Bullock, Michael W. Jennings, Howard Eiland, and Gary Smith, 4 vols (Cambridge, MA: The Belknap Press of Harvard University Press, 1996-2003), I, 62-74.

—— 'The Task of the Translator: An Introduction to the Translation of Baudelaire's *Tableaux parisiens*', in *Illuminations*, ed. Hannah Arendt and trans. Harry Zorn (London: Pimlico, 1999), pp. 70-82.

Berluc-Pérussis, Léon de, *Un document inédit sur Laure de Sade: extrait des Mémoires de l'Académie d'Aix* (Aix-en-Provence: Chez Marius Illy, 1876).

—— and Hippolyte Guillibert, eds, *Fête séculaire et internationale de Pétrarque célébrée en Provence 1874: procès-verbaux & vers inédits* (Aix-en-Provence: Vve Remondet-Aubin, 1875).

Berton, J. Michel, *Éleuthérides: poésies* (Paris: Dumont, 1839).

Bertrand, F., *Laure et Pétrarque: la Fontaine de Vaucluse: rencontre dans les solitudes qui dominant Vaucluse* (Avignon: Librairie H. Chassing, 1883).

Biagioli, Giosafatte, *Traité de la poésie italienne* (Paris: Au magasin de livres italiens, chez Fayolle, 1808).

Boccaccio, Giovanni, *Le Décaméron: traduction nouvelle par Francisque Reynard*, 2 vols (Paris: G. Charpentier, 1879).

—— 'Vite di Petrarca, Pier Damiani e Livio', ed. Renata Fabbri, in Boccaccio, *Tutte le opere*, ed. Vittore Branca, 10 vols in 11 (Milan: Arnoldo Mondadori, 1964-98), V.1 (1992), 898-911.

Boileau, Nicolas, *Œuvres complètes*, ed. Françoise Escal (Paris: Gallimard, 1966).

Boulay-Paty, Évariste, *Sonnets* (Paris: H. Féret, 1851).

—— *Sonnets de la vie humaine* (Paris: Firmin Didot frères, 1852).

Boulmier, Joseph, 'La vraie manière de traduire les poètes', in *La Curiosité littéraire et bibliographique: première série* (Paris: Isidore Liseux, 1880), pp. 77–93.

Bouvard, A.-P.-A., *Fables nouvelles et poésies diverses* (Auxerre: Imprimerie de Gallot-Fournier, 1835).

Brizeux, Auguste, *Œuvres complètes: précédées d'une notice par Saint-René Taillandier*, 2 vols (Paris: Michel Lévy freres, 1860).

Broche, Gaston, *Sur Pétrarque: ses imprécautions contre Avignon* (Avignon: Imprimerie Rullière frères, 1913).

Bruce-Whyte, A., *Histoire des langues romanes et de leur littérature, depuis leur origine jusqu'au XIV siècle*, 3 vols (Paris: Treuttel et Würtz, 1841).

Bujanda, J. M. de, ed., *Index librorum prohibitorum 1600–1966* (Montreal: Médiaspaul, 2002).

—— *Thesaurus de la littérature interdite au XVIe siècle: auteurs, ouvrages, éditions avec addenda et corrigenda* (Geneva: Librairie Droz; Sherbrooke: Centre d'Études de la Renaissance, 1996).

Butler, Judith, *Gender Trouble: Feminism and the Subversion of Identity* (New York: Routledge, 1990).

Chapellon, Alphonse, *Souvenirs* (Odessa: [n. p.], 1848).

Chateaubriand, François-René de, *Essai historique, politique, et moral, sur les révolutions, anciennes et modernes* (London: Henri Colburn, 1815).

—— *Mémoires d'outre-tombe*, ed. Maurice Levaillant and Georges Moulinier, 2 vols (Paris: Gallimard, 1951).

Chatenet, Gustave, *Études sur les poètes italiens Dante, Pétrarque, Alfieri et Foscolo et sur le poète sicilien Giovanni Meli, avec la traduction en vers français des plus belles parties de leurs œuvres* (Paris: Librairie Fischbacher, 1892).

Christophe, J.-B. (abbé), *Histoire de la papauté pendant le XIVe siècle avec des notes et des pièces justificatives*, 2 vols (Paris: Librairie de L. Maison, 1853).

Cochin, Henry, *Le Jubilé de Pétrarque (extrait du 'Correspondant')* (Paris: De Soye et fils, 1904).

Costaing de Pusignan, abbé, *La Muse de Pétrarque dans les collines de Vaucluse, ou Laure des Baux, sa solitude et son tombeau dans le vallon de Galas* (Paris: Chez Rapet; Avignon: Chez Bonnet fils, 1819).

Costantini, P. L., *Nuova scelta di poesie italiane, tratte da' più celebri autori antichi e moderni, con brevi notizie sopra la vita e gli scritti di ciascheduno*, 2 vols (Paris: Bossange, 1823).

Courtet, Victor, *Notice sur Pétrarque, avec une pièce inédite de Mirabeau sur la fontaine de Vaucluse* (Paris: Librairie de Charles Gosselin, 1835).

Crépet, Eugène, ed., *Les Poëtes français: recueil des chefs-d'œuvre de la poésie française depuis les origines jusqu'à nos jours, avec une notice littéraire sur chaque poëte*, 4 vols (Paris: Librairie de L. Hachette, 1861–3).

Delécluze, Étienne-Jean, *Dante Alighieri, ou la poésie amoureuse*, 2 vols (Paris: A. Delahays, 1854).

Delon, Alexandre, *Les Vies de Pétrarque et de Laure, et description de la Fontaine de Vaucluse; et 'Laure et Pétrarque', poème* (Nismes: Buchet, 1788).

Derrida, Jacques, *Le Monolinguisme de l'autre, ou la prothèse d'origine* (Paris: Galilée, 1996).

—— *Monolingualism of the Other; or, The Prosthesis of Origin*, trans. Patrick Mensah (Stanford, CA: Stanford University Press, 1998).

Deschamps, Antony, *Poésies: traduction de Dante Alighieri: les dernières paroles* (Brussels: E. Laurent, 1837).

Désorgues, Théodore, *Épître sur l'Italie, suivie de quelques autres poésies relatives au même pays* (Paris: Marchands de nouveautés, 1796).

Di Negro, J.-C., *Essais poétiques* (Genoa: Imprimerie des sourds-muets, 1840).

Dobson, Susannah, *The Life of Petrarch*, 2 vols (London: James Buckland, 1775).

Duplessis, Philippe, *Œuvres posthumes, imprimées en exécution de son testament*, 5 vols (Paris: Firmin Didot, 1853).

Duprat, Hippolyte, *Pétrarque: opéra en cinq actes: partition piano et chant*, libretto by Duprat and F. Dharmenon (Paris: Brandus & Cie, [n.d.]).

Esménard du Mazet, Camille, *Chants à la Sainte Vierge traduits du bréviaire* (Poissy: A. Bouret, 1867).

Falques, Marianne-Agnès, trans., *Nouvelles fables, avec une traduction de quelques sonnets choisis de Pétrarque et une romance* (London: T. R. Delorme, 1772).

Faure, Gabriel, *Au Ventoux avec Pétrarque, suivi de la Lettre de Pétrarque au P. François Denis, traduite du latin* (Avignon: Aubonel frères, 1928).

Ferri, Louis, *Morceaux choisis, en prose et en vers, des classiques italiens publiés avec une introduction, des notices biographiques et des notes en français* (Paris: Hachette, 1868).

Fournier, Édouard, ed., *Souvenirs poétiques de l'école romantique, 1825 à 1840: précédés d'une notice biographique sur chacun des auteurs* (Paris: Laplace, 1886).

Fowler, Mary, ed., *Cornell University Library Catalogue of the Petrarch Collection bequeathed by Willard Fiske* (London: Oxford University Press, 1916).

Gautier, Théophile, *Histoire du romantisme suivie de Notices romantiques et d'une Étude sur la poésie française 1830–1868* (Paris: Charpentier et Cie, 1874).

—— *Œuvres poétiques complètes*, ed. Michel Brix (Paris: Bartillat, 2004).

Gebhart, Émile, 'Liminaire', in Académie de Vaucluse, *Sixième centenaire de la naissance de Pétrarque célébré à Vaucluse et Avignon les 16, 17, et 18 juillet 1904* (Avignon: François Seguin, 1904), pp. 1–3.

Genlis, Stéphanie-Félicité de, *Pétrarque et Laure*, 2 vols (Paris: Chez l'éditeur des œuvres de Mme de Genlis, 1819).

Glaize, Paul, 'Le centenaire de Pétrarque', *Revue des langues romanes: publiée par la société pour l'étude des langues romanes*, 6 (July and October 1874), 278–91.

Gramont, Ferdinand de, *Les Bébés: texte par le Cte F. de Gramont, vignettes par Oscar Pletsch* (Paris: Hetzel, 1861).

—— *Chant du passé, 1830–1848* (Paris: D. Giraud, 1854).

—— *Olim: sextines et sonnets* (Paris: Paul Ollendorff, 1882).

—— *Sextines précédées de l'histoire de la sextine dans les langues dérivées du latin* (Paris: Alphonse Lemerre, 1872).

—— *Sonnets* (Paris: Imprimerie d'Amédée Gratiot et Cie, 1840).

—— *Les Vers français et leur prosodie* (Paris: J. Hetzel, 1876).

—— and A. de Belloy, trans., *Le Livre de Job traduit en vers par le Cte F.-L. de Gramont, suivi du Livre de Ruth, traduit en vers par le Mis A. de Belloy* (Paris: Waille, 1843).

Hauvette, Henri, 'Ce que nous savons de Laure (lecture faite à la Sorbonne le 6 avril 1927)', in *Pétrarque: mélanges de littérature et d'histoire publiés par l'Union intellectuelle franco-italienne* (Paris: Librairie Ernest Leroux, 1928), pp. 10–25.

Hugo, Victor, 'Le centenaire de Pétrarque', in *Œuvres complètes de Victor Hugo: Actes et paroles: III: Depuis l'exil 1870–1876* (Paris: J. Hetzel & Cie/A. Quantin, 1884), pp. 317–20.

—— *Œuvres poétiques*, ed. Pierre Albouy, 2 vols (Paris: Gallimard, 1964–7).

Jaucourt, Louis de, 'Vaucluse, fontaine de', in *Encyclopédie, ou dictionnaire raisonné des sciences, des arts et des métiers, par une société de gens de lettres*, ed. Diderot and d'Alembert, 5 vols (Neufchastel: Samuel Faulche; Amsterdam: M. M. Rey, 1751–76, reprinted New York: Readex Microprint Corporation, 1969), III, 941.

Julian, Pierre, *Le Pèlerinage littéraire du Mont Ventoux* (Carpentras: Les Éditions du 'Mt Ventoux', 1937).

Jullien, Marc-Antoine, *La France en 1825, ou mes regrets et mes espérances; discours en vers: seconde édition, suivie de quelques autres poésies détachées du même auteur* (Paris: Chez Antoine-Augustin Renouard, 1825).

Krüdener, Barbara Juliane von, *Valérie, ou Lettres de Gustave de Linar à Ernest de G...*, 2 vols (Paris: Henrichs, 1804).

La Harpe, Jean-François, *Correspondance littéraire, adressée à son altesse impériale M.gr le Grand-Duc, aujourd'hui empereur de Russie, et à M. le comte André Schowalow, chambellan de l'impératrice Catherine II, depuis 1774 jusqu'à 1789*, 6 vols (Paris: Migneret, 1801-7).

—— 'Sur une traduction de quelques poésies de Pétrarque', in *Œuvres de La Harpe, de l'Académie française, accompagnée d'une notice sur sa vie et sur ses ouvrages*, 16 vols (Paris: Verdière, 1820-1), XV, 355-67.

La Lande, Jérôme de, *Voyage d'un François en Italie fait dans les années 1765 & 1766*, 8 vols (Venice and Paris: Chez Desaint, 1769).

La Pommeraye, F. de, *Les Souvenirs poétiques, ou recueil de poésies* (Paris: Chez Eymery, 1821).

—— *Souvenirs poétiques et satiriques: deuxieme édition* (Paris: Chez C. J. Trouvé, 1825).

La Rochefoucauld, François Aymard de, *Poésies intimes* (Paris: Didier et Cie, 1877).

Laforêt, Auguste, 'Cinquième centenaire de Pétrarque: fêtes de Vaucluse–Avignon les 18, 19, et 20 juillet 1874', in *Revue de Marseille et de Provence fondée et publiée au profit des pauvres*, 20.7 (July 1874), 361-76.

Lalaing, comtesse de, *Stances de Messer Angelo Poliziano et poésies extraites de Dante, Pétrarque et Leopardi, traduites de l'italien* (Brussels: Imprimerie de J. Stienon, 1853).

Lamartine, Alphonse de, *Correspondance (1830-1867)*, ed. Christian Croisille, 7 vols (Paris: Honoré Champion, 2000-3); *Correspondance: deuxième série (1807-1829)*, ed. Christian Croisille and Marie-Renée Morin, 5 vols (Paris: Honoré Champion, 2004-7).

—— *Cours familier de littérature*, 28 vols (Paris: Chez l'auteur, 1856-69).

—— *Épîtres* (Paris: Urbain Canel, 1825).

—— *Harmonies poétiques et religieuses*, in *Œuvres complètes*, 41 vols (Paris: Chez l'auteur, 1860-6), II (1860), 197-535.

—— *Œuvres complètes*, 41 vols (Paris: Chez l'auteur, 1860-6).

—— *Œuvres poétiques*, ed. Marius-François Guyard (Paris: Gallimard, 1963).

—— *Trois Poètes italiens* (Paris: A. Lemerre, 1893).

Langlois, Louis, *Morceaux choisis: Catulle, Gallus, Properce, Tibulle, Ovide, Maximien, Pétrarque, et Jean Second; précédés d'une notice biographique sur chacun de ces poètes* (Paris: Leclère fils, 1852).

Larousse, Pierre, *Grand dictionnaire universel du XIXe siècle*, 17 vols in 34 (Geneva: Slatkine, 1982 [originally Paris: Administration du Grand dictionnaire universel, 1866-79]).

Le Duc, Philibert, *Sonnets curieux et sonnets célèbres: étude anthologique & didactique, suivie de sonnets inédits* (Paris: L. Willem; Bourg: Francisque Martin, 1879).

Lemerre, Alphonse, ed., *Anthologie des poètes français du XIXème siècle*, 2 vols (Paris: Alphonse Lemerre, 1887-8).

Leroux, Pierre, '*Poésies de Pétrarque, sonnets, canzones, triomphes*. Traduction complète par le comte F.-L. de Gramont', *La Revue indépendante*, 4 (1842), 347-426.

Loise, Ferdinand, *Histoire de la poésie mise en rapport avec la civilisation en Italie depuis les origines jusqu'à nos jours* (Brussels: Alfred Castaigne; Paris: Thorin & fils, A. Fontemoing, 1895).

Mahul, Emma, *Poésies politiques sur les événements de l'Italie* (Turin: Héritiers Botta, 1862).

—— *Traduction inédite de poëtes siciliens: texte en regard* (Livorno: [n.p.], 1876).

Maniani, G., *Morceaux choisis de classiques italiens précédés d'une introduction historique sur la littérature italienne à l'usage des classes supérieures des lycées: prose et vers* (Paris: Jules Delalain et fils, 1866).

Martial, *Epigrams*, trans. D. R. Shackleton Bailey, 3 vols (Cambridge, MA: Harvard University Press, 1993).

Mézières, Alfred, *Pétrarque: étude d'après de nouveaux documents* (Paris: Didier, 1868).

Mistral, Frédéric, *Lou tresor dóu Felibrige, ou, Dictionnaire provençal-français: embrassant les divers dialectes de la langue d'oc moderne*, 2 vols (Aix-en-Provence: Vve Remondet-Aubin, 1878–86).

Monnier, Marc, *La Renaissance, de Dante à Luther* (Paris: Librairie Firmin-Didot, 1884).

Montesquiou, Anatole de, *Chants divers*, 2 vols (Paris: Amyot, 1843).

—— *Hercule, poème épique*, 2 vols (Paris: A. Lemerre, 1873).

—— *Moïse: poëme en vingt-quatre chants*, 2 vols (Paris: Amyot, 1850).

—— *Myrrha, tragédie d'Alfieri, traduite en vers* (Paris: Amyot, 1856).

—— *Poésies*, 2 vols (Paris: F. Didot, 1820–1).

—— *Poésies de Michel-Ange Buonarotti* (Paris: A. Masson, 1875).

Musset, Alfred de, *Le Fils de Titien*, in *Œuvres complètes en prose*, ed. Maurice Allem (Paris: Gallimard, 1951), pp. 428–69.

—— *Œuvres complètes en prose*, ed. Maurice Allem (Paris: Gallimard, 1951).

—— *Poésies complètes*, ed. Maurice Allem (Paris: Gallimard, 1957).

—— 'Salon de 1836', in *Œuvres complètes en prose*, ed. Maurice Allem (Paris: Gallimard, 1951), pp. 969–97.

Musset, Paul de, *Biographie de Alfred de Musset, sa vie et ses œuvres*, 4th edn (Paris: G. Charpentier, 1877).

Nerval, Gérard de, *Poésies allemandes: Klopstock, Goethe, Schiller, Burger: morceaux choisis et traduits* (Paris: Bureau de la Bibliothèque choisie, 1830).

Nolhac, Pierre de, 'L'Année de Pétrarque', in *Pétrarque: mélanges de littérature et d'histoire publiés par l'Union intellectuelle franco-italienne* (Paris: Librairie Ernest Leroux, 1928), pp. 5–8.

—— *Inauguration de la maison de Pétrarque à Vaucluse: le dimanche 7 octobre, 1928: discours de M. Pierre de Nolhac au nom de l'Académie française* (Paris: Typographie de Firmin-Didot et Cie, 1928).

Nostredame, Jean de, *Vies des plus célèbres poètes provençaux: nouvelle édition*, ed. Camille Chabaneau and Joseph Anglade (Paris: Honoré Champion, 1913).

Olivier-Vitalis, Hyacinthe d', *L'Illustre Chatelaine des environs de Vaucluse, la Laure de Pétrarque: dissertation et examen critique* (Paris: Librairie historique et curieuse de J. Teschener, 1842).

Paris, Gaston, *La Poésie du Moyen Âge: leçons et lectures*, 2 vols (Paris: Librairie Hachette, 1885–95).

Péricaud, Antoine (l'aîné), *Curiosités littéraires: Pétrarque & Pétrone; Louis Sygée & Nicolas Chorier* (Lyon: Imprimerie d'Aimé Vingtrinier, 1862).

Pierre, Théodore, *Abrégé de l'histoire de Pétrarque contenant les principaux traits de sa vie et les différents phases de son amour avec la belle Laure d'après ses propres écrits et ceux des meilleurs auteurs et traducteurs anciens* (Vaucluse: Maria Brun; Avignon: Seguin frères, 1879).

Piot, Citoyen, 'Proposition d'ériger à Vaucluse un monument public à la gloire de Pétrarque, le 20 juillet 1804 (1er Thermidor an 12), jour séculaire de sa naissance', in Athénée de Vaucluse, *Mémoires de l'Athénée de Vaucluse, contenant le compte rendu des travaux de cette Société depuis son institution, et le Recueil des ouvrages en prose et en vers, lus à sa séance publique le 2 Brumaire an XII* (Avignon: Alph. Berenguier, an XII (1804)), pp. 105–13.

Planche, Gustave, 'Études sur l'art et la poésie en Italie: II. Pétrarque', *Revue des deux mondes*, 18 (1847), 997–1018.

Proust, Marcel, *À la recherche du temps perdu*, ed. Jean-Yves Tadié, 4 vols (Paris: Gallimard, 1987–9).

—— *Correspondance*, ed. Philip Kolb, 21 vols (Paris: Plon, 1970–93).

Renan, Ernest, *Qu'est-ce qu'une nation? Conférence faite en Sorbonne, le 11 mars 1882*, 2nd edn (Paris: Calmann Lévy Éditeur, 1882).

—— 'What is a nation?', trans. Martin Thom, in *Nation and Narration*, ed. Homi K. Bhabha (Abingdon: Routledge, 1990), pp. 8–22.

Roman, J. J. T. (abbé), *Le Génie de Pétrarque, ou imitation en vers françois, de ses plus belles poésies, précédée de la Vie de cet Homme célèbre, dont les actions & les Écrits sont une des plus singulières époques de l'Histoire & de la Littérature moderne* (Parma and Avignon: Joseph Guichard, 1778; Parma and Paris: Lacombe, 1778).

—— *Vie de François Pétrarque, célèbre poëte italien, dont les actions & les écrits sont une des plus singulières époques de l'histoire & de la littérature moderne ; suivie d'une imitation en vers François de ses plus belles poésies* (Vaucluse and Paris: J. Cussac, 1786).

Roulleaux, Eugène, *Pétrarque et les fêtes du centenaire à Vaucluse et à Avignon (18, 19 et 20 juillet 1874)* (Bourg: Imprimerie P. Comte-Milliet, 1875).

Rousseau, Jean-Jacques, *Julie, ou la Nouvelle Héloïse*, in *Œuvres complètes*, ed. Bernard Gagnebin and Marcel Raymond, 5 vols (Paris: Gallimard, 1959–95), II (1961), 1–793, with notes pp. 1333–829

Sade, Jacques François Paul Aldonce de (abbé), *Mémoires pour la vie de François Pétrarque, tirés de ses œuvres et des auteurs contemporains, avec des notes ou dissertations, & les pieces justificatives*, 3 vols (Amsterdam: Arskée & Mercus, 1764–7).

Sainte-Beuve, Charles-Augustin, *Les Consolations: poésies* (Paris: U. Canel, 1830).

—— *Livre d'amour* (Paris: A. Durel, 1904).

—— *Œuvres: Premiers lundis, Portraits littéraires, Portraits des femmes*, ed. Maxime Leroy, 2 vols (Paris: Gallimard, 1949–51).

—— *Tableau historique et critique de la poésie française et du théâtre français au seizième siècle* (Paris: Sautelet et Compagnie, 1828).

—— *Volupté*, ed. André Guyaux (Paris: Gallimard, 1986).

Saint-Geniès, Léonce de, *Balder, fils d'Odin: poëme scandinave en six chants, suivi de notes sur l'histoire, la religion et les mœurs des nations celtiques* (Paris: L'Éditeur, 1824).

—— and Joseph-Henri de Saur, *Les Aventures de Faust, et sa descente aux enfers*, 3 vols (Paris: Arthus Bertrand, 1825).

Saint-Martin, Jean, *La Fontaine de Vaucluse et ses souvenirs: dessins de Bill, Eysséric, Karl, Paul Saïn et Georges Roux* (Paris: Librairie générale de L. Sauvaitre, 1891).

Sand, George, *Adriani* (Paris: Éditions France-Empire, 1980).

—— *Correspondance*, ed. Georges Lubin, 26 vols (Paris: Éditions Garnier Frères, 1964–95).

—— *Histoire de ma vie*, 10 vols (Saint-Cyr-sur-Loire: Christian Pirot, 1993–2003).

Schlegel, Friedrich, *Literary Notebooks 1797–1801*, ed. Hans Eichner (London: The Athlone Press, 1957).

Seguin, F., *Pèlerinage au Mont Ventoux par F. Seguin suivi de 'Santo-Croux, douas letro a ma bravo sore touneto' par J. Roumanille avec un appendice relatif au Mont Ventoux, comprenant la lettre de Pétrarque, une notice sur M. Requien, et autres documents divers recueillis par F. S.* (Avignon: Chez F. Seguin aîné, 1852).

Sismondi, J. C. L. Simonde de, *De la littérature du Midi de l'Europe*, 4 vols (Paris and Strasbourg: Treuttel et Würtz, 1813).

Soullier, Charles, *Mes Sansonnets: précédés de l'historique du sonnet et de la critique des sonnets célèbres, de diverses pièces de littérature très-curieuses, entre autres le 'Tableau de la vie', ouvrage rare et épuisé* (Paris: Chez l'auteur, 1878).

Staël, Germaine de, *Corinne ou l'Italie*, ed. Simone Balayé (Paris: Gallimard, 1985).

Stendhal, *The Charterhouse of Parma*, trans. C. K. Scott Moncrieff, 2 vols (London: Chatto & Windus, 1926).

—— *La Chartreuse de Parme*, in Stendhal, *Œuvres romanesques complètes*, ed. Yves Ansel, Philippe Berthier, Xavier Bourdenet, and Serge Linkès, 3 vols (Paris: Gallimard, 2005–14), III, 137–597.

—— 'La Comédie est impossible en 1836', in Stendhal, *Œuvres complètes*, ed. Victor Del Litto and Ernest Abravanel, new edn, 50 vols (Geneva: Edito-Service S. A., 1968–74), XLVI (1972), 265–78.

—— *Histoire de la peinture en Italie*, ed. Paul Arbelet, in Stendhal, *Œuvres complètes*, ed. Victor Del Litto and Ernest Abravanel, new edn, 50 vols (Geneva: Edito-Service S. A., 1968–74), XXVI–XXVII (1969).

—— *Journal littéraire*, ed. Victor Del Litto, in Stendhal, *Œuvres complètes*, ed. Victor Del Litto and Ernest Abravanel, new edn, 50 vols (Geneva: Edito-Service S. A., 1968–74), XXXIII–XXXV (1970).

—— *Mémoires d'un touriste*, ed. Louis Royer, in Stendhal, *Œuvres complètes*, ed. Victor Del Litto and Ernest Abravanel, new edn, 50 vols (Geneva: Edito-Service S. A., 1968–74), XV–XVII (1968).

—— *Œuvres complètes*, ed. Victor Del Litto and Ernest Abravanel, new edn, 50 vols (Geneva: Edito-Service S. A., 1968–74).

—— *Promenades dans Rome*, in Stendhal, *Voyages en Italie*, ed. Victor Del Litto (Paris: Gallimard, 1973), pp. 593–1189.

—— 'Rome, Naples et Florence (1826)', in Stendhal, *Voyages en Italie*, ed. Victor Del Litto (Paris: Gallimard, 1973), pp. 285–592.

—— *Souvenirs d'égotisme*, in *Œuvres intimes*, ed. Victor Del Litto, 2 vols (Paris: Gallimard, 1981–2), II, 425–521.

—— *Vie de Henry Brulard*, in *Œuvres intimes*, ed. Victor Del Litto, 2 vols (Paris: Gallimard, 1981–2), II, 523–963.

Terris, Paul, *Le Centenaire de Pétrarque: rapport présenté à la Société littéraire d'Apt dans la Séance du 20 septembre 1874* (Apt: Typographie et lithographie J. S. Jean, 1876).

—— *Pétrarque: ode qui a obtenu la médaille d'argent de l'académie du Gard aux jeux floraux du centenaire 18–20 juillet 1874* (Carpentras: Chez P. Prière, 1874).

Topin, Hippolyte, *Études sur la langue italienne, précédées d'un parallèle entre Dante et Klopstock* (Florence: Typographie Galiléienne; Paris: Chez les principaux libraires, 1855).

Tréverret, Armand-Germain de, 'À M. Ernest Cabadé: lettre pour servir de préface à une traduction en vers des sonnets de Pétrarque', in Ernest Cabadé, *Les Sonnets de Pétrarque traduits en sonnets français avec une préface de M. de Tréverret, professeur de littératures étrangères à la Faculté des Lettres de Bordeaux, et un portrait authentique de Pétrarque (trouvé à la Bibliothèque nationale par M. Pierre de Nolhac)* (Paris: Alphonse Lemerre, 1902), pp. vii–xiii.

Troubat, Jules, *Plume et pinceau: études de littérature et d'art* (Paris: Isidore Liseux, 1878).

Vallon, François, *Écrin de poésies anglaises, allemandes, italiennes et espagnoles* (Paris: Alphonse Lemerre, 1886).

Verlaine, Paul, *Œuvres poétiques complètes*, ed. Yves-Gérard Le Dantec, rev. Jacques Borel (Paris: Gallimard, 1962).

Villemain, A.-F., *Cours de littérature française: tableau de la littérature du Moyen Âge en France, en Italie, en Espagne et en Angleterre: nouvelle édition revue, corrigée et augmentée*, 2 vols (Paris: Didier, 1851 [first edition 1846]).

Virgil, *Eclogues, Georgics, Aeneid 1–6*, trans. H. Rushton Fairclough, rev. G. P. Goold (Cambridge, MA: Harvard University Press, 1999).

Vissac, le baron de, 'Discours du président de l'Académie', in Académie de Vaucluse, *Sixième centenaire de la naissance de Pétrarque célébré à Vaucluse et Avignon les 16, 17, et 18 juillet 1904* (Avignon: François Seguin, 1904), pp. 60–8.

Voltaire *Correspondence and Related Documents*, ed. Theodore Besterman, 51 vols (Oxford: The Voltaire Foundation, 1968–77).

—— *Essai sur les mœurs et l'esprit des nations*, ed. Bruno Bernard, John Renwick, Nicholas Cronk, and Janet Godden, 9 vols (Oxford: Voltaire Foundation, 2009–).

—— 'Lettre aux Auteurs de la *Gazette littéraire*', in 'Supplément à la *Gazette littéraire de l'Europe*: mercredi 6 juin 1764', *Gazette littéraire de l'Europe. Tome premier. Comprenant les mois de mars, avril & mai 1764* (Paris: De l'Imprimerie de la Gazette de France, aux Galeries du Louvre, 1764), pp. 391–6.

Secondary Works

Alduy, Cécile, *Politique des 'Amours': poétique et genèse d'un genre français nouveau (1544–1560)* (Geneva: Droz, 2007).

Alfie, Fabian, 'Old Lady Avignon: Petrarch's *Rerum vulgarium fragmenta* 136 and the topos of *Vituperium in vetulam*', *Italian Culture*, 30.2 (2012), 100–9.

Amadou, Robert, 'Balzac et Saint-Martin', *L'Année balzacienne* (1965), 35–60.

Ascoli, Albert Russell, 'Petrarch's Middle Age: Memory, Imagination, History, and "The Ascent of Mont Ventoux"', *Stanford Italian Review*, 10.1 (1991), 5–43 (repr. in Albert Russell Ascoli, *A Local Habitation and a Name: Imagining Histories in the Italian Renaissance* (New York: Fordham University Press, 2011), pp. 21–58).

Ascoli, Albert Russell, and Unn Falkeid, 'Introduction', in *The Cambridge Companion to Petrarch*, ed. Albert Russell Ascoli and Unn Falkeid (Cambridge: Cambridge University Press, 2015), pp. 1–9.

Ascoli, Albert Russell, and Unn Falkeid, eds, *The Cambridge Companion to Petrarch* (Cambridge: Cambridge University Press, 2015).

Audeh, Aida, and Nick Havely, eds, *Dante in the Long Nineteenth Century: Nationality, Identity, and Appropriation* (Oxford: Oxford University Press, 2012).

Augry-Merlino, Muriel, 'Pétrarque, Stendhal et la souveraineté féminine', in *Dynamique d'une expansion culturelle: Pétrarque en Europe XIVe–XXe siècle: actes du XXVIe congrès international du CEFI, Turin et Chambéry, 11–15 décembre 1995: à la mémoire de Franco Simone*, ed. Pierre Blanc (Paris: Honoré Champion, 2001), pp. 457–64.

Bachelard, Gaston, *La Poétique de la rêverie* (Paris: Presses Universitaires de France, 1960).

Bakhtin, Mikhail, *The Dialogic Imagination: Four Essays*, trans. Michael Holquist (Austin: University of Texas Press, 1981).

Bales, Richard, *Persuasion in the French Personal Novel: Studies of Chateaubriand, Constant, Balzac, Nerval, and Fromentin* (Birmingham, AL: Summa Publications, 1997).

Balibar, René, and Dominique Laporte, *Le Français national: politique et pratiques de la langue nationale sous la Révolution française* (Paris: Hachette, 1974).

Balmas, Enea, 'Prime traduzioni del *Canzoniere* nel cinquecento francese', in *Traduzione e tradizione europea del Petrarca: atti del III convegno sui problemi della traduzione letteraria, Monselice, 9 giugno 1974* (Padua: Antenore Editrice, 1975), pp. 37–54.

Balsamo, Jean, 'Le "premier cercle" du pétrarquisme français (1533–1540)', in *La Postérité répond à Pétrarque: sept siècles de fortune pétrarquienne en France: actes du colloque tenu à l'Hôtel de Sade et à l'Université d'Avignon et des Pays de Vaucluse les 22, 23, 24 janvier 2004*, ed. Ève Duperray (Paris: Beauchesne, 2006), pp. 127–45.

—— ed., *Les Poètes français de la Renaissance et Pétrarque* (Geneva: Droz, 2004).

Barański, Zygmunt G., and Theodore J. Cachey, eds, *Petrarch and Dante: Anti-Dantism, Metaphysics, Tradition* (Notre Dame, IN: University of Notre Dame Press, 2009).

Barolini, Teodolinda, *Dante and the Origins of Italian Literary Culture* (New York: Fordham University Press, 2006).

—— 'The Making of a Lyric Sequence: Time and Narrative in Petrarch's *Rerum vulgarium fragmenta*', *Modern Language Notes*, 140.1 (1989), 1–38 (repr. in Teodolinda Barolini, *Dante and the Origins of Italian Literary Culture* (New York: Fordham University Press, 2006), pp. 193–223).

—— 'Petrarch at the Crossroads of Hermeneutics and Philology: Editorial Lapses, Narrative Impositions, and Wilkins' Doctrine of the Nine Forms of the *Rerum vulgarium fragmenta*', in *Petrarch and the Textual Origins of Interpretation*, ed. Teodolinda Barolini and H. Wayne Storey (Leiden: Brill, 2007), pp. 21–44.

—— and H. Wayne Storey, eds, *Petrarch and the Textual Origins of Interpretation* (Leiden: Brill, 2007).

Barthouil, Georges, 'Traductions françaises du *Canzoniere* de Pétrarque', *Cuadernos de filologia italiana*, Extra 12 (2005), 171–85.

Bartuschat, Johannes, 'Sofonisba e Massinissa. Dall'*Africa* e dal *De viris* ai *Trionfi*', in *Petrarca e i suoi lettori*, ed. Vittorio Caratozzolo and Georges Güntert (Ravenna: Longo, 2000), pp. 110–41.

Behler, Diana, *The Theory of the Novel in Early German Romanticism* (Bern: Peter Lang, 1978).

Bellati, Giovanna, 'Il primo traduttore del *Canzoniere* petrarchesco nel Rinascimento francese: Vasquin Philieul', *Aevum*, 59.2 (1985), 371–98.

Belloni, Gino, *Laura tra Petrarca e Bembo: studi sul commento umanistico-rinascimentale al 'Canzoniere'* (Padua: Antenore Editrice, 1992).

Benedetto, Luigi Foscolo, 'Victor Hugo e Dante', *Lettere italiane*, 20.1 (1968), 40–55.

Bergin, Thomas G., 'Introduction', in *Petrarch's Bucolicum carmen*, ed. and trans. Thomas G. Bergin (New Haven, CT: Yale University Press, 1974), pp. ix–xvii.

Berman, Antoine, *Pour une critique des traductions: John Donne* (Paris: Gallimard, 1995).

—— *Towards a Translation Criticism: John Donne*, trans. and ed. Françoise Massardier-Kenney (Kent, OH: Kent State University Press, 2009).

Bermann, Sandra L., *The Sonnet Over Time: A Study in the Sonnets of Petrarch, Shakespeare and Baudelaire* (Chapel Hill: University of North Carolina Press, 1988).

Bernard-Griffiths, Simone, Pierre Glaudes, and Bertrand Vibert, eds, *La Fabrique du Moyen Âge au XIXe siècle: représentations du moyen âge dans la culture et la littérature françaises du XIXe siècle* (Paris: Honoré Champion, 2006).

Bernardo, Aldo S., *Petrarch, Laura and the 'Triumphs'* (Albany: State University of New York Press, 1974).

—— *Petrarch, Scipio and the 'Africa': The Birth of Humanism's Dream* (Baltimore: Johns Hopkins Press, 1962).

Bersani, Leo, *Balzac to Beckett: Center and Circumference in French Fiction* (New York: Oxford University Press, 1970).

Berthier, Philippe, *Stendhal et la Sainte Famille* (Geneva: Droz, 1983).

Bertolani, Maria Cecilia, *Il corpo glorioso: studi sui 'Trionfi' del Petrarca* (Rome: Carocci, 2001).

—— *Petrarca e la visione dell'eterno* (Bologna: Il Mulino, 2005).

Bertoli, Lide, *La Fortuna del Petrarca in Francia nella prima metà del secolo XIX: note ed appunti* (Livorno: Raffaello Giusti, 1916).

—— 'I traduttori francesi del Petrarca nel secolo XIX', in *Raccolta di studi di storia e critica letteraria dedicata a Francesco Flamini da' suoi discepoli* (Pisa: Mariotti, 1918), pp. 653–79.

Biddick, Kathleen, *The Shock of Medievalism* (Durham, NC: Duke University Press, 1998).

Bishop, Morris, *Petrarch and his World* (London: Chatto & Windus, 1964).

Blanc, Pierre, ed., *Dynamique d'une expansion culturelle: Pétrarque en Europe XIVe–XXe siècle: actes du XXVIe congrès international du CEFI, Turin et Chambéry, 11–15 décembre 1995: à la mémoire de Franco Simone* (Paris: Honoré Champion, 2001).

Blevins, Jacob, ed., *Dialogism and Lyric Self-Fashioning: Bakhtin and the Voices of a Genre* (Selinsgrove, PA: Susquehanna University Press, 2008).

Bloch, R. Howard, and Stephen G. Nichols, eds, *Medievalism and the Modernist Temper* (Baltimore and London: Johns Hopkins University Press, 1996).

Bloncourt-Herselin, Jacqueline, *Lamartine et l'Italie* (Paris: Le Cerf-Volant, 1970).

Borel, Jacques, '*Le Lys dans la vallée' et les sources profondes de la création balzacienne* (Paris: Librairie José Corti, 1961).

Bouquet-Boyer, Marie-Thérèse, 'Franz Liszt: les sonnets de Pétrarque pour piano', in *Dynamique d'une expansion culturelle: Pétrarque en Europe XIVe–XXe siècle: actes du XXVIe congrès international du CEFI, Turin et Chambéry, 11–15 décembre 1995: à la mémoire de Franco Simone*, ed. Pierre Blanc (Paris: Honoré Champion, 2001), pp. 575–9.

Brombert, Victor, *The Hidden Reader: Stendhal, Balzac, Hugo, Baudelaire, Flaubert* (Cambridge, MA: Harvard University Press, 1988).

Bronfen, Elisabeth, *Over Her Dead Body: Death, Femininity and the Aesthetic* (Manchester: Manchester University Press, 1992).

Brooks, Peter, 'L'invention de l'écriture (et du langage) dans *La Chartreuse de Parme*', *Stendhal Club*, 78 (1978), 183–90.

—— 'Virtue-tripping: Notes on *Le Lys dans la vallée*', *Yale French Studies*, 50 (1974), 150–62.

Brovia, Romana, 'Du nouveau sur la fortune du *De remediis* en France (XIVe–XVIe siècles)', in *La Postérité répond à Pétrarque: sept siècles de fortune pétrarquienne en France: actes du colloque tenu à l'Hôtel de Sade et à l'Université d'Avignon et des Pays de Vaucluse les 22, 23, 24 janvier 2004*, ed. Ève Duperray (Paris: Beauchesne, 2006), pp. 87–110.

—— *Itinerari del petrarchismo latino: tradizione e ricezione del 'De remediis utriusque fortune' in Francia e in Borgogna (secc. XIV–XVI)* (Alessandria: Edizioni dell'Orso, 2013).

Brunot, Ferdinand, *Histoire de la langue française des origines à nos jours*, 13 vols (Paris: Librairie Armand Colin, 1967–8).

Bugliani-Knox, Francesca, '"Galeotto fu il libro e chi lo scrisse": Nineteenth-Century English Translations, Interpretations and Reworkings of Dante's Paolo and Francesca', *Dante Studies*, 115 (1997), 221–50.

Cabaillot, Claire, 'Alfred Mézières et la critique du XIXe siècle', in *La Postérité répond à Pétrarque: sept siècles de fortune pétrarquienne en France: actes du colloque tenu à l'Hôtel de Sade et à l'Université d'Avignon et des Pays de Vaucluse les 22, 23, 24 janvier 2004*, ed. Ève Duperray (Paris: Beauchesne, 2006), pp. 197–207.

Cachey, Theodore J., 'From Shipwreck to Port: RVF 189 and the Making of the *Canzoniere*', *Modern Language Notes*, 120 (2005), 30–49.

—— 'Introduction', in *Petrarch's Guide to the Holy Land: Itinerary to the Sepulcher of Our Lord Jesus Christ*, ed. and trans. Theodore J. Cachey (Notre Dame, IN: University of Notre Dame Press, 2002) pp. 1–50.

—— '"Peregrinus (quasi) ubique": Petrarca e la storia del viaggio', *Intersezioni: rivista di storia delle idee*, 27 (1997), 369–84.

Cantor, Norman F., *Inventing the Middle Ages: The Lives, Works, and Ideas of the Great Medievalists of the Twentieth Century* (New York: W. Morrow, 1991).

Cardini, Roberto, and Donatella Coppini, eds, *Petrarca e Agostino* (Rome: Bulzoni, 2004).

Carrara, Enrico, 'La leggenda di Laura (1934)', in *Studi petrarcheschi ed altri scritti: raccolta a cura di amici e discepoli* (Turin: Bottega d'Erasmo, 1959), pp. 77–111.

Casillo, Robert, *The Empire of Stereotypes: Germaine de Staël and the Idea of Italy* (New York: Palgrave Macmillan, 2006).

Cassin, Barbara, *La Nostalgie: quand donc est-on chez soi? Ulysse, Énée, Arendt* (Paris: Librairie Arthème Fayard/Pluriel, 2015).

Catel, Olivier, 'Terre natale et maison onirique: l'expression et la commémoration de soi', in *Lamartine: autobiographie, mémoires, fiction de soi*, ed. Nicolas Courtinat (Clermont-Ferrand: Presses Universitaires Blaise-Pascal, 2009), pp. 63–73.

Cecchetti, Dario, *Il petrarchismo in Francia* (Turin: G. Giappichelli, 1970).

Certeau, Michel de, Dominique Julia, and Jacques Revel, *Une Politique de la langue: la Révolution française et les patois: l'enquête de Grégoire* (Paris: Gallimard, 1975).

Cesareo, G. A., *Su le 'poesie volgari' del Petrarca: nuove ricerche* (Rocca S. Casciano: Licinio Cappelli, 1898).

Challandes, Laure, 'D'Abélard à Julie: un héritage renversé', in *L'Amour dans 'La Nouvelle Héloïse': texte et intertexte: Actes du Colloque de Genève (10-11-12 juin 1999)*, ed. Jacques Berchtold and François Rosset (Geneva: Droz, 2002) (= *Annales de la société Jean-Jacques Rousseau*, 44 (2002)), pp. 55–80.

Cherpack, Clifton, 'Voltaire's Criticism of Petrarch', *The Romanic Review*, 46 (1955), 101–7.

Chevrel, Yves, Lieven D'Hulst, and Christine Lombez, eds, *Histoire des traductions en langue française: XIXe siècle: 1815–1914* (Lagrasse: Éditions Verdier, 2012).

Chines, Loredana, Floriana Calitti, and Roberto Gigliucci, eds, *Il petrarchismo: un modello di poesia per l'Europa*, 2 vols (Rome: Bulzoni, 2006).

Cipollone, Annalisa, 'Peregrinus ubique. Petrarca viaggiatore (nello spazio e nel tempo)', in *Il viaggio e le arti: il contesto italiano*, ed. Lucia Bertolini and Annalisa Cipollone (Pescara: Edizioni dell'Orso, 2009), pp. 61–88.

Clements, Pam, 'Authenticity', in *Medievalism: Key Critical Terms*, ed. Elizabeth Emery and Richard Utz (Cambridge: D. S. Brewer, 2014), pp. 19–26.

Cochin, Henry, 'Les "Epistolae metricae" de Pétrarque: remarques sur le texte et la chronologie', *Giornale storico della letteratura italiana*, 74 (1919), 1–40.

—— *Le Frère de Pétrarque et le livre 'Du repos des religieux'* (Paris: Librairie Émile Bouillon, 1903).

—— 'Les récents progrès des Études Petrarquesques: Arnaldo Foresti', *Études italiennes*, 8 (1926), 85–104 and 140–70.

Condorelli, Emma, 'Emma Mahul des comtes Dejean, une pétrarquiste oubliée', *Revue des études italiennes*, 31 (1985), 103–11.

Contini, Gianfranco, 'Préhistoire de l'*aura* de Pétrarque', in *Actes et mémoires du premier congrès international de langue et littérature du Midi de la France* (Avignon: Palais du Roure, 1957), pp. 113–18.

—— *Varianti e altra linguistica: Una raccolta di saggi 1938–1968* (Turin: Einaudi, 1970).

Cordié, Carlo, *Ricerche stendhaliane* (Naples: Morano Editore, 1967).

Costa, Daniela, 'La ricezione francese del *Secretum*', in *Francesco Petrarca, l'opera latina: tradizione e fortuna: atti del XVI Convegno internazionale (Chianciano-Pienza 19-22 luglio 2004*, ed. Luisa Secchi Tarugi (Florence: Franco Cesati, 2006), pp. 477–84.

Cottino-Jones, Marga, 'The Myth of Apollo and Daphne in Petrarch's *Canzoniere*: The Dynamics and Literary Function of Transformation', in *Francis Petrarch, Six Centuries*

Later: A Symposium, ed. Aldo Scaglione (Chapel Hill: University of North Carolina; Chicago: The Newberry Library, 1975), pp. 152–76.

Counson, Albert, *Dante en France* (Erlangen: Fr. Junge, 1906).

Crouzet, Michel, *Stendhal et l'italianité: essai de mythologie romantique* (Paris: Librairie José Corti, 1982).

Culler, Jonathan, *Theory of the Lyric* (Cambridge, MA: Harvard University Press, 2015).

D'Ovidio, Francesco, *Studii sul Petrarca e sul Tasso* (Rome: Edizioni A.P.E., 1926).

Dakyns, Janine R., *The Middle Ages in French Literature, 1851–1900* (London: Oxford University Press, 1973).

David, Michel, 'La canzone CXXVI', *Lectura Petrarce*, 8 (1988), 111–61.

Davin, Emmanuel, 'Les différentes Laure de Pétrarque', *Bulletin de l'Association Guillaume Budé: lettres d'humanité*, 15 (1956), 83–104.

Davis, Kathleen, and Nadia Altschul, eds, *Medievalisms in the Postcolonial World: The Idea of the 'Middle Ages' Outside Europe* (Baltimore: Johns Hopkins University Press, 2009).

De Sanctis, Francesco, *Saggio critico sul Petrarca*, ed. Ettore Bonora (Bari: Gius. Laterza & figli, 1954).

Dédéyan, Charles, *Lamartine et la Toscane* (Moncalieri: Centro interuniversitario di ricerche sul 'Viaggio in Italia'; Geneva: Slatkine, 1981).

Dejob, Charles, 'Le "Secretum" de Pétrarque', *Bulletin italien*, 3.1 (1903), 261–80.

Delisle, Léopold, *Anciennes traductions françaises du traité de Pétrarque 'Sur les remèdes de l'une et l'autre fortune'* (Paris: Imprimerie nationale, 1891).

Dentith, Simon, *Parody* (London and New York: Routledge, 2000).

D'Hulst, Lieven, ed., *Cent ans de théorie française de la traduction: de Batteux à Littré (1748–1847)* (Lille: Presses Universitaires de Lille, 1990).

Didier, Béatrice, *Stendhal ou la dictée du bonheur: paroles, échos et écritures dans 'La Chartreuse de Parme'* (Paris: Klincksieck, 2002).

Dinshaw, Carolyn, *How Soon is Now? Medieval Texts, Amateur Readers, and the Queerness of Time* (Durham, NC: Duke University Press, 2012).

DiVanna, Isabel, *Reconstructing the Middle Ages: Gaston Paris and the Development of Nineteenth-Century Medievalism* (Newcastle upon Tyne: Cambridge Scholars, 2008).

Domenech, Jacques, 'Saint-Preux et Julie lecteurs du Tasse: connivence érotique et spiritualité amoureuse dans *La Nouvelle Héloïse* (Quand Rousseau "se fait un rempart du Tasse" dans *La Nouvelle Héloïse*)', in *L'Amour dans 'La Nouvelle Héloïse': texte et intertexte: Actes du Colloque de Genève (10–11–12 juin 1999)*, ed. Jacques Berchtold and François Rosset (Geneva: Droz, 2002) (= *Annales de la société Jean-Jacques Rousseau*, 44 (2002)), pp. 119–47.

Donderi, Bruno, 'The French Renaissance Versions of the Canzone "Vergine Bella"', in *Petrarch: The Self and the World*, ed. Supriya Chaudhuri and Sukanta Chaudhuri (Kolkata: Jadavpur University Press, 2012), pp. 226–40.

Dotti, Ugo, *Petrarca a Parma* (Reggio Emilia: Edizioni Diabasis, 2006).

Duperray, Ève, *Galeria d'une triade mythique: Pétrarque, Laure, Vaucluse* (Fontaine-de-Vaucluse: Musée Pétrarque, 1995).

—— 'Le mythe littéraire de Vaucluse dans le roman pétrarquiste de *L'Astrée* (1607–1628) à *Adriani* (1853)', in *Dynamique d'une expansion culturelle: Pétrarque en Europe XIVe–XXe siècle: actes du XXVIe congrès international du CEFI, Turin et Chambéry, 11–15 décembre 1995: à la mémoire de Franco Simone*, ed. Pierre Blanc (Paris: Honoré Champion, 2001), pp. 417–27.

—— *L'Or des mots: une lecture de Pétrarque et du mythe littéraire de Vaucluse des origines à l'orée du XXe siècle: histoire du pétrarquisme en France* (Paris: Publications de la Sorbonne, 1997).

—— 'Le pétrarquisme en Provence (1804–1937): heures de gloire et crépuscule', in *La Postérité répond à Pétrarque: sept siècles de fortune pétrarquienne en France: actes du colloque tenu à l'Hôtel de Sade et à l'Université d'Avignon et des Pays de Vaucluse les 22, 23, 24 janvier 2004*, ed. Ève Duperray (Paris: Beauchesne, 2006), pp. 209–17.

—— ed., *La Postérité répond à Pétrarque: sept siècles de fortune pétrarquienne en France: actes du colloque tenu à l'Hôtel de Sade et à l'Université d'Avignon et des Pays de Vaucluse les 22, 23, 24 janvier 2004* (Paris: Beauchesne, 2006).

Durling, Robert M., 'The Ascent of Mt. Ventoux and the Crisis of Allegory', *Italian Quarterly*, 18 (1974), 7–28.

Edl, Élisabeth, and Wolfgang Matz, 'Un sonnet de Pétrarque dans *La Chartreuse de Parme*', *L'Année stendhalienne*, 7 (2008), 379–84.

Emery, Elizabeth, and Richard Utz, eds, *Medievalism: Key Critical Terms* (Cambridge: D. S. Brewer, 2014).

Enenkel, Karl A. E., and Jan Papy, eds, *Petrarch and his Readers in the Renaissance* (Leiden: Brill, 2006).

Enterline, Lynn, 'Embodied Voices: Petrarch Reading (Himself Reading) Ovid', in *Desire in the Renaissance: Psychoanalysis and Literature*, ed. Valeria Finucci and Regina Schwartz (Princeton, NJ: Princeton University Press, 1994), pp. 120–45.

Fabrizio-Costa, Silvia, 'La prima traduzione francese della *Posteritati*: testo e contesto (1644–1645), in *Francesco Petrarca, l'opera latina: tradizione e fortuna: atti del XVI Convegno internazionale (Chianciano–Pienza 19–22 luglio 2004*, ed. Luisa Secchi Tarugi (Florence: Franco Cesati, 2006), pp. 485–502.

Falconnet, Ernest, *Alphonse de Lamartine: études biographiques, littéraires et politiques* (Paris: Furne et Cie, 1840).

Falkeid, Unn, *The Avignon Papacy Contested: Power and Politics in Fourteenth-Century Literature* (Cambridge, MA: Harvard University Press, forthcoming).

Faxon, Alicia Craig, 'Bath/Bathing', in *Encyclopedia of Comparative Iconography: Themes Depicted in Works of Art*, ed. Helene E. Roberts, 2 vols (Chicago: Fitzroy Dearborn, 1998), I, 109–16.

Fenzi, Enrico, 'Note petrarchesche: R.V.F. XVI, *Movesi il vecchierel*', *Italianistica*, 25.1 (1996), 43–62.

Ferrante, Gennaro, 'Laura de Sade tra leggenda e identificazione storica: la testimonianza inedita di un biografo di Petrarca', *Annali dell'Istituto italiano per gli studi storici*, 24 (2009), 169–99.

Ferré, Vincent, ed., *Médiévalisme, modernité du Moyen Âge* (Paris: L'Harmattan, 2010).

Fontana, Alessio, 'La filologia romanza e il problema del rapporto Petrarca-trovatori (premesse per una ripresa del problema secondo nuove prospettive)', in *Petrarca 1304–1374: Beiträge zu Werk und Wirkung*, ed. Fritz Schalk (Frankfurt am Main: Vittorio Klostermann, 1975), pp. 51–70.

Forster, Leonard, *The Icy Fire: Five Studies in European Petrarchism* (Cambridge: Cambridge University Press, 1969).

Forsyth, Elliott, 'Baudelaire and the Petrarchan Tradition', *Australian Journal of French Studies* 16 (1979), 187–97.

Foster, Kenelm, 'Beatrice or Medusa', in *Italian Studies Presented to E. R. Vincent*, ed. C. P. Brand, K. Foster, and U. Limentani (Cambridge: Heffer, 1962), pp. 41–56.

Foucart, Claude, 'Les grandes tendances du mythe du Moyen Âge dans la littérature française à la fin du XIXème siècle', in *L'Image du Moyen Âge dans la littérature française: colloque organisé par le département de français de l'U.E.R. de Lettres et Langues à l'occasion du 550ème anniversaire de l'Université de Poitiers, 7-8-9 mai 1981*, ed. Michel Autrand, 2 vols (=*La Licorne*, 6.1–2 (1982)), II, 145–75.

Françon, Marcel, 'Vasquin Philieul, traducteur de Pétrarque', *French Studies*, 4.3 (1950), 216–26.

Frappier-Mazur, Lucienne, 'Le régime de l'aveu dans *Le Lys dans la vallée*: formes et fonctions de l'aveu écrit', *Revue des sciences humaines*, 175 (1979), 8–16.

Galbraith, V. H., 'Nationality and Language in Medieval England', *Transactions of the Royal Historical Society*, 23 (1941), 113–28.

Gardair, Jean-Michel, 'Encore sur Emma Mahul', *Revue des études italiennes*, 31 (1985), 112–15.

Gaudon, Jean, 'Le Rouge et le blanc: notes sur *Le Lys dans la vallée*', in *Balzac and the Nineteenth Century: Studies in French Literature Presented to Herbert J. Hunt by Pupils, Colleagues, and Friends*, ed. D. G. Charlton, J. Gaudon, and Anthony R. Pugh (Leicester: Leicester University Press, 1972), pp. 71–8.

Gégou, Fabienne, 'Stendhal et l'amour en "Provence" au Moyen Âge', *Stendhal Club*, 72 (1976), 316–26.

Gellner, Ernest, *Nations and Nationalism* (Oxford: Basil Blackwell, 1983).

Genette, Gérard, *Palimpsestes: la littérature au second degré* (Paris: Éditions du Seuil, 1982).

Gidel, Charles, *Les troubadours et Pétrarque: thèse présentée à la Faculté des lettres de Paris* (Angers: Cosnier et Lachèse, 1857).

Gillingham, Susan, 'Biblical Studies on Holiday? A Personal View of Reception History', in *Reception History and Biblical Studies: Theory and Practice*, ed. William John Lyons and Emma England (London: Bloomsbury, 2015), pp. 17–30.

Ginguené, Pierre-Louis, *Histoire littéraire de l'Italie*, 14 vols (Paris: Chez Michaud frères, 1811–35).

Girard, René, *Mensonge romantique et vérité romanesque* (Paris: Bernard Grasset, 1961).

Giraud, Yves, 'Un admirateur de Pétrarque au XVIIIe siècle: les romances de l'abbé Roman', in *Dynamique d'une expansion culturelle: Pétrarque en Europe XIVe–XXe siècle: actes du XXVIe congrès international du CEFI, Turin et Chambéry, 11–15 décembre 1995: à la mémoire de Franco Simone*, ed. Pierre Blanc (Paris: Honoré Champion, 2001), pp. 383–400.

Giudici, Enzo, 'Bilancio di un'annosa questione: Maurice Scève e "la scoperta" della tomba di Laura', *Quaderni di filologia e lingue romanze*, 2 (1980), 3–70.

Giunta, Claudio, 'Memoria di Dante nei *Trionfi*', *Rivista di letteratura italiana*, 11 (1993), 411–52.

Gorni, Guglielmo, 'Beatrice agli inferi', in *Omaggio a Beatrice 1290–1990*, ed. Rudy Abardo (Florence: Le Lettere, 1997), pp. 143–58.

—— 'Petrarca Virgini (Lettura della canzone CCCLXVI "Vergine bella")', *Lectura Petrarce*, 7 (1987), 201–18.

Gossman, Lionel, *Medievalism and the Ideologies of the Enlightenment: The World and Work of La Curne de Sainte-Palaye* (Baltimore: Johns Hopkins University Press, 1968).

Goulbourne, Russell, '"Bizarre, mais brillant de beautés naturelles": Voltaire and Dante's *Commedia*', in *Dante in France*, ed. Russell Goulbourne, Claire Honess, and Matthew Treherne (= *La Parola del testo: rivista internazionale di letteratura italiana e comparata*, 17.1–2 (2013)), pp. 31–43.

—— 'Voltaire, Dante and the Dynamics of Influence', in *Questions of Influence in Modern French Literature*, ed. Thomas Baldwin, James Fowler, and Ana de Medeiros (Houndmills: Palgrave Macmillan, 2013), pp. 18–31.

Gragnolati, Manuele, Fabio Camilletti, and Fabian Lampart, eds, *Metamorphosing Dante: Appropriations, Manipulations, and Rewritings in the Twentieth and Twenty-First Centuries* (Vienna: Turin + Kant, 2011).

Greene, Roland, *Post-Petrarchism: Origins and Innovations of the Western Lyric Sequence* (Princeton, NJ: Princeton University Press, 1991).

Greene, Thomas M., *The Vulnerable Text: Essays on Renaissance Literature* (New York: Columbia University Press, 1986).

Guérin, Jean, *Pétrarque considéré comme amant, poëte et philosophe* (Avignon: [n.p.], 1804).

Guillemin, Henri, *Le Jocelyn de Lamartine: étude historique et critique avec des documents inédits* (Paris: Boivin et Cie, 1936).

Guy, Anselme, *Notice historique et littéraire sur M. le comte Anatole de Montesquiou-Fezensac* (Paris: Au Bureau central de la publication, 1847).

Hainsworth, Peter, 'The Myth of Daphne in the *Rerum vulgarium fragmenta*', *Italian Studies*, 34.1 (1979), 28–44.

Hauvette, Henri, 'Laure de Noves?', *Bulletin italien*, 2 (1902), 15–22.

Havely, Nick, 'Francesca Observed: Painting and Illustration, c. 1790–1840', in *Dante on View: The Reception of Dante in the Visual and Performing Arts*, ed. Antonella Braida and Luisa Calè (Aldershot: Ashgate, 2007), pp. 95–107.

—— ed., *Dante in the Nineteenth Century: Reception, Canonicity, Popularization* (Oxford: Peter Lang, 2011).

Hayes, Julie Candler, 'Petrarch/Sade: Writing the Life', in *Representations of the Self from the Renaissance to Romanticism*, ed. Patrick Coleman, Jayne Lewis, and Jill Kowalik (Cambridge: Cambridge University Press, 2000), pp. 117–34.

Heathcote, Owen, 'Balzac's "mal d'archive"? "Lieux de mémoire" in *Le Lys dans la vallée*', in *Mapping Memory in Nineteenth-Century French Literature and Culture*, ed. Susan Harrow and Andrew Watts (Amsterdam: Rodopi, 2012), pp. 193–207.

Hendrix, Harald, 'The Early Modern Invention of Literary Tourism: Petrarch's Houses in France and Italy', in *Writers' Houses and the Making of Memory*, ed. Harald Hendrix (New York and London: Routledge, 2008), pp. 15–29.

—— 'From Early Modern to Romantic Literary Tourism: A Diachronical Perspective', in *Literary Tourism and Nineteenth-Century Culture*, ed. Nicola Watson (Basingstoke: Palgrave Macmillan, 2009), pp. 13–24.

—— 'Petrarch 1804–1904: Nation-Building and Glocal Identities', in *Commemorating Writers in Nineteenth-Century Europe: Nation-Building and Centenary Fever*, ed. Joseph Leerssen and Ann Rigney (Basingstoke: Palgrave Macmillan, 2014), pp. 117–33.

—— ed., *Writers' Houses and the Making of Memory* (New York and London: Routledge, 2008).

Hoffmeister, Gerhart, 'The Petrarchan Mode in European Romanticism', in *European Romanticism: Literary Cross-Currents, Modes, and Models*, ed. Gerhart Hoffmeister (Detroit: Wayne State University Press, 1990), pp. 97–111.

Hollander, Robert, and Albert L. Rossi, 'Dante's Republican Treasury', *Dante Studies*, 104 (1986), 59–82.

Holmes, Olivia, *Assembling the Lyric Self: Authorship from Troubadour Song to the Italian Poetry Book* (Minneapolis: University of Minnesota Press, 2000).

House, John, 'Impressionist Painting: *esquisse* or *ébauche*?', in *Esquisses/Ébauches: Projects and Pre-Texts in Nineteenth-Century French Culture*, ed. Sonya Stephens (New York: Peter Lang, 2007), pp. 222–9.

Houston, Jason M., *Building a Monument to Dante: Boccaccio as Dantista* (Toronto: University of Toronto Press, 2010).

Hutcheon, Linda, *A Theory of Parody: The Teachings of Twentieth-Century Art Forms* (New York and London: Methuen, 1985).

Iknayan, Marguerite, *The Idea of the Novel in France: The Critical Reaction, 1815–1848* (Geneva: Droz, 1961).

Janson, Tore, *Speak: A Short History of Languages* (Oxford: Oxford University Press, 2002).

Jasinski, Max, *Histoire du sonnet en France: thèse présentée à la Faculté des Lettres de Paris* (Douai: Imprimerie H. Brugère, A. Dalsheimer et Cie, 1903).

Jefferson, Ann, *Reading Realism in Stendhal* (Cambridge: Cambridge University Press, 1988).

——— Stendhal, 'La Chartreuse de Parme' (London: Grant & Cutler, 2003).

Jones, Frederic J., 'Further Evidence of the Identity of Laura', *Italian Studies*, 39 (1984), 27–46.

——— 'I rapporti tra la Laure de Sade e la Laura del Petrarca', *Italianistica: rivista di letteratura italiana*, 21.2–3 (1992), 485–501.

Kay, Sarah, *Parrots and Nightingales: Troubadour Quotations and the Development of European Poetry* (Philadelphia: University of Pennsylvania Press, 2013).

Keller, Barbara G., *The Middle Ages Reconsidered: Attitudes in France from the Eighteenth Century through the Romantic Movement* (New York: Peter Lang, 1994).

Kennedy, William J., *Authorizing Petrarch* (Ithaca, NY: Cornell University Press, 1994).

——— 'The Economy of Invective and a Man in the Middle: *De sui ipsius et multorum ignorantia*', in *Petrarch: A Critical Guide to the Complete Works*, ed. Victoria Kirkham and Armando Maggi (Chicago: University of Chicago Press, 2009), pp. 63–73.

——— *The Site of Petrarchism: Early Modern National Sentiment in Italy, France, and England* (Baltimore: Johns Hopkins University Press, 2003).

Kim, Ji-hyun Philippa, *Pour une littérature médiévale moderne: Gaston Paris, l'amour courtois et les enjeux de la modernité* (Paris: Honoré Champion, 2012).

Kirkham, Victoria, and Armando Maggi, eds, *Petrarch: A Critical Guide to the Complete Works* (Chicago: University of Chicago Press, 2009).

Labarthe, Patrick, 'Balzac et Sainte-Beuve, ou de l'inimitié créatrice', *L'Année balzacienne*, 9 (2008), 7–23.

——— 'Expérience intimiste et politique dans *Volupté*', in *La Pensée du paradoxe: approches du romantisme: hommage à Michel Crouzet*, ed. Fabienne Bercegol and Didier Philippot (Paris: Presses de l'université de Paris-Sorbonne, 2006), pp. 107–40.

Laforgue, Pierre, *L'Œdipe romantique: le jeune homme, le désir et l'histoire en 1830* (Grenoble: ELLUG, 2002).

Laignel, M.-Th., *La Littérature italienne* (Paris: Armand Colin, 1926).

Leerssen, Joseph, and Ann Rigney, eds, *Commemorating Writers in Nineteenth-Century Europe: Nation-Building and Centenary Fever* (Basingstoke: Palgrave Macmillan, 2014).

Lepschy, Giulio, 'Mother Tongues in the Middle Ages and Dante', in *Dante's Plurilingualism: Authority, Knowledge, Subjectivity*, ed. Sara Fortuna, Manuele Gragnolati, and Jürgen Trabant (London: Legenda, 2010), pp. 16–23.

Lombez, Christine, 'Poésie', in *Histoire des traductions en langue française: XIXe siècle: 1815–1914*, ed. Yves Chevrel, Lieven D'Hulst, and Christine Lombez (Lagrasse: Éditions Verdier, 2012), pp. 345–442.

——— 'Théories en marge de la pratique: l'art de la préface chez les traducteurs français de poésie au XIXe siècle', in *L'Art de la préface*, ed. Philippe Forest (Nantes: Éditions Cécile Defaut, 2006), pp. 159–75.

Looney, Dennis, 'The Beginnings of Humanistic Oratory: Petrarch's *Coronation Oration*', in *Petrarch: A Critical Guide to the Complete Works*, ed. Victoria Kirkham and Armando Maggi (Chicago: University of Chicago Press, 2009), pp. 131–40.

Mackenzie, Louisa, *The Poetry of Place: Lyric, Landscape, and Ideology in Renaissance France* (Toronto: University of Toronto Press, 2011).

M'Enesti, Ana-Maria, 'The Representation of Petrarch in the Eighteenth-Century *Encyclopédie*', *Humanist Studies and the Digital Age*, 1.1 (2011), 136–44.

Majewski, Henry F., *Paradigm and Parody: Images of Creativity in French Romanticism: Vigny, Hugo, Balzac, Gautier, Musset* (Charlottesville: University Press of Virginia, 1989).

——— *Transposing Art into Texts in French Romantic Literature* (Chapel Hill: North Carolina Studies in the Romance Languages and Literatures, 2002).

Malkin, Shira, 'Tableau et coup de théâtre: le pathétique dans *Adriani*', *Études littéraires*, 35.2–3 (2003), 107–22.

Mann, Nicholas, 'La fortune de Pétrarque en France: recherches sur le *De remediis*', *Studi francesi*, 37 (1969), 1–15.

Marie, Aristide, *Le Peintre poète Louis Boulanger* (Paris: H. Floury, 1925).

Marix-Spire, Thérèse, *Les Romantiques et la musique: le cas George Sand 1804–1838* (Paris: Nouvelles Éditions latines, 1954).

Marshal, David, ed., *Mass Market Medieval: Essays on the Middle Ages in Popular Culture* (Jefferson, NC: McFarland, 2007).

Marshall, David, 'Ut pictura poesis', in *The Cambridge History of Literary Criticism*, ed. H. B. Nisbet and Claude Rawson, 9 vols (Cambridge: Cambridge University Press, 1989–2001), IV: *The Eighteenth Century* (1997), 681–99.

Martinez, Ronald L., 'The Book Without a Name: Petrarch's Open Secret', in *Petrarch: A Critical Guide to the Complete Works*, ed. Victoria Kirkham and Armando Maggi (Chicago: University of Chicago Press, 2009), pp. 291–9.

Masséna, Victor, prince d'Essling, and Eugène Müntz, *Pétrarque: ses études d'art, son influence sur les artistes, ses portraits et ceux de Laure, l'illustration de ses écrits* (Paris: Gazette des Beaux-Arts, 1902).

Matthews, David, 'Chaucer's American Accent', *American Literary History* 22.4 (2010), 758–72.

Mazzotta, Giuseppe, *The Worlds of Petrarch* (Durham, NC: Duke University Press, 1993).

McLaughlin, Martin, 'Nineteenth-Century British Biographies of Petrarch', in *Petrarch in Britain: Interpreters, Imitators, and Translators Over 700 Years*, ed. Martin McLaughlin and Letizia Panizza with Peter Hainsworth (Oxford: Oxford University Press for the British Academy, 2007), pp. 319–40.

—— and Letizia Panizza, with Peter Hainsworth, eds, *Petrarch in Britain: Interpreters, Imitators, and Translators Over 700 Years* (Oxford: Oxford University Press for the British Academy, 2007).

Ménager, Daniel, 'Le "Triomphe de la mort" dans deux traductions françaises du seizième siècle', in *Dynamique d'une expansion culturelle: Pétrarque en Europe XIVe–XXe siècle: actes du XXVIe congrès international du CEFI, Turin et Chambéry, 11–15 décembre 1995: à la mémoire de Franco Simone*, ed. Pierre Blanc (Paris: Honoré Champion, 2001), pp. 347–61.

Milbank, Alison, *Dante and the Victorians* (Manchester: Manchester University Press, 1998).

Miller, David, *On Nationality* (Oxford: Clarendon Press, 1995).

Miller, Nancy K., '"Tristes Triangles": *Le Lys dans la vallée* and Its Intertext', in *Pre-Text, Text, Context: Essays on Nineteenth-Century French Literature*, ed. Robert L. Mitchell (Columbus: Ohio State University Press, 1980), pp. 66–77.

Millet, Olivier, 'Le tombeau de la morte et la voix du poète: la mémoire de Pétrarque en France autour de 1533', in *Regards sur le passé dans l'Europe des XVIe et XVIIe siècles: actes du colloque organisé par l'Université de Nancy II (14 au 16 décembre 1995)*, ed. Francine Wild (Bern: Peter Lang, 1997), pp. 183–95.

Minta, Stephen, ed., *Petrarch and Petrarchism: The English and French Traditions* (Manchester: Manchester University Press, 1980).

Moevs, Christian, 'Subjectivity and Conversion in Dante and Petrarch', in *Petrarch and Dante: Anti-Dantism, Metaphysics, Tradition*, ed. Zygmunt G. Barański and Theodore J. Cachey (Notre Dame, IN: University of Notre Dame Press, 2009), pp. 226–59.

Montoya, Alicia C., *Medievalist Enlightenment from Charles Perrault to Jean-Jacques Rousseau* (Cambridge: D. S. Brewer, 2013).

Moulinas, René, *Histoire de la Révolution d'Avignon* (Avignon: Aubanel, 1986).

Mouret, François J.-L., *Les Traducteurs anglais de Pétrarque 1754–1798* (Paris: Didier, 1976).

Naselli, Carmelina, *Il Petrarca nell'ottocento* (Naples: Società anonima editrice Francesco Perrella, 1923).

Niederer, Christoph, 'La bipartizione *in vita/in morte* del "Canzoniere" di Petrarca', in *Petrarca e i suoi lettori*, ed. Vittorio Caratozzolo and Georges Güntert (Ravenna: Longo, 2000), pp. 19–41.

Niess, Robert J., 'Sainte-Beuve and Balzac: *Volupté* and *Le Lys dans la vallée*', *Kentucky Romance Quarterly*, 20.1 (1973), 113–24.

Nolhac, Pierre de, *Le Canzoniere autographe de Pétrarque* (Paris: C. Klincksieck, 1886).

—— 'Le *De viris illustribus* de Pétrarque', *Notices et extraits des manuscrits de la Bibliothèque nationale et autres bibliothèques*, 34.1 (1891), 61–148.

—— *Pétrarque et l'humanisme*, 2 vols (Paris: Honoré Champion, 1907).

—— 'Préface', in G. Finzi, *Pétrarque: sa vie et son œuvre: traduit avec l'autorisation de l'auteur par Mme Thiérard-Baudrillart* (Paris: Perrin et Cie, 1906), pp. 5–11.

Nora, Pierre, ed., *Les Lieux de mémoire*, 4 vols (Paris: Gallimard, 1984–6).

O'Grady, Deirdre, 'Francesca da Rimini from Romanticism to Decadence', in *Dante Metamorphoses: Episodes in a Literary Afterlife*, ed. Eric C. Haywood (Dublin: Four Courts Press, 2003), pp. 221–39.

Paden, William D., 'Petrarch as a Poet of Provence', in *Petrarch and the European Lyric Tradition*, ed. Dino S. Cervigni (= *Annali d'Italianistica*, 22 (2004)), pp. 19–44.

Pakscher, Arthur, *Die Chronologie der Gedichte Petrarcas* (Berlin: Weidmannsche Buchhandlung, 1887).

Pasquini, Emilio, 'Il mito polemico di Avignone nei poeti italiani del trecento', in *Aspetti culturali della società italiana nel periodo del papato Avignonese: 15–18 ottobre 1978* (Todi: L'Accademia tudertina, 1981), pp. 257–309.

Pavet-Jörg, Pierrette, 'Les erreurs amoureuses. La poétique pétrarquiste et la poétique du ridicule dans *De l'amour*', in *La Pensée du paradoxe: approches du romantisme: hommage à Michel Crouzet*, ed. Fabienne Bercegol and Didier Philippot (Paris: Presses de l'Université Paris-Sorbonne, 2006), pp. 249–70.

Pearson, Roger, *Stendhal's Violin: A Novelist and his Reader* (Oxford: Clarendon Press, 1988).

—— *Unacknowledged Legislators: The Poet as Lawgiver in Post-Revolutionary France: Chateaubriand–Staël–Lamartine–Hugo–Vigny* (Oxford: Oxford University Press, 2016).

Perugi, Maurizio, 'Petrarca provenzale', *Quaderni petrarcheschi*, 7 (1990), 109–81.

—— *Trovatori a Valchiusa: un frammento della cultura provenzale del Petrarca* (Padua: Editrice Antenore, 1985).

Picone, Michelangelo, 'Il sonetto CLXXXIX', *Lectura Petrarce*, 9 (1989), 151–77.

Piéri, Marius, *Le Pétrarquisme au XVIe siècle: Pétrarque & Ronsard, ou, De l'influence de Pétrarque sur la Pléiade française* (Marseille: Lafitte, 1896).

Pitwood, Michael, *Dante and the French Romantics* (Geneva: Droz, 1985).

Poli, Annarosa, 'George Sand et l'opéra italien', in *Présences de l'Italie dans l'œuvre de George Sand* (Moncalieri: Centro interuniversitario di ricerche sul 'Viaggio in Italia', 2004), pp. 113–47.

Ponzetto, Valentina, 'Musset et les écrivains italiens du Moyen Âge et de la Renaissance', in *Poétique de Musset*, ed. Sylvain Ledda, Frank Lestringant, and Gisèle Séginger (Mont-Saint-Aignan: Presses universitaires de Rouen et du Havre, 2013), pp. 29–52.

Powell, David A., *While the Music Lasts: The Representation of Music in the Works of George Sand* (Lewisburg, PA: Bucknell University Press; London: Associated University Presses, 2001).

Quiller-Couch, Arthur, 'Foreword on the Gentle Art', in *Parodies and Imitations Old and New*, ed. J. A. Stanley Adam and Bernard C. White (London: Hutchinson and Co., 1912), pp. v–xvi.

Ramazani, Jahan, *Poetry and Its Others: News, Prayer, Song, and the Dialogue of Genres* (Chicago: University of Chicago Press, 2013).

Reynolds, Matthew, *The Poetry of Translation: From Chaucer & Petrarch to Homer & Logue* (Oxford: Oxford University Press, 2011).

Rico, Francisco, '"Rime sparse", "Rerum vulgarium fragmenta": sul titolo e sul primo sonetto del *Canzoniere*', trans. S. Bogliolo, in *Il 'Canzoniere' di Francesco Petrarca: la critica contemporanea*, ed. Gennaro Barbarisi and Claudia Berra (Milan: Edizioni Universitarie di Lettere Economia Diritto, 1992), pp. 117–44.

Roche, Alphonse V., 'Petrarch and the Felibres', *Italica*, 30.1 (1953), 1–18.

Roche, Thomas P., *Petrarch in English* (London: Penguin, 2005).

Roubaud, Jacques, *La Fleur inverse: essai sur l'art formel des troubadours* (Paris: Éditions Ramsay, 1986).

Rougemont, Denis de, *L'Amour et l'Occident* (Paris: Plon, 1939).

Rouget, François, 'La fortune du *De vita solitaria* de Pétrarque dans la littérature française de la Renaissance: Peletier, Ronsard, Pibrac et Montaigne', in *Francesco Petrarca, l'opera latina: tradizione e fortuna: atti del XVI Convegno internazionale (Chianciano–Pienza 19–22 luglio 2004*, ed. Luisa Secchi Tarugi (Florence: Franco Cesati, 2006), pp. 461–76.

Rowell, Diana, *Paris: The 'New Rome' of Napoleon I* (London: Bloomsbury Academic, 2012).

Rushworth, Jennifer, *Discourses of Mourning in Dante, Petrarch, and Proust* (Oxford: Oxford University Press, 2016).

Sade, Thibault de, 'Les Sade et Pétrarque', in *La Postérité répond à Pétrarque: sept siècles de fortune pétrarquienne en France: actes du colloque tenu à l'Hôtel de Sade et à l'Université d'Avignon et des Pays de Vaucluse les 22, 23, 24 janvier 2004*, ed. Ève Duperray (Paris: Beauchesne, 2006), pp. 187–96.

Santagata, Marco, *Amate e amanti: figure della lirica amorosa fra Dante e Petrarca* (Bologna: Il Mulino, 1999).

—— 'Introduzione', in Petrarch, *Canzoniere*, ed. M. Santagata, 4th edn (Milan: Arnoldo Mondadori, 2010), pp. xix–ci.

Scanlon, Mara, and Chad Engbers, eds, *Poetry and Dialogism: Hearing Over* (Basingstoke: Palgrave Macmillan, 2014).

Scott, Clive, *Translating Baudelaire* (Exeter: University of Exeter Press, 2000).

Scott, David, *Pictorialist Poetics: Poetry and the Visual Arts in Nineteenth-Century France* (Cambridge: Cambridge University Press, 1988).

—— *Sonnet Theory and Sonnet Practice in Nineteenth-Century France: Sonnets on the Sonnet* (Hull: University of Hull Publications, 1977).

Séché, Léon, *Études d'histoire romantique: Lamartine de 1816 à 1830: Elvire et les 'Méditations' (documents inédits), avec le portrait d'Elvire en héliogravure* (Paris: Société de Mercure de France, 1906).

Séité, Yannick, *Du livre au lire: 'La Nouvelle Héloïse', roman des lumières* (Paris: Honoré Champion, 2002).

Simmons, Clare A., 'Introduction', in *Medievalism and the Quest for the 'Real' Middle Ages*, ed. Clare A. Simmons (Oxford: Taylor and Francis, 2001), pp. 1–28.

Singleton, Charles, *An Essay on the 'Vita nuova'* (Cambridge, MA: Publication for the Dante Society by Harvard University Press, 1949).

Snell, Robert, *Théophile Gautier: A Romantic Critic of the Visual Arts* (Oxford: Clarendon Press, 1982).

Southerden, Francesca, 'Between Autobiography and Apocalypse: The Double Subject of Polemic in Petrarch's *Liber sine nomine* and *Rerum vulgarium fragmenta*', in *Polemic: Language as Violence in Medieval and Early Modern Discourse*, ed. Almut Suerbaum, George Southcombe, and Benjamin Thompson (Farnham: Ashgate, 2015), pp. 17–42.

—— 'The Ghost of a Garden: Seeds of Discourse and Desire in Petrarch's *Triumphus Mortis II*', *Le Tre corone: rivista internazionale di studi su Dante, Petrarca, Boccaccio*, 1 (2014), 131–51.

Sozzi, Lionello, '*Un cœur sensible*: Petrarca in Francia nel settecento', in *Dynamique d'une expansion culturelle: Pétrarque en Europe XIVe–XXe siècle: actes du XXVIe congrès international du CEFI, Turin et Chambéry, 11–15 décembre 1995: à la mémoire de Franco Simone*, ed. Pierre Blanc (Paris: Honoré Champion, 2001), pp. 441–9.

Squarotti, Giorgio Bàrberi, 'Il vecchio Romeo: Petrarca, 16', *Critica letteraria*, 22.1 (1994), 43–52.

Stackelberg, Jürgen, 'Du paysage de l'amour au paysage de l'âme: Rousseau et Pétrarque', in *Vérité et littérature au XVIIIe siècle: mélanges rassemblés en l'honneur de Raymond Trousson*, ed. Paul Aron et al. (Paris: Champion, 2001), pp. 265–70.

Stahuljak, Zrinka, *Bloodless Genealogies of the French Middle Ages: Translatio, Kinship, and Metaphor* (Gainesville: University Press of Florida, 2005).

—— 'Genealogy', in *Medievalism: Key Critical Terms*, ed. Elizabeth Emery and Richard Utz (Cambridge: D. S. Brewer, 2014), pp. 71–8.

—— *Pornographic Archeology: Medicine, Medievalism, and the Invention of the French Nation* (Philadelphia: University of Pennsylvania Press, 2013).

Steinberg, Justin, 'Dante *Estravagante*, Petrarca *Disperso*, and the Spectre of the other Woman', in *Petrarch and Dante: Anti-Dantism, Metaphysics, Tradition*, ed. Zygmunt G. Barański and Theodore J. Cachey (Notre Dame, IN: University of Notre Dame Press, 2009), pp. 263–89.

Stephens, Sonya, ed., *Esquisses/Ébauches: Projects and Pre-Texts in Nineteenth-Century French Culture* (New York: Peter Lang, 2007).

Storey, H. Wayne, 'All'interno della poetica grafico-visiva di Petrarca', in Petrarch, *Rerum vulgarium fragmenta, codice Vat. Lat. 3195: commentario all'edizione in fac-simile*, ed. Gino Belloni, Furio Brugnolo, H. Wayne Storey, and Stefano Zamponi (Padua: Antenore Editrice, 2004), pp. 131–71.

—— 'Canzoniere e petrarchismo: un paradigma di orientamento formale e materiale', in *Il petrarchismo: un modello di poesia per l'Europa*, ed. Loredana Chines, Floriana Calitti, and Roberto Gigliucci, 2 vols (Rome: Bulzoni, 2006), I, 291–310.

—— 'The Economies of Authority: Bembo, Vellutello, and the Reconstruction of "Authentic Petrarch"', in '*Accessus ad Auctores*': *Studies in Honor of Christopher Kleinhenz*, ed. Fabian Alfie and Andrea Dini (Tempe: Arizona Center for Medieval and Renaissance Studies, 2011), pp. 493–506.

Stroppa, Sabrina, '"Obscuratus est sol". Codice lirico e codice biblico in RVF III', *Lettere italiane*, 56.2 (2004), 165–89.

Sturm-Maddox, Sara, 'The French Petrarch', in *Petrarch and the European Lyric Tradition*, ed. Dino S. Cervigni (= *Annali d'Italianistica*, 22 (2004)), pp. 171–87.

—— *Ronsard, Petrarch and the 'Amours'* (Gainesville: University Press of Florida, 1999).

Suitner, Franco, 'L'invettiva antiavignonese del Petrarca e la poesia infamante medievale', *Studi petrarcheschi*, n.s., 2 (1985), 201–10.

Swain, Virginia E., 'Le sublime et le grotesque: la lettre du Valais et la théorie esthétique de Rousseau', in *L'Amour dans 'La Nouvelle Héloïse': texte et intertexte: Actes du Colloque de Genève (10–11–12 juin 1999)*, ed. Jacques Berchtold and François Rosset (Geneva: Droz, 2002) (= *Annales de la société Jean-Jacques Rousseau*, 44 (2002)), pp. 101–18.

Tastu, Amable, *Tableau de la littérature italienne depuis l'établissement du christianisme jusqu'à nos jours* (Tours: Mame, 1843).

Tateo, Francesco, *Dialogo interiore e polemica ideologica nel 'Secretum' del Petrarca* (Florence: Le Monnier, 1965).

Théophile Gautier: l'art et l'artiste: actes du colloque international, 2 vols (Montpellier: La Société Théophile Gautier, 1982).

Thomas, James W., 'Dante and the Provençal Renaissance', in *Dante in France*, ed. Russell Goulbourne, Claire Honess, and Matthew Treherne (= *La Parola del testo: rivista internazionale di letteratura italiana e comparata*, 17.1–2 (2013)), pp. 71–83.

Toesca, Maurice, *Lamartine ou l'amour de la vie* (Paris: Albin Michel, 1969).

Toswell, M. J., 'Lingua', in *Medievalism: Key Critical Terms*, ed. Elizabeth Emery and Richard Utz (Cambridge: D. S. Brewer, 2014), pp. 117–24.

Trapp, J. B., 'Petrarchan Places: An Essay in the Iconography of Commemoration', *Journal of the Warburg and Courtauld Institutes*, 69 (2006), 1–50.

—— 'Petrarch's Laura: The Portraiture of an Imaginary Beloved', *Journal of the Warburg and Courtauld Institutes*, 64 (2001), 55–192.

—— 'The Poet Laureate: Rome, *Renovatio* and *Translatio Imperii*', in *Rome in the Renaissance: The City and the Myth: Papers of the Thirteenth Annual Conference of the Center for Medieval & Early Renaissance Studies*, ed. P. A. Ramsey (Binghamton, NY: Medieval & Renaissance Texts and Studies, 1982), pp. 93–130.

Trompeo, Pietro Paolo, *Incontri di Stendhal* (Naples: Edizioni scientifiche italiane, 1963).

Trousson, Raymond, *Balzac, disciple et juge de Jean-Jacques Rousseau* (Geneva: Droz, 1983).

Utz, Richard, 'Coming to Terms with Medievalism', *European Journal of English Studies*, 15.2 (2011), 101–13.

Van Nuffel, Robert O. J., 'Note e rassegne: per la fortuna del Petrarca in Francia', *Studi petrarcheschi*, 6 (1956), 225–31.

Venuti, Lawrence, *The Translator's Invisibility: A History of Translation* (London: Routledge, 1995).

Veyne, Paul, 'Parme et Modène: un premier jet de la *Chartreuse*', *Annales de la faculté des lettres d'Aix*, 38 (1964), 161–6.

Viala, Alain, 'Un temps de querelles', *Littératures classiques*, 8 (2013), 5–22.

Vianey, Joseph, *Le Pétrarquisme en France au XVIe siècle* (Montpellier: Coulet et fils, 1909).

Vierne, Simone, 'George Sand et le dialogue: d'une forme à une philosophie', in *George Sand, l'écriture du roman: actes du XIe colloque international George Sand*, ed. Jeanne Goldin (Montréal: Département d'Études françaises, Université de Montréal, 1996) (= *Paragraphes*, 12 (1996)), pp. 133–41 (repr. in Simone Vierne, *George Sand, la femme qui écrivait la nuit* (Clermont-Ferrand: Presses Universitaires Blaise Pascal, 2004), pp. 247–58).

Ward, Marvin J., 'Fabrice del Dongo et Perceval le Gallois: intertextualité?', *Stendhal Club*, 119 (1988), 209–22.

Ward, Patricia A., *The Medievalism of Victor Hugo* (University Park: Pennsylvania State University Press, 1975).

Watson, Nicola, ed., *Literary Tourism and Nineteenth-Century Culture* (Basingstoke: Palgrave Macmillan, 2009).

Weinmann, Heinz, 'Bachelard et l'analyse du roman: structure des thèmes et des images dans *Le Lys dans la vallée* de Balzac', *Revue des sciences humaines*, 157 (1975), 122–41.

Wilkins, E. H., *The Life of Petrarch* (Chicago: University of Chicago Press, 1961).

—— 'Peregrinus Ubique', *Studies in Philology*, 45.3 (1948), 445–53 (repr. in E. H. Wilkins, *The Making of the 'Canzoniere' and Other Petrarchan Studies* (Rome: Edizioni di storia e letteratura, 1951), pp. 1–8).

—— *Studies in the Life and Works of Petrarch* (Cambridge, MA: The Mediaeval Academy of America, 1955).

Wolff, Étienne, 'Victor Develay, les études néo-latines et Pétrarque', *Latomus*, 58.1 (1999), 172–8.

Workman, Leslie J., 'Editorial', *Studies in Medievalism* 1.1 (1979), 1–3.

Yousefzadeh, Mahnaz, *City and Nation in the Italian Unification: The National Festivals of Dante Alighieri* (Basingstoke: Palgrave Macmillan, 2011).

Zantedeschi, Francesca, 'Petrarch 1874: Pan-National Celebrations and Provençal Regionalism', in *Commemorating Writers in Nineteenth-Century Europe: Nation-Building and Centenary Fever*, ed. Joseph Leerssen and Ann Rigney (Basingstoke: Palgrave Macmillan, 2014), pp. 134–51.

Zuccato, Edoardo, *Petrarch in Romantic England* (Houndmills: Palgrave Macmillan, 2008).

Index

CPSIA information can be obtained
at www.ICGtesting.com
Printed in the USA
BVOW06*1638120317
478249BV00007B/36/P